THE Traditional Games

OF ENGLAND, SCOTLAND, AND IRELAND

THE Traditional Games

OF ENGLAND, SCOTLAND, AND IRELAND

collected and annotated by
Alice Bertha Gomme

Introduction by
Fr. Damian Webb O.S.B.

 THAMES AND HUDSON

First published in Great Britain in two volumes, 1894–98

Printed in Great Britain
at the University Press, Oxford

INTRODUCTION

It is just ninety years since Lady Gomme published her remarkable two-volume dictionary, with its eight hundred or so titles of children's games collected from England, Ireland and Scotland. Her pioneer work provides a unique 'snapshot' of the games, and the chants they embody, of a century ago. Yet it is in the period since then, more than any other, that we have experienced the most profound changes in our civilization. It has been suggested that anyone born during the First World War has seen in his or her lifetime greater changes than are embodied in the whole previous history of mankind. It is inevitable that such a dramatic evolution should influence the content of children's games, though not necessarily the way they play. To define the changes is a challenging problem and would be difficult even if it concerned the impact of the last decade. I cannot attempt here a comprehensive analysis, for this is the territory of the antiquarian, but I shall try to convey impressions and conclusions from my personal experience.

In the Preface to her first volume (published four years before the second) Lady Gomme wisely comments that 'Children do not invent, but they imitate or mimic very largely'. And this poses an immediate problem: they are liable to pick up a game from friends with garbled versions of the words so that 'titles' – opening words – of games proliferate, making comparisons with the past somewhat laborious. A game may be widespread in England today, but with a variety of titles: take, for example, the game listed in Gomme as 'Three Dukes'. She lists thirty versions, most of which begin 'Here come three Dukes a-riding', though variations include 'One duck comes a-ridin', 'Here comes a Jew a-riding', 'Five dukes comes here a-ridin', as well as several others. Now I have found this game to be widespread in the north of England, where it turns up in a vast variety of forms, most of which start off either as 'There came a Duke a-riding', or as 'There came a Gipsy riding', according to the region (roughly, 'Duke' in the south and 'Gipsy' in the north). Thus it must be remembered that Lady Gomme's collection, with its huge range of variations, includes several games which have considerable popularity today, but with a different title.

There is a second and more fundamental problem in the search to establish an authentic picture of a century ago, which I shall come to via some specific examples. Gomme gives no less than thirty-seven games under the general title of 'Three Knights from Spain'. I have found this game only once – and that as long ago as the early 1960s – in Cumbria, played by a group of girls who sung it with a plaintive little tune, in the following version:

Sister Jane and brother Jim, sister Jane and brother Jim
Sister Jane is far too young to marry a man of twenty-one
Fly away, O fly away, come again another day;
Face to face and back to back, choose the one you
love the best.

When I contacted one of the mothers of this group, she gave me a version she used to play as a child, containing the lines common – more or less – to all the Gomme versions: 'My daughter Jane, she is too young,/She cannot bear your flattering tongue'.

In both 'Three Dukes' and 'Three Knights from Spain' the basic description as to how the games are played (and there are plenty of other examples in Lady Gomme's volumes) reads as follows: 'The players stand in two lines, facing one another, three boys on one side and the girls (any number) on the other. The boys advance and retire dancing, and saying the first two lines. . . .' The text concludes, after a long description: 'Then the last boy in the line puts his arms round the chosen girl's waist and carries her off.' In searching for a reliable picture as to how children played traditional games at the time the Gomme collection was made, there is a question to be answered: to what extent did boys and girls at that time play together? This is the problem on which I shall try to shed some light. Firstly, Lady Gomme makes it clear that she has collected her information from a variety of sources. These sources include both earlier writings and published accounts, and also her own correspondents in various parts of the country. The trouble is that in general none of these sources give specific details: what sort of children were playing the games in what sort of place and what were their ages? Were they the urban poor singing and dancing in their own back streets and cul-de-sacs, or were they organized groups of children playing under adult supervision?

The answer, which is vital to finding out what has happened in the last century, can only be guessed at; but there are some significant clues in the text. The first is found in Volume I and is representative of a number of similar phrases in which a clear hint is given that the game is played indoors. Miss E. Cadman is quoted as describing how 'They [i.e., a line of boys facing a line of girls] cross the *room* to each other's places.' It is true that today children go to parties and play organized games of 'Oranges and lemons', 'Sir Roger de Coverley' (children don't distinguish between games and country dances), 'Tom Tiddler's ground', 'Nuts in May' and 'Grandmother's footsteps', to name but a few. But these can hardly be described as part of the real child folk tradition. Again, children of both sexes play singing games at school under the care and instruction of teachers. But left to themselves boys and girls above infant age rarely play singing games together. And the memoir at the end of Volume II of Lady Gomme's work mentions that Strutt 'records none of those interesting dialogue games which we now know as singing games. It may be that these games were in his day, as now, the property more of girls than of boys.' While it remains clear that today mixed groups of infants in Britain will play garbled versions of games they have been taught at school (after they get home and 'play out', as they say, in the street), it is very rare indeed to find the age range of eight to twelve playing together. And eight to twelve is the short age range during which the singing games flourish and are passed to another generation of children.

This period in a child's life has been described as the 'Flight of the sexes' and normally extends into the lower teens. School teachers will be well aware that during it boys will bend over backwards (sometimes literally) to avoid contact with girls. Though boys may enjoy the romp of a good country dance, they object to girl partners, for this involves physical contact: and even in a classroom when a ring has to be formed, the boys stand together and try to avoid joining hands with the girls. It is true that I once came across a group of junior boys and girls in Leyland, Lancashire, dancing a superb action game to 'Green grow the rushes-O', but as I was making a tape recording it is likely that the boys simply wanted to be in on the act. So one way or another, we simply have to suspend judgment about boys and girls playing singing games together in the street a century ago, and to view with deep suspicion the frequent references in the dictionary to equal numbers of boys and girls facing each other to sing a dialogue.

In the Preface to the first volume Lady Gomme states: 'Unless we have a scientific arrangement of the enormously scattered material and a close comparison of the details of each item of folk-lore, it is next to impossible to expect that the full truth which lies hidden in these remnants of the past may be revealed.' The memoir which concludes Volume II is entirely concerned with the theme of tracing children's games back to mysterious tribal instincts, tribal conflicts and customs and superstitions. I suspect that the boy-and-girl descriptions of how the games were played is vital to the argument of trying to trace every word and action to primitive man. Of course many of the games, both then and now, contain fascinating fragments of history which antiquarians painstakingly sort out (and none more successfully than Iona and the late Peter Opie); but to extend this backwards to remote and often sinister tribal conflict seems to me to be dangerous because it colours one's attitude in collecting games.

These reservations apart, the Gomme Dictionary remains an outstanding work by any standards and gives us a unique link with the past in the world of children's games. But what seems to be happening to the tradition now? Games without singing or dialogue, most of which are associated with boys, though by no means exclusively, seem relatively unaffected by the passage of time. Ball games (such as King of the ring), Conkers, Tiggy (in its various forms), Marbles (I once met a girl champion marble player of twelve staggering round with a sack of over six hundred marbles she had won), together with other seasonal games (such as Tops and Whips), continue to flourish with varying degrees of popularity more or less everywhere. It is in the field of the singing games that major changes appear to be taking place. These are the games normally associated with girls, though again not exclusively so, or with a sprinkling of infant boys. However, I came across a junior school for boys in Kenya which had a very lively singing game tradition, and some of these games were quite frightening to watch. Two lines advanced and retired as they threatened each other to do battle. Here, indeed, was a truly primitive tribal ritual. One game in particular had nothing of the humour and fun contained in the British 'battle game' of 'We are the Roman Soldiers'.

I should explain that I have never collected games through correspondents. The first games I collected were recorded on tape recorders in the early 1950s. I wanted a sound track to go with colour slides of children playing in Portugal – where the singing game tradition was outstanding – and it was only later on that I found that there was plenty going on round me in England. Parents said that I was forty years too late, but I soon found out how wrong they were. I collected and recorded for ten years in Cumbria, then in Lancashire, and to a lesser extent in Yorkshire, with a few isolated recordings from different parts of the country. I used to make expeditions to Scotland from Cumbria, and once only spent a holiday collecting in Ireland. On the other hand, I have a very considerable amount of material recorded, again on holiday, from Madeira and the Azores, in addition to mainland Portugal; from Italy, both north and central, as well as the island of Sardinia; and from the Maltese Island of Gozo. If my collection from the British Isles is strictly limited, there is an abundance of material to compare it with from Europe, together with a good selection from Kenya, collected during a nine-month stint in East Africa.

In this Introduction I am mainly concerned with these singing games. I divide them up as follows: (1) games in which a ballad is sung and acted out, usually with distinct characters taking solo parts; (2) games in which someone is chosen from a ring or from an opposite line, usually to invite them to marry (or 'choose the one you love the best'); (3) games which have action imitations in them; (4) dance routines with actions such as hand clapping and high kicks; these may involve a dialogue between two sides, or soloists, or there may be choruses. This grouping may not be entirely satisfactory, but it will be helpful in making some assessment of the fate of many games. Indeed, it would have been useful if Lady Gomme had divided the singing games from the rest and adopted some sort of similar classification. There is, incidentally, no fundamental difference between ring games and those played in lines: in fact it seems that there is a tendency for ring games to 'deteriorate' – if that is the right word – into line games against a wall.

Now I have already suggested that some of the games in the Gomme Dictionary have a remarkable popularity in recent times. 'Three Dukes' and its variants has been mentioned. This game, far from following the normal pattern of gradual loss of words and overall contraction, has experienced expansion: a sure sign that it is increasing in popularity and in a very healthy state. I put its popularity down to: (a) the ever-popular theme of choosing someone to marry; (b) the opportunities it offers for the players mildly to insult each other within the strict limits of the verses; and (c) the fact that it involves many such actions as flicking up of skirts or kicking up heels. All kinds of actions may be introduced, but I particularly like the dialogue that runs:

> We've come to marry one of you (Will you come?)
> Why won't your marry one of us?
> Because you're stiff as a poker
> We can bend as well as you . . .

All delightfully inconsequential.

I have found that all the countries in which I have recorded have a version of 'Oranges and lemons'. Normally in England this game is organized by adults at parties for small children, but I once recorded it in a street at Workington in the north-west, and on that occasion boys were involved with girls. Italy has a version with the same actions, with a choice of oranges or lemons leading to a tug of war; but both words and melody are quite different, and it is called 'Siamo sette cavalieri'. Portugal too has its own game with chopper and tug of war, but this time the game is called 'O Senhor Barqueiro'. Whatever its title, in both Italy and Portugal the game belongs very much to the street tradition.

The very old game of 'Cock Robin [or Old Roger] is dead and lays in his grave' is a good example of a ballad game which remains popular. This is a game with a long and distinguished pedigree, and has a good mixture of action and repose – always important – as well as special characters: Old Roger, The Apple tree and the old woman picking up the apples. Other games of similar antiquity have become very rare, or even extinct. I have only once, for example, come across the game 'I've come to see your Janie Jones', and that was in Nelson, Lancashire. The verses take the ailing Janie through growing pale and ill, and finally to death and burial. It is interesting to observe that in all the countries where I have made a collection of games, there is always one game which involves death. Of course there are others which go right through life and death to resurrection – games like 'I am a little Dutch girl', or one I encountered in Gozo in which Maltese children end up as devils; but in these examples death is not the central issue.

Another rarity, which I came across in Dearham, Cumberland, was 'There were three jolly Sailor boys who lately came ashore'. This game was played in the school playground under the eye of the headmaster, and on this occasion, under some pressure, the three sailors were boys who each had to kiss the girl of their choice at the end. The bell for end of playtime saved the third sailor.

From time to time games with a fine pedigree turn up in places hundreds of miles apart. I found in the 1960s some small children singing a dance in a ring on a new estate in Workington. It started like this, with a distinctive tune:

Mary Malloga she lifted her leg she lifted her
                                    leg so high-yow
All of a sudden a great surprise came floating
                                    through the air-o
Yaw-saw Magamozoni [× 3] Early in the morning.

I have only heard of one other record of this quaint little game. Iona Opie sent me a longer but equally zany version from Glasgow that she had discovered ten years earlier. How can one explain the fact that this game has survived in isolation so far apart?

If, as is usually admitted, there has been a tremendous decline in the number of traditional singing games within the British Isles, has anything entered the tradition to replace them? I found, again in the 1960s and 70s, that girls had a tremendous repertoire of games, but there was a marked shift to newcomers involving a snappy dance routine, with hand clapping and other actions, derived from a variety of sources. Of these newer games, the 'Bow-legged chicken' is typical. It contains, in common with many others, a simple dance routine and plenty of fun. The long and often serious Gomme ballads, with many verses to remember, are abandoned: the emphasis is on a simple verse with a catchy tune which provides the lilt for the steps and actions. Such games are woven from any material to hand, from current pop songs to musicals of ten, twenty or forty years ago. Added to this there is often a sprinkling of naughty lines of the kind collected by the Opies under the heading of 'Parody and Impropriety' in their masterly book, *The Lore and Language of School Children.*

A good example from the modern period, which I have found to be fairly widespread (at least in Southern Ireland and Yorkshire), is 'She sat 'neath the Lilaac and played her guitar . . .'. This highly cynical ballad ends up with the suitor sitting on the tomb of his wife, and then . . .

He sat on the tombstone and laughed 'til he cried
The tombstone fell on him and squish-squash he died
She went up to heaven and flip-flop she flied
He went down to Hell and frizzled and fried.

I believe this was once popular at Scout jamborees, but I do not have the original.

Among an abundance of modern games, 'Sunnyside' deserves pride of place. Here is one of several different versions:

> Keep the sunnyside up, up
> And the other side too, too
> See the soldiers marching along
> See the drummers drumming along
> See Tom Fenny sucking his thumb
> See Sabrina waggle her bum
> So keep the Sunnyside up, up [× 3] . . . O-lay.

Sunnyside up is the title of a 20th Century-Fox film which came out in 1929 and also of its theme tune. The film and the song were both poor, but the tune stayed alive in dance halls during the 1930s because it was used for the 'Palais Glide'. I have no idea when it first became a popular children's game, but the Opies tell me that their first record of it dates from 1961 and that in the next five to ten years it spread all over the British Isles. The children's words vary enormously, but are a vast improvement on the original, and many kinds of famous characters may be incorporated.

I find this incubation period fascinating. Pop characters of yesterday suddenly take on a new lease of life and become, for the time being, immortalized in a singing game. We cannot tell what song will achieve this distinction: I can remember no song that won in its day a popularity comparable to that of 'The Ballad of Davy Crockett' in the 1950s. Davy Crockett souvenirs, and especially hats, became the rage among British children, and in some cities cats vanished from the streets to supply the need. Yet it never became a singing game.

Nevertheless, one thing is certain: a game will flourish and spread only if it is fun *now*. Children have no sense of preserving a game because it is of historical interest. It is therefore surprising that, with such a very short handing on overlap period of about five years from one generation to another, so many have lasted for so long.

But now I have to draw this Introduction to a rather sombre conclusion. For some twenty years I remained convinced that children sang and danced as much as they ever did, and possibly more; that the changing content of their special tradition reflected a changing civilization without diminishing their repertoire. I was convinced that the singing game represented a living folk tradition at its best, uninhibited by becoming fossilized in 'authentic versions'. If I play recordings of a game to children from different parts of the country, they have no interest in the variation. Their comment is usually, 'they are doing it all wrong'. For them the only authentic version is the one they enact now.

And yet, in recent years I have to admit that there does seem to have been a steady decline in both the content and distribution of such games. I would willingly have put this down to my lack of contact with other parts of the country until the following events persuaded me otherwise. Twenty years ago I used to stay with a fisherman and his family in a village in the Algarve of southern Portugal. Every night as the sun went down, children from the neighbouring streets came to the flat, cobbled space in front of our cottage and sang and danced for an hour. I collected sufficient singing games to fill a book on its own. Today, following the building of several luxury hotels and the tourist explosion, the fleet of fishing boats has vanished and the vast majority of cottages have been bought for holiday apartments. The narrow streets are clogged with parked cars. I visited an old lady who lived next door to our cottage, and one evening she collected a dozen or more children to come and do their singing games in the street. They did not know a single one. I asked a girl what they liked playing best, to which she replied: 'Raiding the hotel dustbins for empty lipstick holders.' In less than two decades an entire tradition had been wiped out.

Are we to experience a similar catastrophe in England? I don't think it will happen on such a scale but I do believe the process is going on around us. And that brings me to the most difficult judgment of all: if the singing game tradition is on the decline in the British Isles, what are the root causes? This must inevitably be a matter of impression and personal judgment. My own view is that several different factors have contributed. These include increased traffic on the roads and far fewer places to play, the weekend habit of going away, television removing the stimulant to 'play out', and more recently the addition of the video. There is also the pressure on both girls and boys to learn adult games rather than create their own. But there remains in my mind one single factor which impresses itself as being of even greater significance than all the suggestions above – it is the loss of the single sex playgrounds. Many child customs – such as the Easter Pace Egg Mummers' Play, long kept alive at Far Sawrey, near Windermere – vanished when local schools for children of all ages closed and older children were taken by bus to larger centres. Whatever the financial or educational criteria, the fact remains that the imposition of mixed sex schooling has dealt a terrible blow to traditional children's games. When I recorded the singing games of Workington during the 1960s there were two junior girls' schools and two for boys. And it was in the crowded playgrounds of these single sex schools that the tradition flourished. I am convinced that nothing in this century has done more to destroy our ancient and precious heritage of the singing game tradition than to force boys and girls to play together on the very limited area most junior schools possess.

Here is an interesting, if controversial, insight into the modern tendency to confuse equality of sexes with identity of sexes, the wider effects of which have done so much to alter – in my view, to damage – society as a whole.

Fr. Damian Webb O.S.B.   *April 1983*
St Benedict's Priory
Garforth, Leeds

Volume
1

A DICTIONARY

OF

BRITISH FOLK-LORE

EDITED BY

G. LAURENCE GOMME, Esq., F.S.A.
PRESIDENT OF THE FOLK-LORE SOCIETY, ETC.

PART I.

TRADITIONAL GAMES

BY THE SAME EDITOR.

---◆◆---

Small 4to.   In Specially Designed Cover.

ENGLISH SINGING GAMES.

A Collection of the best Traditional Children's Singing
Games, with their Traditional Music harmonised, and
Directions for Playing.   Each Game, Text and Music,
is written out and set within a Decorative Border by
WINIFRED SMITH, who has also designed Full-page
Illustrations to each Game, and Initials and Decora-
tive Border to the playing directions.

THE

TRADITIONAL GAMES

Of England, Scotland, and Ireland

WITH

TUNES, SINGING-RHYMES, AND METHODS OF PLAYING
ACCORDING TO THE VARIANTS EXTANT AND
RECORDED IN DIFFERENT PARTS
OF THE KINGDOM

COLLECTED AND ANNOTATED BY

ALICE BERTHA GOMME

VOL. I.

ACCROSHAY—NUTS IN MAY

LONDON
DAVID NUTT, 270–71 STRAND
1894

TO

MY HUSBAND

PREFACE

SOON after the formation of the Folk-lore Society in 1878 my husband planned, and has ever since been collecting for, the compilation of a dictionary of British Folk-lore. A great deal of the material has been put in form for publication, but at this stage the extent of the work presented an unexpected obstacle to its completion.

To print the whole in one alphabet would be more than could be accomplished except by the active co-operation of a willing band of workers, and then the time required for such an undertaking, together with the cost, almost seemed to debar the hope of ever completing arrangements for its publication. Nevertheless, unless we have a scientific arrangement of the enormously scattered material and a close comparison of the details of each item of folk-lore, it is next to impossible to expect that the full truth which lies hidden in these remnants of the past may be revealed.

During my preparation of a book of games for children it occurred to me that to separate the whole of the games from the general body of folk-lore and to make them a section of the proposed dictionary would be an advantageous step, as by arranging the larger groups of folk-lore in independent sections the possibility of publishing the contemplated dictionary again seemed to revive. Accordingly, the original plan has been so far modified that these volumes will form the first section of the dictionary, which, instead of being issued in one alphabet throughout, will now be issued in sections, each section being arranged alphabetically.

The games included in this collection bear the important qualification of being nearly all Children's Games : that is to say, they were either originally children's games since developed into games for adults, or they were the more serious avocations of adults, which have since become children's games only. In both cases the transition is due to traditional circumstances, and not to any formal arrangements. All invented games of skill are therefore excluded from this collection, but it includes both indoor and outdoor games, and those played by both girls and boys.

The bulk of the collection has been made by myself, greatly through the kindness of many correspondents, to whom I cannot be sufficiently grateful. In every case I have acknowledged my indebtedness, which, besides being an act of justice, is a guarantee of the genuineness of the collection. I have appended to this preface a list of the collectors, together with the counties to which the games belong; but I must particularly thank the Rev. W. Gregor, Mr. S. O. Addy, and Miss Fowler, who very generously placed collections at my disposal, which had been prepared before they knew of my project ; also Miss Burne, Miss L. E. Broadwood, and others, for kindly obtaining variants and tunes I should not otherwise have received. To the many versions now printed for the first time I have added either a complete transcript of, where necessary, or a reference to, where that was sufficient, printed versions of games to be found in the well-known collections of Halliwell and Chambers, the publications of the Folk-lore and Dialect Societies, Jamieson's, Nares', and Halliwell's Dictionaries, and other printed sources of information. When quoting from a printed authority, I have as far as possible given the exact words, and have always given the reference. I had hoped to have covered in my collection the whole field of games as played by children in the United Kingdom, but it will be seen that many counties in each country are still unrepresented; and I shall be greatly indebted for any games from other places, which would help to make this collection more complete. The tunes of the games have been taken down, as sung by the children, either by myself or correspondents (except where otherwise stated), and are unaltered.

The games consist of two main divisions, which may be called descriptive, and singing or choral. The descriptive games are arranged so as to give the most perfect type, and, where they occur, variable types in succession, followed, where possible, by any suggestions I have to make as to the possible origin of the game. The singing games are arranged so as to give, first, the tunes; secondly, the different versions of the game-rhymes; thirdly, the method of playing; fourthly, an analysis of the game-rhymes on a plan arranged by my husband, and which is an entirely novel feature in discussing the history of games; fifthly, a discussion of the results of the analysis of the rhymes so far as the different versions allow; and sixthly, an attempt to deduce from the evidence thus collected suggestions as to the probable origin of the game, together with such references to early authorities and other facts bearing upon the subject as help to elucidate the views expressed. Where the method of playing the game is involved, or where there are several changes in the forms, diagrams or illustrations, which have been drawn by Mr. J. P. Emslie, are inserted in order to assist the reader to understand the different actions, and in one or two instances I have been able to give a fac-simile reproduction of representations of the games from early MSS. in the Bodleian and British Museum Libraries.

Although none of the versions of the games now collected together are in their original form, but are more or less fragmentary, it cannot, I think, fail to be noticed how extremely interesting these games are, not only from the point of view of the means of amusement (and under this head there can be no question of their interest), but as a means of obtaining an insight into many of the customs and beliefs of our ancestors. Children do not invent, but they imitate or mimic very largely, and in many of these games we have, there is little doubt, unconscious folk-dramas of events and customs which were at one time being enacted as a part of the serious concerns of life before the eyes of children many generations ago. As to the many points of interest under this and other heads there is no occasion to dwell at length here, because the second volume will contain an appendix giving a complete analysis of the incidents mentioned in the games, and an attempt to tell the story of their origin and development, together with a comparison with the games of children of foreign countries.

The intense pleasure which the collection of these games has given me has been considerably enhanced by the many expressions of the same kind of pleasure from correspondents who have helped me, it not being an infrequent case for me to be thanked for reviving some of the keenest pleasures experienced by the collector since childhood; and I cannot help thinking that, if these traditional games have the power of thus imparting pleasure after the lapse of many years, they must contain the power of giving an equal pleasure to those who may now learn them for the first time.

ALICE BERTHA GOMME.

BARNES COMMON, S.W.,
    Jan. 1894.

LIST OF AUTHORITIES

ENGLAND.

Halliwell's *Nursery Rhymes.*
Halliwell's *Dictionary*, ed. 1889.
Holloway's *Dictionary*, ed. 1838.
Strutt's *Sports and Pastimes*, ed. 1831.
Brand's *Popular Antiquities*, ed. 1875.
Nares' *Glossary*, ed. 1872.

Grose's *Dictionary*, 1823.
Notes and Queries.
Reliquary.
English Dialect Society Publications.
Folk-lore Society Publications, 1878–1892.

BEDFORDSHIRE—
    Luton . . . . . Mrs. Ashdown.
    Roxton . . . . . Miss Lumley.
BERKSHIRE . . . . Lowsley's *Glossary.*
    Enborne . . . Miss Kimber.
    Fernham, Longcot . . Miss I. Barclay.
    Newbury . . . Mrs. S. Batson, Miss Kimber.
    Sulhampstead . . Miss Thoyts (*Antiquary*, vol. xxvii.)
CAMBRIDGESHIRE—
    Cambridge . . . . Mrs. Haddon.
CHESHIRE . . . . { Darlington's, Holland's, Leigh's, and Wilbraham's *Glossaries.*
    Congleton . . . Miss A. E. Twemlow.
CORNWALL . . . . *Folk-lore Journal*, v., Courtney's *Glossary.*
    Penzance . . . Miss Courtney, Mrs. Mabbott.
CUMBERLAND . . . Dickinson's *Glossary.*
DERBYSHIRE . . . { *Folk-lore Journal*, vol. i., Mrs. Harley, Mr. S. O. Addy.
    Dronfield, Eckington, Egan . Mr. S. O. Addy.
DEVONSHIRE . . . Halliwell's *Dictionary.*
DORSETSHIRE . . . Barnes' *Glossary, Folk-lore Journal*, vol. vii.
DURHAM . . . . Brockett's *North Country Words*, ed. 1846.
    Gainford . . . Miss Eddleston.
    South Shields . . Miss Blair.
ESSEX—
    Bocking . . . . *Folk-lore Record*, vol. iii. pt. 2.
    Colchester . . . Miss G. M. Francis.
GLOUCESTERSHIRE . . Holloway's *Dictionary, Midland Garner.*
    Shepscombe, Cheltenham . Miss Mendham.
    Forest of Dean . . Miss Matthews.
HAMPSHIRE . . . . Cope's *Glossary*, Miss Mendham.
    Bitterne . . . . Mrs. Byford.
    Liphook . . . Miss Fowler.

HAMPSHIRE—
    Hartley, Winchfield, Witney .   Mr. H. S. May.
    Southampton .   .   .   .   Mrs. W. R. Carse.
ISLE OF MAN   .   .   .   Mr. A. W. Moore.
ISLE OF WIGHT—
    Cowes .   .   .   .   Miss E. Smith.
KENT .   .   .   .   .   Pegge's *Alphabet of Kenticisms.*
    Bexley Heath   .   .   Miss Morris.
    Crockham Hill, Deptford   Miss Chase.
    Platt .   .   .   .   Miss Burne.
    Wrotham   .   .   .   Miss D. Kimball.
LANCASHIRE .   .   .   { Nodal and Milner's *Glossary*, Harland and Wilkinson's *Folk-lore*, ed. 1882, Mrs. Harley.
    Monton .   .   .   .   Miss Dendy.
LEICESTERSHIRE .   .   .   Evan's *Glossary.*
    Leicester   .   .   .   Miss Ellis.
LINCOLNSHIRE .   .   .   { Peacock's, Cole's, and Brogden's *Glossaries*, Rev. — Roberts.
    Anderby, Botterford, Brigg, Frodingham, Horncastle, North Kelsey, Stixwould, Winterton .   .   .   .   { Miss Peacock.
    East Kirkby .   .   .   Miss K. Maughan.
    Metheringham   .   .   Mr. C. C. Bell.
MIDDLESEX .   .   .   .   Miss Collyer.
    Hanwell   .   .   .   Mrs. G. L. Gomme.
    London .   .   .   .   { Miss Chase, Miss F. D. Richardson, Mr. G. L. Gomme, Mrs. G. L. Gomme, Mr. J. P. Emslie, Miss Dendy, Mr. J. T. Micklethwaite (*Archæological Journal*, vol. xlix.), *Strand Magazine*, vol. ii.
NORFOLK .   .   .   .   { Forby's *Vocabulary*, Spurden's *Vocabulary*, Mr. J. Doe.
    Sporle, Swaffham .   .   Miss Matthews.
NORTHAMPTONSHIRE .   .   { Baker's *Glossary*, *Northants Notes and Queries*, *Revue Celtique*, vol. iv., Rev. W. D. Sweeting.
    Maxey .   .   .   .   Rev. W. D. Sweeting.
NORTHUMBERLAND   .   .   Brockett's *Provincial Words*, ed. 1846.
    Hexham   .   .   .   Miss J. Barker.
NOTTINGHAMSHIRE   .   .   Miss Peacock.
    Long Eaton .   .   .   Miss Youngman.
    Nottingham .   .   .   Miss Winfield, Miss Peacock.
    Ordsall .   .   .   .   Miss Matthews.
OXFORDSHIRE   .   .   .   Aubrey's *Remains*, ed. 1880.
    Oxford .   .   .   .   Miss Fowler.
    Summertown .   .   .   *Midland Garner*, vol. ii.
SHROPSHIRE   .   .   .   Burne's *Shropshire Folk-lore.*
    Madeley, Middleton   .   Miss Burne.
    Tong .   .   .   .   Miss R. Harley.

SOMERSETSHIRE .	Elworthy's *Dialect, Somerset and Dorset Notes and Queries*, Holloway's *Dictionary*.
Bath	Miss Large.
STAFFORDSHIRE—	
Hanbury . . .	Miss E. Hollis.
Cheadle	Miss Burne.
Tean, North Staffordshire Potteries	Miss Keary, Miss Burne, Mrs. T. Lawton.
Wolstanton . . .	Miss Keary.
SUFFOLK	Moor's *Suffolk Words*, Forby's *Vocabulary*, Lady C. Gurdon's *Suffolk County Folk-lore*.
SURREY—	
Barnes	Mrs. G. L. Gomme.
Clapham . . .	Miss F. D. Richardson.
Hersham . . .	*Folk-lore Record*, vol. v.
Redhill	Miss G. Hope.
SUSSEX	Parish's *Dialect*, Holloway's *Dictionary*, Toone's *Dictionary*.
Hurstmonceux . .	Miss Chase.
Shipley, Horsham, West Grinstead	Miss R. H. Busk (*Notes and Queries*).
Ninfield . . .	Mr. C. Wise.
WARWICKSHIRE . . .	Northall's *Folk Rhymes, Notes and Queries*, *Northants Notes and Queries*, Mr. C. C. Bell.
WILTSHIRE—	
Marlborough, Manton, Ogbourne . . .	Mr. H. S. May.
WORCESTERSHIRE . .	Chamberlain's *Glossary*.
Upton-on-Severn . .	Lawson's *Glossary*.
YORKSHIRE	Atkinson's, Addy's, Easther's, Hunter's, Robinson's, Ross and Stead's *Glossaries*, Henderson's *Folk-lore*, ed. 1879.
Almondbury . . .	Easther's *Glossary*.
Epworth, Lossiemouth .	Mr. C. C. Bell.
Earls Heaton, Haydon, Holmfirth	Mr. H. Hardy.
Settle	Rev. W. S. Sykes.
Sharleston . . .	Miss Fowler, Rev. G. T. Royds.
Sheffield . . .	Mr. S. O. Addy, Miss Lucy Garnett.
Wakefield . . .	Miss Fowler.

SCOTLAND.

Chambers' *Popular Rhymes*, ed. 1870.
Mactaggart's *Gallovidian Encyclopædia*, ed. 1871.

Jamieson's *Etymological Dictionary*, ed. 1872–1889.
Folk-lore Society Publications.

ABERDEEN—
Pitsligo . . . . . Rev. W. Gregor.

BANFFSHIRE—
    Duthil, Keith, Strathspey   .   Rev. W. Gregor.
ELGIN—
    Fochabers   .   .   .   Rev. W. Gregor.
KIRKCUDBRIGHT—
    Auchencairn .   .   .   Prof. A. C. Haddon.
LANARKSHIRE—
    Biggar   .   .   .   Mr. Wm. Ballantyne.
    Lanark   .   .   .   Mr. W. G. Black.
NAIRN—
    Nairn   .   .   .   Rev. W. Gregor.

IRELAND.

Folk-lore Society Publications.   *Notes and Queries.*

ANTRIM AND DOWN .   .   Patterson's *Glossary.*
CLARE—
    Kilkee   .   .   .   G. H. Kinahan (*Folk-lore Journal,* vol. ii.)
CORK—
    Cork   .   .   .   Mrs. B. B. Green, Miss Keane.
DOWN—
    Ballynascaw .   .   .   Miss C. N. Patterson.
    Belfast .   .   .   Mr. W. H. Patterson.
    Holywood   .   .   Miss C. N. Patterson.
DUBLIN—
    Dublin .   .   .   Mrs. Lincoln.
LOUTH—
    Annaverna, Ravendale .   .   Miss R. Stephen.
QUEEN'S COUNTY—
    Portarlington .   .   .   G. H. Kinahan (*Folk-lore Journal,* vol. ii.)
WATERFORD—
    Lismore .   .   .   Miss Keane.

WALES.

Byegones.   Folk-lore Society Publications.

CARMARTHENSHIRE—
    Beddgelert   .   .   .   Mrs. Williams.

LIST OF GAMES

ERRATA.

On page 15, line 12, *for* "Eggatt" *read* "Hats in Holes."

On pp. 24, 49, 64, 112, *for* "*Folk-lore Journal*, vol. vi." *read* "vol. vii."

On page 62, last line, *insert* "vol. xix." *after* "*Journ. Anthrop. Inst.*"

On page 66, line 4, *delete* "Move All."

On page 224, fig. 3 of "Hopscotch" should be reversed.

On page 332, diagram of "London" omitted.

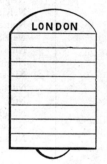

LONDON

CHILDREN'S GAMES.

Accroshay

A cap or small article is placed on the back of a stooping boy by other boys as each in turn jumps over him. The first as he jumps says "Accroshay," the second "Ashotay," the third "Assheflay," and the last "Lament, lament, Leleeman's (or Leleena's) war." The boy who in jumping knocks off either of the things has to take the place of the stooper.—Cornwall (*Folk-lore Journal*, v. 58).

See "Leap-frog."

All-hid

"A meere children's pastime" (*A Curtaine Lecture*, 1637, p. 206). This is no doubt the game of "Hide and Seek," though Cotgrave apparently makes it synonymous with "Hoodman Blind." See Halliwell's *Dictionary*. It is alluded to in Dekker's *Satiromastix*, "Our unhansomed-fac'd Poet does play at Bo-peepes with your Grace, and cryes All-hidde, as boyes doe." Tourneur, *Rev. Trag.*, III., v. 82, "A lady can at such Al-hid beguile a wiser man," is quoted in Murray's *Dictionary* as the first reference.

All a Row

> All a row, a bendy bow,
> Shoot at a pigeon and kill a crow ;
> Shoot at another and kill his brother ;
> Shoot again and kill a wren,
> And that 'll do for gentlemen.
> —Northall's *English Folk Rhymes*, p. 386.

This is a marching game for very little children, who follow each other in a row.

(*b*) Halliwell gives the first two lines only (*Nursery Rhymes*, No. dxv., p. 101), and there is apparently no other record of

this game. It is probably ancient, and formerly of some significance. It refers to days of bows and arrows, and the
allusion to the killing of the wren may have reference to the
Manx and Irish custom of hunting that bird.

All in the Well

A juvenile game in Newcastle and the neighbourhood. A
circle is made, about eight inches in diameter, termed the well,
in the centre of which is placed a wooden peg four inches long,
with a button balanced on the top. Those desirous of playing
give buttons, marbles, or anything else, according to agreement,
for the privilege of throwing a short stick, with which they are
furnished, at the peg. Should the button fly out of the ring,
the player is entitled to double the stipulated value of what
he gives for the stick. The game is also practised at the Newcastle Races and other places of amusement in the North with
three pegs, which are put into three circular holes made in the
ground about two feet apart, and forming a triangle. In this
case each hole contains a peg about nine inches long, upon
which are deposited either a small knife or some copper. The
person playing gives so much for each stick, and gets all the
articles that are thrown off so as to fall on the outside of the
holes.—Northumberland (Brockett's *North Country Glossary*).

All the Birds in the Air

A Suffolk game, not described (Moor's *Suffolk Glossary*).
Jamieson also gives it without description. Compare the rhyme
in the game " Fool, fool, come to School," "Little Dog, I call you."

All the Boys in our Town

I.   All the boys in our town
      Shall lead a happy life,
      Except 'tis ——, and he wants a wife.
      A wife he shall have, and a-courting he shall go,
      Along with ——, because he loves her so.
      He huddles her, he cuddles her,
      He sits her on his knee;
      He says, My dear, do you love me?
      I love you, and you love me,

And we shall be as happy
As a bird upon a tree.

The wife makes the pudding,
And she makes it nice and soft—
In comes the husband and cuts a slice off.
Tas-el-um, Tos-el-um, don't say Nay,
For next Monday morning shall be our wedding day;
The wife in the carriage,
The husband in the cart.

—Hampshire (from friend of Miss Mendham).

II.   All the boys in our town
      Leads a happy life,
      Excepting [Charley Allen],
      And he wants a wife;
      And a-courting he shall go
      Along with [girl's name],
      Because he loves her so.

      He kisses her, he cuddles her,
      He sets her on his knee,
      And says, My dearest darling,
      Do you love me?
      I love you and you love me;
      We'll both be as happy
      As birds on the tree.

      Alice made a pudding,
      She made it nice and sweet,
      Up came Charley, cut a slice off—
      A slice, a slice, we don't say No;
      The next Monday morning the wedding goes
            (or "is our wedding day").
      I've got knives and forks,
      I've got plates and dishes,
      I've got a nice young man,
      He breaks his heart with kisses.

      If poor Alice was to die,
      Wouldn't poor Charley, he *would* cry.

He would follow to the grave
With black buttons and black crape,
And a guinea for the church,
And the bell shall ring.

Up came the doctor, up came the cat,
Up came the devil with a white straw hat.
Down went the doctor, down went the cat,
Down went the devil with a white straw hat.*

—Deptford (Miss Chase).

III. Up the heathery mountains and down the rushy glen
We dare not go a-hunting for Connor and his men ;
They are all lusty bachelors but one I know,
And that's [Tom Mulligan], the flower of the flock ;
He is the flower of the flock, he is the keeper of the glen,
He courted [Kate O'Neill] before he was a man ;
He huggled her, he guggled her, he took her on his knee,
Saying, My bonnie [Kate O'Neill], won't you marry me ?

So —— made a pudding so nice and so sweet,
Saying, Taste, love, taste, and don't say no,
For next Sunday morning to church we will go.

With rings on our fingers and bells on our toes,
And a little baby in her arms, and that's the way she goes.
And here's a clap, and here's a clap, for Mrs. ——'s
daughter.

—Belfast (W. H. Patterson).

IV. Up the plain and down the plain,
As stippy [slippery] as a glass,
We will go to Mrs. ——
To find a pretty lass.

[Annie] with her rosy cheeks,
Catch her if you can,
And if you cannot catch her
I'll tell you who's the man.

[Annie] made a pudding,
She made it very sweet ;

* Miss Chase says, " I think the order of verses is right ; the children hesitated
a little."

> She daren't stick a knife in
> Till George came home at neet [night].

> Taste [George], taste, and don't say Nay!
> Perhaps to-morrow morning'll be our wedding day.
> [The bells shall ring, and we shall sing,
> And all clap hands together.] *
>   —Earls Heaton (Herbert Hardy).

(*b*) A full description of this game could not be obtained in each case. The Earls Heaton game is played by forming a ring, one child standing in the centre. After the first verse is sung, a child from the ring goes to the one in the centre. Then the rest of the verses are sung. The action to suit the words of the verses does not seem to have been kept up. In the Hampshire version, after the line "As a bird upon a tree," the two children named pair off like sweethearts while the rest of the verse is being sung.

(*c*) The analysis of the game rhymes is as follows :—

	Hants.	Deptford (Kent).	Belfast.	Earls Heaton (Yorks.).
1.	Village life.	Village life.	Hunting life.	Roving life.
2.	All the boys happy.	All the boys happy.	All lusty bachelors.	—
3.	Except [ ], who wants a wife.	Except [ ], who wants a wife.	Except [ ], who courts [ ].	—
4.	He shall court [ ].	He shall court [ ].	He courted [ ].	Seeks for a bride.
5.	Huddles and cuddles, and sits on his knee.	Kisses and cuddles, and sits on his knee.	Huggled and guggled, and took on his knee.	—
6.	—	—	—	Catch the bride.
7.	Mutual expressions of love.	Mutual expressions of love.	—	—
8.	—	—	Asking to marry.	
9.	Wife makes a pudding.	Girl makes a pudding.	Girl makes a pudding.	Girl makes a pudding.
10.	Husband cuts a slice.	Boy cuts a slice.	Asks boy to taste.	Asks boy to taste.
11.	Fixing of wedding day.	Fixing of wedding day.	Fixing of wedding day.	Fixing of wedding day.
12.	Wife in carriage, husband in cart.	Wife with domestic utensils.	Bride with rings on fingers and bells on toes.	—
13.	—	Grief if wife should die.	—	—
14.	—	—	Bride with a baby.	—
15.	—	Doctor, cat, and devil.	—	—
16.	—	—	Applause for the bride.	Applause for the bride.

* Mr. Hardy says, "This was sung to me by a girl at Earls Heaton or Soothill Nether. Another version commences with the last verse, continues with the first, and concludes with the second. The last two lines inserted here belong to that version."

It appears by the analysis that all the incidents of the Hants version of this game occur in one or other of the versions, and these incidents therefore may probably be typical of the game.   This view would exclude the important incidents of bride capture in the Earls Heaton version; the bride having a baby in the Belfast version, and the two minor incidents in the Deptford version (Nos. 13 and 15 in the analysis), which are obviously supplemental.   Chambers, in his *Popular Rhymes of Scotland*, pp. 119, 137, gives two versions of a courtship dance which are not unlike the words of this game, though they do not contain the principal incidents.   Northall, in his *English Folk Rhymes*, p. 363, has some verses of a similar import, but not those of the game.   W. Allingham seems to have used this rhyme as the commencement of one of his ballads, " Up the airy mountain."

(*d*) The game is clearly a marriage game.   It introduces two important details in the betrothal ceremony, inasmuch as the " huddling and cuddling " is typical of the rude customs at marriage ceremonies once prevalent in Yorkshire, the northern counties, and Wales, while the making of the pudding by the bride and the subsequent eating together, are clearly analogies to the bridal-cake ceremony.   In Wales, the custom known as " bundling " allowed the betrothing parties to go to bed in their clothes (Brand, ii. 98).   In Yorkshire, the bridal cake was always made by the bride. The rudeness of the dialogue seems to be remarkably noticeable in this game.

See " Mary mixed a Pudding up," " Oliver, Oliver, follow the King."

All the Fishes in the Sea

A Suffolk game, not described.—Moor's *Suffolk Glossary*. See " Fool, fool, come to School," " Little Dog, I call you."

All the Soldiers in the Town

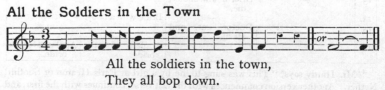

All the soldiers in the town,
They all bop down.
—Sporle, Norfolk (Miss Matthews).

The children form into a ring and sing the above words. They "bop down" at the close of the verse. To "bop" means in the Suffolk dialect "to stoop or bow the head."—Moor.

Allicomgreenzie

A little amusing game played by young girls at country schools. The same as "Drop Handkerchief," except that the penalty for not following exactly the course of the child pursued is to "stand in the circle, face out, all the game afterwards; if she succeed in catching the one, the one caught must so stand, and the other take up the cap and go round as before" (Mactaggart's *Gallovidian Encyclopedia*). No explanation is given of the name of this game.

See "Drop Handkerchief."

Alligoshee

I.   Betsy Blue came all in black,
     Silver buttons down her back.
     Every button cost a crown,
     Every lady turn around.
     Alligoshi, alligoshee,
     Turn the bridle over my knee.
               —Middleton (Burne's *Shropshire Folk-lore*, p. 523).

II. Barbara, Barbara, dressed in black,
     Silver buttons all up your back.
     Allee-go-shee, allee-go-shee,
     Turn the bridle over me.
               —Shepscombe, Gloucestershire (Miss Mendham).

III. All-i-go-shee, alligoshee,
     Turn the bridle over my knee.
     My little man is gone to sea,
     When he comes back he'll marry me.
               —Warwickshire (Northall's *Folk Rhymes*, p. 394).

IV. Darby's son was dressed in black,
     With silver buttons down his back.
     Knee by knee, and foot by foot,
     Turn about lady under the bush.
               —Hersham, Surrey (*Folk-lore Record*, v. 87).

V.   Darby and Joan were dressed in black,
Sword and buckle behind their back.
Foot for foot, and knee for knee,
Turn about Darby's company.
                    —Halliwell's *Nursery Rhymes*, p. 121.

(*b*) The children form pairs, one pair following the other, with their arms linked behind. While the first four lines are repeated by all, they skip forward, and then skip back again. At the end of the last line they turn themselves about without loosing hands.

(*c*) Miss Burne includes this among obscure and archaic games, and Halliwell-Phillips mentions it as a marching game. The three first versions have something of the nature of an incantation, while the fourth and fifth versions may probably belong to another game altogether. It is not clear from the great variation in the verses to which class the game belongs.

Almonds and Reasons

An old English game undescribed.—*Useful Transactions in Philosophy*, 1709, p. 43.

Angel and Devil

One child is called the "Angel," another child the "Devil," and a third child the "Minder." The children are given the names of colours by the Minder. Then the Angel comes over and knocks, when the following dialogue takes place.

Minder: "Who's there?"

Answer: "Angel."

Minder: "What do you want?"

Angel: "Ribbons."

Minder: "What colour?"

Angel: "Red."

Minder retorts, if no child is so named, "Go and learn your A B C." If the guess is right the child is led away. The Devil then knocks, and the dialogue and action are repeated.—Deptford, Kent (Miss Chase).

See "Fool, fool, come to School."

Auntieloomie

The children join hands, and dance in a circle, "with a front step, a back step, and a side step, round an invisible May-pole," singing—

> Can you dance the Auntieloomie?
> Yes, I can; yes, I can.

Then follows kissing.—Brigg, Lincolnshire (Miss Peacock).

Babbity Bowster

—Biggar (Wm. Ballantyne).

> Wha learned you to dance,
>   You to dance, you to dance?
> Wha learned you to dance
>   Babbity Bowster brawly?
>
> My minnie learned me to dance,
>   Me to dance, me to dance;
> My minnie learned me to dance
>   Babbity Bowster brawly.
>
> Wha ga'e you the keys to keep,
>   Keys to keep, keys to keep?
> Wha ga'e you the keys to keep,
>   Babbity Bowster brawly?
>
> My minnie ga'e me the keys to keep,
>   Keys to keep, keys to keep;
> My minnie ga'e me the keys to keep,
>   Babbity Bowster brawly.
>
> One, twa, three, B, ba, Babbity,
>   Babbity Bowster neatly;
> Kneel down, kiss the ground,
>   An' kiss your bonnie lassie [or laddie].

—Biggar (W. H. Ballantyne).

(*b*) Mr. Ballantyne describes the dance as taking place at the end of a country ball. The lads all sat on one side and the girls on the other. It began with a boy taking a handkerchief and dancing before the girls, singing the first verse (fig. 1). Selecting one of the girls, he threw the handkerchief into her lap, or put it round her neck, holding both ends himself. Some spread the handkerchief on the floor at the feet of the girl. The object in either case was to secure a kiss, which, however, was not given without a struggle, the girls cheering their companion at every unsuccessful attempt which the boy

Fig 1   Fig 2

Fig 3   Fig 4

made (fig. 2). A girl then took the handkerchief, singing the next verse (fig. 3), and having thrown the handkerchief to one of the boys, she went off to her own side among the girls, and was pursued by the chosen boy (fig. 4). When all were thus paired, they formed into line, facing each other, and danced somewhat like the country dance of Sir Roger.

(*c*) Chambers' *Popular Rhymes*, p. 36, gives a slightly different version of the verses, and says they were sung by children at their sports in Glasgow. Mactaggart alludes to this game as "'Bumpkin Brawly,' an old dance, the dance which always ends balls; the same with the 'Cushion' almost."

> Wha learned you to dance,
> You to dance, you to dance,
> Wha learned you to dance
> A country bumpkin brawly?
>
> My mither learned me when I was young,
> When I was young, when I was young,
> My mither learned me when I was young,
> The country bumpkin brawly."

The tune of this song is always played to the dance, says Mactaggart, but he does not record the tune. *To bab*, in Lowland Scottish, is defined by Jamieson to mean "to play backward and forward loosely; to dance." Hence he adds, "Bab at the bowster, or Bab wi' the bowster, a very old Scottish dance, now almost out of use; formerly the last dance at weddings and merry-makings." Mr. Ballantyne says that a bolster or pillow was at one time always used. One correspondent of *N. and Q.*, ii. 518, says it is now (1850) danced with a handkerchief instead of a cushion as formerly, and no words are used, but later correspondents contradict this. See also *N. and Q.*, iii. 282.

(*d*) Two important suggestions occur as to this game. First, that the dance was originally the indication at a marriage ceremony for the bride and bridegroom to retire with "the bowster" to the nuptial couch. Secondly, that it has degenerated in Southern Britain to the ordinary "Drop Handkerchief" games of kiss in the ring. The preservation of this "Bab at the Bowster" example gives the clue both to the origin of the present game in an obsolete marriage custom, and to the descent of the game to its latest form. See "Cushion Dance."

Bad

A rude kind of "Cricket," played with a bat and a ball, usually with wall toppings for wickets. "Bad" seems to be the pronunciation or variation of "Bat." Halliwell says it was a rude game, formerly common in Yorkshire, and probably resembling the game of "Cat." There is such a game played now, but it is called "Pig."—Easther's *Almondbury Glossary*.

Baddin

The game of " Hockey " in Cheshire.—Holland's *Glossary*.

Badger the Bear

A rough game, sometimes seen in the country. The boy who personates the Bear performs his part on his hands and knees, and is prevented from getting away by a string. It is the part of another boy, his Keeper, to defend him from the attacks of the others.—Halliwell's *Dictionary*.

This is a boys' game, and is called "Buffet the Bear." It may be taken part in by any number. One boy—the Bear—goes down on all fours, and lowers his head towards his breast as much as possible. Into his hand is placed one end of a piece of cord, and another boy, called the Keeper, takes hold of the other end in one hand, while he has in the other his cap. The other boys stand round, some with their caps in hand, and others with their neckties or pocket-handkerchiefs, and on a given signal they rush on the Bear and pelt him, trying specially to buffet him about the ears and face, whilst the Keeper does his best to protect his charge. If he happens to strike a boy, that boy becomes the Bear, and the former Bear becomes the Keeper, and so on the game goes.—Keith, Banff-shire (Rev. W. Gregor).

I saw this game played on Barnes Green, Surrey, on 25th August 1892. The boys, instead of using their hats, had pieces of leather tied to a string, with which they struck the Bear on the back. They could only begin when the Keeper cried, "My Bear is free." If they struck at any other time, the striker became the Bear. It is called "Baste the Bear."—A. B. Gomme.

Chambers (*Popular Rhymes*, p. 128) describes this game under the title of "The Craw." It was played precisely in the same way as the Barnes game. The boy who holds the end of the long strap has also a hard twisted handkerchief, called the *cout;* with this cout he defends the Craw against the attacks of the other boys, who also have similar couts. Before beginning, the Guard of the Craw must call out—

Ane, twa, three, my Craw's free.

The first one he strikes becomes the Craw. When the Guard wants a respite, he calls out—

> Ane, twa, three, my Craw's no free.

(*b*) Jamieson defines "Badger-reeshil" as a severe blow; borrowed, it is supposed, from the hunting of the badger, or from the old game of "Beating the Badger."

> Then but he ran wi' hasty breishell,
> And laid on Hab a badger-reishill. —*MS. Poem.*

Mr. Emslie says he knows it under the name of "Baste the Bear" in London, and Patterson (*Antrim and Down Glossary*) mentions a game similarly named. It is played at Marlborough under the name of "Tom Tuff."—H. S. May.

See "Doncaster Cherries."

Bag o' Malt

> A bag o' malt, a bag o' salt,
> Ten tens a hundred.
> —Northall's *English Folk Rhymes*, p. 394.

Two children stand back to back, linked near the armpits, and weigh each other as they repeat these lines.

See "Weigh the Butter."

Ball

> I. Stottie ba', hinnie ba, tell to me
>   How mony bairns am I to hae?
>   Ane to live, and ane to dee,
>   And ane to sit on the nurse's knee!
>   —Chambers' *Pop. Rhymes of Scotland*, p. 115.
>
> II. Toss-a-ball, toss-a-ball, tell me true,
>   How many years I've got to go through!
>   —Burne's *Shropshire Folk-lore*, p. 530.

(*b*) Children throw a ball in the air, repeating the rhyme, and divine the length of their lives by the number of times they can catch it again. In some places this game is played with a cowslip ball, thence called a "tissy-ball."

(*c*) I have heard other rhymes added to this, to determine whether the players shall marry or not, the future husband's calling, dress to be worn, method of going to church, &c. (A. B.

Gomme). Strutt describes a handball game played during the Easter holidays for Tansy cakes (*Sports*, p. 94). Halliwell gives rhymes for ball divination (*Popular Rhymes*, p. 298) to determine the number of years before marriage will arrive. Miss Baker (*Northamptonshire Glossary*) says, "The May garland is suspended by ropes from the school-house to an opposite tree, and the Mayers amuse themselves by throwing balls over it. A native of Fotheringay, Mr. C. W. Peach," says Miss Baker, "has supplied me with the reminiscences of his own youth. He says the May garland was hung in the centre of the street, on a rope stretched from house to house. Then was made the trial of skill in tossing balls (small white leather ones) through the framework of the garland, to effect which was a triumph."

See "Cuck Ball," "Keppy Ball," "Monday."

Ball and Bonnets

This is a boys' game. The players may be of any number. They place their caps or bonnets in a row. One of the boys takes a ball, and from a fixed point, at a few yards' distance from the bonnets, tries to throw it into one of the caps (fig. 1).

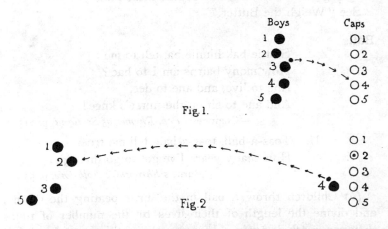

If the ball falls into the cap, all the boys, except the one into whose cap the ball has fallen, run off. The boy into whose cap the ball has been thrown goes up to it, lifts the ball from it, and calls out "Stop!" The other boys stop. The boy with the ball tries to strike one of the other boys (fig. 2).   If he does so, a small stone is put into the cap of the boy struck.   If he misses, a stone is put into his own cap.   If the boy who is to pitch the ball into the cap misses, a stone is put into his own cap, and he makes another trial.   The game goes on till six stones are put into one cap.   The boy in whose cap are the six stones has to place his hand against a wall, when he receives a certain number of blows with the ball thrown with force by one of the players.   The blows go by the name of "buns."   The game may go on in the same way till each player gets his "buns."—Nairn (Rev. W. Gregor).

See "Eggatt."

Ball in the Decker

A row of boys' caps is set by a wall.   One boy throws a ball into one of the caps.   The owner of the cap runs away, and is chased by all the others till caught.   He then throws the ball. —Dublin (Mrs. Lincoln).

Ball of Primrose

We'll wear yellow ribbons, yellow ribbons, yellow ribbons,
We'll wear yellow ribbons at the Ball of Primrose;
We'll all go a-waltzing, a-waltzing, a-waltzing,
We'll all go a-waltzing at the Ball of Primrose.
—Epworth, Doncaster ; and Lossiemouth, Yorkshire
(Charles C. Bell).

(*b*) The children form a ring, joining hands, and dance round singing the two first lines.   Then loosing hands, they waltz in couples, singing as a refrain the last line.   The game is continued, different coloured ribbons being named each time.

(*c*) This game was played in 1869, so cannot have arisen from the political movement.

Baloon

A game played with an inflated ball of strong leather, the ball being struck by the arm, which was defended by a bracer of wood.—Brand's *Pop. Antiq.*, ii. 394.

(*b*) It is spelt "balloo" in Ben Jonson, iii. 216, and "baloome" in Randolph's *Poems*, 1643, p. 105. It is also mentioned in Middleton's *Works*, iv. 342, and by Donne.

> " 'Tis ten a clock and past; all whom the mues,
>   *Baloun*, tennis, diet, or the stews
>   Had all the morning held."
>   —Donne's *Poems*, p. 133.

Toone (*Etymological Dict.*) says it is a game rather for exercise than contention; it was well known and practised in England in the fourteenth century, and is mentioned as one of the sports of Prince Henry, son of James I., in 1610. Strutt (*Sports and Pastimes*, p. 96) gives two illustrations of what he considers to be baloon ball play, from fourteenth century MSS.

Bandy-ball

A game played with sticks called "bandies," bent and round at one end, and a small wooden ball, which each party endeavours to drive to opposite fixed points. Northbrooke in 1577 mentions it as a favourite game in Devonshire (Halliwell's *Dict. of Provincialisms*). Strutt says the bat-stick was called a "bandy" on account of its being bent, and gives a drawing from a fourteenth century MS. book of prayers belonging to Mr. Francis Douce (*Sports*, p. 102). The bats in this drawing are nearly identical with modern golf-sticks, and "Golf" seems to be derived from this game. Peacock mentions it in his *Glossary of Manley and Corringham Words*. Forby has an interesting note in his *Vocabulary of East Anglia*, i. 14. He says, "The bandy was made of very tough wood, or shod with metal, or with the point of the horn or the hoof of some animal. The ball is a knob or gnarl from the trunk of a tree, carefully formed into a globular shape. The adverse parties strive to beat it with their bandies through one or other of the goals."

Bandy Cad or Gad

A game played with a nurr and crooked stick, also called "Shinty," and much the same as the "Hockey" of the South of England. "Cad" is the same as "cat" in the game of "Tip-cat;" it simply means a cut piece of wood.—Nodal and Milner's *Lancashire Glossary*.

Bandy-hoshoe

A game at ball common in Norfolk, and played in a similar manner to "Bandy" (Halliwell's *Dictionary*). Toone (*Etymological Dictionary*) says it is also played in Suffolk, and in West Sussex is called "Hawky."

Bandy-wicket

The game of "Cricket," played with a bandy instead of a bat (Halliwell's *Dictionary*). Toone mentions it as played in Norfolk (*Dict.*), and Moor as played in Suffolk with bricks usually, or, in their absence, with bats in place of bails or stumps (*Suffolk Words*).

Banger

Each boy provides himself with a button. One of the boys lays his button on the ground, near a wall. The other boys snap their buttons in turn against the wall. If the button drops within one span or hand-reach of the button laid down, it counts two (fig. 2); if within two spans, it counts one.

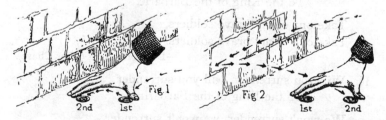

When it hits the button and bounces within one span, it counts four (fig. 1); within two spans, three; and above three spans, one. Each player snaps in turn for an agreed number; the first to score this number wins the game.—Deptford, Kent, and generally in London streets (Miss Chase).

This game is known in America as "Spans."—Newell, p. 188.

Bar

To play at "Bar," a species of game anciently used in Scotland.—Jamieson.

This game had in ancient times in England been simply denominated "Bars," or, as in an Act of James IV., 1491, edit. 1814, p. 227: "That na induellare within burgh . . . play at bar," "playing at Bars."

See "Prisoner's Base."

Barbarie, King of the

I. O will you surrender, O will you surrender
　　To the King of the Barbarie?

We won't surrender, we won't surrender
　　To the King of the Barbarie.

I'll go and complaint, I'll go and complaint
　　To the King of the Barbarie.

You can go and complaint, you can go and complaint
　　To the King of the Barbarie.

Good morning, young Prince, good morning, young Prince,
　　I have a complaint for you.

What is your complaint?
What is your complaint?

They won't surrender, they won't surrender
　　To the King of the Barbarie.

Take one of my brave soldiers,
Take one of my brave soldiers.
　　　　　　　　　—Deptford, Kent (Miss Chase).

II. Will you surrender, will you surrender
　　To the King of the Barbarines?

We won't surrender, we won't surrender
　　To the King of the Barbarines.

We'll make you surrender, we'll make you surrender
　　To the King of the Barbarines.

You can't make us surrender, you can't make us surrender
　　To the King of the Barbarines.

We'll go to the King, we'll go the King,
　To the King of the Barbarines.

You can go to the King, you can go to the King,
　To the King of the Barbarines.
　　　　　—Clapham, Surrey (Miss F. D. Richardson).

III. Will you surrender, will you surrender
　　　The Tower of Barbaree?

We won't surrender, we won't surrender
　The Tower of Barbaree.

We will go and tell the Queen,
Go and tell the Queen of Barbaree.

Don't care for the Queen, don't care for the Queen,
　The Queen of Barbaree.

Good morning, young Queen, good morning, young Queen,
　I have a complaint to thee.

Pray what is your complaint to me?

They won't surrender, they won't surrender
　The Tower of Barbaree.

Take one of my brave soldiers.
　　　—Lady Camilla Gurdon's *Suffolk County Folk-lore*, p. 63.

IV. You must surrend' me, you must surrend' me
　　　To the Queen of Barbaloo.

No, we'll not surrend' you, no, we'll not surrend' you
　To the Queen of Barbaloo.

We'll complain, we'll complain, &c.
　[To the Queen of Barbaloo.]

You can complain, you can complain, &c.
　[To the Queen of Barbaloo.]
　　　　　　—Penzance (Mrs. Mabbott).

(*b*) Two children stand together joining hands tightly, to personate a fortress; one child stands at a distance from these to personate the King of Barbarie, with other children standing behind to personate the soldiers (fig. 1). Some of the soldiers go to the fortress and surround it, singing the first verse (fig. 2). The children in the fortress reply, the four first verses being thus sung alternately. The soldiers then go to the King singing the fifth verse (fig. 3), the remaining verses being thus sung alternately. One of the soldiers then goes to the fortress and endeavours by throwing herself on the clasped hands of the children forming the fortress to break down the guard

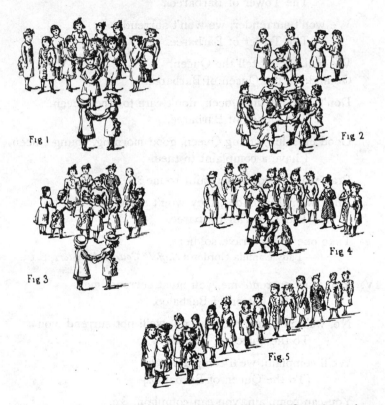

(fig. 4). All the soldiers try to do this, one after the other; finally the King comes, who breaks down the guard. The whole troop of soldiers then burst through the parted arms (fig. 5).

This is the Deptford version. The Clapham version is almost identical; the children take hold of each others' skirts and make a long line. If the brave soldier is not able to break the clasped hands he goes to the end of the line of soldiers.

The soldiers do not surround the fortress. In the Suffolk version the soldiers try to break through the girls' hands. If they do they have the tower. The Cornwall version is not so completely an illustration of the capture of a fortress.

Barley-break

Barley-break, or the Last Couple in Hell, was a game played by six people, three of each sex, who were coupled by lot. A piece of ground was then chosen, and divided into three compartments, of which the middle one was called Hell. It was the object of the couple condemned to this division to catch the others who advanced from the two extremities (figs. 1, 2), in which case a change of situation took place, and Hell was filled by the couple who were excluded by pre-occupation from

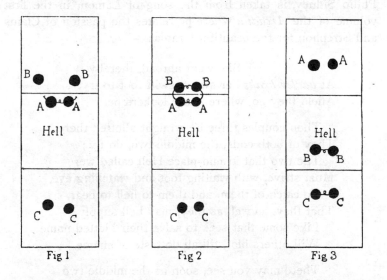

Fig 1   Fig 2   Fig 3

the other place (fig. 3). In this catching, however, there was some difficulty, as by the regulations of the game the middle couple were not to separate before they had succeeded, while the others might break hands whenever they found themselves hard pressed. When all had been taken in turn, the last couple was said to be "in Hell," and the game ended.— Dekker's *Works*, iv. 434.

Jamieson calls this "a game generally played by young people in a corn-yard. Hence called *barla-bracks about the stacks*, S. B." (*i.e.*, in the North of Scotland). "One stack is fixed on as the *dule* or goal; and one person is appointed to catch the rest of the company, who run out from the *dule*. He does not leave it till they are all out of sight. Then he sets off to catch them. Any one who is taken cannot run out again with his former associates, being accounted a prisoner; but is obliged to assist his captor in pursuing the rest. When all are taken the game is finished; and he who was first taken is bound to act as catcher in the next game. This innocent sport seems to be almost entirely forgotten in the South of Scotland. It is also falling into desuetude in the North."

(*b*) The following description of Barley-break, written by Sir Philip Sidney, is taken from the song of Lamon, in the first volume of the *Arcadia*, where he relates the passion of Claius and Strephon for the beautiful Urania :—

> She went abroad, thereby,
> At *barley-brake* her sweet, swift foot to try. . . .
> Afield they go, where many lookers be.

> Then couples three be straight allotted there,
> They of both ends, the middle two, do fly;
> The two that in mid-place Hell called were
> Must strive, with waiting foot and watching eye,
> To catch of them, and them to hell to bear,
> That they, as well as they, may hell supply;
> Like some that seek to salve their blotted name
> Will others blot, till all do taste of shame.

> There may you see, soon as the middle two
> Do, coupled, towards either couple make,
> They, false and fearful, do their hands undo;
> Brother his brother, friend doth friend forsake,
> Heeding himself, cares not how fellow do,
> But of a stranger mutual help doth take;
> As perjured cowards in adversity,
> With sight of fear, from friends to friends do fly.

Sir John Suckling also has given a description of this pastime with allegorical personages, which is quoted by Brand. In Holiday's play of the *Marriages of the Arts*, 1618, this sport is introduced, and also by Herrick (*Hesperides*, p. 44). Barley-break is several times alluded to in Massinger's plays : see the *Dramatic Works of Philip Massinger*, 1779, i. 167. "We'll run at barley-break first, and you shall be in hell" (Dekker's *The Honest Whore*). "Hee's at barli-break, and the last couple are now in hell" (Dekker's *The Virgin Martir*). See Gifford's *Massinger*, i. 104, edit. 1813. See also Browne's *Britannia's Pastorals*, published in 1614, Book I., Song 3, p. 76.

Randle Holme mentions this game as prevailing in his day in Lancashire. Harland and Wilkinson believe this game to have left its traces in Yorkshire and Lancashire. A couple link hands and sally forth from *home*, shouting something like

> Aggery, ag, ag,
> Ag's gi'en warning,

and trying to tick or touch with the free hand any of the boys running about separately. These latter try to slip behind the couple and throw their weight on the joined hands to separate them without being first touched or ticked ; and if they sunder the couple, each of the severed ones has to carry one home on his back. Whoever is touched takes the place of the toucher in the linked couple (*Legends of Lancashire*, p. 138). The modern name of this game is "Prison Bars" (*Ibid.*, p. 141). There is also a description of the game in a little tract called *Barley Breake ; or, A Warning for Wantons*, 1607. It is mentioned in Wilbraham's *Cheshire Glossary* as "an old Cheshire game." Barnes, in his *Dorsetshire Glossary*, says he has seen it played with one catcher on hands and knees in the small ring (Hell), and the others dancing round the ring crying "Burn the wold witch, you barley breech." Holland (*Cheshire Glossary*) also mentions it as an old Cheshire game.

See " Boggle about the Stacks," " Scots and English."

Barnes (Mr.)

> Mr. Barnes is dead and gone,
> And left his widder,

> Three poor children in her arms;
> What will you give her?
>
> Where did you come from?
>> —Played about 1850 at Hurstmonceaux,
>> Sussex (Miss Chase).

This is probably a forfeit game, imperfectly remembered.
See "Old Soldier."

Base-ball

An undescribed Suffolk game.—Moor's *Suffolk Words*.
See "Rounders."

Basket

>> —London (A. B. Gomme).

In this game the children all follow one who is styled the
"mother," singing:
> I'll follow my mother to market,
> To buy a silver basket.

The mother presently turns and catches or pretends to beat
them.—Dorsetshire (*Folk-lore Journal*, vi. 231).

> We'll follow our mother to market,
> To buy herself a basket;
> When she comes home she'll break our bones,
> We'll follow our mother to market.
>> —Hersham, Surrey (*Folk-lore Record*, v. 84).

A version familiar to me is the same as above, but ending
with
> For tumbling over cherry stones.

The mother then chased and beat those children she caught.
The idea was, I believe, that the children were imitating or
mocking their mother (A. B. G.). In Warwickshire the four

lines of the Surrey game are concluded by the additional
lines—

> We don't care whether we work or no,
> We'll follow our mother on tipty-toe.

When the mother runs after them and buffets them.—Northall's
English Folk Rhymes, p. 393.

Battledore and Shuttlecock

See "Shuttlefeather."

Bedlams or Relievo

A number of boys agree to play at this game, and sides are
picked. Five, for example, play on each side. A square is
chalked out on a footpath by the side of a road, which is called
the "Den;" five of the boys remain by the side of the Den, one
of whom is called the "Tenter;" the Tenter has charge of the
Den, and he must always stand with one foot in the Den and the

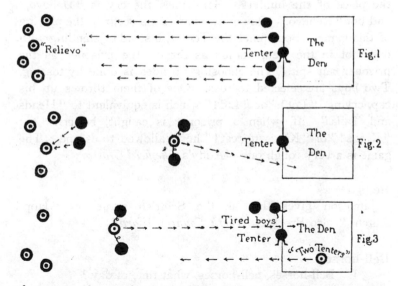

other upon the road; the remaining five boys go out to field,
it being agreed beforehand that they shall only be allowed
to run within a prescribed area, or in certain roads or streets
(fig. 1). As soon as the boys who have gone out to field have
reached a certain distance—there is no limit prescribed—they

shout "Relievo," and upon this signal the four boys standing by the side of the Den pursue them, leaving the Tenter in charge of the Den (fig. 2). When a boy is caught he is taken to the Den, where he is obliged to remain, unless the Tenter puts both his feet into the Den, or takes out the one foot which he ought always to keep in the Den. If the Tenter is thus caught tripping, the prisoner can escape from the Den. If during the progress of the game one of the boys out at field runs through the Den shouting "Relievo" without being caught by the Tenter, the prisoner is allowed to escape, and join his comrades at field. If one of the boys out at field is tired, and comes to stand by the side of the Den, he is not allowed to put his foot into the Den. If he does so the prisoner calls out, "There are two Tenters," and escapes if he can (fig. 3). When all the boys out at field have been caught and put into the Den, the process is reversed—the boys who have been, as it were, hunted, taking the place of the hunters. Sometimes the cry is "Delievo," and not "Relievo." One or two variations occur in the playing of this game. Sometimes the Tenter, instead of standing with one foot in the Den, stands as far off the prisoner as the prisoner can spit. The choosing of sides is done by tossing. Two boys are selected to toss. One of them throws up his cap, crying, "Pot!" or "Lid!" which is equivalent to "Heads and Tails." If, when a prisoner is caught, he cries out "Kings!" or "Kings to rest!" he is allowed to escape. The game is a very rough one.—Addy's *Sheffield Glossary*.

Beds

Jamieson gives this as the Scottish name for "Hopscotch;" also Brockett, *North Country Words*.

Bell-horses

I. Bell-horses, bell-horses, what time of day?
    One o'clock, two o'clock, three, and away!
    Bell-horses, bell-horses, what time of day?
    Two o'clock, three o'clock, four, and away!
    Five o'clock, six o'clock, now time to stay!
    —Stanton Lacey (Burne's *Shropshire Folk-lore*, p. 520).

II.   Bellasay, bellasay, what time of day ?
    One o'clock, two o'clock, three, and away.
           —Halliwell's *Nursery Rhymes*, p. 283.

(*b*) The children form long trains, standing one behind the other.   They march and sing the first four lines, then the fifth line, when they stand and begin again as before.

(*c*) Miss Burne suggests a connection with the old pack-horses.   Mr. Addy (*Sheffield Glossary*) gives the first two lines as a game.   He says, "The first horse in a team conveying lead to be smelted wore bells, and was called the bell-horse."   I remember when a child the two first lines being used to start children a race (A. B. G.).   Chambers (*Pop. Rhymes*, p. 148) gives a similar verse, used for starting a race :—

    Race horses, race horses, what time of day ?
    One o'clock, two o'clock, three, and away ;

and these lines are also used for the same purpose in Cheshire (Holland's *Glossary*) and Somersetshire (Elworthy's *Glossary*). Halliwell, on the strength of the corrupted word "Bellasay," connects the game with a proverbial saying applied to the family of Bellasis ; but there is no evidence of such a connection except the word-corruption.   The rhyme occurs in *Gammer Gurton's Garland*, 1783, the last words of the second line being "time to away."

Bellie-mantie

The name for "Blind Man's Buff" in Upper Clydesdale.   As anciently in this game he who was the chief actor was not only hoodwinked, but enveloped in the skin of an animal.— Jamieson.

See "Blind Man's Buff."

Belly-blind

The name for "Blind Man's Buff" in Roxburgh, Clydesdale, and other counties of the border.   It is probable that the term is the same with "Billy Blynde," said to be the name of a familiar spirit or good genius somewhat similar to the brownie.— Jamieson.

See "Blind Man's Buff."

Bend-leather

A boys' phrase for a slide on a pond when the ice is thin and bends. There is a game on the ice called playing at "Bend-leather." Whilst the boys are sliding they say "Bend-leather, bend-leather, puff, puff, puff."—Addy's *Sheffield Glossary*.

Betsy Bungay

Hi, Betsy Bungay, all day on Sunday;
You're the lock and I'm the key,
All day on Monday. —Kent (J. P. Emslie).

Two children cross their hands in the fashion known as a "sedan chair." A third child sits on their hands. The two sing the first line. One of them sings, "You're the lock," the other sings, "and I'm the key," and as they sang the words they unclasped their hands and dropped their companion on the ground. Mr. J. P. Emslie writes, "My mother learned this from her mother, who was a native of St. Laurence, in the Isle of Thanet. The game possibly belongs to Kent."

Bicky

In Somersetshire the game of "Hide and Seek." *To bik'ee* is for the seekers to go and lean their heads against a wall, so as not to see where the others go to hide.—Elworthy's *Dialect*. See "Hide and Seek."

Biddy-base

A Lincolnshire name for "Prisoner's Base."—Halliwell's *Dictionary*; Peacock's *Manley and Corringham Glossary*; Cole's *S. W. Lincolnshire Glossary*.

Biggly

Name for "Blind Man's Buff."—Dickinson's *Cumberland Glossary*.

Billet

The Derbyshire name for "Tip-cat."—Halliwell's *Dictionary*.

Billy-base

A name for " Prisoner's Base."—Halliwell's *Dictionary*.

Bingo

—Leicestershire.

—Hexham.

—Derbyshire.

—Earls Heaton, Yorks.

—Enborne.

I. The miller's mill-dog lay at the mill-door,
    And his name was Little Bingo.
    B with an I, I with an N, N with a G, G with an O,
    And his name was Little Bingo.

The miller he bought a cask of ale,
And he called it right good Stingo.
S with a T, T with an I, I with an N, N with a G,
    G with an O,
And he called it right good Stingo.

The miller he went to town one day,
And he bought a wedding Ring-o!
R with an I, I with an N, N with a G, G with an O,
And he bought a wedding Ring-o!
—Monton, Lancashire (Miss Dendy).

II.   A farmer's dog lay on the floor,
    And Bingo was his name O!
B, i, n, g, o, B, i, n, g, o,
    And Bingo was his name O!

The farmer likes a glass of beer,
    I think he calls it Stingo!
S, t, i, n, g, o, S, t, i, n, g, o!
    I think he calls it Stingo!
S, t, i, n, g, O! I think he calls it Stingo!
—Market Drayton, Ellesmere, Oswestry (Burne's
Shropshire Folk-lore, p. 513).

III.   There was a jolly farmer,
    And he had a jolly son,
    And his name was Bobby Bingo.
BINGO, BINGO, BINGO,
    And Bingo was his name.
—Liphook, Hants; Wakefield, Yorks (Miss Fowler).

IV.   There <i>was</i> a farmer <i>had</i> a dog,
    His name was Bobby Bingo.
B-i-n-g-o, B-i-n-g-o, B-i-n-g-o,
    His name was Bobby Bingo.
—Tean, Staffs.; and North Staffs. Potteries (Miss Keary).

V.   The farmer's dog lay on the hearth,
    And Bingo was his name oh!
B-i-n-g-o, B-i-n-g-o, B-i-n-g-o,
    And Bingo was his name oh!
—Nottinghamshire (Miss Winfield).

VI. The miller's dog lay on the wall,
    And Bingo was his name Oh!
    B-i-n-g-o,
    And Bingo was his name Oh!
        —Maxey, Northants (Rev. W. D. Sweeting).

VII. The shepherd's dog lay on the hearth,
    And Bingo was his name O.
    B i n g o, Bi, n, g, o, Bi-n-g-o,
    And Bingo was his name O.
        —Eckington, Derbyshire (S. O. Addy).

VIII. Pinto went to sleep one night,
    And Pinto was his name oh!
    P-i-n-t-o, P-i-n-t-o,
    And Pinto was his name oh.
        —Enbourne, Berks (Miss Kimber).

(*b*) In the Lancashire version, one child represents the Miller. The rest of the children stand round in a circle, with the Miller in the centre. All dance round and sing the verses. When it comes to the spelling part of the rhyme, the Miller points at one child, who must call out the right letter. If the child fails to do this she becomes Miller. In the Shropshire version, a ring is formed with one player in the middle. They dance round and sing the verses. When it comes to the spelling part, the girl in the middle cries B, and signals to another, who says I, the next to her N, the third G, the fourth "O! his name was Bobby Bingo!" Whoever makes a mistake takes the place of the girl in the middle. In the Liphook version, at the fourth line the children stand still and repeat a letter each in turn as quickly as they can, clapping their hands, and at the last line they turn right round, join hands, and begin again. In the Tean version, the one in the centre points, standing still, to some in the ring to say the letters B.I.N.G; the letter O has to be sung; if not, the one who says it goes in the ring, and repeats it all again until the game is given up. In the other Staffordshire version, when they stop, the one in the middle points to five of the others in turn, who have to say the letters forming "Bingo," while the one to whom O comes has to sing it on the note on which the others left off. Any one who says the wrong letter, or fails to sing the O right, takes the place of the middle one. The Northants version follows the Lancashire version, but if the answers are all made correctly, the last line is sung by the circle, and the game begins again. In the Metheringham version the child in the centre is blindfolded. When the song is over the girls say, " Point with your finger as we go round." The girl in the centre points accordingly, and whichever of the others happens to be opposite to her when she says " Stop ! " is caught. If the blindfolded girl can identify her captive they exchange places, and the game goes on as before. The Forest of Dean and the Earls Heaton versions are played the same as the Lancashire. In the West Cornwall version, as seen played in 1884, a ring is formed, into the middle of which goes a child holding a stick ; the others with joined hands run round in a circle, singing the verses. When they have finished singing they cease running, whilst the one in the centre, pointing with his stick, asks them in turn to spell Bingo. If they all spell it correctly they again move round singing ; but should either of them make a mistake, he or she has to take the place of the middle man (*Folk-lore Journal*, v. 58). In the Hexham version they sing a second verse, which is the same as the first with the name spelt *backwards*. The Berks version is practically the same as the Tean version. The Eckington (Derbyshire) version is played as follows :—A number of young women form a ring. A man stands within the ring, and they sing the words. He then makes choice of a girl, who takes his arm. They both walk round the circle while the others sing the same lines again. The girl who has been chosen makes choice of a young man in the ring, who in his turn chooses another girl, and so on till they have all paired off.

(*c*) The first verse of the Shropshire version is also sung at Metheringham, near Lincoln (C. C. Bell), and Cowes, I.W. (Miss E. Smith). The Staffordshire version of the words is sung in Forest of Dean, Gloucestershire (Miss Matthews), West Cornwall (*Folk-lore Journal*, v. 58), Earls Heaton, Yorkshire (H. Hardy), Hexham, Northumberland (Miss Barker),

Leicester (Miss Ellis). Miss Peacock says, "A version is known in Lincolnshire." Tunes have also been sent from Tean, North Staffs. (Miss Keary), and Epworth, Doncaster (Mr. C. C. Bell), which are nearly identical with the Leicester tune; from Market Drayton (Miss Burne), similar to the Derbyshire tune; from Monton, Lancashire (Miss Dendy), which appears to be only the latter part of the tune, and is similar to those given above. The tune given by Rimbault is not the same as those collected above, though there is a certain similarity.

The editor of *Northamptonshire Notes and Queries*, vol. i. p. 214, says, "Some readers will remember that Byngo is the name of the 'Franklyn's dogge' that Ingoldsby introduces into a few lines described as a portion of a primitive ballad, which has escaped the researches of Ritson and Ellis, but is yet replete with beauties of no common order." In the *Nursery Songs* collected by Ed. Rimbault from oral tradition is "Little Bingo." The words of this are very similar to the Lancashire version of the game sent by Miss Dendy. There is an additional verse in the nursery song.

Bird-apprentice

A row of boys or girls stands parallel with another row opposite. Each of the first row chooses the name of some bird, and a member of the other row then calls out all the names of birds he can think of. If the middle member of the first row has chosen either of them, he calls out "Yes," and all the guessers immediately run to take the place of the first row, the members of which attempt to catch them. If any succeed, they have the privilege of riding in on their captives' backs.—Ogbourne, Wilts (H. S. May).

Birds, Beasts, and Fishes

$$B \times \times \times \times \times \times h = \text{Bullfinch}$$
$$E \times \times \times \times \times t = \text{Elephant}$$
$$S \times \times \times \times \times \times h = \text{Swordfish}$$

This is a slate game, and two or more children play. One writes the initial and final letters of a bird's, beast's, or fish's

name, making crosses (×) instead of the intermediate letters of
the word, stating whether the name is that of bird, beast, or fish.
The other players must guess in turn what the name is.   The
first one who succeeds takes for himself the same number of
marks as there are crosses in the word, and then writes the
name of anything he chooses in the same manner.   If the
players are unsuccessful in guessing the name, the writer takes
the number to his own score and writes another.   The game is
won when one player gains a certain number of marks previously decided upon as "game."—Barnes (A. B. Gomme).

Bittle-battle

The Sussex game of "Stoolball."   There is a tradition that
this game was originally played by the milkmaids with their
milking-stools, which they used for bats; but this word makes
it more probable that the stool was the wicket, and that it was
defended with the bittle, which would be called the bittle-bat.—
Parish's *Sussex Dialect*.

See "Stoolball."

Bitty-base

Bishop Kennet (in *MS. Lansd.* 1033) gives this name as a
term for "Prisoner's Base."—Halliwell's *Dictionary*.

Black Man's Tig

A long rope is tied to a gate or pole, and one of the players
holds the end of the rope, and tries to catch another player.
When he succeeds in doing so the one captured joins him (by
holding hands) and helps to catch the other players.   The
game is finished when all are caught.—Cork (Miss Keane).

Black Thorn

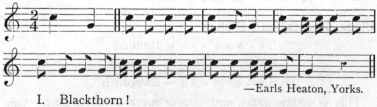

—Earls Heaton, Yorks.

I.   Blackthorn!
    Butter-milk and barley-corn;

How many geese have you to-day ?
As many as you can catch and carry away.
                    —Monton, Lancashire (Miss Dendy).

II.   Blackthorn ! Blackthorn !
Blue milk and barley-corn ;
How many geese have you to-day ?
More than you can catch and carry away.
    —Harland and Wilkinson's *Lancashire Folk-lore*, p. 150.

III.   Blackthorn !
New milk and barley-corn ;
How many sheep have you to sell ?
More nor yo can catch and fly away wi'.
    —Addy's *Sheffield Glossary*.

IV.   Blackthorn !
Butter-milk and barley-corn ;
How many sheep have you to-day ?
As many as you catch and carry away.
    —Earls Heaton, Yorkshire (Herbert Hardy).

(*b*) One set of children stand against a wall, another set stand opposite, facing them. The first set sing the first line, the others replying with the second line, and so with the third and fourth lines. The two sides then rush over to each other, and the second set are caught. The child who is caught last becomes one of the first set for another game. This is the Earls Heaton version. The Lancashire game, as described by Miss Dendy, is : One child stands opposite a row of children, and the row run over to the opposite side, when the one child tries to catch them. The prisoners made, join the one child, and assist her in the process of catching the others. The rhyme is repeated in each case until all are caught, the last one out becoming "Blackthorn" for a new game. Harland and Wilkinson describe the game somewhat differently. Each player has a mark, and after the dialogue the players run over to each other's marks, and if any can be caught before getting home to the opposite mark, he has to carry his captor to the mark, when he takes his place as an additional catcher.

(*c*) Miss Burne's version (*Shropshire Folk-lore*, p. 521) is practically the same as the Earls Heaton game, and Easther in his *Almondbury Glossary* gives a version practically like the Sheffield. Mr. Hardy says it is sometimes called "Black-butt," when the opposite side cry "Away we cut." Miss Dendy quotes an old Lancashire rhyme, which curiously refers to the different subjects in the Lancashire game rhyme. It is as follows :—

> Little boy, little boy, where were you born ?
> Way up in Lancashire, under a thorn,
> Where they sup butter-milk in a ram's horn.

Another version is given in *Notes and Queries*, 3rd Series, vii. 285.

(*d*) This is a dramatic game, in which the children seem to personate animals, and to depict events belonging to the history of the flock. Miss Burne groups it under her "dramatic games."

Blind Bell

A game formerly common in Berwickshire, in which all the players were hoodwinked except the person who was called the Bell. He carried a bell, which he rung, still endeavouring to keep out of the way of his hoodwinked partners in the game. When he was taken, the person who seized him was released from the bandage, and got possession of the bell, the bandage being transferred to him who was laid hold of.— Jamieson.

(*b*) In "The Modern Playmate," edited by Rev. J. G. Wood, this game is described under the name of "Jingling." Mr. Wood says there is a rougher game played at country feasts and fairs in which a pig takes the place of the boy with the bell, but he does not give the locality (p. 7). Strutt also describes it (*Sports*, p. 317).

Blind Bucky-Davy

In Somersetshire the game of "Blind Man's Buff." Also in Cornwall (see Couch's *Polperro*, p. 173). Pulman says this means "Blind buck and have ye" (Elworthy's *Dialect*).

Blind Harie
A name for "Blind Man's Buff."—Jamieson.

Blind Hob
 The Suffolk name for "Blind Man's Buff.—Halliwell's *Dictionary;* Moor's *Suffolk Glossary.*

Blind Man's Buff
I. Come, shepherd, come, shepherd, and count your sheep.
   I canna come now, for I'm fast asleep.
   If you don't come now they'll all be gone.
   What's in my way?
   A bottle of hay.
   Am I over it?
                  —Shrewsbury (Burne's *Shropshire Folk-lore*, p. 525).

   II. How many fingers do I hold up?
       Four, three, &c. [at random in reply].
       How many horses has your father?
       Three [fixed reply].
       What colour?
       White, red, and grey.
       Turn you about three times;
       Catch whom you may!   —Deptford (Miss Chase).

III. How many horses has your father got in his stables?
     Three.
     What colour are they?
     Red, white, and grey.
     Then turn about, and twist about, and catch whom you
        may.
                  —Cornwall (*Folk-lore Journal*, v. 57, 58).

IV. Antony Blindman kens ta me
    Sen I bought butter and cheese o' thee?
    I ga' tha my pot,
    I ga' tha my pan,
    I ga' tha a' I hed but a rap ho'penny I gave a poor oald
       man.   —Cumberland (Dickinson's *Glossary*).

(*b*) In the Deptford version one of the players is blindfolded. The one who blindfolds ascertains that the player cannot see by putting the first question. When the players are satisfied that the blindfolding is complete, the dialogue follows, and the blind man is turned round three times. The game is for him to catch one of the players, who is blindfolded in turn if the blind man succeeds in guessing who he is. Players are allowed to pull, pinch, and buffet the blind man.

(*c*) This sport is found among the illuminations of an old missal formerly in the possession of John Ives, cited by Strutt in his *Manners and Customs*. The two illustrations are fac-similes from drawings in one of the Bodleian MSS., and they

indicate the complete covering of the head, and also the fact that the game was played by adults. Gay says concerning it—

As once I play'd at *blindman's-buff*, it hap't,
About my eyes the towel thick was wrapt.
I miss'd the swains, and seiz'd on Blouzelind.

And another reference is quoted by Brand (ii. 398)—

Sometyme the one would goe, sometyme the other,
Sometymes all thre at once, and sometyme neither;
Thus they with him play at boyes blynde-man-bluffe.
—*The Newe Metamorphosis*, 1600, MS.

Other names for this game are "Belly Mantie," "Billy Blind," "Blind Bucky Davy," "Blind Harie," "Blind Hob," "Blind Nerry Mopsey," "Blind Palmie," "Blind Sim," "Buck Hid,"

" Chacke Blynd Man," " Hoodle-cum-blind," " Hoodman Blind,"
" Hooper's Hide," " Jockie Blind Man."

(d) There is some reason for believing that this game can
be traced up to very ancient rites connected with prehistoric
worship. The name " Billy Blind " denoted the person who
was blindfolded in the game, as may be seen by an old poem
by Lyndsay, quoted by Jamieson :

> War I ane King
> I sould richt sone mak reformatioun
> Farlyeand thairof your grace sould richt sone finde
> That Preistis sall leid yow lyke ane bellye blinde.

And also in Clerk's *Advice to Luvaris :*

> Sum festnit is and ma not flé,
> Sum led is lyk.the belly blynd
> With luve, war bettir lat it be.

" It is probable," says Jamieson, " that the term is the same
as Billy Blynde, said to be the name of a familiar spirit or good
genius somewhat similar to the brownie." Professor Child
identifies it with Odin, the blind deity. Another name in Scotland is also " Blind Harie," which is not the common Christian name " Harry," because this was not a name familiar in
Scotland. Blind Harie may therefore, Jamieson thinks, arise
from the rough or hairy attire worn by the principal actor.
Auld Harie is one of the names given to the devil, and also
to the spirit Brownie, who is represented as a hairy being.
Under " Coolin," a curious Highland custom is described by
Jamieson, which is singularly like the game of " Belly Blind,"

and assists in the conclusion that the game has descended from a rite where animal gods were represented. Sporting with animals before sacrificing them was a general feature at these rites. It is known that the Church opposed the people imitating beasts, and in this connection it is curious to note that in South Germany the game is called *blind bock*, i.e., "blind goat," and in German *blinde kuhe*, or "blind cow." In Scotland, one of the names for the game, according to A. Scott's poems, was "Blind Buk":

> Blind buk! but at the bound thou schutes,
> And them forbeirs that the rebutes.

It may therefore be conjectured that the person who was hoodwinked assumed the appearance of a goat, stag, or cow by putting on the skin of one of those animals.

He who is twice crowned or touched on the head by the taker or him who is hoodwinked, instead of once only, according to the law of the game, is said to be *brunt* (burned), and regains his liberty.—Jamieson.

Blind Man's Stan

A boys' game, played with the eggs of small birds. The eggs are placed on the ground, and the player who is blindfolded takes a certain number of steps in the direction of the eggs; he then slaps the ground with a stick thrice in the hope of breaking the eggs; then the next player, and so on.—Patterson's *Antrim and Down Glossary*.

Blind Nerry-Mopsey

The Whitby name for "Blind Man's Buff.—Robinson's *Glossary*.

Blind Palmie or Pawmie

One of the names given to the game of "Blindman's Buff." —Jamieson.

Blind Sim

Suffolk name for "Blind Man's Buff."—Forby's *Vocabulary of East Anglia*.

Block, Haimmer (Hammer), and Nail

This is a boys' game, and requires seven players. One boy, the Block, goes down on all fours; another, the Nail, does the same behind the Block, with his head close to his *a posteriori* part. A third boy, the Hammer, lies down on his back behind the two. Of the remaining four boys one stations himself at each leg and one at each arm of the Hammer, and he is thus lifted. He is swung backwards and forwards three times in this position by the four, who keep repeating "Once, twice, thrice." When the word "Thrice" is repeated, the *a posteriori* part of the Hammer is knocked against the same part of the Nail. Any number of knocks may be given, according to the humour of the players.—Keith (Rev. W. Gregor).

A fellow lies on all fours—this is the Block; one steadies him before—this is the Study; a third is made a Hammer of, and swung by boys against the Block (Mactaggart's *Gallovidian Encyclopædia*). Patterson (*Antrim and Down Glossary*) mentions a game, "Hammer, Block, and Bible," which is probably the same game.

Blow-point

Strutt considers this to have been a children's game, played by blowing an arrow through a trunk at certain numbers by way of lottery (*Sports*, p. 403). Nares says the game was blowing small pins or points against each other, and probably not unlike "Push-pin." Marmion in his *Antiquary*, 1641, says: "I have heard of a nobleman that has been drunk with a tinker, and of a magnifico that has played at blow-point." In the *Comedy of Lingua*, 1607, act iii., sc. 2, Anamnestes introduces Memory as telling "how he played at blowe-point with Jupiter when he was in his side-coats." References to this game are also made in *Apollo Shroving*, 1627, p. 49; and see Hawkins' *English Drama*, iii. 243.

See "Dust-Point."

Bob Cherry

A children's game, consisting in jumping at cherries above their heads and trying to catch them with their mouths (Halliwell's *Dictionary*). It is alluded to in Herrick's

Hesperides as "Chop Cherry." Major Lowsley describes the game as taking the end of a cherry-stalk between the teeth, and holding the head perfectly level, trying to get the cherry into the mouth without using the hands or moving the head

(*Berkshire Glossary*). It is also mentioned in Peacock's *Manley and Corringham Glossary*. Strutt gives a curious illustration ·of the game in his *Sports and Pastimes*, which is here reproduced from the original MS. in the British Museum.

The Staffordshire St. Clement Day custom (Poole's *Staffordshire Customs, &c.*, p. 36) and the northern Hallowe'en custom (Brockett's *North-Country Words*) probably indicate the origin of this game from an ancient rite.

Boggle about the Stacks

A favourite play among young people in the villages, in which one hunts several others (Brockett's *North-Country Words*). The game is alluded to in one of the songs given by Ritson (ii. 3), and Jamieson describes it as a Scottish game.

See "Barley-break."

Boggle-bush

The child's play of finding the hidden person in the company. —Robinson's *Whitby Glossary*. See "Hide and Seek."

Bonnety

This is a boys' game. The players place their bonnets or caps in a pile. They then join hands and stand in a circle round it. They then pull each other, and twist and wriggle round and round and over it, till one overturns it or knocks a bonnet off it. The player who does so is hoisted on the back of another, and pelted by all the others with their bonnets. —Keith, Nairn (Rev. W. Gregor).

Booman

                                                        —Norfolk.

Dill doule for Booman, Booman is dead and gone,
Left his wife all alone, and all his children.

Where shall we bury him ?   Carry him to London ;
By his grandfather's grave grows a green onion.

Dig his grave wide and deep, strow it with flowers ;
Toll the bell, toll the bell, twenty-four hours.
                              —Norfolk, 1825–30 (J. Doe).

(*b*) One boy lies down and personates Booman. Other boys form a ring round him, joining hands and alternately raising and lowering them, to imitate bell-pulling, while the girls who play sit down and weep. The boys sing the first verse. The girls seek for daisies or any wild flowers, and join in the singing of the second verse, while the boys raise the prostrate Booman and carry him about. When singing the third verse the boys act digging a grave, and the dead boy is lowered. The girls strew flowers over the body. When finished another boy becomes Booman.

(*c*) This game is clearly dramatic, to imitate a funeral. Mr. Doe writes, "I have seen somewhere [in Norfolk] a tomb with a crest on it—a leek—and the name Beaumont," but it does not seem necessary to thus account for the game.

Boss-out

A game at marbles.   Strutt describes it as follows :—" One bowls a marble to any distance that he pleases, which serves as a mark for his antagonist to bowl at, whose business it is to hit the marble first bowled, or lay his own near enough to it for him to span the space between them and touch both the marbles.   In either case he wins.   If not, his marble remains where it lay, and becomes a mark for the first player, and so alternately until the game be won."—*Sports*, p. 384.

Boss and Span

The same as " Boss-out."   It is mentioned, but not described, in Baker's *Northamptonshire Glossary*.

Boys and Girls

—*The Dancing Master*, 1728, vol. ii., p. 138.

> Boys, boys, come out to play,
> The moon doth shine as bright as day ;
> Come with a whoop, come with a call,
> Come with a goodwill or don't come at all ;
> Lose your supper and lose your sleep,
> So come to your playmates in the street.
> —*Useful Transactions in Philosophy*, p. 44.

This rhyme is repeated when it is decided to begin any game, as a general call to the players.   The above writer says it occurs in a very ancient MS., but does not give any reference to it. Halliwell quotes the four first lines, the first line reading "Boys and girls," instead of "Boys, boys," from a curious ballad written about the year 1720, formerly in the possession of Mr. Crofton Croker (*Nursery Rhymes*). Chambers also gives this rhyme (*Popular Rhymes*, p. 152).

Branks

A game formerly common at fairs, called also "Hit my Legs and miss my Pegs."—Dickinson's *Cumberland Glossary*.

Bridgeboard

A game at marbles. The boys have a board a foot long, four inches in depth, and an inch (or so) thick, with squares as in the diagram; any number of holes at the ground edge, numbered irregularly. The board is placed firmly on the ground, and each player bowls at it. He wins the number of marbles denoted by the figure above the opening through which his marble passes. If he misses a hole, his marble is lost to the owner of the Bridgeboard.—Earls Heaton (Herbert Hardy). [The owner or keeper of the Bridgeboard presumably pays those boys who succeed in winning marbles.]

See "Nine Holes."

Broken-down Tradesmen

A boys' game, undescribed.—Patterson's *Antrim and Down Glossary*.

Brother Ebenezer

Ebenezer is sent out of the room, and the remainder choose one of themselves. Two children act in concert, it being understood that the last person speaking when Ebenezer goes out of the room is the person to be chosen. The medium left in the room causes the others to think of this person without letting them know that they are not choosing of their own free will. The medium then says, "Brother Ebenezer, come in," and asks him in succession, "Was it William, or Jane," &c., mentioning several names before saying the right one, Ebenezer saying "No!" to all until the one is mentioned who last spoke.—Bitterne, Hants (Mrs. Byford).

Bubble-hole

A child's game, undescribed.—Halliwell's *Dictionary*.

Bubble-justice

The name of a game probably the same as "Nine Holes."—Halliwell's *Dictionary*.

Buck, Buck

A boy stoops so that his arms rest on a table; another boy sits on him as he would on a horse. He then holds up (say) three fingers, and says—

> Buck, buck, how many horns do I hold up?

The stooping boy guesses, and if he says a wrong number the other says—

> [Two] you say and three there be;
> Buck, buck, how many horns do I hold up?

When the stooping boy guesses rightly the other says—

> [Four] you say and [four] there be;
> Buck, buck, rise up.

The boy then gets off and stoops for the other one to mount, and the game is played again.—London (J. P. Emslie).

Similar action accompanies the following rhyme:—

> Inkum, jinkum, Jeremy buck,
> Yamdy horns do au cock up?
> Two thà sès, and three there is,
> Au'll lea'n thee to la'ke at Inkum.
> —Almondbury (Easther's *Glossary*).

A different action occurs in other places. It is played by three boys in the following way:—One stands with his back to a wall; the second stoops down with his head against the stomach of the first boy, "forming a back;" the third jumps on it, and holds up his hand with the fingers distended, saying—

> Buck shee, buck shee buck,
> How many fingers do I hold up?

Should the stooper guess correctly, they all change places, and the jumper forms the back. Another and not such a rough way of playing this game is for the guesser to stand with his face towards a wall, keeping his eyes shut.—Cornwall (*Folklore Journal*, v. 59).

In Nairn, Scotland, the game is called Post and Rider. One boy, the Post, takes his stand beside a wall. Another boy stoops down with his head touching the Post's breast. Several other boys stoop down in the same way behind the first boy, all in line. The Rider then leaps on the back of the boy at the end of the row of stooping boys, and from his back to that of the one in front, and so on from back to back till he reaches the boy next the Post. He then holds up so many fingers, and says—

Buck, buck, how many fingers do I hold up?

The boy makes a guess. If the number guessed is wrong, the Rider gives the number guessed as well as the correct number, and again holds up so many, saying—

[Four] you say, but [two] it is;
Buck, buck, how many fingers do I hold up?

This goes on till the correct number is guessed, when the guesser becomes the Rider. The game was called "Buck, Buck" at Keith. Three players only took part in the game—the Post, the Buck, and the Rider. The words used by the Rider were—

Buck, buck, how many horns do I hold up?

If the guess was wrong, the Rider gave the Buck as many blows or kicks with the heel as the difference between the correct number and the number guessed. This process went on till the correct number was guessed, when the Rider and the Buck changed places.—Rev. W. Gregor.

(*b*) Dr. Tylor says: "It is interesting to notice the wide distribution and long permanence of these trifles in history when we read the following passage from Petronius Arbiter, written in the time of Nero:—'Trimalchio, not to seem moved by the loss, kissed the boy, and bade him get up on his back. Without delay the boy climbed on horseback on him, and slapped him on the shoulders with his hand, laughing and calling out,

"Bucca, bucca, quot sunt hic ?" '—*Petron. Arbitri Satiræ*, by Buchler, p. 84 (other readings are *buccæ* or *bucco*)."—*Primitive Culture*, i. 67.

Buck i' t' Neucks

A rude game amongst boys.—Dickinson's *Cumberland Glossary*.

Buckerels

"A kind of play used by boys in London streets in Henry VIII.'s time, now disused, and I think forgot" (Blount's *Glossographia*, p. 95). Hall mentions this game, temp. Henry VIII., f. 91.

Buckey-how

For this the boys divide into sides. One "stops at home," the other goes off to a certain distance agreed on beforehand and shouts "Buckey-how." The boys "at home" then give chase, and when they succeed in catching an adversary, they bring him home, and there he stays until all on his side are caught, when they in turn become the chasers.—Cornwall (*Folk-lore Journal*, v. 60).

Buff

1st player, thumping the floor with a stick : "Knock, knock!"
2nd ditto : "Who's there ? "
1st : "Buff."
2nd : "What says Buff ? "
1st : "Buff says Buff to all his men,
    And I say Buff to you again ! "
2nd : "Methinks Buff smiles ? "
1st : "Buff neither laughs nor smiles,
    But looks in your face
    With a comical grace,
    And delivers the staff to you again" (handing it over).
    —Shropshire (Burne's *Shropshire Folk-lore*, p. 526).

Same verses as in Shropshire, except the last, which runs as follows :—

Buff neither laughs nor smiles,
But strokes his face
With a very good grace,
And delivers his staff to you.
—Cheltenham (Miss E. Mendham).

Same verses as in Shropshire, except the last, which runs as follows :—

Buff neither laughs nor smiles,
But strokes his face for want of grace,
And sticks his staff in the right place.
—London (J. P. Emslie).

(*b*) Five or six children stand in a row. Another child comes up to the first of the row, and strikes smartly on the ground with a stick. The child facing him asks the first question, and the one with the stick answers. At "strokes his face" he suits the action to the words, and then thumps with his stick on the ground at the beginning of the last line. The object of all the players is to make Buff smile while going through this absurdity, and if he does he must pay a forfeit.

Another version is for one child to be blindfolded, and stand in the middle of a ring of children, holding a long wand in his hand. The ring dance round to a tune and sing a chorus [which is not given by the writer]. They then stop. Buff extends his wand, and the person to whom it happens to be pointed must step out of the circle to hold the end in his hand. Buff then interrogates the holder of the wand by grunting three times, and is answered in like manner. Buff then guesses who is the holder of the wand. If he guesses rightly, the holder of .the stick becomes Buff, and he joins the ring (*Winter Evening's Amusements*, p. 6). When I played at this game the ring of children walked in silence three times only round Buff, then stopped and knelt or stooped down on the ground, strict silence being observed. Buff asked three questions (anything he chose) of the child to whom he pointed the stick, who replied by imitating cries of animals or birds (A. B. Gomme).

(*c*) This is a well-known game. It is also called "Buffy Gruffy," or "Indian Buff." The Dorsetshire version in *Folk-lore Journal*, vi. 238, 239, is the same as the Shropshire version.

Halliwell (*Nursery Rhymes*, cclxxxii.) gives a slight variant. It is also given by Mr. Addy in his *Sheffield Glossary*, the words being the same except the last two lines, which run—

> But shows his face with a comely grace,
> And leaves his staff at the very next place.

Buk-hid

This seems to be an old name for some game, probably "Blindman's Buff," Sw. "Blind-bock," q. "bock" and "hufwud head" (having the head resembling a goat). The sense, however, would agree better with "Bo-peep" or "Hide and Seek." —Jamieson.

Bull in the Park

One child places himself in the centre of a circle of others. He then asks each of the circle in turn, "Where's the key of the park?" and is answered by every one, except the last, "Ask the next-door neighbour." The last one answers, "Get out the way you came in." The centre one then makes a dash at the hands of some of the circle, and continues to do so until he breaks through, when all the others chase him. Whoever catches him is then Bull.—Liphook, Hants (Miss Fowler).

"The Bull in the Barn" is apparently the same game. The players form a ring; one player in the middle called the Bull, one outside called the King.

Bull: "Where is the key of the barn-door?"
Chorus: "Go to the next-door neighbour."
King: "She left the key in the church-door."
Bull: "Steel or iron?"

He then forces his way out of the ring, and whoever catches him becomes Bull.—Berrington (Burne's *Shropshire Folk-lore*, pp. 519, 520).

Another version is that the child in the centre, whilst the others danced around him in a circle, saying, "Pig in the middle and can't get out," replies, "I've lost my key but I will get out," and throws the whole weight of his body suddenly on the clasped hands of a couple, to try and unlock them. When he had succeeded he changed the words to, "I've broken your locks, and I have got out." One of the pair whose hands he had opened took his place, and he joined the ring.—Cornwall (*Folk-lore Journal*, v. 50).

(*b*) Mr. S. O. Addy says the following lines are said or sung in a game called " T' Bull 's i' t' Barn," but he does not know how it is played :—

> As I was going o'er misty moor
> I spied three cats at a mill-door ;
> One was white and one was black,
> And one was like my granny's cat.
> I hopped o'er t' style and broke my heel,
> I flew to Ireland very weel,
> Spied an old woman sat by t' fire,
> Sowing silk, jinking keys ;
> Cat's i' t' cream-pot up to t' knees,
> Hen's i' t' hurdle crowing for day,
> Cock's i' t' barn threshing corn,
> I ne'er saw the like sin' I was born.

Bulliheisle

A play amongst boys, in which, all having joined hands in a line, a boy at one of the ends stands still, and the rest all wind round him. The sport especially consists in an attempt to heeze or throw the whole mass on the ground.—Jamieson.

See " Eller Tree," " Wind up Jack," " Wind up the Bush Faggot."

Bummers

A play of children. " Bummers—a thin piece of wood swung round by a cord " (*Blackwood's Magazine*, Aug. 1821, p. 35). Jamieson says the word is evidently denominated from the booming sound produced.

Bun-hole

A hole is scooped out in the ground with the heel in the shape of a small dish, and the game consists in throwing a marble as near to this hole as possible. Sometimes, when several holes are made, the game is called " Holy."—Addy's *Sheffield Glossary ; Notes and Queries*, xii. 344.

Bunch of Ivy

Played by children in pairs (one kneeling and one standing) in a ring. The inner child of each pair kneels. The following dialogue begins with the inner circle asking the first question, which is replied to by the outer circle.

"What time does the King come home?"

"One o'clock in the afternoon."

"What has he in his hand?"

"A bunch of ivy."

The rhyme is repeated for every hour up to six, the outer circle running round the inner as many times as the number named. The children then change places and repeat.—Monton, Lancashire (Miss Dendy).

Bung the Bucket

—London (J. P. Emslie).

A number of boys divide themselves into two sides. One side, the Buckets, stoop down, as for "Leap-frog," arranging themselves one in front of the other. The hindmost supports himself against the one in front of him, and the front one

supports himself against a wall (fig.). They thus make an even and solid row of their backs. The other side, the Bungs, leap on to the backs of the Buckets, the first one going as far up the row as possible, the second placing himself close behind the first, and so on. If they all succeed in getting a secure place, they cry out twice the two first lines—

> Bung the Bucket,
> One, two, three.
> Off, off, off!

If no breakdown occurs, the Buckets count one in their favour, and the Bungs repeat the process. When a breakdown occurs the Bungs take the place of the Buckets.—Barnes, Surrey (A. B. Gomme).

(*b*) Mr. Emslie, to whom I am indebted for the tune to this game, gives me the words as—

Jump a little nag-tail,
One, two, three.

He says, "I once heard this sung three times, followed by 'Ha! ha! he!' to the tune of the last bar." Mr. W. R. Emslie says the game is known at Beddgelert as "Horses, Wild Horses," he believes, but is not quite certain.

Northall (*Rhymes*, p. 401) describes a game very similar to this under "Buck," in which the rhyme and method of play is the same as in that game. He continues, "This is closely allied to a game called in Warwickshire 'Jack upon the Mopstick.' But in this there is no guessing. The leaping party must maintain their position whilst their leader says—

Jack upon the mopstick,
One, two, three, four, five, six, seven, eight, nine, ten,
Count 'em off again."

Bunting

Name for "Tip-cat."—Cole's *S. W. Lincolnshire Glossary*.

Burly Whush

A game played at with a ball. The ball is thrown up by one of the players on a house or wall, who cries on the instant it is thrown to another to catch or kep it before it falls to the ground. They all run off but this one to a little distance, and if he fails in kepping it he bawls out "Burly Whush;" then the party are arrested in their flight, and must run away no farther. He singles out one of them then, and throws the ball at him, which often is directed so fair as to strike; then this one at which the ball has been thrown is he who gives "Burly Whush" with the ball to any he chooses. If the corner of a house be at hand, as is mostly the case, and any of the players escape behind it, they must still show one of their hands past its edge to the Burly Whush man, who sometimes hits it such a whack with the ball as leaves it dirling for an hour afterwards.—Mactaggart's *Gallovidian Encyclopædia*.

See " Ball," " Keppy Ball," " Monday."

Buttons

Two or more boys take two buttons in their right hands, and try to throw them both into a small hole in the ground about two yards off. The boy who succeeds in getting both buttons in begins first next game, and takes a button as prize. [This seems merely a mild form of marbles.]—Lincolnshire (Rev. — Roberts).

There were several games played with buttons—some on level ground, in a ring or square; but the most approved was with a hole dug in the earth near a wall, or near the trunk of a large tree. The hole should be about the cavity of a small tea-cup, the players toeing a scratched line about four or five feet from the hole, after tossing for first innings. Each of the players (mostly two) contribute an equal number of buttons, say from two to ten, and of equal value or quality. The one having first turn takes the whole of them in his hand, and by an under-throw, or rather a pitch, endeavours to get the whole, or as many as possible, into the hole. If all 'go clean into the hole, he wins the game, and takes the whole of the buttons started with ; but if one or more of the buttons are left outside the hole, the non-player has then the choice of selecting one which he considers difficult to be hit, and requesting the player to hit it with his *nicker*. This is made of solid lead, about the size of a florin, but twice its substance, and each player is provided with one of his own. Much judgment is required in making this selection, the object being to make it most difficult not only to hit it, but to prevent it being hit without being knocked into the hole, or sending the nicker in, or sending another button in, or even not striking one at all. In any one of these cases the player loses the game, and the non-player takes the whole of the stakes. In playing the next game, the previous non-player becomes the player.—London (C. A. T. M.).

The following was the value of the buttons :—

(1.) The plain metal 3 or 4-holed flat button, called a Sinkie, say, value 1 point.

(2.) The same kind of button, with letters or inscription on the rim, valued at 2 points.

(3.) The small metal shank button, called a Shankie, without any inscription, valued at 3 points; if with inscription, at 4 points; the large sizes and corresponding description were valued relatively 4 and 5 points.

(4.) The small Shankies, with a crest (livery waistcoat buttons), 6 points, and the large corresponding, 7 points.

(5.) The small Shankies, with coat of arms, value 8 points, and the large corresponding, 9 points.

(6.) Ornamental and various other buttons, such as regimental, official, mounted and engraved in flowers, and other designs according to arrangement, up to 20 points.

See " Banger," " Cots and Twisses."

Buzz and Bandy

A local name for " Hockey," which was formerly a very popular game among the young men of Shrewsbury and Much Wenlock. Called simply " Bandy " at Ludlow and Newport. —*Shropshire Folk-lore*, p. 525.

Cache-pole

The game of " Tennis."—Jamieson.

Caiche

The game of " Handball."

> Thocht I preich nocht I can play at the caiche.
> I wait thair is nocht ane among you all
> Mair ferilie can play at the fute ball.
> —Lyndsay's *S. P. Repr.*, ii. 243.

This language Lyndsay puts into the mouth of a Popish parson. The game seems to be that of ball played with the hand, as distinguished from " Football."—Jamieson.
See " Ball."

Call-the-Guse

This game is supposed by Jamieson to be equivalent to

"Drive the Goose," and the game seems to be the same with one still played by young people in some parts of Angus, in which one of the company, having something that excites ridicule unknowingly pinned behind, is pursued by all the rest, who still cry out, "Hunt the Goose!"—Jamieson.

Camp

A game formerly much in use among schoolboys, and occasionally played by men in those parts of Suffolk on the sea coast—more especially in the line of Hollesley Bay between the Rivers Orwell and Alde, sometimes school against school, or parish against parish. It was thus played: Goals were pitched at the distance of 150 or 200 yards from each other; these were generally formed of the thrown-off clothes of the competitors. Each party has two goals, ten or fifteen yards apart. The parties, ten or fifteen on a side, stand in line, facing their own goals and each other, at about ten yards distance, midway between the goals, and nearest that of their adversaries. An indifferent spectator, agreed on by the parties, throws up a ball, of the size of a common cricket-ball, midway between the confronted players, and makes his escape. It is the object of the players to seize and convey the ball between their own goals. The rush is therefore very great: as is sometimes the shock of the first onset, to catch the falling ball. He who first can catch or seize it speeds therefore home, pursued by his opponents (thro' whom he has to make his way), aided by the jostlings and various assistances of his own *sidesmen*. If caught and held, or in imminent danger of being caught, he *throws* the ball—but must in no case *give* it—to a less beleaguered friend, who, if it be not arrested in its course, or he jostled away by the eager and watchful adversaries, catches it; and he hastens homeward, in like manner pursued, annoyed, and aided, winning the notch (or snotch) if he contrive to *carry*, not *throw*, it between his goals. But this in a well-matched game is no easy achievement, and often requires much time, many doublings, detours, and exertions. I should have noticed, that if the holder of the ball be caught with the ball in his possession, he loses a *snotch*; if, therefore, he be hard pressed, he *throws* it to a convenient friend, more free and in breath than himself. At the loss (or gain) of a *snotch*, a recommence takes place, arranging which gives the parties time to take breath. Seven or nine notches are the game—and these it will sometimes take two or three hours to win. Sometimes a large football was used—and the game was then called "Kicking Camp"—and if played with the shoes on, "Savage Camp."—Moor's *Suffolk Words*.

(*b*) The sport and name are very old. The "Camping pightel" occurs in a deed of the 30 Henry VI.—about 1486; Cullum's *Hawstead*, p. 113, where Tusser is quoted in proof, that not only was the exercise manly and salutary, but good also for the *pightel* or meadow:

> In meadow or pasture (to grow the more fine)
> Let campers be camping in any of thine;
> Which if ye do suffer when low is the spring,
> You gain to yourself a commodious thing.—P. 65.

And he says, in p. 56:

> Get campers a ball,
> To camp therewithall.

Ray says that the game prevails in Norfolk, Suffolk, and Essex. The Rev. S. Arnot, in *Notes and Queries*, 8th series, vol. ii. p. 138, who was rector of Ilket's Hall, in the county of Suffolk, says the ball was about the size of a cricket-ball, and was driven through a narrow goal; and from the evidence of the parish clerk it seems certain that it was not "Football." See also Spurden's *East Anglian Words*, and *County Folk-lore*, *Suffolk*, pp. 57–59.

There are Upper Campfield and Lower Campfield at Norton Woodseats. They are also called Camping fields. This field was probably the place where football and other village games were played. These fields adjoin the Bocking fields. In Gosling's Map of Sheffield, 1736, Campo Lane is called *Camper Lane*. The same map shows the position of the old Latin school, or grammar school, and the writing school. These schools were at a very short distance from Campo Lane, and it seems probable that here the game of football was played (Addy's *Sheffield Glossary*). "The camping-land appropriated to this game occurs in several instances in authorities of the fifteenth century" (Way's Note in *Prompt. Parv.*, p. 60). In Brinsley's *Grammar Schoole*, cited by Mr. Furnivall in *Early English Meals and Manners*, p. lxii., is this passage: "By this meanes also the schollars may be kept euer in their places, and hard to their labours, without that running out to the Campo (as they tearme it) at school times, and the mani-folde disorders thereof; as watching and striuing for the clubbe and loytering then in the fields."

See " Football."

Canlie

A very common game in Aberdeen, played by a number of boys, one of whom is by lot chosen to act the part of Canlie. A certain portion of a street or ground, as it may happen, is marked off as his territory, into which, if any of the other boys presume to enter, and be caught by Canlie before he can get off the ground, he is doomed to take the place of Canlie, who becomes free in consequence of the capture. The game is prevalent throughout Scotland, though differently denominated: in Lanarkshire and Renfrewshire it is called "Tig," and in Mearns "Tick."—Jamieson.

See "Tig."

Capie-Hole

A hole is made in the ground, and a certain line drawn, called a Strand, behind which the players must take their stations. The object is at this distance to throw the bowl into the hole. He who does this most frequently wins. It is now more generally called "The Hole," but the old designation is not quite extinct. It is otherwise played in Angus. Three holes are made at equal distances. He who can first strike his bowl into each of these holes thrice in succession wins the game (Jamieson). It is alluded to in *The Life of a Scotch Rogue*, 1722, p. 7.

See "Bun-hole."

Carrick

Old name for "Shinty" in Fife.—Jamieson.

Carry my Lady to London

> I. Give me a pin to stick in my thumb
>   To carry my lady to London.
> Give me another to stick in my other
>   To carry her a little bit farther.
> —Belfast (W. H. Patterson).

> II. London Bridge is broken,
>   And what shall I do for a token ?
> Give me a pin to stick in my thumb
> And carry my lady to London.
> —*Notes and Queries*, 4th series, xii. 479.

> III. Give me a pin to stick in my chin (? cushion)
>   To carry a lady to London ;
> London Bridge is broken down
> And I must let my lady down.
> —Northall's *English Folk Rhymes*, p. 353.

(*b*) In this game two children cross hands, grasping each other's wrists and their own as well: they thus form a seat on which a child can sit and be carried about. At the same time they sing the verse.

Carrying the Queen a Letter

The King and Queen have a throne formed by placing two chairs a little apart, with a shawl spread from chair to chair. A messenger is sent into the room with a letter to the Queen, who reads it, and joins the King in a courteous entreaty that the bearer of the missive will place himself between them. When he has seated himself on the shawl, up jumps the King and Queen, and down goes the messenger on the floor.— Bottesford and Anderly (Lincolnshire), and Nottinghamshire (Miss M. Peacock).

(*b*) This is virtually the same game as "Ambassador," described by Grose as played by sailors on some inexperienced fellow or landsman. Between the two chairs is placed a pail of water, into which the victim falls.

Cashhornie

A game played with clubs by two opposite parties of boys, the aim of each party being to drive a ball into a hole belonging to their antagonists, while the latter strain every nerve to prevent this.—Jamieson.

Castles

A game at marbles. Each boy makes a small pyramid of three as a base, and one on the top. The players aim at these from a distant stroke with balsers, winning such of the castles as they may in turn knock down (Lowsley's *Glossary of Berkshire Words*). In London, the marble alluded to as "balser" was called "bonsor" or "bouncer" (J. P. Emslie).

See "Cockly Jock," "Cogs."

Cat and Dog

An ancient game played in Angus and Lothian. Three play, and they are provided with clubs. These clubs are called "dogs." The players cut out two holes, each about a foot in diameter, and seven inches in depth. The distance between them is about twenty-six feet. One stands at each hole with a club. A piece of wood about four inches long and one inch in diameter, called a Cat, is thrown from the one hole towards the other by a third person. The object is to prevent the Cat from getting into the hole. Every time that it enters the hole, he who has the club at that hole loses the club, and he who threw the Cat gets possession both of the club and of the hole, while the former possessor is obliged to take charge of the Cat. If the Cat be struck, he who strikes it changes places with the person who holds the other club; and as often as these positions are changed one is counted in the game by the two who hold the clubs, and who are viewed as partners.—Jamieson.

(*b*) This is not unlike the "Stool-Ball" described by Strutt (*Sports and Pastimes*, p. 76), but it more nearly resembles "Club-Ball," an ancient English game (ibid., p. 83). The game of "Cat," played with sticks and a small piece of wood, rising in the middle, so as to rebound when struck on either side, is alluded to in *Poor Robin's Almanack* for 1709, and by Brand. Leigh (*Cheshire Glossary*) gives "Scute" as another name for the game of "Cat," probably from *scute* (O.W.), for boat, which it resembles in shape.

See "Cudgel," "Kit-cat," "Tip-cat."

Cat-Beds

The name of a game played by young people in Perthshire. In this game, one, unobserved by all the rest, cuts with a knife the turf in very unequal angles. These are all covered, and each player puts his hand on what he supposes to be the smallest, as every one has to cut off the whole surface of his division. The rate of cutting is regulated by a throw of the knife, and the person who throws is obliged to cut as deep as the knife goes. He who is last in getting his bed cut up is bound to carry the whole of the clods, crawling on his hands and feet, to a certain distance measured by the one next to him, who throws the knife through his legs. If the bearer of the clods let any of them fall, the rest have a right to pelt him with them. They frequently lay them very loosely on, that they may have the pleasure of pelting.—Jamieson.

Cat's Cradle

One child holds a piece of string joined at the ends on his upheld palms, a single turn being taken over each, and by inserting the middle finger of each hand under the opposite turn, crosses the string from finger to finger in a peculiar form. Another child then takes off the string on his fingers in a rather different way, and it then assumes a second form. A repetition of this manœuvre produces a third form, and so on. Each of these forms has a particular name, from a fancied resemblance to the object—barn-doors, bowling-green, hour-glass, pound, net, fiddle, fish-pond, diamonds, and others.—*Notes and Queries*, vol. xi. p. 421.

The following forms are those known to me, with their names. They are produced seriatim.

1. The cradle.
2. The soldier's bed.
3. Candles.
4. The cradle inversed, or manger.
5. Soldier's bed again, or diamonds.
6. Diamonds, or cat's eyes.
7. Fish in dish.
8. Cradle as at first.

The different orders or arrangements must be taken from the hands of one player by another without disturbing the arrangement.—A. B. Gomme.

(*b*) Nares suggests that the proper name is "Cratch Cradle," and is derived from the archaic word *cratch*, meaning a manger. He gives several authorities for its use. The first-made form is not unlike a manger. Moor (*Suffolk Words*) gives the names as cat's cradle, barn-doors, bowling-green, hour-glass, pound,

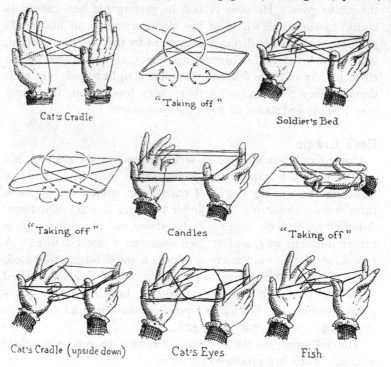

Cat's Cradle　　　　　"Taking off"　　　　　Soldier's Bed

"Taking off"　　　　　Candles　　　　　"Taking off"

Cat's Cradle (upside down)　　　　　Cat's Eyes　　　　　Fish.

net, diamonds, fish-pond, fiddle. A supposed resemblance originated them. Britton (*Beauties of Wiltshire*, Glossary) says the game in London schools is called "Scratch-scratch" or "Scratch-cradle."

The game is known to savage peoples. Professor Haddon noted it among the Torres Straits people, who start the game in the same manner as we do, but continue it differently (*Journ. Anthrop. Inst.*, p. 361); and Dr. Tylor has pointed out the significance of these string puzzles among savage peoples in *Journ. Anthrop. Inst.*, ix. 26.

Cat-gallows

A child's game, consisting of jumping over a stick placed at right angles to two others fixed in the ground.—Halliwell's *Dictionary*.

(*b*) In Ross and Stead's *Holderness Glossary* this is called "Cat-gallas," and is described as three sticks placed in the form of a gallows for boys to jump over. So called in consequence of being of sufficient height to hang cats from. Also mentioned in Peacock's *Manley and Corringham Glossary* and Elworthy's *West Somerset Words*, Brogden's *Provincial Words*, *Lincs.*, Dickinson's *Cumberland Glossary*, Atkinson's *Cleveland Glossary*, Brockett's *North Country Words*, Evans' *Leicestershire Glossary*, Baker's *Northants Glossary*, and Darlington's *South Cheshire Glossary*. On one of the stalls in Worcester Cathedral, figured in Wright's *Archæological Essays*, ii. 117, is a carving which represents three rats busily engaged in hanging a cat on a gallows of this kind.

Cat i' the Hole

A game well known in Fife, and perhaps in other counties. If seven boys are to play, six holes are made at certain distances. Each of the six stands at a hole, with a short stick in his hand; the seventh stands at a certain distance holding a ball. When he gives the word, or makes the sign agreed upon, all the six change holes, each running to his neighbour's hole, and putting his stick in the hole which he has newly seized. In making this change, the boy who has the ball tries to put it into an empty hole. If he succeeds in this, the boy who had not his stick (for the stick is the Cat) in the hole to which he had run is put out, and must take the ball. There is often a very keen contest whether the one shall get his stick, or the other the ball, or Cat, first put into the hole. When the Cat *is in the hole*, it is against the laws of the game to put the ball into it.—Jamieson.

(*b*) Kelly, in his *Scottish Proverbs*, p. 325, says, "'Tine cat, tine game;' an allusion to a play called 'Cat i' the Hole,' and the English 'Kit-cat.' Spoken when men at law have lost their principal evidence."

See "Cat and Dog," "Cudgel," "Kit-cat."

Cat after Mouse

This game, sometimes called "Threading the Needle," is played by children forming a ring, with their arms extended and hands clasped; one—the Mouse—goes outside the circle and gently pulls the dress of one of the players, who thereupon becomes the Cat, and is bound to follow wherever the Mouse chooses to go—either in or out of the ring—until caught, when he or she takes the place formerly occupied in the ring by the Cat, who in turn becomes Mouse, and the game is recommenced.—Dorsetshire (*Folk-lore Journal*, vi. 214).

(*b*) Played at Monton, Lancashire (Miss Dendy); Clapham Middle-Class School (Miss Richardson); and many other places. It is practically the same game as "Drop Handkerchief," played without words. It is described by Strutt, p. 381, who considers "Kiss-in-the-Ring" is derived from this "Cat and Mouse."

Catchers

One bicken is required in this game, and at this a lad must stand with a bat and ball in hand. He hits the ball away along the sand. Another boy picks it up and asks the striker "How many?" who replies—

> Two a good scat,
> Try for the bat.

The ball is then thrown to the bicken, and if it does not come within the distance named—two bats—the striker again sends the ball away, when the question is again asked—

> Three a good scat,
> Try for the bat.

And so on until the boy standing out throws the ball in to the required distance.—Old newspaper cutting without date in my possession (A. B. Gomme).

Chacke-Blyndman

Scotch name for "Blindman's Buff."—Jamieson.

Chance Bone

In Langley's abridgment of *Polydore Vergile*, f. l., we have a description of this game: "There is a game also that is played with the posterne bone in the hinder foote of a sheepe, oxe, gote, fallow, or redde dere, whiche in Latin is called *talus*. It hath foure chaunces: the ace point, that is named Canis, or Canicula, was one of the sides; he that cast it leyed doune a peny, or so muche as the gamers were agreed on; the other side was called Venus, that signifieth seven. He that cast the chaunce wan sixe and all that was layd doune for the castyng of Canis. The two other sides were called Chius and Senio. He that did throwe Chius wan three. And he that cast Senio gained four. This game (as I take it) *is used of children in Northfolke*, and they cal it the Chaunce Bone; they playe with three or foure of those bones together; it is either the same or very lyke to it."

See "Dibs," "Hucklebones."

Change Seats, the King's Come

In this game as many seats are placed round a room as will serve all the company save one. The want of a seat falls on an individual by a kind of lot, regulated, as in many other games, by the repetition of an old rhythm. All the rest being seated, he who has no seat stands in the middle, repeating the words "Change seats, change seats," &c., while all the rest are on the alert to observe when he adds, "the king's come," or, as it is sometimes expressed, change their seats. The sport lies in the bustle in consequence of every one's endeavouring to avoid the misfortune of being the unhappy individual who is left without a seat. The principal actor often slily says, "The king's *not* come," when, of course the company ought to keep their seats; but from their anxious expectation of the usual summons, they generally start up, which affords a great deal of merriment.—Brand's *Pop. Antiq.*, ii. 409.

(*b*) Dr. Jamieson says this is a game well-known in Lothian and in the South of Scotland. Sir Walter Scott, in *Rob Roy*, iii. 153, says, "Here auld ordering and counter-ordering—but patience! patience!—We may ae day play at *Change seats, the king's coming.*"

This game is supposed to ridicule the political scramble for places on occasion of a change of government, or in the succession.

See "Move All," "Musical Chairs," "Turn the Trencher."

Checkstone

Easther's *Almondbury Glossary* thus describes this game. A set of checks consists of five cubes, each about half an inch at the edge, and a ball the size of a moderate bagatelle ball: all made of pot. They are called checkstones, and the game is played thus. You throw down the cubes all at once, then toss the ball, and during its being in the air gather up one stone in your right hand and catch the descending ball in the same. Put down the stone and repeat the operation, gathering two stones, then three, then four, till at last you have "summed up" all the five at once, and have suceeeded in catching the ball. In case of failure you have to begin all over again.

(*b*) In Nashe's *Lenten Stuff* (1599) occurs the following: "Yet towards cock-crowing she caught a little slumber, and then she dreamed that Leander and she were playing at checkstone with pearls in the bottom of the sea."

A game played by children with round small pebbles (Halliwell's *Dictionary*). It is also mentioned in the early play of *Apollo Shroving*, 1627, p. 49.

See "Chucks," "Fivestones."

Cherry Odds

A game of "Pitch and Toss" played with cherry-stones (Elworthy's *West Somerset Words*). Boys always speak of the stones as "ods."

Cherry-pit

"Cherry-pit" is a play wherein they pitch cherry-stones into a little hole. It is noticed in the *Pleasant Grove of New Fancies*, 1657, and in Herrick's *Hesperides*. Nares (*Glossary*) mentions it as still practised with leaden counters called Dumps, or with money.

Chicamy

> Chicamy, chickamy, chimey O,
> Down to the pond to wash their feet;
> Bring them back to have some meat,
> Chickamy, chickamy, chimey O.
> —Crockham Hill, Kent (Miss Chase).

The children sing the first line as they go round and round. At the second line they move down the road a little, and turn round and round as they end the rhyme.

Chickidy Hand

> Chickidy hand,
> Chickidy hand,
> The Warner, my Cock,
> Crows at four in the morning.

Several boys, placing their clasped fists against a lamp-post, say these lines, after which they run out, hands still clasped. One in the middle tries to catch as many as possible, forming them in a long string, hand in hand, as they are caught. Those still free try to break through the line and rescue the prisoners. If they succeed in parting the line, they may carry one boy pig-a-back to the lamp-post, who becomes " safe." The boy caught last but one becomes " it " in the next game.—Deptford, Kent (Miss Chase).

See " Hunt the Staigie," " Stag Warning," " Whiddy."

Chinnup

A game played with hooked sticks and a ball, also called " Shinnup." Same as " Hockey."

Chinny-mumps

A school-boys' play, consisting in striking the chin with the knuckles; dexterously performed, a kind of time is produced. —Addy's *Sheffield Glossary*.

Chock or Chock-hole

A game at marbles played by " chocking " or pitching marbles in a hole made for the purpose, instead of shooting at a ring

(Northamptonshire, Baker's *Glossary*).　　Clare mentions the game in one of his poems.

Chow

A game played in Moray and Banffshire.　The ball is called the Chow.　The game is the same as "Shinty."　The players are equally divided.　After the Chow is struck off by one party, the aim of the other is to strike it back, that it may not reach the limit or goal on their side, because in this case they lose the game, and as soon as it crosses the line the other party cry Hail! or say that it is hail, as denoting that they have gained the victory.　In the beginning of each game they are allowed to raise the ball a little above the level of the ground, that they may have the advantage of a surer stroke.　This is called the "deil-chap," perhaps as a contraction of "devil," in reference to the force expended on the stroke.　It may, however, be "dule-chap," the blow given at the "dule" or goal.—Jamieson.

See "Hockey."

Chuck-farthing

Strutt says this game was played by boys at the commencement of the last century, and probably bore some analogy to "Pitch and Hustle."　He saw the game thus denominated played with halfpence, every one of the competitors having a like number, either two or four; a hole being made in the ground, with a mark at a given distance for the players to stand, they pitch their halfpence singly in succession towards the hole, and he whose halfpenny lies the nearest to it has the privilege of coming first to a second mark much nearer than the former, and all the halfpence are given to him; these he pitches in a mass toward the hole, and as many of them as remain therein are his due; if any fall short or jump out of it, the second player—that is, he whose halfpenny in pitching lay nearest to the first goer's—takes them and performs in like manner; he is followed by the others as long as any of the halfpence remain (*Sports*, pp. 386, 387).　There is a letter in the *Spectator*, supposed to be from the father of a romp, who, among other complaints of her conduct, says, "I have catched her once at eleven years old at 'Chuck-farthing' among the boys."

Chuck-hole, Chuck-penny

Same game as "Chuck-farthing," with this difference, that if the pennies roll outside the ring it is a "dead heat," and each boy reclaims his penny.—Peacock's *Manley and Corringham Glossary;* and see Brogden's *Lincolnshire Words.*

Chucks

A game with marbles played by girls (Mactaggart's *Gallovidian Encyclopædia*). A writer in *Blackwood's Magazine,* August 1821, p. 36, says "Chucks" is played with a bowl and chucks—a species of shells (*Buccinum lapillus*) found on the sea-shore ["bowl" here probably means a marble]. Brockett (*North Country Words*) says this game is played by girls with five sea-shells called chucks, and sometimes with pebbles, called chuckie-stanes. Jamieson says a number of pebbles are spread on a flat stone; one of them is tossed up, and a certain number must be gathered and the falling one caught by the same hand.

See "Checkstones," "Fivestones."

Church and Mice

A game played in Fifeshire; said to be the same with the "Sow in the Kirk."—Jamieson.

Click

Two Homes opposite each other are selected, and a boy either volunteers to go Click, or the last one in a race between the Homes does so. The others then proceed to one of the Homes, and the boy takes up his position between them. The players then attempt to run between the Homes, and if the one in the middle holds any of them while he says "One, two, three, I catch thee; help me catch another," they have to stay and help him to collar the rest until only one is left. If this one succeeds in getting between the Homes three times after all the others have been caught, he is allowed to choose the one to go Click in the next game; if he fails, he has to go himself.—Marlborough, Wilts (H. S. May).

See "Cock."

Click, Clock, Cluck

A man called Click came west from Ireland,
A man called Click came west from Ireland,
A man called Click came west from Ireland,
Courting my Aunt Judy.

A man called Clock came west from Ireland,
A man called Clock came west from Ireland,
A man called Clock came west from Ireland,
Courting my Aunt Judy.

A man called Cluck came west from Ireland,
A man called Cluck came west from Ireland,
A man called Cluck came west from Ireland,
Courting my Aunt Judy.

—Isle of Man (A. W. Moore).

These verses and the game are now quite forgotten, both in English and Manx. It was sung by children dancing round in a ring.

Clowt-clowt

"A kinde of playe called clowt-clowt, to beare about, or my hen hath layd."—*Nomenclator*, p. 299.

Clubby

A youthful game something like "Doddart."—Brockett's *North Country Words*.

Coal under Candlestick

A Christmas game mentioned in *Declaration of Popish Impostures*, p. 160.

Cob

A game at marbles played by two or three boys bowling a boss marble into holes made in the ground for the purpose, the number of which is generally four.—Baker's *Northamptonshire Glossary*.

Cobbin-match

A school game in which two boys are held by the legs and arms and bumped against a tree, he who holds out the longest being the victor.—Ross and Stead's *Holderness Glossary*.

Cobble

A name for "See-saw."—Jamieson.

Cobbler's Hornpipe

This was danced by a boy stooping till he was nearly in a sitting posture on the ground, drawing one leg under him until its toe rested on the ground, and steadying himself by thrusting forward the other leg so that the heel rested on the ground; the arms and head being thrown forwards as far as possible in order to maintain a balance.  The thrust-out leg was drawn back and the drawn-in leg was shot out at the same time. This movement was repeated, each bringing down to the ground of the toe and heel causing a noise like that of hammering on a lapstone. The arms were moved backwards and forwards at the same time to imitate the cobbler's sewing.—London (J. P. Emslie).

Cob-nut

The children in Yorkshire have a game which is probably an ancient English pastime. Numerous hazel-nuts are strung like the beads of a rosary. The game is played by two persons, each of whom has one of these strings, and consists in each party striking alternately, with one of the nuts on his own string, a nut of his adversary's. The field of combat is usually the crown of a hat. The object of each party is to crush the nuts of his opponent. A nut which has broken many of those of the adversary is a Cob-nut.—Brand, ii. 411; Hunter's *Hallamshire Glossary*.

(*b*) This game is played in London with chestnuts, and is called "Conquers." In Cornwall it is known as "Cock-haw."

The boys give the name of Victor-nut to the fruit of the common hazel, and play it to the words: "Cockhaw! First blaw! Up hat! Down cap! Victor!" The nut that cracks another is called a Cock-battler (*Folk-lore Journal*, v. 61). Halliwell describes this game differently. He says "it consists in pitching at a row of nuts piled up in heaps of four, three at the bottom and one at the top of each heap. The nut used for the pitching is called the Cob. All the nuts knocked down are the property of the pitcher." Alluding to the first described form, he says it "is probably a more modern game," and quotes Cotgrave *sub voce* "Chastelet" as authority for the earlier form in the way he describes it (*Dictionary*). Addy says the nuts were hardened for the purpose. When a nut was broken it was said to be "cobbered" or "cobbled" (*Sheffield Glossary*). Evans' *Leicestershire Glossary* also describes it. Darlington (*South Cheshire Words*) says this game only differs from "Cobblety-cuts" in the use of small nuts instead of chestnuts. George Eliot in *Adam Bede* has, "Gathering the large unripe nuts to play at 'Cob-nut' with" (p. 30). Britton's *Beauties of Wiltshire* gives the Isle of Wight and Hants as other places where the game is known.

See "Conquerors."

Cock

One boy is chosen Cock. The players arrange themselves in a line along one side of the playground. The Cock takes his stand in front of the players. When everything is ready, a rush across the playground is made by the players. The Cock tries to catch and "croon"—*i.e.*, put his hand upon the head of—as many of the players as he can when running from one side of the playground to the other. Those caught help the Cock in the rush back. The rush from side to side goes on till all are captured. To "croon" was the essential point in capturing. When a boy was being pursued to be taken prisoner, his great object was, when he came to close quarters with his pursuers, to save his head from being touched on the crown by one of them.—Nairn (Rev. W. Gregor).

At Duthil, Strathspey, this game goes by the name of

" Rexa-boxa-King." When the players have ranged themselves on one side of the playground, and the King has taken
his stand in front of them, he calls out " Rexa-boxa-King," or
simply " Rexa," when all the players rush to the other side.
The rush from side to side goes on till all are captured. The
one last captured becomes King in the next game.—Rev. W.
Gregor.

See " Click."

Cock-battler

Children, under the title of " Cock-battler," often in country
walks play with the hoary plantain, which they hold by the
tough stem about two inches from the head ; each in turn tries
to knock off the head of his opponent's flower.—Cornwall (*Folk-
lore Journal*, v. 61).

In the North, and in Suffolk, it is called " Cocks," " a puerile
game with the tough tufted stems of the ribwort plantain "
(Brockett's *North Country Words*). Moor (*Suffolk Words*)
alludes to the game, and Holloway (*Dictionary of Provincialisms*) says in West Sussex boys play with the heads of rib
grass a similar game. Whichever loses the head first is conquered. It is called " Fighting-cocks."

Cock-fight

This is a boys' game. Two boys fold their arms, and then,
hopping on one leg, butt each other with their shoulders till one
lets down his leg. Any number of couples can join in this
game.—Nairn (Rev. W. Gregor).

Cock-haw.

See " Cob-nut."

Cock-stride

One boy is chosen as Cock. He is blindfolded, and stands
alone, with his legs as far apart as possible. The other boys
then throw their caps as far as they are able between the extended legs of the Cock (fig. 1). After the boys have thrown
their caps, and each boy has taken his stand beside his cap,
the Cock, still blindfolded, stoops down and crawls in search

of the caps (fig. 2). The boy whose cap he first finds has to run about twenty yards under the buffeting of the other boys, the

Fig. 1   Fig. 2

blows being directed chiefly to the head. He becomes Cock at the next turn of the game.—Rosehearty, Pitsligo (Rev. W. Gregor).

Cockertie-hooie

This game consists simply of one boy mounting on the neck of another, putting a leg over each shoulder and down his breast. The boy that carries takes firm hold of the legs of the one on his neck, and sets off at a trot, and runs hither and thither till he becomes tired of his burden. The bigger the one is who carries, the more is in the enjoyment to the one carried.—Keith (Rev. W. Gregor).

See "Cock's-headling."

Cockle-bread

Young wenches have a wanton sport, which they call moulding of Cocklebread; viz. they gett upon a Table-board, and then gather-up their knees and their coates with their hands as high as they can, and then they wabble to and fro with their Buttocks as if the[y] were kneading of Dowgh, and say these words, viz. :—

My Dame is sick and gonne to bed,
And I'le go mowld my cockle-bread.

In Oxfordshire the maids, when they have put themselves into the fit posture, say thus :—

My granny is sick, and now is dead,
And wee'l goe mould some cockle-bread.

Up with my heels, and down with my head,
And this is the way to mould cocklebread.
                              —*Aubrey's Remains*, pp. 43, 44.

To make "Barley bread" (in other districts, "Cockley bread")
this rhyme is used in West Cornwall :—

Mother has called, mother has said,
Make haste home, and make barley bread.
Up with your heels, down with your head,
That is the way to make barley bread.
                              —*Folk-lore Journal*, v. 58.

The Westmoreland version is given by Ellis in his edition
of Brand as follows :—

My grandy's seeke,
And like to dee,
And I'll make her
Some cockelty bread, cockelty bread,
And I'll make her
Some cockelty bread.

The term "Cockelty" is still heard among our children
at play. One of them squats on its haunches with the hands
joined beneath the thighs, and being lifted by a couple of others
who have hold by the bowed arms, it is swung backwards and
forwards and bumped on the ground or against the wall, while
continuing the words, "This is the way we make cockelty
bread."—Robinson's *Whitby Glossary*, p. 40.

The moulding of "Cockelty-bread" is a sport amongst
hoydenish girls not quite extinct. It consists in sitting on
the ground, raising the knees and clasping them with the hand,
and then using an undulatory motion, as if they were kneading
dough.

My granny is sick and now is dead,
And we'll go mould some cocklety bread ;
Up with the heels and down with the head,
And that is the way to make cocklety bread.
                              —Hunter's MSS. ; Addy's *Sheffield Glossary*.

(*b*) The *Times* of 1847 contains a curious notice of this
game. A witness, whose conduct was impugned as light and

unbecoming, is desired to inform the court, in which an action for breach of promise was tried, the meaning of "mounting cockeldy-bread;" and she explains it as "a play among children," in which one lies down on the floor on her back, rolling backwards and forwards, and repeating the following lines:—

> Cockeldy bread, mistley cake,
> When you do that for our sake.

While one of the party so laid down, the rest sat around; and they laid down and rolled in this manner by turns.

These lines are still retained in the modern nursery-rhyme books, but their connection with the game of "Cockeldy-bread" is by no means generally understood. There was formerly some kind of bread called "cockle-bread," and *cocille-mele* is mentioned in a very early MS. quoted in Halliwell's *Dictionary*. In Peele's play of the *Old Wives Tale*, a voice thus speaks from the bottom of a well:—

> Gently dip, but not too deep,
> For fear you make the golden beard to weep.
> Fair maiden, white and red,
> Stroke me smooth and comb my head,
> And thou shalt have some *cockell-bread*.

Cockly-jock

A game among boys. Stones are loosely placed one upon another, at which other stones are thrown to knock the pile down.—Dickinson's *Cumberland Glossary*.

See "Castles."

Cock's-headling

A game where boys mount over each other's heads.—Halliwell's *Dictionary*.

See "Cockertie-hooie."

Cock-steddling

A boyish game mentioned but not described by Cope in his *Hampshire Glossary*. He gives as authority *Portsmouth Telegraph*, 27th September 1873.

Codlings

A game among youngsters similar to "Cricket," a short piece

of wood being struck up by a long stick instead of a ball by a bat. Also called "Tip and Go" or "Tip and Slash."—Robinson's *Whitby Glossary*.

See "Cudgel."

Cogger

A striped snail shell. It is a common boyish pastime to hold one of these shells between the last joints of the bent fingers, and forcibly press the apex against another held in a similar manner by an opponent, until one of them, by dint of persevering pressure, forces its way into the other; and the one which in these contests has gained the most victories is termed the Conqueror, and is highly valued (Northamptonshire, Baker's *Glossary*). The game is known as "Fighting Cocks" in Evans' *Leicestershire Glossary*. In London it was played with walnut shells.

Cogs

The top stone of a pile is pelted by a stone flung from a given distance, and the more hits, or "cogglings off," the greater the player's score.—Robinson's *Whitby Glossary*.

Apparently the same game as "Cockly-jock."

Common

A game played with a ball and crooked stick (cut from a tree or hedge), with a crook at the end (same game as "Hurl"). —Dublin (Mrs. Lincoln).

Mr. Patterson (*Antrim and Down Glossary*) mentions this as "Hockey;" the same as "Shinney." "Called in some districts," he adds, "'Comun' and 'Kamman,' from the Irish name for the game."

Conkers

The same game as "Cogger." The game is more generally called "playin at sneel-shells."—Ross and Stead's *Holderness Glossary*.

Conquerors or Conkers

I.   Cobbly co!
       My first blow!

Put down your black hat,
And let me have first smack !
　　　　　　—Burne's *Shropshire Folk-lore*, p. 531.

II.　Obli, obli O, my first go ;
　　　And when the nut is struck,
　　　Obli, obli onker, my nut will conquer.
　　　　　　—*Notes and Queries*, 5th series, x. 378.

III.　Cobblety cuts,
　　　 Put down your nuts.
　　　　　　—Darlington's *Folk-speech of South Cheshire*.

IV.　Obbly, obbly onkers, my first conquers ;
　　　Obbly, obbly O, my first go.
　　　　　　—Lawson's *Upton-on-Severn Words and Phrases*.

V.　Hobley, hobley, honcor, my first conkor ;
　　 Hobbley, hobbley ho, my first go ;
　　 Hobley, hobley ack, my first crack.
　　　　　　—Chamberlain's *West Worcestershire Glossary*.

(*b*) This game is played with horse chestnuts threaded on a
string.　Two boys sit face to face astride of a form or a log of
timber.　If a piece of turf can be procured so much the better.
One boy lays his chestnut upon the turf, and the other strikes
at it with his chestnut ; and they go on striking alternately till
one chestnut splits the other.　The chestnut which remains
unhurt is then "conqueror of one."　A new chestnut is substituted for the broken one, and the game goes on.　Whichever chestnut now proves victorious becomes "conqueror of
two," and so on, the victorious chestnut adding to its score all
the previous winnings.　The chestnuts are often artificially
hardened by placing them up the chimney or carrying them in
a warm pocket ; and a chestnut which has become conqueror
of a considerable number acquires a value in schoolboys' eyes ;
and I have frequently known them to be sold, or exchanged for
other toys (Holland's *Cheshire Glossary*).　The game is more
usually played by one boy striking his opponent's nut with his
own, both boys standing and holding the string in their hands.
It is considered bad play to strike the opponent's *string*.　The
nut only should be touched.　Three tries are usually allowed.

(*c*) For information on various forms of this game, see *Notes and Queries*, 1878. See also Elworthy's *West Somerset Words*. The boy who first said the rhyme has first stroke at Oswestry. The game is elsewhere called "Cobbet" (Meole Brace) and "Cobbleticuts" (Burne's *Shropshire Folk-lore*, p. 531). In "Conquer-nuts" "obbly" was probably "nobbly" or "knobbly," expressing the appearance of the string of nuts; and "onkers" was probably invented as a rhyme to "conquers" (*Upton-on-Severn Words and Phrases*, by R. Lawson).

Contrary, Rules of

    I.   Here I go round the rules of contrary,
          Hopping about like a little canary.
          When I say "Hold fast," leave go;
          When I say "Leave go," hold fast.
                    —Cornwall (*Folk-lore Journal*, v. 52).

    II.   Here we go round the rules of contrary,
          When I say "Hold fast!" let go, and when I say
          "Let go!" hold fast.   —London (A. B. Gomme).

(*b*) A ring is formed by each child holding one end of a handkerchief. One child stands in the centre and acts as leader. The ring moves round slowly. The leader says the words as above while the ring is moving round, and then suddenly calls out whichever he chooses of the two sayings. If he says "Hold fast!" every one must immediately let go the corner of the handkerchief he holds. They should all fall to the ground at once. When he says "Let go!" every one should retain their hold of the handkerchief. Forfeits are demanded for every mistake.

This game, called "Hawld Hard," is commonly played about Christmas-time, where a number hold a piece of a handkerchief. One then moves his hand round the handkerchief, saying, "Here we go round by the rule of Contrairy; when I say 'Hawld hard,' let go, and when I say 'Let go,' hawld hard." Forfeits are paid by those not complying with the order.— Lowsley's *Berkshire Glossary*.

Cop-halfpenny

The game of " Chuck-farthing."—Norfolk and Suffolk (Holloway's *Dict. of Provincialisms*).

Corsicrown

A square figure is divided by four lines, which cross each other in the crown or centre. Two of these lines connect the opposite angles, and two the sides at the point of bisection. Two players play; each has three men or flitchers. Now there are seven points for these men to move about on, six on the edges of the square and one at the centre. The men belonging to each player are not set together as at draughts, but mingled with each other. The one who has the first move may always have the game, which is won by getting the three men on a line.—Mactaggart's *Gallovidian Encyclopædia*.

See " Kit Cat Cannio," " Noughts and Crosses."

Cots and Twisses

A flat stone is obtained called a Hob, upon which those who are playing place equal shares of Cots and Twisses. Cots are brass buttons, and Twisses bits of brass—a Twiss of solid brass being worth many Cots. Each player provides himself with a nice flat [key] stone, and from an agreed pitch tosses it at the Hob. If he knocks off any of the Cots and Twisses nearer to the players than the Hob is, he claims them. The other players try to knock the Hob away with their key-stones from any Cots and Twisses that may not have been claimed; and if any key-stone touches Hob after all have thrown, the owner cannot claim any Cots and Twisses.—Earls Heaton (Herbert Hardy).

Each player selects a Cast or stone to pitch with; on another stone, called the Hob, the Cots and Twys are placed; at some distance Scops are set in the ground. First the players pitch from the Hob to the Scop, and the one who gets nearest goes first. He then pitches at the Hob, and if he knocks off the stakes he has them, provided his Cast is nearer to them than the Hob is; in failure of this, the other player tries. In pitching up, one Cast may rest on another, and if the boy whose stone is underneath can lift it up to knock the other Cast away, it has to remain at the place to which it has been struck ; if he does not succeed in doing this, the second player may lift off his Cast and place it by the side of the first. Whoever knocks off the stakes, they go to the boy whose Cast is nearest to them. The Hob and Scop are usually three yards apart. The Cot was a button off the waistcoat or trousers, the Twy one off the coat, and, as its name implies, was equal to two Cots. Formerly, when cash was much more rare than now it is amongst boys, these formed their current coin. The game about 1820 seems to have been chiefly one of tossing, and was played with buttons, then common enough. Now, metal buttons being rare, it is played with pieces of brass or copper of any shape. The expression, "I haven't a cot," is sometimes used to signify that a person is without money.— Easther's *Almondbury and Huddersfield Glossary*.

See "Banger," "Buttons."

Course o' Park

The game of "Course of the Park" has not been described, but is referred to in the following verse :—

"Buff"'s a fine sport,
And so's "Course o' Park."

—*The Slighted Maid*, 1663. p. 50.

Crab-sowl, Crab-sow

A game played with a bung or ball struck with sticks (Brogden's *Provincial Words, Lincolnshire*). This is played on Barnes Common, and is apparently a form of "Hockey" (A. B. Gomme).

Crates

The game of "Nine Holes." This is the game described by John Jones, M.D., in his book called *The Benefit of the Auncient Bathes of Buckstones*, 1572, p. 12, as having been played by ladies at Buxton for their amusement in wet weather. See Pegge's *Anonymiana*, 1818, p. 126, and Addy's *Sheffield Glossary*.

Cricket

A description of this game is not given here; its history and rules and regulations are well known, and many books have been devoted to its study. The word "Cricket" is given in Lawson's *Upton-on-Severn Words and Phrases* as a low wooden stool. He continues, "The game of 'Cricket' was probably a development of the older game of 'Stool-ball,' a dairymaid's stool being used for the wicket." Wedgwood (*Etym. Dict.*) suggests that the proper name for the bat was "cricket-staff," A.-S. *criec*, a staff.

See "Bittle-battle," "Stool-ball."

Crooky

An old game called "Crooky" was formerly played at Portarlington, Queen's co., and Kilkee, co. Clare. Fifty years ago it was played with wooden crooks and balls, but about twenty-five years ago, or a little more, mallets were introduced at Kilkee; while subsequently the name was changed to "Croquet." I have heard it stated that this game was introduced by the French refugees that settled at Portarlington. —G. H. Kinahan (*Folk-lore Journal,* ii. 265).

Cross and Pile

The game now called "Heads and Tails" (Halliwell's *Dictionary*). See *Nomenclator,* p. 299; Addy's *Sheffield Glossary.* Strutt points out that anciently the English coins were stamped on one side with a cross. See also Harland's *Lancashire Legends,* p. 139.

Cross-bars

A boys' game.—Halliwell's *Dictionary*.

Cross-questions

Nares (*Glossary*) mentions this game in a quotation from Wilson's *Inconstant Lady,* 1614. "Cross Questions and Crooked Answers" was a popular game àt juvenile parties. The players sit in a circle, and each is asked in a whisper a question by the one on his left, and receives also in a whisper an answer to a question asked by himself of the person on his right. Each player must remember both the question he was asked and the answer he received, which have at the conclusion of the round to be stated aloud. Forfeits must be given if mistakes are made.—A. B. Gomme.

Cross Tig

One of the players is appointed to be Tig. He calls out the name of the one he intends to chase, and runs after him. Another player runs across between Tig and the fugitive, and then Tig runs after this cross-player until another player runs across between Tig and the fugitive; and so on. Each time a player crosses between Tig and the player he is following he leaves the original chase and follows the player who has crossed. When he captures, or, in some places, touches one of the players he is following, this player becomes Tig, and the game begins again.—Ireland (Miss Keane).

This game is known in and near London as "Cross Touch."

Cry Notchil

This is an old game where boys push one of their number into a circle they have made, and as he tries to escape push him back, crying, "No child of mine!" (Leigh's *Cheshire Glossary*). He adds, "This may be the origin of the husband's disclaimer of his wife when he 'notchils' her." To "cry notchil" is for a man to advertise that he will not be answerable for debts incurred by his wife.

Cuck-ball

A game at ball. The same as "Pize-ball." It is sometimes called "Tut-ball."—Addy's *Sheffield Glossary*.

See "Ball."

Cuckoo

A child hides and cries "Cuckoo." The seekers respond—

Cuckoo cherry-tree,
Catch a bird and bring it me.
—Burne's *Shropshire Folk-lore*, p. 222.

Halliwell calls this a game at ball, and the rhyme runs—

Cuckoo cherry tree,
Catch a bird and bring it me;

Let the tree be high or low,
Let it hail, rain or snow.
See " Hide and Seek."

Cuddy and the Powks

Two boys join hands and feet over the back of a third, the
which creeps away with them on hands and knees to a certain
distance; and if able to do this, he, the Cuddy, must have a
ride as one of the powks on some other's back.—Mactaggart's
Gallovidian Encyclopædia.

Cudgel

Four or more boys can play this game, and sides are chosen.
Two holes are made in the ground at a distance of about eight
or ten feet apart. A ring about a foot in diameter is made
round each hole. A boy stands at each hole with a stick,
which he puts into the hole to guard it. Two other boys stand
behind the holes, who act as bowlers. One of these throws a
small piece of wood shaped like a Cat, and tries to pitch it into
the hole. The boy guarding the hole tries to hit it with his

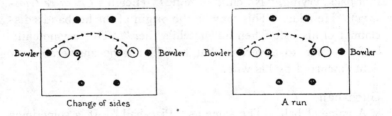

Change of sides   A run

stick. If he succeeds, he and the boy at the other hole run to
each other's places. Should the boy who throws the piece of
wood succeed in getting it into the hole, the batsmen are out.
Should the Cat fall into the ring or a span beyond, one of the
bowlers picks it up, and both run to a hiding-place. They then
agree as to which of them should hold the Cat. This must be
carried in such a way that it cannot be seen by the batsmen,
both boys assuming the same attitude. Both boys then resume
their previous places. They kneel down, still keeping the same
attitudes. The batsmen, keeping their sticks in the holes,
then agree which of the two holds the Cat. One batsman

runs across and puts his stick into the hole behind which the boy kneels whom they consider has the Cat, the other then running to his place.   If they are right in their guess, the holder of the Cat throws it across the ground for the opposite bowler to put it in the hole before the second batsman reaches it.   If they guess wrongly, the holder of the Cat puts it into the hole as soon as the batsman runs, and they then become the batsmen for the next game.   If the batsmen leave their holes unguarded with the stick, the catsmen can at any time put them "out," by putting the Cat in a hole.   If more than two boys on a side play, the others field as in "Cricket."—Barnes (A. B. Gomme).

See "Cat and Dog."

Curcuddie

I.   Will ye gang to the lea, Curcuddie,
And join your plack wi' me, Curcuddie ?
I lookit about and I saw naebody,
And linkit awa' my lane, Curcuddie.
                    —Chambers' *Popular Rhymes*, p. 139.

II.   Will ye gang wi' me, Curcuddie,
Gang wi' me o'er the lea ?
I lookit roun', saw naebody ;
Curcuddie, he left me.
                    —Biggar (William Ballantyne).

(*b*) This is a grotesque kind of dance, performed in a shortened posture, sitting on one's hams, with arms akimbo, the dancers forming a circle of independent figures.   It always excites a hearty laugh among the senior bystanders ; but, ridiculous as it is, it gives occasion for the display of some spirit and agility, as well as skill, there being always an inclination to topple over.   Each performer sings the verse (Chambers ; Mactaggart's *Gallovidian Encyclopædia*).

Mr. Ballantyne says that each one apart tried to dance by throwing out their feet and jumping sideways.

(*c*) The first syllable of this word is, says Jamieson, undoubtedly the verb *curr*, to sit on the houghs or hams.   The second may be from Teut. *kudde*, a flock ; *kudd-en*, coire,

convenire, congregari, aggregari; *kudde wijs*, gregatim, cater-
vatim, q. to curr together. The same game is called *Harry
Hurcheon* in the North of Scotland, either from the resemblance
of one in this position to a *hurcheon*, or hedge-hog, squatting
under a bush; or from the Belg. *hurk-en*, to squat, to *hurkle*.
—Jamieson.

See "Cobbler's Hornpipe," "Cutch-a-Cutchoo."

Curly Locks

    I. Curly locks, curly locks,
        Wilt thou be mine?
    Thou shalt not wash dishes
        Nor yet feed the swine;
    But sit on a fine cushion
        And sew a fine seam,
    And feed upon strawberries,
        Sugar and cream.
              —Earls Heaton (Herbert Hardy).

    II. Bonny lass, canny lass,
        Wilta be mine?
    Thou's nowder wesh dishes
        Nor sarra the swine:
    But sit on thy crippy, &c.
           —Dickinson's *Cumberland Glossary*.

(*b*) Two children, a girl and a boy, separate from their
fellows, who are not particularly placed, the boy caressing the
girl's curls and singing the verses.

(*c*) This game is evidently a dramatic representation of

wooing, and probably the action of the game has never been quite completed in the nursery. The verses are given as "nursery rhymes" by Halliwell, Nos. cccclxxxiii. and ccccxciv. The tune is from Rimbault's *Nursery Rhymes*, p. 70. The words given by him are the same as the Earls Heaton version.

Currants and Raisins

> Currants and raisins a penny a pound,
> Three days holiday.

This is a game played "running under a handkerchief;" "something like 'Oranges and Lemons.'"—Lincoln (Miss M. Peacock).

Cushion Dance

This strain twice.   This once.

Play this as oft as is required.

—Dancing Master, 1686.

This music is exactly as it is printed in the book referred to.

(*b*) The following is an account of the dance as it was known in Derbyshire amongst the farmers' sons and daughters and the domestics, all of whom were on a pretty fair equality, very different from what prevails in farm-houses of to-day. The "Cushion Dance" was a famous old North-country amusement, and among the people of Northumberland it is still commonly observed. The dance was performed with boisterous fun, quite unlike the game as played in higher circles, where the conditions and rules of procedure were of a more refined order.

The company were seated round the room, a fiddler occupying a raised seat in a corner. When all were ready, two of the young men left the room, returning presently, one carrying a large square cushion, the other an ordinary drinking-horn, china bowl, or silver tankard, according to the possessions of the family. The one carrying the cushion locked the door, putting the key in his pocket. Both gentlemen then went to the fiddler's corner, and after the cushion-bearer had put a coin in the vessel carried by the other, the fiddler struck up a lively tune, to which the young men began to dance round the room, singing or reciting to the music:—

> Frinkum, frankum is a fine song,
> An' we will dance it all along;
> All along and round about,
> Till we find the pretty maid out.

After making the circuit of the room, they halted on reaching the fiddler's corner, and the cushion-bearer, still to the music of the fiddle, sang or recited:—

> Our song it will no further go!

The Fiddler: Pray, kind sir, why say you so?

The Cushion-bearer: Because Jane Sandars won't come to.

The Fiddler: She must come to, she shall come to,
> An' I'll make her whether she will or no.

The cushion-bearer and vessel-holder then proceeded with the dance, going as before round the room, singing "Frinkum, frankum," &c., till the cushion-bearer came to the lady of his choice, before whom he paused, placed the cushion on the floor at her feet, and knelt upon it. The vessel-bearer then offered the cup to the lady, who put money in it and knelt on the cushion in front of the kneeling gentleman. The pair kissed, arose, and the gentleman, first giving the cushion to the lady with a bow, placed himself behind her, taking hold of some portion of her dress. The cup-bearer fell in also, and they danced on to the fiddler's corner, and the ceremony was again gone through as at first, with the substitution of the name of "John" for "Jane," thus:—

The Lady: Our song it will no further go!

The Fiddler: Pray, kind miss, why say you so?

The Lady: Because John Sandars won't come to.

The Fiddler: He must come to, he shall come to,
> An' I'll make him whether he will or no!

The dancing then proceeded, and the lady, on reaching her choice (a gentleman, of necessity), placed the cushion at his

feet. He put money in the horn and knelt. They kissed and
rose, he taking the cushion and his place in front of the lady,
heading the next dance round, the lady taking him by the coat-
tails, the first gentleman behind the lady, with the horn-bearer
in the rear. In this way the dance went on till all present,
alternately a lady and gentleman, had taken part in the ceremony. The dance concluded with a romp in file round the
room to the quickening music of the fiddler, who at the close
received the whole of the money collected by the horn-
bearer.

At Charminster the dance is begun by a single person (either
man or woman), who dances about the room with a cushion in
his hand, and at the end of the tune stops and sings :—

Man :   This dance it will no further go.
Musician : I pray you, good sir, why say you so ?
Man :   Because Joan Sanderson will not come to.
Musician : She must come to, and she shall come to,
            And she must come whether she will or no.

Then the following words are sung as in the first example :—

Man : Welcome, Joan Sanderson, welcome, welcome.
Both : Prinkum-prankum is a fine dance,
        And shall we go dance it once again,
            And once again,
        And shall we go dance it once again ?
Woman : This dance it will no further go.
Musician : I pray you, madam, why say you so ?
Woman : Because John Sanderson will not come to.
Musician : He must come to, and he shall come to,
            And he must come whether he will or no.

And so she lays down the cushion before a man, who,
kneeling upon it, salutes her, she singing—

        Welcome, John Sanderson, &c.

Then, he taking up the cushion, they take hands and dance
round singing as before ; and this they do till the whole company is taken into the ring. Then the cushion is laid down
before the first man, the woman singing, "This dance," &c., as
before, only instead of "come to," they sing "go fro," and instead of "Welcome, John Sanderson," &c., they sing "Farewell,

John Sanderson, farewell," &c., and so they go out one by one as they came in.—Charminster (*Notes and Queries*, ii. 517, 518).

This description is almost the same as a seventeenth century version. The dance is begun by a single person (either man or woman), who, taking a cushion in his hand, dances about the room, and at the end of the tune he stops and sings :—

> This dance it will no further go.

The Musician answers :

> I pray you, good sir, why say you so ?

Man :   Because Joan Sanderson will not come to.

Musician : She must come to, and she shall come to,

> And she must come whether she will or no.

Then he lays down the cushion before a woman, on which she kneels, and he kisses her, singing—

> Welcom, Joan Sanderson, welcom, welcom.

Then he rises, takes up the cushion, and both dance, singing—

> Prinkum-prankum is a fine dance,
> And shall we go dance it once again,
> Once again, and once again,
> And shall we go dance it once again.

Then, making a stop, the wo(man) sings as before—

> This dance, &c.

Musician : I pray you, madam, &c.

Woman :   Because John Sanderson, &c.

Musician : He must, &c.

And so she lays down the cushion before a man, who, kneeling upon it, salutes her, she singing—

> Welcom, John Sanderson, &c.

Then, he taking up the cushion, they take hands and dance round, singing as before. And thus they do till the whole company are taken into the ring. And then the cushion is laid before the first man, the woman singing, "This dance," &c. (as before), only instead of "come to," they sing "go fro," and instead of "Welcom, John Sanderson," &c., they sing "Farewel, John Sanderson, farewel, farewel;" and so they go out one by one as they came in. *Note*, that the woman is kiss'd by all the men in the ring at her coming in and going out, and the like of the man by the woman.—*The Dancing Master:* London, printed by J. P., and sold by John Playford at his shop near the Temple Church, 1686, 7th edition.

Another version gives the words as follows :—

> We've got a new sister in our degree,
> And she's welcome into our companee, companee.
> Mrs. Sargesson says she weänt come to,
> We'll make her whether she will or no,
>   Will or no, will or no,
> We'll maäke her whether she will or no.

Children form a ring with one in the middle, who lays a cushion on the ground. They sing the first two lines, and the child in the centre points at one, and the others dance round singing the other lines, the centre child dragging the imaginary Mrs. Sargesson on to the cushion by force, kissing her, and leaving her in the centre. Then Mrs. Sargesson points at one in the ring, and the game begins again.—East Kirkby, Lincolnshire (Miss Maughan). The tune sung is the same as the " Mulberry Bush."

Miss Baker (*Northamptonshire Glossary*) says the Cushion Dance is still continued, with some variations, and generally closes the evening's amusements. One of the young men endeavours secretly to bring in a cushion, and locks the doors, to prevent the escape of the young maidens ; then all the party unite hands and dance round three times to the left and three times to the right, after which the company all seat themselves, except the young man who holds the cushion. He advances to the fiddler, and says—

> This dance it will no further go.

Fiddler :   Why say you so ? why say you so ?
Cushion-holder : Because the young women will not come to.
Fiddler :   They must come to, they shall come to,
               And tell them I say so.

The cushion-holder then goes to the girl he fancies most, and drops the cushion at her feet. She kneels down with him on the cushion, and he salutes her, and they then rise and dance round and round to the fiddler. The girls then go through the same thing, saying, "young men," and then "a young man," &c., until the whole company have gone through the same ceremony, which concludes with all dancing round three times, as at the commencement.

The Norfolk and London versions are reduced to a simple "Kiss in the Ring" game, with the following verse :—

> Round the cushion we dance with glee,
> Singing songs so merrily ;
> Round the cushion we dance with glee,
> Singing songs so merrily ;
> Yet the punishment you must bear
> If you touch the cushion there.
> —Sporle, Norfolk (Miss Matthews).

(c) Selden, in his *Table Talk*, thus refers to this game :— "The Court of England is much altered. At a solemn dancing first you have the grave measures, then the Cervantoes and the Golliards, and this is kept up with ceremony. At length to Trenchmore and the *Cushion Dance ;* and then all the company dance, lord and groom, lady and kitchen-maid, no distinction. But in King Charles's time there has been nothing but Trenchmore and the Cushion Dance," &c. The "Whishin Dance" (an old-fashioned dance, in which a cushion is used to kneel upon), mentioned by Dickinson (*Cumberland Glossary*), is probably the same game or dance, "whishin" meaning cushion. Brockett (*North Country Words*) mentions "Peas Straw," the final dance at a rustic party ; something similar to the ancient "Cushion Dance" at weddings. It is also recorded in Evans' *Leicestershire Glossary*, and by Burton in the following passage from the *Anatomy of Melancholy :* "A friend of his reprehended him for dancing beside his dignity, belike at some cushen dance." In the version from East Kirkby, Lincolnshire, the expression "in our degree" in the first line of the verse is apparently meaningless, and it is probably a corruption of "highdigees, highdegrees," a dialect word for roystering, high spirits, merriment, dancing, romping. Elworthy (*Somerset Words*) gives this word, and quotes the following line from Drayton :—

> Dance many a merry round and many a highdegy.
> —*Polyolbion*, Bk. xxv., l. 1162.

(d) The transition from a dance to a pure game is well

illustrated by the different versions, and the connection of the dance with the ceremony of marriage is obvious. A curious account of the merry-makings at marriages is given in Coverdale's *Christen State of Matrimony*, 1543: "After the banket and feast there beginneth a mad and unmannerly fashion; for the bride must be brought into an open dauncing-place. Then is there such a running, leaping, and flinging among them that a man might think all these dauncers had cast all shame behinde them, and were become starke mad, and out of their wits, and that they were sworne to the devil's daunce. Then must the bride keep foote with all dauncers, and refuse none, how scabbed, foule, drunken, rude, and shameless soever he be. . . . After supper must they begin to pipe and daunce again of anew. And though the young persons come once towards their rest, yet can they have no quietness."—1575 edit., fol. 59, rev. 60. Edward L. Rimbault, writing in *Notes and Queries*, vi. 586, says it was formerly the custom at weddings, both of the rich as well as the poor, to dance after dinner and supper. In an old Court masque of James I.'s time, performed at the marriage ceremony of Philip Herbert and Lady Susan (MS. in the writer's possession), it is directed that, at the conclusion of the performance, "after supper" the company " dance a round dance." This was "dancing the bride to bed." William Chappell (*Notes and Queries*, ii. 442) says, "I have a tune called 'A round dance to dance the bride to bed.' It dates from about 1630, or earlier, and resembles that of 'The Hunt is up.'" Dancing was considered so essential at weddings (according to Grose) that if in a family the youngest daughter should chance to be married before her elder sisters, they must dance at her wedding without shoes. May not the custom of throwing of old and worn-out shoes after the bride have arisen from the practice of dancing? The danced-out shoes may have been the ones used. It is curious that the cushion is used in the marriage ceremonies of the Brahmins. Mr. Kearns, in his *Marriage Ceremonies of the Hindoos of the South of India*, p. 6, says that a stool or cushion is one of the preparations for the reception of the bridegroom, who on entering the apartment sits down on the stool which is presented to him. He says,

"I step on this for the sake of food and other benefits, on this variously splendid footstool." The bride's father then presents to him a cushion made of twenty leaves of cúsa grass, holding it up with both hands and exclaiming, "The cushion! the cushion! the cushion!" The bridegroom replies, "I accept the cushion," and taking it, places it on the ground under his feet, while he recites a prayer. It is probable that we may have in the "Cushion Dance" the last relics of a very ancient ceremony, as well as evidence of the origin of a game from custom.

Cutch-a-Cutchoo

Children clasp their hands under their knees in a sitting posture, and jump thus about the room. The one who keeps up longest wins the game.—Dublin (Mrs. Lincoln).

(*b*) In *Notes and Queries*, x. 17, "E. D." says this amusement was fashionable sixty years ago, and from the low dresses worn then by ladies he mentions its indecency. He gives extracts from a satire called *Cutchacutchoo, or the Jostling of the Innocents*, 2nd ed., Dublin, in which the game and position are mentioned—

> Now she with tone tremendous cries
> Cutchacutchoo.
> Let each squat down upon her ham,
> Jump like a goat, puck like a ram.

"Uneda," at same reference (x. 17), speaks of it as a known game in Philadelphia. The analogy which this game has to some savage dances is curious; a correspondent in *Notes and Queries*, ix. 304, draws attention to the illustration, in Richardson's *Expedition to Arctic Shores* (vol. i. p. 397), of a dance by the "Kutchin-Kutcha" Indians, a parallel to the name as well as the dance which needs some research in America.

See "Curcuddie," "Hop-frog."

Cutters and Trucklers

A remembrance of the old smuggling days. The boys divide into two parties; the Trucklers try to reach some given point before the Cutter catches them.—Cornwall (*Folk-lore Journal*, v. 60).

Dab

> Dab a prin in my lottery book;
> Dab ane, dab twa, dab a' your prins awa'.

A game in which a pin is put at random in a school-book, between the leaves of which little pictures are placed. The successful adventurer is the person who puts the pin between two leaves including a picture which is the prize, and the pin itself is the forfeit (*Blackwood's Magazine*, Aug. 1821, p. 36). This was a general school game in West London in 1860–1866 (G. L. Gomme).

Dab-an-thricker

A game in which the *dab* (a wooden ball) is caused to spring upwards by a blow on the *thricker* (trigger), and is struck by a flat, bottle-shaped mallet fixed to the end of a flexible wand, the distance it goes counting so many for the striker.—Ross and Stead's *Holderness Glossary*.

This is the same as "Knur and Spell."

Dab-at-the-hole

A game at marbles (undescribed).—Patterson's *Antrim and Down Glossary*.

Dalies

A child's game, played with small bones or pieces of hard wood. The *dalies* were properly sheep's trotters.—Halliwell's *Dictionary*.

Evidently the same game as "Fivestones" and "Hucklebones."

Davie-drap

Children amuse themselves on the braesides i' the sun, playing at "Hide and Seek" with this little flower, accompanying always the hiding of it with this rhyme, marking out the circle in which it is hid with the forefinger:—

> Athin the bounds o' this I hap,
> My black and bonny davie-drap;
> Wha is here the cunning yin
> My davie-drap to me will fin.
> —Mactaggart's *Gallovidian Encyclopædia*.

The davie-drap is a little black-topped field-flower.

Deadily

A school game, not described.—Mactaggart's *Gallovidian Encyclopædia*.

Diamond Ring

My lady's lost her diamond ring;
I pitch upon you to find it!

Children sit in a ring or in a line, with their hands placed together palm to palm, and held straight, the little finger downmost between the knees. One of them is then chosen to represent a servant, who takes a ring, or some other small article as a substitute, between her two palms, which are pressed flat together like those of the rest, and goes round the circle or line placing her hands into the hands of every player, so that she is enabled to let the ring fall wherever she pleases without detection. After this she returns to the first child she touched, and with her hands behind her says the above words. The child who is thus addressed must guess who has the ring, and the servant performs the same ceremony with each of the party. They who guess right escape, but the rest forfeit. Should any one in the ring exclaim "I have it!" she also forfeits; nor must the servant make known who has the ring until all have guessed under the same penalty. The forfeits are afterwards cried as usual.—Halliwell's *Nursery Rhymes*, p. 223.

(*b*) This game was a general favourite at juvenile parties years ago. The hands were held in the posture described by Halliwell, but any child was pitched upon for the first finder, and afterwards the child in whose hands the ring was found had to be finder. There was no guessing; the closed hands were looked into (A. B. Gomme). Mr. Addy has collected a similar game called "My lady's lost a gold ring," and Mr. Newell (*Games and Songs of American Children*, p. 150) has another, "Hold fast my gold ring."

Dibbs

A game played with the small knuckle-bones taken from legs of mutton; these bones are themselves called "dibs" (Lowsley's

Glossary of Berkshire Words). Holloway's *Dictionary* says five of these bones are used by boys, with which they play a game called "Dibs" in West Sussex.

See "Check-stones," "Fivestones," "Hucklebones."

Dinah

No one in the house but Dinah, Dinah,
No one in the house I know, I know;
No one in the house but Dinah, Dinah,
Playing on the old banjo.

A ring is formed, and a girl stands blindfolded inside. As the verse is sung and finished, Dinah goes to any one in the ring, and, if successful in guessing her name, takes her place, the other taking the place of Dinah, the game going on as before.—Earls Heaton (Herbert Hardy).

"Dinah" was a Christy Minstrel song in the "fifties." It is probable that the game, which resembles "Buff," has been played to the tune of the song. Singing a chorus would soon follow.

See "Buff," "Muffin Man."

Dip o' the Kit

A rustic game, undescribed and marked as obsolescent.—Peacock's *Manley and Corringham Glossary*.

Dish-a-loof

A singular rustic amusement. One lays his hand down on a table, another clashes his upon it, a third his on that, and so on (fig. 1). When all the players have done this, the one who has his hand on the board pulls it out and lays it on the one uppermost (fig. 2): they all follow in rotation, and so a continual clashing and dashing is kept up; hence the name "Dish." Those who win the game are those who stand out longest—viz., those who are best at enduring pain. Tender hands could not stand it a moment: one dash of a rustic "loof" would make the blood spurt from the tip of every finger. It is a piece of pastime to country lads of the same nature as "Hard Knuckles" (Mactaggart's *Gallovidian Encyclopædia*). This is a well-known game for small children in

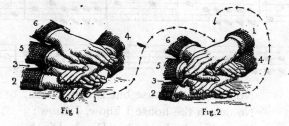

Fig 1   Fig.2

London. After each child's hands have been withdrawn and replaced on top as many times as possible without deranging the order, a general scramble and knocking of hands together ends the game (A. B. Gomme). Jamieson (*Etymological Dict.*) gives this as a sport of children.

See "Dump," "Green Grass," "Hot Cockles."

Doddart

A game played in a large level field with a bent stick called "doddart." Two parties, headed by two captains, endeavour to drive a wooden ball to their respective boundaries (Halliwell's *Dictionary*). Brockett (*North Country Words*) adds to this that the captains are entitled to choose their followers by alternate votes. A piece of globular wood called an "orr" or "coit" is thrown down in the middle of the field and driven to one of two opposite hedges—the alley, hail-goal, or boundary. The same game as "Clubby," "Hockey," "Shinney," "Shinneyhaw."

Doncaster Cherries

One boy kneels, holding a long rope, the other end of which is held by another boy; the other players stand round about with handkerchiefs in hands, knotted. The one who holds the rope-end and standing cries out—

Doncaster cherries, ripe and sound ;
Touch 'em or taste 'em—
Down, you dogs !
—Earls Heaton, Yorkshire (H. Hardy).

This is evidently a version of " Badger the Bear," with a different and apparently degraded formula.

Dools

A school game. The dools are places marked with stones, where the players always remain in safety—where they dare neither be caught by the hand nor struck with balls. It is only when they leave these places of refuge that those out of the doons have any chance to gain the game and get in; and leave the doons they frequently must—this is the nature of the game. Now this game seems to have been often played in reality by our ancestors about their doon-hills.—Mactaggart's *Gallovidian Encyclopædia*.

Down in the Valley

I. Down in the valley where the green grass grows
  Stands E—— H——, she blows like a rose.
  She blows, she blows, she blows so sweet.
  In came F—— S—— and gave her a kiss.
  E—— made a pudding, she made it nice and sweet,
  F—— took a knife and fork and cut a little piece.
  Taste of it, taste of it, don't say nay,
  For next Sunday morning is our wedding day.
  First we'll buy a money box,
  Then we'll buy a cradle ;
  Rock, rock the bottom out,
  Then we'll buy another.
  Bread and cheese all the week, cork on Sunday,
  Half a crown on Saturday night, and a jolly good dance on
    Monday.   —Cowes, Isle of Wight (Miss E. Smith).

II. Down in the meadows where the green grass grows,
  To see —— blow like a rose.
  She blows, she blows, she blows so sweet.

Go out, ——; who shall he be?
—— made a pudding,
She made it so sweet,
And never stuck a knife in
Till —— came to eat.
Taste, love, taste, love, don't say nay,
For next Monday morning is your wedding day.
He bought her a gown and a guinea gold ring,
And a fine cocked hat to be married in.

—West Haddon, Northamptonshire; Long Itchington,
Warwickshire (*Northants Notes and Queries*, ii. 105).

III. Down in the valley the violets grow.
Dear little ——, she blows like a rose.
She blows, she blows, she blows so sweet.
    Come along in.
Buy a shawl, buy a new black shawl,
A bonnet trimmed with white and a new parasol.
Oh dear, oh dear, what can I do,
For next Monday morning is my wedding due.

—Shipley, Horsham; *Notes and Queries*,
8th series, i. 210 (Miss Busk).

(*b*) The children form a ring by joining hands, one child standing in the centre. They dance round. At the mention of the second name one from the ring goes into the centre. The two kiss at the end of the verse, and the first child takes the place in the ring, and the game begins again.

See "All the Boys," "Oliver, Oliver, follow the King."

Drab and Norr

A game similar to "Trippit and Coit."—Halliwell's *Dict*.

Draw a Pail of Water

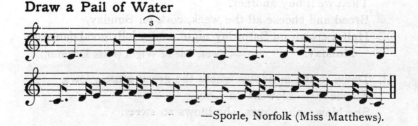

—Sporle, Norfolk (Miss Matthews).

I. Draw a pail of water
    For my lady's daughter;
    My father's a king and my mother's a queen,
    My two little sisters are dressed in green,
    Stamping grass and parsley,
    Marigold leaves and daisies.
    One rush, two rush,
    Pray thee, fine lady, come under my bush.
            —Halliwell's *Nursery Rhymes*, Games, cclxxxvii.

II. Draw a pail of water,
     Send a lady a daughter;
     One o' my rush, two o' my rush,
     Please, young lady, creep under the briar bush.
                —Liphook, Hants (Miss Fowler).

III. Draw, draw water,
      For my lady's daughter;
        One in a rush,
        Two in a bush,
      Pretty my lady, pop under the bush.
              —Berrington and Ellesmere (*Shropshire
              Folk-lore*, p. 521).

IV. Draw a bucket o' water
     For a lady's daughter;
     One and a hush, two and a rush,
     Please, young lady, come under my bush.
                —Fochabers (Rev. W. Gregor).

V. Draw a bucket of water
    For a lady's daughter;
      One in a bush,
      Two in a bush,
      Three in a bush,
      Four in a bush,
        And out you go.
                —Crockham Hill, Kent (Miss Chase).

VI. Drawing a bucket of water
     For my lady's daughter;

Put it in a chestnut tree,
And let it stay an hour.
One of you rush, two may rush,
Please, old woman, creep under the bush ;
The bush is too high, the bush is too low,
Please, old woman, creep under the bush.

—Hampshire (Miss Mendham).

VII.   Draw a pail of water
For a lady's daughter ;
Give a silver pin for a golden ring—
Oh pray, young lady, pop under.

—Northants (Rev. W. D. Sweeting).

VIII.   Draw a bucket of water
For my lady's daughter ;
One go rush, and the other go hush,
Pretty young lady, bop under my bush.

—Sporle, Norfolk (Miss Matthews).

IX.   Draw a bucket of water
For the farmer's daughter ;
Give a gold ring and a silver watch,
Pray, young lady, pop under.

—Sporle, Norfolk (Miss Matthews).

X.   Draw a bucket of water
For my lady's daughter ;
A guinea gold ring
And a silver pin,
So pray, my young lady, pop under.

—Haydon (Herbert Hardy).

XI.   Draw a bucket of water
To wash my lady's garter ;
A guinea gold ring
And a silver pin,
Please, little girl, pop under.

—Earls Heaton (Herbert Hardy).

XII.   See-saw, a bucket of water,
To wash my lady's garter.

One in a rush, and two in a bush,
To see a fine lady pop under a bush.
                    —Anderby, Lincolnshire, and Nottinghamshire
                            near the Trent (Miss Peacock).

XIII.   One we go rush,
        Two we go push;
        Lady come under the corner bush.
                            —Shepscombe, Gloucestershire
                                    (Miss Mendham).

XIV.   Sift the lady's oaten meal, sift it into flour,
        Put it in a chest of drawers and let it lie an hour.
            One of my rush,
            Two of my rush,
        Please, young lady, come under my bush.
        My bush is too high, my bush is too low,
        Please, young lady, come under my bow.
        Stir up the dumpling, stir up the dumpling.
                            —Belfast (W. H. Patterson).

XV.   Sieve my lady's oatmeal,
            Grind my lady's flour;
        Put it in a chestnut,
            Let it stand an hour.
        One may rush, two may rush;
        Come, my girls, walk under the bush.
                    —Halliwell's *Nursery Rhymes*, Games, cclxxxviii.

(*b*) The Berrington version of this game is played as
follows:—Two girls face each other, holding each other by
both hands. Two others face each other, holding both hands
across the other two. They see-saw backwards and forwards,
singing the lines (fig. 1). One girl gets inside the enclosing
hands (fig. 2), and they repeat till all four have "popped
under" (fig. 3), when they "jog" up and down till they fall on
the floor! (fig. 4). At Ellesmere only *two* girls join hands,
and as many "pop under" as they can encircle. The
Lincolnshire and Norfolk versions are played practically in
the same way. In the Liphook version the children stand
in two and two opposite to each other; the children on

one side of the square hold hands up at the third line, and the other two children run under the hands of the first two. There is no pause, but the verse is sung time after time, so that the four children are nearly always moving. In the other Hampshire version four girls stand in a square, each holding the hands of the one opposite to her, pulling each other's hands backwards and forwards singing the lines. Two arms are then raised, and one girl comes under; this is repeated till all four girls have come under the arms, then

Fig. 1   Fig. 2

Fig. 3   Fig. 4

their arms encircle each other's waists and they dance round. In the Scottish version there are only two girls who join hands and pull each other backwards and forwards, repeating the words. Halliwell describes a different action to any of these. A string of children, hand in hand, stand in a row. A child stands in front of them as leader; two other children form an arch, each holding both of the hands of the other. The string of children pass under the arch, the last of whom is taken captive by the two holding hands. The verses are repeated until all are taken.—Halliwell's *Nursery Rhymes*, cclxxxvii.

(c) The analysis of the game rhymes is as follows:—

No.	Halliwell's Version.	Liphook (Hants).	Shropshire.	Fochabers (Scotland).	Hampshire.	Northants.	Norfolk (1).	Norfolk (2).
1.	Draw a pail of water.	Draw a pail of water.	Draw, draw water.	Draw a bucket o' water.	Drawing a bucket of water.	Draw a pail of water.	Draw a bucket of water.	Draw a bucket of water.
2.	—	—	—	—	—	—	—	—
3.	For my lady's daughter.	Send a lady a daughter.	For my lady's daughter.	For a lady's daughter.	For my lady's daughter.	For a lady's daughter.	For my lady's daughter.	For the farmer's daughter.
4.	—	—	—	—	—	—	—	—
5.	My father's a king and my mother's a queen.				Put it in a chestnut tree.			
6.				—	Let it stay an hour.			
7.	My father's a king and my mother's a queen.							
8.	—						—	
9.	My two little sisters are dressed in green.	—				—		
10.	Stamping grass and parsley.							
11.	Marigold leaves and daisies.	—				—		
12.	One rush, two rush.	One o' my rush, two o' my rush.	One in a rush, two in a bush.	One and a hush, two and a rush.	One of you rush, two may rush.	—	One go rush and the other go hush.	—
13.	—			—		Give a silver pin for a golden ring.	—	Give a gold ring and a silver watch.
14.	Pray, thee, fine lady, come under my bush.	Please, young lady, creep under the briar bush.	Pretty my lady, pop under the bush.	Please, young lady, come under my bush.	Please, old woman, creep under the bush.	Pray, young lady, pop under.	Pretty young lady, bop under my bush.	Pray, young lady, pop under.
15.	—	—	—	—	The bush is too high, the bush is too low.	—	—	—
16.	—	—			Please, old woman, creep under the bush.			
17.	—	—	—	—	—	—	—	—
18.								

No.	Haydon.	Earls Heaton.	Lincolnshire and Nottinghamshire.	Gloucestershire.	Belfast.	Halliwell's Version (No. 2).	Crockham Hill.
1.	Draw a bucket of water.	Draw a bucket of water.	See saw, a bucket of water.	—	—	—	Draw a bucket of water.
2.	—	—	—	—	Sift the lady's oatmeal.	Sieve my lady's oatmeal.	—
3.	—	—	—	—	Sift it into flour.	Grind my lady's flour.	—
4.	For my lady's daughter.	—	—	—	—	—	For a lady's daughter.
5.	—	To wash my lady's garter.	To wash my lady's garter.	—	—	—	—
6.	—	—	—	—	Put it in a chest of drawers.	Put it in a chest-nut.	—
7.	—	—	—	—	Let it lie an hour.	Let it stand an hour.	—
8.	—	—	—	—	—	—	—
9.	—	—	—	—	—	—	—
10.	—	—	—	—	—	—	—
11.	—	—	—	—	—	—	—
12.	—	—	One in a rush and two in a bush.	One we go rush, two we go push.	One of my rush, two of my rush.	One may rush, two may rush.	One in a bush, two in a bush, three in a bush, four in a bush.
13.	A guinea gold ring and a silver pin.	A guinea gold ring and a silver pin.	—	—	—	—	—
14.	Pray, young lady, pop under.	Please, little girl, pop under.	To see a fine lady pop under a bush.	Lady, come under the corner bush.	Please, young lady, come under my bush.	Come, my girls, walk under the bush.	—
15.	—	—	—	—	My bush is too high, my bush is too low.	—	—
16.	—	—	—	—	Please, young lady, come under my bow.	—	—
17.	—	—	—	—	Stir up the dumpling.	—	—
18.	—	—	—	—	—	—	And out you go.

The analysis shows that the majority of the variants retain four principal incidents of what must have been the original form of the game, and the fact of the Gloucestershire version having come down with only two of the incidents, namely, the two most common to all the variants (12 and 14), shows that the game has been in a state of decadence. The four principal incidents, Nos. 1, 4, 12, and 14, point distinctly to some water ceremonial; and if it may be argued that the incidents which occur in only one or two of the variants may be considered to have belonged to the original type, we shall be able to suggest that this game presents a dramatic representation of ancient well-worship. The incidents which occur in one version only are those given by Mr. Halliwell, and unfortunately the locality from which he obtained this variant is unknown. Still it is an earlier version than those which are now printed for the first time, and may without doubt be looked upon as genuine. Taking all the incidents of the various versions as the means by which to restore the earliest version, it would appear that this might have consisted of the following lines:—

Draw a pail of water
For a lady's daughter;
Her father's a king, her mother's a queen,
Her two little sisters are dressed in green,
Stamping grass and parsley, marigold leaves and daisies;
Sift the lady's oatmeal, sift it into flour,
Put it in a chestnut tree, let it lie an hour;
Give a silver pin and a gold ring,
One and a hush! two and a rush!
Pray, young lady, pop under a bush;
My bush is too high, my bush is too low,
Please, young lady, come under my bow!

(*d*) This restoration of the words, though it probably is far from complete, and does not make so good a game rhyme as the reduced versions, nevertheless shows clearly enough that the incidents belong to a ceremonial of primitive well-worship. The pulling of the hands backwards and forwards may be taken to indicate the raising of water from a well. If this is conceded, the incidents might be grouped as follows:—

(1.) Drawing of water from a well.

(2.) For a devotee at the well.

(3.) Collecting flowers for dressing the well.

(4.) Making of a cake for presentation.

(5.) Gifts to the well [the silver pin, gold ring, and probably the garter].

(6.) Command of silence.

(7.) The presence of the devotee at the sacred bush.

All these are incidents of primitive well-worship (see Gomme's *Ethnology and Folk-lore*, pp. 82–103). Garland dressing is very general; cakes were eaten at Rorrington well, Shropshire (Burne's *Shropshire Folk-lore*, p. 433); pins and portions of the dress are very general offerings; silence is strictly enforced in many instances, and a sacred tree or bush is very frequently found near the well.

The tune of the Hampshire game (Miss Mendham's version) is practically the same as that of the "Mulberry Bush."

Newell (*Games of American Children*, p. 90) gives a version of this game.

Drawing Dun out of the Mire

Brand, quoting from "an old collection of satires, epigrams, &c.," says this game is enumerated among other pastimes :

> At shove-groat, venter-point, or crosse and pile,
> At leaping o'er a Midsummer bone-fier,
> Or at *the drawing Dun out of the myer.*

So in the *Dutchesse of Suffolke*, 1631 :

> Well done, my masters, lends your hands,
> *Draw Dun out of the ditch,*
> Draw, pull, helpe all, so, so, well done.
>
> [*They pull him out.*

They had shoved Bishop Bonner into a well, and were pulling him out.

We find this game noticed at least as early as Chaucer's time, in the *Manciple's Prologue* :

> Then gan our hoste to jape and to play,
> And sayd, sires, what ? *Dun is in the mire.*

Nares (*Glossary*) says this game was a rural pastime, in

which *Dun* meant a dun horse, supposed to be stuck in the mire, and sometimes represented by one of the persons who played.

Gifford (*Ben Jonson*, vol. vii. p. 283), who remembered having played at the game (doubtless in his native county, Devonshire), thus describes it :—"A log of wood is brought into the midst of the room : this is Dun (the cart horse), and a cry is raised that he is stuck in the mire. Two of the company advance, either with or without ropes, to draw him out. After repeated attempts they find themselves unable to do it, and call for more assistance. The game continues till all the company take part in it, when Dun is extricated of course ; and the merriment arises from the awkward and affected efforts of the rustics to lift the log, and sundry arch contrivances to let the ends of it fall on one another's toes."

Drop Handkerchief

This is a game similar to Cat and Mouse, but takes its name from the use of the handkerchief to start the pursuit. Various rhyming formulæ are used in some places. In Monton, Lancashire (Miss Dendy), no rhyme is used.

The children stand in a ring. One runs round with a handkerchief and drops it ; the child behind whom it is dropped chases the dropper, the one who gets home first takes the vacant place, the other drops the handkerchief again.

In Shropshire the two players pursue one another in and out of the ring, running under the uplifted hands of the players who compose it : the pursuer carefully keeping on the track of the pursued (Burne's *Shropshire Folk-lore*, p. 512).

The Dorsetshire variant is accompanied by a rhyme :

I wrote a letter to my love ;
I carried water in my glove ;
And by the way I dropped it—
I dropped it, I dropped it, I dropped it, &c.

This is repeated until the handkerchief is stealthily dropped immediately behind one of the players, who should be on the alert to follow as quickly as possible the one who has dropped it, who at once increases her speed and endeavours to take the place left vacant by her pursuer. Should she be caught before she can succeed in doing this she is compelled to take the handkerchief a second time. But if, as it more usually happens, she is successful in accomplishing this, the pursuer in turn takes the handkerchief, and the game proceeds as before.—Symondsbury (*Folk-lore Journal*, vi. 212).

> Jack lost his supper last night,
> And the night before; if he does again to-night,
> He never will no more—more—more.
>
> I wrote a letter to my love,
> And on the way I dropt it;
> Some of you have picked it up,
> And got it in your pocket—pocket—pocket—pocket.
>
> I have a little dog, it won't bite you—
> It won't bite you—it won't bite you—
> It *will* bite you. —Leicestershire (Miss Ellis).

The Forest of Dean version is the same as the Dorsetshire, except that the child who is unsuccessful in gaining the vacant place has to stand in the middle of the ring until the same thing happens to another child.—Miss Matthews.

In Nottinghamshire the children form in a ring; one walks round outside the ring singing and carrying a handkerchief:

> I wrote a letter to my love, and on the way I dropt it;
> One of you has picked it up and put it in your pocket.
> It isn't you, it isn't you, &c. &c.; it is you.

The handkerchief is then dropped at some one's back, the one at whose back the handkerchief was dropped chasing the other.

Or they say:

> I lost my supper last night, I lost it the night before,
> And if I lose it again to-night, I'll knock at somebody's door.
> It isn't you, it isn't you, &c. &c.; it's you.
> —Miss Winfield.

At Winterton and Lincoln the children form a circle, standing arms-length apart. A child holding a handkerchief occupies the centre of the ring and sings:

Wiskit-a-waskit,
A green leather basket ;
I wrote a letter to my love,
And on the way I lost it ;
Some of you have picked it up,
And put it in your pocket.
I have a little dog at home,
And it shan't bite you,
(Here the singer points to each child in turn)
Nor you, nor you, nor you ;
But it shall bite *you*.

Then she drops the handkerchief before her chosen playmate, who chases her in and out of the ring under the arms of the other children until she is captured. The captor afterwards takes the place in the centre, and the original singer becomes a member of the circle.—Miss M. Peacock.

The Deptford version of the verse is as follows :—

I had a little dog whose name was Buff,
I sent him up the street for a penny'orth of snuff,
He broke my box and spilt my snuff,
I think my story is long enough—
'Tain't you, and 'tain't you, and 'tis you !

—Deptford, Kent (Miss Chase).

A Staffordshire and Sharleston version gives some altogether different formulæ :—

What colour's the sky ?
Blue.
Look up again.
Like a W.

Follow me through every little hole that I go through.

—Staffordshire (Rev. G. T. Royds, Rector of Haughton).

At Sharleston the centre child says, "What colour is t' sky ?" The other answers, "Blue." Centre child says, "Follow me true." Here the centre child runs in and out between the others until the one who was touched catches her, when they change places, the first joining the children in the ring.—Sharleston (Miss Fowler).

At Beddgelert, Wales (Mrs. Williams), this game is called Tartan Boeth. It is played in precisely the same manner as the English game, but the words used are:

Tartan Boeth, Oh ma'en llosgi, Boeth iawn

Hot Tart. Oh, it burns! very hot!

At the words, "Very hot!" the handkerchief is dropped.

(*b*) In this game no kissing takes place, and that this is no mere accidental omission may be shown by Mr. Udal's description of the Dorsetshire game. He was assured by several persons who are interested in Dorset Children's Games that the indiscriminate kissing (that is, whether the girl pursued runs little or far, or, when overtaken, whether she objects or not) with which this game is ordinarily associated, as played now both in Dorset and in other counties, was not indigenous to this county, but was merely a pernicious after-growth or outcome of later days, which had its origin in the various excursion and holiday fêtes, which the facilities of railway travelling had instituted, by bringing large crowds from the neighbouring towns into the country. He was told that thirty years ago such a thing was unknown in the country districts of Dorset, when the game then usually indulged in was known merely as "Drop the Handkerchief" (*Folk-lore Journal*, vi. 212).

In other cases the rhymes are used for a purely kissing game, for which see "Kiss in the Ring."

Dropping the Letter

An undescribed Suffolk boys' game.—Moor's *Suffolk Words*, p. 238.

Duck under the Water

Each child chooses a partner, and form in couples standing one before the other, till a long line is formed. Each couple holds a handkerchief as high as they can to form an arch. The couple standing at the end of the line run through the arch just beyond the last couple standing at the top, when they stand still and hold their handkerchief as high as possible, which is the beginning of the second arch; this is repeated by every last couple in succession, so that as many arches as are wanted can be formed.—East Kirkby, Lincolnshire (Miss K. Maughan).

Miss Baker (*Northamptonshire Glossary*) says the game is played in that county. Formerly in the northern part of the county even married women on May Day played at it under the May garland, which was extended from chimney to chimney across the village street.

Duck at the Table

A boys' game, played with round stones and a table-shaped block of stone.—Patterson's *Antrim and Down Glossary*.

Probably the same as Duckstone.

Duck Dance

Last verse only.

—London (A. B. Gomme).

I saw a ship a sailin',
A sailin' on the sea,
And oh, it was laden
With pretty things for me [thee].

There were comfits in the cabin,
And apples in the hold;
The sails were made of silk,
And the masts were made of gold.

Four and twenty sailors
That sat upon the deck,
Were four and twenty white mice
With chains about their necks.

The captain was a duck,
With a packet on his back;
And when the ship began to move,
The captain cried "Quack! quack!"

—Northamptonshire, *Revue Celtique*, iv. 200;
Halliwell's *Nursery Rhymes*, No. ccclxxvii.

(*b*) A number of little girls join hands and form a ring. They all jump round and sing the verses. The game ends by the girls following one of their number in a string, all quacking like ducks.—Northamptonshire.

(*c*) Halliwell does not include it among his games, but simply as a nursery paradox. The tune given is that to which I as a child was taught to sing the verses as a song. We did not know it as a game. The "Quack, quack!" was repeated as another line to the notes of the last bar given, the notes gradually dying away (A. B. Gomme).

Duck Friar

The game of "Leap-frog."—*Apollo Shroving*, 1627, p. 83.

Ducks and Drakes

A pastime in which flat stones or slates are thrown upon the surface of a piece of water, so that they may dip and emerge several times without sinking (Brockett's *North Country Words*). "Neither cross and pile nor ducks and drakes are quite so ancient as hand dandy" (Arbuthnot and Pope, quoted in Todd's *Johnson*).

Halliwell gives the words used in the game both formerly and at the present day. If the stone emerges only once it is a duck, and increasing in the following order :—

> 2. A duck and a drake,
> 3. And a halfpenny cake,
> 4. And a penny to pay the old baker,
> 5. A hop and a scotch is another notch,
> 6. Slitherum, slatherum, take her.
>
>   —Halliwell's *Dictionary*.

> Hen-pen,
> Duck and mallard,
> Amen.
>
> —Somersetshire (Holloway's *Dict. of Provincialisms*).

> A duck and a drake
> And a white penny cake.
>
> —Hampshire (Holloway's *Dict. of Provincialisms*).

> A duck and a drake
> And a penny white cake,
> And a skew ball.
> —Peacock's *Manley and Corringham Glossary.*

Moor (*Suffolk Words and Phrases*) gives the names for the number of times the stone emerges, as (1) "a duck;" (2) "a duck an' a drake;" if thrice, "a duck an' a drake an' a fi'epenny cake;" four times is "a duck an' a drake an' a fi'epenny cake, an' a penny to pah the baker." If more than four, "a duck," "a duck an' a drake," &c., are added. These distinctions are iterated quickly to correspond in time as nearly as may be with the dips of the stone. A flattish stone is evidently the best for this sport.

(*b*) This game is also given by Mr. Addy in his *Sheffield Glossary*, and by Holland (*Cheshire Glossary*), Brogden (*Provincial Words, Lincolnshire*), Lowsley (*Berkshire Glossary*), Nares' *Glossary*, and Baker's *Northants Glossary*. Miss Courtenay gives "Scutter" and "Tic Tac Mollard" as Cornish names for the game (*West Cornwall Glossary*). See also Halliwell's *Nursery Rhymes*, p. 139, and Strutt's *Sports and Pastimes*, p. 326.

Butler, in his *Hudibras* (p. ii. canto iii. l. 302), makes it one of the important qualifications of his conjurer to tell—

> What figur'd slates are best to make
> On wat'ry surface *duck* or *drake*.

The following description of this sport is given by Minucius Felix, ed. 1712, p. 28, which evinces its high antiquity : " Pueros videmus certatim gestientes, testarum in mare jaculationibus ludere. Is lusus est, testam teretem, jactatione fluctuum lævigatam, legere de litore : eam testam plano situ digitis comprehensam, inclinem ipsum atque humilem, quantum potest, super undas irrorare : ut illud jaculum vel dorsum maris raderet, vel enataret, dum leni impetu labitur ; vel summis fluctibus tonsis emicaret, emergeret, dum assiduo saltu sublevatur. Is se in pueris victorem ferebat, cujus testa et procurreret longius, et frequentius exsiliret."

"From this pastime," says Moor, "has probably arisen the application of the term to a spendthrift—of whose approaching ruin we should thus speak: 'Ah, he'ave made fine ducks and drakes of a's money, that a' have.'"—*Suffolk Words*.

Duckstone

A large stone called the Duckstone or Duck-table is placed on the ground, generally with a wall for a background, but this is of little consequence. Several boys take a stone each, and a place pretty near the Duckstone is chosen for "home." One of the boys puts his stone on the Duckstone, and he is called the Tenter. He has to guard the home and catch the other boys if he can. Each boy in turn throws his stone at the stone on the Duck-table and immediately runs home. The Tenter tries to catch him before he can touch the wall or post or whatever is chosen for the home. If the Tenter can catch him he becomes Tenter, and puts his stone on the Duckstone, and the original Tenter takes his turn in throwing. One rule of the game is that the Tenter's stone must always be on the Duck-table when he is trying to catch a boy, so if it is knocked off it must be replaced before he can try to catch the boy running "home." The chance of getting home is increased for the boy who knocks it off.—North-West Lincolnshire (Rev. — Roberts and Miss Peacock).

(*b*) Similar versions are from Earls Heaton (Herbert Hardy), Ireland (*Folk-lore Journal*, ii. 265), Peacock (*Manley and Corringham Glossary*). Addy (*Sheffield Glossary*) gives this game with the following addition: If a duck falls short of the Duckstone, and the one whose duck is on the stone sees that he can *wand* or *span* with his hand the distance between the duck thus thrown and the Duckstone, he shouts out "Wands," and if he can wand or span the distance he takes his duck off, and the duck thus thrown is put on. Holland (*Cheshire Glossary*), Darlington (South Cheshire), Baker (*Northants Glossary*), and Brogden (*Provincial Words, Lincolnshire*), also give this game. Elworthy (*West Somerset Words*) calls it "Duck," and "Ducks off" and "Cobbs off" in Dorsetshire. In London the boy repeats the words, "Gully, gully, all round the hole, one duck on," while he is playing (*Strand Magazine*, November 1891). Newell (*Games*, p. 188) calls it "Duck on a Rock."

Duffan Ring

Name for "Cat and Mouse" in Cornwall. — *Folk-lore Journal*, v. 57.

Dumb Crambo

An undescribed game mentioned in Moor's *Suffolk Words*, p. 238.

Dumb Motions

Two sides are chosen, which stand apart from each other inside the line of their den. One side chooses a trade, and goes to the opposite side imitating working at the trade and giving the initial letters of it. If the opposite side guesses the name of the trade, the players run to their own den, being chased by their opponents. If any of the players are caught they must go to the opposite side. In turn the opposite side chooses a trade, and imitates the actions practised.—Cork, Ireland (Miss Keane).

This is called "An Old Woman from the Wood" in Dorsetshire. The children form themselves into two ranks.

The first rank says :

Here comes an old 'oman from the wood.

The second party answers :

What cans't thee do ?

First Party :   Do anythin'.

Second Party :   Work away.

This the children proceed to do, some by pretending to sew, some to wash, some to dig, some to knit, without any instruments to do it with. If the opposite side guess what they are doing, they change sides. This game, Miss Summers believes, is very old, and has been played by several generations in the village of Hazelbury Bryan.—Dorsetshire (*Folk-lore Journal*, vii. 230).

See "Trades."

Dump

A boys' amusement in Yorkshire, in vogue about half a century ago, but now believed to be nearly obsolete. It is played in this manner.   The lads crowd round and place their fists endways, the one on the other, till they form a high pile of hands.   Then a boy, who has one hand free, knocks the piled fists off one by one, saying to every boy as he strikes his fist away, "What's there, Dump?"   He continues this process till he comes to the last fist, when he exclaims :—

What's there ?
Cheese and bread, and a mouldy halfpenny !
Where's my share ?
I put it on the shelf, and the cat got it.
Where's the cat ?
She's run nine miles through the wood.
Where's the wood ?
T' fire burnt it.
Where's the fire ?
T' waters sleekt (extinguished) it.
Where's the water ?
T' oxen drank it.
Where's the oxen ?
T' butcher killed 'em.
Where's the butcher ?

Upon the church tops cracking nuts, and you may go and eat the shells; and them as speaks first shall have nine nips, nine scratches, and nine boxes over the lug !

Every one then endeavours to refrain from speaking in spite of mutual nudges and grimaces, and he who first allows a word to escape is punished by the others in the various methods adopted by schoolboys.   In some places the game is played differently.   The children pile their fists in the manner described above; then one, or sometimes all of them, sing :

I've built my house, I've built my wall ;
I don't care where my chimneys fall !

The merriment consists in the bustle and confusion occasioned by the rapid withdrawal of the hands (Halliwell's *Nursery Rhymes*, p. 225).   Compare Burne's *Shropshire Folk-lore*, p. 529.

Northall (*Folk Rhymes*, p. 418) gives the following rhymes as said in Warwickshire while the fists are being piled on one another :—

Here's one hammer on the block,
My men, my men ;
There's one hammer, &c., my man John.
Dibble the can, blow bellows, blow,
Fire away, lads, for an hour or so.
See " Dish-a-loof," " Sacks."

Dumps

A game at marbles or taw, played with holes scooped in the ground (Roxburgh, Jamieson). Grose gives *dump* as signifying " a deep hole of water " (*Provincial Glossary*).

Dust-point

A game in which boys placed their points in a heap, and threw at them with a stone. Weber and Nares give wrong explanations. It is alluded to in Cotton's Works, 1734, p. 184.

I'll venter on their heads my brindled cow,
With any boy at dust-point they shall play.
—Peacham's *Thalia's Banquet*, 1620.

Nares (*Glossary*) suggests that this game and blow-point resembled the game of Push-pin. See also Halliwell's *Dictionary*.

Eller Tree

A number of young men and women stand in a line, a tall girl at one end of the line representing the tree. They then begin to wrap round her, saying, " The old eller tree grows thicker and thicker." When they have all got round her (the tree), they jump all together, calling out, " A bunch of rags, a bunch of rags," and try to tread on each other's toes.—Sheffield, Yorks (S. O. Addy).

(*b*) The tree is the alder. It abounds in the North of England more than in any other part of the kingdom, and seems always to have been there held in great respect and veneration. Many superstitions also attach to the tree. It is possible from these circumstances that the game descends from an old custom of encircling the tree as an act of worship, and the allusion to the " rags " bears at least a curious relationship to tree worship.

If this conclusion is correct, the particular form of the game preserved by Mr. Addy may be the parent form of all games

in which the act of winding is indicated. There is more reason for this when we consider how easy the notion of clock-winding would creep in after the old veneration for the sacred alder tree had ceased to exist.

See "Bulliheisle," "Wind up the Bush Faggot," "Wind up the Watch."

Ezzeka

Old Ezzeka did one day stand
Upon a barrel top;
The bung flew out, and all at once
It went off with a pop.   —Dronfield (S. O. Addy).

This game is usually played in a house or schoolroom, by boys and girls. A boy or girl is chosen who is considered to be able to stand a joke. He sits on a chair. A stool is put behind, upon which a boy called "Ezzeka" stands. Then the other boys and girls in the room sing the lines. As they are finished, Ezzeka, who has a bottle of water in his hand, takes out the cork, and pours the water upon his victim's head. This game may be compared with the game of "King Arthur" mentioned by Brand (*Pop. Antiq.*, ii. 393).

Father's Fiddle

This is a boys' game. One boy says to another, "Divv (do) ye ken (know) aboot my father's fiddle?" On replying that he does not, the questioner takes hold of the other's right hand with his left, and stretches out the arm.   With his right hand he touches the arm gently above the elbow, and says, "My father had a fiddle, an' he brook (broke) it here, an' he brook it here" (touching it below the elbow), "an' he brook it throw the middle," and comes down with a sharp stroke on the elbow-joint.—Keith, Fochabers (Rev. W. Gregor).

This is probably the same game as that printed by Halliwell, No. cccxxxv., to which the following rhyme applied :—

> My father was a Frenchman,
> He bought for me a fiddle ;
> He cut me here, he cut me here,
> He cut me right in the middle.

Feed the Dove

An undescribed game mentioned in an old poem called *Christmas* (i. 285), quoted in Ellis's Brand, i. 517 : "Young men and maidens now at 'Feed the Dove' (with laurel leaf in mouth) play."

Find the Ring

> O the grand old Duke of York
> He had ten thousand men,
> He marched them up the hill ago
> And he marched them down again.
> And when they were up they were up,
> And when they were down they were down,
> And when they were half-way up the hill
> They were neither up nor down.
>
> —Sheffield (S. O. Addy).

A ring of chairs is formed, and the players sit on them. A piece of string long enough to go round the inner circum-ference of the chairs is procured.   A small ring is put upon the string, the ends of which are then tied.   Then one of the players gets up from his chair and stands in the centre.   The players sitting on the chairs take the string into their hands and pass the ring round from one to another, singing the lines. If the person standing in the centre can find out in whose hand the ring is, he sits down, and his place is taken by the one who had the ring. The game is sometimes played round a haycock in the hayfield.

Miss Dendy sends a similar rhyme from Monton, Lancashire, where it is known simply as a marching game. For similar rhymes, see Halliwell's *Nursery Rhymes*, p. 3.

See " Paddy from Home," " Tip it."

Fippeny Morrell

" Twice three stones, set in a crossed square, where he wins the game that can set his three along in a row, and that is fippeny morrell I trow."—*Apollo Shroving*, 1626.

See " Nine Men's Morice," " Noughts and Crosses."

Fire, Air, and Water

The players seat themselves in a circle. One of the players has a ball, to which a string is fastened. He holds the string that he may easily draw the ball back again after it is thrown. The possessor of the ball then throws it to one in the circle, calling out the name of either of the elements he pleases. This player must, before ten can be counted, give the name of an inhabitant of that element. When " Fire " is called, strict silence must be observed or a forfeit paid.—Cork, Ireland (Miss Keane).

The players were seated in a half-circle, and the possessor of the ball faced the others. There was no string attached to the ball, but it was necessary that it should hit the child it was thrown to. When " Fire " was called, " Salamander " and " Phœnix " were allowed to be said. . The third time " Fire " was called, silence was observed, and every player bowed the head. We called it " Earth, Air, Fire, and Water." A forfeit had to be paid for every mistake.—London (A. B. Gomme).

It seems probable that a survival of fire-worship is shown by this game.

Fivestones

This game was played by a newspaper boy at Richmond Station for me as follows :—He had five square pieces of tile or

stone about the size of dice. He took all five pieces in the
palm of the hand first, then threw them up and caught them on
the back of the hand, and then from the back of the hand into
the palm. Four of the stones were then thrown on the ground;
the fifth was thrown up, one stone being picked up from the
ground, and the descending fifth stone caught in the same hand;
the other three pieces were next picked up in turn. Then two
were picked up together in the same manner twice, then one,
then three, then all four at once, the fifth stone being thrown up
and caught with each movement. All five were then thrown up
and caught on the back of the hand, and then thrown from
the back and caught in the palm. When he dropped one, he
picked it up between his outstretched fingers while the other
stones remained on the back of the hand; then he tossed and
caught it likewise. Then after throwing up the five stones and
catching them on the back of the hand and the reverse, all five
being kept in the palm, one was thrown up, and another deposited on the ground before the descending stone was caught.
This was done to the three others in turn. Then with two at a
time twice, then one and three, then all four together, then from
the palm to the back of the hand, and again to the palm. This
completed one game. If mistakes were made another player
took the stones. Marks were taken for successful play. This
boy called the game "Dabs."—A. B. Gomme.

In South Notts this game was called "Snobs." It was
played with small stones or marbles. There were nine sets of
tricks. First One-ers (of which there were five in the set),
then Two-ers (two in set), Three-ers (three in set), Four-ers
(four in set), Four Squares (four in set), Trotting Donkeys
(eight in set, I believe), Fly-catchers (six or seven in set), Magic
(five in set), and Magic Fly-catchers (five in set). One-ers
is played thus:—The five stones are thrown into the air
and caught on the back of the hand. If all are caught they
are simply tossed up again and caught in the hollow of the
hand, but if any are not caught they have to be picked up,
one by one, another stone being at the same time thrown into
the air and caught with the one picked up in the hand.
Two-ers, Three-ers, and Four-ers, are played in the same way,

except that the stones not caught on the back of the hand have
to be arranged in twos, threes, and fours respectively by the
hand on which the caught stones are lying meanwhile, and
then each lot has to be picked up altogether. If the number
that fall when the stones are first thrown up won't allow of
this, the player has to drop the required number (but no more)
from his hand. In Magic the play is just the same as in
One-ers, except that instead of only throwing up a single
stone and catching it as the others are in turn picked up, the
whole number, except those remaining to be picked up, are
thrown and caught. In Four Squares, four of the stones are
arranged in a square, each of them is then picked up, whilst the
remaining stone is flung upwards and caught ; the one picked up
is then tossed up, and the one originally tossed up is put down
in the place of the other, which is caught as it descends, and the
process repeated " all round the square." Trotting Donkeys is
similarly played, except that the four stones are arranged in a
line—not in a square—and I believe there is some other slight
difference, but I forget what. Fly-catchers is played like
One-ers, except that the stone thrown into the air while the
others are being picked up, is not simply caught by being
allowed to fall into the hand, but by an outward movement of
the hand is *pounced on*, hawk-fashion, from above. Magic Fly-
catchers is played in precisely the same way, except that as
in simple Magic, not one stone, but all are thrown up and
caught—that is, if there are four on the ground one only is
thrown up for the first, two for the second, three for the third,
and so on until they are all picked up. This is, of course, the
most difficult part of all, and, in fact, only experts were expected
to do it. Every failure means " out," and then your opponent
has his turn. The winner is the one who gets through first.
Such is the game as I remember it, but I have an uneasy
suspicion that I have missed something out. I seem to remember one trick in which all the stones on the ground had to
be picked up at once *where they lay*—scrambled up so to speak.
Or it may be (and, in fact, I think it was) that sometimes, to
add to the difficulty of the game, we picked up the groups of
two, three, and four in Two-ers, Three-ers, and Four-ers in

this fashion, instead of first placing them together.—Epworth, Doncaster (C. C. Bell).

In Wakefield the set of pot checks, which represents five hucklebones, now consists of four checks and a ball about the size of a large marble. The checks are something like dice, but only two opposite sides are plain, the other four being fluted. The table played on is generally a doorstep, and it is made ready by drawing a ring upon it with anything handy which will make a mark. There are twelve figures or movements to be gone through as follows. Some have special names, but I do not learn that all have.

1. The player, taking the checks and ball in the right hand, throws down the checks, keeping the ball in the hand. If any check fall outside the ring the player is "down." There is skill needed in the throwing of the checks in this and the following movements, so that they may be conveniently placed for taking up in the proper order. The checks being scattered, the player throws up the ball, takes up one check, and catches the ball as it comes down, or, as it is sometimes played, after it has bounced once from the step. This is repeated till all the checks are taken up.

2. As the last figure, but the checks are taken up two at a throw.

3. As the last, but at the first throw one check, called the Horse, is taken up, and at the second the remaining three checks at once, called the Cart.

4. As before, but all the checks taken up together.

5. Called Ups and Downs. The checks are taken up at one throw, and set down outside the ring at the next. This is done first with one, then with two, and so on.

6. Each check is touched in turn as the ball is thrown.

7. The checks are separately pushed out of the ring.

8. Each check in turn is taken up and knocked against the ground.

9. Each check is taken up and tapped upon another.

10. The checks are first arranged three in a line, touching each other, and the fourth placed at the top of that at one end of the row. This is called the Cradle. It has to be taken

down check by check, and if, in taking one, another is moved, the player is out.

11. Like the last, but the checks are put one above another to make a Chimney.

12. Called the Dish-clout—I know not why, unless it be that it wipes up the game. The movement used in taking up the checks is thus described :—"Take hold of the sleeve of the right hand with the left ; throw up the ball, and twist your right hand underneath and over your left, and catch the ball. With the hand still twisted throw up the ball and untwist and catch it." The checks are picked up in the course of the twisting.

These I am told are the orthodox movements ; and I do not doubt that in them there is much of very old tradition, although the tenth and eleventh must have been either added or modified since pot checks came into use, for the figures could not be built up with the natural bones. Some other movements are sometimes used according to fancy, as for example the clapping of the ground with the palm of the hand before taking up the checks and catching the ball.—J. T. Micklethwaite (*Arch. Journ.*, xlix. 327–28).

I am told that in the iron districts of Staffordshire, the round bits of iron punched out in making rivet holes in boiler plates are the modern representatives of hucklebones.—*Ibid.*

In Westminster four stones are held in the right hand, a marble is thrown up, and all four stones thrown down, and the marble allowed to bounce on the hearthstone or pavement, and then caught in the same hand after it has rebounded. The marble is then thrown up again, and one of the four stones picked up, and the marble caught again after it has rebounded. This is done separately to the other three, bringing all four stones into the hand. The marble is again bounced, and all four stones thrown down and the marble caught. Two stones are then picked up together, then the other two, then one, then three together, then all four together, the marble being tossed and caught with each throw. An arch is then formed by placing the left hand on the ground, and the four stones are again thrown down, the marble tossed, and the four stones put separately into the arch, the marble being caught after it has rebounded each time; or the four stones are separately put between the fingers of the left hand in as straight a row as possible. Then the left hand is taken away, and the four stones caught up in one sweep of the hand. Then all four stones are thrown down, and one is picked up before the marble is caught. This is retained in the hand, and when the second stone is picked up the first one is laid down before the marble is caught; the third is picked up and the second laid down, the fourth picked up and the third laid down, then the fourth laid down, the marble being tossed and caught again each time. The stones have different names or marks (which follow in rotation), and in picking them up they must be taken in their proper order, or it is counted as a mistake. The game is played throughout by the right hand, the left hand only being used when "arches" is made. The marble should be thrown up about the same height each toss, and there should be little or no interval between the different figures.—Annie Dicker.

I saw this game played in Endell Street, London, W.C., by two girls. Their game was not so long nor so complete as the above. They did not throw all four stones down as a preliminary stage, but began with the second figure, the four gobs being placed in a square ⦂ ⦂ , nor were they particular as to which stones they picked up. They knew nothing of numbering or naming them. Their marble was called a "jack." They had places chalked on the pavement where they recorded their successful "goes," and the game was played in a ring.—A. B. Gomme.

An account sent me from Deptford (Miss Chase) is doubtless the same game. It begins with taking two "gobs" at once, and apparently there are eight stones or gobs to play with. The marble or round stone which is thrown up is called a "tally." The directions for playing are—

> We take twoses,
> We take threeses,
> We take fourses,
> We take sixes,
> We take eights.

Chain eggs—*i.e.*, to pick up one and drop it again until this has been done to each stone. Arches—*i.e.*, gobs in a row. This was described by the player as "while the tally is up to sweep the whole row or line off the ground into the arch of the finger and thumb before catching the tally."

(*b*) These games are variants of one common original. It is the same game as that described by F. H. Low in the *Strand Magazine*, ii. 514, as played in the London streets. The marble there is called a "buck." "Pegsy" was the name of the No. 5 stage of the Wakefield version, and this varies too, inasmuch as it was the same gob which is picked up and then laid down before catching the buck.

Mr. Kinahan says, "'Jackstones,' played with three or four small stones that are thrown up in the air and caught again, seems to have been a very ancient game, as the stones have been found in the *crannogs* or lake-dwellings in some hole near the fireplaces, similar to where they are found in a cabin at the present day. An old woman, or other player, at the present time puts them in a place near the hob when they stop their game and go to do something else" (*Folk-lore Journal*, ii. 266). In the Græco-Roman saloon, British Museum, is a statue originally composed of two boys quarrelling at the game of "Tali" (see *Townley Gallery*, i. 305; Smith's *Dict. Greek and Roman Antiq.*, s.v. *Talus*), and it is interesting to note that in the Deptford game the marble is called a "Tally."

Mr. Kinahan's note suggests that "Fivestones" may be an independent game, instead of a derivative from "Hucklebones." If this is so, we have interesting evidence of the spread or transmission of one game from at least two centres. Professor Attwell, in *Notes and Queries*, 8th ser., iv. 201, suggests that "Hucklebones" was introduced into Europe by the Romans, and was spread throughout the countries which formed the empire by means of Roman colonists and soldiers. Mr. Newell (*Games*, pp. 190–93) describes a similar game to "Fivestones" played in Boston under the name of "Otadama," or "Japanese Jacks." This game is of Japanese origin, "Tedama" (that is, "Handballs") being its proper name. He says there can be no doubt that the two forms of this amusement are branches of the same root; and we thus have an example of a game which, having preserved its essential characteristics for thousands of years, has fairly circumnavigated the globe, so that the two currents of tradition, westward and eastward, from Europe and Asia, have met in America.

See "Checkstones," "Dibs," "Hucklebones," "Jack-stones."

Flowers

Sides are chosen; each side must have a "home" at the top and bottom of the ground where the children are playing. One side chooses a flower and goes over to the other side, the members of which stand in a row facing the first side. The first side states the initial letters of the flower it has chosen, and when the second side guesses the right flower they run and try to catch as many of the opposite side as they can before they reach their home. The captives then become members of the side which captured them.—Bitterne, Hants (Mrs. Byford).

Follow my Gable

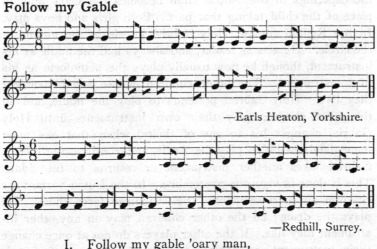

—Earls Heaton, Yorkshire.

—Redhill, Surrey.

I.   Follow my gable 'oary man,
     Follow my gable 'oary man,
     I'll do all that ever I can
     To follow my gable 'oary man.

We'll borrow a horse and steal a gig,
And round the world we'll have a jig,
And I'll do all that ever I can
To follow my gable 'oary man.

> —Earls Heaton, Yorks (Herbert Hardy).

II.   Holy Gabriel, holy man,
Rantum roarum reeden man,
I'll do all as ever I can
To follow my Gabriel, holy man.*

> —Redhill, Surrey (Miss G. Hope).

III.   I sell my bat, I sell my ball,
I sell my spinning-wheel and all;
And I'll do all that ever I can
To follow the eyes of the drummer man.

> —Luton, Bedfordshire (Mrs. Ashdown).

(*b*) In the Yorkshire version a ring is formed with one child in the middle as the 'Oary Man. Whatever he, or she, does, all in the ring must mimic, going round and singing at the same time. Any one found late in changing the action or idle in obeying the caperings of the central child becomes the 'Oary Man in place of the child taking that part. Both girls and boys play. In the Redhill version, Holy Gabriel kneels in the middle of the circle. He acts as leader, and always had the fiddle as his instrument, though he now usually plays the pianoforte as his first instrument. The other children choose any instrument they like. Holy Gabriel pretends to play the fiddle, and all the other children play their own instruments until Holy Gabriel changes his to one of theirs, when that one must immediately begin to play the fiddle, and continue until Holy Gabriel takes another instrument or returns to the fiddle. This is done in vigorous pantomime. In the Luton variant the children sit in a semicircle, the Drummer faces them. He plays the drum; all the other children play on any other instrument they like. If the other players do not at once change their instrument, or neglect to sing the lines, a forfeit is demanded.

* A variant of the second line is, "Ranting, roaring, heely man." "I suppose he was Irish," said my informant, "as he was named 'Healey'" (Miss G. Hope).

(c) Mr. Hardy says some sing this game, "Follow my game an holy man." Mr. Hardy once thought it was the remnant of a goblin story of a hoary man of the gable or house-roof, who presided over the destinies of poor cottagers, and he had begun to make out the folk tale. The fairy would sometimes come down, and, playing his antics, compel whomsoever observed him to follow him in a mimicking procession. Miss Hope writes of "Holy Gàbriel" that the game is played at Mead Vale, a small village in Surrey, but is unknown at larger villages and towns a few miles off. Some of the women who played it in their youth say that it began in the Primitive Methodist school at Mead Vale. It is played at Outword, also a remote village, and was introduced there by a stonemason, who stated that he had learned it from a cousin who had been in America. Further inquiry by Miss Hope elicited the fact that the cousin had learned the game, when a boy, in his native place in Lancashire. He did not know whether it was a well-known game there. This information points perhaps to a modern origin, but in such cases it must be borne in mind that people are very fond of suggesting recent circumstances as the cause of the most ancient traditions or customs. The obvious analogy to the incident in the myth of the Pied Piper, and to the Welsh custom at St. Almedha Church, near Brecknock, recorded by Giraldus Cambrensis, where the imitation of a frenzied leader is carried out as a religious ceremony, rather suggests that in this game we may have a survival of a ceremonial so common among early or uncultured people, the chief incident of which is the frenzied dancing of a god-possessed devotee.

Follow my Leader

This is a boys' game. Any number can take part in it. It requires a good extent of country to play it well. The boy who is the swiftest runner and the best jumper is chosen as Leader. He sets out at a good speed over the fields, tries to jump as many ditches or burns, jumping such from one side to the other again and again, to scramble over dykes, through hedges, over palings, and run up braes. The others have to follow him as they can. This steeplechase continues till the followers are all tired out.—Keith (Rev. W. Gregor).

This is a very general game among schoolboys, but in Hereford it was a town custom occurring once in seven years on 11th October (*Folk-lore Journal*, v. 75).

Fool, Fool, come to School

This game is played under the name of "Foolie, Foolie" at Duthil, Strathspey. The players are placed in a row, either standing or sitting. Two are chosen, the one as Namer and the other as Foolie. Foolie withdraws, if not out of sight, at least out of range of hearing. The Namer then gives a name secretly to each player. When this is done, he calls on Foolie—Foolie, Foolie, come to your schoolie.

Foolie pays no attention to this call. It is again repeated, but with the same results. This goes on for several times. At last the Namer calls out—

Foolie, Foolie, come to your schoolie ;
Your bannocks are burnin' an' ready for turnin'.

Foolie always obeys this call, comes and stations himself beside the Namer. A little chaffing generally goes on against Foolie. The Namer says, "Come chise me oot, come chise me in, tae" so and so, naming one by the assumed fancy name. Foolie makes choice of one. If the choice falls right, the one so chosen steps from the line and stands beside Foolie. If the choice falls wrong, the one named remains in the line. All the players' names are called out in this way. If any stand unchosen by Foolie, the Namer then goes up to each and asks if he wants, *e.g.*, "an aipple," "an orange," "a kirk," "a cottage," &c. Each one whispers what he wants. The same question is put to Foolie. If he answers, *e.g.*, "orange," the one so named steps out and stands beside Foolie. All not first chosen are gone over in this way. Those left unchosen take their stand beside the Namer. There is then a tug-of-war, with the Namer and Foolie as the leaders.—Keith (Rev. W. Gregor).

In Hants the children stand *vis-à-vis*, as in a country dance. One of the number is sent out of earshot, and the others decide with the Captain as to the name of the bird each wishes to personate. The Captain then calls to the child who is out, "Tom Fool, Tom Fool, come home from school, and pick me out a blackbird," "cuckoo," or other bird. If Tom Fool is wrong in his guessing after three trials, he is condemned to run the gauntlet, being pelted with gloves or handkerchiefs not too mercifully.—Bitterne, Hants (Miss Byford).

In Sussex there is the same action with the following words, but there is no chasing or hitting—

> Of all the birds in the air,
> Of all the fishes in the sea,
> You can pick me out [   ].

If the children fail to do so, they say—

> Poor fool, been to school,
> Learn more in a week;
> Been there seven years
> And hasn't learnt a bit.
> —Hurstmonceux, Sussex (Miss Chase).

The same game is played indoors in Cornwall, the reply being—

> Fool, fool, go back to school
> And learn your letters better.
> —Cornwall (*Folk-lore Journal*, v. 99-80).

See "Namers and Guessers."

Foot and Over

One boy out of a number stoops in the position for "Leap-frog" at an agreed fixed line. From the players he chooses a Leader and a Foot. The Leader first leaps over the stooping boy at a foot from the line; the other players then leap in turn each at a foot further from the line, the stooping boy moving forward from the line for each player; finally the Foot leaps as far as the distance leapt by the last boy. If this is accomplished, the Leader hops from the line and then leaps; the followers hop and leap each a foot further than each other; finally the Foot hops and leaps as far as the distance covered by the last boy. If this is accomplished, the Leader hops twice and then leaps; the same process going on until one of the boys fails, who then takes the place of the stooping boy, and the game begins again. If the Foot covers any longer distance than the Leader, the Leader stoops down.—Earls Heaton, Yorks. (H. Hardy).

This game is general. Mr. Emslie describes the London version somewhat differently. After all the boys had jumped over the first boy's back, a cry of "Foot it" was raised, and the boy who had given the back placed one of his feet at a right

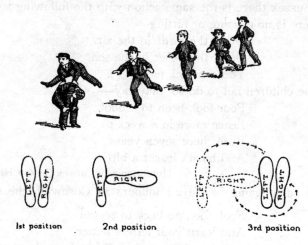

| 1st position | 2nd position | 3rd position |

angle to the other, and in this way measured a "foot's length" from the starting-place. All the boys then "overed" his back from the original line, the last one crying "Foot it," and then the measuring ceremony was again gone through, and the game commenced again, and continued in the same manner until one of the boys failed to "over" the back, when he became Back.

Football

The modern game of "Football" is too well known to need description here, and, like "Cricket," it has become no longer a children's game. As to its origin, there are many ball games, such as "Camping," which have been suggested as the original form of "Football." Every school almost had some peculiarity in the method of playing, and Eton, Winchester, Uppingham, and Rugby are well-known examples. It is not a little interesting to note, now that "Football" has settled down into a national game organised by county committees, that one of the forms of play officially recognised is the old Rugby game, the other form, known as the "Association," being arrived at by agreement of those interested in the game.

To illustrate the ancient origin of the game, and its serious import as a local contest rather than a sport, some examples may be given. It is still (1877) keenly contested at Workington on Easter Tuesday on the banks of, and not unfrequently in, the river Derwent (Dickinson's *Cumberland Glossary*). At Derby there was a football contest between the parishes of All Saints' and St. Peter's. The ball was thrown into the market-place from the Town Hall. The moment it was thrown the "war cries" of the rival parishes began, and the contest, nominally that of a football match, was in reality a fight between the two sections of the town; and the victors were announced by the joyful ringing of their parish bells (Dyer's *Popular Customs*, p. 75). At Chester-le-Street the game was played between what were termed "up-streeters" and "down-streeters," one side endeavouring to get the ball to the top of the town, whilst their opponents tried to keep it near the lower or north end. At one o'clock the ball was thrown out from near the old commercial hotel, the Queen's Head, in the centre of the town, and it has often been received by over three and four hundred people, so great was the interest taken in this ancient sport. At Asborne the struggle was between the "up'ards" and "down'ards." At Dorking the divisions were between the east and west ends of the town, and there was first a perambulation of the streets by the football retinue composed of grotesquely dressed persons. At Alnwick the divisions were the parishes of St. Michael's and St. Paul's. At Kirkwall the contest was on New Year's Day, and was between "up the gates" and "down the gates," the ball being thrown up at the Cross. At Scarborough, on the morning of Shrove Tuesday, hawkers paraded the streets with parti-coloured balls, which were purchased by all ranks of the community. With these, and armed with sticks, men, women, and children repaired to the sands below the old town and indiscriminately commenced a contest. The following graphic account of Welsh customs was printed in the *Oswestry Observer* of March 2, 1887: "In South Cardiganshire it seems that about eighty years ago the population, rich and poor, male and female, of opposing parishes, turned out on Christmas Day and indulged in the game of 'Football' with such vigour that it became little short of a serious fight. The parishioners of Cellan and Pencarreg were particularly bitter in their conflicts; men threw off their coats and waistcoats and women their gowns, and sometimes their petticoats. At Llanwenog, an extensive parish below Lampeter, the inhabitants for football purposes were divided into the Bros and the Blaenaus. A man over eighty, an inmate of Lampeter Workhouse, gives the following particulars :—In North Wales the ball was called the Bêl Troed, and was made with a bladder covered with a Cwd Tarw. In South Wales it was called Bél Ddu, and was usually made by the shoemaker of the parish, who appeared on the ground on Christmas Day with the ball under his arm. The Bros, it should be stated, occupied the high ground of the parish. They were nicknamed 'Paddy Bros,' from a tradition that they were descendants from Irish people who settled on the hills in days long gone by. The Blaenaus occupied the lowlands, and, it may be presumed, were pure-bred Brythons. The more devout of the Bros and Blaenaus joined in the service at the parish church on Christmas morning. At any rate, the match did not begin until about mid-day, when the service was finished. Then the whole of the Bros and Blaenaus, rich and poor, male and female, assembled on the turnpike road which divided the highlands from the lowlands. The ball having been redeemed from the Crydd, it was thrown high in the air by a strong man, and when it fell Bros and Blaenaus scrambled for its possession, and a quarter of an hour frequently elapsed before the ball was got out from among the struggling heap of human beings. Then if the Bros, by hook or by crook, could succeed in taking the ball up the mountain to their hamlet of Rhyddlan they won the day; while the Blaenaus were successful if they got the ball to their end of the parish at New Court. The whole parish was the field of operations, and sometimes it would be dark before either party scored a victory. In the meantime many kicks would be given and taken, so that on the following day some of the competitors would be unable to walk, and sometimes a kick on the shins would lead the two men concerned to abandon the game until they had decided which was the better pugilist. There do not appear to have been any rules for the regulation of the game; and the art of football playing in the olden time seems to have been to reach the goal. When once the goal was reached, the victory was celebrated by loud hurrahs and the firing of guns, and was not disturbed until the following Christmas Day. Victory on Christmas Day, added the old man, was so highly esteemed by the whole countryside, that a Bro or Blaenau would as soon lose a cow from his cow-house as the football from his portion of the parish."

(*b*) In Gomme's *Village Community*, pp. 241–44, the position of football games as elements in the traditions of race is discussed, and their relationship to a still earlier form of tribal games, where the element of clan feuds is more decidedly preserved, is pointed out.

Forfeits

Forfeits are incurred in those games in which penalties are exacted from players for non-compliance with the rules of the game; "Buff," "Contrary," "Crosspurposes," "Fire, Air, and Water," "Follow my Gable," "Genteel Lady," "Jack's Alive," "Old Soldier," "Twelve Days of Christmas," "Turn the Trencher," "Wadds," and others. These games are described under their several titles, and the formula for forfeits is always the same. Small articles belonging to the players must be given by them every time a forfeit is incurred, and these must be redeemed at the close of the game. They are "cried" in the following manner:—One of the players sits on a chair having the forfeits in her lap. A child kneels on the ground and buries his face in his hands on the lap of the person who holds the forfeits. The "crier" then takes up indiscriminately one of the forfeits, and holding it up in the sight of all those who have been playing the games (without the kneeling child seeing it), says—

Here's a very pretty thing and a very pretty thing,

And what shall be done to [*or*, by] the owner of this very
pretty thing?

The kneeling child then says what the penance is to be. The owner of the forfeit must then perform the penance before the other players, and then another forfeit is "cried."

The more general penances imposed upon the owners of the forfeits are as follows, but the list could be very much extended :—

Bite an inch off the poker.

Kneel to the prettiest, bow to the wittiest, and kiss the one you love best.

Stand in each corner of the room, sigh in one, cry in another, sing in another, and dance in the other.

Put yourself through the keyhole.

Place two chairs in the middle of the room, take off your shoes, and jump over them.

Measure so many yards of love ribbon.

Postman's knock.

Crawl up the chimney.

Spell Opportunity.

Miss Burne mentions one penance designed to make the victim ridiculous, as when he is made to lie on his back on the floor with his arms extended, and declare—

Here I lie!
The length of a looby,
The breadth of a booby,
And three parts of a jackass!

—Shropshire Folk-lore, pp. 526–27.

(c) Halliwell gives, in his *Nursery Rhymes*, pp. 324–26, some curious verses, recorded for the first time by Dr. Kenrick in his Review of Dr. Johnson's Shakespeare, 1765, on "rules for seemly behaviour," in which the forfeits imposed by barbers as penalties for handling razors, &c., are set forth. Although "barbers' forfeits" are not of the same nature as the nursery forfeits, it is possible that this general custom among so important a class of the community in early times as barbers may have suggested the game. Both Forby in his *Vocabulary of East Anglia* and Moor in his *Suffolk Words* bear testimony to the general prevalence of barbers' forfeits, and it must be borne in mind that barbers were also surgeons in early days.

A curious custom is also recorded in another East Anglian word-list, which may throw light upon the origin of the game from popular custom. "A forfeit is incurred by using the word 'water' in a brew-house, where you must say 'liquor;' or by using the word 'grease' in a chandlery, where it is 'stuff' or 'metal.' The forfeit is to propitiate the offended *genius loci*" (Spurden's *East Anglian Vocabulary*). The element of divination in the custom is perhaps indicated by a curious note from Waldron, in his *Description of the Isle of Man* (*Works*, p. 55), "There is not a barn unoccupied the whole twelve days, every parish hiring fiddlers at the public charge. On Twelfth Day the fiddler lays his head on some of the wenches' laps, and a third person asks who such a maid or such a maid shall marry, naming the girls then present one after another; to which he answers according to his own whim, or agreeable to the intimacies he has taken notice of during this time of merriment. But whatever he says is as absolutely depended on as an oracle; and if he happen to couple two people who have an aversion to each other, tears and vexation succeed the mirth. This they call cutting off the fiddler's head; for after this he is dead for the whole year." Redeeming the forfeits is called "Crying the Weds," in Burne's *Shropshire Folk-lore*, p. 526. See "Wadds."

Fox

> Fox, a fox, a brummalary
> How many miles to Lummaflary? Lummabary?
> Eight and eight and a hundred and eight.
> How shall I get home to-night?
> Spin your legs and run fast.

Halliwell gives this rhyme as No. ccclvii. of his *Nursery Rhymes*, but without any description of the game beyond the words, "A game of the fox." It is probably the same game as "Fox and Goose."

Fox and Goose (1)

In Dorsetshire one of the party, called the Fox, takes one end of the room or corner of a field (for the game was equally played indoors or out); all the rest of the children arrange themselves in a line or string, according to size, one behind the other, the smallest last, behind the tallest one, called Mother Goose, with their arms securely round the waist of the one in front of them, or sometimes by grasping the dress.

The game commences by a parley between the Fox and Goose to this effect, the Goose beginning.

"What are you after this fine morning?"

"Taking a walk."

"With what object?"

"To get an appetite for a meal."

"What does [will] your meal consist of?"

"A nice fat goose for my breakfast."

"Where will you get it?"

"Oh, I shall get a nice morsel somewhere; and as they are so handy, I shall satisfy myself with one of yours."

"Catch one if you can."

A lively scene follows. The Fox and Mother Goose should be pretty evenly matched; the Mother with extended arms seeking to protect her Brood, while the Fox, who tries to dodge under, right and left, is only allowed in case of a successful foray or grasp to secure the last of the train. Vigorous efforts are made to escape him, the Brood of course supplementing the Mother's exertions to elude him as far as they are able, but without breaking the link. The game may be continued until all in turn are caught.—*Folk-lore Journal*, vii. 217–18.

In Lancashire the children stand in line behind each other, holding each other by the waist. One stands facing them and calls out—

> My mother sits on yonder chimney,
> And she says she *must* have a chicken.

The others answer—

> She *can't* have a chicken.

The one then endeavours to catch the last child of the tail, who when caught comes behind the captor; repeat until all have changed sides.—Monton, Lancashire (Miss Dendy).

A version of this game played at Eckington, Derbyshire, is played as follows:—A den is chalked out or marked out for the Fox. A larger den, opposite to this, is marked out for the

Geese. A boy or a girl represents the Fox, and a number of others the Geese. Then the Fox shouts, "Geese, Geese, gannio," and the Geese answer, "Fox, Fox, fannio." Then the Fox says, "How many Geese have you to-day?" The Geese reply, "More than you can catch and carry away." Then the Geese run out of the den, and the Fox tries to catch them. He puts as many as he catches into his den (S. O. Addy).

(*b*) This game is a very general one at Christmas time. It is practically the same as "Gled Wylie," and "Hen and Chickens," and the "Hawk and Chickens" of Mr. Newell's *Games and Songs of American Children*, pp. 155–56. By referring to these games it will be seen that the whole group are mimic representatives of farmyard episodes, though the animal characters are giving way to more domestic affairs, as shown in the Pins and Needles version of "Hen and Chickens." It is possible that the different animals which are victims to the Fox appearing in the different games may arise from local circumstances, and that in this case a real distinction exists between the various names by which this game is known. A game called "Wolf and Deer," similar to "Fox and Geese," is given in *Winter Evening Amusements*, by R. Revel. The last one at the end of the tail may, if she has no other chance of escape, try and place herself before the Deer or Hen. She is then no longer to be hunted; all the others must then follow her example until the deer becomes the last of the line. The game then terminates by exacting a forfeit for each lady whom the Wolf has suffered to escape his clutches (pp. 64, 65).

See "Gled Wylie," "Hen and Chickens," "Old Dame."

Fox and Geese (2)

A game known by this name is played with marbles or pegs on a board on which are thirty-three holes, or on the pavement, with holes scraped out of the stones. To play this game there are seventeen pieces called Geese, and another one either larger or distinguished from the Geese by its colour, which is called the Fox. The Fox occupies the centre hole, and the Geese occupy nine holes in front, and four on each side of him.

The vacant holes behind are for the Geese and Fox to move in. The game is for the Geese to shut up the Fox so that he cannot move. All the pieces can be moved from one spot to another in the direction of the lines, but cannot pass over two holes at once. The Geese are not permitted to take the Fox. The Fox's business is to take all, or as many of the Geese as will prevent him from being blockaded. The Fox can take the Geese whenever there is a vacant space behind them, which he passes to, then occupies.

This game has been very popular among schoolboys in all ages. Mr. Micklethwaite, in a paper on the Indoor Games of School Boys in the Middle Ages (*Arch. Journ.* xlix. 322), gives instances of finding figures of this game cut "in the cloister benches of Gloucester Cathedral and elsewhere, and there are several on the twelfth century tomb at Salisbury, miscalled Lord Stourton's," and also at Norwich Castle. For the date of these boards, Mr. Micklethwaite says for the last three centuries and a half cloisters everywhere in England have been open passages, and there have generally been schoolboys about. It is therefore not unlikely that they should have left behind them such traces as these play-boards. But if they are of later date they would not be found to be distributed in monastic cloisters with respect to the monastic arrangement, and we do find them so. Strutt describes the game (*Sports*, p. 319).

See "Nine Men's Morris," "Noughts and Crosses."

Fox in the Fold

"The Tod (Fox) i' the Faul (Fold)." This game is commonly played by boys. Any number of boys join hands and stand in a circle to form the Faul. The boy that represents the Tod is placed within the circle. His aim is to escape. To effect this he rushes with all his force, increased by a run, against the joint hands of any two of the players. If the rush does not unloose the grasp, he hangs on the two arms with all his weight, pressing and wriggling. If he fails he makes a rush at another two, always selecting those players he thinks weakest. When he does break through he rushes off at the top of his speed, with all the players in full cry, till he is caught and brought back. The game begins anew with another boy as Tod.—Keith (Rev. W. Gregor).

See " Bull in the Park," " Frog in the Middle."

Fox in the Hole

All the players are armed with handkerchiefs. One of the players is chosen for Fox, who has his den marked out. The Fox hops out on one leg, with his handkerchief ready to strike. The players gather round him and attack him. If he can strike one of his assailants without putting his foot to the ground from his hopping position, the player so struck is chased by the others into the den, and he then becomes the Fox for another round of the game.—Cork (Miss Keane).

Halliwell (*Nursery Rhymes*, p. 228) describes the game in practically the same manner, but adds that when the Fox is coming out he says—

The Fox gives warning
It's a cold and frosty morning,

after which he is at liberty to hop out and use his handkerchief.

(*b*) This game is alluded to in *Soliman and Perseda*, 1599; *Florio*, p. 480; *Herrick*, i. 176. See Halliwell's *Dictionary*. Professor Mayor communicated to the *Gentleman's Magazine* of 1848 (ii.), p. 147, the following early allusions to the game from old dictionaries :—

Gouldman, London, MDCLXIV. — "*Ascoliasmus*, Empusæ ludus : a kind of play wherein boys lift up one leg and hop with the other, where they beat one another with bladders tied to the end of strings. Fox to thy hole."

Holyoke, MDCLXXVII.—"*Empusa*. παρὰ τὸ ἐνὶ ποδίζειν, quòd uno incedat pede. Hence *empusam agere* is used for a play, hopping on one leg ; with us, Fox to his hole."

Id. "*Ascoliasmus*. A kind of play that children use when they hop on one leg, called Fox to thy hole."

Cambridge Dict. MDCXCIII. — "*Ascol*. A kind of play wherein boys hopping on one leg beat one another with gloves or pieces of leather, and is called Fox to thy hole."

Coles, 7th ed. 1711.—"*Ascol*. The play called Fox to the

hole.—*Empus*. Ludus Empusæ. Scotch hoppers, or Fox in the hole."

A similar game to this is played at Earls Heaton, Yorkshire (Mr. Hardy), and called "Goose and Gander." Two players, the Goose and the Gander, stand in a ring, each on one leg. They hop out in turn, and try to catch one of the other players without letting their other leg touch the ground. If they fail in this they get "strapped" back to the ring. When either are successful, the player who is caught takes the place of either Goose or Gander in turn. The game is also mentioned in *Useful Transactions in Philosophy*, 1708–9.

French Jackie

This game is played either by boys or girls or by both together. One is chosen to stand alone; the other players join hands and form a circle. The one outside the circle goes round it and touches on the back one of the circle. He then runs off round the circle, and the one who was touched runs off in the opposite direction round the circle. The aim of each player is to reach the vacant place in the circle first. The one left out has to repeat the same action. The game may go on for any length of time.—Keith (Rev. W. Gregor).

At Barnes this game is called "Gap." It is known as "French Tag" in the Forest of Dean, Gloucestershire (Miss Matthews), and "Tap-back" at Bitterne, Hants (Mrs. Adam).

French and English

The children choose sides under a leader, and a boundary line is made in the middle of the ground dividing the French and English territory. A handkerchief is then placed in the back part of each territory to represent a flag. The object is to obtain as many flags from the opposite side as possible. If a person is captured before having seized a flag, he is taken prisoner, and must be rescued by one of his own side. Thus, for instance, an Englishman enters the French territory and tries to reach the flag. If he is seen by the French before he reaches the flag, he is taken prisoner and is placed near the flags, and the next Englishman rescues him instead of taking a flag. As soon as the flag is taken, one of the party must put another handkerchief in its place. A player cannot be taken prisoner after having obtained the handkerchief or flag. The winning side is decided by counting the flags and prisoners. —Bitterne, Hants (Mrs. Byford).

This is a very general game, and is known as "Scotch and English" in the north, where some interesting details occur, for which see "Scotch and English."

French Blindman's Buff

The children kneel in a circle, one standing blindfolded in the middle. The kneeling children shout, "Come point to me with your pointer."—Monton, Lancashire (Miss Dendy).

See "Buff," "Dinah," "Muffin Man."

Friar-rush

A Christmas game, mentioned in the *Declaration of Popish Impostures*, 1603.

Frincy-francy

A game played between the dances at balls in farm-houses. A chair was placed in the middle of the barn or room; the master of the ceremonies led to the chair a young woman, who sat down and named the young man whom she was willing should kiss her. This he did, and then took the seat which the lady vacated. He then called out the name of some favourite girl, who was led up to him; there was another kiss. The girl then took the seat, and so on (county of Down). The same game is called "Frimsey-framsey" in parts of the county of Antrim.—Patterson's *Antrim and Down Glossary*.

Compare "Cushion Dance."

Frog-lope

Name for "Leap-frog."—Addy's *Sheffield Glossary*.

Frog in the Middle

One child is seated on the ground with his legs under him; the other players form a ring round. They then pull or buffet the centre child or Frog, who tries to catch one of them without rising from the floor.   The child who is caught takes the place of the centre child.   Another method of playing the game is similar to "Bull in the Park."   The child in the centre tries to break out of the ring, those forming it keeping the Frog in the ring by any means in their power, while still keeping their hands clasped.   They sometimes sing or say—

Hey! hey! hi! Frog in the middle and there shall lie;

He can't get out and he shan't get out—hey! hey! hi!

They dance round when saying this, all keeping a watch on the

Frog, who suddenly makes a rush, and tries to break through the ring.—London (A. B. Gomme).

Strutt describes this game, and gives an illustration from a fourteenth century MS. which is here reproduced from the original (*Sports*, p. 303).   Newell (*Games of American Children*, p. 171) also mentions it, and gives the rhyme as—

Frog in the sea, can't catch me!

Gap

The same as "French Jackie."   This game is called "Tap-back" or "Tat-back" at Bitterne, Hants.

Garden Gate

Children join hands and form a ring.   One child stands inside the ring; this child walks round and asks one of the circle, called the Keeper—

Have you the key of the garden gate?

Open and let me go through.

The Keeper replies—

> My next-door neighbour's got the key;
> Ask him and he'll give it to you.

This is repeated by each one in the circle.   Then the inside child comes again to the Keeper and says—

> None of the neighbours have got the key,
> So you must let me go through.

The Keeper answers—

> I've lost the key of the garden gate,
> And cannot let you through.

Then all the ring say—

> You must stop all night within the gate,
> Unless you have strength to break through.

The child inside then attempts to break through, and if he succeeds in breaking any of the clasped hands the one who first gives way has to take the place in the centre.—Roxton, St. Neots (Miss Lumley).

See "Bull in the Park."

Gegg

"To smuggle the Gegg," a game played by boys in Glasgow, in which two parties are formed by lot, equal in number, the one being denominated the Outs, the other Ins.   The Outs are those who go out from the den or goal, where those called the Ins remain for a time.   The Outs get the Gegg, which is anything deposited, as a key, a penknife, &c.   Having received this, they conceal themselves, and raise the cry, "Smugglers!" On this they are pursued by the Ins; and if the Gegg (for the name is transferred to the person who holds the deposit) be taken, they exchange situations—the Outs become Ins and the Ins Outs.   This play is distinguished from "Hy-spy" only by the use of the Gegg.   One of the Ins who is touched by one of the Outs is said to be taken, and henceforth loses his right to hold the Gegg.   If he who holds the Gegg gets in the den, the Outs are winners, and have the privilege of getting out again.   The Outs, before leaving the den, shuffle the Gegg, or smuggle it so between each other that the Ins do not know which person has it.   He who is laid hold of, and put to the question, is supposed to deny that he has the Gegg: if he escapes with it, he gets out again.—Jamieson.

Genteel Lady

A player begins thus:—"I, a genteel lady (or gentleman) came from that genteel lady (or gentleman) to say that she (or he) owned a tree." The other players repeat the words in turn, and then the leader goes over them again, adding, "with bronze bark." The sentence goes round once more, and on the next repetition the leader continues, "with golden branches." He afterwards adds, "and silver leaves," "and purple fruit," "and on the top a milk-white dove," and, finally, "mourning for the loss of his lady-love."

If a player should fail in repeating the rigmarole, there is a fine to pay. A "pipe-lighter" is stuck in her hair, and she must say "one-horned lady" instead of "genteel lady." When a second horn is added, of course she says "two-horned," and so forth. Some players wear half-a-dozen before the conclusion of the game. The game is called "The Wonderful Tree." —Anderby, Lincolnshire (Miss M. Peacock).

In some parts of Yorkshire it is customary to say "no-horned lady" instead of "genteel lady" at the beginning of the game.

When we played this game we said "always genteel" after "genteel lady," and varied the formula. For instance, the first player would say, "I, a genteel lady, always genteel, come from a genteel lady, always genteel, to say she lives in a house with twelve windows," or words were used beginning with the letter A. Each player must repeat this, and add something else in keeping with a house; or sentences had to be made in which words beginning with the letter A must be said, the other players doing the same alphabetically.—London (A. B. Gomme).

Mr. Newell, in writing of this game, says that the "lamp-lighter" or "spill" was lighted when placed in the hair of the players who made mistakes. He does not mention forfeits being exacted.—*Games*, p. 139.

Ghost at the Well

One of the party is chosen for Ghost (if dressed in white so much the better); she hides in a corner; the other children are a mother and daughters. The eldest daughter says:—

"Mother, mother, please give me a piece of bread and butter."

M. "Let me (or 'leave me') look at your hands, child. Why, they are very dirty."

E. D. "I will go to the well and wash them."

She goes to the corner, the Ghost peeps up, and she rushes back, crying out—

"Mother! mother! I have seen a Ghost."

M. "Nonsense, child! it was only your father's nightshirt I have washed and hung out to dry. Go again."

The child goes, and the same thing happens. She returns, saying—

"Yes! mother! I have seen a ghost."

M. "Nonsense, child! we will take a candle, and all go together to search for it."

The mother picks up a twig for a candle, and they set off. When they come near to the Ghost, she appears from her hiding-place, mother and children rush away in different directions, the Ghost chases them until she has caught one, who in her turn becomes Ghost.—West Cornwall (Miss Courtney, *Folk-lore Journal*, v. 55).

This game was "Ghost in the Copper" in London. It was played in the same way as above. Chairs formed the copper, and the ghost crouched down behind. The "Mother" was "washing" at a tub, also formed with two chairs. The eldest daughter was told she could not go to school to-day; she must stop at home and help hang up the clothes. The other children go to play. The Mother said, "Here, Jane, take this (pretending to give her a garment out of the wash-tub) and put it in the copper, and push it down well with the stick." Jane goes to the copper and pretends to take off the lid. When she puts the washed garment in, and pokes down with the stick, the Ghost jumps up. She cries out as above, the Mother saying, "Nonsense, child! it's only some of the boiling clothes."

The child goes again, and the game proceeds as above. It is generally played now as "Ghost."—A. B. Gomme. It is mentioned by Newell (*Games*, p. 223).

Giants

A Giant is chosen, and he must be provided with a cave. A summer-house will do, if there is no window for the Giant to see out of. The others then have to knock at the door with their knuckles separately. The Giant rushes when he thinks all the children have knocked, and if he succeeds in catching one before they reach a place of safety (appointed beforehand) the captured one becomes Giant.—Bitterne, Hants (Mrs. Byford). See "Wolf."

Giddy

Giddy, giddy, gander,
Who stands yonder?
Little Bessy Baker,
Pick her up and shake her;
Give her a bit of bread and cheese,
And throw her over the water.
—Warwickshire.

(*b*) A girl being blindfolded, her companions join hands and form a ring round her. At the word "Yonder" the blindfolded girl points in any direction she pleases, and at line three names one of the girls. If the one pointed at and the one named be the same, she is the next to be blinded; but, curiously enough, if they be not the same, the one named is the one. Meanwhile, at line four, she is not "picked up," but is shaken by the shoulders by the still blindfolded girl; and at line five she is given by the same "bread and cheese," *i.e.*, the buds or young leaves of what later is called "May" (*Cratægus oxyacantha*); and at line six she is taken up under the blinded girl's arm and swung round. — Warwickshire (*Notes and Queries*, 6th Ser., viii. 451).

Gilty-galty (or gaulty)

A boy's game. One boy is chosen, who says:—
Gilty-galty four-and-forty,
Two tens make twenty.

He then counts one, two, three, four, &c., up to forty, having his eyes covered by his hands, and the others hide while he is saying the "nominy." At the conclusion he uncovers his eyes, and if he sees any boys not yet hidden they have to stand still. He seeks the rest, but if he moves far away from his place, called the "stooil" (stool), one of the hidden boys may rush out and take it, provided he can get there first. Should he fail in this he also has to stand aside; but if any one succeeds, then all run out as before, and the same boy has to say the "nominy" again. On the other hand, if he finds all the boys without loosing his "stooil," the boy first caught has to take his place and say the "nominy." The game was thus played in 1810, and is so still, both here and at Lepton.—Easther's *Almondbury and Huddersfield Glossary.*

Gipsy

> I charge my children, every one,
> To keep good house while I am gone.
> You, and you [points], but specially you
> [or sometimes, but specially Sue],
> Or else I'll beat you black and blue.

One child is selected for Gipsy, one for Mother, and one for Daughter Sue. The Mother says the lines, and points to several children to emphasise her words. During her absence the Gipsy comes in, entices a child away, and hides her. This process is repeated till all the children are hidden, when the mother has to find them.—Halliwell (*Nursery Rhymes*, p. 228).

See " Mother, Mother, the Pot Boils Over," " Witch."

Gled-wylie

The name of a singular game played at country schools. One of the largest of the boys steals away from his comrades, in an angry-like mood, to some dykeside or sequestered nook, and there begins to work as if putting a pot on a fire. The others seem alarmed at his manner, and gather round him, when the following dialogue takes place :—

They say first to him—

> What are ye for wi' the pot, gudeman ?
> Say what are ye for wi' the pot ?

We dinna like to see ye, gudeman,
  Sae thrang about this spot.

We dinna like ye ava, gudeman,
  We dinna like ye ava.
Are ye gaun to grow a gled, gudeman ?
And our necks draw and thraw ?

He answers—
  Your minnie, burdies, ye maun lae ;
  Ten to my nocket I maun hae ;
  Ten to my e'enshanks, and or I gae lye,
  In my wame I'll lay twa dizzen o' ye by.

The mother of them, as it were, returns—
  Try't than, try't than, do what ye can,
  Maybe ye maun toomer sleep the night, gudeman ;
  Try't than, try't than, Gled-wylie frae the heugh,
  Am no sae saft, Gled-wylie, ye'll fin' me bauld and teugh.

After these rhymes are said the chickens cling to the mother
all in a string. She fronts the flock, and does all she can to
keep the kite from her brood, but often he breaks the row and
catches his prey.—Mactaggart's *Gallovidian Encyclopedia.*

Evidently denominated from the common mode of designat-
ing the kite among the vulgar (Jamieson). " The Greedy
Gled's seeking ye," is one of the lines of a rhyme used in
" Hide and Seek " in Edinburgh. Glead, or Gled, is also a
Yorkshire and Cheshire name for a kite. " As hungry as a
Glead " (*Glossary*, by an Old Inhabitant).—Leigh (*Cheshire
Glossary*).

See " Fox and Goose," " Hen and Chickens," " Hide and
Seek."

Glim-glam

The play of " Blind Man's Buff."—Banffshire, Aberdeen
(Jamieson).

Gobs

A London name for the game of " Hucklebones."
See " Fivestones."

Green Grass

Spoken.
"Will you come?" "No!"

Spoken.
"Will you come?" "Yes!"

—Middlesex (Miss Collyer).

"Will you come?" "No!"
"Will you come?" "Yes!"

—London (A. B. Gomme).

—Congleton (Miss A. E. Twemlow).

I.   A dis, a dis, a green grass,
        A dis, a dis, a dis;
     Come all you pretty fair maids
        And dance along with us.

     For we are going roving,
        A roving in this land;
     We'll take this pretty fair maid,
        We'll take her by the hand.

     Ye shall get a duke, my dear,
        And ye shall get a drake;
     And ye shall get a young prince,
        A young prince for your sake.

     And if this young prince chance to die,
        Ye shall get another;
     The bells will ring, and the birds will sing,
        And we'll clap hands together.
                —Chamber's *Popular Rhymes*, pp. 137–38.

II. A-diss, a-diss, a-green grass,
        A-diss, a-diss, a-dass;
     Come, my pretty fair maid,
        And walk along with us.

     For you shall have a dik-ma-day,
        You shall have a drāgon;
     You shall have a nice young man
        With princes for his thēgan (or sēgan).
                    —Lanarkshire (W. G. Black).

III. A dish, a dish, a green grass,
        A dish, a dish, a dish,
     Come all you pretty maidens
        And dance along wi' us.

For we are lads a roving,
  A roving through the land,
We'll take this pretty fair maid
  By her lily white hand.

Ye sall get a duke, my dear,
  An ye sall get a drake,
An ye sall get a bonny prince
  For your ain dear sake.

And if they all should die,
  Ye sall get anither;
The bells will ring, the birds will sing,
  And we'll clap our hands together.
                    —Biggar (W. Ballantyne).

IV.   Dissy, dissy, green grass,
        Dissy, dissy, duss,
      Come all ye pretty fair maids
        And dance along with us.

      You shall have a duck, my dear,
        And you shall have a drake,
      And you shall have a nice young man
        To love you for your sake.

      If this young man should chance to die
        And leave the girl a widow,
      The birds shall sing, the bells shall ring,
        Clap all your hands together.
              —Yorkshire (Henderson's *Folk-lore, Northern
                      Counties*, p. 27).

V.   Dossy, dossy green grass,
        Dossy, dossy, doss,
      Come all ye pretty fair maids
        And dance upon the grass.

      I will give you pots and pans,
        I will give you brass,
      I will give you anything
        For a pretty lass.

I will give you gold and silver,
    I will give you pearl,
I will give you anything
    For a pretty girl.

Take one, take one, the fairest you can see.

You shall have a duck, my dear,
    You shall have a drake,
You shall have a young man
    Apprentice for your sake.

If this young man shall wealthy grow
    And give his wife a feather,
The bells shall ring and birds shall sing
    And we'll all clap hands together.
                    —Roxton, St. Neots (Miss Lumley).

VI. Walking up the green grass,
        A dust, a dust, a dust!
    We want a pretty maiden
        To walk along with us.

    We'll take this pretty maiden,
        We'll take her by the hand,
    She shall go to Derby,
        And Derby is the land!

    She shall have a duck, my dear,
        She shall have a drake,
    She shall have a nice young man
        A-fighting for her sake!

    Suppose this young man was to die,
        And leave the poor girl a widow;
    The bells would ring and we should sing,
        And all clap hands together!
            —Berrington (*Shropshire Folk-lore*, p. 511).

VII. Tripping up the green grass,
        Dusty, dusty, day,
    Come all ye pretty fair maids,
        Come and with me play.

You shall have a duck, my dear,
　And you shall have a swan,
And you shall have a nice young man
　A waiting for to come.

Suppose he were to die
　And leave his wife a widow,
Come all ye pretty fair maids,
　Come clap your hands together!

　　Will you come?
　　No!

Naughty man, he won't come out,
　He won't come out, he won't come out,
Naughty man, he won't come out,
　To help us in our dancing.

　　Will you come?
　　Yes!

Now we've got our bonny lad,
　Our bonny lad, our bonny lad,
Now we've got our bonny lad,
　To help us in our dancing.
　　　　　　—Middlesex (Miss Collyer).

VIII.　Stepping on the green grass
　　　Thus, and thus, and thus;
　　Please may we have a pretty lass
　　　To come and play with us?
　　We will give you pots and pans,
　　　We will give you brass,

　　　　No!

　　We will give you anything
　　　For a bonny lass.

　　　　No!

　　We will give you gold and silver,
　　　We will give you pearl,
　　We will give you anything
　　　For a pretty girl.

Yes!

You shall have a goose for dinner,
　　You shall have a darling,
You shall have a nice young man
　　To take you up the garden.

But suppose this young man was to die
　　And leave this girl a widow?
The bells would ring, the cats would sing,
　　So we'll all clap together.
　　　　　—Frodingham and Nottinghamshire (Miss
　　　　　　　M. Peacock).

IX.　Stepping up the green grass,
　　　　Thus, and thus, and thus;
　　Will you let one of your fair maids
　　　　Come and play with us?
　　We will give you pots and pans,
　　　　We will give you brass,
　　We will give you anything
　　　　For a pretty lass.

　　　　No!

We won't take your pots and pans,
　　We won't take your brass,
We won't take your anything
　　For a pretty lass.

Stepping up the green grass,
　　Thus, and thus, and thus;
Will you let one of your fair maids
　　Come and play with us?
We will give you gold and silver,
　　We will give you pearl,
We will give you anything
　　For a pretty girl.

　　　　Yes!

Come, my dearest [Mary],
　　Come and play with us,

You shall have a young man
  Born for your sake.
And the bells shall ring
  And the cats shall sing,
And we'll all clap hands together.
           —Addy's *Sheffield Glossary.*

X. Up and down the green grass,
    This, and that, and thus;
  Come all you fair maids
    And walk along with us.

Some will give you silver,
  Some will give you gold,
Some will give you anything
  For a pretty lass.

Don't you think [*boy's name*]
  Is a handsome young man?
Don't you think Miss [*child who has been choosing*]
  Is as handsome as he?

Then off with the glove
  And on with the ring;
You shall be married
  When you can agree.

Take hold of my little finger,
  Maycanameecan,
Pray tell me the name
  Of your young man.
           —Hurstmonceux, Sussex (Miss Chase).

XI. Here we come up the green grass,
    Green grass, green grass,
  Here we come up the green grass,
    Dusty, dusty, day.

Fair maid, pretty maid,
  Give your hand to me,
I'll show you a blackbird,
  A blackbird on the tree.

We'll all go roving,
    Roving side by side,
I'll take my fairest ——,
    I'll take her for my bride.

        Will you come?
No!

Naughty miss, she won't come out,
    Won't come out, won't come out,
Naughty miss, she won't come out,
    To help us with our dancing.

        Will you come?
Yes!

Now we've got our bonny lass,
    Bonny lass, bonny lass,
Now we've got our bonny lass,
    To help us with our dancing.
                —London (A. B. Gomme).

XII. Here we go up the green grass,
      The green grass, the green grass;
      Here we go up the green grass,
      So early in the morning.

          Fair maid, pretty maid,
      Give your hand to me,
          And you shall see a blackbird,
      A blackbird on the tree;
          All sorts of colours
      Lying by his side,
          Take me, dearest [——],
      For to be my bride—

              Will you come?
      No!

      Naughty old maid, she won't come out,
      She won't come out,
      To help us with our dancing—

              Will you come?
      Yes!

Now we've got the bonny lass,
Now we've got the bonny lass,
To help us with our dancing.
—Liphook, Hants (Miss Fowler).

XIII. Trip trap over the grass,
If you please, will you let one of your [eldest] daughters
come,
Come and dance with me?
I will give you pots and pans,
I will give you brass,
I will give you anything
For a pretty lass—
No!
I will give you gold and silver,
I will give you pearl,
I will give you anything
For a pretty girl.

Take one, take one, the fairest you may see.

The fairest one that I can see
Is pretty [Nancy], come to me;
You shall have a duck, my dear,
And you shall have a drake,
And you shall have a young man,
Apprentice for your sake.

If this young man should happen to die,
And leave this poor woman a widow,
The bells shall all ring and the birds shall all sing,
And we'll clap hands together.
—Halliwell's *Popular Nursery Rhymes*, cccxxxii.

XIV. Will you take gold and silver, or will you take brass,
Will you take anything for a pretty lass?

No! we'll not take gold and silver, no! we'll not take brass;
We'll not take anything for a pretty lass.

Will you take the keys of school, or will you take brass?
Will you take anything for a pretty lass?

Yes! we'll take the keys of school; yes! we will take brass;
We will take anything for a pretty lass.

Come, my dear [Mary Anne], and give me your right hand,

    And you shall have a duck, my dear,
      You shall have a drake;
    You shall have a nice young man
      To fiddle for your sake.

    The birds will sing, the bells will ring,
    And we'll all clap hands together.
    —Congleton Workhouse School (Miss A. E. Tremlow).

(*c*) The popular version of this game is played by the greater number of the children forming a line on one side with joined hands, and one child (sometimes two or more) facing them, advancing and retiring while singing the verses. When he asks the question, " Will you come ? " one girl on the opposite side answers " No!" and afterwards " Yes!" When this is said, she goes to the opposite side, and the two dance round together while singing the next verse. The game begins again by the two singing the verses, and thus getting a third child to join them, when the game proceeds for a fourth, and so on.

The Congleton and London versions are played by two lines of children of about equal numbers. In the Lincolnshire version the above description answers, except that when the last line is sung every one claps hands. In the Sussex version the child at the end of the line is taken over by the child who sings the verses, and they lock their little fingers together while singing the remainder.

Addy (*Sheffield Glossary*) says :—" Two children advance and retire on one side. When the opposite side says 'Yes!' the two take the first child in the row and dance round with her, singing the remaining verse. This is called ' the wedding.' "

The Lanarkshire version is quite a different one, and contains rather remarkable features. Mr. Black says that the game was played entirely by girls, never by boys, and generally in the months of May or June, about forty years ago. The children sang with rather mincing and refined voices, evidently making an effort in this direction. They walked, with their hands clasped behind their backs, up and down the road. Each child was crowned with rushes, and also had sashes or girdles of rushes.

Mr. Ballantyne says in his boyhood it was played by a row of boys on one side and another of girls opposite. The boys selected a girl when singing the third verse.

In the Roxton version, one child at the end of the line of children acts as "mother." One child advances as "suitor," and says the three first verses. The "mother" replies with the next line. The "suitor" chooses a girl and says the next verse, and then all the children sing the last verse. This is the same action as in Halliwell's version.

(*d*) The analysis of the game-rhymes is on pp. 164–67. This analysis presents us with a very good example of the changes caused by the game-rhymes being handed down by tradition among people who have forgotten the original meaning of the game. The first line in the Scotch version contains the word "dis," which is not known to the ordinary vocabulary. Another word, of similar import, is "dik-ma-day" in the Lanarkshire version. Two other words occur, namely, "thegan" in the Lanarkshire, and "maycanameecan" in the Sussex versions, which are also not to be found in ordinary vocabularies. The two last words appear only once, and cannot, therefore, be used for the purpose of tracing out an original form of the game-rhyme, because on the system of analysis adopted they may be arbitrary introductions and totally unconnected with the original rhymes. This, however, is not the case with the two first-mentioned words, and I am inclined to consider them as forming part of the earliest version. The word "dis" is carried through no less than ten out of the fourteen variants, the gradation in the forms being as follows :—

dis
dass
dish
diss[y]—duss
dossy
this—thus
—dust
—dust[y]

No.	Scotland (Chambers).	Lanarkshire.	Biggar.	Yorkshire.	Roxton.	Shropshire.
1.	A-dis, a-dis, a green grass.	A-dis, a-dis, a green grass.	A dish, a dish, a green grass.	Dissy, dissy, green grass.	Dossy, dossy, green grass.	—
2.	—	—	—	—	—	Walking up the green grass.
3.	A-dis, a-dis, a-das.	A-dis, a-dis, a-dass.	A dish, a dish, a dish.	Dissy, dissy, duss.	Dossy, dossy, doss.	Adust, adust, a dust.
4.	—	—	—	—	—	We want a pretty maiden.
5.	—	Come my pretty fair maid.	—	—	—	To walk along with us.
6.	Come all ye pretty maids,	And walk along with us.	Come all ye pretty maids.	Come all ye pretty maids.	Come all ye pretty maids.	—
7.	And dance along with us.	—	And dance along with us.	And dance along with us.	Dance upon the grass.	—
8.	For we are going a-roving.	—	For we are lads a roving.	—	—	—
9.	We'll take this maid by the hand.	—	We'll take this pretty fair maid by the hand.	—	—	We'll take her by the hand.
10.	—	—	—	—	—	—
11.	—	—	—	—	—	She shall go to Derby.
12.	You shall have a duke, my dear.	You shall have a dik-ma-day.	Ye sall get a duke.	You shall have a duck.	You shall have a duck (after No. 19)	She shall have a duck, my dear.
13.	—	—	—	—	I will give pots and pans.	—
14.	—	—	—	—	...... brass.	—
15.	—	—	—	—	...... gold and silver.	—
16.	—	—	—	—	...... pearl.	—
17.	—	—	—	—	...... anything.	—
18.	—	—	—	—	—	—
19.	—	—	—	—	For a pretty lass.	—
20.	You shall have a drake.	You shall have a dragon.	Ye sall get a drake.	You shall have a drake.	You shall have a drake.	She shall have a drake.
21.	—	—	—	—	—	—
22.	—	—	—	—	—	—

	And ye shall get a young prince.	You shall have a nice young man.	Ye sall get a bonny prince.	You shall have a nice young man.	You shall have a young man.	She shall have a nice young man.
23. [8.] 24.	—	—	—	—	—	—
25. 26.	A young prince for your sake.	—	For your ain sake.	To love you for your sake.	Apprentice for your sake.	A fighting for her sake.
27.	—	—	—	—	—	—
28.	If this young prince should die.	—	If they all should die.	If this young man should chance to die.	If this young man should wealthy grow.	Suppose this young man was to die.
29. 30.	—	—	—	—	—	—
31.	—	—	—	—	—	—
32. 33.	Ye shall get another.	—	Ye sall get anither.	And leave the girl a widow.	And give his wife a feather.	And leave the girl a widow.
34.	—	—	—	—	—	—
35.	Bells will ring and birds sing.	—	The bells will ring, birds will sing.	Birds shall sing and bells ring.	Bells shall ring and birds sing.	Bells ring and we shall sing.
36. 37.	We'll all clap hands together.	With princes for his thegan.	We'll clap hands together.	Clap all your hands together.	We'll all clap hands together.	And all clap hands together.
38.	—	—	—	—	—	—
39. 40. 41. 42. 43. 44. 45. 46.	— — — — — — — —	— — — — — — — —	— — — — — — — —	— — — — — — — —	— — — — — — — —	— — — — — — — —

No.	Lincolnshire, Frodingham.	Sussex, Hurstmonceux.	Middlesex.	London.	Hants, Liphook.	Halliwell.	Sheffield.
1.	—	—	—	—	—	—	—
2.	Stepping up the green grass.	Up and down the green grass.	Tripping up the green grass.	Here we come up the green grass.	Here we go up the green grass.	Trip, trap, over the grass.	Stepping up the green grass.
3.	Thus, and thus, and thus.	This, and that, and thus.	—	—	—	—	Thus, and thus, and thus.
4.	—	—	Dusty, dusty day.	On a dusty, dusty day.	So early in the morning.	—	—
5.	—	—	—	Fair maid, pretty maid.	Fair maid, pretty maid.	—	Will you let one of your fair maids.
6.	Please may we have a pretty lass.	Come all ye fair maids.	Come all ye pretty maids.	—	—	Please let one of your daughters come.	—
7.	To come and play with us.	And walk along with us.	Come and with us play.	—	—	Come and dance with me.	Come and play with us.
8.	—	—	—	[See below.]	—	—	—
9.	—	—	—	Give your hand to me.	Give your hand to me.	Take one, take the fairest you can see.	—
10.	—	—	—	—	—	Pretty [ ] come to me.	—
11.	—	—	—	—	—	—	—
12.	—	—	You shall have a duck.	—	—	You shall have a duck, my dear.	—
13.	We will give you pots and pans.	—	—	—	—	I will give you pots and pans.	We will give you pots and pans.
14.	...... brass.	—	—	—	—	...... brass.	...... brass.
15.	......gold and silver.	Some will give us silver ...... gold.	—	—	—	...... gold and silver.	......gold and silver.
16.	...... pearl.	—	—	—	—	...... pearl.	...... pearl.
17.	...... anything.	—	—	—	—	...... anything.	...... anything.
18.	—	—	—	I'll show you a blackbird.	You shall see a blackbird.	—	—
19.	For a pretty lass.	—	—	—	—	For a pretty girl.	For a pretty lass.
20.	You shall have a goose for dinner.	—	You shall have a swan.	—	—	You shall have a drake.	—
21.	—	Take hold of my finger. Maycanameecan.	—	—	—	—	—
22.	—	—	—	We'll all go roving.	All sorts of colours lying by his side.	—	—
23.	—	—	—	—	—	—	—
[8.]	—	—	—	—	—	—	—
24.	You shall have a nice young man.	—	You shall have a nice young man.	—	—	You shall have a young man.	You shall have a nice young man.

No.		Pray tell me the name of your young man.					
25.	—	—	—	I'll take [ ] my bride.	Take [ ] for my bride.	—	—
26.	—	—	A waiting for to come.	—	—	—	—
27.	To take you up the garden.	—	—	—	—	—	—
28.	—	—	—	—	—	Apprentice for your sake.	Born for your sake.
29.	Suppose this young man was to die.	—	Suppose he were to die.	—	—	—	—
30.	—	—	—	—	—	If this young man should happen to die.	—
31.	—	—	—	—	—	—	—
32.	—	—	—	—	—	—	—
33.	And leave the girl a widow.	—	And leave his wife a widow.	—	—	And leave the poor woman a widow.	—
34.	Bells would ring, cats would sing.	—	—	—	—	Bells shall ring, birds shall sing.	Bells shall ring, cats shall sing.
35.							
36.	—	—	Come all ye pretty fair maids.	—	—	—	—
37.	So we'll all clap hands together.	—	Come clap your hands together.	—	—	We'll all clap hands together.	We'll all clap hands together.
38.	—	Don't you think [ ] a nice young man?	—	—	—	—	—
39.		Don't you think [ ] as handsome as he?					
40.	—	—	—	—	—	—	—
41.	—	Then off with the glove, on with the ring,	—	—	—	—	—
42.	—	You shall be married when you can agree,	—	—	—	—	—
43.	—	—	Naughty miss, she won't come out. To help us with our dancing.	Naughty miss, she won't come out. To help us with our dancing.	Naughty old maid, she won't come out. To help us with our dancing.	—	—
44.	—	—	Now we've got our bonny lass, To help us with our dancing.	Now we've got our bonny lass, To help us with our dancing.	Now we'll get our bonny lass, To help us with our dancing.	—	—
45.	—	—	—	—	—	—	—
46.	—	—	—	—	—	—	—

What the meaning of this word is it may be impossible to ascertain, though probably Mr. Newell may be correct in his suggestion that it represents the old English word "adist," the opposite of "ayont," meaning "this way," "come hither" (*Games of American Children*, p. 51). But the point really is, that the version which contains the oldest word-forms would probably be the purest in other respects. The analysis of the whole game confirms this view, as the Scottish and Yorkshire versions are nearly parallel, while the discrepancies begin to creep in with the Shropshire version, reaching their last stage in the versions recorded by Halliwell and from Congleton. Following this line of argument, "dik-ma-day" becomes first "duke, my dear," and then "duck, my dear." Turning next to the import of the rhymes, apart from special words used, it is curious to note that "dis" is only converted into "dusty," and hence into "dusty day," in two versions out of the fourteen. The Lincolnshire version agrees with Halliwell's version in making some curious offers for a pretty lass, but these rhymes are probably an innovation. In the same way the incidents numbered 39–40, occurring in the Sussex version, and 43–46 occurring in the London and Hants versions, are borrowings from other games, and not original portions of this. The Congleton version is evidently incomplete.

(*e*) Henderson, in describing the curious rites accompanying the saining or blessing of a corpse in the Scottish Lowlands, states that empty dishes are arranged on the hearth as near as possible to the fire, and after certain ceremonies in connection therewith have been performed, the company join hands and dance round the dishes, singing this burden :—

> A dis, a dis, a dis,
> A green griss ;
> A dis, a dis, a dis.
> —*Folk-lore of Northern Counties*, p. 54.

This rhyme is, it will be seen, the same as the first two lines of the game, the word "griss" in the burial-rhyme becoming "grass" in the game-rhyme, "grisse" being the old form for "grass" or herb (Halliwell, *Provincial Glossary*, quotes a MS. authority for this). This identification of the game-rhyme would suggest that the game originally was a child's dramatic imitation of an old burial ceremony, and it remains to be seen whether the signification of the words would carry out this idea.

In the first place, the idea of death is a prominent incident in the game, appearing in seven out of the fourteen versions. In all these cases the death is followed by the clapping of hands and bell-ringing, and in five cases by the singing of birds. Clapping of hands occurs in two other cases, and bell-ringing in one other case, not accompanied by the death incident. Now it is singular that the burial-rite which has just been quoted is called Dish-a-loof; and a reference to the game of "Dish-a-loof" [under that title], will show that it derives its name from the clapping of hands. In the ceremony, as described by Henderson, although songs and games are part of the burial-ceremony, there is no specific mention of hand-clapping; but it is conceivable that the action at one time formed part of the ceremony, and hence the name "Dish-a-loof." This would not account for the promise of a duck, drake, &c., as in incidents Nos. 12 and 20; nor for the promise of a young prince or young man; but these incidents might very well be variants of some earlier forms which are not now discoverable, especially as love-games were played at funerals, and as the tendency, in the less complete forms of the game as they have come down to us, is in the direction of transposing the game into a complete love-game. The use of rushes in the Lanarkshire game might indicate the funeral garland (Aubrey's *Remaines*, pp. 109, 139). For clapping of hands to indicate bell-tolling or bell-ringing at times of death see Napier's *Folk-lore*, p. 66. Henderson (p. 63) says the "passing bell" was supposed in former times to serve two purposes: it called on all good Christians within hearing to pray for the departing spirit, and it scared away the evil spirits who were watching to seize it, or at least to scare and terrify it.

On the whole evidence from the rhymes, therefore, I should be disposed to class this game as originally belonging to burial, and not love, rites.

Green Gravel

—Madeley, Shropshire (Miss Burne).

—Earls Heaton (H. Hardy).

—Sporle, Norfolk (Miss Matthews).

—Redhill, Surrey (Miss G. Hope).

—Lancashire (Mrs. Harley).

—Derbyshire (Mrs. Harley).

I. Green gravel, green gravel, your grass is so green,
The fairest young damsel that ever was seen ;
We washed her, we dried her, we rolled her in silk,
And we wrote down her name with a glass pen and ink.
Dear Annie, dear Annie, your true love is dead,
And we send you a letter to turn round your head.
                                    —Belfast (W. H. Patterson).

II. Green gravel, green gravel, the grass is so green,
The fairest young lady that ever was seen ;
I'll wash you in milk,
And I'll clothe you with silk,
And I'll write down your name with a gold pen and ink.
O Sally, O Sally, your true love is dead,
He sent you a letter to turn round your head.
                —Berrington, Oswestry (*Shropshire Folk-lore*, p. 510).

III. Around the green gravel the grass is so green,
All the pretty fair maids are plain to be seen ;

Wash them in milk, and clothe them in silk,
Write their names down with a gold pen and ink.
All but Miss " Jenny," her sweetheart is dead ;
She's left off her wedding to turn back her head.

O mother, O mother, do you think it is true ?
O yes, child ! O yes, child !
Then what shall I do ?
We'll wash you in milk, and dress you in silk,
And write down your name with a gold pen and ink.
> —Derbyshire and Worcestershire (Mrs. Harley).

IV.   Green gravel, green gravel,
The grass is so green,
Such beautiful flowers
As never were seen.
O Annie [or any name], O Annie,
Your sweetheart is dead !
He has sent you a letter
To turn back your head.
> —Earls Heaton, Yorkshire (H. Hardy).

V.   Green gravel, green gravel,
The grass is so green,
The fairest young damsels
As ever were seen.
O ——, O ——, your true love is dead ;
He sent you a letter
To turn round your head.

Green gravel, green gravel,
The grass is so green,
The dismalest damsels
As ever were seen.
O ——, O ——, your true love's not dead ;
He sends you a letter
To turn back your head.
> —Lincoln, Winterton, and Wakefield
> (Miss Fowler and Miss Peacock).

VI.   Green gravel, green gravel, the grass is so green,
The fairest young lady [damsel] that ever was seen.

O ——, O ——, your true love is dead;
He's sent you a letter to turn round your head.

> —Redhill, Surrey (Miss G. Hope);
> Lancashire (Mrs. Harley).

VII. Green meadows, green meadows, your grass is so green,
The fairest young damsel that ever was seen;
O Mary, O Mary, your sweetheart is dead;
We've sent you a letter to turn back your head.

Or, Green gravel, green gravel, the grass is so green,
and following on as above.

> —Sporle, Norfolk (Miss Matthews).

VIII. Green grover, green grover, your grass is so green,
The prettiest young lady that ever was seen.
O ——, O ——, your true love is dead;
I send you this letter, so turn round your head.

> —Gainford, Durham (Miss Eddleston).

IX. Green gravels, green gravels,
The grass is so green,
And all the pretty maidens
Are not to be seen,
Except —— (said twice),
And she's not [?] to be seen,
So I send you a letter to turn round your head.

> —Hampshire (Miss E. Mendham).

X. Green gravels, green gravels, the grass is so green,
Fine pencils, fine pencils, as ever were seen.
O Mary! O Mary! your true love is dead,
And he's sent you a letter to turn round your head.

> —Wales (*Byegones*, 1890).

XI. Yellow gravel, yellow gravel,
The grass is so green,
The fairest young lady
That ever was seen.
O ——, O ——,
Your true love is dead;
I send you a letter to turn round your head.

> —Cowes, Isle of Wight (Miss E. Smith).

XII.   Green gravel, green gravel, the grass is so green,
         Said the fairest young damsel that ever I've seen.
         O mother, O mother, my true-love is dead,
         He sent me this letter to turn round my head.
         O mother, O mother, do you think this is true?
         O yes, love! O yes, love!
         And what shall I do?
         I'll wash you in butter-milk, I'll dress you in silk,
         I'll write down your name with my gold pen and ink.
                              —Isle of Man (A. W. Moore).

XIII.   Green gravel, green gravel, the grass is so green,
         The flowers are all faded and none to be seen.
         O [Dolly], O [Dolly], your sweetheart is dead,
         He's sent you a letter to turn back your head.

         Wallflowers, wallflowers, growing up so high,
         We are but little, and we shall have to die!
         Excepting [Dolly Turner], she's the youngest girl.
         O for shame, and fie for shame, and turn your back to
               home again.   —Madeley, Shropshire (Miss Burne).

XIV.   Green gravel, green gravel, the grass is so green,
         The fairest young lady that ever was seen.
         As I went up Miss Betsey's stairs to buy a frying-pan,
         There sat Miss Betsey a-kissing her young man.

         She pulled off her glove and showed me her ring,
         And the very next morning the bells did ring.
         Dear Betsey, dear Betsey, your true love is dead,
         He's sent you a letter to turn back your head.
                              —Summertown, Oxford (A. H. Franklin,
                                 Midland Garner, vol. ii. p. 32).

XV.   Round the green gravel the grass grows green,
         All pretty fair maids are fit to be seen ;
         Wash them in milk, and clothe them in silk,
         And write down their names with pen and black ink—
         Choose one, choose two, choose the fairest daughter.

         Now, my daughter, married to-day,
         Like father and mother they should be,

To love one another like sister and brother—
I pray you now to kiss one another.

Now my daughter Mary's gone,
With her pockets all lined with gold;
On my finger a gay gold ring—
Good-bye, Mary, good-bye.

Now this poor widow is left alone,
Nobody could marry a better one;
Choose one, choose two—
Choose the fairest daughter.　　—Sheffield (S. O. Addy).

XVI.　Round the green gravel the grass is so green,
And all the fine ladies that ever were seen;
Washed in milk and dressed in silk,
The last that stoops down shall be married.

[Johnnie Smith] is a nice young man,
And so is [Bessie Jones] as nice as he;
He came to the door with his hat in his hand,
Inquiring for [Miss Jones].

She is neither within, she is neither without,
She is up in the garret a-walking about.
Down she came, as white as milk,
With a rose in her bosom as soft as silk.

Silks and satins be ever so dear,
You shall have a kiss [gown ?], my dear,
So off with the glove and on with the ring—
To-morrow, to-morrow, the wedding begins.
　　　　—Forest of Dean, Gloucestershire (Miss Matthews).

XVII.　Around a green gravill
The grass is so green,
And all the fine ladies
Ashamed to be seen.
They wash 'em in milk
And dress 'em in silk—
We'll all cou' don' together.

My elbow, my elbow,
My pitcher and my can ;
Isn't ——
A nice young gell ?
Isn't ——
As nice as her—
They shall be married with a guinea-gold ring.

I peep'd through the window,
I peep'd through the door,
I seed pretty ——
A-dancin on the floor ;
I cuddled her an' fo'dled her,
I set her on my knee ;
I says pretty ——
Won't [ëe ?] you marry me.

A new-swept parlour,
An' a new-made bed,
A new cup and saucer
Again we get wed.
If it be a boy, he shall have a hat,
To follow with his mammy to her na', na', na' ;
If he be a gell, she shall have a ring,
To follow with her mammy to her ding, ding, ding.
—Wakefield (Miss Fowler).

(c) The more general way of playing this game is to form a
ring of children simply. The children walk round singing the
verse as in the Belfast version, and when the last line is sung, the
child whose name is mentioned turns round, facing the outside
of the ring and having her back to the centre. She continues to
hold hands with the others, and dances round with them in that
position. This is repeated until all the children have "turned"
their backs to the inside of the ring. Here the game ends in
many cases, but another verse is sung in the Lincoln, Winterton, and Wakefield versions from Miss Peacock, and this was
sung also in the London version. The second verse thus terminates the game, with the players one by one reversing their
position and facing the centre of ring as at first. In the

Forest of Dean and Wakefield versions the action of the game
is somewhat different.   A child stands in the centre of the ring
of children, without apparently taking much part in the game,
except to name the children in turn.   In the Wakefield version, however (Miss Fowler, No. xvii.), a little boy stands in the
middle of a circle of girls who sing the first verse.   At " We'll
all cou' don' together," all crouch down, as if in profound
respect, then rising slowly, sing the next verse.   After " My
pitcher and my can," each child mentions her own name.   At
" Isn't —— as nice as her ? " each mentions her sweetheart's
name, and the child thus chosen goes into the circle.   At the
end of the fourth verse they all clap hands, and the one that is
sweetheart to him in the middle kisses him.   The " crouching
down " is also done in the Forest of Dean version when singing the fourth line.   The last one to stoop has to name her
sweetheart.   When this is done, the children all dance round
and sing the other lines.

(*d*) The analysis of the game-rhymes is on pp. 178–181.
The most constant formulæ of this game-rhyme are shown
by this analysis to be Nos. 1, 6, 7, 13, 15, 18, 23, and the
variants, though important, are not sufficient to detract from
the significance of the normal version.   It is evidently a funeral
game.   The green gravel and the green grass indicate the
locality of the scene ; " green," as applied to gravel, may mean
freshly disturbed, just as green grave means a freshly made
grave.   The tenant of the new grave is the well-loved lady
of a disconsolate lover, and probably the incidents of washing and dressing the corpse, and putting an inscription on
the place where it is laid, are indicated by Nos. 13 and 15.
The dirge, or singing to the dead, is indicated by Nos. 18,
23, and 26, and the beauty of the first line is in complete
accord with the mournful music.   That No. 26 occurs in only
two variants, Derbyshire and the Isle of Man, is curious, as
the pathos of this appeal is very apparent in the movement
of the game.   The communion with the dead which is indicated by No. 23 is by no means considered impossible by the
peasantry.   In confirmation of this being a representation of
an old funeral ceremony, it may be pointed out that the action

No.	Belfast.	Shropshire.	Derbyshire.	Earls Heaton, Yorks.	Lincolnshire.	Redhill, Surrey.	Sporle, Norfolk.	Gainford, Durham.	Hants.
1.	Green gravel.	Green gravel.	—	Green gravel.	Green gravel.	Green gravel.	—	—	Green gravels.
2.	—	—	Around the green gravel.	—	—	—	—	—	—
3.	—	—	—	—	—	—	Green meadows.	Green grover.	—
4.	Your grass is so green.	The grass is so green.	The grass is so green.	The grass is so green.	The grass is so green.	The grass is so green.	Your grass is so green.	Your grass is so green.	The grass is so green.
5.									
6.									
7.	The fairest damsel ever seen.				Fairest damsel ever seen.	Fairest damsel ever seen.	Fairest damsel ever seen.		
8.	—	The fairest young lady ever seen.	—	—	—	—	—	Prettiest young lady ever seen.	—
9.	—	—	All pretty maids are plain to be seen.	—	—	—	—	—	All pretty maidens are *not* to be seen.
10.	—	—	—	Such beautiful flowers ever seen.	—	—	—	—	—
11.	—	—	—	—	—	—	—	—	—
12.	Washed her, dried her, rolled her in silk.	Wash you in milk, clothe in silk.	Wash them in milk, clothe in silk.	—	—	—	—	—	—
13.									
14.	—	—		—	—	—	—	—	—

No.									
15.	—	—	—	—	—	—	—	—	Wrote name in glass pen and ink.
16.	—	—	—	—	—	—	Write names in gold pen and ink.	Write name in gold pen and ink.	—
17.	—	True love is dead.	Sweetheart is dead.	True love is dead.	True love is dead.	Sweetheart is dead.	Her sweetheart is dead.	True love is dead.	Your true love is dead.
18.	Except —— she's not to be seen.	—	—	—	—	—	—	—	—
19.	—	—	—	—	—	—	—	—	—
20.	—	—	—	—	—	—	—	—	—
21.	—	—	—	—	—	—	—	—	—
22.	I send letter to turn round your head.	I send letter to turn your head.	We sent letter to turn your head.	He sent letter to turn your head.	He sent letter to turn your head.	He sent letter to turn your head.	—	He sent letter to turn your head.	He sent letter to turn your head.
23.	—	—	—	—	—	—	—	—	—
24.	—	—	—	—	—	—	She's left off her wedding to turn back her head.	—	—
25.	—	—	—	—	—	—	Mother, is it true; What shall I do? [Then repeat Nos. 14 & 16.]	—	—
26.									
27.	—	—	—	—	True love not dead, he sends letter to turn your head.	—	—	—	—
28.	—	—	—	—	—	—	—	—	—
29.	—	—	—	—	—	—	—	—	—
30.	—	—	—	—	—	—	—	—	—
31.	—	—	—	—	—	—	—	—	—

No.	Wales.	Isle of Wight.	Isle of Man.	Madeley.	Oxfordshire.	Sheffield.	Forest of Dean.	Wakefield.
1.	Green gravel.	—	Green gravel.	Green gravel.	Green gravel.	Round the green gravel.	Round the green gravel.	Around the green gravill.
2.	—	—	—	—	—	—	—	—
3.	—	—	—	—	—	—	—	—
4.	—	—	—	—	—	—	—	—
5.	The grass is so green.	Yellow gravel.	The grass is so green.	The grass is so green.	The grass is so green.	The grass grows green.	The grass is so green.	The grass is so green.
6.		The grass is so green.	Fairest damsel ever I've seen.	—	—	—	—	—
7.	—	—	—	—	Fairest young lady ever seen.	—	All fine ladies ever were seen.	—
8.	—	Fairest young lady ever seen.	—	—	—	All pretty fair maids are fit to be seen.	—	—
9.	—	—	—	Flowers all faded, none to be seen.	—	—	—	—
10.	—	—	—	—	—	—	—	—
11.	—	—	—	—	—	—	—	All fine ladies ashamed to be seen.
12.	Fine pencil as ever was seen.	—	—	—	—	—	—	—
13.	—	—	[Wash you in butter-milk, dress in silk.] (After No. 26.)	—	—	Wash them in milk, clothe in silk.	Washed in milk, dressed in silk.	Wash 'em in milk, dress in silk.
14.	—	—		—	—			
15.	—	—	Write name with my gold pen and ink.] (After No. 26.)	—	—	—	—	—
16.	—	—		—	—	—	—	—
17.	—	—	—	—	—	Write names with pen and black ink.	—	—

No.	1	2	3	4	5	6	7
18.	True love is dead.	True love is dead.	True love is dead.	Sweetheart is dead.	[True love is dead.] (After No. 25.)		
19. 20.					Betsy kissing her young man.		
21.					Choose the fairest daughter.	Choose the fairest daughter.	
22.						Last to stoop down shall be married.	We'll all cow down together.
23.	He's sent letter to turn head.	I send you letter to turn round your head.	He sent this letter to turn my head.	I've sent letter to turn your head.	[He sent letter to turn back your head.] (After No. 25.)	He came to inquire, down she came, so off with glove and on with ring, to-morrow the wedding begins.	
24. 25.				[Wallflowers verses follow.]	She showed her ring and bells did ring.	Married to-day, so kiss one another.	They shall be married with gold ring.
26.			Mother, is it true? What shall I do?				
27. 28.							
29.					Poor widow left alone, and choose the fairest daughter.	Poor widow left alone, and choose the fairest daughter.	
30.							[Dancing, cuddling, asking to marry.] [Furnishing.] [If a boy, he's to have a hat; if a girl, a ring.]
31. 32.							

of turning backwards during the singing of the dirge is also
represented in the curious funeral ceremony called "Dish-a-
loof," which is described in Henderson's *Folk-lore of the Northern
Counties*, p. 53.   Henderson's words are : "All the attendants,
going out of the room, return into it backwards, repeating this
rhyme of 'saining.'"   The additional ceremony of marriage in
four of the games is clearly an interpolation, which may have
arisen from the custom of playing love and marriage games
at funerals and during the watching with the corpse, or may
be a mere transition to the more pleasant task of love-making
as the basis of a game.   The Derbyshire incident (No. 24) may
indicate indeed that the funeral is that of a young bride, and
in that case the tendency to make the game wholly a marriage
game is accounted for.   The decay which has set in is apparent by the evident attempt to alter from "green gravel" to
"green grover" and "yellow gravel" (Nos. 4 and 5), and to
introduce pen and black ink (No. 17).   The addition of the
incongruous elements from other games (Nos. 27–31) is a frequent occurrence in modern games, and is the natural result of
decadence in the original form of the game.   Altogether this
game-rhyme affords a very good example of the condition of
traditional games among the present generation of children.

(*e*) Other versions, actually or practically identical with the
Redhill (Surrey) version, have been sent by Miss Blair (South
Shields); Mr. H. S. May, Ogbourne and Manton (Wilts);
Mrs. Haddon (Cambridge); Mrs. Harley (Lancashire); and
Miss Burne, Platt, near Wrotham (Kent).   There are also
similar printed versions in *Folk-lore Journal*, vi. 214 (Dorsetshire); *Folk-lore Record*, v. 84 (Hersham, Surrey).   Northall
prints a version in his *Folk Rhymes*, 362–3, identical with
No. 17.   The tune of the Platt version sent by Miss Burne,
and the Ogbourne and Manton (H. S. May), are almost identical,
except the termination.   This seems to be the most general
tune for the game.   The Lancashire tune is the same as the
London version.

Miss Burne says of the Madeley version : "I never knew
'Green Gravel' and 'Wallflowers' played together as in this
way elsewhere (I had not got this variant when I wrote *Shrop-*

shire Folk-lore), except at Much Wenlock, where they reverse the two verses, and only sing *one line* (the last) of 'Green Gravel.' But I feel sure they must have been *meant* to go together (see my note in *Shropshire Folk-lore*, p. 510), and I can explain them, I think. The ring of girls are dancing on the green grass plot in the middle of an old-fashioned sixteenth-century walled garden : each gets the news of her lover's death, and 'turns her face to the wall,' the old token of hopeless sorrow. Then they apostrophise the wallflowers in the border surrounding the grass plot against the old high wall ; and here another variant explains the lament (second line)—

Wallflowers, wallflowers, growing up so high,
We shall all be maidens [and so], we shall all die ;
Except the youngest (who will meet with another lover), whether as an instance of the proverbial luck of the 'youngest born,' or as a piece of juvenile giddiness and inconstancy, I cannot say ; but considering the value set on true love and hopeless constancy in the ballad-lore, and the special garland which distinguished the funerals of bereaved but constant maidens, and the solemnity of betrothal in old days, the latter seems probable, especially considering the 'for shame.'"

The incidents of *washing* a corpse in milk and *dressing* it in silk occur in "Burd Ellen," Jamieson's *Ballads*, p. 125.

"Tak up, tak up my bonny young son,
Gar *wash* him wi' the *milk ;*
Tak up, tak up my fair lady,
Gar row her in the *silk.*"

Green Grow the Leaves (1)

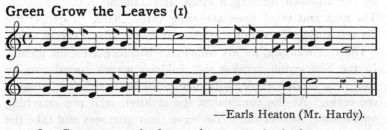

—Earls Heaton (Mr. Hardy).

I. Green grow the leaves (or grows the ivy)
round the old oak tree,
Green grow the leaves round the old oak tree,

Green grow the leaves round the old oak tree,
    As we go marching on.

Bless my life I hardly knew you,
Bless my life I hardly knew you,
Bless my life I hardly knew you,
    As we go marching on.

—Lincolnshire and Nottinghamshire
(Miss Peacock).

II.   Green grow the leaves on the old oak tree,
    I love the boys and the boys love me,
        As we go marching on.

—Sharleston (Miss Fowler).

III.   I love the boys and the boys love me,
    I love the boys and the boys love me,
    I love the boys and the boys love me,
        As we go marching home.

Glory, glory, hallelujah !
Glory, glory, hallelujah !
Glory, glory, hallelujah !
    As we go marching home.

The old whiskey bottle lies empty on the shelf,
The old whiskey bottle lies empty on the shelf,
The old whiskey bottle lies empty on the shelf,
    As we go marching home.

—Earls Heaton, Yorkshire (Herbert).

(*b*) In Lincolnshire and Nottinghamshire the game is played by the children forming a circle and dancing round, singing. The first and third lines are sung three times. Partners are chosen during the singing of the last line. Miss Peacock adds, " The rest wanting, as my informant had forgotten the game." In the Sharleston version the children march round two by two, in a double circle, with one child in the centre, singing the verse. At the conclusion, the children who are marching on the inner side of the circle leave their partners and take the place of one in front of them, while the centre child endeavours to get one of the vacant places, the child turned out taking the place of the one in the centre, when the game begins again.

In the Earls Heaton version there is the circle of children, with one child in the centre, who chooses a partner after the lines have been sung.

(c) From this it would seem that while the Lincolnshire and Nottinghamshire words appear to be the most complete, the action has been preserved best at Sharleston. The acting of this version is the same as that of " The Jolly Miller." The third variant is evidently an imitation of the song, " John Brown."

Green Grow the Leaves (2)

—Northants (R. S. Baker).

Green grow the leaves on the hawthorn tree,
Green grow the leaves on the hawthorn tree,
We jangle and we wrangle and we never can agree,
But the tenor of our song goes merrily, merrily, merrily,
The tenor of our song goes merrily.
—R. S. Baker (*Northants Notes and Queries*, ii. 161).

(b) One couple is chosen to lead, and they go off, whither they will, followed by a long train of youths and maidens, all singing the refrain. Sometimes the leaders part company, and branch off to the right or left; the others have to do the same, and not until the leaders meet can they join again. They march arm in arm.

(c) Mr. R. S. Baker, who records this, says a Wellingborough lady sent him the tune and words, and told him the game was

more like a country dance than anything else, being a sort of
dancing " Follow My Leader."

Gully

A sink, or, failing that, a particular stone in the pavement
was the " Gully."   Some boy chosen by lot, or one who volun-
teered in order to start the game, laid his top on the ground at
some distance from the " Gully."   The first player then spun
his top, pegging at the recumbent top, so as to draw it towards
the " Gully."   If he missed the top, he stooped down and took
up his own top by pushing his hand against it in such a
manner that the space between his first and second finger
caught against the peg and forced the top into the palm of his
hand.   He then had " a go " at the recumbent top (I forget
what this was called), and sent his own top against it so as to
push it towards the " Gully."   If he missed, he tried again and
again, until his own top could spin no longer.   If he did not
hit the top with his own while it was spinning, his top had to
be laid down and the other one taken up, and its owner took
his turn at pegging.   When a spinning-top showed signs of
exhaustion, and the taking it up might kill it, and it was not
very far from the down-lying top, its owner would gently push
it with his finger, so as to make it touch the other top, and so
avoid putting it into the other's place.   This was called " kissing," and was not allowed by some players.   When one player
succeeded in sending the top into the " Gully," he took it up
and fixed it by its peg into a post, mortar of a wall, or the best
place where it could be tolerably steady.   Holding it by one
hand, he drove the peg of his own top as far as he could into
the crown of the victim top.   This was called " taking a grudge."
He then held either his own or the victim top and knocked the
other against the wall, the object being to split the victim.   He
was allowed three " grudges."   If the top did not give way,
the other players tried in turn.   If the top did not split, it was
returned to its owner, but any boy who succeeded in splitting
it through the middle, so that the peg fell out, took possession
of the peg.   I have seen a top split at the side in such a way
as to be quite useless as a top, though no peg was gained.   I

remember, too, a schoolfellow of mine drawing from his pocket some seven or eight pegs, the trophied memorials of as many tops.—London (J. P. Emslie).

See "Hoatie," "Hoges," "Peg-top."

Hairry my Bossie

This is a game of chance. The players are two, and may be boys or girls, or a boy and a girl. The stakes may be pins, buttons, marbles, or anything for which children gamble. One player puts a number, one, two, three or more, of the articles to be gambled for into the hollow of the closed hand, and says, "Hairry my bossie;" the other answers, "Knock 'im down," upon which he puts his closed hands down with a blow on his knees, and continues to strike them upwards and downwards on the knee, so as to give the opponent in play an idea of the number of objects concealed by the sound given forth. He then says, "How many blows?" and gets the reply, "As many's goes." A guess is then made. If the guess is correct the guesser gets the objects. If the guess is incorrect the guesser has to make up the difference between the number guessed and the real number. The players play alternately. This game was played for the most part at Christmas.—Keith (Rev. W. Gregor).

(b) Hairry = "rob," Bossie = "a wooden bowl," commonly used for making the leaven in baking oat-cakes, and for making "brose."

This is a very general game amongst schoolboys.

Half-Hammer

The game of "Hop-step-and-jump," Norfolk. This game is played in the west of Sussex, but not in the east. It is played thus by two or more boys. Each boy in his turn stands first on one leg and makes a hop, then strides or steps, and lastly, putting both feet together, jumps. The boy who covers the most ground is the victor.—Halliwell's *Dictionary*.

Han'-and-Hail

A game common in Dumfries, thus described by Jamieson. Two goals called hails, or dules, are fixed on at about a distance of four hundred yards. The two parties then place themselves in the middle between the goals or dules, and one of the players, taking a soft elastic ball, about the size of a man's fist, tosses it into the air, and, as it falls, strikes it with his palm towards his antagonists. The object of the game is for either party to drive the ball beyond the goal which lies before them, while their opponents do all in their power to prevent this. As soon as the ball is gowf't, that is, struck away, the opposite party endeavour to intercept it in its fall. This is called keppan' the ba'. If they succeed in this attempt, the player who does so is entitled to throw the ball with all his might towards his antagonists. If he kep it in the first bound which it makes off the ground, called a stot, he is allowed to haunch, that is, to throw the ball by bringing his hand with a sweep past his thigh, to which he gives a stroke as his hand passes, and discharging the ball at the moment when the stroke is given. If the ball be caught in the second bounce, the catcher may hoch the ball, that is, throw it through below one of his houghs. If none of the party catch the ball, it must be gowf't in the manner before described. As soon as either of the parties succeed in driving the ball, or, as it is called, hailin' the dules, the game then begins by one of the party which was successful throwing the ball towards the opposing goal and the other party striving to drive it back.

Hand in and Hand out

A game played by a company of young people who are drawn up in a circle, when one of them, pitched upon by lot, walks round the band, and, if a boy, hits a girl, or, if a girl, she strikes a boy whom she chooses, on which the party striking and the party struck run in pursuit of each other till the latter is caught, whose lot it then becomes to perform the same part. A game so called was forbidden by statute of Edward IV.—Halliwell's *Dictionary*.

See " Drop Handkerchief."

Handy-Croopen

A game in which one of the players turns his face to the wall, his hand resting upon his back.   He must continue in position until he guesses who struck his hand, when the striker takes his place.—Orkney and Shetland (Jamieson's *Dictionary*.

See "Hot Cockles."

Handy Dandy

I.   Handy dandy,
    Sugary candy—
    Top or bottom ?

    Handy spandy,
    Jack a dandy—
    Which good hand will you have ?
    —Halliwell's *Dictionary : Nursery Rhymes*, p. 216.

II.   Handy dandy riddledy ro—
    Which will you have, high or low ?
    —Halliwell's *Nursery Rhymes*, p. 216.

III.   Handy pandy,
    Sugary candy,
    Which will you have—
    Top or bottom ?   —London (A. B. Gomme).

IV.   Handy pandy, Jack a dandy,
    Which hand will you have ?
    —Burne's *Shropshire Folk-lore*, p. 530.

(*b*) The hands are closed, some small article is put in one of them behind the back of the player.   The closed fists are then turned rapidly round one another while the rhyme is being said, and they are then placed one on top of the other.   A guess is then made by any one of the players as to which hand the object is in.   If correct, the guesser obtains the object; if incorrect, the player who performs "Handy dandy" keeps it.

(*c*) This game is mentioned in *Piers Plowman*, p. 69 of Wright's edition.   Douce quotes an ancient MS. which curiously mentions the game as "men play with little children at 'handye-dandye,' which hand will you have" (ii. 167).   Johnson says : "' Handy dandy,' a play in which children change hands and places : ' See how yon justice rails upon yon simple thief !   Hark, in thine ear : change places, and, handy dandy, which is the justice, which is the thief?" (*King Lear*, iv. 6). Malone says, "'Handy dandy' is, I believe, a play among children, in which something is shaken between two hands, and then a guess is made in which hand it is retained." See Florio's *Italian Dictionary*, 1598: "Bazzicchiare, to shake between the hands; to play 'Handy dandy.'" Pope, in his *Memoirs of Cornelius Scriblerus*, in forbidding certain sports to his son Martin till he is better informed of their antiquity, says: "Neither cross and pile, nor ducks and drakes, are quite so ancient as 'Handy dandy,' though Macrobius and St. Augustine take notice of the first, and Minutius Foelix describes the latter; but 'Handy dandy' is mentioned by Aristotle, Plato, and Aristophanes." Browne, in *Britannia's Pastorals* (i. 5), also alludes to the game.

See "Neiveie-nick-nack."

Hap the Beds

A singular game, gone through by hopping on one foot, and with that foot sliding a little flat stone out of an oblong bed, rudely drawn on a smooth piece of ground. This bed is divided into eight parts, the two of which at the farther end of it are called the Kail-pots. If the player then stands at one end, and pitches the smooth stone into all the divisions one after the other, following the same on a foot (at every throw), and bringing it out of the figure, this player wins not only the game, but is considered a first-rate daub at it; failing, however, to go through all the parts so, without missing either a throw or a hop, yet keeping before the other gamblers (for many play at one bed), still wins the curious rustic game.— Mactaggart's *Gallovidian Encyclopædia*.

A game called "The Beds," mentioned by a writer in *Blackwood's Magazine*, August 1821, p. 36, as played in Edinburgh when he was a boy by girls only, is described as a game where a pitcher is kicked into chalked divisions of the pavement, the performer being on one leg and hopping.

See "Hop-scotch."

Hard Buttons

Several boys place one button each close together on a line.

The game consists in hitting a particular button out of this line with the nicker without touching the others. This is generally played in London streets, and is mentioned in the *Strand Magazine*, ii. 515.

See "Banger," "Buttons."

Hare and Hounds

A boys' game. One boy is chosen as the Hare. He carries with him a bag filled with strips of paper. The rest of the boys are the Hounds. The Hare has a certain time (say fifteen minutes) allowed him for a start, and he goes across country, scattering some paper on his way in order to indicate his track. He may employ any manœuvre in order to deceive his pursuers, but must keep up the continuity of his paper track-signs. The Hounds follow him and try to catch him before he gets home, which is a place agreed upon beforehand. —London (G. L. Gomme).

In Cornwall the leader, when at fault, says—

> Uppa, uppa, holye! If you don't speak
> My dogs shan't folly.
> > —Courtney (*Folk-lore Journal*, v. 73).

Other versions of this holloa are—

> Whoop, whoop, and hollow!
> Good dogs won't follow
> Without the hare cries, Peewit.
> > —Halliwell's *Nursery Rhymes*, p. 66.

> Sound your holler,
> Or my little dog shan't foller.
> > —Northall's *English Folk Rhymes*, p. 357.

This game is played in Wales under the name of "Hunt the Fox." The Fox has a certain time given him for a start, the other players then go after him.—Beddgelert (Mrs. Williams).

Harie Hutcheon

A game among children, in which they hop round in a ring, sitting on their hams.—Jamieson.

See "Curcuddie," "Cutch-a-cutchoo," "Hirtschin Hairy."

Hark the Robbers

—Tong, Shropshire (Miss R. Harley).

I.   Hark the robbers coming through,
      Coming through,
    Hark the robbers coming through,
      My fair lady.

    What have the robbers done to you,
      Done to you,
    What have the robbers done to you,
      My fair lady ?

    You have stole my watch and chain,
      Watch and chain,
    You have stole my watch and chain,
      My fair lady.

    Half-a-crown you must pay,
      You must pay,
    Half-a-crown you must pay,
      My fair lady.

    Half-a-crown we cannot pay,
      Cannot pay,
    Half-a-crown we cannot pay,
      My fair lady.

    Off to prison you must go,
      You must go,
    Off to prison you must go,
      My fair lady.   —Deptford, Kent (Miss Chase).

II.   Here are the robbers coming through,
      Coming through, coming through,
    Here are the robbers coming through,
      My fair lady.

What will the robbers do to you,
  Do to you, do to you,
What will the robbers do to you,
    My fair lady ?

Steal your watch and break your chain,
  Break your chain, break your chain,
Steal your watch and break your chain,
    My fair lady.

Then they must go to jail,
  Go to jail, go to jail,
Then they must go to jail,
      My fair lady.   —Belfast (W. H. Patterson).

III.   Hark the robbers
    Coming through, coming through,
      My fair lady.

They have stolen my watch and chain,
  Watch and chain, watch and chain.

Off to prison they shall go,
  They shall go, they shall go,
    My fair lady.
—Wolstanton, Stoke-on-Trent (Miss A. A. Keary).

IV.   Hark the robbers coming through,
    Coming through, coming through,
  Hark the robbers coming through,
      My fair lady.

What's the robbers done to you,
  Done to you, done to you,
What's the robbers done to you,
    My fair lady ?

They have stole my watch and chain,
  Watch and chain, watch and chain,
They have stole my watch and chain,
    My fair lady.

What's the price will set you free,
  Set you free, set you free,
What's the price will set you free,
    My fair lady?

Half-a-guinea will set me free,
  Will set me free, will set me free,
Half-a-guinea will set me free,
    My fair lady.

Half-a-guinea you shall not have,
  Shall not have, shall not have,
Half-a-guinea you shall not have,
    My fair lady.

Let's join hands, it is too late,
  'Tis too late, 'tis too late,
Let's join hands, it is too late,
    My fair lady.

        —Tong, Shropshire (Miss R. Harley).

V. Hark at the robbers going through,
    Through, through, through; through, through, through;
  Hark at the robbers going through,
    My fair lady.

  What have the robbers done to you,
    You, you, you; you, you, you?
  What have the robbers done to you,
    My fair lady?

  Stole my gold watch and chain,
    Chain, chain, chain; chain, chain, chain;
  Stole my gold watch and chain,
    My fair lady.

  How many pounds will set us free,
    Free, free, free; free, free, free?
  How many pounds will set us free,
    My fair lady?

A hundred pounds will set you free,
  Free, free, free ; free, free, free ;
A hundred pounds will set you free,
    My fair lady.

We have not a hundred pounds,
  Pounds, pounds, pounds ; pounds, pounds, pounds ;
We have not a hundred pounds,
    My fair lady.

Then to prison you must go,
  Go, go, go ; go, go, go ;
Then to prison you must go,
    My fair lady.

To prison we will not go,
  Go, go, go ; go, go, go ;
To prison we will not go,
    My fair lady.

          —Shipley, Horsham (*Notes and Queries*,
            8th Series, i. 210, Miss Busk).

VI. See the robbers coming through,
    Coming through, coming through,
  See the robbers coming through,
    A nice young lady.

Here's a prisoner we have got,
  We have got, we have got,
Here's a prisoner we have got,
    A nice young lady.

How many pounds to set her free,
  Set her free, set her free,
How many pounds to set her free,
    A nice young lady ?

A hundred pounds to set her free,
  Set her free, set her free,
A hundred pounds to set her free,
    A nice young lady.

A hundred pounds we cannot give,
    We cannot give, we cannot give,
‚A hundred pounds we cannot give,
    A nice young lady.

Then to prison she must go,
    She must go, she must go,
Then to prison she must go,
    A nice young lady.

If she goes we'll go too,
    We'll go too, we'll go too,
If she goes we'll go too,
    A nice young lady.

Round the meadows we will go,
 . We will go, we will go,
Round the meadows we will go,
    A nice young lady.
                    —Settle, Yorks. (Rev. W. S. Sykes).

VII.   O what has this poor prisoner done,
       Poor prisoner done, poor prisoner done?
  O what has this poor prisoner done,
       So early in the morning?

  She stole my watch and lost my key,
       Lost my key, lost my key,
  She stole my watch and lost my key,
       So early in the morning.

  How many pounds to set her free,
       Set her free, set her free?
  How many pounds to set her free,
       So early in the morning?

  Five hundred pounds to set her free,
       Set her free, set her free,
  Five hundred pounds to set her free,
       So early in the morning.

Five hundred pounds we have not got,
Have not got, have not got,
Five hundred pounds we have not got,
So early in the morning.

So off to prison she must go,
She must go, she must go,
So off to prison she must go,
So early in the morning.

If she go then I'll go too,
I'll go too, I'll go too,
If she go then I'll go too,
So early in the morning.

So round the meadows we must go,
We must go, we must go,
So round the meadows we must go,
So early in the morning.

—Sporle, Norfolk (Miss Matthews).

(*b*) In the Deptford version two girls join hands, holding them up as an arch for the other players to tramp through. The first two verses are sung first by one and then by the other of the two girls. At the finish of these the girl then going through the arch is stopped, and the third, fourth, and fifth verses are sung by the two girls alternately. Then finally both girls sing the last verse, and the child is sent as prisoner behind one or other of the two girls. The verses are then begun again, and repeated afresh for each of the troop marching through the arch until all of them are placed behind one or other of the two girls. The two sides thus formed then proceed to tug against each other, and the strongest side wins the game.

The Belfast version is practically the same, except that the verses are not sung as a dialogue, but by all the players together, and the prisoner, when caught, has the choice of sides, by being asked, "Which will you have, a golden apple or golden pear?" and according to the answer given is sent behind one of the leaders. The Norfolk and Shropshire games are different. Miss Matthews thus describes the Norfolk game: "Two girls take hold of hands, and another, the prisoner, stands between them. The rest form themselves into a line opposite, and advance and retreat while singing the first verse, the gaolers singing the next verse, and so on alternately. [At the end of the last verse but one] the children break the line, form themselves into a ring, and dance round the prisoner, singing the final verse." Miss Harley describes the Shropshire version as follows: "The first six verses are sung by the alternate parties, who advance and retire, tramping their feet, at first, to imitate the robbers. The last verse is sung altogether going round in a ring." In the Shipley version, Miss Busk says: "The children form themselves into two lines, while two or three, representing the robbers, swagger along between them. When the robbers sing the last verse they should have attained the end of the lines [of children], as during the parley they were safe; having pronounced the defiance they run away. The children in the lines rush after them, and should catch them and put them in prison."

(c) The analysis of this game is easy. The Deptford, Belfast, and Wolstanton versions are clearly enough dramatic representations of the capture of a robber, and probably the game dates from the period of the prevalence of highway robbery. The Wolstanton version shows us that the game is breaking up from its earlier form, while the Norfolk and Shropshire versions show a fresh development into the mere game for children, apart from its original significance. The action of the game confirms this view. The Norfolk action seems to be the most nearly perfect in its dramatic significance, and the Shropshire action comes next. The action of the other games seems to have been grafted on to the superior form of "Oranges and Lemons." It is probable that this fact has preserved the words more completely than in the other cases, where the force of the robber action would become less and less as actual experience of robbers and robbery died out. Altogether, this game supplies a very good example of the change produced in games by changes in the actual life which gave rise to them. It is singular that the verses of this game also enter into the composition of "London Bridge is broken down." It is probable, therefore, that it may be an altered form of the game of "London Bridge." The refrain, "My fair lady," occurs in both games.

See "London Bridge."

Hats in Holes

A boys' game. The players range their hats in a row against the wall, and each boy in turn pitches a ball from a line at some twenty-five feet distance into one of the hats. The boy into whose hat it falls has to seize it and throw it at one or other of the others, who all scamper off when the ball is "packed in." If he fails to hit he is out, and takes his cap up. The boy whose cap is left at the last has to "cork" the others, that is, to throw the ball at their bent backs, each in turn stooping down to take his punishment.—Somerset (Elworthy's *Dialect*).

See "Balls and Bonnets."

Hattie

A game with preens, pins, on the crown of a hat. Two or more may play. Each lays on a pin, then with the hand they strike the side of the hat time about, and whoever makes the pins by a stroke cross each other, lifts those so crossed.—Mactaggart's *Gallovidian Encyclopædia*.

Hawkey

A game played by several boys on each side with sticks called "hawkey bats," and a ball. A line is drawn across the middle of the ground from one side to the other; one party stands on one side of the line and the opposite party on the other, and neither must overstep this boundary, but are allowed to reach over as far as their bats will permit to strike the ball. The object is to strike the ball to the farther end to touch the fence of the opposing party's side, when the party so striking the ball scores one, and, supposing nine to be the game, the party obtaining that number first of course wins the game.— West Sussex (Holloway's *Dict. of Provincialisms*).

See "Bandy," "Doddart," "Hockey."

Headicks and Pinticks

This game was played only at Christmas. The number of

players was two. The stakes were pins. One player laid in the hollow of the hand, or on one of the forefingers, a pin, and then placed the other forefinger over it so as to conceal it. He then held up his hand to his opponent and said, "Headicks or pinticks?" His opponent made a guess by pointing with his finger and saying "Headicks," or "Pinticks." If the guess was correct he gained the pin, but if it was incorrect he forfeited one. The players played alternately.—Keith (Rev. W. Gregor).

Another version seems to be "Headim and Corsim." Pins are hid with fingers in the palms of the hands; the same number is laid alongside them, and either "Headim" or "Corsim" called out by those who do so. When the fingers are lifted, if the heads of the pins hid and those beside them be lying one way when the crier cried "Headim," then that player wins; but if "Corsim," the one who hid the pins wins. This is the king of all the games at the preens.—Mactaggart's *Gallovidian Encyclopædia.*

The editors of Jamieson's *Dictionary* say that the name should be "Headum and Corsum."

Heads and Tails

That plan for deciding matters by the "birl o' a bawbee." The one side cries "Heads" (when the piece is whirling in the air) and the other "Tails," so whichever is uppermost when the piece alights that gains or settles the matter, heads standing for the King's head and tails for the figure who represents Britannia.—Mactaggart's *Gallovidian Encyclopædia.* This is a general form of determining sides or beginning a game all over the country.

Hecklebirnie

A play among children in Aberdeenshire. Thirty or forty children in two rows, joining opposite hands, strike smartly with their hands thus joined on the head or shoulders of their companion as he runs the gauntlet through them. This is called "passing through the mires of Hecklebirnie."—Jamieson.

The editors of Jamieson append a lengthy note connecting

the name of this game with the northern belief that the wicked were condemned to suffer eternal punishment in Hecla, the volcanic mountain in Iceland.

See "Namers and Guessers."

Hen and Chicken

> Chickery, chickery, cranny crow,
> I went to the well to wash my toe,
> When I got back a chicken was dead.

This verse is said by the Hen to her Chickens, after which they all go with the Hen to search for the dead Chicken. On their way they meet the Fox. The following dialogue between the Fox and Hen ensues, the Hen beginning:—

> What are you doing ?
> Picking up sticks.
> What for ?
> To make a fire.
> What's the fire for ?
> To boil some water.
> What's the water for ?
> To boil some chickens in.
> Where do you get them from ?
> Out of your flock.
> That I'm sure you won't.
> —Derbyshire (*Folk-lore Journal*, i. 386).

The game is played in the usual manner of "Fox and Goose" games. One is chosen to be the Hen, and one to be the Fox. The rest are the Chickens. The Chickens take hold of each other's waists, the first one holding the Hen's waist. At the end of the dialogue the Fox tries to get hold of one of the chickens. If he succeeds in catching them, they all with the Fox try to dodge the Hen, who makes an effort to regain them.

It is known at Winterton under the name of "Pins and Needles." The players stand in a row, one behind another, with one of the party as their Leader. Another player, called "Outsider," pretends to scratch the ground. The Leader asks the questions, and the Outsider replies—

What are you scratching for ?
Pins and needles.
What do you want your pins and needles for ?
To mend my poke.
What do you want your poke for ?
To put some sand in.
What do you want your sand for ?
To sharpen knives with.
What do you want your knives for ?
To cut all the little chickens' heads off with.

Here the Outsider tries to dodge past the Leader to catch one of the children at the further end of the row, the Leader meanwhile attempting to bar her progress. When at last she succeeds, the child caught takes her place, and the game is recommenced.—Winterton (Miss M. Peacock).

See " Fox and Goose," " Gled-wylie."

Here comes a Lusty Wooer

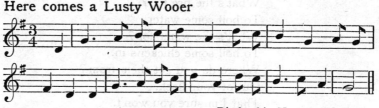

—Rimbault's *Nursery Rhymes*.

Here comes a lusty wooer,
My a dildin, my a daldin ;
Here comes a lusty wooer,
Lily bright and shine a'.

Pray who do you woo ?
My a dildin, my a daldin ;
Pray who do you woo ?
Lily bright and shine a'.

For your fairest daughter,
My a dildin, my a daldin ;
For your fairest daughter,
Lily bright and shine a'.

> Then there she is for you,
> My a dildin, my a daldin ;
> Then there she is for you,
> Lily bright and shine a'.
>> —Ritson (*Gammer Gurton's Garland*, 1783).

Northall says this game is played after the manner of the "Three Dukes" (*Folk Rhymes*, p. 383). Halliwell (*Nursery Rhymes*, p. 98) has a version, and Rimbault (*Nursery Rhymes*) gives both words and tune. It is also contained in *The Merrie Heart* (p. 47). See "Jolly Hooper," "Jolly Rover."

Here comes One Virgin

> Here comes one Virgin on her knee,
> On her knee, on her knee,
> Here comes one Virgin on her knee,
> Pray what will you give her ?
>
> When did you come ?
>
> I came by night and I came by day,
> I came to steal poor Edie away.
>
> She is too old, she is too young,
> She hasn't learnt her virgin tongue.
>
> Let her be old or let her be young,
> For her beauty she must come.
>
> In her pocket a thousand pounds,
> On her finger a gay gold ring.
>
> Good-bye, good-bye, my dear.
>> —Hurstmonceux, Sussex (Miss Chase).

One child stands by herself, and the rest of the players range themselves in line. The child sings the first verse and the line replies, the four succeeding verses being alternately sung. After the last line the girl tries to pull one whom she has chosen from the line toward her. If not successful, she must try again. If she is, they both stand in the middle, and commence singing the words again with—

> Here come *two* virgins on their knees, &c.

Probably a degraded version of "Three Lords from Spain."

Here I sit on a Cold Green Bank

Here I sit on a cold green bank
On a cold and frosty morning.

We'll send a young man [*or* woman] to take you away,
To take you away,
We'll send a young man to take you away,
On a cold and frosty morning.

Pray tell me what his name shall be ? [*or*]
Pray, whom will you send to take me away ?

We'll send Mr. —— to take you away.

The children form a ring around one of the party, who sits in the middle, and says the two first lines. Then those in the circle dance round her, singing the next four lines. This is repeated three times, with the refrain, "On a cold," &c., after which the dancing and singing cease, and the child is asked, "Sugar, sweet, or vinegar, sour ? " Her answer is always taken in a contrary sense, and sung, as before, three times, whilst the children circle round. The one in the middle then rises to her feet. The boy (or girl) named advances and kisses her, they change places, and the game begins again.—Cornwall (*Folk-lore Journal*, v. 56–57).

Here stands a Young Man

I. Here stands a young man who wants a sweetheart,
With all his merry maids round him ;

He may choose from east, he may choose from west,
He may choose the prettiest girl that he loves best.

Now this young couple is married together,
We propose they kiss each other.
—Glapthorn (*Northants Notes and Queries*,
i. 214, A. Palmer).

II. Here stands a young lady [lass] who wants a sweetheart,
Wants a sweetheart, wants a sweetheart,
And don't know where to find one, find one, find one.
Choose the prettiest that you loves best.

Now you're married I wish you joy,
First a girl and then a boy,
Seven years after son and daughter,
Pray you come to kiss together.
—Longcot, Berkshire (Miss I. Barclay).

(*b*) A ring is formed by the players joining hands, one child
standing in the centre. The ring dance round singing the
first four lines. At the fourth line the child in the centre
chooses one from the ring, who goes into the centre with her.
The marriage formula or chorus is then sung, the two kiss,
and the one who was first in the centre joins the ring, the
second one choosing another in her turn. Played by both
boys and girls.
See "Sally Water," "Silly Old Man."

Here we go around, around

Our shoes are made of leather,
Our stockings are made of silk,
Our pinafores are made of calico,
As white as any milk.

Here we go around, around, around,
And we shall touch the ground.
—Barnes and London Streets (A. B. Gomme).

A ring is formed by the children joining hands. They walk
round singing the first four lines. They then dance round
quickly and sit down suddenly, or touch the ground with their
clothes.
A version of this game from Liphook, Hants, almost identical in words, has been sent by Miss Fowler, and another
from Crockham Hill, Kent, by Miss Chase.

Here's a Soldier

Here's a soldier left his lone [*qy.* alone],
Wants a wife and can't get none.

Merrily go round and choose your own,
Choose a good one or else choose none ;
Choose the worst or choose the best,
Or choose the very one you like best.

What's your will, my dilcy dulcy officer ?
What's your will, my dilcy dulcy dee ?

My will is to marry, my dilcy dulcy officer ;
My will is to marry, my dilcy dulcy dee.

Come marry one of us, my dilcy dulcy officer ;
Come marry one of us, my dilcy dulcy dee.

You're all too old and ugly, my dilcy dulcy officer ;
You're all too old and ugly, my dilcy dulcy dee.

Thrice too good for you, sir, my dilcy dulcy officer ;
Thrice too good for you, sir, my dilcy dulcy dee.

This couple got married, we wish them good joy,
Every year a girl and a boy,
And if that does not do, a hundred and two,
We hope the couple will kiss together.

　　　　　　　　—Annaverna, co. Louth (Miss R. Stephen).

(*b*) One child stands in the middle, the others dance round singing. The one in the middle chooses another before the four last lines are sung. Then the rest dance round singing these lines, and kiss each other.

(*c*) It is evident that these words comprise two distinct games, which have become mixed in some inexplicable fashion. The first six lines and the last four are one game, a ring form, with the marriage formula and blessing. The other portion of the game is a dialogue game, evidently having had two lines of players, questions being asked and answers given. It is, in fact, a part of the "Three Dukes" game. The first part is a kiss-in-the-ring game, a version of "Here stands a Young Man," "Silly Old Man," and "Sally Water."

Hewley Puley Take this! What's this?
Hewley Puley.
Where's my share?
About the kite's neck.
Where's the kite?
Flown to the wood.
Where's the wood?
The fire has burned it.
Where's the fire?
The water's quenched it.
Where's the water?
The ox has drunk it.
Where's the ox?
The butcher has killed it.
Where's the butcher?
The rope has hanged him.
Where's the rope?
The rat has gnawed it.
Where's the rat?
The cat has killed it.
Where's the cat?

Behind the door, cracking pebble-stones and marrow-bones for yours and my supper, and the one who speaks first shall have a box on the ear. —Halliwell's *Nursery Rhymes*, p. 222.

The children are seated, and the questions are put by one of the party who holds a twisted handkerchief or something of the sort in the hand. The handkerchief was called "hewley puley," and the questions are asked by the child who holds it. If one answers wrongly, a box on the ear with the handkerchief was the consequence; but if they all replied correctly, the one who broke silence first had that punishment.

For similar rhymes see "Dump," "Mother, may I go out?"

Hey Wullie Wine

I. Hey Wully wine, and How Wully wine,
I hope for hame ye'll no incline;
Ye'll better light, and stay a' night,
And I'll gie thee a lady fine.

Wha will ye gie, if I wi' ye bide,
To be my bonny blooming bride,
And lie down lovely by my side?

I'll gie thee Kate o' Dinglebell,
A bonny body like yersell.

I'll stick her up in the pear-tree
Sweet and meek, and sae is she:
I lo'ed her ance, but she's no for me,
Yet I thank ye for your courtesy.

I'll gie thee Rozie o' the Cleugh,
I'm sure she'll please thee weel eneugh.

Up wi' her on the bane dyke,
She'll be rotten or I'll be ripe:
She's made for some ither, and no me,
Yet I thank ye for your courtesy.

Then I'll gie ye Nell o' sweet Sprinkell,
Owre Galloway she bears the bell.

I'll set her up in my bed-head,
And feed her wi' milk and bread;
She's for nae ither, but jist for me,
Sae I thank ye for your courtesy.
—Mactaggart's *Gallovidian Encyclopædia.*

II. I maun ride hame, I maun gang hame,
       And bide nae langer here;
     The road is lang, the mirk soon on,
       And howlets mak' me fear.

     Light doon and bide wi' us a' night,
       We'll choose ye a bonnie lass;
     Ye'll get your wull and pick o' them a',
       And the time it soon wull pass.

     Which ane will ye choose,
       If I with you will bide?

     The fairest and rarest
       In a' the kintra side.

A girl's name was then mentioned. If the lad was pleased with the choice made, he replied—

> I'll set her up on a bonnie pear-tree,
> It's tall and straight, and sae is she;
> I'd keep wauken a' night her love to be.

If he was not pleased, he replied in one or other of the next three verses—

> I'll set her up ayont the dike,
> She'll be rotten ere I be ripe,
> The corbies her auld banes wull pike.

> I'll set her up on a high crab-tree,
> It's sour and dour, and so is she;
> She may gang to the mools unkissed by me.

> Though she be good and fair to see,
> She's for another, and no for me;
> But I thank you for your courtesie.

When a girl took the place of the lad, she replied in one or other of the three following, according as she was angry or pleased—

> I'll put him in a riddle
> And riddle him o'er the sea,
> And sell to Johnny Groat's
> For a Scotch bawbee.

> I'll set him up on my lum-head [chimney],
> And blaw him up wi' pouther and lead;
> He'll never be kissed though he be dead.

> I'll set him up at my table head,
> Feed him wi' sweet milk and bread,
> If he likes gang hame on his fine steed.
>
> —Biggar (Wm. Ballantyne).

(*b*) In Biggar, all the players were seated round the hearth-stone, lads on one side, lassies the other; one lad rising up said the first verse, then one acting as "maister" said the next verse. The young man then said the next two lines, to which the other replied in the two following, and naming at the close any girl he thought would be acceptable. If the lad was pleased he sang the next verse. If he was not pleased with the girl offered him he replied in either of the three following verses. The first of the three was generally said if the girl was thought to be too old ; if bad-tempered, the second. If the lad found no fault, but wished to politely refuse, he sang the last verse. The girl then was asked in her turn, and the same formula gone through, she saying either of the three last verses given. Forfeits were demanded for every refusal, and were cried at the end of the game.

(c) Mr. Ballantyne writes : "This game was a great favourite in my father's house. This was a forfeit game, forfeits being called 'wadds.'" Chambers, *Popular Rhymes*, p. 124, gives a version of this game. It is practically the same as Mr. Ballantyne's version, with only a few verbal differences. Mactaggart says, "The chief drift of this singular game seemed to be to discover the sweethearts of one another," and such discoveries are thought valuable, but not so much as they were anciently. In any case, it appears to me that the game is an early one, or, at all events, a reflection of early custom.

Hickety, Bickety

> Hickety, bickety, pease-scone,
> Where shall this poor Scotchman gang ?
> Will he gang east, or will he gang west,
> Or will he gang to the craw's nest ?
>
> —Chambers (*Popular Rhymes*, p. 122).

One boy stands with his eyes bandaged and his hands against a wall, with his head resting on them. Another stands beside him repeating the rhyme, whilst the others come one by one and lay their hands upon his back, or jump upon it. When he has sent them all to different places he turns round and calls, "Hickety, bickety!" till they have all rushed back to the place, the last in returning being obliged to take his place, when the game goes on as before.

Chambers adds, "The 'craw's nest' is close beside the eye-bandaged boy, and is therefore an envied position." Newell, *Games*, p. 165, refers to this game.

See "Hot Cockles."

Hickety-hackety

The game of Hop-scotch, played with a piece of tile, which has to be kicked by the player with the foot on which he hops over lines into various squares marked on the ground.—Somersetshire (Elworthy's *Dialect*).

See "Hop-scotch."

Hick, Step, and Jump

The game of " Hop, step, and jump."—Somerset (Holloway's *Dict. of Provincialisms*).

See " Half-Hammer."

Hide and Seek (1)

A writer in *Blackwood's Magazine*, August 1821, p. 36, mentions this as a summer game. It was called " Ho, spy ! " the words which are called out by those boys who have hidden. He says the watchword of " Hide and seek " was " hidee," and gives as the rhyme used when playing—

> Keep in, keep in, wherever you be,
> The greedy gled's seeking ye.

This rhyme is also given by Chambers (*Popular Rhymes*, p. 122). Halliwell gives the rhyme as—

> Hitty titty indoors,
> Hitty titty out,
> You touch Hitty titty,
> And Hitty titty will bite you.
> —*Nursery Rhymes*, p. 213.

At Ashford-in-the-Water the words used were—

> One a bin, two a bin, three a bin, four,
> Five a bin, six a bin, seven, gie o'er ;
> A bunch of pins, come prick my shins,
> A loaf brown bread, come knock me down.
> I'm coming !   —*Reliquary*, viii. 57.

The words are said by the one who has to find the person hidden.

In Scotland the game is called " Hospy," and is played by boys only, and it can be played only in a village or hamlet in which there is the means of hiding. A Spy is chosen, and a spot, called Parley, is fixed upon at which the Spy stands till all the other players are hid, and to which he can run when pursued. When the players are hid, the cry, "Hospy," *i.e.*, "Ho! spy!" is raised by them. The Spy then sets out to find them. The moment he detects one he turns and runs with all his might to the Parley, pursued by the one he has discovered. If he is overtaken, he must carry on his back the pursuer to the Parley. The same thing is gone through till all the players are discovered.—Keith (Rev. W. Gregor).

Jamieson says, "'Hy Spy,' a game resembling 'Hide and Seek,' but played in a different manner. The station, which in England is called Home, is here the Den, and those who keep it are the Seekers, and are called the Ins. Those who hide themselves, instead of crying 'Hoop,' as in England, cry 'Hy spy;' and they are denominated the Outs. The business of the Ins is, after the signal is given, to lay hold of the Outs before they can reach the den. The captive then becomes one of the Ins; for the honour of the game consists in the privilege of hiding oneself." Jamieson adds, "Hy is still used in calling after a person, to excite attention, or when it is wished to warn him to get out of the way." Strutt describes it as "Harry-Racket," or "Hide and Seek" (*Sports*, p. 381).

At Cork two sides are chosen for Spy; one side hides while the other side hunts. When the hunters see one of the hidden players, they call out, "I spy ——," and the child's name. The player called must run after the Spy and try to catch him before he reaches his Den; if he succeeds, the one caught must go to the opposite side of players, then next time the spies hide, and those who have been hiding, spy (Miss Keane). A more general form of the game is for one child to hide, and to make a noise in a disguised voice to give notice of his where-abouts, or to call out "Whoop!" or "Coo!" Until this noise or call is made, the searchers may not seek him. If when spied or discovered the hider cannot reach home before being caught, he again has to hide (A. B. Gomme).

(*b*) In the parish church of Bawdrip is a monument to Edward Lovell, his wife Eleanor (*née* Bradford), and their two daughters Maria and Eleanor. The inscription touching the latter is :—

"Eleanora . . . obiit Jun. 14, 1681. Hanc, subito et imma-turo (ipsos pene inter hymenæos) fato correptam, mœstissimus luxit maritus, et in gratam piamq. parentum sororis et dilec-tissimæ conjugis memoriam, monumentum hoc erigi voluit." Tradition connects this sudden death—"ipsos pene inter hymenæos"—with the story of the bride playing at "Hide and Seek." It is curious that, in Haynes Bayly's song, the bride-groom's name should be Lovell. There is no mention on the monument of the name of the bereaved husband. The father, Edward Lovell, was fourteen years rector of Bawdrip and fellow of Jesus College, Cambridge, and died in 1675, and so could not have been present at the wedding, as represented in the song. He came from Batcombe, near Castle-Cary; at which latter place the Lovells were seated in very early days.— *Notes and Queries*, 4th Ser., ix. 477.

Cope (*Hampshire Glossary*) calls the game "I spy I." Lowsley (*Berkshire Glossary*) says, "In playing this game, the seeker has to call out 'I spy!' to the one he finds before he may start for home." It is called "Hy Spy" in Patterson's *Antrim and Down Glossary;* Evans' *Leicestershire Glossary*, "Hide and Wink;" Barnes' *Dorset Glossary*, "Hidy Buck."

In Pegge's *Alphabet of Kenticisms* the game is given as "Hide and Fox." *Cf.* "Hide Fox, and all after," *i.e.*, let the fox hide and the others go to seek him; Hamlet, iv. 2, 32. In Stead's *Holderness Glossary*, "Hed-o." In the North Riding it is "Lam-pie-sote-it," also called "Felto" in Robin-son's *Whitby Glossary*. He also mentions that the hidden child cries "How-ly" to the finder. Apparently the same as the south country "Whoop," a signal to the finder to begin the search. Addy (*Sheffield Glossary*) says this game is called "Felt and Laite." Holland (*Cheshire Glossary*) speaks of it as "I Spy."

See "Davie Drap."

Hide and Seek (2)

—London.

I.   Beans and butter,
     Come home to supper,
     'Tis all ready done.
                        —Hampshire (Miss Mendham).

II. Little pigs come to supper,
     Hot boiled beans and ready butter.
                        —Northall's *Folk Rhymes*, p. 409.

III. Hot beans and butter!
     Please to come to supper!
                        —Much Wenlock (*Shropshire Folk-
                        lore*, p. 525).

IV. Hot boiled beans, and very good butter,
     Ladies and gentlemen, come to supper.
                        —London (A. B. Gomme).

V.   Vesey vasey vum,
     Buck aboo has come!
     Find it if you can and take it home,
     Vesey vasey vum.
                        —Newlyn West, near Penzance
                        (*Folk-lore Journal*, v. 49).

One child hides an article, while those who are to search
for it go in another room (or out of the way somewhere). When
it is hidden, they are called to find it by one of the above
rhymes being sung or said. The searchers are enabled more
readily to find the hidden article by being told "hot," "very
hot," "scorching," "burning," or "cold," "very cold," and
"freezing," when near to or far from the hidden article.
Sometimes several may agree to hide the article, and only one
to be the finder. In the Penzance game one child is blindfolded,
other children hide something, then shout the words. Search
is then made for the hidden object: when found, the finder in
his turn is blindfolded. There appears to be some mistake in
the description of this game.

Hinch-Pinch

The name of an old Christmas game mentioned in *Declaration of Popish Impostures*, 1603.

Hinmost o' Three

A game played on village greens.—Dickinson's *Cumberland Glossary, Supplement*.

Hirtschin Hairy

The players (boy or girl) cower down on their haunches, "sit doon curriehunkers," and hop round and round the floor like a frog, clapping the hands first in front and then behind, and crying out, "Hirtschin Hairy." It is sometimes called "Hairy Hirtschin." In Lothian the players try to knock each other over by hustling against one another.—Rev. W. Gregor.

Same game as "Harie Hutcheon."

See "Curcuddie," "Cutch-a-cutchoo," "Hop-frog."

Hiry-hag

A boys' game, in which several, joining hands, endeavour to catch another, who, when caught, is beaten with caps, the captors crying out—

Hiry-hiry-hag,
Put him in a bag, &c.

—Ross and Stead's *Holderness Glossary*.

Hiss and Clap

All the boys are requested to leave the room, when the girls take their seats, leaving a vacant place on the right side of each girl for the gentleman of her choice. Each boy in turn is then summoned by another who acts as doorkeeper, and asked to guess which lady he imagines has chosen him for her partner. Should he guess rightly he is allowed to take his seat by the lady who has chosen him, while the other girls loudly clap hands. Should he guess wrongly he is hissed, and sent out of the room by the doorkeeper.—Cork, Ireland (Miss Keane).

At Long Eaton in Nottinghamshire Miss Youngman records a similar game to this, with a rhyme that is probably taken from a popular song or ballad. The successful candidate for the girl's choice claims a kiss, but if unsuccessful he is beaten out of the room with knotted handkerchiefs.

Hitch Jamie; Hitch Jamie, Stride and Loup

The boyish play of "Hop, Step, and Jump."—Atkinson's *Cleveland Glossary*.

Brockett (*North Country Words*) calls this "Hitch."

See "Half-Hammer," "Hick, Step, and Jump."

Hitchapagy

An undescribed Suffolk game.—Halliwell's *Dictionary*.

Hitchy Cock Ho

An undescribed Suffolk game.—Moor's *Suffolk Words*.

Hity Tity

The Somerset name for "See-Saw."

Hoatie, Hots

When a number of boys agree to have a game at the Pearie or peg-top, a circle is drawn on the ground, within which all the tops must strike and spin. If any of them bounce out of the circle without spinning, it is called a Hoatie. The punishment to which the Hoatie is subjected consists in being placed in the ring, while all the boys whose tops ran fairly have the privilege of striking—or, as it is called, "deggin"—it till it is either split or struck out of the circle. If either of these take place, the boy to whom the Hoatie belonged has the privilege of playing again.—Upper Lanarkshire (Jamieson).

See "Gully," "Hoges."

Hob-in-the-Hall

An old game mentioned by Wycherley (*Plain Dealer*, 1677).

Hockerty Cokerty

The same game as "Cockerty-hooie."

Hockey

This game is played with a solid indiarubber ball from two to two and a half inches in diameter. The players each have a bent or hooked stick or "hockey." They take opposite sides. The object of the game is for each side to drive the ball through

their opponents' goal. The goals are each marked by two poles
standing about eight to ten feet apart, and boundaries are
marked at the sides. The ball is placed in the middle of the
ground. It is started by two players who stand opposite each
other, the ball lying between their two sticks. They first touch
the ground with their hockey-sticks, then they touch or strike
their opponents' stick. This is repeated three times. At the
third stroke they both try to hit the ball away. The ball may
only be played by a hockey-stick, and a goal is gained when
the ball is played between the posts by the opposing party.—
Barnes (A. B. Gomme).

(b) In Ross and Stead's *Holderness Glossary* this game is
described under the name of "Shinnup." Robinson (*Mid
Yorkshire Glossary*) gives it under "Shinnops," a youth's game
with a ball and stick, heavy at the striking end, the player
manœuvring to get as many strokes as possible and to drive
the ball distances. "Shinnoping" is also used for the game in
operation. "Jowling," or "Jowls," is given in Robinson's
Whitby Glossary, as a game played much the same as
"Hockey." "Baddin" is the name given to it in Holland's
Cheshire Glossary. Another name is "Doddart" (Brockett,
North Country Words).

(c) An old custom in vogue in bygone days was Rotherham
Fair, or what was called "Whipping Toms," which took place in
the Newarkes every Shrove Tuesday. So soon as the pancake
bell rang men and boys assembled with sticks having a knob
or hook at the end. A wooden ball was thrown down, and two
parties engaged in striving which could get the ball by striking
it with their sticks to one end of the Newarke first—those who
did so were the victors. This game was called "Shinney," or
"Hockey." About one o'clock the Whipping Toms appeared on
the scene of action. These were three men clad in blue smock
frocks, with very long waggon whips, who were accompanied by
three men with small bells. They commenced driving the men
and boys out of the Newarkes. It was very dangerous sometimes; they would lash the whip in such a manner round the
legs of those they were pursuing as to throw them down, which
produced laughter and shouting. Some would stop, and turn

to the whipper and say, "Let's have a pennyworth," and he
would guard and parry off the lashes with his shinney stick.
When the whipper was successful in lashing him he demanded
his penny, and continued lashing until he paid. This was
continued until five o'clock, then the game terminated. This
was suppressed, I believe, in 1847. At that period it was a
prevalent idea that it could not be abolished, as it was connected with an "old charter." It is believed in the town that
this custom was to commemorate the driving out of the Danes
from the Newarkes at the time they besieged Leicester.—
Leicester (Robert Hazlewood).

See "Bandy," "Camp," "Football," "Hood," "Hurling."

Hoges

"The hoges," a boy's game played with "peeries" (peg-
tops). The victor is entitled to give a certain number of
blows with the spike of his peerie to the wood part of his
opponent's.—Patterson's *Antrim and Down Glossary*.

See "Gully," "Hoatie."

Ho-go

A game played with marbles. The first player holds up a
number in his closed hand and says, "Ho-go;" the second
says, "Handfull;" the first then says, "How many?" The
other guesses. If he should guess correctly he is entitled to
take them all; but otherwise he must give the difference between the number he guessed and the number actually held
up to make.—Lowsley's *Berkshire Words*. It is also called
"How many eggs in a basket?"—London (J. P. Emslie).

See "Hairry my Bossie."

Hoilakes

The name of a game of marbles which are cast into a hole in
the ground.—Easther's *Almondbury and Huddersfield Glossary*.

Holy Bang

A game with marbles, which consists in placing a marble in
a hole and making it act as a target for the rest. The marble

which can hit it three times in succession, and finally be shot
into the hole, is the winning ball, and its owner gets all the
other marbles which have missed before he played.—London
(*Strand Magazine*, ii. 519).

See "Bridgeboard," "Capie Hole," "Hundreds."

Honey Pots

Staccato

—London (J. P. Emslie).

A number of children stoop down in a row, clasping their
hands under their legs.   One child stands in front of them, and
acts as owner or seller; another acts as purchaser (fig. 1).
The purchaser inquires—

 Have you any honey pots for sale?

 Yes, plenty; will you walk round and taste them?

The purchaser goes round, pretending to taste each one in
turn, inquiring the price and weight; finds fault with several,
one being too sweet and the other not fresh enough, and so on.
When one honey pot is discovered to the purchaser's taste, she

Fig 1   Fig. 2

is lifted by the purchaser and owner, or by two children who
act as weights or scales, and then swung by her arms backwards and forwards to estimate her weight and price (fig. 2).
As long as the child can keep her hands clasped, so long is the
swinging kept up; and as many times as they count, so many

is the number of pounds she weighs. The seller sometimes said, when each one was bought—

>Take her and bake her,
>And into pies make her,
>And bring her back
>When she is done.

They were not brought back, and the "owner" had to catch and bring back each one. When sold, the honey pot is taken to the other side, or "home" of the purchaser. The game goes on till all the honey pots are sold. — London (A. B. Gomme).

In Sporle, a girl clasps her hands under her legs to form a seat, and two others swing her by the arms, saying—

>Honey pot, honey pot, over the river;
>When the old cat dies you shall have the liver.

>—Miss Matthews.

In a version sent by Miss Chase, and told her by a London maidservant, the children sit as in "Hunt the Slipper." One steps in a corner out of earshot; the rest are named "Gooseberry Tart," "Cherry Tart," &c., by another, who recalls the child in the corner with—

>Fool, fool, come to school,
>Pick me out a [cherry tart, as the case may be].

If he chooses the wrong one he is told—

>Go back and learn your A, B, C.

If rightly—

>Take him and bake him,
>And give me a piece
>When he's done.

The child is then led off in a squatting position. Later the one who named them pretends tasting, and says, "Very nice," or "You must be baked longer," when another squatting walk and wait takes place.

A version sent by Mr. J. P. Emslie is similar to the other London versions—

>"Buy my fine honey to-day.
>Which shall I buy?
>Taste 'em and try.

The child would then go round, pretending to taste, saying,

' Don't like that one,' till one was approved. That one was then swung round to the tune given, the words being—

An apple for the king and a pear for the queen,
And a good jump over the bowling green.

At the last bar they swung the child higher and higher, and at the last note they swung it as high as they could. I believe the last note in the music should be G, but it was raised to give effect."

In Scotland the game is called " Hinnie Pigs," and is played as follows. The boys sit down in rows, hands locked beneath their hams. Round comes one of them, the honey merchant, who feels those who are sweet and sour, by lifting them by the arm-pits and giving them three shakes. If they stand these without the hands unlocking below they are then sweet and saleable, fit for being office-bearers of other ploys.—Mactaggart's *Gallovidian Encyclopædia*.

In Ross and Stead's *Holderness Glossary* this is described as a girls' game, in which two carry a third as a pot of honey to market. It is mentioned by Addy (*Sheffield Glossary*) and by Holland (*Cheshire Glossary*). Mr. Holland adds, "If the hands give way before twenty is reached it is counted a bad honey pot; if not, it is a good one."

In Dublin the seller sings out—

Honey pots, honey pots, all in a row,
Twenty-five shillings wherever you go—
Who'll buy my honey pots ?   —Mrs. Lincoln.

The game is mentioned by a writer in *Blackwood's Magazine*, August 1821, p. 36, as being played in Edinburgh when he was a boy.

Hood

A game played at Haxey, in the Isle of Axholme, on the 6th of January. The Hood is a piece of sacking, rolled tightly up and well corded, and which weighs about six pounds. This is taken into an open field on the north side of the church, to be contended for by the youths assembled for that purpose. When the Hood is about to be thrown up, the Plough-bullocks or Boggins, as they are called, dressed in scarlet jackets, are

placed amongst the crowd at certain distances. Their persons
are sacred, and if amidst the general row the Hood falls into
the hands of one of them, the sport begins again. The object
of the person who seizes the Hood is to carry off the prize to
some public-house in the town, where he is rewarded with
such liquor as he chooses to call for. This pastime is said to
have been instituted by the Mowbrays, and that the person
who furnished the Hood did so as a tenure by which he held
some land under the lord. How far this tradition may be
founded on fact I do not know, but no person now acknow-
ledges to hold any land by that tenure.—Stonehouse's *Isle of
Axholme*, p. 291.

W. J. Woolhouse (*Notes and Queries*, 2nd series, v. 95)
says when the Hood is thrown up by the Chief of the Boggons
or by the officials, it becomes the object of the villagers to get
the Hood to their own village, the other eleven men, called
Boggons, being stationed at the corners and sides of the field,
to prevent, if possible, its being thrown out of the field; and
should it chance to fall into any of their hands, it is " bog-
goned," and forthwith returned to the chief, who again throws
it up, as at the commencement of the game. The next day is
occupied by the Boggons going round the villages singing as
waits, and they are regaled with hot furmenty; from some
they get coppers given them, and from others a small measure
of wheat. The day after that they assume the character of
Plough-bullocks, and at a certain part of Westwood-side they
" smoke the Fool "—that is, straw is brought by those who
like, and piled in a heap, a rope being tied or slung over the
branches of the tree next to the pile of straw; the other end of
the rope is fastened round the waist of the Fool, and he is
drawn up and fire is put to the straw, the Fool being swung
to and fro through the smoke until he is well-nigh choked,
after which he goes round and collects whatever the spectators
choose to give him. The sport is then at an end till the next
year. The land left by Lady Mowbray was forty acres, which
are known by the name of " Hoodlands," and the Boggons'
dresses and the Hood are made from its proceeds.

In the contiguous parish of Epworth a similar game is played under the same name, but with some variations. The Hood is not here carried away from the field, but to certain goals, against which it is struck three times and then declared free. This is called "wyking" the Hood, which is afterwards thrown up again for a fresh game.—*Notes and Queries*, 6th series, vii. 148.

See "Football," "Hockey."

Hoodle-cum-blind

Name for "Blind Man's Buff."—Baker's *Northamptonshire Glossary*.

Hoodman Blind

Name for "Blind Man's Buff." Mentioned in *Hamlet*, iii. 4; *Merry Devil of Edmonton;* and *Wise Women of Hogsden.*

Hooper's Hide

Name for "Blind Man's Buff."—Nares' *Glossary*.

Hop-crease

The game of "Hop-scotch."—Halliwell's *Dictionary*.

Hop-frog

The players bend as though about to sit on a *very low* stool, then spring about with their hands resting on their knees.—Dorsetshire (*Folk-lore Journal*, vii. 234).

Miss Peacock says that a game called "Hop-frog over the Dog" is played at Stixwould, Lincolnshire, in the same way as "Leap-frog."

See "Curcuddie," "Cutch-a-cutchoo," "Harie Hutcheon," "Hirtschin Hairy."

Hop-score

Game of "Hop-scotch."—Hunter's *Glossary of Hallamshire*.

Hop-scotch

A game, the object of which is to eject a stone, slate, or "dump" out of a form linearly marked on the ground in different directions, by hopping without touching any of the lines.—Halliwell's *Dictionary*.

In the plan (fig. 8) the players first lay the stone on the back of the hand, and *walk* through the plan, stepping into each division, throw it up and catch it. Then the stone is *thrown* back from No. 7 outside No. 1. Now it is placed on the toe, and the child walks through again, throwing up the foot when out, to catch the stone in the hand. Another way, done on the same plan, is for the player to place the stone in No. 1, leave it there, and hop into each division and back, then place it in No. 2, and repeat the hopping, and so on through all the figures. There is no *kicking* of the stone, as is usual in London.—Roxton, St. Neots (Miss Lumley).

From Crockham Hill, Kent, Miss Chase sends four versions.

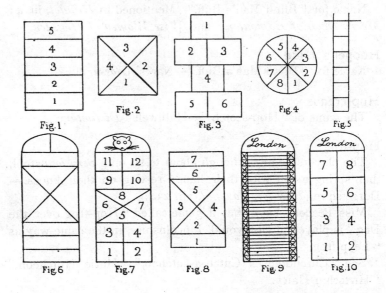

In the first plan (fig. 1) the game is :—Throw stone into No. 1. Hop from No. 1 to No. 5 and back. Then pick it up. So on successively. After having thrown it into No. 5, begin to reverse by throwing stone into No. 1 while standing at No. 5—return with it on your thumb. Throw into No. 2—return with stone on your eye. Throw into No. 3—return with stone in your palm. Throw into No. 4—return with stone on your head. Throw into No. 5—return with stone on your back. In each case, upon reaching the goal without dropping it, throw up and catch it as it falls.

In the second plan (fig. 2) the game is :—Throw stone into No. 1. Pick it up. Hop, not touching lines, from No. 1 to No. 4, and "out." Throw stone into No. 2. Do as before. And so successively into Nos. 3 and 4. Next balance stone on shoe, then on the palm of hand, then on the back of hand, then on the head, then on the shoulder, then on the eye (tilt head back to keep it from falling). In each case walk round once with it so balanced and catch at end.

In the third plan (fig. 3) the game is :—Put pebble in No. 1. Pick up. Hop, having one foot in No. 2 and the other in No. 3. Step into No. 4. Hop, having one foot in No. 5 and the other in No. 6. Jump round. Go back as you came. Then with stone on shoe, walk through the figure, kick it up and catch at the close. Place stone on eyelid; walk through the same figure, dropping it off into hand at close. This is called "jumping."

In the fourth plan (fig. 4) the game is :—Throw stone into No. 1. Pick it up. Hop from No. 1 to No. 8, not touching lines. So successively into Nos. 2, 3, 4, &c. Walk into No. 1 with stone on foot, and out at No. 8. Kick it up and catch it. The same with stone on thumb. Toss it up and catch. Again with stone on your back. Straighten up, let it slide into your hand.

In Stead's *Holderness Glossary*, this is described as a boys' or girls' game, in which the pavement is chalked with numbered crossed lines, and a pebble or piece of crockery is propelled onward by the foot, the performer hopping on one leg, the number reached on the chalk-line being scored to him or her. At Whitby it is called "Pally-ully," and played with rounded pieces of pot the size of a penny. Divisions are chalked on the pavement, and the "pally-ullies" are impelled within the lines by a hop on one leg, and a side shuffle with the same foot (*Whitby Glossary*). It is sometimes called "Tray-Trip." Atkinson describes the figure as oblong, with many angular compartments (*Cleveland Glossary*). Jamieson defines "Beds" as "Hop-scotch," a game denominated from the form, sometimes by strangers called squares. In Aberdeen the spaces marked out are sometimes circular.

Mrs. Lincoln sends a diagram of the game from Dublin (fig. 6). Addy (*Sheffield Glossary*) under the name of "Hop-score" says it is a game in which certain squares are drawn or *scored* on the ground. The piece of stone which is pushed with the foot is called the "scotch." Elworthy (*West Somerset Words*) says a piece of tile is kicked over lines and into squares marked on the ground. It is called "Hickety-Hackety," also "Huckety." Cope (*Hampshire Glossary*) says it is played in Hants. Moor (*Suffolk Words and Phrases*) describes this game under the name of "Scotch-hob," by hopping and kicking a bit of tile from bed to bed of a diagram which he gives (fig. 5, here printed). Brockett (*North Country Words*) calls it "Beds." Barnes (*Dorset Glossary*) only says "hopping over a parallelo-gram of scotches or chalk-lines on the ground." F. H. Low, in *Strand Magazine*, ii. 516, says the divisions are respectively named onesie, twosie, threesie, foursie, and puddings. It is called "Hop-bed" at Stixwold in Lincolnshire (Miss Peacock), "Hop-score" in Yorkshire (Halliwell, *l.c.*), and "Hitchibed" in Cleveland, Yorks. (*Glossary of Cleveland Words*). Strutt describes it (*Sports*, p. 383); and Wood's *Modern Playmate*, p. 32, gives a diagram similar to one seen on a London pave-ment by A. B. Gomme (see fig. 7). Mr. Emslie has sent me figs. 9 and 10, also from London streets. Newell (*Games*, p. 188) speaks of it as a well-known game in America.

Mr. Elworthy (*West Somerset Words*) says, "Several of these (diagrams marked on the ground) are still to be seen, scratched on the ancient pavement of the Roman Forum." Mr. J. W. Crombie says, "The game of 'Hop-scotch' was one of considerable antiquity, having been known in England for more than two centuries, and it was played all over Europe under different names. Signor Pitré's solar explanation of its origin appeared improbable to him, for not only was the evidence in its favour extremely weak, but it would require the original number of divisions in the figure to have been twelve instead of seven, which was the number indicated by a considerable body of evidence. It would seem more probable that the game at one time represented the progress of the soul from earth to heaven through various intermediate states, the name given to the last court being most frequently paradise or an equivalent, such as crown or glory, while the names of the other courts corresponded with the eschatological ideas prevalent in the early days of Christianity." Some such game existed before Christianity, and Mr. Crombie considered that it had been derived from several ancient games. Possibly the strange myths of the labyrinths might have had something to do with "Hop-scotch," and a variety of the game played in England, under the name of "Round Hop-scotch," was almost identical with a game described by Pliny as being played by the boys of his day. Mr. Crombie also said he "believed that the early Christians adopted the general idea of the ancient game, but they not only converted it into an allegory of heaven, with Christian beliefs and Christian names; they Christianised the figure also; they abandoned the heathen labyrinth and replaced it by the form of the Basilicon, the early Christian church, dividing it into seven parts, as they believed heaven to be divided, and placing paradise, the inner sanctum of heaven, in the position of the altar, the inner sanctum of their earthly church."

See " Hap the Beds."

Hop, Step, and Jump
See " Half-Hammer."

Hornie
A game among children in which one of the company runs after the rest having his hands clasped and his thumbs pushed out before him in resemblance of horns. The first person whom he touches with his thumbs becomes his property, joins hands with him, and aids in attempting to catch the rest: and so on until they are all made captives. Those who are at liberty still cry out, "Hornie, Hornie."—Lothian (Jamieson).

Jamieson says: "Whether this play be a vestige of the very ancient custom of assuming the appearance and skins of animals, especially in the sports of Yule, or might be meant to symbolise the exertions made by the devil (often called ' Hornie') in making sinful man his prey, and employing fellow-men as his coadjutors in this work, I cannot pretend to determine."

See "Hunt the Staigie," "Whiddy."

Hornie Holes

A game in which four play, a principal and an assistant on each side. A. stands with his assistant at one hole, and throws what is called a Cat (a piece of stick, and frequently a sheep's horn), with the design of making it alight in another hole at some distance, at which B. and his assistant stand ready to drive it aside. The bat or driver is a rod resembling a walking-stick.

The following unintelligible rhyme is repeated by a player on the one side, while they on the other are gathering in the Cats, and is attested by old people as of great antiquity :—

> Jock, Speak, and Sandy,
> W' a' their lousy train
> Round about by Errinborra,
> We'll never meet again.
> Gae head 'im, gae hang 'im,
> Gae lay 'im in the sea ;
> A' the birds o' the air
> Will bear him companee.
> With a nig-nag, widdy- [or worry-] bag,
> And an e'endown trail, trail ;
> Quoth he.
> —Jamieson.

The game is also called "Kittie-cat."
See "Cat and Dog," "Cudgel," "Tip-cat."

Horns

"A' Horns to the Lift," a game of young people. A circle is formed round a table, and all placing their forefingers on the table, one cries, "A' horns to the lift! Cat's horns upmost!" If on this any one lift his finger, he owes a wad, as cats have no horns. In the same manner, the person who does not raise his fingers when a horned animal is named is subjected to a forfeit.—Jamieson.

Hot Cockles

At Sheffield a boy is chosen for a Stump, and stands with his back against a wall. Another boy bends his back as in "Leap-frog," and puts his head against the Stump. The cap of the boy who bends down is then taken off, and put upon his back upside down. Then each of the other boys who are playing puts the first finger of his right hand into the cap. When all the fingers are put into the cap, these lines are sung—

> The wind blows east, the wind blows west,
> The wind blows o'er the cuckoo's nest.
> Where is this poor man to go?
> Over yond cuckoo's hill I O.

Then the boy whose back is bent jumps up, and the others run away crying out, "Hot cockles." The boy who is caught by the one whose back was first bent has to bend his back next time, and so on.—S. O. Addy.

At Cork a handkerchief is tied over the eyes of one of the company, who then lays his head on a chair, and places his hand on his back with the palm uppermost. Any of the party come behind him and give him a slap on his hand, he in the meantime trying to discover whose hand it is that strikes.—Miss Keane.

"Hot Cockles" is an old game, practised especially at Christmas. One boy sits down, and another, who is blindfolded, kneels and lays his head on his knee, placing at the same time his open hand on his own back. He then cries, "Hot cockles, hot!" Another then strikes his open hand, and the sitting boy asks who strikes. If the boy guessed wrongly, he made a forfeit; but if rightly, he was released.—*Notes and Queries*, 4th series, ix. 262.

The sport is noticed by Gay—

> As at hot-cockles once I laid me down,
> I felt the weighty hand of many a clown;
> Buxoma gave a gentle tap, and I
> Quick rose and read soft mischief in her eye.

Halliwell describes it rather differently. The blindfolded boy lies down on his face, and, being struck, must guess who it is that hit him. A good part of the fun consisted in the hardness of the slaps, which were generally given on the throne of honour. He quotes from a MS. play as follows—

> It is edicted that every Grobian shall play at Bamberye hott cockles at the four festivals.
> Indeed a verye usefull sport, but lately much neglected to the mollefieinge of the flesh.   —Halliwell's *Dictionary*.

Nares' *Glossary* also contains quotations from works of 1639, 1653, and 1697 which illustrate the game. Mr. Addy says " that this game as played in Sheffield is quite different from that described under the same title in Halliwell's *Dictionary*. Aubrey (p. 30) speaks of ' Hot Cockles ' as a game played at funerals in Yorkshire, and the lines here given show that this was the game. The lines—

> Where is this poor man to go ?
> Over yond cuckoo's hill I O,

embodies the popular belief that the soul winged its way like a bird, and they remind one of the passing of the soul over Whinny Moor (see funeral dirge in Aubrey's *Remains of Gen-*

tilisme, p. 31). Grimm mentions the cuckoo hill (Gauchsberg). He says, ' Originally in Gauchsberg the bird himself may very well have been meant in a mystic sense which has fallen dark to us now ' (*Teut. Myth.*, ii. 681). We know, too, the old belief that the cuckoo tells children how many years they have to live. These lines are also sometimes said, in addition to those given above—

> Elder belder, limber lock,
> Three wives in a clock ;
> Sit and sing, and call a spring,
> O-u-t spells out.

The boy who bends down is supposed to be undergoing a great penalty." Strutt (*Sports*, p. 394) describes this game, and gives an illustration which is here reproduced from the original MSS. in the Bodleian.

This game may have originated from a custom at funerals of practising spells for the safe and speedy passage of the departing spirit to its destination, or from divination mysteries to foretell who would be the next among the mourners to follow the dead body to the grave. The spirit of prophecy was believed to exist in a dying person. See " Handy Croopen."

How many Miles to Babylon

> I.   King and Queen of Cantelon,
>   How many miles to Babylon ?
>   Eight and eight and other eight.
>   Will I get there by candle-light ?
>   If your horse be good and your spurs be bright.
>   How mony men have ye ?
>   Mae nae ye daur come and see.
>   —Chambers' *Popular Rhymes*, p. 124 ;
>   Mactaggart's *Gallovidian Encyclopædia.*

> II.   How many miles to Babylon ?
>   Three score and ten.
>   Will we be there by candle-light ?
>   Yes, and back again.
>   Open your gates and let us go through.
>   Not without a beck and a boo.
>   There's a beck, and there's a boo,
>   Open your gates and let us go through.
>   —Nairn, Scotland (Rev. W. Gregor).

> III. How far to Banbury Cross ?
>   Four score and ten.
>   Can I get there by candle-light ?
>   Yes, if your legs are long and light.

Please to let me go ?
Not without you bend and bow [pronounced bo].
Here's my bend [curtseys],
And here's my bow [touches forehead],
Now will you let me go ?
                    —Fernham and Longcot (Miss I. Barclay).

IV.   How many miles to Babylon ?
      Three score and ten.
      Can we get there by candle-light ?
      Yes, and back again.
      Open your gates as wide as you can,
      And let King George and his family go through.
      Not without a back, not without a bow,
      Not without a curtsey, and then I'll let you through.
                    —South Shields (Miss Blair).

V.   How many miles to Babylon ?
      Three score and ten.
      Can I get there o' candle-light ?
      There and back again.
      Here's my black [raising one foot],
      And here's my blue [raising the other],
      Open the gates and let me through.
                    —Annaverna, Ravendale, co. Louth, Ireland
                              (Miss R. Stephen).

VI.   How many miles to Barney Bridge ?
      Three score and ten.
      Will I be there by candle-light ?
      Yes, if your legs are long.
      A curtsey to you, another to you,
      If you please will you let the king's horses go through ?
      Yes, but take care of your hindmost man.
                    —Belfast (W. H. Patterson).

VII. How many miles to Gandigo ?
      Eighty-eight almost, or quite.
      Can I [we] get there by candle-light ?
      Yes, if your legs are long and light.

Open the gate as high as the sky,
And let the king and his queen go by.
                    —Dorsetshire (*Folk-lore Journal*, vii. 230, 231).

VIII.   How many miles to Banbury?
        Three score and ten.
        Can I get there by candle-light?
        Yes, and back again.
        But mind the old witch doesn't catch you.
                              —London (Miss Dendy).

 IX.   How many miles to Barley Bridge?
        Three score and ten.
        Can I get there by candle-light?
        Yes, if your legs be long.
        A courtesy to you, and a courtesy to you,
        If you please will you let the king's horses through?
        Through and through shall they go,
        For the king's sake;
        ·But the one that is the hindmost
        Will meet with a great mistake.
                    —Halliwell's *Popular Rhymes*, p. 217.

  X.   How many miles to Barney Bridge?
        Three score and ten.
        Will I be there by Candlemass?
        Yes, and back again.
        A curtsey to you, another to you,
        And pray, fair maids, will you let us through?
        Thro' and thro' shall you go for the king's sake,
        But take care the last man does not meet a mistake.
                              —Dublin (Mrs. Lincoln).

 XI.   How many miles to Burslem?
        Three score and ten.
        Can we get there by candle-light?
        Yes, and back again.
        Open the gates so wide, so wide,
        And let King George aside, aside;
        The night is so dark we cannot see,
        Thread the needle and go through.
                              —Isle of Man (A. W. Moore).

XII.   How many miles to Banbury Cross?
       Three score and ten.
       Shall we get there by midnight?
       Yes, if you run well.
       Then open your gates as wide as the sky,
       And let King George and his men pass by.
       It is so dark we cannot see, so thread the needle Nancy,
       Thread the needle Nancy.
       One, two, three.
                    —Warwick (from a little girl living near Warwick,
                         through Mr. C. C. Bell).

XIII. How many miles to London?
       Three score ten.
       Can I get there by candle-light?
       Yes, and back again.
       Open the gate and let me through.
       Not unless you're black and blue.
       Here's my black and here's my blue,
       Open the gates and let me through.
       Dan, Dan, thread the needle; Dan, Dan, sew.
                         —*Suffolk County Folk-lore*, p. 63.

XIV.   How many miles to Babylon?
       Three score and ten.
       Shall I be there by candle-light?
       Yes, there and back again.
       Open the gates as wide as high,
       And let King George and his family pass by.
                         —Wales (*Folk-lore Record*, v. 88).

                                   ⎧ Barley Bridge?
XV.   How many miles to ⎨ Banbury?
                                   ⎩ London?
       Four score and ten [*or*, Fifty miles and more].
       Shall we be there by candle-light?
       Oh, yes, and back again.
            [*Or, at Market Drayton.*
       Shift your feet with nimble light,
       And you'll be there by candle-light.]

Open the gates as wide as the sky,
And let King George and his lady go by.
—Market Drayton, Ellesmere, Whitchurch,
(Burne's *Shropshire Folk-lore*, p. 522).

XVI.   How many miles to Bethlehem?
Three score and ten.
Shall we get there by candle-light?
Yes, there and back again.
So open the gates and let King George and his family
go through.   —Hayton, near York (H. Hardy).

XVII.   How far is it to Babylon?
Three score miles and ten.
Can I get there by candle-light?
Yes, there and back again.
—Sporle, Norfolk (Miss Matthews).

XVIII.   How many miles to Babylon?
Three score and ten.
Can you get there by candle-light?
O yes, and back again.
—Hanbury, Staffordshire (Miss E. Hollis).

XIX.   Open the gates as wide as high,
And let King George and I go by;
It is so dark I cannot see
To thread my grandmother's needle.
—Surrey (*Folk-lore Record*, v. 88).

(*b*) There are two methods of playing this game, one in which a King and Queen are represented, and the other in which gates of a city are represented. Of the first Chambers and Mactaggart practically give the same account. The latter says, "Two of the swiftest boys are placed between two 'doons' or places of safety; these, perhaps, are two hundred yards distant. All the other boys stand in one of these places or doons, when the two fleet youths come forward and address them with the rhyme. When out, they run in hopes to get to Babylon or the other doon, but many get not near that place before they are caught by the runners, who 'taens' them, that is, lay their hands upon their heads, when they are not allowed to run any more in that game, that is, until they all be taened or taken."

The Norfolk game seems to resemble the Scotch, though in a much less complete form. Miss Matthews describes it as follows :—" A line of children is formed, and the two standing opposite it sing the questions, to which the line reply ; then the two start off running in any direction they please, and the others try to catch them."

The second method of playing is best described by the Rev. Walter Gregor, from the Nairn game, which is known as " The Gates of Babylon." Mr. Gregor writes as follows :—" This game may be played either by boys or girls. Two of the players join hands, and stand face to face, with their hands in front as if forming a gate. Each of these has a secret name. The other players form themselves into a line by clasping each

Fig 1   Fig 2

other round the waist from behind. They go up to the two that form the gate, and the leader asks the first question, as in version No. 2. The dialogue then proceeds to the end. The two then lift their arms as high as they can, still joined, and the line of players passes through. All at once the two bring their arms down on one and make him (or her) prisoner. The prisoner is asked in a whisper, so as not to disclose the secret name, which of the two is to be chosen. The one so captured takes his (or her) stand behind the one chosen. The same process is gone through till all the players are taken captive, and have stationed themselves behind the one or the other of the two forming the gate. The last one of the line goes through three times. The first time the word 'breakfast' is pronounced; the second time 'dinner;' and the third time 'supper.' The player then chooses a side. The two sides have then a tug of war. The game ends at this point with girls. With boys the conquered have to run the gauntlet. The victors range themselves in two lines, each boy with his cap or handkerchief tightly plaited in his hand, and pelt with all their might the vanquished as they run between the lines. The boys of Nairn call this running of the gauntlet, 'through fire an' watter.'"

The method of playing the Warwick, Fernham, and Louth versions is practically the same. The children stand in half-circle beginning with the two tallest at either end. All clasp hands. The two at one end question those at the other end alternately (fig. 1). At the last line the two that have been answering hold their hands up to form a bridge, and all the others thread through, still holding hands (the bridge advancing slowly) (fig. 2). The Louth version is also sometimes played as "Oranges and Lemons." This is also the case with the Belfast, South Shields, Ellesmere, and Dublin versions. Miss Burne also gives a second method of playing this game at Ellesmere: she says, "The whole number of players stand in two rows facing each other, each player joining hands with the one opposite. The pair at the lower end parley with the pair at the top, and then run under the extended arms of the others, receiving thumps on the back as they go, till they reach the upper end, and become the top couple in their turn." The Hanbury version is played in a similar way. Two lines stand close together holding handkerchiefs across. The questions are asked and answered by the top and bottom players. Then two children run under the line of handkerchiefs. The Dorset version is played by as many as like standing, two and two, opposite each other, each of them taking with the right hand the right hand of the other; then the two that are the King and Queen say or sing the first question, to which the others reply, and the dialogue ends in this manner. Then all the other pairs hold up their hands as high as they can, and the King and Queen run through the archway and back again, and so on with the next pair, and other pairs in turn. The Isle of Man version is played, Mr. Moore says, the same as other "Thread the Needle" games.

(*c*) The game is evidently dramatic in form, and perhaps is illustrative of some fact of history, such as the toll upon merchandise entering a walled town. The changes in the words of the different versions are not very great, but they show the influence of modern history upon the game. The appearance of King George evidently points to the date when it was frequently played, though the older versions are doubtless those in which his Majesty does not do duty. Mactaggart has the following quaint note which perhaps may supply the origin, though it seems a far cry to the Crusaders:—"This sport has something methinks of antiquity in it; it seemeth to be a pantomime of some scenes played off in the time of the Crusades. 'King and Queen o' Cantilon' evidently must be King and Queen of Caledon, but slightly changed by time. Then Babylon in the rhyme, the way they had to wander and hazard being caught by the infidels, all speak as to the foundation of the game" (Mactaggart's *Gallovidian Encyclopædia*).

In the *Gentleman's Magazine* for December 1849, in a review of the *Life of Shirley*, it is stated that in many parts of England the old game of "Thread the Needle" is played to the following words, which refer to the gate of the city of Hebron, known as the "needle's eye."

How many miles to Hebron?
Three score and ten.
Shall I be there by midnight?
Yes, and back again.
Then thread the needle, &c.

The game is also described in *Notes and Queries*, iv. 141, as played in the same way as above, and the writer adds there are subsequent evolutions by which each couple becomes in succession the eye of the needle.

Howly

A street game played by boys in a town, one of them hiding behind a wall or house-end, and crying "Howly" to the seekers.—Atkinson's *Cleveland Glossary*.

See "Hide and Seek."

Huckie-buckie down the Brae

Children in Lothian have a sport in which they slide down a hill, sitting on their hunkers (Jamieson). The well-known custom at Greenwich is probably the same game, and there are examples at Tumbling Hill, a few miles from Exeter, at May Pole Hill, near Gloucester, and other places.

Huckle-bones

Holloway (*Dict. of Provincialisms*) says that the game is called "Huckle-bones" in East Sussex and "Dibs" in West Sussex. Parish (*Dict. of Sussex Dialect*) mentions that huckle-bones, the small bone found in the joint of the knee of a sheep, are used by children for playing the game of "Dibs;" also Peacock's *Manley and Corringham Glossary*. Barnes (*Dorset Glossary*) says, "A game of toss and catch, played mostly by two with five dibs or huckle-bones of a leg of mutton, or round pieces of tile or slate." Halliwell's description is clearly wrong. He says it was a game formerly played by throwing up the hip-bone of some animal, on one side of which was a head of Venus and on the other that of a dog. He who turned up the former was the winner (*Dictionary*). Miss J. Barker writes that "Huckle-bones" is played in Hexham; and Professor Attwell (Barnes) played the game as a boy, and is still a proficient in it; he played it recently for my benefit with his set of real huckle-bones (A. B. Gomme); and see *Notes and Queries*, 9th ser., iv. 378, 379.

The figures or sets are practically the same as those described under "Fivestones." The game is very ancient. In the *Sanctuarie of Salvation*, &c., translated from the Latin of Levinus Lemnius by Henry Kinder (8vo, London, printed by H. Singleton), p. 144, we read, "These bones are called 'huckle-bones' or 'coytes.'" For further information relating to this game, as played by the ancients, the reader may consult *Joannis Meursii Ludibunda, sive de Ludis Græcorum, Liber singularis* (8vo, Lugd. Bat. 1625), p. 7, and *Dan. Souterii Palamedes*, p. 81; but more particularly, *I Tali ed altri Strumenti lusori degli antichi Romani, discritti da Francesco de 'Ficoroni*, 4to, Rom. 1734. Against the suggestion that the modern game is derived directly from the Romans, is the fact that it is known in countries never traversed or occupied by the Romans. Thus Dr. Clarke, in his *Travels in Russia*, 1810, p. 106, says: "In all the villages and towns from Moscow to Woronetz, as in other parts of Russia, are seen boys, girls, and sometimes even old men, playing with the joint-bones of sheep. This game is called 'Dibbs' by the English. It is of very remote antiquity; for I have seen it very beautifully represented on Grecian vases; particularly on a vase in the collection of the late Sir William Hamilton, where a female figure appeared most gracefully delineated kneeling upon one knee, with her right arm extended, the palm downwards, and the bones ranged along the back of her hand and arm. In this manner the Russians play the game."

See "Dalies," "Fivestones."

Hummie

The game otherwise called "Shinty." The shinty or hummie is played by a set of boys in two divisions who attempt to drive with curved sticks a ball, or what is more common, part of the vertebral bone of a sheep, in opposite directions (*Blackwood's Magazine*, August 1821, p. 36). If one of the adverse party happens to stand or run among his opponents, they call out "Hummie, keep on your own side."—Jamieson.

Hundreds

A game at marbles, which is carried on until one of the players scores 100 or some other high number agreed upon. Any number can play, but it is best described for two players, A. and B. First the players taw up to a hole; if both get in, they repeat the process until one is left out, say B.; then A. counts 10. Should both fail, the nearest goes first. He may now lay his taw about the hole or fire at the other, on hitting which he counts another 10. He now goes for the hole again, and failing, lies where he happens to stop. If he misses, B. from his present position tries to get into the hole, and failing, lies still; but if he reaches the hole, he counts 10, and proceeds as A. had done. The one who first gets the 100 (or other number) now goes in for his "pizings," which performance takes place thus:—The loser, so far, is lying about, and the winner goes back to "drakes," and again tries to lodge in the hole; and if he succeeds, the game is up. If not, he lies still, and the loser tries for the hole; if he gets in he counts another 10, or if he should succeed in hitting the winner he scores his adversary's 100 to his own number, and then goes on for his "pizings" as the other had done. In failure of either securing the game thus, the process is repeated at "drakes." When, however, the one who is on for his "pizings" manages to taw into the hole, the game is concluded.—Easther's *Almondbury and Huddersfield Glossary*.

Hunt the Hare

A game among children, played on the ice as well as in the fields (Brockett's *North Country Words*). Strutt (*Sports*, p. 381) says "Hunt the Hare" is the same game as "Hunt the Fox." In this game one boy is permitted to run out, and having law given to him—that is, being permitted to go to a certain distance from his comrades before they pursue him— their object is to take him, if possible, before he can return home.

See "Hare and Hounds."

Hunt the Slipper

—Lancashire (Mrs. Harley).

All the players but one sit on the floor in a circle with their legs crossed (Turkish fashion), one acting as Chief, all pretending to work at making or mending shoes. The other player brings a slipper to the Chief Cobbler, and desires it to be mended, saying—

> Cobbler, cobbler, mend my shoe,
> Get it done by half-past two.

The child walks away, and returns in a few moments and asks whether the shoe is ready. The Cobbler says, "Not quite; call again in an hour's time," or makes any other excuse which occurs to him. When the child calls again, she is told it has been sent home. After several pretences the child declares an intention to search for it. The Cobblers in the ring then all place their hands under their knees, and pass the slipper secretly from one to another in such a way as to prevent the owner of the shoe getting it for some time. The Cobbler from whom the slipper is taken becomes the owner next time (Barnes, A. B. Gomme). In the Nottinghamshire version (Miss Peacock) the rhyme is—

Cobbler, cobbler, mend my shoe,
Give it a stitch and that will do.

Versions from Wakefield, Liphook, Ellesmere, and other places are practically the same as the Barnes game, but Mr. Udal gives an elaboration of the Dorsetshire game in the *Folklore Journal*, vii. 238. One Lancashire version (Miss Dendy) reverses the characters by making the Cobbler run round the ring, and the children requiring the shoe to be mended, call out, "Blackie, come mend my slipper." Mrs. Harley, in another Lancashire version, gives the words sung to the tune printed as—

Pass on, pass on, passy on the slipper;
The best fun we ever had was passing on the slipper.

Holloway (*Dict. of Provincialisms*) says this game was well known in Somerset, Hants, Sussex, but now is almost out of fashion. He describes it as being played without words. The child who has to find the shoe stands in the centre of the circle. The chief amusement arises from the one in the circle who has the slipper striking the one who stands up (the searcher) while he or she is steadily looking for it in an opposite direction. Strutt (*Sports*, p. 387) also describes this game.

Hunt the Staigie

A boys' game. One is chosen to be the Staigie (little stallion). The other players scatter themselves over the playground. The Staigie locks his fingers into each other. He then repeats the words—

Hunt the Staigie,
Huntie, untie, staige,
Ailleman, ailleman, aigie,

and rushes off with his hands locked, and tries to touch one of
the players. He must not unlock his hands till he has caught
one. When he has captured one, the two join hands and hunt

for another. When another is caught, he joins the two. This
goes on till all are hunted down.—Keith (Rev. W. Gregor).
See "Chickidy Hand," "Whiddy."

Hunting

—Earls Heaton (Herbert Hardy).

—Epworth (C. C. Bell).

I.   Oh, a-hunting we will go, a-hunting we will go;
    We'll catch a little fox and put him in a box,
        And never let him go.   —Bath (Miss Large).

II.   Hunting we will go, brave boys,
    Hunting we will go;

We'll catch an old fox
And put him in a box,
For a-hunting we will go.
Halt! shoulder arms! fire!
—Horncastle, North Kelsey, Lincoln (Miss Peacock).

III. O have you seen the Shah,
O have you seen the Shah?
He lights his pipe on a star-light night,
O have you seen the Shah?
For a-hunting we will go,
A-hunting we will go;
We'll catch a fox and put him in a box,
A-hunting we will go.
—Epworth, Doncaster (C. C. Bell).

(*b*) The players march two by two, all singing. The first pair let go hands, separate, and skip widely apart, still singing. Gradually, in this manner, two separate lines are formed, until, following each other and singing, the pairs come together again, join hands, and march and sing in couplets linked.

The Bath game is played by the children standing in two rows facing each other, and clapping hands and singing the verse. At the same time the two children facing each other at the top of the lines join hands and trip down and up between the lines. Their hands are unclasped, and the two children run down the outside of the lines, one running on each side, and meet at the bottom of the lines, where they stand. The two children now standing at the top proceed in the same way: this is continued until all the children have done the same. A ring is then formed, when the children again clap and sing. Any number can play at this game.

In the Epworth version the children range themselves in double rank at one end of the room or playground, and march down to the other end hand in hand. At the bottom they loose hands and divide, the first rank turning right, the second left, and march back in two single files to the other end again, where they re-form as at first, and repeat their manœuvre, singing the verses alternately.

The Lincolnshire game is played by the children walking two and two in a circle round one of their companions, singing. The players then stand facing the child in the centre, and place their hands on their partners' shoulders. After the lines are sung the centre child cries out, " Halt ! Shoulder arms ! Fire ! " at which words each child kisses his partner. If the commander sees any one hesitate, or avoid kissing, he runs forward and takes the defaulter's place, leaving him to fill the middle position.

Similar versions are played at Earls Heaton (Mr. Hardy), Forest of Dean (Miss Matthews), Ellesmere (Burne, *Shropshire Folk-lore*, p. 574), Derbyshire (*Folk-lore Journal*, i. 386).

Hurling

A game played with a ball. The players are divided into two equal parties, each of which tries to secure and keep the ball in their possession. The prize is a ball made of cork, covered with silver.—Courtney's *West Cornwall Glossary*.

In Taylor's *Antiquitates Curiosæ*, p. 144, it is stated :—" The game of hurling consisted in throwing or hurling a ball of wood about three inches in diameter, and covered with plated silver, sometimes gilt. On the ball was frequently a Cornish motto allusive to the game, and signifying that fair play was best. Success depended on catching the ball dexterously when dealt, and conveying it away through all the opposition of the adverse party, or, if that was impossible, to throw it into the hands of a partner, who, in his turn, was to exert his utmost efforts to convey it to his own goal, which was often three or four miles distant from that of his adversaries."

T. Durfey's *Collin's Walk through London*, 1690, p. 192, says : " Hurling is an ancient sport us'd to this day in the countys of Cornwall and Devon, when once a year the hardy young fellows of each county meet; and a cork ball thinly plated with silver being thrown up between 'em, they run, bustle, and fight for it, to the witty dislocating of many a shrew'd neck, or for the sport of telling how bravely their arms or legs came to be broke, when they got home." It is fully described by Carew in his *Survey of Cornwall*, 1602, p. 73.

It is also a very ancient Irish game, and Mr. Kinahan says: "Many places are called after it: such as, Killahurla, the hurlers' church; Gortnahurla, the field of the hurlers; Greenanahurla, the sunny place of the hurlers; this, however, is now generally corrupted into hurling-green. The hurling-green where the famous match was played by the people of Wexford against those of Cather (now divided into the counties of Carlow and Wicklow), and where the former got the name of yellow bellies, from the colour of the scarfs they wore round their waist, is a sunny flat on the western side of North Wicklow Gap, on the road from Gorey to Trinnahely. There are also many other different names that record the game."—*Folk-lore Journal*, ii. 266.

See "Bandy," "Camp," "Football," "Hockey," "Hood," "Shinty."

Hurly-burly

An undescribed boys' game. In it the following rhyme is used—

> Hurly-burly, trumpy trace,
> The cow stands in the market-place;
> Some goes far, and some goes near,
> Where shall this poor sinner steer?
> —*Patterson's Antrim and Down Glossary.*

For a similar rhyme see "Hot Cockles."

Huss

Children play a game which is accompanied by a song beginning—

> Hussing and bussing will not do,
> But go to the gate, knock, and ring—
> Please, Mrs. Brown, is Nellie within?
> —*Parish's Dictionary of the Sussex Dialect.*

Hustle Cap

A boys' game, played by tossing up halfpence. It is mentioned in *Peregrine Pickle*, cap. xvi. Cope (*Hampshire Glossary*) says, "Halfpence are placed in a cap and thrown up, a sort of 'pitch-and-toss.'"

Hynny-pynny

A peculiar game at marbles, sometimes called " Hyssy-pyssy," played in some parts of Devon and Somerset. A hole of some extent was made in an uneven piece of ground, and the game was to shoot the marbles at some object beyond the hole without letting them tumble into it. The game occasionally commenced by a ceremony of no very delicate description, which sufficed to render the fallen marble still more ignominious.— Halliwell's *Dictionary*.

Isabella

—Ogbourne, Wilts (H. S. May).

—Earls Heaton (H. Hardy).

—London (A. B. Gomme).

I.   Isabella, Isabella, Isabella, Farewell!!
     Last night when we parted
     I left you broken-hearted,
     And on a green mountain,
     There stands a young man.

     Could you love him?
     Could you love him?
     Could you love him?   Farewell!

     Choose one, love,
     Choose one, love,
     Choose one, love, Farewell!

     Take a walk, love,
     Take a walk, love,
     Take a walk, love, Farewell!

     In the ring, love,
     In the ring, love,
     In the ring, love, Farewell!

     Put the ring on,
     Put the ring on,
     Put the ring on, Farewell!

     Go to church, love,
     Go to church, love,
     Go to church, love, Farewell!

     Take a kiss, love,
     Take a kiss, love,
     Take a kiss, love, Farewell!

Shake hands, love,
Shake hands, love,
Shake hands, love, Farewell!
                    —Enborne, Newbury (M. Kimber).

II. Isabella, Isabella, Isabella, Farewell!
     Last night when I departed
     I left her broken-hearted;
     Upon the steep mountain
     There stands a young man.

     Who'll you choose, love?
     Who'll you choose, love?
     Who'll you choose, love?   Farewell!

     Go to church, love,
     Go to church, love,
     Go to church, love, Farewell!

     Say your prayers, love,
     Say your prayers, love,
     Say your prayers, love, Farewell!

     Put your ring on,
     Put your ring on,
     Put your ring on, Farewell!

     Come back, love,
     Come back, love,
     Come back, love, Farewell!

     Roast beef and plum pudding,
     Roast beef and plum pudding,
     Roast beef and plum pudding,
     For our dinner to-day.

     Kiss together, love,
     Kiss together, love,
     Kiss together, love, Farewell!
                    —Ogbourne, Wilts (H. S. May).

III.   Isabella, Isabella, Isabella, Farewell!
       Last night when I departed
       I left you broken-hearted
       Broken-hearted on the mountain,
       On the mountain, Farewell!

       Choose your loved one, choose your loved one,
       Choose your loved one, Farewell!

       Kiss your hand, love, kiss your hand, love,
       Kiss your hand, love, Farewell!

       Go to church, love, go to church, love,
       Go to church, love, Farewell!

       Say your prayers, love, say your prayers, love,
       Say your prayers, love, Farewell!

       Come to dinner, love, come to dinner, love,
       Come to dinner, love, Farewell!

       What have you for dinner, for dinner, for dinner,
       What have you for dinner, for dinner to-day?

       Roast beef and plum pudding, plum pudding, plum
          pudding,
       Roast beef and plum pudding, plum pudding to-day.
                    —Southampton (Mrs. W. R. Carse).

IV.   Isabella, Isabella, Isabella, Farewell!
       Last night I met you downhearted and sad,
       And down by the river I met your young man.

       Choose a lover, choose a lover,
       Choose a lover, Farewell!

       Walk to church, love, walk to church, love,
       Walk to church, love, Farewell!

       Come to the ring, love, come to the ring, love,
       Come to the ring, love, Farewell!

       Give a kiss, love, give a kiss, love,
       Give a kiss, love, Farewell!
               —West Grinstead, Sussex (*Notes and Queries*,
                     8th Series, i. 249, Miss Busk).

V.   Arabella!
      Arabella!
      Arabella!   Farewell!

Last night when we parted
I left you broken-hearted
Down by the mill-side.

Who'll you have, love?
Who'll you have, love?
Who'll you have, love?   Farewell!

Go to church, love,
Go to church, love,
Go to church, love, Farewell!

Come back, love,
Come back, love,
Come back, love, Farewell!

Shake hands, love,
Shake hands, love,
Shake hands, love, Farewell!

Take a kiss, love,
Take a kiss, love,
Take a kiss, love, Farewell!
     —Platt School, near Wrotham, Kent (Miss Burne).

VI.   Isabella, Isabella, Isabella, Farewell!
      Last night when we parted
      I left you broken-hearted,
      And on the green meadow
      You was standing alone.

Choose a sweetheart, choose a sweetheart,
Choose a sweetheart, fair maid.

Take her hand, love, take her hand, love,
Take her hand, love, fair maid.

Kneel down, love, kneel down, love,
Kneel down, love, fair maid.

Take a kiss, love, take a kiss, love,
Take a kiss, love, fair maid.

Now you're married I wish you joy,
First a girl and then a boy,
Seven years after son and daughter;
Pray, young couple, come kiss together.

Kiss her once, kiss her twice, kiss her three times over.
—From a London nursemaid, 1878 (A. B. Gomme).

VII. Isabella, Isabella, Isabella, Farewell!
Last night when we parted
I believed you broken-hearted,
As on the green mountain
You stands [*qy.* sang] like a lark.

Go to church, love, go to church, love,
Go to church, love, Farewell!

In the ring, love, in the ring, love,
In the ring, love, Farewell!

Give a kiss, love, give a kiss, love,
Give a kiss, love, Farewell!

Isabella, Isabella, Isabella, Farewell!
—Fernham and Longcot (Miss I. Barclay).

VIII. Isabella, Isabella, Isabella, Farewell!
Last night when I departed I left her broken-hearted;
On the hill yonder there stands your young man.

Fetch him here, love, fetch him here, love,
Fetch him here, love, Farewell!

Shut the gates, love, shut the gates, love,
Shut the gates, love, Farewell!

Open the gates, love, open the gates, love,
Open the gates, love, Farewell!

Go to church, love, go to church, love,
Go to church, love, Farewell!

Show your ring, love, show your ring, love,
Show your ring, love, Farewell!
                    —Hanbury, Staffs. (Miss E. Hollis).

IX. The trees are uncovered, uncovered, uncovered,
     The trees are uncovered, Isabella, for me!

     Last night when we parted we were all broken-hearted,
     Isabella, Isabella, Isabella, for me!

     Then give me your hand, love, your hand, love, your
          hand, love,
     Then give me your hand, love, and a sweet kiss from you.
                    —Earls Heaton (Herbert Hardy).

X. When the trees are uncovered, Isabellow, for me.
    Last night when we parted
    She was nigh broken-hearted,
    Isabellow, Isabellow, Isabellow, for me.

    Your hand, love, your hand, love,
    Then give me your hand, love,
    Take a sweet kiss from me.
                    —Winterton, Nottinghamshire and Yorkshire (Miss Peacock).

XI. Isabella, Isabella, Isabella, Farewell!
     Last night when we parted I left you broken-hearted,
     And down by the river you saw your young man.

     In the stream, love, in the stream, love,
     In the stream, love, Farewell!

     Go to church, love, go to church, love,
     Go to church, love, Farewell.

     In the ring, love, in the ring, love,
     In the ring, love, Farewell!
                    —Long Eaton, Nottinghamshire (Miss Youngman).

XII. Elizabella, Farewell!
      Last night as we parted
      She left me broken-hearted,
      And on a green mountain
      She looked like a dove.

Choose your loved one,
Choose your loved one,
Choose your loved one, Farewell!

Go to church, love, Farewell!
Say your prayers, love, Farewell!
In the ring, love, Farewell!

Shake hands, loves,
Shake hands, loves, Farewell!

Give a kiss, loves,
Give a kiss, loves, Farewell!
—Liphook, Hants (Miss Fowler).

XIII.   Last night when we parted
She was nigh broken-hearted,
To-morrow we gather
And a bright welcome be.
Then give me your hand, love,
Your hand, love, your hand, love,
Then give me your hand, love,
     Isabella for me.
     Isabella, Isabella,
     Isabella for me.
—North Derbyshire (S. O. Addy).

(*b*) In the Enborne, Newbury, version (Miss Kimber) a ring is formed by the children (boys and girls) joining hands. Another child stands in the centre. The ring of children walk round while singing the verses. The singing is confined to the ring. When the centre child is told to "choose," she selects a boy from the ring, who goes into the centre and they stand together. At the next verse these two children walk out of the ring arm-in-arm. When the next verse is sung they return, and again stand in the centre. At the next verse the boy pretends to put a ring on the girl's finger. They walk out of the ring when told to go to church (two children in the ring unclasping hands to let them walk out, and again clasping hands after they return), and kiss each other and shake hands when the two next verses are sung.

The child who was first in the centre then joins the ring, and the game proceeds in the same way with the second child, who chooses in his turn. All the other versions follow the same rules, suiting their actions to the words, except Ogbourne, Wilts, in which the two children in the centre sing the verse, "roast beef and plum pudding." They stand face to face, take hold of each other's hands, and sway their arms from side to side. The ring then sing the concluding verse. In those versions where "say your prayers" and "kneel down" occur, the two centre children kneel, and hold their open hands together in front of them to imitate a book. In the London version (A. B. Gomme) a handkerchief was laid on the ground, and the two children stood on each side of it and clasped hands across it. In the Fernham and Longcot version the one child leads the other out of the ring at "go to church," with a graceful half-dancing motion, and back again in the same way. The first child joins the ring while the refrain is sung. In the Hanbury version the centre child pretends to be weeping; another child stands outside the ring and goes into it; when the two meet they kiss. In the North Derbyshire version (Mr. S. O. Addy) a ring is formed of young men and women, a young man being in the centre. He chooses a young woman at the singing of the fifth line, and then joins the ring, the girl remaining in the centre.

(c) The tunes of all versions are very similar. The tune of the Newbury game (Miss Kimber) is the same as the *first* part of the Ogbourne tune printed (Mr. H. S. May); that from Nottingham (Miss Youngman) is the same as the first part of the London version. This is also the case with the Hanbury, Staffs. (Miss E. Hollis) and Fernham and Longcot game. What difference there is is very slight. The Platt, Kent, game (Miss Burne), is sung to the same tune as "Green Gravel," given *ante*, p. 170. The *first* portion only of the tune is repeated for all verses sung after the first verse. The Barnes game is sung to the same tune as the Earls Heaton (Mr. Hardy), which is printed *ante*. A version played at Barnes is almost identical with the Southampton version, and another collected by Miss Thoyts in Berkshire (*Antiquary*, vol. xxvii. p. 193) is similar to the Hanbury version. The first lines run—Choose your lover; Open the gates; Go to church, love; Kneel down, love; Say your prayers, love; Put on the ring; Stand up, love; In the ring, love; Kiss together, love.

(d) The words of all the versions are sufficiently similar to analyse without a special form. The game appears to be purely a love and marriage game, and has probably had its origin in a ballad, and this idea is strengthened by the fact that only one version (London) has the marriage formula sung at the end, and this is probably an arbitrary addition. The lover is represented as lonely and disconsolate, and the remedy suggested is to choose a sweetheart. The marriage ceremony is of the simplest description—the clasping of hands and the kissing within the circle probably implying the betrothal at a spot sacred to such functions, similar to the Standing Stones of Stenness. Whatever may have been the original intention of these stones, they came in more recent times to be the resort of lovers, who joined their right hands through the hole in the altar stones in the belief that this ceremony would add additional solemnity to the betrothal. Miss Gordon Cumming, in her *Tour in the Hebrides*, mentions the fact of the marriage ceremony being of the simplest—a man and woman standing facing each other and clasping hands over a particular stone. Walking arm-in-arm is a sign in Dorsetshire that a couple are married. The mention of the "roast beef and plum pudding" for dinner has probably had its origin in the wedding dinner or breakfast, and the inviting of friends to assemble for the wedding dinner. The word "Isabella" may have been originally something quite different from the name of a girl. I am inclined to think the word was not the name of a person at all; possibly it was something addressed to a particular person in words the sense of which are now lost, and the nearest idea to it was this name. The same thing may also apply to the word "farewell," and hence the incongruity of the first few lines in nearly all versions.

Jack's Alive.

A number of people sit in a row, or on chairs round a

parlour. A lighted wooden spill or taper is handed to the first, who says—

> Jack's alive, and likely to live;
> If he dies in your hand you've a forfeit to give.

The one in whose hand the light expires has to pay a forfeit. As the spill is getting burnt out the lines are said very quickly, as everybody is anxious not to have to pay the forfeit.—Addy's *Sheffield Glossary*.

At Egan, in Derbyshire, a number of persons sit round a fire; one of them lights a stick, twirls it round, and says—

> Little Nanny Cockerthaw,
> What if I should let her fa'?

The others reply—

> Nine sticks and nine stones
> Shall be laid on thy bare back bones
> If thou shouldst let fa'
> Little Nanny Cockerthaw.

If the ember or lighted stick goes out whilst any one is twirling it round, and whilst the lines are being said, he has to lie on the floor, when stones, chairs, or other articles of furniture are piled upon him.—S. O. Addy.

Mactaggart calls it " Preest Cat," and says that it is an ingleside game. A piece of stick is made red in the fire; one hands it to another, saying—

> About wi' that, about wi' that,
> Keep alive the preest cat.

Then round is handed the stick, and whomsoever's hand it goes out in, that one is in a wad, and must kiss the crook, the cleps, and what not, ere he gets out of it.

> Lilly cuckoo, lilly cuckoo,
> Sticks and stanes lie at thy weary banes
> If thou fa', for a' I blaw,
> Lilly cuckoo, lilly cuckoo.

This rhyme is common in the " Preest Cat" sport toward the border. Anciently, when the priest's cat departed this life, wailing began in the country side, as it was thought it became some supernatural being—a witch, perhaps, of hideous form—

so to keep it alive was a great matter.—Mactaggart's *Gallo-vidian Encyclopædia.*

He also refers to a game called "Robin-a-Ree," much like "Preest Cat," only in passing the burnt stick round the ring the following rhyme is said—

> Robin-a-Ree, ye'll no dee wi' me,
> Tho' I birl ye roun' three times and three;
> O Robin-a-Ree, O Robin-a-Ree,
> O dinna let Robin-a-Reerie dee.

Robin-a-Ree occurs in an old song.—Mactaggart's *Gallovidian Encyclopædia.*

In Cornwall it is known as "Robin's a-light," and is played around the fire. A piece of stick is set on fire and whirled around rapidly in the hand of the first player, who says, "Robin's a-light, and if he go out I will saddle your back." It is then passed to the next, who says the same thing, and so on. The person who lets the spark die out has to pay a forfeit.—Scilly (Courtney's *West Cornwall Glossary*). A rhyme at Lostwithiel is known as follows—

> Jack's alive, and likely to live;
> If he die in my hand a pawn (forfeit) I'll give.
>
> —(J. W.)

Jamieson (*Dictionary*) says, "To do 'Dingle-dousie,' a stick is ignited at one end and given as a plaything to a child." Elworthy (*West Somerset Words*) does not give this as a game, but says a burning stick was whirled round and round very quickly, so as to keep up the appearance of a ribbon of fire. Miss Burne (*Shropshire Folk-lore*, p. 530), says, "Children wave a burning stick in the air, saying—

> A girdle o' gold, a saddle o' silk,
> A horse for me as white as milk,

an evident relic of divinations or incantations practised with bonfires." Halliwell (*Nursery Rhymes*, p. 213) gives the rhyme as— Jack's alive, and in very good health,

> If he dies in your hand you must look to yourself;

the game being played in the same way as the Sheffield version (see also Halliwell's *Dictionary* and Moor's *Suffolk Words*).

(*b*) This is a very significant game, and its similarity in miniature to the old tribal custom of carrying the fiery cross to rouse the clans at once suggests the possible origin of it. The detention of the fiery cross through neglect or other impediment was regarded with much dread by the inhabitants of the place in which it should occur. This subject is discussed in Gomme's *Primitive Folkmoots*, p. 279 *et seq.*

Jack, Jack, the Bread's a-burning

> Jack, Jack, the bread's a-burning,
> All to a cinder;
> If you don't come and fetch it out
> We'll throw it through the winder.

These lines are chanted by players that stand thus. One places his back against a wall, tree, &c., grasping another, whose back is toward him, round the waist; the second grasps a third, and so on. The player called Jack walks apart until the conclusion of the lines. Then he goes to the others and pokes at or pats them, saying, " I don't think you're done yet," and walks away again. The chant is repeated, and when he is satisfied that the bread is "done" he endeavours to pull the foremost from the grasp of the others, &c.—Warwickshire (Northall's *Folk Rhymes*, p. 390).

See " Mother Mop."

Jack upon the Mopstick

See " Bung the Bucket."

Jackysteauns

A game among school-girls, played with small pebbles, and sometimes with plum or cherry stones (Dickinson's *Cumberland Glossary*). "A children's game, played with five white pebbles called Jackstones," says Mr. Patterson (*Antrim and Down Glossary*). The game is called " Jack."

See " Fivestones," " Hucklebones."

Jauping Paste-eggs

A youthful amusement in Newcastle and the neighbourhood at Easter. One boy, holding an egg in his hand, challenges another to give blow for blow. One of the eggs is sure to be fractured in the conflict, and its shattered remains become the spoil of the conqueror.

See "Conkers."

Jenny Jones

—Platt, near Wrotham, Kent (Miss Burne).

—Northants (Rev. W. D. Sweeting).

—Belfast (W. H. Patterson).

I. I'm come to court Janet jo,
    Janet jo, Janet jo,
    I'm come to court Janet jo,
    How's she the day ?

    She's up the stair washin',
    Washin', washin',
    She's up the stair washin',
    Ye canna see her the day.

[Then follow verses, the words of which are not given by Chambers, representing Jenny as bleaching, drying, and ironing clothes. At last they say—]

Janet jo's dead and gane,
Dead and gane, dead and gane;
Janet jo's dead and gane,
She'll never come hame!
—Chambers' *Popular Rhymes*, pp. 140-41.

II.   I'm come to court Janet jo, Janet jo, Janet jo,
Come to court Janet jo,
     How is she the day?

She's butt the house washing, washing, washing
She's butt the house washing,
     You can't see her to-day.

Fare ye well, ladies, ladies, ladies,
Fare ye well, ladies,
     For I must away.
       —West Scotland (*Folk-lore Record*, iv. 474).

III.   We've come to court Jinny jo,
    Jinny jo, Jinny jo,
    We've come to court Jinny jo,
    Is she within?

    Jinny jo's washing clothes,
    Washing clothes, washing clothes,
    Jinny jo's washing clothes,
    You can't see her to-day.

    So fare ye well, ladies,
    O ladies, O ladies,
    So fare ye well, ladies
    And gentlemen too.

[These verses are repeated for—

        (1) drying clothes,
        (2) starching,
        (3) ironing,
        (4) ill,
        (5) dying.

Then—]   Jinny jo's lying dead,
Lying dead, lying dead,
Jinny jo's lying dead,
You can't see her to-day.

So turn again, ladies,
Ladies, ladies, ladies,
So turn again, ladies,
And gentlemen too.

What shall we dress her in?
Dress her in, dress her in?
What shall we dress her in?
Shall it be red?

Red's for the soldiers,
The soldiers, the soldiers,
Red's for the soldiers,
And that will not do.

[Various other colours are suggested in the same way, but are found unsuitable—black because " black's for the mourners," green because " green's for the croppies," and so on till at last white is named.]

White's for the dead people,
Dead people, the dead people,
White's for the dead people,
And that will just do.

                      —Belfast (*Notes and Queries*, 7th series,
                              xii. 492, W. H. Patterson).

IV.   I came to see Jenny jo, Jenny jo, Jenny jo,
I came to see Jenny jo, is she within?

Jenny jo's washing clothes, washing clothes, washing clothes,
Jenny jo's washing clothes, and ye can't see her to-day.

Oh but I'm sorry, I'm sorry, I'm sorry,
Oh but I'm sorry, I can't see her to-day.

Farewell ladies, O ladies, O ladies,
Farewell ladies, and gentlemen too.

[Then the same verses are repeated for—
            (1) starching clothes,
            (2) smoothing clothes,
            (3) dead,
the four lines above being repeated after each, and the verses
proceed with—]

What shall we dress her in, dress her in, dress her in?
What shall we dress her in?   Shall it be black?

Black for the sweeps, the sweeps, the sweeps,
Black for the sweeps, and that shall not do.

What shall we dress her in, dress her in, dress her in?
What shall we dress her in?   Shall it be blue?

Blue for the sailors, sailors, sailors,
Blue for the sailors, and that shall not do.

What shall we dress her in, dress her in, dress her in?
What shall we dress her in?   Shall it be red?

Red for the soldiers, soldiers, soldiers,
Red for the soldiers, and that shall not do.

What shall we dress her in, dress her in, dress her in?
What shall we dress her in?   Shall it be orange?

Orange for the Orange-men, Orange-men, Orange-men,
Orange for the Orange-men, and that shall not do.

What shall we dress her in, dress her in, dress her in?
What shall we dress her in?   Shall it be white?

White for the corpse, the corpse, the corpse,
White for the corpse, and that will just do.

We have lost a soldier, soldier, soldier,
We have lost a soldier, and the Queen has lost a man.
We will bury him in the bed of glory, glory, glory,
We will bury him in the bed of glory, and we'll never
     see him any more.
            —Holywood, co. Down (Miss C. N. Patterson).

V. I've come to see Jenny jo, Jenny jo, Jenny jo,
      I've come to see Jenny jo,
        How is she now ?

Jenny jo is washing clothes, washing clothes, washing
      clothes,
      Jenny jo is washing clothes,
        You can't see her now.

I've come to see Jenny jo, Jenny jo, Jenny jo,
      I've come to see Jenny jo,
        How is she now ?

Jenny jo is ironing clothes, ironing clothes, ironing clothes,
      Jenny jo is ironing clothes,
        You can't see her now.

I've come to see Jenny jo, Jenny jo, Jenny jo,
      I've come to see Jenny jo,
        How is she now ?

Jenny jo is sick, my dear, sick, my dear, sick, my dear,
      Jenny jo is sick, my dear,
        You can't see her now.

I've come to see Jenny jo, Jenny jo, Jenny jo,
      I've come to see Jenny jo,
        How is she now ?

Jenny jo is underboard, underboard, underboard,
      Jenny jo is underboard,
        You can't see her now.

          —Lismore (Miss F. Keane, collected from Miss
               Ward, National Schoolmistress).

VI. We've come to see Jenny Jones,
     Jenny Jones, Jenny Jones,
     We've come to see Jenny Jones,
     And how is she now ?

       O Jenny is washing,
       O washing, O washing,
       O Jenny is washing,
       And you can't see her now.

Very well, ladies, ladies, ladies,
Very well, ladies, and gentlemen too.

We've come to see Jenny Jones,
Jenny Jones, Jenny Jones,
We've come to see Jenny Jones,
And how is she now?

O Jenny is starching,
O starching, O starching,
O Jenny is starching,
And you can't see her now.

Very well, ladies, ladies, ladies,
Very well, ladies, and gentlemen too.

We've come to see Jenny Jones,
Jenny Jones, Jenny Jones,
We've come to see Jenny Jones,
And how is she now?

O Jenny is ironing,
O ironing, O ironing,
O Jenny is ironing,
And you can't see her now.

Very well, ladies, ladies, ladies,
Very well, ladies, and gentlemen too.

We've come to see Jenny Jones,
Jenny Jones, Jenny Jones,
We've come to see Jenny Jones,
And how is she now?

O Jenny is ill,
O ill, O ill,
O Jenny is ill,
And you can't see her now.

Very well, ladies, ladies, ladies,
Very well, ladies, and gentlemen too.

We've come to see Jenny Jones,
Jenny Jones, Jenny Jones,
We've come to see Jenny Jones,
And how is she now?

O Jenny is dying,
O dying, O dying,
O Jenny is dying,
And you can't see her now.

Very well, ladies, ladies, ladies,
Very well, ladies, and gentlemen too.

We've come to see Jenny Jones,
Jenny Jones, Jenny Jones,
We've come to see Jenny Jones,
And how is she now?

O Jenny is dead,
Is dead, is dead,
O Jenny is dead,
And you can't see her now.

Very well, ladies, ladies, ladies,
Very well, ladies, and gentlemen too.

What shall we lay her in, lay her in, lay her in?
What shall we lay her in?   Shall it be red?

Red is for soldiers, soldiers, soldiers,
Red is for soldiers, and that won't do.

Very well, ladies, ladies, ladies,
Very well, ladies, and gentlemen too.

What shall we lay her in, lay her in, lay her in?
What shall we lay her in?   Shall it be blue?

Blue is for sailors, sailors, sailors,
Blue is for sailors, and that won't do.

Very well, ladies, ladies, ladies,
Very well, ladies, and gentlemen too.

What shall we lay her in, lay her in, lay her in ?
What shall we lay her in ?   Shall it be black ?

Black is for mourners, mourners, mourners,
Black is for mourners, and that won't do.

Very well, ladies, ladies, ladies,
Very well, ladies, and gentlemen too.

What shall we lay her in, lay her in, lay her in ?
What shall we lay her in ?   Shall it be white ?

White's what the dead wear, dead wear, dead wear,
White's what the dead wear, and that will just do.
                    —Hanwell, Middlesex, 1878 (A. B. Gomme).

VII. We've come to see poor Jenny Jones, poor Jenny Jones,
         poor Jenny Jones,
      We've come to see poor Jenny Jones, how is she to-day ?

Poor Jenny is washing, washing, washing,
Poor Jenny is washing, washing hard to-day.

What time can we see her ?
At one o'clock.   (Clock strikes one.)

We've come to see poor Jenny Jones, poor Jenny Jones,
     poor Jenny Jones,
We've come to see poor Jenny Jones, how is she to-day ?

Poor Jenny is starching, starching, starching,
Poor Jenny is starching, you can't see her to-day.

When can we see her ?
At two o'clock.   (Clock strikes two.)

We've come to see poor Jenny Jones, poor Jenny Jones,
     poor Jenny Jones,
We've come to see poor Jenny Jones, how is she to-day ?

Poor Jenny is folding, folding, folding,
Poor Jenny is folding, you can't see her to-day.

When can we see her ?
At three o'clock.   (Clock strikes three.)

We've come to see poor Jenny Jones, poor Jenny Jones,
    poor Jenny Jones,
We've come to see poor Jenny Jones, how is she to-day?

Poor Jenny is ironing, ironing, ironing,
Poor Jenny is ironing, you can't see her to-day.

When can we see her?
At four o'clock.   (Clock strikes four.)

We've come to see poor Jenny Jones, poor Jenny Jones,
    poor Jenny Jones,
We've come to see poor Jenny Jones, how is she to-day?

Poor Jenny is poorly, poorly, poorly,
Poor Jenny is poorly, you can't see her to-day.

When can we see her?
At five o'clock.   (Clock strikes five.)

We've come to see poor Jenny Jones, poor Jenny Jones,
    poor Jenny Jones,
We've come to see poor Jenny Jones, how is she to-day?

Poor Jenny is dying, dying, dying,
Poor Jenny is dying, you can't see her to-day.

When shall we see her?
(Come) at six o'clock.   (Clock strikes six.)

We've come to see poor Jenny Jones, poor Jenny Jones,
    poor Jenny Jones,
We've come to see poor Jenny Jones, how is she to-day?

Poor Jenny is dead, dead, dead,
Poor Jenny is dead, you can't see her to-day.

What colour will you have for the funeral for poor
    Jenny Jones?

Red?

Red is for the soldiers, soldiers, soldiers,
Red is for the soldiers, and that won't do.

Blue?

Blue is for the sailors, sailors, sailors,
Blue is for the sailors, and that won't do.

Pink ?

Pink is for the babies, babies, babies,
Pink is for the babies, and that won't do.

White ?

White is for a wedding, a wedding, a wedding,
White is for a wedding, and that won't do.

Black ?

Black is for the mourners, mourners, mourners,
Black is for the mourners, and that will do.

Poor Jenny Jones is dead, dead, dead,
Poor Jenny Jones is dead, and lies in her grave.
—Southampton (from nursemaid of Mrs. W. R. Carse).

VIII. We've come to see Jenny Jones, Jenny Jones, Jenny
Jones,
We've come to see Jenny Jones, is she at home ?

Jenny Jones is scrubbing, scrubbing, scrubbing,
Jenny Jones is scrubbing, you can't see her now.

[Then follow verses asking alternately " Is she at home ? "
in the same words as the first verse, and answering that she is
(1) washing,
(2) ill,
(3) dying,
(4) dead ;
all of them in the same form as the second verse.   Then the
verses continue with—]

Jenny Jones is dead, she is dead, she is dead,
Jenny Jones is dead, you can't see her now.

We'll come to the funeral, funeral, funeral,
We'll come to the funeral, and how shall we dress ?

You can come in yellow, in yellow, in yellow,
You can come in yellow, that's how you can dress.

Yellow's for jealousy, jealousy, jealousy,
Yellow's for jealousy, so *that* won't do.

You can come in green, in green, in green,
You can come in green, that's how you can dress.

Green's forsaken, forsaken, forsaken,
Green's forsaken, so *that* won't do.

You can come in white, in white, in white,
You can come in white, that's how you can dress.

White's for weddings, weddings, weddings,
White's for weddings, so that won't do.

You can come in black, in black, in black,
You can come in black, that's how you can dress.

Black is for funerals, funerals, funerals,
Black is for funerals, so black will do.
          —Colchester (from Miss G. M. Frances, Colchester,
                    through Miss Morris).

IX.   We've come to see Jenny Jones, Jenny Jones,
      We've come to see Jenny Jones.   How is she now?

Jenny is washing, washing, washing,
Jenny is washing, you can't see her now.

[Then follow the alternate question and answer; the questions in the same words as the first verse, and the answers in the same form as the second verse, stating that Jenny is

                    (1) folding,
                    (2) starching,
                    (3) ironing,
                    (4) ill,
                    (5) dying,
                    (6) dead;
then the verses proceed with—]

May we come to the funeral?
Yes.

May we come in red?
Red is for soldiers, you can't come in red.

May we come in blue?
Blue is for sailors, you can't come in blue.

May we come in white?
White is for weddings, you can't come in white.

May we come in black?
Black is for funerals, so you can come in that.
                    —Bocking, Essex (*Folk-lore Record*, iii. 471).

X.   I come to see poor Jenny Joe,
      Jenny Joe, Jenny Joe,
      I come to see poor Jenny Joe,
      And how is she now?

      She's washing, she's washing,
      And you can't see her now.

      Very well, ladies, ladies, ladies,
      Very well, ladies, and gentlemen too.

      I come to see poor Jenny Joe,
      Jenny Joe, Jenny Joe,
      I come to see poor Jenny Joe,
      And how is she now?

      She's folding, she's folding,
      And you can't see her now.

      Very well, ladies, ladies, ladies,
      Very well, ladies, and gentlemen too.

      I come to see poor Jenny Joe,
      Jenny Joe, Jenny Joe,
      I come to see poor Jenny Joe,
      And how is she now?

      She's ironing, she's ironing,
      And you can't see her now.

      Very well, ladies, ladies, ladies,
      Very well, ladies, and gentlemen too.

[Then follow alternate questions and answers in the same
manner for—   (1) dying,
                             (2) dead.

Then—]

> I come in my white dress, white dress, white dress,
> I come in my white dress, and how will that do?

> White is for wedding, wedding, wedding,
> White is for wedding, and that won't do.

> Very well, ladies, ladies, ladies,
> Very well, ladies, and gentlemen too.

> I come in my blue dress, blue dress, blue dress,
> I come in my blue dress, and how will that do?

> Blue is for sailors, sailors, sailors,
> Blue is for sailors, and that won't do.

[Then follow verses as before, beginning—

> Very well, ladies.
> I come in my red dress.
> Red is for soldiers,
> Very well, ladies.

Then—]

> I come in my black dress, black dress, black dress,
> I come in my black dress, and how will that do?

> Black is for funeral,
> And that will do
> To carry poor Jenny to the grave.
>   —Sporle, Norfolk (Miss Matthews).

XI. We're come to see Jenny Jones, Jenny Jones, Jenny
        Jones,
     Come to see Jenny Jones, how is she now?

> Jenny is a-washing, a-washing, a-washing,
> Jenny is a-washing, you can't see her now.

> Very well, ladies, very well, ladies,
> Very well, ladies, we can't see her now.

[Then follow the same verses for—
                (1) ironing,
                (2) badly,
                (3) dead;

And the singing proceeds with—]
>   Please, will white do, white do, white do ?
>   Please, will white do, please, will it do ?
>
>   White's for the weddingers, the weddingers,
>   White's for the weddingers, that won't do.
>
>   Please, will blue do, blue do, blue do ?
>   Please, will blue do, please will it do ?

[Then follow verses as before, beginning—
>   Blue's for the sailors, the sailors, the sailors.
>   Please, will red do, red do ?
>   Red's for the soldiers.

Then—]
>   Please, will black do, black do, black do ?
>   Black's for the funeral, black will do.
>   —Northamptonshire (Rev. W. D. Sweeting).

XII.   I've come to see how Jenny Jones is to-day.
>   You can't see her, she's washing.
>   I've come to see how Jenny Jones is to-day.
>   You can't see her, she's ironing [she's starching, she's
>   brewing, she's baking, *successively*].
>   I've come to see how Jenny Jones is to-day.
>   You can't see her, she's ill [then she's worse].
>   I've come to see how Jenny Jones is to-day.
>   You can't see her, she's dead !

Chorus. There's red for the soldiers,
>   Blue for the sailors,
>   White for the angels [for the *baby*, Chirbury],
>   And black for the mourners [of poor Jenny Jones].
>   —Berrington, Chirbury (*Shropshire Folk-lore*, p. 577).

XIII.   We've come to see poor Jenny Jones.
>   Poor Jenny Jones is washing, you can't see her.
>   We've come to see poor Jenny Jones.
>   Poor Jenny Jones is drying, you can't see her.
>   We've come to see poor Jenny Jones.
>   Poor Jenny Jones is starching, you can't see her.

We've come to see poor Jenny Jones.
Poor Jenny Jones is ironing, you can't see her.
We've come to see poor Jenny Jones.
Poor Jenny Jones is dead, you can't see her.
What shall we follow, in red, blue, or black ?
Red's for the soldier, blue for the sailor,
Black for the dead.

—Enborne School, Berks (Miss M. Kimber).

XIV.   Come to see Miss Jenny Jones,
Miss Jenny Jones, Miss Jenny Jones ;
Come to see Miss Jenny Jones,
And how is she to-day ?

Miss Jenny Jones is washing, washing, washing,
Miss Jenny Jones is washing,
You can't see her to-day.

Farewell, ladies, ladies, ladies, and gentlemen too.

[Miss Jenny Jones is drying, starching, ironing, ill, worse,
dying, and dead in turn.   Then—]

What shall we dress her in,
Dress her in, dress her in ?
What shall we dress her in,
Dress her in red?

Red's what the soldiers wear,
The soldiers wear, the soldiers wear,
Red's what the soldiers wear,
And that won't do.

What shall we dress her in,
Dress her in, dress her in ?
What shall we dress her in,
Dress her in blue ?

Blue's what the sailors wear,
Sailors wear, sailors wear ;
Blue's what the sailors wear,
And that won't do.

What shall we dress her in,
Dress her in, dress her in?
What shall we dress her in,
Dress her in black?

Black's what the mourners wear,
The mourners wear, the mourners wear;
Black's what the mourners wear,
And that won't do.

What shall we dress her in,
Dress her in, dress her in?
What shall we dress her in,
Dress her in white?

White's what the dead wear,
The dead wear, the dead wear;
White's what the dead wear,
And that will do.   —Liphook, Hants (Miss Fowler).

XV.   Come to see Jinny Jones, Jinny Jones,
    Come to see Jinny Jones,
        And where is she now?

Jinny is washing, is washing,
Jinny is washing,
    And you can't see her now.

Very well, very well, lady, lady,
Very well, lady,
    That will do.

[Then follow—   (1) starching,
        (2) ironing,
        (3) dying,
        (4) dead.]

What shall we follow in, follow in?
What shall we follow in?
    We'll follow in blue.

Blue is for sailors, for sailors,
Blue is for sailors,
And that won't do.
[*or*, You can't follow her so.]

[Then follow—Red is for soldiers,
White is for weddings,
Yellow is for babies.]

Black is not deep enough, deep enough,
That won't do.

What shall we follow in, follow in ?

We'll follow her in crape, crape [pronounced
cray-ape].

You may follow her in crape, crape,
You may follow her in crape,
That will do.   —Deptford (Miss E. Chase).

XVI. I've come to see Georgina, Georgina, Georgina,
I've come to see Georgina, how's she to-day ?

She's upstairs washing, washing, washing,
She's upstairs washing, and can't get away.

O very well, ladies, ladies, ladies,
We'll come another day.

We've come to see Georgina, Georgina, Georgina,
We've come to see Georgina, how's she to-day ?

She's upstairs ironing, ironing, ironing,
She's upstairs ironing, and can't get away.

[Then the two verses are repeated—
O very well, ladies.
We've come to see Georgina.
Then follows—]

She was coming downstairs with a basin of water, and
she fell down and broke her toe, and she's dead.

And what shall we dress her in, dress her in, dress
her in ?
And what shall we dress her in ?   Dress her in red.

Red for the soldiers, soldiers, soldiers,
Red for the soldiers, and that shan't do.

[Then follow blue for the sailors, black for the mourners, and finally—]

What shall we dress her in, dress her in, dress her in ?
What shall we dress her in ?   Dress her in white.

White for the dead people, dead people, dead people,
White for the dead people, and that will do.
                    —Auchencairn, Kirkcudbright (A. C. Haddon).

XVII.   How's poor Jenny jo, Jenny jo, Jenny jo ?
        He's very ill.
        Oh, very good, very good, very good.
        How's poor Jenny jo, Jenny jo, Jenny jo ?
        He's fallen downstairs and broken his neck.
        Oh, very good, very good, very good.
        How's poor Jenny jo, Jenny jo, Jenny jo ?
        He's dead.
        Oh, very good, very good, very good.
                    —Annaverna, Louth, Ireland (Miss R. Stephen).

(b) Two children stand apart; one, who personates the Mother, stands still and holds out her skirts with both hands; the other personates Jenny Jones, and kneels or stoops down in a crouching position behind her companion's outstretched skirts.   The other players form a line by joining hands.   They sing the first, third, and every alternate verse, advancing and retiring in line while doing so.   The Mother sings the answers to their questions, standing still and hiding Jenny Jones all the time from view.   When the verses are finished, Jenny Jones lies down as if she were dead, and the Mother stands aside. Two of the other players then take up Jenny Jones, one by the shoulders and the other by the feet, and carry her a little distance off, where they lay her on the ground.   All the players follow, generally two by two, with their handkerchiefs at their eyes and heads lowered, pretending to grieve.

This is the more general way of playing the game.   In those versions where the reply, " Very well, ladies," occurs, this is sung by the line of children just before they sing, "We've come to see Jenny Jones." Sometimes, as in the Berrington and Chirbury game, two lines of children facing each other advance and retire, singing the verses. They then carry Jenny Jones to a corner, lay her down, stand in a circle round, and sing to her the last verse. In the Hants versions sent by Miss Mendham, six or eight children carry Jenny stretched out and flat, lay her down, cover her over, and then sing the last lines. The rest of the children follow them. In the Irish (Belfast) version the game is played in the same way; the funeral is arranged, when Jenny suddenly comes to life again (W. H. Patterson). In the Southampton version, after the carrying of Jenny by her head and feet to the grave, and the other children following and standing round, Jenny Jones rises up and pursues the children. She is called the Ghost. The children run away in affected terror, calling out, "The Ghost!" Whoever she catches becomes Jenny Jones in the next game. This incident is also played in the Barnes, Northants, Annaverna, co. Louth, Enborne and Liphook versions.

(c) This game is played very generally throughout the country, and I have other versions collected from Earls Heaton (Mr. H. Hardy), Barnes (A. B. Gomme), Cambridge (Mrs. Haddon), Hampshire (Miss Mendham), Frodingham (Miss Peacock), Cowes, Isle of Wight (Miss E. Smith), Sulhampstead, Berks (Miss Thoyts), and Platt, Kent (Miss Burne). These versions are so similar to the Hanwell version, with the exception of the "Very well, ladies," that it is needless to print them in full; special differences are noted hereafter. In some places the game is said in a sing-song manner.

Some of the versions differ from the general type in two ways—first, in the method of playing; secondly, in the wording of the verses. The differences in the method of playing direct attention to the connection of the game with ancient custom. The game is always played by the players taking sides; but one method is for one side to consist of only two children (Mother and Jenny Jones), and the other side to consist of all the other players; while the other method is for the players to be divided into two sides of about equal numbers, each side advancing and retiring in line when singing their part. Jenny Jones in some cases walks with the girls in her line until the funeral, when she is carried to the grave, and in others she stands alone behind the line. The way of performing the funeral also differs. Generally two of the players carry Jenny to the grave, the rest following two by two; but in one Hampshire version six or eight children carry Jenny, stretched out and flat, to the grave, and cover her over; in Holywood, co. Down, she is carried sitting on the crossed hands of two players; while in some versions no funeral is apparently performed, the words only being sung. Another significant incident is the Ghost. An additional incident occurs in the Liphook version, which represents her being "swung to life again" by two of the players.

These differences may perhaps be immaterial to the meaning and origin of the game, but they are sufficiently indicative of early custom to suggest the divergence of the game in modern times towards modern custom. Thus the players divided line-by-line follow the general form for children playing singing games, and it would therefore suggest itself as the earlier form for this game. The change of the game from the line-by-line action to the mother-and-line action would indicate a corresponding change in the prevailing custom which influenced the game. This custom was the wooing by a band of suitors of girls surrounded by their fellow-villagers, which became obsolete in favour of ordinary marriage custom. The dropping out of this custom would cause the game to change from a representation of both wooing and burial to one of burial only. As burial only the mother-and-line action is sufficient, but the presence of a wooing incident in the earlier form of the game is plainly revealed by the verse which sings, "Fare ye well, ladies," or, as it has become in the English variant, "Very well, ladies."

The difference in the wording of the versions is slight, and does not need formal analysis. Domestic occupation is shown throughout, washing and its attendants, drying, folding, starching and ironing being by far the most numerous, brewing, and baking only occurring in one. Illness, dying, and death are the usual forms for the later verses, but illness and dying are lost in several versions. The choosing of colours is in some versions not for the mourners but for the dead maiden, and in these cases (six) white is the colour chosen, for "white's what the dead wear."

This question of colours for the dead is a very important one. The dressing of the dead body of a maiden in white by her girl companions, and the carrying of the body by them to the grave, are known village customs, the whole village being invited to the funeral. The rising of the dead lover, and the belief that excessive mourning over a loved one disturbs his or her rest in the grave, thus causing the dead to rise and speak, are shown in old ballads; the belief that spirits of the dead haunt churchyards and places of their former abode may also be adduced in illustration of the ghost incident.

(d) The methods of playing, and the incidents revealed by the verses sung, show that this is perhaps the most realistic of all the singing games, the daily occupation, the illness, death, and burial being portrayed, first, in the words of the rhymes, and secondly, by the accompanying action. The Scottish versions make the opening incident that of a lover coming to the house of the loved one, then proceed to the domestic occupation, and finally to the death incident; while the English versions give the idea of village friends calling upon a favourite companion, and subsequently attending her funeral. That the former is the older of the two versions is confirmed by the great probability of the name "Jenny Jones" being a degraded form of "Janet jo." There is some evidence for this. The Sporle version gives it as "Jenny Joe," which is clearly a misunderstood rendering of "Jenny jo." The corruption of this into "Jenny Jones" is exactly what might be expected from modern English ignorance of the pretty meaning of the word jo, "dear;" and to what lengths this corruption may proceed under such influences may be seen by versions from Earls Heaton, where we have "Jingy Jog;" Leeds, where we get "Jilly Jog;" and the Edinburgh version, where we have "Georgina."

This would be an argument for the Scottish home of the

rhymes, and for the direct borrowing of the name from Scotland by the English villagers. In furtherance of this view the following passage from Chambers may be quoted :—

In the Stewartry of Kirkcudbright, "Janet Jo" is a dramatic entertainment amongst young rustics. Suppose a party has met in a harvest or winter evening round a good peat fire, and it is resolved to have "Janet Jo" performed. Two undertake to personate a goodman and a goodwife; the rest a family of marriageable daughters. One of the lads, the best singer of the party, retires, and equips himself in a dress proper for representing an old bachelor in search of a wife. He comes in, bonnet in hand, bowing, and sings—

> Guid e'en to ye, maidens a',
> Maidens a', maidens a',
> Guid e'en to ye, maidens a',
> Be ye or no.

> I'm come to court Janet jo,
> Janet jo, Janet jo,
> I'm come to court Janet jo,
> Janet, my jo.

Goodwife sings—What'll ye gie for Janet jo,
> Janet jo, Janet jo?
> What'll ye gie for Janet jo,
> Janet, my jo?

Wooer—I'll gie ye a peck o' siller,
> A peck o' siller, peck o' siller,
> I'll gie ye a peck o' siller,
> For Janet, my jo.

Goodwife says—Gae awa', ye auld carle!

Then sings—Ye'se never get Janet jo,
> Janet jo, Janet jo,
> Ye'se never get Janet jo,
> Janet, my jo.

The wooer hereupon retires, singing a verse expressive of mortification, but soon re-enters with a reassured air, singing—

I'll gie ye a peck o' gowd,
A peck o' gowd, a peck o' gowd,
I'll gie ye a peck o' gowd,
For Janet, my jo.

The matron gives him a rebuff as before, and he again retires discomfited, and again enters, singing an offer of " twa pecks o' gowd," which, however, is also refused. At his next entry he offers " three pecks o' gowd," at which the good wife brightens up and sings—

Come ben beside Janet jo,
Janet jo, Janet jo,
Ye're welcome to Janet jo,
Janet, my jo.

The suitor then advances gaily to his sweetheart, and the affair ends in a scramble for kisses.—*Popular Rhymes*, pp. 141, 142.

On the other hand, it must not be overlooked that this game-drama and the game of " Janet Jo " have no connection beyond the name of the heroine and the wooing incident; so that the borrowing, if borrowing there be, might have been by Scotland, who improved the commonplace " Jenny Jones " into the pretty sweetness of her Scottish namesake. The Scottish version of the game leaves out the question of the colours for mourning, but, on the other hand, it contains the very important incident of the restoration of the dead. Chambers (*Popular Rhymes*, p. 141) suggests that this incident was introduced for the purpose of beginning the game again, but this seems extremely doubtful, in consideration of the Liphook variant, in which Miss Fowler says, " It is no uncommon thing for 'Jenny Jones' to be swung into life again;" and the still more significant Southampton version, where "'Jenny Jones' appears in the character of the Ghost, and scatters and pursues the surrounding mourners." This detail is also used by the Northants and Barnes children, the version of whose game is very like the Southampton one. On the whole, the analysis would suggest that there has been a game played by the children of both England and Scotland, the leading incidents of which have been varied in accordance with the conditions of life. Mr. Napier (*Folk-lore Record*, iv. 474), in his description of the West Scotland example, evidently considered the game to be thoroughly representative of Scottish life, and this, indeed, seems to be the most striking feature of the game in all the variants. The domestic economy which they reveal is in no case out of keeping with the known facts of everyday peasant life, and many a mother has denied to her child's friends the companionship they desired because of the work to be done.

In most cases the burden of the song rests upon the question of health, but in two cases, namely, Colchester and Deptford, the question is put as to where " Jenny Jones" is at the time of the visit. It is curious that the refrain of "Farewell, ladies," should appear in such widely separated districts as Scotland, Northamptonshire, Norfolk, Middlesex, Hants, Lincoln, and Barnes.

With reference to the colours for mourning, there is an obvious addition of crape introduced into the Deptford version which is very suggestive of the decadence going on. The four colours used in most versions are red, blue, white, and black, colours which have been known to the people from ancient times. Black is accepted as the correct colour in all versions except five, where white is declared to be the colour which the dead wear. The method of question and answer is adopted for all the rhyme-movements. The tune of the game, with but slight variation, in all the versions is the same as that given from Platt, near Wrotham, except the two which are printed from Northants and Belfast.

Jenny Mac

> Jenny Mac, Jenny Mac, Jenny Macghie,
> Turn your back about to me ;
> And if you find an ill baubee,
> Lift it up and gie't to me.

Two girls cross their arms behind their backs, and .thus taking hold of each other's hands, parade along together, by daylight or moonlight, occasionally turning upon their arms, as indicated in the rhyme. Another rhyme for this amusement is—

> A basket, a basket, a bonny penny basket,
> A penny to you, and a penny to me,
> Turn about the basket.
>
> —Chambers's *Popular Rhymes*, p. 123.

See " Basket."

Jib-Job-Jeremiah

An undescribed Suffolk game.—Moor's *Suffolk Words*, p. 238.

Jiddy-cum-jiddy

A northern name for " See Saw."

Jingle-the-bonnet

A game in which two or more put a halfpenny each, or any piece of coin, into a cap or bonnet. After jingling or shaking them together, they are thrown on the ground; and he who has most heads when it is his turn to jingle, gains the stakes which were put into the bonnet.—Jamieson.

Halliwell (*Dictionary*) says this is a northern name for the game of " Shake Cap," and Brockett (*North Country Words*) speaks of it as a game much practised among the young pitmen and keelmen.

Jingo-ring

> Here we go by jingo-ring, jingo-ring, jingo-ring,
> Here we go by jingo-ring, and round by merry-ma-tansy.
>
> —Sporle, Norfolk (Miss Matthews).

Sung to the " Mulberry or " Ivy bush " tune.

The children form a ring and dance round singing. At the last word they all fall down.

See " Merry-ma-tansa.

Jinkie

A game among children, in which they run round a table trying to catch one whose business is by quick turns to elude them.—Jamieson.

Jock and Jock's Man

A juvenile sport in which the *bon camarada* is to repeat all the pranks which the leader can perform.—Brockett's *North Country Words*.

See "Follow my Gable," "Follow my Leader."

Jockie Blind-man

Scotch name for "Blind Man's Buff."—Jamieson.

See "Blind Man's Buff."

Joggle along

I.   Come all you young men
      In your youthful ways,
   And sow your wild oats
      In your youthful days.
   Then you'll be happy,
   Then you'll be happy,
      As you grow old.
   For the day's far spent,
      And the night's coming on,
   So give us your arm, and
      We'll joggle along.
               —Penzance, Cornwall (Mrs. Mabbott).

II.   Come all ye young men, with your wicked ways,
    Sow all your wild oats in your youthful days,
    That we may live happy, that we may live happy,
    That we may live happy when we grow old.
    The day is far spent, the night's coming on,
    Give us your arm, and we'll joggle along,
    That we may live happy, &c., &c.
              —Cornwall (*Folk-lore Journal*, v. 57).

(*b*) There must be an odd number of players at this game. They form into couples, each standing behind the other, making a ring, the girls inside, one boy standing alone in the middle. As they go round they sing the verse. At the end each boy leaves hold of his partner's arm and catches the arm of the girl in front, the one who is standing in the centre trying in the confusion to get into a place. If he succeeds, the child left out has to be the one in the centre the next time.

(*c*) Mr. Newell (*Games*, p. 101) says this game was called the "Baptist Game" in Virginia, where it is said to be enjoyed by pious people who will not dance. The American game is played in the same way as the English one. Mr. Newell gives the tune to which the game was sung. The words are almost identical. This game is played in the same way as "Jolly Miller," which see.

Johnny Rover

One boy is chosen to be Johnny Rover. The other players stand near him. Rover cries out—

> A [I] warn ye ance, A warn you twice;
> A warn ye three times over;
> A warn ye a' t' be witty an' wise
> An flee fae Johnny Rover.

While the words are being repeated all the players are putting themselves on the alert, and when they are finished they run off in all directions, with Rover in full pursuit. If a player is hard pressed he has the privilege of running to " Parley," the place from which the players started, and which in all games is an asylum. If he is caught before he reaches it, he becomes Johnny Rover for the next game. The one first captured becomes Rover.—Keith (Rev. W. Gregor).

Jolly Fishermen

—Tean, North Staffs. (Miss Burne).

I. They were two jolly fishermen,
They were two jolly fishermen,

They were two jolly fishermen,
And just come from the sea,
And just come from the sea.
They cast their nets into the sea,
And jolly fish caught we,
And jolly fish caught we,
And jolly fish caught we,
They cast their nets into the sea,
And jolly fish caught we.
            —Tean and Cheadle, North Staffs. (Miss Burne).

II.   There was three jolly fishermen,
        And they all put out to sea.
    They cast their nets into the sea,
        And the [three ?] jolly fish caught we.
            —North Staffs. Potteries (Mrs. Thomas Lawton).

(b) A circle is formed by joining hands, and two children stand in the centre. They walk round. At the seventh line the two in the centre each choose one child from the ring, thus making four in the centre. They then sing the remaining four lines. The two who were first in the centre then go out, and the game begins again, with the other two players in the centre.

(c) Miss Burne says this game is more often played as "Three Jolly Fishermen." At Cheadle, North Staffs., a few miles distant from Tean, this game is played by grown-up men and women.

Jolly Hooper

I.   Here comes a [or one] jolly hooper,
        Ring ding di do do,
        Ring ding di do do.

    And who are you looking for,
        In a ring ding di do do,
        In a ring ding di do do ?

    I am looking for one of your daughters,
        In a ring ding di do do,
        In a ring ding di do do.

What shall her name be,
In a ring ding di do do,
In a ring ding di do do ?

Her name shall be [Sarah],
In a ring ding di do do,
In a ring ding di do do.

Sarah shall ramble,
In a ring ding di do do,
In a ring ding di do do,
All around the chimney [jubilee] pot in 1881.
—Deptford, Kent (Miss Chase).

II.   I've come for one of your daughters,
       With a ring a ding a my dolly;
       I've come for one of your daughters
       On this bright shining night.

       Pray, which have you come for,
       With a ring a ding a my dolly?
       Pray which have you come for
       On this bright shining night?

       I've come for your daughter Mary,
       With a ring a ding a my dolly;
       I've come for your daughter Mary
       On this bright shining night.

       Then take her, and welcome,
       With a ring a ding a my dolly;
       Then take her, and welcome,
       On this bright shining night [incomplete].
                       —Sheffield (S. O. Addy).

(*b*) A number of children stand against a wall, and a row of other children face them. They walk backwards and forwards, singing the first and third verses. Then the children who are standing still (against the wall) answer by singing the second and fourth verses. When these are sung the moving line of children take Mary and dance round, singing " some lines which my informant," says Mr. Addy, " has forgotten."

(*c*) I have no description of the way Miss Chase's game is played. It, too, is probably an incomplete version. The words "Ring ding di do do" show a possible connection between this and games of the "Three Dukes a-riding" type. They may or may not be variants of the same game.

See "Here comes a Lusty Wooer," "Here comes a Virgin," "Jolly Rover," "Three Dukes."

Jolly Miller

—Epworth, Doncaster (C. C. Bell).

—Earls Heaton (H. Hardy).

—Derbyshire (Mrs. Harley).

I.   There was a jolly miller, and he lived by himself,
     As the wheel went round he made his pelf;
     One hand in the hopper, and the other in the bag,
     As the wheel went round he took his grab.
                              —Leicester (Miss Ellis).

II. There was a jolly miller, he lived by himself,
     As the mill went round he made his wealth;
     One hand in the hopper, another in his bag,
     As the wheel went round he made his grab.
                         —Liphook, Hants (Miss Fowler).

III. There was a jolly miller, and he lived by himself,
     As the wheel goes round he makes his wealth;
     One hand in his hopper, and the other in his bag,
     As we go round he makes his grab.
                      —Monton, Lancashire (Miss Dendy).

IV. There was a jolly miller, and he lived by himself,
     As the mill went round he gained his wealth;
     One hand in the hopper, and the other in the bag,
     As the mill went round he made his grab.

     Sandy he belongs to the mill,
     And the mill belongs to Sandy still,
     And the mill belongs to Sandy.
                         —Addy's *Sheffield Glossary*.

V.   There was a jolly miller, and he lived by himself,
     As the wheel went round he made his wealth;
     One hand in the upper and the other in the bank,
     As the wheel went round he made his wealth.
                      —Earls Heaton, Yorks. (Herbert Hardy).

VI. There was a jolly miller, and he lived by himself,
     As the wheel went round he made his grab;
     One hand in the other, and the other in the bag,
     As the wheel went round he made his grab.
                      —Nottinghamshire (Miss Winfield).

VII.   There was a jolly miller, and he lived by himself (or by
the Dee),
The sails went round, he made his ground ;
One hand in his pocket, the other in his bag.
—North Staffs. Potteries (Miss A. A. Keary).

(*b*) This game requires an uneven number of players.   All
the children except one stand in couples arm in arm, each
couple closely following the other.   This forms a double ring or
wheel (fig. 1).   The odd child stands in the centre.   The children
forming the wheel walk round in a circle and sing the verse.
When they come to the word "grab," those children standing
on the *inside* of the wheel leave hold of their partners' arms,
and try to catch hold of the one standing immediately in front
of their previous partners.   The child in the centre (or Miller)

Fig. 1

Fig. 2

tries (while they are changing places) to secure a partner and
place (fig. 2).   If he succeeds in doing this, the one then left out
becomes the Miller.   At Leicester the "odd" child, or "miller,"
stands *outside* the wheel or ring, instead of being in the centre,
and it is the outside children who change places.   Mr. Addy,
in the Sheffield version, says, "The young men stand in the
outer ring, and the young women in the inner.   A man stands
within the inner circle, quite near to it.   The men try and grasp
the arm of the girl in front of them, and the man in the centre
also tries to grasp one ; the man he displaces taking his place
as Miller.   Then the three last lines are sung."

(*c*) Versions of this game, almost identical with the Leicester
version given here (with the exception that the word "wealth"
ends the second line instead of "pelf"), have been sent me
from East Kirkby, Lincolnshire (Miss K. Maughan) ; Epworth,

Doncaster (Mr. C. C. Bell); Settle, Yorks. (Rev. W. S. Sykes); Derbyshire (Mrs. Harley); Redhill, Surrey (Miss G. Hope); Ordsall, Nottinghamshire (Miss Matthews); Brigg, Lincolnshire (Miss J. Barker); and there are other versions from Hersham, Surrey (*Folk-lore Record*, v. 86); Cornwall (*Folk-lore Journal*, v. 57); Derbyshire (*Folk-lore Journal*, i. 385); Oswestry, Ellesmere (*Shropshire Folk-lore*, p. 512). Miss Peacock sends a version which obtains at Lincoln, Horncastle, Winterton, and Anderby, Lincolnshire, and in Nottinghamshire; it is identical with the Liphook version. Two versions from Sporle, Norfolk, which vary slightly from the Leicester, have been sent by Miss Matthews. The versions given from Lancashire, Yorks., Nottingham, and North Staffs. have been selected to show the process of decadence in the game. "Hopper" has first become "upper," and then "other." Of the North Staffs. Potteries version Miss Keary says, " How it ends I have never been able to make out; no one about here seems to know either." With the exception of these few variants, it is singular how stereotyped the words of the rhyme have become in this game.

(*d*) This game may owe its origin to the fact of the miller in olden times paying himself in kind from the corn brought to him to be ground. The miller is a well-known object of satire in old ballads and mediæval writers. It is, however, probable that the custom which formerly prevailed at some of the public festivals, of catching or "grabbing" for sweethearts and wives, is shown in this game. For instance, to account for a Scottish custom it is said that St. Cowie, patron saint of two parishes of Campbeltown, proposed that all who did not find themselves happy and contented in the marriage state, should be indulged with an opportunity of parting and making a second choice. For that purpose he instituted an annual solemnity, at which all the unhappy couples in his parish were to assemble at his church; and at midnight all present were blindfolded and ordered to run round the church at full speed, with a view of mixing the lots in the urn. The moment the ceremony was over, without allowing an instant for the people present to recover from their confusion, the word

"Cabbay (seize quickly) was pronounced, upon which every man laid hold of the first female he met with. Whether old or young, handsome or ugly, good or bad, she was his wife till the next anniversary of this custom (Guthrie's *Scottish Customs*, p. 168). Another old wedding superstition is alluded to by Longfellow :—

"While the bride with roguish eyes,
    Sporting with them, now escapes and cries,
    'Those who catch me, married verily this year will be.'"

See "Joggle Along."

Jolly Rover

—Derbyshire (Mrs. Harley).

Here comes one jolly rover, jolly rover, jolly rover,
Here comes one jolly rover, jolly rover, jolly rover,
A roving all day.

And what do you rove for, rove for, rove for?
And what do you rove for?
Lily white and shining.

I rove for my pleasure, my pleasure, my pleasure,
I rove for my pleasure, my pleasure, my pleasure,
Lily white and shining.

And what is your pleasure, your pleasure, your pleasure?
What is your pleasure?
Lily white and shining.

My pleasure's for to marry you, to marry you, to marry you,
My pleasure's for to marry you,
Lily white and shining.

So through the kitchen and through the hall,
I choose the fairest of them all,
The fairest one that I can see
Is ——, so come to me.

—Derbyshire (Mrs. Harley).

(*b*) A long row of children walk to and fro. One child, facing them on the opposite side, represents the Rover. He sings the first, third, and fifth verses. The row of children sing the second and fourth in response. After the fifth verse is sung the Rover skips round the long row, singing the sixth verse to the tune of "Nancy Dawson," or "Round the Mulberry bush." He chooses one of them, who goes to the opposite side with him, and the game goes on until all are rovers like himself.

See "Here comes a Lusty Wooer," "Jolly Hooper."

Jolly Sailors

I.   Here comes one [some] jolly, jolly sailor boy,
Who lately came on shore;
He [they] spent his time in drinking wine
As we have done before.

We are the Pam-a-ram-a-ram,
We are the Pam-a-ram-a-ram,
And those who want a pretty, pretty girl,
Must kiss her on the shore,
Must kiss her on the shore.

—Warwick (from a little girl, through Mr. C. C. Bell).

II.   He was a jolly, jolly sailor boy,
Who had lately come ashore;
He spent his time in drinking wine
As he had done before.

Then we will have a jolly, jolly whirl,
Then we will have a jolly, jolly whirl,
And he who wants a pretty little girl
Must kiss her on the shore.

—Forest of Dean, Gloucestershire (Miss Matthews).

III.   Here comes one jolly sailor,
    Just arrived from shore,
    We'll spend our money like jolly, jolly joes,
    And then we'll work for more.

    We'll all around, around and around,
    And if we meet a pretty little girl
    We'll call her to the shore.
             —Northants (Rev. W. D. Sweeting).

IV.   Here comes four jolly sailor boys,
    Just lately come ashore;
    They spend their days in many merry ways,
    As they have done before.

    Round, round the ring we go,
    Round, round the ring,
    And he that choose his bonny, bonny lass
    Must kiss her on the floor.
             —Raunds (*Northants Notes and Queries*, i. 232).

V.   Here come three jolly, jolly, jolly boys
    As lately come from shore;
    We will spend our time on a moonlight night
    As we have done before.

    We will have a round, a round, a round,
    We will have a round, a round, a round;
    Let the lad that delights in a bonny, bonny lass,
    Let him kiss her on the ground.
             —Earls Heaton, Yorks. (Herbert Hardy).

VI.   Here comes three jolly, jolly sailors,
    Just arrived on shore;
    We'll spend our money like merry, merry men,
    And then we'll work for more.

    Hurrah for the round, round ring,
    Hurrah for the round, round ring;
    And he that loves a pretty, pretty girl,
    Let him call her from the ring.
             —Shipley, Horsham (*Notes and Queries*,
                8th series, i. 210, Miss Busk).

(*b*) This game is played at Warwick as follows :—The children form a large ring, clasping hands and standing still. One child walks round inside the ring, singing the verses. This child then chooses another from the ring, bending on one knee and kissing her hand. The lines are then repeated, the two walking arm in arm round the inside of the ring. Another child is chosen out of the ring by the one who was chosen previously. This goes on until all are chosen out of the ring, walking two by two round inside. When the ring will no longer hold them, the two walk round outside. At Northants the ring walks round, and the child is *outside* the ring. Partners are chosen, and the two walk round outside the ring. The first two walk together till there is a third, then the three walk together till there is a fourth, then they go in couples. In the Northants version, from Raunds, four boys stand in the centre of the ring. When the verses are sung they choose four girls, and then take their places in the ring. The four girls then choose four lads, and so on. At Earls Heaton the children stand against a wall in a line. Another child walks up and down singing the verses, and chooses a partner. He spreads a handkerchief on the ground, and they kneel and kiss.

(*c*) The Shipley version is a " Kiss in the Ring " game. A version sent by the Rev. W. Slater Sykes from Settle, Yorkshire, is almost identical with the Earls Heaton version. Northall (*Folk Rhymes*, p. 369) says " to kiss on the floor " —*i.e.*, not in secret. He gives the words of a sort of musical catch, sung in the Midlands, similar in character to this game, which may once have been used in some courting game. Mr. Newell (*Games*, p. 124) gives a version sung in the streets of New York, and considers it to be a relic of antiquity, a similar round being given in *Deuteromelia*, 1609.

Jowls

A game played by boys, much the same as " Hockey," and taking its name, no doubt, from the mode of playing, which consists in striking a wooden ball or knorr from the ground in any given direction with a sufficiently heavy stick, duly curved at the striking end.—Atkinson's *Cleveland Glossary*.

It is also given in *Yorkshire Glossary* (Whitby).

See "Bandy," "Doddart," "Hockey."

Jud

A game played with a hazel nut bored and run upon a string.—Dickinson's *Cumberland Glossary*.

Probably the same game as "Conkers."

See "Conkers."

Keeling the Pot

Brockett mentions that a friend informed him that he had seen a game played amongst children in Northumberland the subject of which was "Keeling the Pot." A girl comes in exclaiming, "Mother, mother, the pot's boiling ower." The answer is, "Then get the ladle and keel it." The difficulty is to get the ladle, which is "up a height," and the "steul" wants a leg, and the joiner is either sick or dead (*Glossary North Country Words*). A sentence from *Love's Labour's Lost*, "While greasy Joan doth keel the pot," illustrates the use of the term "keel."

See "Mother, Mother, the Pot Boils over."

Keppy Ball

In former times it was customary every year, at Easter and Whitsuntide, for the mayor, aldermen, and sheriff of Newcastle, attended by the burgesses, to go in state to a place called the Forth, a sort of mall, to countenance, if not to join in the play of "Keppy ba" and other sports. This diversion is still in part kept up by the young people of the town (Brockett's *North Country Words*). It is also mentioned in Peacock's *Manley and Corringham Glossary*, and in Ross and Stead's *Holderness Glossary*.

Mr. Tate (*History of Alnwick*) says that a favourite pastime of girls, "Keppy ball," deserves a passing notice, because accompanied by a peculiar local song. The name indicates the character of the game; "kep" is from *cepan*, Anglo-Saxon,

" kappan," Teut., " to catch or capture ; " for when the game
was played at by several, the ball was thrown into the air and
" kepped," or intercepted, in its descent by one or other of the
girls, and it was then thrown up again to be caught by some
other.　But when the song was sung it was played out by one
girl, who sent the ball against a tree and drove it back again as
often as she could, saying the following rhymes, in order to
divine her matrimonial future :—

> Keppy ball, keppy ball, Coban tree,
> Come down the long loanin' and tell to me,
> The form and the features, the speech and degree
> Of the man that is my true love to be.
>
> Keppy ball, keppy ball, Coban tree,
> Come down the long loanin' and tell to me
> How many years old I am to be.
>
> One a maiden, two a wife,
> Three a maiden, four a wife, &c.

The numbers being continued as long as the ball could be kept
rebounding against the tree.

The following from Halliwell's *Nursery Rhymes*, p. 298, is
also used for ball divination.　To " cook " is to toss or throw.

> Cook a ball, cherry tree ;
> Good ball, tell me
> How many years I shall be
> Before my true love I do see ?
> One and two, and that makes three ;
> Thankee, good ball, for telling of me.

See " Ball," " Cuckoo," " Monday."

Kibel and Nerspel

This game was played at Stixwold seventy years ago.　It
resembled " Trap, Bat, and Ball."　*Kibel* = bat, *ner* = ball of
maplewood, *spel* = trap, with a limock (pliant) stick fastened to
it.　The score was made by hitting the *ner* a certain distance,
but not by the striker running, as in " Rounders."—Miss M.
Peacock.

See " Nur and Spell."

King by your leave

"A playe that children have, where one sytting blyndefolde in the midle, bydeth so tyll the rest have hydden themselves, and then he going to seeke them, if any get his place in the meane space, that same is kynge in his roome."—Huloet, 1572.

See "Hide and Seek."

King Cæsar

One player is chosen to be King Cæsar by lot or naming. All the others stand in two rows, one row at each end of the ground. A line is drawn on the ground in front of them to mark "dens." All the players must keep within this line. King Cæsar stands in the middle of the ground. Any number of the players can then rush across the ground from one den to another. King Cæsar tries to catch one as they run. When he catches a boy he must count from one to ten in succession before he leaves hold of the boy, that boy in the meantime trying to get away. If King Cæsar succeeds in holding a boy, this boy stays in the centre with him and assists in catching the other players (always counting ten before a captive is secured). The dens must always be occupied by some players. If all the players get into one den, King Cæsar can go into the empty den and say, "Crown the base, one, two, three," three times before any of the other players get across to that den. If he succeeds in doing this, he can select a boy to run across from one den to the other, which that boy must do, King Cæsar trying to catch him. Other and bigger boys can help this one to get across, to save him from being captured, either by carrying him or running across with him. The game ends when all have been captured and are in the centre. King Cæsar and the other captured boys can leave the centre if they each successively catch three players.—Barnes (A. B. Gomme).

This game is called "King-sealing" in Dorsetshire.

See "King of Cantland," "Lamploo."

King Come-a-lay

A game played by boys. Two sets of boys, or sides, strive which can secure most prisoners for the King.—Shetland (Jamieson).

King of Cantland

A game of children, in which one of a company, being chosen King o' Cantland, and two goals appointed at a considerable distance from each other, all the rest endeavoured to run from one goal to the other; and those whom the King can seize in their course, so as to lay his hand upon their heads (which operation is called winning them), become his subjects, and assist him in catching the remainder.—Dumfries (Jamieson). Jamieson adds: "This game is called 'King's Covenanter' in Roxburgh." He also refers to the game of "King and Queen of Cantelon," recorded by Mactaggart. He considers the origin of this game to be representative of the contentions about the "Debatable Lands" on the border. This game was played at University Coll. School, London, under the name of "Kings" (A. Nutt).

See "How many miles to Barley Bridge?" "King Cæsar."

King o' the Castle

One boy is chosen as King. He mounts on any convenient height, a knoll, or dyke, or big stone, and shouts—

A'm King o' the Castle,
An' fah (who) 'll ding (knock) me doon?

The players make a rush at the King, and try to pull him down. A tussle goes on for a longer or a shorter time, according to the strength of the King and his skill in driving off his assailants. The boy that displaces the King becomes King, and is in his turn assaulted in the same way. The game may go on for any length of time. Another form of words is—

I'm the King o' the Castle,
An' nane can ding me doon.
—Keith (Rev. W. Gregor).

Other words sung by the Scotch children are—

I, Willy Wastle,
Stand on my castle,
And a' the dogs o' your toon
Will no drive Willie Wastle doon.

Chambers (*Popular Rhymes*, p. 114) records the tradition that when Oliver Cromwell lay at Haddington he sent to require the governor of Home Castle, in Berwickshire, to surrender;

the governor is said to have replied in the above quatrain of juvenile celebrity.

The London version is for the boys to run up a hillock, when one of them declares as follows—

> I'm the King of the Castle ;
> Get down, you dirty rascal,

whereupon he pushes down his companions. If another boy succeeds in getting his place he becomes King, and repeats the doggerel (G. L. Gomme). This is a very popular boys' game. Newell (*Games*, 164) mentions it as prevalent in Pennsylvania.

See "Tom Tiddler's Ground."

King Plaster Palacey

The players are a King and his three sons named White Cap, Red Cap, Brown Cap. Red Cap says, " Plaster Palacey had a son, whose name was old daddy White Cap." White Cap, in an injured voice, says, "Me, sir ?" The King says, "Yes, sir." White Cap answers, "You're a liar, sir." The King then says, "Who then, sir ?" White Cap answers, " Old daddy Red Cap."—Deptford, Kent (Miss Chase).

The game as given above is obviously incomplete, and no description as to how the game was played was sent me. Newell (*Games*, p. 145), describes a game, "The Cardinal's Hat," which is probably a variant of the original game, of which the above is only a fragment. I remember once witnessing a game in which a ball was passed from player to player, and in which the dialogue was similar. When one player was told that the ball was in his possession, the answer was, "What, me, sir ? " "Yes, you, sir." "Not I, sir." "Who then, sir ?" "White Cap, sir ;" the questions and answers were again repeated for Red Cap, and Blue Cap. When it was Black Cap's turn, I think the ball was thrown by this player to some one else ; whoever was hit by the ball had to chase and capture one, who became questioner ; but my recollection of the game is too slight for me to be certain either of the dialogue or the way the game terminated (A. B. Gomme). A game described in *Suffolk County Folk-lore*, p. 62, is apparently a version of this. It is there described as a forfeit game.

King William

—Earls Heaton, Yorks. (H. Hardy).

I. King William was King David's son,
    And all the royal race is run ;
    Choose from the east, choose from the west,
    Choose the one you love the best.

    Down on this carpet you shall kneel
    While the grass grows in yonder field ;
    Salute your bride and kiss her sweet,
    Rise again upon your feet.
                                  —Hanging Heaton, Yorks. (H. Hardy).

II. King William was King David's son,
    All the royal race is run ;
    Choose from the east, choose from the west,
    Choose the one that you love best ;
    If she's not here to take her part,
    Choose another with all your heart.
                                  —Sheffield (S. O. Addy).

(*b*) In Sheffield a ring of young men and women is formed. A man goes inside the ring and walks round within it, whilst the others sing the verse. The young man then chooses a sweetheart, and the two walk round arm-in-arm within the ring, whilst the same verses are sung. When the singing is ended, the girl picks a young man, and so they all pair off.

(*c*) Mr. Addy entitles this game " Kiss in the Ring." It appears, however, from this description to lack the two principal elements of most " kiss-in-the-ring " games—the chase between pursued and pursuer, and the kissing in the ring when the capture is made. In the Hanging Heaton version two children kneel and kiss in the middle of the ring. Mr. Newell (*Games*, p. 73), in describing a game with a similar rhyme, mentions a version which had been sent him from

Waterford, Ireland. He says, "We learn from an informant that in her town it was formerly played in this peculiar manner. Over the head of a girl who stood in the centre of a ring was held a shawl, sustained by four others grasping the corners." The game then proceeded as follows—

> King William was King George's son,
> From the Bay of Biscay O!
> Upon his breast he wore a star—
> Find your way to English schools.
> Down on the carpet you must kneel;
> As the grass grows in the field,
> Salute your bride and kiss her sweet,
> And rise again upon your feet.

Then followed the game-rhyme, repeated with each stanza—

> Go choose you east, go choose you west,

apparently the same as last four lines of Sheffield version. King William is then supposed to enter—

> The first girl that I loved so dear,
> Can it be she's gone from me?
> If she's not here when the night comes on,
> Will none of you tell me where she's gone?

He then recognises the disguised girl—

> There's heart beneath the willow tree,
> There's no one here but my love and me.

"He had gone to the war, and promised to marry her when he came back. She wrapped a shawl about her head to see if he would recognise her." This was all the reciter could recollect; the lines of the ballad were sung by an old woman, the ring answering with the game-rhyme.

This version seems to indicate clearly that in this game we have preserved one of the ceremonies of a now obsolete marriage-custom—namely, the disguising of the bride and placing her among her bridesmaids and other young girls, all having veils or other coverings alike over their heads and bodies. The bridegroom has to select from among these maidens the girl whom he wished to marry, or whom he had already married, for until this was done he was not allowed to depart with his bride. This custom was continued in sport as one of the ceremonies to be gone through after the marriage was over, long after the custom itself was discontinued. For an instance of this see a "Rural Marriage in Lorraine," in *Folk-lore Record*, iii. 267–268. This ordeal occurs in more than one folk-tale, and it usually accompanies the incident of a youth having travelled for adventures, sometimes in quest of a bride. He succeeds in finding the whereabouts of the coveted girl, but before he is allowed by the father to take his bride away he is required to perform tasks, a final one being the choosing of the girl with whom he is in love from among others, all dressed alike and disguised. Our bridal veil may probably originate in this custom.

In the ballad from which Mr. Newell thinks the game may have originated, a maid has been given in marriage to another than her chosen lover. He rides to the ceremony with a troop of followers; the bride, seeing him approach, calls on her maidens to "take off her gold crown and coif her in linen white," to test her bridegroom's affection. This incident, I think, is not to test "affection," but the ordeal of recognising his bride, however disguised, and the fact that "the hero at once recognises his love, mounts with her on horseback, and flees to Norway," may be considered to support my view.

See also Brand, vol. ii. p. 141, under "Care Cloth."

King's Chair

Two children join hands, by crossing their arms, so as to form a seat. A third mounts on the crossed arms, and clasps the carriers round their necks, while they move on saying—

> King, King Cairy (carry)
> London lairy,
> Milk an bread,
> In the King's chairie.

This game is played at Keith, without the words. The words are used at Fochabers.—Rev. W. Gregor.

Jamieson says, "Lothian children, while carrying one of their number in this manner, repeat the following rhyme—

> Lend me a pin to stick i' my thumb,
> To carry the lady to London town."

He says this method of carrying is often used as a substitute for a chair in conveying adult persons from one place to another, especially when infirm. In other counties it is called " Queen's Cushion " and " Queen's Chair," also " Cat's Carriage."

Brockett (*North Country Words*) says, " ' King's Cushion,' a sort of seat made by two persons crossing their hands, in which to place a third. The thrones on the reverses of the early Royal Seals of England and Scotland consist of swords, spears, snakes, &c., placed in the manner of a ' King's Cushion.' "

The method used is for both children to grasp the wrist of his left hand with the right, while he lays hold of the right wrist of his companion with his left hand. This way of hoisting or carrying is still used by schoolboys when they desire to honour a boy who has distinguished himself in the playground or schoolroom.

See " Carry my Lady to London."

Kirk the Gussie

A sort of play. The Gussie is a large ball, which one party endeavours to beat with clubs into a hole, while another party strives to drive it away. When the ball is lodged in the hole it is said to be " Kirkit."—Jamieson.

Kiss in the Ring

—Nottingham (Miss Youngman).

—Lancashire (Mrs. Harley).

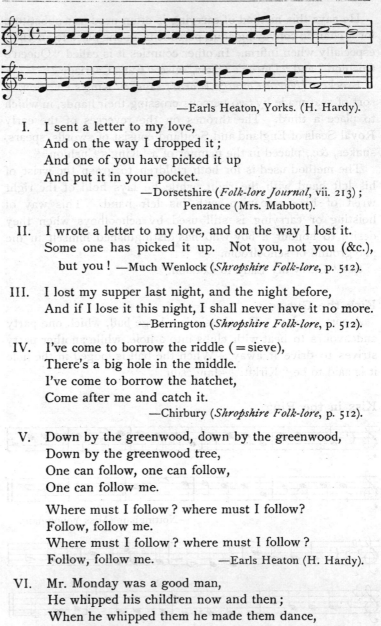

—Earls Heaton, Yorks. (H. Hardy).

I.   I sent a letter to my love,
      And on the way I dropped it;
      And one of you have picked it up
      And put it in your pocket.
                    —Dorsetshire (*Folk-lore Journal*, vii. 213);
                    Penzance (Mrs. Mabbott).

II.   I wrote a letter to my love, and on the way I lost it.
      Some one has picked it up.   Not you, not you (&c.),

      but you! —Much Wenlock (*Shropshire Folk-lore*, p. 512).

III. I lost my supper last night, and the night before,
      And if I lose it this night, I shall never have it no more.
                    —Berrington (*Shropshire Folk-lore*, p. 512).

IV.   I've come to borrow the riddle (= sieve),
      There's a big hole in the middle.
      I've come to borrow the hatchet,
      Come after me and catch it.
                    —Chirbury (*Shropshire Folk-lore*, p. 512).

V.   Down by the greenwood, down by the greenwood,
      Down by the greenwood tree,
      One can follow, one can follow,
      One can follow me.

      Where must I follow? where must I follow?
      Follow, follow me.
      Where must I follow? where must I follow?
      Follow, follow me.   —Earls Heaton (H. Hardy).

VI.   Mr. Monday was a good man,
      He whipped his children now and then;
      When he whipped them he made them dance,
      Out of Scotland into France;

Out of France into Spain,
Back to dear old England again.
O-u-t spells " out,"
If you please stand out.
I had a little dog and his name was Buff,
I sent him after a penn'orth of snuff,
He broke the paper and smelled the snuff,
And that's the end of my dog Buff.
He shan't bite you—he shan't bite you—he shan't bite
you, &c., &c.—he *shall* bite you all over.
— Dorsetshire (*Folk-lore Journal*, vii. 213).

VII.   I sent a letter to my love,
I carried water in my glove,
And by the way I dropped it.
   I did so!   I did so!

I had a little dog that said " Bow! wow!"
I had a little cat that said " Meow! meow!"
Shan't bite you—shan't bite you—
Shall bite you.   —Cornwall (*Folk-lore Journal*, v. 52).

VIII.   I sent a letter to my love,
I carried water in my glove,
I dript it, I dropped it, and by the way I lost it.
   —Hersham, Surrey (*Folk-lore Record*, v. 87).

IX.   I have a pigeon in my pocket,
If I have not lost it ;
   Peeps in, peeps out,
By the way I've lost it ;
   Drip, drop,
By the way I've lost it.   —Earls Heaton (H. Hardy).

X.   I have a pigeon in my pocket,
It peeps out and in,
And every time that I go round
I give it a drop of gin.
Drip it, drop it, drip it, drop it.
   —Settle, Yorkshire (Rev W. S. Sykes).

XI. I sent a letter to my love,
   I thought I put it in my glove,
   But by the way I dropped it.
   I had a little dog said "Bow, wow, wow!"
   I had a little cat said "Mew, mew, mew!"
   It shan't bite you,
   It *shall* bite *you*.   —Bexley Heath (Miss Morris).

XII. I sent a letter to my love,
   And by the way I droppt it;
   I dee, I dee, I dee, I droppt it,
   And by the way I droppt it. —Keith (Rev. W. Gregor).

XIII. I had a little dog, it shan't bite you,
   Shan't bite you, shan't bite you,
   Nor you, nor you, nor you.
   I had a little cat, it shan't scratch you,
   Shan't scratch you, nor you, nor you.

   I wrote a letter to my love, and on the way I dropped it.
   And one of you have picked it up and put it in your
     pocket.
   It wasn't you, it wasn't you, nor you, nor you, but it
     was *you*.   —London (A. B. Gomme).

XIV. I have a little dog and it lives in my pocket.
   It shan't bite you, &c.

   Now you're married I hope you'll enjoy
   First a girl and then a boy;
   Seven years gone, and two to come,
   So take her and kiss her and
   Send her off home. —Wolstanton, North Staffs. Potteries
             (Miss A. A. Keary).

(*b*) In Dorsetshire a ring is formed by all the players joining
hands except one. The odd player, carrying a handkerchief,
commences to walk slowly round the outside of the ring,
repeating the words; then, touching each one with her hand-

kerchief as she passes, she says, "Not you," "not you," "not you," &c., &c., till the favoured individual is reached, when it is changed to "But you!" and his or her shoulder lightly touched at the same time. The first player then runs round the ring as fast as he can, pursued by the other, who, if a capture is effected (as is nearly always the case), is entitled to lead the first player back into the centre of the ring and claim a kiss. The first player then takes the other's place in the ring, and in turn walks round the outside repeating the same formula.—*Folk-lore Journal*, vii. 212; Penzance (Mrs. Mabbott).

In Shropshire, as soon as the player going round the ring has dropped the handkerchief on the shoulder of the girl he chooses, both players run *opposite ways* outside the ring, each trying to be the first to regain the starting-point. If the one who was chosen gets there first, no kiss can be claimed. It is often called "Drop-handkerchief," from the signal for the chase. The more general way of playing (either with or without words), as seen by me on village greens round London, is, when the handkerchief has been dropped, for the player to dart through the ring and in and out again under the clasped hands; the pursuer must follow in and out through the same places, and must bring the one he catches into the ring before he can legally claim the kiss.

Elworthy (*West Country Words*), in describing this game, says : "The person behind whom the handkerchief is dropped is entitled to kiss the person who dropped it, if he or she can catch him or her, before the person can get round the ring to the vacant place. Of course, when a girl drops it she selects a favoured swain, and the chase is severe up to a point, but when a girl is the pursuer there often is a kind of donkey race lest she should have to give the kiss which the lad takes no pains to avoid." Mr. Elworthy does not mention any words being used, and it is therefore probable that this is the "Drop-hand-kerchief" game, which generally has no kissing. It also, in the way it is played, resembles "French Jackie." In the Wolstanton game, Miss Keary says: "If the owner of the handkerchief overtakes the one who is bitten as they run round, they shake hands and go into the middle of the ring, while the others sing the marriage formula.   In Berkshire (*Antiq.* xxvii. 255) the game is played without words, and apparently no handkerchief or other sign is used.   Miss Thoyts says the young man raises his hat when he embraces the young woman of his choice.   To "throw (or fling) the handkerchief" is a common expression for an expected proposal of marriage which is more of a condescension than a complimentary or flattering one to the girl.   "Kiss in the Ring" is probably a relic of the earliest form of marriage by choice or selection. The custom of dropping or sending a glove as the signal of a challenge may have been succeeded by the handkerchief in this game.   Halliwell, p. 227, gives the game of "Drop Glove," in which a glove is used.   For the use of handkerchiefs as love-tokens see Brand, ii. 92.

See "Drop Handkerchief," "French Jackie."

Kit-Cat

A game played by boys.   Three small holes are made in the ground, triangularly about twenty feet apart, to mark the position of as many boys, each of whom holds a small stick, about two feet long.   Three other boys of the adverse side pitch successively a piece of stick, a little bigger than one's thumb, called Cat, to be struck by those holding the sticks. On its being struck, the boys run from hole to hole, dipping the ends of their sticks in as they pass, and counting one, two, three, &c., as they do so, up to thirty-one, which is game.   Or the greater number of holes gained in the innings may indicate the winners, as at cricket.   If the Cat be struck and caught, the striking party is out, and another of his sidesmen takes his place, if the set be strong enough to admit of it.   If there be only six players, it may be previously agreed that three *put outs* shall end the innings.   Another mode of putting out is to throw the Cat home, after being struck, and placing or pitching it into an unoccupied hole, while the in-party are running.   A certain number of misses (not striking the Cat) may be agreed on to be equivalent to a put out.   The game may be played by two, placed as at

cricket, or by four, or I believe more.—Moor's *Suffolk Words ;*
Holloway's *Dict. of Provincialisms.*

Brockett (*North Country Words*, p. 115) calls this "'Kitty-
Cat,' a puerile game.

> Then in his hand he takes a thick bat,
> With which he used to play at 'Kit-Cat.'"
>
> —Cotton's *Works*, 1734, p. 88.

See "Cat and Dog," "Cudgel," "Munshets," "Tip-Cat."

Kit-Cat-Cannio

A sedentary game, played by two, with slate and pencil, or
pencil and paper. It is won by the party who can first get
three marks (o's or x's) in a line; the marks being made
alternately by the players o or x in one of the nine spots
equidistant in three rows, when complete. He who begins
has the advantage, as he can contrive to get his mark in the
middle.—Moor's *Suffolk Words.*

The same game as "Nought and Crosses," which see.

Kittlie-cout

A game mentioned but not described by a writer in *Blackwood's Magazine*, August 1821, as played in Edinburgh. He
mentions that the terms "hot" and "cold" are used in the
game. The game of "Hide and Seek."—Jamieson.

Knapsack

One boy takes another by the feet, one foot over each
shoulder, with his head downwards and his face to his back,
and sets off running as fast as he can. He runs hither and
thither till one or other of the two gets tired.—Keith (Rev. W.
Gregor).

Knights

Two big boys take two smaller ones on their shoulders. The
big boys act as horses, while the younger ones seated on their
shoulders try to pull each other over. The "horses" may
push and strike each other with their shoulders, but must not
kick or trip up with their feet, or use their hands or elbows.
The game is usually won by the Horse and Knight who
throw their opponents twice out of three times (G. L. Gomme).

Strutt (*Sports*, p. 84) describes this, and says, "A sport of this kind was in practice with us at the commencement of the fourteenth century." He considers it to bear more analogy to wrestling than to any other sport. He gives illustrations, one

of which is here reproduced from the original MS. in the British Museum. The game is also described in the Rev. J. G. Wood's *Modern Playmate*, p. 12.

Knocked at the Rapper

The girl who spoke of this game, says Miss Peacock, could only remember its details imperfectly, but as far as she recollects it is played as follows:—The players dance round a centre child, leaving one of their number outside the circle. The dancers sing to the one in their midst—

Here comes ——,

He knocked at the rapper, and he pulled at the string,

Pray, Mrs. ——, is —— within?

At "is —— within," the child outside the circle is named. The centre child says—

O no, she has gone into the town:

Pray take the arm-chair and sit yourself down.

The ring of children then sing—

> O no, not until my dearest I see,
> And then one chair will do for we.

Then all sing—

> My elbow, my elbow,
> My pitcher, and my can :
> Isn't —— —— a nice young girl ?

Mentioning the supposed sweetheart.

> Isn't —— —— as nice as she ?

Mentioning the outside child.

> They shall be married when they can agree.

Then the inside and outside children each choose a companion from the circle, and the rest repeat :—

> My elbow, my elbow, &c.

When the words have been sung a second time, the four children kiss, and the two from the circle take the places of the other, after which change the game begins again.—North Kelsey, Lincolnshire (Miss M. Peacock).

Knor and Spell

See " Nur and Spell."

Lab

A game of marbles (undescribed).—Patterson's *Antrim and Down Glossary*.

See " Lag."

Lady of the Land

Tong, Shropshire (Miss R. Harley).

I. Here comes the lady of the land,
    With sons and daughters in her hand ;
    Pray, do you want a servant to-day ?

    What can she do ?

She can brew, she can bake,
She can make a wedding cake
Fit for you or any lady in the land.

Pray leave her.

I leave my daughter safe and sound,
And in her pocket a thousand pound,
And on her finger a gay ring,
And I hope to find her so again.
—*Somerset and Dorset Notes and Queries*, i. 133.

II. There camed a lady from other land,
With all her children in her hand—
Please, do you want a sarvant, marm?

Leave her.

I leaves my daughter zafe and zound,
And in her pocket a thousan pound,
And on her finger a goulden ring,
And in her busum a silver pin.
I hopes when I return,
To see her here with you.
Don't'e let her ramble; don't'e let her trot;
Don't'e let her car' the mustard pot.

The Mistress says softly—
She shall ramble, she shall trot,
She shall carry the mustard pot.
—*Dorset County Chronicle*, April 1889 ;
Folk-lore Journal, vii. 228.

III. Here comes an old woman from Baby-land,
With all her children in her hand.
Pray take one of my children in.

[Spoken] What can your children do?

[Sung] One can bake, one can brew,
And one can bake a lily-white cake.
One can sit in the parlour and sing,
And this one can do everything.
—Tong, Shropshire (Miss R. Harley).

IV. Here comes a poor woman from Baby-land
   With three small children in her hand.
   One can brew, the other can bake,
   The other can make a pretty round cake.
   One can sit in the garden and spin,
   Another can make a fine bed for the king;
   Pray, ma'am, will you take one in?
   —Halliwell's *Nursery Rhymes*, p. 72.

V. Here is a poor widow from Sandy Row,
   With all her children behind her.
   One can knit and one can sew,
   And one can make the winder go.
   Please take one in.

   Now poor Nellie she is gone
   Without a farthing in her hand,
   Nothing but a guinea gold ring.
   Good-bye, Nellie, good-bye!
   —Belfast (W. H. Patterson).

VI. Here comes an old woman from Baby-land,
   With six poor children by the hand.
   One can brew, one can bake,
   And one can make a lily-white cake;
   One can knit, one can spin,
   And one can make a bed for a king.
   Please will you take one in? [choose out one]

   Now poor —— she is gone
   Without a farthing in her hand,
   Nothing but a gay gold ring.
   Good-bye! Good-bye!
   Good-bye, mother, good-bye!
   —Isle of Man (A. W. Moore)

VII. Here comes a poor widow from Sandalam,
   With all her children at her hand;
   The one can bake, the other can brew,
   The other can make a lily-white shoe;
   Another can sit by the fire and spin,
   So pray take one of my daughters in.

The fairest one that I can see
Is pretty [Mary] come to me.

And now poor [Mary] she is gone
Without a guinea in her hand,
And not so much as a farthing.   Good-bye!
Good-bye, my love, good-bye!
> —Forest of Dean, Gloucester (Miss Matthews).

VIII.   Here comes an old woman from Cumberland,
With seven poor children in her hand;
One can sing, the other can sew;
One can sit up in the corner and cry, Alleluia!
Choose the fairest you can see.
The fairest one that I can see is ——, come to me.
Now my daughter —— gone,
A thousand pound in her pocket and a gold ring on her
finger.
Good-bye, mother, good-bye!
> —Berkshire (Miss Thoyts, *Antiquary*, xxvii. 254).

IX.   There was an old woman from Sandyland
With all her children in her hand.
One can knit and one can sow [sew],
One can make a lily-white bow.
Please take one in.

When all the children have been taken in, the Old Woman
says—   There was an old woman from Sandiland
With no children by the hand.
Will you give me one?
> —Ballynascaw School, co. Down (Miss C. N. Patterson).

(*b*) The first Dorsetshire game is played as follows:—Two
girls are chosen, the one to represent a lady and the other a
mother, who is supposed to be taking her children out to service.
She has one or more of them in each hand, and leads them up
to the lady, saying or singing the first verse. The dialogue
then proceeds, and the verse is repeated until all the children
are similarly disposed of. A few days are supposed to pass,
after which the mother calls to see her children, when the lady

tells her she cannot see them. At last she insists upon seeing them, and the children are all "sat down" behind the lady, and the mother asks one child what the lady has done to her; and she tells her "that the lady has cut off her nose, and made a nose-pie, and never give her a bit of it." Each one says she has done something to her and made a pie, and when all have told their tale "they all turn on her and put her to prison."

The second Dorsetshire game somewhat differs. One child takes seven or eight others whom she pretends are her children. Another child, presumably a mistress in want of servants, stands at a distance. The first child advances, holding the hand of her children, saying the first verse. The dialogue is concluded, and as the woman and her children are supposed to be out of hearing, the last couplet is said or sung. This process is gone through again until the mistress has engaged all the children as her servants, when she is supposed to let them all out to play with the mustard pots, which are represented by sticks or stones, in their hands.

The other versions are played as follows:—The children form a line, the one in the middle being the mother, or widow; they advance and retire, the mother alone singing the first verse. One child, who is standing alone on the opposite side, who has been addressed by the widow, then asks [not sings] the question. The mother, or widow, sings the reply, and points to one child when singing the last line, who thereupon crosses over to the other side, joining the one who is standing alone. This is continued till all have been selected. The Bally-nascaw version (Miss Patterson) is played in a similar way. One child sits on a bank, and the others come up to her in a long line. The "old woman" says the first five lines. No question is asked by the "lady," she simply takes one child. The "old woman" shakes hands with this child, and says good-bye to her. When all the children have been "taken in" by the one who personates the "lady," the "old woman" says the other three lines, and so one by one gets all the children back again. The Berkshire version (Miss Thoyts) is said, not sung, and is played with two leaders, "old woman" and "lover." As the lover chooses a child, that one is sent behind him,

holding round his waist. Each child as she goes says, "Good-
bye, mother, good-bye," and pretends to cry. Finally they all
cry, and the game ends in a tug of war. This tug is clearly
out of place unless only half the children are selected by one
side. Miss Thoyts does not say how this is done.

(c) This game is called "School-teacher" in Belfast. The
corruption of "Lady of the Land," to "Babyland," "Babylon,"
and "Sandiland," is manifest. It appears to be only fragmentary in its present form, but the versions undoubtedly indicate
that the origin of the game arises from the practice of hiring
servants. Mr. Halliwell has preserved another fragmentary
rhyme, which he thinks may belong to this game.

> I can make diet bread
> Thick and thin,
> I can make diet bread
> Fit for the king ; (No. cccxliv.)

which may be compared with the rhyme given by Chambers
(*Popular Rhymes*, p. 136), and another version given by
Halliwell, p. 229.

If these rhymes belong to this game it would have probably been played by each child singing a verse descriptive of
her own qualifications, and I have some recollection, although
not perfect, of having played a game like this in London,
where each child stated her ability to either brew, bake, or
churn. It is worth noting that the Forest of Dean and
Berkshire versions have absorbed one of the "selection"
verses of the love-games. Mr. Halliwell, in recording the
Nursery Rhymes, Nos. cccxliii. and cccxliv., as quoted above,
says, "They are fragments of a game called 'The Lady of
the Land,' a complete version of which has not fallen in my
way." Mr. Udal's versions from Dorsetshire are not only
called "The Lady of the Land," but are fuller than all the
other versions, though probably these are not complete. Mr.
Newell (*Games*, pp. 56–58) gives some versions of this game.
He considers the original to have been a European game (he
had not found an English example) in which there were two
mothers, a rich and a poor one ; one mother begging away, one
by one, all the daughters of the other.

(*d*) This game no doubt originates from the country practice of hiring servants at fairs, or from a dramatic " Hirings " being acted at Harvest Homes. The "Good-bye" of mother and daughters belongs, no doubt, to the original game and early versions, and is consistent with the departure of a servant to her new home. The "lover" incident is an interpolation, but there may have been a request on the part of the "mother" to the "lady" not to allow the girl followers or sweethearts too soon. As to the old practice of hiring servants, Miss Burne has noted how distinctly it stamps itself upon local custom (*Shropshire Folk-lore*, pp. 461, 464). That the practice forms the groundwork of this game is well illustrated by the following descriptive passage. " They stay usually two or three dayes with theire friends, and then aboute the fifth or sixth day after Martynmasse will they come to theire newe masters; they will depart from theire olde services any day in the weeke, but theire desire (hereaboutes) is to goe to theire newe masters eyther on a Tewsday or on a Thursday; for on a Sunday they will seldome remoove, and as for Monday, they account it ominous, for they say—

> Monday flitte,
> Neaver sitte;

but as for the other dayes in the weeke they make no greate matter. I heard a servant asked what hee could doe, whoe made this answeare—

> I can sowe,
> I can mowe,
> And I can stacke;
> And I can doe,
> My master too,
> When my master turnes his backe."
> —Best's *Rural Economy of Yorks.*, 1641 ;
> Surtees Society, pp. 135-136.

In *Long Ago*, ii. 130, Mr. Scarlett Potter mentions that in South Warwickshire it was customary at harvest-homes to give a kind of dramatic performance. One piece, called "The Hiring," represents a farmer engaging a man, in which work done by the man, the terms of service, and food to be supplied, are stated in rhymes similar to the above. See "Lammas."

Lady on the Mountain

—Barnes, Surrey (A. B. Gomme).

I.   There stands a lady on the mountain,
      Who she is I do not know;
      All she wants is gold and silver,
      All she wants is a nice young man.
      Choose one, choose two, choose the fairest one of the two.
      The fairest one that I can see,
      Is pretty ——, walk with me.

—Barnes, Surrey (A. B. Gomme).

II.   There lives a lady on the mountain,
      Who she is I do not know;
      All she wants is gold and silver,
      All she wants is a nice young man.

      Choose one, choose two,
      Choose the fairest of the few.

      Now you're married I wish you joy,
      Father and mother you must obey;
      Love one another like sister and brother,
      And pray, young couple, come kiss one another.

—Colchester (Miss G. M. Frances).

III.   Here stands a lady on a mountain,
      Who she is I do not know;
      All she wants is gold and silver,
      All she wants is a nice young man.

Choose you east, and choose you west,
Choose you the one as you love best.

Now Sally's got married we wish her good joy,
First a girl and then a boy;
Twelve months a'ter a son and da'ter,
Pray young couple, kiss together.
> —Berrington (*Shropshire Folk-lore*, pp. 509, 510).

IV.   Stands a lady on the mountain,
Who she is I do not know;
All she wants is gold and silver,
All she wants is a nice young beau.
Take her by the lily-white hand,
Lead her across the water;
Give her kisses, one, two, three,
For she is her mother's daughter.
> —Shipley, Horsham (*Notes and Queries*,
> 8th series, i. 210, Miss Busk).

V.   There stands a lady on a mountain,
Who she is I do not know;
All she wants is gold and silver,
All she wants is a nice young man.

Now she's married I wish her joy,
First a girl and then a boy;
Seven years after son and daughter,
Pray young couple kiss together.

Kiss her once, kiss her twice,
Kiss her three times three.
> —Wrotham, Kent (Miss D. Kimball).

VI.   There stands a lady on the ocean [mountain],
Who she is I do not know her;
All she wants is gold or silver,
All she wants is a nice young man.

Choose once, choose twice,
Choose three times over.

Now you're married I wish you joy,
First a girl and then a boy;
Seven years old a son and daughter,
Play and cuddle and kiss together.

Kiss her once, kiss her twice,
Kiss her three times over.   —Deptford (Miss Chase).

VII. There stands a lady on the mountain,
Who she is I do not know:
Oh! she wants such gold and silver!
Oh! she wants such a nice young man!

Now you're married I wish you joy,
First a girl and then a boy;
Seven years after a son and a daughter,
Kiss your bride and come out of the ring.
              —Berkshire (Miss Thoyts, *Antiquary*, xxvii. 254).

(*b*) A ring is formed, one child in the centre. The ring sing the first verse, and then the centre child chooses one from the ring. The chosen pair kiss when the ring has sung the second. The first child then joins the ring, and the game begins again. In the Barnes version the centre child calls one to her from the ring by singing the second verse and naming the child she chooses.

(*c*) A version from Lady C. Gurdon's *Suffolk County Folk-lore* (p. 62) is the same as previous versions, except that it ends—

Now you're married you must be good,
Make your husband chop the wood;
Chop it fine and bring it in,
Give three kisses in the ring.

Other versions are much the same as the examples given.

(*d*) This game has probably had its origin in a ballad. Miss Burne draws attention to its resemblance to the "Disdainful Lady" (*Shropshire Folk-lore*, p. 561), and Halliwell mentions a nursery rhyme (No. cccclxxix.) which is very similar. Mr. Newell (*Games*, p. 55) prints words and tune of a song which is very similar to that ballad, and he mentions the fact that he has seen it played as a round by the "Arabs of the street."

He considers it to be an old English song which has been fitted for a ring game by the addition of a verse.

See "Lady on Yonder Hill."

Lady on Yonder Hill

I.   Yonder stands a lovely lady,
     Whom she be I do not know;
     I'll go court her for my beauty,
     Whether she say me yea or nay.
     Madam, to thee I humbly bow and bend.
     Sir, I take thee not to be my friend.
     Oh, if the good fairy doesn't come I shall die.

          —Derbyshire (*Folk-lore Journal*, i. 387).

II.   There stands a lady on yonder hill,
     Who she is I cannot tell;
     I'll go and court her for her beauty,
     Whether she answers me yes or no.
     Madam, I bow vounce to thee.
     Sir, have I done thee any harm?
     Coxconian!
     Coxconian is not my name; 'tis Hers and Kers, and
        Willis and Cave.
     Stab me, ha! ha! little I fear. Over the waters there
        are but nine, I'll meet you a man alive. Over
        the waters there are but ten, I'll meet you there
        five thousand.
     Rise up, rise up, my pretty fair maid,
     You're only in a trance;
     Rise up, rise up, my pretty fair maid,
     And we will have a dance.

          —Lady C. Gurdon's *Suffolk County Folk-lore*, p. 65.

(*b*) In the Suffolk game the children form a ring, a boy and girl being in the centre. The boy is called a gentleman and the girl a lady. The gentleman commences by singing the first verse. Then they say alternately the questions and answers. When the gentleman says the lines commencing, "Stab me," he pretends to stab the lady, who falls on the

ground. Then he walks round the lady and sings the last
verse, "Rise up," and lifts up the lady. In the Derbyshire
game only three children play, the lover, lady, and fairy. The
girl stands a little distance off. The lover says the first four
lines, then approaches the lady, falls on one knee, and says the
next line. The lady replies, and retires further away. The
lover then falls on the ground and says the next line. As this
is said the good fairy appears, touches the fallen lover with her
hand, and he is immediately well again.

(c) This is a curious game, and is perhaps derived from a
ballad which had been popular from some more or less local
circumstance, or more probably it may be a portion of an old
play acted in booths at fair times by strolling players. It is
not, as far as I can find out, played in any other counties.
The lines—

> Over the water at the hour of ten,
> I'll meet you with five thousand men;
> Over the water at the hour of five,
> I'll meet you there if I'm alive,

are portions of a dialogue familiar to Mr. Emslie, and also
occur in some mumming plays. It may also be noted that the
curing of illness or death from a stab is an incident in these
plays, as is also the method of playing. The first lines are
similar to those of "Lady on the Mountain," which see.

Lag

A number of boys put marbles in a ring, and then they all
bowl at the ring. The one who gets nearest has the first
shot at the marbles. He has the option of either "knuckling
doon" and shooting at the ring from the prescribed mark, or
"ligging up" (lying up)—that is, putting his taw so near the
ring that if the others miss his taw, or miss the marbles in the
ring, he has the game all to himself next time. If, however, he
is hit by the others, he is said to be "killed."—Addy's *Sheffield
Glossary*.

Lammas

A party of boys take a few straws, and endeavour to hold

one between the chin and the turned-down under-lip, pro-
nouncing the following rhyme—

I bought a beard at Lammas fair,

It's a' awa' but ae hair ;

Wag, beardie, wag !

He who repeats this oftenest without dropping the straw is
held to have won the game (Chambers' *Popular Rhymes*, p. 115).
This game-rhyme has an interesting reference to Lammas, and
it may also refer to the hiring of servants. Brockett (*North
Country Words*, p. 221) says, "At a fair or market where
country servants are hired, those who offer themselves stand
in the market-place with a piece of straw or green branch in
their mouths to distinguish them."

Lamploo

A goal having been selected and bounds determined, the
promoters used to prepare the others by calling at the top of
their voices—

Lamp ! Lamp ! Laa-o !

Those that don't run shan't play-o !

Then one of the "spryest" lads is elected to commence,
thus :—First touching the goal with his foot or leaning against
it, and clasping his hands so as to produce the letter W in the
dumb alphabet, he pursues the other players, who are not so
handicapped, when, if he succeeds in touching one without
unclasping his hands, they both make a rush for the goal.
Should either of the other boys succeed in overtaking one of
these before reaching that spot, he has the privilege of riding
him home pick-a-back. Then these two boys (*i.e.*, the original
pursuer and the one caught), joining hands, carry on the game
as before, incurring a similar penalty in case of being overtaken
as already described. Each successive boy, as he is touched
by the pursuers, has to make for the goal under similar risks,
afterwards clasping hands with the rest, and forming a new
recruit in the pursuing gang, in whose chain the outside players
alone have the privilege of touching and thus adding to their
numbers. Should the chain at any time be broken, or should
the original pursuer unclasp his hands, either by design or

accident, the penalty of carrying a capturer to the goal is incurred and always enforced. In West Somerset the pursuing boys after starting were in the habit of crying out the word "Brewerre" or "Brewarre;" noise appearing to be quite as essential to the game as speed.—*Somerset and Dorset Notes and Queries*, i. 186 (1888).

Another correspondent to the same periodical (i. 204) says that an almost identical game was played at the King's School, Sherborne, some fifty years ago. It was called "King-sealing," and the pursuing boy was obliged by the rules to retain his hold of the boy seized until he had uttered—

One, two, three, four, five, six, seven, eight, nine, ten.

You are one of the king-sealer's men.

If the latter succeeded in breaking away before the couplet was finished, the capture was incomplete.

The second game described is almost identical with "King Cæsar," played at Barnes.

About twenty years ago the game was common in some parts of Bedfordshire and Hertfordshire, where it was sometimes called "Chevy Chase."—*Folk-lore Journal*, vii. 233.

See "Chickidy Hand," "Hunt the Staigie," "King Cæsar," "Whiddy."

Lang Larence

That is, "Long Lawrence," an instrument marked with signs, a sort of teetotum. A "Long Lawrence" is about three inches long, something like a short ruler with eight sides; occasionally they have but four. On one side are ten x's, or crosses, forming a kind of lattice-work; on the next, to the left, three double cuts, or strokes, passing straight across in the direction of the breadth; on the third, a zig-zag of three strokes one way, and two or three the other, forming a W, with an additional stroke or a triple V; on the fourth, three single bars, one at each end and one in the middle, as in No. 2, where they are doubled; then the four devices are repeated in the same order. The game, formerly popular at Christmas, can be played by any number of persons. Each has a bank of pins or other small matters. A pool is formed; then in turn each rolls the

"Long Lawrence." If No. 1 comes up the player cries "Flush," and takes the pool; if No. 2, he puts down two pins; if No. 3, he says "Lave all," and neither takes nor gives; if No. 4, he picks up one. The sides are considered to bear the names, "Flush," "Put doan two," "Lave all," "Sam up one." It has been suggested that the name "Lawrence" may have arisen from the marks scored on the instrument, not unlike the bars of a gridiron, on which the saint perished.—Easthers's *Almondbury Glossary.*

See "Teetotum."

Leap Candle

The young girls in and about Oxford have a sport called "Leap Candle," for which they set a candle in the middle of a room in a candlestick, and then draw up their coats into the form of breeches, and dance over the candle back and forth, saying the words—

> The taylor of Bicester he has but one eye,
> He cannot cut a pair of green galagaskins
> If he were to die.

This sport, in other parts, is called "Dancing the Candle-rush" (Aubrey's *Remaines of Gentilisme and Judaisme*, p. 45). Halliwell (*Rhymes*, p. 65) has a rhyme—

> Jack be nimble,
> And Jack be quick,
> And Jack jump over
> The candlestick,

which may refer to this game. Northall (*Folk Rhymes*, p. 412) says in Warwickshire a similar game is called "Cock and Breeches."

Leap-frog

One boy stoops down sideways, with his head bent towards his body, as low as possible. This is called "Tucking in your Tuppeny." Another boy takes a flying leap over the "frog," placing his hands on his back to help himself over. He then proceeds to a distance of some four or five yards, and, in his turn, stoops in the same manner as the first boy, as another frog. A third boy then leaps first over frog No. 1, and then over frog No. 2, taking his place as frog No. 3, at about the same distance onwards. Any number of boys may play in the game. After the last player has taken his leap over all the frogs successively, frog No. 1 has his turn and leaps over his companions, taking his place as the last in the line of frogs. Then No. 2 follows suit, and so on, the whole line of players in course of time covering a good distance.—London (G. L. Gomme).

Leap-frog is known in Cornwall as "Leap the Long-mare" (*Folk-lore Journal*, v. 60), and in Antrim and Down as "Leap the Bullock" (Patterson's *Glossary*).

See "Accroshay," "Loup the Bullocks," "Spanish Fly."

Leap the Bullock

See "Leap-frog," "Loup the Bullocks."

Leaves are Green

> The leaves are green, the nuts are brown,
> They hang so high they will not come down;
> Leave them alone till frosty weather,
> Then they will all come down together.
> —Berkshire (Miss Thoyts, *Antiquary*, xxvii. 254).

These lines are sung while the children dance round in a circle. When the last words are sung, the children flop down upon the ground. The tune sung is, Miss Thoyts says, that of "Nuts in May."

Lend Me your Key

> Please will you lend us your key?
> What for?
> Please, our hats are in the garden.
> Yes, if you won't steal any beans.
> Please, we've brought the key back; will you lend
>   us your frying-pan?
> What to do with?
> To fry some beans.
> Where have you got them?
> Out of your garden.   —Earls Heaton (H. Hardy).

One child represents an old woman, and the other players carry on the dialogue with her. At the end of the dialogue the children are chased by the old woman.

See "Mother, Mother, may I go out to Play," "Witch."

Letting the Buck out

This game was played seventy years ago. A ring being formed, the "Buck" inside has to break out, and reach his "home," crying "Home!" before he can be caught and surrounded. Afterwards these words were sung—

Circle: Who comes here?

Buck: Poor Johnny Lingo.

Circle: Don't steal none of my black sheep, Johnny Lingo,
     For if you do
     I shall put you in the pinder pin-fold.
          —Stixwold, Lincs. (Miss M. Peacock).

See "Who goes round my Stone Wall?"

Level-coil

Nares, in his *Glossary*, says this is "a game of which we seem to know no more than that the loser in it was to give up his place to be occupied by another." Minshew gives it thus: "To play at *levell coil*, G. jouer à cul léve: *i.e.*, to play and lift up your taile when you have lost the game, and let another sit down in your place." Coles, in his *English Dictionary*, seems to derive it from the Italian *leva il culo*, and calls it also "Pitch-buttock." In his *Latin Dictionary* he has "*level-coil*, alternation, cession;" and "to play at *level coil*, vices ludendi præbere." Skinner is a little more particular and says, "Vox tesseris globulosis ludentium propria:" an expression belonging to a game played with little round tesseræ. He also derives it from French and Italian. It is mentioned by Jonson, *Tale of a Tub*, iii. 2:—

    "Young Justice Bramble has kept *level-coyl*
    Here in our quarters, stole away our daughter."

Gifford says that, in our old dramatists, it implies riot and disturbance. The same sport is mentioned by Sylvester, *Dubartas*, IV. iv. 2, under the name of *level-sice*:—

    "By tragick death's device
    Ambitious hearts do play at *level-sice*."

In the margin we have this explanation: "A kinde of
Christmas play, wherein each hunteth the other from his seat.
The name seems derived from the French *levez sus*, in English,
arise up." Halliwell's *Dictionary* says that Skelton, ii. 31,
spells it *levell suse*.

Libbety, Libbety, Libbety-lat

A child stands before a hassock, and as if he were going up
stairs; he puts on it first his right and then his left foot,
gradually quickening his steps, keeping time to the words—

> Libbety, libbety, libbety-lat,
> Who can do this? and who can do that?
> And who can do anything better than that?

> —Cornwall (*Folk-lore Journal*, v. 59).

Limpy Coley

A boy's game undescribed.—Patterson's *Antrim and Down
Glossary*.

Little Dog I call you

A number of girls stand in a line with their backs to a wall.
One of their number is sent away to a distance, but remains
within call. Another girl, who stands in front of the line, asks
the girls one by one what they would like if they could obtain
their desires. After she has asked every one, she tells them
to turn their faces to the wall, and calls after the girl who was
sent away, saying, "Little Dog, I call you." The girl replies,
"I shan't come to please you." "I'll get a stick and make
you," is the rejoinder. "I don't care for that." "I've got a
rice pudding for you." "I shan't come for that." "I've got
a dish of bones." "I'll come for that." The Dog then comes.
The girls have been previously told not to laugh whilst the
one who stands out is talking to the Dog. Then the girl says
to the Dog—

> All the birds in the air,
> All the fishes in the sea,
> Come and pick me out (for example)
> The girl with the golden ball.

If the girl who desired the golden ball laughs, the Dog picks
her out. If nobody laughs, he guesses who the girl is that has
wished for the golden ball. If the Dog guesses correctly, she

goes and stands behind him, and if he guesses incorrectly she goes and stands behind the one who has been asking the questions. They continue this until they get to the last girl or girl at the end of the row, who *must* have desired to be—

> A brewer or a baker,
> Or a candlestick maker,
> Or a penknife maker.

Then the questioner says—

> All the birds in the air,
> All the fishes in the sea,
> Come pick me out
> A brewer or a baker,
> Or a candlestick maker,
> Or penknife maker.

If the Dog guesses the right one, he takes that girl on his side, she standing behind him. Then they draw a line and each side tries to pull the other over it.—Sheffield (S. O. Addy). The game, it will be seen, differs in several ways from the other games of "Fool, Fool, come to School" type. The "fool" becomes a definite Dog, and the players *wish* for any thing they choose; the Dog has apparently to find out their wishes. See "All the Birds," "Fool, Fool."

Lobber

There are three or more players on each side, two stones or holes as stations, and one Lobber. The Lobber lobs either a stick about three inches long or a ball—(the ball seems to be a new institution, as a stick was always formerly used)—while the batsman defends the stone or hole with either a short stick or his hand. Every time the stick or ball is hit, the boys defending the stones or holes must change places. Each one is out if the stick or ball lodges in the hole or hits the stone; or if the ball or stone is caught; or if it can be put in the hole or hits the stone while the boys are changing places. This game is also played with two Lobbers, that lob alternately from each end. The game is won by a certain number of runs. —Ireland (*Folk-lore Journal*, ii. 264).

See "Cat," "Cudgel," "Kit-Cat," "Rounders."

Loggats

An old game, forbidden by statute in Henry VIII.'s time.
It is thus played, according to Stevens. A stake is fixed in the
ground; those who play throw Loggats at it, and he that is
nearest the stake wins. Loggats, or loggets, are also small
pieces or logs of wood, such as the country people throw at
fruit that cannot otherwise be reached. "Loggats, little logs
or wooden pins, a play the same with ninepins, in which the
boys, however, often made use of bones instead of wooden
pins" (Dean Miles' MS.; Halliwell's *Dictionary*). Strutt refers
to this game (*Sports*, p. 272).

London

A diagram (similar to Fig. 9 in "Hopscotch") is drawn on a
slate, and two children play. A piece of paper or small piece of
glass or china, called a "chipper," is used to play with. This
is placed at the bottom of the plan, and if of *paper*, is *blown*
gently towards the top; if of glass or china, it is *nicked* with
the *fingers*. The first player blows the paper, and in whichever
space the paper stops makes a small round o with a slate pencil,
to represent a man's head. The paper or chipper is then put
into the starting-place again, and the same player blows, and
makes another "man's head" in the space where the paper
stops. This is continued until all the spaces are occupied. If
the paper goes a second time into a space already occupied by
a "head," the player adds a larger round to the "head," to
represent a "body;" if a third time, a stroke is drawn for a
leg, and if a fourth time, another is added for the second leg;
this completes a "man." If three complete men in one space can
be gained, the player makes "arms;" that is, two lines are
drawn from the figures across the space to the opposite side of
the plan. This occupies that space, and prevents the other player
from putting any "men" in it, or adding to any already there.
When all the spaces are thus occupied by one player, the game
is won. Should the paper be blown on to a line or *outside* the
plan, the player is out; the other player then begins, and makes
as many "men" in her turn, until she goes on a line or outside. Should the paper go into "London," the player is entitled

to make a "head" in every space, or to add another mark to those already there.—Westminster (A. B. Gomme). This game resembles one described by F. H. Low in *Strand Mag.*, ii. 516.

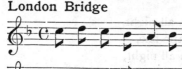

London Bridge

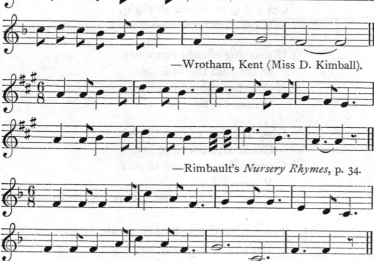

—Wrotham, Kent (Miss D. Kimball).

—Rimbault's *Nursery Rhymes*, p. 34.

—Enborne School, Berks. (Miss M. Kimber).

I. London Bridge is broken down,
       Grant said the little bee,*
    London Bridge is broken down,
       Where I'd be.

    Stones and lime will build it up,
       Grant said the little bee,
    Stones and lime will build it up,
       Where I'd be.

    Get a man to watch all night,
       Grant said the little bee,
    Get a man to watch all night,
       Where I'd be.

* Another informant gives the refrain, "Grand says the little Dee."

Perhaps that man might fall asleep,
    Grant said the little bee,
Perhaps that man might fall asleep,
    Where I'd be.

Get a dog to watch all night,
    Grant said the little bee,
Get a dog to watch all night,
    Where I'd be.

If that dog should run away,
    Grant said the little bee,
If that dog should run away,
    Where I'd be.

Give that dog a bone to pick,
    Grant said the little bee,
Give that dog a bone to pick,
    Where I'd be.
               —Belfast, Ireland (W. H. Patterson).

II.   London Bridge is broken down,
      Dance o'er my lady lee,
   London Bridge is broken down,
      With a gay lady.

   How shall we build it up again ?
      Dance o'er my lady lee,
   How shall we build it up again ?
      With a gay lady.

   Silver and gold will be stole away,
      Dance o'er my lady lee,
   Silver and gold will be stole away,
      With a gay lady.

   Build it up with iron and steel,
      Dance o'er my lady lee,
   Build it up with iron and steel,
      With a gay lady.

Iron and steel will bend and bow,
    Dance o'er my lady lee,
Iron and steel will bend and bow,
    With a gay lady.

Build it up with wood and clay,
    Dance o'er my lady lee,
Build it up with wood and clay,
    With a gay lady.

Wood and clay will wash away,
    Dance o'er my lady lee,
Wood and clay will wash away,
    With a gay lady.

Build it up with stone so strong,
    Dance o'er my lady lee,
Huzza! 'twill last for ages long,
    With a gay lady.
      —[London]* (Halliwell's *Nursery Rhymes*, clii.).

III. London Bridge is broaken down,
    Is broaken down, is broaken down,
    London Bridge is broaken down,
      My fair lady.

    Build it up with bricks and mortar,
    Bricks and mortar, bricks and mortar,
    Build it up with bricks and mortar,
      My fair lady.

    Bricks and mortar will not stay,
    Will not stay, will not stay,
    Bricks and mortar will not stay,
      My fair lady.

    Build it up with penny loaves,
    Penny loaves, penny loaves,
    Build it up with penny loaves,
      My fair lady.

* I have identified this with a version played at Westminster and another taught
to my children by a Hanwell girl.—A. B. G.

Penny loaves will mould away,
Mould away, mould away,
Penny loaves will mould away,
     My fair lady.

What have this poor prisoner done,
Prisoner done, prisoner done,
What have this poor prisoner done ?
     My fair lady.

Stole my watch and lost my key,
Lost my key, lost my key,
Stole my watch and lost my key,
     My fair lady.

Off to prison you must go,
You must go, you must go,
Off to prison you must go,
     My fair lady.
                         —Liphook, Hants (Miss Fowler).

IV.   Where are these great baa-lambs going,
      Baa-lambs going, baa-lambs going,
      Where are these great baa-lambs going ?
           My fair lady.

We are going to London Bridge,
London Bridge, London Bridge,
We are going to London Bridge,
     My fair lady.

London Bridge is broken down,
Broken down, broken down,
London Bridge is broken down,
     My fair lady.

[Then verses follow, sung in the same way and with the same refrain, beginning with—]

Mend it up with penny loaves.

Penny loaves will wash away.

Mend it up with pins and needles.

Pins and needles they will break.

Mend it up with bricks and mortar,

Bricks and mortar, that will do.

[After these verses have been sung—]

What has this great prisoner done,
Prisoner done, prisoner done,
What has this great prisoner done ?
     My fair lady.

Stole a watch and lost the key,
Lost the key, lost the key,
Stole a watch and lost the key,
     My fair lady.

Off to prison you must go,
You must go, you must go,
Off to prison you must go,
     My fair lady.

          —Hurstmonceux, Sussex (Miss Chase).

V.   Over London Bridge we go,
Over London Bridge we go,
Over London Bridge we go,
     Gay ladies, gay !

London Bridge is broken down,
London Bridge is broken down,
London Bridge is broken down,
     Gay ladies, gay !

Build it up with lime and sand,
Build it up with lime and sand,
Build it up with lime and sand,
     Gay ladies, gay !

[Then follow verses sung in the same manner and with the same refrain, beginning with—]

Lime and sand will wash away.

Build it up with penny loaves.

Penny loaves 'll get stole away.

O, what has my poor prisoner done?

Robbed a house and killed a man.

What will you have to set her free?

Fourteen pounds and a wedding gown.

Stamp your foot and let her go!
—Clun (Burne's *Shropshire Folk-lore*, pp. 518–19).

VI.   London Bridge is broken down,
    Broken down, broken down,
    London Bridge is broken down,
        My fair lady.

    Build it up with iron bars,
    Iron bars, iron bars,
    Build it up with iron bars,
        My fair lady.

[Then follow verses with the same refrain, beginning with—]

    Build it up with pins and needles.

    Pins and needles rust and bend.

    Build it up with penny loaves.

    Penny loaves will tumble down.

    Here's a prisoner I have got.

    What's the prisoner done to you?

    Stole my watch and broke my chain.

    What will you take to let him out?

    Ten hundred pounds will let him out.

    Ten hundred pounds we have not got.

    Then off to prison he must go.
—Kent (Miss Dora Kimball).

VII.   London Bridge is falling down,
    Falling down, falling down,
    London Bridge is falling down,
        My fair lady.

Build it up with mortar and bricks,
Mortar and bricks, mortar and bricks,
Build it up with mortar and bricks,
 My fair lady.

[Then follow verses in the same style and with the same refrain, beginning with—]

Bring some water, we'll wash it away.

Build it up with silver and gold.

Silver and gold will be stolen away.

We'll set a man to watch at night.

Suppose the man should fall asleep?
Give him a pipe of tobacco to smoke.

Suppose the pipe should fall and break?
We'll give him a bag of nuts to crack.

Suppose the nuts were rotten and bad?
We'll give him a horse to gallop around, &c.
   —Enborne School, Berks (M. Kimber).

VIII. London Bridge is broken down,
  Gran says the little D,
  London Bridge is broken down,
   Fair la-dy.
  Build it up with lime and stone,
  Gran says the little D,
  Build it up with lime and stone,
   Fair la-dy.

[Then follow verses beginning with the following lines—]

Lime and stone would waste away.

Build it up with penny loaves.

Penny loaves would be eaten away.

Build it up with silver and gold.

Silver and gold would be stolen away.

Get a man to watch all night.

If the man should fall asleep?

Set a dog to bark all night.

If the dog should meet a bone?

Set a cock to crow all night.

If the cock should meet a hen?

Here comes my Lord Duke,
And here comes my Lord John;
Let every one pass by but the very last one,
And catch him if you can.
                            —Cork (Mrs. B. B. Green).

IX. London Bridge is broken down,
    Broken down, broken down,
    London Bridge is broken down,
        My fair lady.

[Other verses commence with one of the following lines, and are sung in the same manner—]

Build it up with penny loaves.

Penny loaves will melt away.

Build it up with iron and steel.

Iron and steel will bend and bow.

Build it up with silver and gold.

Silver and gold I have not got.

What has this poor prisoner done?

Stole my watch and broke my chain.

How many pounds will set him free?

Three hundred pounds will set him free.

The half of that I have not got.

Then off to prison he must go.
                    —Crockham Hill, Kent (Miss E. Chase).

(*b*) This game is now generally played like " Oranges and Lemons," only there is no " tug-of-war" at the end.   Two children hold up their clasped hands to form an arch. The other children form a long line by holding to each other's dresses or waists, and run under. Those who are running under sing the first verse; the two who form the arch sing the second and alternate verses. At the words, "What has this poor prisoner done?" the girls who form the arch catch one of the line (generally the last one). When the last verse is sung the prisoner is taken a little distance away, and the game begins again. At Clun the players form a ring, moving round. They sing the first and alternate verses, and chorus, "London Bridge is broken down." Two players outside the ring run round it, singing the second and alternate verses. When singing "Penny loaves 'll get stole away," one of the two outside children goes into the ring, the other remains and continues her part, singing the next verse. When the last verse is sung the prisoner is released. The Berkshire game (Miss Kimber) is played by the children forming two long lines, each line advancing and retiring alternately while singing their parts. When the last verse is begun the children form a ring and gallop around, all singing this last verse together. In the Cork version (Mrs. Green) the children form a circle by joining hands. They march round and round, singing the verses to a sing-song tune. When singing, "If the cock should meet a hen," they all unclasp hands; two hold each other's hands and form an arch. The rest run under, saying the last verse. The "arch" lower their hands and try to catch the last child.

(c) The analysis of the game-rhymes is on pp. 342–45. It appears from this analysis that the London version is alone in its faithful reflection of an actual building episode. Three other versions introduce the incident of watching by a man, and failing him, a dog or cock; while five versions introduce a prisoner. This incident occurs the greatest number of times. It is not surprising that the London version seems to be the most akin to modern facts, being told so near the spot indicated by the verses, and on this account it cannot be considered as the oldest of the variants. There remain the other two groups. Both are distinguished by the introduction of a

ANALYSIS OF GAME-RHYMES.

No.	Belfast.	Halliwell.	Liphook.	Hurstmonceux.	Shropshire.	Kent.	Enborne.	Cork.	Crockham Hill.
1.				Where are these great baa-lambs going?					
2.				My fair lady.					
3.				We are going to L. B.					
4.					Over L. B. we go.				
5.	L. B. is broken down.	L. B. is broken down.	L. B. is broken down.	L. B. is broken down.	L. B. is broken down.	L. B. is broken down.		L. B. is broken down.	L. B. is broken down.
6.							L. B. is falling down.	Says the little D.	
7.	Grant said the little bee.	Dance o'er my lady lee.							
8.		With a gay lady.							
9.			My fair lady.	My fair lady.	Gay ladies, gay.	My fair lady.	My fair lady.	Fair lady.	My fair lady.
10.									
11.	Where I'd be.								
12.		How shall we build it up again?							
13.	Stones and lime will build it up.		Build it up with bricks and mortar.	Mend it up with bricks and mortar.	Build it up with lime and sand.		Build it up with mortar and bricks.	Build it up with lime and stone.	
14.			Bricks and mortar will not stay.		Lime and sand will wash away.		Mortar and bricks will waste away.	Lime and stone would waste away.	

No.	1	2	3	4	5	6	7	8
15.	Build it up with penny loaves, Penny loaves will melt away.	—	—	Build it up with penny loaves, Penny loaves will tumble down.	Build it up with penny loaves, Penny loaves 'll get stole away.	Mend it up with penny loaves, Penny loaves will wash away.	Build it up with penny loaves, Penny loaves will mould away.	—
16.	—	—	—	—	—	—	—	—
17.	Build it up with silver and gold, Silver and gold I have not got.	Build it up with silver and gold, Silver and gold would be stolen away.	Build it up with silver and gold, Silver and gold will be stolen away.	—	—	—	—	Silver and gold will be stole away.
18.	—	—	—	—	—	—	—	Build it up with iron and steel.
19.	—	—	—	—	—	—	—	Iron and steel will bend and bow.
20.	—	—	—	—	—	—	—	—
21.	—	—	—	Build it up with pins and needles. Pins and needles rust and bend.	—	Mend it up with pins and needles. Pins and needles they will break.	—	—
22.	—	—	—	—	—	—	—	—
23.	—	—	—	—	—	—	—	Build it up with wood and clay.
24.	—	—	—	—	—	—	—	Wood and clay will wash away.
25.	—	—	—	—	—	—	—	Build it up with stone so strong.
26.	—	Set a man to watch all night.	We'll set a man to watch all night.	—	—	—	—	Get a man to watch all night.

ANALYSIS OF GAME-RHYMES—*continued.*

No.	Belfast.	Halliwell.	Liphook.	Hurstmonceux.	Shropshire.	Kent.	Enborne.	Cork.	Crockham Hill.
27.	Perhaps that man might fall asleep.	—	—	—	—	—	Suppose the man should fall asleep.	If the man should fall asleep.	—
28.	—	—	—	—	—	Here's a prisoner I have got.	—	—	—
29.	—	—	What has this poor prisoner done?	What has this great prisoner done?	O, what has my poor prisoner done?	What's the prisoner done to you?	—	—	What has this poor prisoner done?
30.	—	—	Stole my watch and lost my key.	Stole a watch and lost the key.	—	Stole my watch and broke my chain.	—	—	Stole my watch and broke my chain.
31.	—	—	—	—	Robbed a house and killed a man.	—	—	—	—
32.	—	—	—	—	—	—	Give him a pipe of tobacco to smoke.	—	—
33.	—	—	—	—	—	—	Suppose the pipe should fall and break.	—	—
34.	—	—	—	—	—	—	We'll give him a bag of nuts to crack.	—	—
35.	—	—	—	—	—	—	Suppose the nuts were rotten and bad.	—	—
36.	Get a dog to watch all night.	—	—	—	—	—	—	Set a dog to bark all night.	—
37.	If that dog should run away.	—	—	—	—	—	—	If the dog should meet a bone,	—

38.	—	—	—	—	—	—	—	Give that dog a bone to pick.
39.	—	Set a cock to crow all night.	—	—	—	—	—	—
40.	—	If the cock should meet a hen.	—	—	—	—	—	—
41.	How many pounds will set him free?	—	What will you take to let him out?	What will you have to set her free?	—	—	—	—
42.	Three hundred pounds will set him free.	—	Ten hundred pounds will let him out.	F o u r t e e n pounds and a wedding gown.	—	—	—	—
43.	The half of that I have not got.	—	Then a hundred pounds we have not got.	—	—	—	—	—
44.	Then off to prison he must go.	—	Then off to prison you must go.	—	Off to prison you must go.	—	—	—
45.	—	—	—	Stamp your foot and let her go.	—	—	Huzza! it will last for ages long.	—
46.	—	—	—	—	—	Off to prison you must go.	—	—
47.	—	—	—	—	—		—	—
48.	—	—	We'll give him a horse to gallop around.	—	—	—	—	—
49.	Here comes my lord Duke, let everyone pass by but the very last one.	—	—	—	—	—	—	—

human element, one as watchman, the other as prisoner. The watchman incident approaches nearer to modern facts; the prisoner incident remains unexplained by any appeal to modern life, and it occurs more frequently than the others. In only one case, the Shropshire, is the prisoner ransomed; in the others he is sent to prison. Besides this main line of criticism brought out by the analysis there is little to note. The Hurstmonceux version begins with taking lambs over London Bridge, and the Shropshire version with the players themselves going over; but these are doubtless foreign adjuncts, because they do not properly prefix the main incident of the bridge being broken. The Belfast version has a curious line, "Grant said the little bee or dee," which the Cork version renders, "Gran says the little D." To these there is now no meaning that can be traced, but they help to prove that the rhyme originated from a state of things not understood by modern players. In all the versions with the prisoner incident it comes quite suddenly, without any previous indication, except in the Kent version, which introduces the exclamation, " Here's a prisoner I have got!" As the analysis shows the prisoner incident to be a real and not accidental part of the game, and the unmeaning expressions to indicate an origin earlier than modern players can understand, we can turn to other facts to see if the origin can be in any way traced.

(*d*) This game is universally acknowledged to be a very ancient one, but its origin is a subject of some diversity of opinion. The special feature of the rhymes is that considerable difficulty occurs in the building of the bridge by *ordinary* means, but without exactly suggesting that extraordinary means are to be adopted, a prisoner is suddenly taken. The question is, What does this indicate?

Looking to the fact of the widespread superstition of the foundation sacrifice, it would seem that we may have here a tradition of this rite. So recently as 1872, there was a scare in Calcutta when the Hooghly Bridge was being constructed. The natives then got hold of the idea that Mother Ganges, indignant at being bridged, had at last consented to submit to the insult on condition that each pier of the structure was founded on a layer of children's heads (Gomme's *Early Village Life*, p. 29). Formerly, in Siam, when a new city gate was being erected, it was customary for a number of officers to lie in wait and seize the first four or eight persons who happened to pass by, and who were then buried alive under the gate-posts to serve as guardian angels (Tylor's *Primitive Culture*, i. 97). Other instances of the same custom and belief are given in the two works from which these examples are taken; and there is a tradition about London Bridge itself, that the stones were bespattered with the blood of little children. Fitzstephen, in his well-known account of London of the twelfth century, mentions that when the Tower was built the mortar was tempered with the blood of beasts. Prisoners heads were put on the bridge after execution down to modern times, and also on city gates.

These traditions about London, when compared with the actual facts of contemporary savagery, seem to be sufficient to account for such a game as that we are now examining having originated in the foundation sacrifice. Mr. Newell, in his examination of the game, gives countenance to this theory, but he strangely connects it with other games which have a tug-of-war as the finish. Now in all the English examples it is remarkable that the tug-of-war does not appear to be a part of the game; and if this evidence be conclusive, it would appear that this incident got incorporated in America. It is this incident which Mr. Newell dwells upon in his ingenious explanation of the mythological interpretation of the game. But apart from this, the fact that the building of bridges was accompanied by the foundation sacrifice is a more likely origin for such a widespread game which is so intimately connected with a bridge.

This view is confirmed by what may be called the literary history of the game. The verses, as belonging to a game, have only recently been recorded, and how far they go back into tradition it is impossible to say. Dr. Rimbault is probably right when he states "that they have been formed by many fresh additions in a long series of years, and [the game] is perhaps almost interminable when received in all its different versions" (*Notes and Queries*, ii. 338). In *Chronicles of London Bridge*, pp. 152, 153, the author says he obtained the following note from a Bristol correspondent:—"About forty years ago, one moonlight night in the streets of Bristol, my attention was attracted by a dance and chorus of boys and girls, to which the words of this ballad gave measure. The breaking down of the Bridge was announced as the dancers moved round in a circle hand in hand, and the question, 'How shall we build it up again?' was chanted by the leader while the rest stood still." This correspondent also sent the tune the children sang, which is printed in the *Chronicles of London Bridge*. This was evidently the same game, but it would appear that the verses have also been used as a song, and it would be interesting to find out which is the more ancient of the two—the song or the game; and to do this it is necessary that we should know something of the history of the song. A correspondent of *Notes and Queries* (ii. 338) speaks of it as a "lullaby song" well known in the southern part of Kent and in Lincolnshire. In the *Gentleman's Magazine* (1823, Part II. p. 232) appeared the following interesting note:—

The projected demolition of London Bridge recalls to my mind the introductory lines of an old ballad which more than seventy years ago I heard plaintively warbled by a lady who was born in the reign of Charles II., and who lived till nearly the end of that of George II. I now transcribe the lines, not as possessing any great intrinsic merit, but in the hope of learning from some intelligent correspondent the name of the author and the story which gave rise to the ballad, for it probably originated in some accident that happened to the old bridge. The " Lady Lea " evidently refers to the river of that name, the favourite haunt of Isaac Walton, which, after fertilising the counties of Hertford, Essex, and Middlesex, glides into the Thames.

London Bridge is broken down,
Dance over the Lady Lea;
London Bridge is broken down,
With a gay lady [la-dee].

Then we must build it up again.
What shall we build it up withal ?
Build it up with iron and steel,
Iron and steel will bend and break.
Build it up with wood and stone,
Wood and stone will fall away.
Build it up with silver and gold,
Silver and gold will be stolen away.
Then we must set a man to watch,
Suppose the man should fall asleep ?
Then we must put a pipe in his mouth,
Suppose the pipe should fall and break ?
Then we must set a dog to watch,
Suppose the dog should run away ?
Then we must chain him to a post.

The two lines in *italic* are all regularly repeated after each line.—M. Green.

Another correspondent to this magazine, in the same volume, p. 507, observes that the ballad concerning London Bridge "formed, in my remembrance, part of a Christmas Carol, and commenced thus—

Dame, get up and bake your pies,
On Christmas-day in the morning.

The requisition goes on to the dame to prepare for the feast, and her answer is—

London Bridge is fallen down,
On Christ-mas day in the morning, &c.

The inference always was, that until the bridge was rebuilt some stop would be put to the Dame's Christmas operations; but why the falling of London Bridge should form part of a Christmas Carol at Newcastle-upon-Tyne I am at a loss to know." Some fragments were also printed in the *Mirror* for November 1823; and a version is also given by Ritson, *Gammer Gurton's Garland*. The *Heimskringla* (Laing, ii. 260, 261) gives an animated description of the Battle of London Bridge, when Ethelred, after the death of Sweyn, was assisted by Olaf in retaking and entering London, and it is curious that the first line of the game-rhyme appears—

> London Bridge is broken down,
> Gold is won and bright renown ;
>   Shields resounding,
>   War-horns sounding,
> Hild is shouting in the din ;
>   Arrows singing,
>   Mail-coats ringing,
> Odin makes our Olaf win.

If this is anything more than an accidental parallel, we come back to an historical episode wherein the breaking down and rebuilding of London Bridge occur, and it looks as if the two streams down which this tradition has travelled, namely, first, through the game, and second, through the song, both refer to the same event.

Dr. Rimbault has, in his *Nursery Rhymes*, p. 34, reconstructed a copy of the original rhyme from the versions given by Halliwell and the *Mirror*, and gives the tune to which it was sung, which is reprinted here. The tune from Kent is the one generally used in London versions. The tune of a country dance called " London Bridge " is given in Playford's *Dancing Master*, 1728 edition.

Long-duck

A number of children take hold of each other's hands and form a half-circle. The two children at one end of the line lift up their arms, so as to form an arch, and call " Bid, bid, bid," the usual cry for calling ducks. Then the children at the other end pass in order through the arch. This process is repeated, and they go circling round the field.—Addy's *Sheffield Glossary*.

See " Duck Dance."

Long Tag

See " Long Terrace."

Long-Tawl

A game at marbles where each takes aim at the other in turn, a marble being paid in forfeit to whichever of the players may make a hit.—Lowsley's *Berkshire Glossary*.

Long Terrace

Every player chooses a partner. The couples stand immediately in front of each other, forming a long line, one remaining outside of the line on the right-hand side, who is called the "Clapper." The object of the game is for the last couple to reach the top of the line, each running on different sides, and keeping to the side on which they are standing. The object of the Clapper is to hit the one running on the right side of the line, which, if he succeeds in doing, makes him the Clapper, and the Clapper takes his place. [The next *last* couple would then presumably try and reach the top.]— East Kirkby, Lincs. (Miss K. Maughan).

A similar game to this is played at Sporle, Norfolk (Miss Matthews). It is there called "Long Tag." The players stand in line behind one another, and an odd one takes her place somewhere near the front; at a given signal, such as clapping of hands, the two at the back separate and try to meet again in front before the one on the watch can catch them; they may run where they please, and when one is caught that one becomes the one "out."

See "French Jackie."

Loup the Bullocks

Young men go out to a green meadow, and there on all-fours plant themselves in a row about two yards distant from each other. Then he who is stationed farthest back in the "bullock rank" starts up and leaps over the other bullocks before him, by laying his hands on each of their backs; and when he gets over the last one leans down himself as before, whilst all the others, in rotation, follow his example; then he starts and leaps again.

I have sometimes thought that we (the Scotch) have borrowed this recreation from our neighbours of the "Green Isle," as at their wakes they have a play much of the same kind, which they call "Riding Father Doud." One of the wakers takes a stool in his hand, another mounts that one's back, then Father Doud begins rearing and plunging, and if he unhorses his rider with a dash he does well. There is another play (at these wakes) called "Kicking the Brogue," which is even ruder than "Riding Father Doud," and a third one called "Scuddieloof."—Mactaggart's *Gallovidian Encyclopædia*.

Patterson(*Antrim and Down Glossary*)mentions a game called "Leap the Bullock," which he says is the same as "Leap-frog."

Dickinson's *Cumberland Glossary Supplement*, under "Lowp," says it means a leap or jump either running or standing. The various kinds include "Catskip"—one hitch, or hop, and one jump; "Hitch steppin"—hop, step, and lowp; a hitch, a step, and a leap; "Otho"—two hitches, two steps, and a leap; "Lang spang"—two hitches, two steps, a hitch, a step, and a leap.

See "Accroshay," "Knights," "Leap-frog."

Lubin

—Hexham (Miss J. Barker).

—Doncaster (Mr. C. Bell).

—London (A. B. Gomme).

—Dorsetshire (Miss M. Kimber).

—Sporle, Norfolk (Miss Matthews).

I.   Here we dance lubin, lubin, lubin,
        Here we dance lubin light,
     Here we dance lubin, lubin, lubin,
        On a Saturday night.

     Put all the right hands in,
        Take all the right hands out,
     Shake all the right hands together,
        And turn yourselves about.

     Here we dance lubin, lubin, lubin,
        Here we dance lubin light,
     Here we dance lubin, lubin, lubin,
        On a Saturday night.

     Put all your left hands in,
        Take all your left hands out,
     Shake all your left hands together,
        And turn yourselves about.

     Here we dance lubin, lubin, lubin,
        Here we dance lubin light,

Here we dance lubin, lubin, lubin,
  On a Saturday night.

Put all your right feet in,
  Take all your right feet out,
Shake all your right feet together,
  And turn yourselves about.

Here we dance lubin, lubin, lubin,
  Here we dance lubin light,
Here we dance lubin, lubin, lubin,
  On a Saturday night.

Put all your left feet in,
  Take all your left feet out,
Shake all your left feet together,
  And turn yourselves about.

Here we dance lubin, lubin, lubin,
  Here we dance lubin light,
Here we dance lubin, lubin, lubin,
  On a Saturday night.

Put all your heads in,
  Take all your heads out,
Shake all your heads together,
  And turn yourselves about.

Here we dance lubin, lubin, lubin,
  Here we dance lubin light,
Here we dance lubin, lubin, lubin,
  On a Saturday night.

Put all the [Marys] in,
  Take all the [Marys] out,
Shake all the [Marys] together,
  And turn yourselves about.

Here we dance lubin, lubin, lubin,
  Here we dance lubin light,
Here we dance lubin, lubin, lubin,
  On a Saturday night.

Put all yourselves in,
 Take all yourselves out,
Shake all yourselves together,
 And turn yourselves about.
     —Oxford and Wakefield (Miss Fowler).

II. Now we dance looby, looby, looby,
  Now we dance looby, looby, light;
  Shake your right hand a little,
   And turn you round about.

  Now we dance looby, looby, looby;
  Shake your right hand a little,
  Shake your left hand a little,
   And turn you round about.

  Now we dance looby, looby, looby;
  Shake your right hand a little,
  Shake your left hand a little,
  Shake your right foot a little,
   And turn you round about.

  Now we dance looby, looby, looby;
  Shake your right hand a little,
  Shake your left hand a little,
  Shake your right foot a little,
  Shake your left foot a little,
   And turn you round about.

  Now we dance looby, looby, looby;
  Shake your right hand a little,
  Shake your left hand a little,
  Shake your right foot a little,
  Shake your left foot a little,
  Shake your head a little,
   And turn you round about.
     —Halliwell (*Popular Rhymes*, p. 226).

III. Fal de ral la, fal de ral la,
   Hinkumbooby round about.

Right hands in and left hands out,
Hinkumbooby round about;
Fal de ral la, fal de ral la,
Hinkumbooby round about.

Left hands in and right hands out,
Hinkumbooby round about;
Fal de ral la, fal de ral la,
Hinkumbooby round about.

Right foot in and left foot out,
Hinkumbooby round about;
Fal de ral la, fal de ral la,
Hinkumbooby round about.

Left foot in and right foot out,
Hinkumbooby round about;
Fal de ral la, &c.

Heads in and backs out,
Hinkumbooby round about;
Fal de ral la, &c.

Backs in and heads out,
Hinkumbooby round about;
Fal de ral la, &c.

A' feet in and nae feet out,
Hinkumbooby round about;
Fal de ral la, &c.

Shake hands a', shake hands a',
Hinkumbooby round about;
Fal de ral la, &c.

Good night a', good night a',
Hinkumbooby round about;
Fal de ral la, &c.

—Chambers (*Popular Rhymes*, pp. 137-139).

IV. This is the way we wash our hands,
Wash our hands, wash our hands,
To come to school in the morning.

This is the way we wash our face,
Wash our face, wash our face,
To come to school in the morning.

Here we come dancing looby,
Lewby, lewby, li.

Hold your right ear in,
Hold your right ear out,
Shake it a little, a little,
And then turn round about.

Here we come dancing lewby,
Lewby, lewby, li, &c.
                    —Eckington, Derbyshire (S. O. Addy).

  V. How do you luby lue,
   How do you luby lue,
   How do you luby lue,
   O'er the Saturday night?

   Put your right hand in,
   Put your right hand out,
   Shake it in the middle,
   And turn yourselves about.
—Lady C. Gurdon's Suffolk *County Folk-lore*, p. 64.

[Repeat this for "left hand," "right foot," "left foot,"
"heads," and "put yourselves in."]

  VI. Can you dance looby, looby,
   Can you dance looby, looby,
   Can you dance looby, looby,
   All on a Friday night?

   You put your right foot in,
   And then you take it out,
   And wag it, and wag it, and wag it,
   Then turn and turn about.
      Addy's *Sheffield Glossary*.

VII.   Here we dance luby, luby,
      Here we dance luby light,
      Here we dance luby, luby,
      All on a Wednesday night.
          —Ordsall, Nottinghamshire (Miss Matthews).

VIII.   Here we go lubin loo,
      Here we go lubin li,
      Here we go lubin loo,
      Upon a Christmas night.
          —Epworth, Doncaster (C. C. Bell).

IX.   Here we go looby loo,
      Here we go looby li,
      Here we go looby loo,
      All on a New-Year's night.
          —Nottingham (Miss Winfield).

X.   Here we come looby, looby,
      Here we come looby light,
      Here we come looby, looby,
      All on a Saturday night.
          —Belfast (W. H. Patterson).

XI.   Here we come looping, looping [louping ?],
      Looping all the night;
      I put my right foot in,
      I put my right foot out,
      I shake it a little, a little,
      And I turn myself about.
          —Hexham (Miss J. Barker).

XII.   Christian was a soldier,
      A soldier, a soldier,
      Christian was a soldier, and a brave one too.
      Right hand in, right hand out,
      Shake it in the middle, and turn yourself about.
          —Sporle, Norfolk (Miss Matthews).

XIII.   Friskee, friskee, I was and I was
        A-drinking of small beer.
        Right arms in, right arms out,
        Shake yourselves a little, and little,
        And turn yourselves about.
                    —Cornwall (*Folk-lore Journal*, v. p. 49).

XIV.   I love Antimacassar,
        Antimacassar loves me.
        Put your left foot in,
        Put your right foot out,
        Shake it a little, a little, a little,
        And turn yourself about.
                    —Dorsetshire (Miss M. Kimber).

(*b*) A ring is formed and the children dance round, singing the first verse. They then stand till, sing the next verse, and, while singing, suit the action to the word, each child turning herself rapidly round when singing the last line. The first verse is then repeated, and the fourth sung in the same way as the second, and so on.

Another way of playing is that the children do not dance round and round. They form a ring by joining hands, and they then all move in one direction, about half way round, while singing the first line, "lubin;" then back again in the opposite direction, while singing the second line, "light," still keeping the ring form, and so on for the third and fourth lines. In each case the emphasis is laid upon the "Here" of each line, the movement being supposed to answer to the "Here."

The Dorsetshire version (Miss M. Kimber) is played by the children taking hands in pairs, forming a ring, and dancing round. At Eckington (S. O. Addy) the children first pretend to wash their hands, then their face, while singing the words; then comb their hair and brush their clothes; then they join hands and dance round in a ring singing the words which follow, again suiting their actions to the words sung.

In the Scottish version a ring is formed as above. One sings, and the rest join, to the tune of "Lillibullero," the first line. As soon as this is concluded each claps his hand and wheels grotesquely, singing the second line. They then sing the third line, suiting the action to the word, still beating the time; then the second again, wheeling round and clapping hands. When they say "A' feet in, and nae feet out," they all sit down with their feet stretched into the centre of the ring.

(c) The other variants which follow the Halliwell version are limited to the first verse only, as the remainder of the lines are practically the same as those given in Miss Fowler's version which is written at length, and three or four of these apparently retain only the verse given. A London version, collected by myself, is nearly identical with that of Miss Fowler, except that the third line is "Shake your —— a little, a little," instead of as printed. This is sung to the tune given.

The incidents in this game are the same throughout. The only difference in all the versions I have collected being in the number of the different positions to be performed, most of them being for right hands, left hands, right feet, left feet, and heads; others, probably older forms, having "ears," "yourselves," &c. One version, from Eckington, Derbyshire, curiously begins with "washing hands and face," "combing hair," &c., and then continuing with the "Looby" game, an apparent "mix-up" of "Mulberry Bush" and "Looby." Three more versions, Sporle, Cornwall, and Dorsetshire, also have different beginnings, one (Dorsetshire) having the apparently unmeaning "I love Antimacassar."

(d) The origin and meaning of this game appears somewhat doubtful. It is a choral dance, and it may owe its origin to a custom of wild antic dancing in celebration of the rites of some deity in which animal postures were assumed. The Hexham version, "Here we come louping [leaping]" may probably be the oldest and original form, especially if the conjecture that this game is derived from animal rites is accepted. The term "looby," "lubin," or "luby" does not throw much light on the game. Addy (*Sheffield Glossary*) says, "Looby is an old form of the modern 'lubber,' a 'clumsy fellow,' 'a dolt.'" That a stupid or ridiculous meaning is attached to the word "looby" is also shown by one of the old penances for redeeming a forfeit,

where a player has to lie stretched out on his back and
declare,

> Here I lie
> The length of a looby,
> The breadth of a booby,
> And three parts of a jackass.

The Scottish forms of the game bear on the theory of the
game being grotesque. The fact of the players having both
their arms extended at once, one behind and one in front of
them, and the more frequent spinning round, suggest this.
Then, too, there is the sudden "sit down" posture, when "all
feet in" is required.

In the version given by Halliwell there is more difficulty in
the game, and possibly more fun. This version shows the
game to be cumulative, each player having to go through an
additional antic for each verse sung. This idea only needs to
be carried a little further to cause the players to be ridiculous
in their appearance. This version would be more difficult to
perform, and they would be exhausted by the process, and the
constant motion of every member of the body. Attention, too,
might be drawn to the word "Hinkumbooby" occurring in
Chambers's version. Newell (*Games*, p. 131) mentions that
some sixty years ago the game was danced deliberately and
decorously, as old fashion was, with slow rhythmical movement.

Lug and a Bite

A boy flings an apple to some distance. All present race
for it. The winner bites as fast as he can, his compeers
lugging at his ears in the meantime, who bears it as well as
he can, and then he throws down the apple, when the sport is
resumed (Halliwell's *Dictionary*). Brogden's *Lincolnshire Provincial Words* says "Luggery-bite" is a game boys play with
fruit. One bites the fruit, and another pulls his hair until he
throws the fruit away. The game is also played in Lancashire
(*Reliquary*).

See "Bob-Cherry."

Luggie

A boys' game. In this game the boys lead each other about

by the "lugs," *i.e.*, ears; hence the name (Patterson's *Antrim and Down Glossary*). Jamieson says that the leader had to repeat a rhyme, and if he made a mistake, he in turn became Luggie. The rhyme is not recorded.

Luking

The West Riding name for "Knor and Spell." Playing begins at Easter.—Henderson's *Folk-lore*, p. 84.

See "Nur and Spell."

Mag

A game among boys, in which the players throw at a stone set up on edge.—Barnes (*Dorset Glossary*).

Magic Whistle

All the players but three sit on chairs, or stand in two long rows facing each other. One player sits at one end of the two rows as president; another player is then introduced into the room by the third player, who leads him up between the two rows. He is then told to kneel before the one sitting at the end of the row of players. When he kneels any ridiculous words or formula can be said by the presiding boy, and then he and those players who are nearest to the kneeling boy rub his back with their hands for two or three minutes. While they are doing this the boy who led the victim up to the president fastens a string, to which is attached a small whistle, to the victim's coat or jacket. It must be fastened in such a way that the whistle hangs loosely, and will not knock against his back. The whistle is then blown by the player who attached it, and the kneeling boy is told to rise and search for the Magic Whistle. The players who are seated in the chairs must all hold their hands in such a way that the victim suspects it is in their possession, and proceeds to search. The whistle must be blown as often as possible, and in all directions, by those players only who can do so without the victim being able to either see or feel that he is carrying the whistle with him.—London (A. B. Gomme).

This game is also called "Knight of the Whistle." The boy who is to be made a Knight of the Order of the Whistle, when led up between the two rows of players, has a cloak put round his shoulders and a cap with a feather in it on his head. The whistle is then fastened on to the cloak. This is described by the Rev. J. G. Wood (*Modern Playmate*, p. 189). Newell (*Games*, p. 122) gives this with a jesting formula of initiation into knighthood. He says it was not a game of children, but belonged to an older age.

See "Call-the-Guse."

Magical Music

A pleasant drawing-room evening amusement. — Moor's *Suffolk Words*.

Probably the same as "Musical Chairs."

Malaga, Malaga Raisins

A forfeit game. The players sat in a circle. One acquainted with the trick took a poker in his right hand, made some eccentric movements with it, passed it to his left, and gave it to his next neighbour on that side, saying, "Malaga, Malaga raisins, very good raisins I vow," and told him to do the same. Should he fail to pass it from right to left, when he in his turn gave it to his neighbour, without being told where the mistake lay, he was made to pay a forfeit.—Cornwall (*Folk-lore Journal*, v. 50).

"Malaga raisins are very good raisins, but I like Valencias better," is the saying used in the London version of this game, and instead of using a poker a paper-knife is used, and it is played at the table. Other formulæ for games of this kind are, "As round as the moon, has two eyes, a nose, and a mouth." These words are said while drawing on a table with the forefinger of the *left* hand an imaginary face, making eyes, nose, and mouth when saying the words. The fun is caused through those players who are unacquainted with the game drawing the imaginary face with the right hand instead of the left. Another formula is to touch each finger of the right hand with the forefinger of the left hand, saying to each finger in succession, "Big Tom, Little Tom, Tommy, Tom, Tom." The secret in this case is to say, "Look here!" before commencing the formula. It is the business of those players who know the game to say the words in such a way that the uniniated imagine the saying of the words correctly with particular accents on particular words to be where the difficulty lies. If this is well done, it diverts suspicion from the real object of these games. —A. B. Gomme.

Marbles

Brand considers that marbles had their origin in bowls, and received their name from the substance of which the bowls were formerly made. Strutt (*Sports*, p. 384) says, "Marbles have been used as a substitute for bowls. I believe originally nuts, round stones, or any other small things that could easily be bowled along were used as marbles." Rogers notices "Marbles" in his *Pleasures of Memory*, l. 137 :—

> "On yon gray stone that fronts the chancel-door,
>   Worn smooth by busy feet, now seen no more,
>   Each eve we shot the marble through the ring."

Different kinds of marbles are alleys, barios, poppo, stonies. Marrididdles are marbles made by oneself by rolling and baking common clay. By boys these are treated as spurious and are always rejected. In barter, a bary = four stonies; a common white alley = three stonies. Those with pink veins being considered best. Alleys are the most valuable and are always reserved to be used as "taws" (the marble actually used by the player). They are said to have been formerly made of different coloured alabaster. See also Murray's *New English Dict*.

For the different games played with marbles, see "Boss Out," "Bridgeboard," "Bun-hole," "Cob," "Hogo," "Holy Bang," "Hundreds," "Lag," "Long-Tawl," "Nine Holes," "Ring Taw."

Mary Brown

I.   Here we go round, ring by ring,
        To see poor Mary lay in the ring;
        Rise up, rise up, poor Mary Brown,
        To see your dear mother go through the town.

        I won't rise, I won't rise [from off the ground],
        To see my poor mother go through the town.

Rise up, rise up, poor Mary Brown,
To see your dear father go through the town.

I won't rise, I won't rise [from off the ground],
To see my dear father go through the town.

Rise up, rise up, poor Mary Brown,
To see your dear sister go through the town.

I won't rise, I won't rise from off the ground,
To see my dear sister go through the town.

Rise up, rise up, poor Mary Brown,
To see your dear brother go through the town.

I won't rise, I won't rise up from off the ground,
To see my dear brother go through the town.

Rise up, rise up, poor Mary Brown,
To see your dear sweetheart go through the town.

I will rise, I will rise up from off the ground,
To see my dear sweetheart go through the town.
                          —Barnes, Surrey (A. B. Gomme).

II.   Rise up, rise up, Betsy Brown,
      To see your father go through the town.

      I won't rise up upon my feet,
      To see my father go through the street.

      Rise up, rise up, Betsy Brown,
      To see your mother go through the town.

      I won't rise up upon my feet,
      To see my mother go through the street.

[Then follow verses for sister, brother, and lover.   When
this last is sung, she says—]

      I will rise up upon my feet,
      To see my lover go through the street.
                          —Ninfield, Sussex, about sixty years ago
                              (Charles Wise).

III. Rise daughter, rise daughter, off of your poor feet,
      To see your dear mother lie dead at your feet.

I won't rise, I won't rise off of my poor feet,
To see my dear mother lie dead at my feet.

Rise daughter, rise daughter, off of your poor feet,
To see your poor father lie dead at your feet.

I won't rise, I won't rise off of my poor feet,
To see my poor father lie dead at my feet.

Rise daughter, rise daughter, off of your poor feet,
To see your dear sister lie dead at your feet.

I won't rise, I won't rise off of my poor feet,
To see my poor sister lie dead at my feet.

Rise daughter, rise daughter, off of your poor feet,
To see your poor brother lie dead at your feet.

I won't rise, I won't rise off of my poor feet,
To see my poor brother lie dead at my feet.

Rise daughter, rise daughter, off of your poor feet,
To see your dear sweetheart lie dead at your feet.

I will rise, I will rise off of my poor feet,
To see my dear sweetheart lie dead at my feet.
　　　　　　　　　　　—Barnes, Surrey (A. B. Gomme).

IV.　Rise daughter, rise daughter,
　　　　Rise from off your knees,
　　　To see your poor father lie
　　　　Down at yonder trees.

　　　I won't rise, I won't rise,
　　　　From off my knees,
　　　To see my poor father lie
　　　　Down at yonder trees.

[The verses are then repeated for mother, sister, brother, and sweetheart.　When this is said the girl sings—]

　　　I will rise, I will rise,
　　　　From off my knees,
　　　To see my sweetheart lie
　　　　Down at yonder trees.
　　　　　　　　—Hurstmonceux, Sussex (Miss Chase).

V.   Here we all stand round the ring,
      And now we shut poor Mary in;
      Rise up, rise up, poor Mary Brown,
      And see your poor mother go through the town.

[Then follow verses the same as in the Barnes version, No. 1, and then—]

      Rise up, rise up, poor Mary Brown,
      To see the poor beggars go through the town.

      I will not stand up upon my feet
      To see the poor beggars go through the street.

[Two other verses are sometimes added, introducing gentleman and ladies. All versions, however, conclude with the girl saying—]

      Rise up, rise up, poor Mary Brown,
      And see your poor sweetheart go through the town.

      I will get up upon my feet,
      To see my sweetheart go through the street.
              —Halliwell's *Nursery Rhymes*, p. 218.

(*b*) The children form a ring, one child laying or kneeling down in the centre. The ring sing the first, third, fifth, and alternate verses; the girl in the middle answers with the second, fourth, and so on alternately. At the last verse the girl jumps up and breaks through the ring by force; another girl takes her place in the ring, and the game begins again. The Sussex version of " Mary Brown " (Chas. Wise) is played by the children standing in line and advancing and retiring towards the lying or kneeling child. The Barnes version of " Rise, Daughter " is also played in this way. The "daughter" lays down, and at the end of the game joins the line, and another lays down. In the Hurstmonceux version, when the last verse is sung, the girl in the middle rises and picks a boy out of the ring; he goes in the middle with her, and they kiss. The version given by Halliwell is played in the same way as the Barnes version.

(*c*) Halliwell (*Game Rhymes*, p. 219) gives a version of a

Swedish ballad or ring dance-song, entitled "Fair Gundela," he considers this may be a prototype of the English game, or that they may both be indebted to a more primitive original. The Swedish game rather gives the idea of a maiden who has sought supernatural assistance from a wise woman, or witch, to ask after the fate of those dear to her, and the English versions may also be dramatic renderings of a ballad of this character. Mr. Jacobs' *More English Fairy Tales*, p. 221, considers this game to have originated from the Tale of the "Golden Ball."

Mary mixed a Pudding up

Mary mixed a pudding up,
She mixed it very sweet,
She daren't stick a knife in
Till John came home at neet [=night].
Taste John, taste John, don't say nay,
Perhaps to-morrow morning will be our wedding-day.

The bells shall ring and we shall sing,
And all clap hands together (round the ring).

Up the lane and down,
It's slippery as a glass,
If we go to Mrs. ——
We'll find a nice young lass.
Mary with the rosy cheeks,
Catch her if you can ;
And if you cannot catch her,
We'll tell you her young man.
—Hanging Heaton (Herbert Hardy).

A ring is formed by the children joining hands, one child in the centre. The first verse is sang. Two children from the ring go to the one in the centre and *ask* her who is her love, or as they say here [Yorks.], "who she goes with ;" after that the rest is sung.

See "All the Boys."

Merrils

See "Nine Men's Morris."

Merritot, or the Swing

This sport, which is sometimes called "Shuggy-shew" in the North of England, is described as follows by Gay:—

"On two near elms the slackened cord I hung,
Now high, now low, my Blouzalinda swung."

So Rogers, in the *Pleasures of Memory*, l. 77:—

"Soar'd in the swing, half pleas'd and half afraid,
Through sister elms that wav'd their summer shade."

Speght, in his *Glossary*, says, "'Meritot,' a sport used by children by swinging themselves in bell-ropes, or such like, till they are giddy." In *Mercurialis de Arte Gymnastica*, p. 216, there is an engraving of this exercise.

Halliwell quotes from a MS. *Yorkshire Glossary*, as follows:—"'Merrytrotter,' a rope fastened at each end to a beam or branch of a tree, making a curve at the bottom near the floor or ground in which a child can sit, and holding fast by each side of the rope, is swung backwards and forwards."

Baker (*Northamptonshire Glossary*) calls "Merrytotter" the game of "See-saw," and notes that the antiquity of the game is shown by its insertion in Pynson, "Myry totir, child's game, oscillum."

Chaucer probably alludes to it in the following lines of the *Miller's Tale*—

"What eileth you? some gay girle (God it wote)
Hath brought you thus on the merry tote."

Merry-ma-tansa

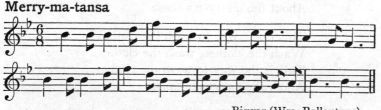

—Biggar (Wm. Ballantyne).

I. Here we go round by jingo-ring,
    Jingo-ring, and jingo-ring,
    Here we go round by jingo-ring,
    About the merry-ma-tansa.

Come name the lad you like the best,
Like the best, like the best,
Come name the lad you like the best,
About the merry-ma-tansa.

Guess ye wha's the young gudeman,
The young gudeman, the young gudeman,
Come guess ye wha's the young gudeman
About the merry-ma-tansa.

Honey's sweet and so is he,
So is he, so is he,
Honey's sweet and so is he,
About the merry-ma-tansa.

[Or—   Crab-apples are sour and so is he,
So is he, so is he,
Crab-apples are sour and so is he,
About the merry-ma-tansa.]

Can she bake and can she brew?
Can she shape and can she sew,
'Boot a house can a' things do?
About the merry-ma-tansa?

She can bake and she can brew,
She can shape and she can sew,
'Boot a house can a' things do,
About the merry-ma-tansa.

This is the way to wash the clothes,
Wash the clothes, wash the clothes,
This is the way to wash the clothes,
About the merry-ma-tansa.

[Then follows verses for wringing clothes, ironing, baking bread, washing hands, face, combing hair, washing and sweeping the house, and a number of other things done in housekeeping. The boy then presents the girl with a ring, and they all sing—]

Now she's married in a goud ring,
A gay goud ring, a gay goud ring,
Now she's married in a goud ring,
About the merry-ma-tansa.

A gay goud ring is a dangerous thing,
A cankerous thing, a cankerous thing,
A gay goud ring is a dangerous thing,
About the merry-ma-tansa.

Now they're married we wish them joy,
Wish them joy, wish them joy,
Now they're married we wish them joy,
About the merry-ma-tansa.

Father and mother they must obey,
Must obey, must obey,
Father and mother they must obey,
About the merry-ma-tansa.

Loving each other like sister and brother,
Sister and brother, sister and brother,
Loving each other like sister and brother,
About the merry-ma-tansa.

We pray this couple may kiss thegither,
Kiss thegither, kiss thegither,
We pray this couple may kiss thegither,
About the merry-ma-tansa.

[If any lad was left without a partner, the ring sing—]

Here's a silly auld man left alone,
Left alone, left alone,
He wants a wife and can't get none,
About the merry-ma-tansa.
                           —Biggar (William Ballantyne).

II.   Here we go the jingo-ring,
      The jingo-ring, the jingo-ring,
      Here we go the jingo-ring,
      About the merry-ma-tansie.

Twice about, and then we fa',
Then we fa', then we fa',
Twice about, and then we fa',
About the merry-ma-tansie.

Guess ye wha's the young goodman,
The young goodman, the young goodman,
Guess ye wha's the young goodman,
About the merry-ma-tansie.

Honey is sweet, and so is he,
So is he, so is he,
Honey is sweet, and so is he,
About the merry-ma-tansie.

[Or—   Apples are sour, and so is he,
So is he, so is he,
Apples are sour, and so is he,
About the merry-ma-tansie.]

He's married wi' a gay gold ring,
A gay gold ring, a gay gold ring,
He's married wi' a gay gold ring,
About the merry-ma-tansie.

A gay gold ring's a cankerous thing,
A cankerous thing, a cankerous thing,
A gay gold ring's a cankerous thing,
About the merry-ma-tansie.

Now they're married, I wish them joy,
I wish them joy, I wish them joy,
Now they're married, I wish them joy,
About the merry-ma-tansie.

Father and mother they must obey,
Must obey, must obey,
Father and mother they must obey,
About the merry-ma-tansie.

Loving each other like sister and brother,
Sister and brother, sister and brother,
Loving each other like sister and brother,
About the merry-ma-tansie.

We pray this couple may kiss together,
Kiss together, kiss together,
We pray this couple may kiss together,
About the merry-ma-tansie.
—Chambers' *Popular Rhymes*, pp. 132–134.

(*b*) At Biggar (Mr. Ballantyne) this game was generally played on the green by boys and girls. A ring is formed by all the children but one, joining hands. The one child stands in the centre. The ring of children dance round the way of the sun, first slowly and then more rapidly. First all the children in the ring bow to the one in the centre, and she bows back. Then they dance round singing the first and second verses, the second verse being addressed to the child in the centre. She then whispers a boy's name to one in the ring. This girl then sings the third verse. None in the ring are supposed to be able to answer, and the name of the chosen boy is then said aloud by the girl who asked the question. If the name is satisfactory the ring sing the fourth verse, and the two players then retire and walk round a little. If the name given is not satisfactory the ring sing the fifth verse, and another child must be chosen. When the two again stand in the centre the boys sing the sixth verse. The girls answer with the seventh. Then all the ring sing the next verses, imitating washing clothes, wringing, ironing, baking bread, washing hands, combing hair, &c., suiting their actions to the words of the verses sung. The boy who was chosen then presents a ring, usually a blade of grass wrapped round her finger, to the girl. The ring then sing the ninth, tenth, eleventh, and twelfth verses. When all have chosen, if any lad is left without a partner, the last verse is sung.

The version recorded by Chambers is similar in action, but there are some important differences in detail. The centre child acts as mistress of the ceremonies. The ring of children dance round her, singing the verses. At the end of the first line of the second verse they all courtesy to her, and she returns the compliment.   At the conclusion of this verse she selects a girl from the ring and asks her her sweetheart's name, which is imparted in a whisper.   Upon this the child in the centre sings the third verse, the ring dancing round as before.   If the ring approves her choice, they sing the fourth verse as in the Biggar version, and if they disapprove, the fifth.   Chambers does not say whether another child is selected, if this is the case; but it is probable, as he says, the marriage is finally concluded upon and effected by the ring singing the verses which follow. When singing the first line of the eighth verse all the ring unclasps hands for a moment, and each child performs a pirouette, clapping her hands above her head.

(c) It seems very clear from both the versions given that this is a ceremonial dance, round or at a place sacred to such ceremonies as betrothal and marriage.   The version given by Chambers suggests this the more strongly, as the child in the centre acts as mistress of the ceremonies, or "go-between," the person who was the negotiator between the parents on either side in bringing a marriage about.   The courtesying and bowing of those in the ring to her may show respect for this office.   On the other hand, there is the more important office of priest or priestess of "the stones" suggested by the action of the game, and the reverence to the centre child may be a relic of this.   The fact that she asks a girl to tell her her sweetheart's name, and then announces the name of the girl's choice for approval or disapproval by the ring in both versions, points to the time when consent by relations and friends on both sides was necessary before the marriage could be agreed upon —the inquiry regarding the qualifications of the proposed wife, the recital of her housewifely abilities, and the giving of the ring by the boy to the girl are also betrothal customs.   It is to be noted that it was a popular belief in ancient times that to wed with a rush-ring was a legal marriage, without the intervention of a priest or the ceremonies of marriage.   Poore, Bishop of Salisbury (circa 1217), prohibited the use of them—

" With gaudy girlonds or fresh flowers dight
   About her necke, or rings of rushes plight."
                                                —Spenser's *Queen.*

And Shakespeare alludes to the custom in the lines—"As fit as ten groats for the hand of an attorney, as Tib's rush for Tom's forefinger."—*All's Well that Ends Well.* The rejoicing and bestowal of the blessing by the ring of friends give an almost complete picture of early Scotch marriage custom. A version of this game, which appeared in the *Weekly Scotsman* of October 16, 1893, by Edgar L. Wakeman, is interesting, as it confirms the above idea, and adds one or two details which may be important, *i.e.*, the "choose your maidens one by one," and "sweep the house till the bride comes home." This game is called the "Gala Ship," and the girls, forming a ring, march round singing—

> Three times round goes the gala, gala ship,
> And three times round goes she;
> Three times round goes the gala, gala ship,
> And sinks to the bottom of the sea.

They repeat this thrice, courtesying low. The first to courtesy is placed in the centre of the circle, when the others sing:—

> Choose your maidens one by one,
> One by one, one by one;
> Choose your maidens one by one—
> And down goes (all courtesy)
> Merrima Tansa!

She chooses her maidens. They take her to a distance, when she is secretly told the name of her lover. The remainder of the girls imitate sweeping, and sing several stanzas to the effect that they will "sweep the house till the bride comes home," when the bride is now placed within the circle, and from a score to a hundred stanzas, with marching and various imitations of what the lucky bride accomplishes or undergoes, are sung. Each one closes with "Down goes Merrima Tansa" and the head-ducking; and this wonderful music-drama of childhood is not concluded until the christening of the bride's first-born, with—

> Next Sunday morn to church she must gae,
> A babe on her knee, the best of 'a—
> And down goes Merrima Tansa!

Jamieson gives the game as a ring within which one goes round with a handkerchief, with which a stroke is given in succession to every one in the ring; the person who strikes, or the taker, still repeating this rhyme :—

> Here I gae round the jingie ring,
> The jingie ring, the jingie ring,
> Here I gae round the jingie ring,
> And through my merry-ma-tanzie.

Then the handkerchief is thrown at one in the ring, who is obliged to take it up and go through the same process. He also mentions another account of the game which had been sent him, which describes the game as played in a similar manner to the versions given by Chambers.

Stewart, in his *Ben Nevis and Glencoe*, p. 361, records the following rhyme :—

> Here we go with merry shout,
> Up and down and round about,
> And dance a merry-ma-tandy,

but he does not describe the game in detail.

Milking Pails

Last bar only. London version.

—Monton, Lancashire (Miss Dendy);
London (A. B. Gomme).

—Earls Heaton, Yorks. (H. Hardy).

I. Mary's gone a-milking,
   Mother, mother,
Mary's gone a-milking,
   Gentle sweet mother o' mine.

Take your pails and go after her,
　Daughter, daughter,
Take your pails and go after her,
　Gentle sweet daughter o' mine.

Buy me a pair of new milking pails,
　Mother, mother,
Buy me a pair of new milking pails,
　Gentle sweet mother o' mine.

Where's the money to come from,
　Daughter, daughter,
Where's the money to come from,
　Gentle sweet daughter o' mine?

Sell my father's feather bed,
　Mother, mother,
Sell my father's feather bed,
　Gentle sweet mother o' mine.

What's your father to sleep on,
　Daughter, daughter,
What's your father to sleep on,
　Gentle sweet daughter o' mine?

Put him in the truckle bed,
　Mother, mother,
Put him in the truckle bed,
　Gentle sweet mother o' mine.

What are the children to sleep on,
　Daughter, daughter,
What are the children to sleep on,
　Gentle sweet daughter o' mine?

Put them in the pig-sty,
　Mother, mother,
Put them in the pig-sty,
　Gentle sweet mother o' mine.

What are the pigs to lie in,
  Daughter, daughter,
What are the pigs to lie in,
  Gentle sweet daughter o' mine?

Put them in the washing-tubs,
  Mother, mother,
Put them in the washing-tubs,
  Gentle sweet mother o' mine.

What am I to wash in,
  Daughter, daughter,
What am I to wash in,
  Gentle sweet daughter o' mine?

Wash in the thimble,
  Mother, mother,
Wash in the thimble,
  Gentle sweet mother o' mine.

Thimble won't hold your father's shirt,
  Daughter, daughter,
Thimble won't hold your father's shirt,
  Gentle sweet daughter o' mine.

Wash in the river,
  Mother, mother,
Wash in the river,
  Gentle sweet mother o' mine.

Suppose the clothes should blow away,
  Daughter, daughter,
Suppose the clothes should blow away,
  Gentle sweet daughter o' mine?

Set a man to watch them,
  Mother, mother,
Set a man to watch them,
  Gentle sweet mother o' mine.

Suppose the man should go to sleep,
    Daughter, daughter,
Suppose the man should go to sleep,
    Gentle sweet daughter o' mine ?

Take a boat and go after them,
    Mother, mother,
Take a boat and go after them,
    Gentle sweet mother o' mine.

Suppose the boat should be upset,
    Daughter, daughter,
Suppose the boat should be upset,
    Gentle sweet daughter o' mine ?

Then that would be an end of you,
    Mother, mother,
Then that would be an end of you,
    Gentle sweet mother o' mine.
          —London Nursemaid, 1876 (A. B. Gomme).

II.   Mary's gone a-milking, a-milking, a-milking,
     Mary's gone a-milking, mother, dear mother of mine.

Where did she get her money from, daughter, daughter ?
Where did she get her money from, daughter, dear
    daughter of mine ?

[Then follow verses sung in the same manner, beginning
with the following lines—]

Sold her father's feather bed, feather bed.
What will your father lie on, lie on ?
Lay him in the pig-sty, pig-sty.
Where will the pigs lie, daughter ?
Lay them in the wash-tub, mother.
What shall I wash in, wash in ?
Wash in a thimble, mother.
A thimble won't hold my night-cap.
Wash by the sea-side, mother.

Suppose the clothes should blow away?
Get a boat and go after them, mother.
But suppose the boat should turn over?
Then that would be an end of you, mother.
—Bocking, Essex (*Folk-lore Record*, iii. 169).

III. Mother, please buy me a milking-can,
    A milking-can, a milking-can!
Mother, please buy me a milking-can,
    With a humpty-dumpty-daisy!

[Then follow verses sung in the same manner, beginning—]

Where's the money to come from, to come from?
Sell my father's feather bed.
Where's your father going to lie?
Lie on the footman's bed.
Where's the footman going to lie?
Lie in the cowshed.
Where's the cows going to lie?
Lie in the pig-sty.
Where's the pig going to lie?
Lie in the dolly-tub.
And what am I to wash in?
Wash in a thimble.
A thimble wunna hold a cap.
Wash in an egg-shell.
An egg-shell wunna hold a shirt.
Wash by the river-side.
Suppose the clothes should float away?
Get a boat and fetch them back.
Suppose the boat should overthrow?
Serve you right for going after them!
—Berrington, Oswestry, Chirbury (Burne's
Shropshire Folk-lore, p. 515).

IV. Mother, will you buy me a milking-can,
    A milking-can, a milking-can?
Mother, will you buy me a milking-can,
    To me, I, O, OM?

Where's the money to buy it with,
To buy it with, to buy it with,
Where's the money to buy it with,
    To me, I, O, OM ?

[Then the following verses—]

    Sell my father's feather bed.
    Where will your father sleep ?
    My father can sleep in the boys' bed.
    Where will the boys sleep ?
    The boys can sleep in the pig-sty.
    Where will the pigs sleep ?
    The pigs can sleep in the wash-tub.
    Where shall I wash my clothes ?
    You can wash them in a thimble.
    A thimble is not large enough.
    You can wash them in an egg-shell.
    An egg-shell would not hold them.
    You can wash them by the river side.
    But what if I should fall in ?
    We'll get a rope and pull you out,
        To me, I, O, OM.   —Sheffield (S. O. Addy).

V.   Mother, come buy me two milking-pails,
    Two milking-pails, two milking-pails,
    Mother, come buy me two milking-pails,
    O sweet mother o' mine.

[Then verses beginning with the following lines—]

    Where shall I get my money from,
    O sweet daughter o' mine ?

    Sell my father's feather beds.
    Where shall your father sleep ?
    Sleep in the servant's bed.
    Where shall the servant sleep ?
    Sleep in the washing-tub.
    Where shall I wash the clothes ?
    Wash them in the river.

Suppose the clothes float away ?
Take a boat and go after them.
Suppose the boat upsets ?
Then you will be drownded.

—London (Miss Dendy).

VI.   Mother, come buy me a milking-can,
       Milking-can, milking-can,
       Mother, come buy me a milking-can,
       O mother o' mine.

       Where can I have my money from,
       O daughter o' mine ?

       Sell my father's bedsteads.
       Where must your father sleep ?
       Sleep in the pig-sty.
       Where must the pig sleep ?
       Sleep in the washing-tub.
       What must I wash in ?
       Wash in your thimble.
       What must I sew with ?
       Sew with your finger.
       What will you say if I prick me ?
       Serve you right, serve you right.

       —Monton, Lancashire (Miss Dendy).

VII.   Mother, will you buy me a pair of milking-cans,
       Milking-cans, milking-cans,
       Mother, will you buy me a pair of milking-cans,
       O gentle mother of mine ?

       But where shall I get the money from ?
       Sell my father's feather bed.
       But where, O where, will your father lie ?
       Father can lie in the girls' bed.
       But where, O where, shall the girls then lie ?
       The girls can lie in the boys' bed.
       But where, O where, shall the boys lie ?
       The boys may lie in the pig-sty.

Then where, O where, will the pigs lie ?
The pigs may lie in the washing-tub.
Then where, O where, shall we wash our clothes ?
We can wash by the river side.
The tide will wash the clothes away.
Get the prop and follow them.
—Sheffield (Miss Lucy Garnett).

VIII.   Mother, buy some milking-cans,
        Milking-cans, milking-cans.

        Where must our money come from ?
        Sell our father's feather bed.

[This goes on for many more verses, articles of furniture
being mentioned in each succeeding verse.]
—Earls Heaton (Herbert Hardy).

IX.   Buy me a milking-pail, my dear mother.
      Where's the money to come from, my dear daughter ?
      Sell father's feather bed.
      Where could your father sleep ?
      Sleep in the pig-sty.
      What's the pigs to sleep in ?
      Put them in the washing-tub.
      What could I wash the clothes in ?
      Wash them in your thimble.
      Thimble isn't big enough for baby's napkin.
      Wash them in a saucer.
      A saucer isn't big enough for father's shirt.
      Wash by the river side, wash by the river side.
—Crockham Hill, Kent (Miss Chase).

X.   Please, mother, buy me a milking-can,
     Milking-can, milking-can,
     Please, mother, buy me a milking-can,
     My dear mother.

     Where can I get the money from ?
     Sell father's feather bed.

Where shall your father sleep?
Sleep in the boys' bed.
Where shall the boys sleep?
Sleep in the pig-sty.
Where shall the pigs sleep?
Sleep in the washing-tub.
What shall I wash with?
Wash in an egg-shell.
The egg-shell will break.
Wash in a thimble.
Thimble's not big enough.
Wash by the river side.
Suppose the things should float away?
Get a boat and go after them.
Suppose the boat should be upset?
Then you'll be drowned,
Drowned, drowned,
Then you'll be drowned,
And a good job too.

> —Enborne, Berks. (Miss M. Kimber).

XI.   Please, mother, buy me a milk-can,
A milk-can, a milk-can,
   Please, mother, do.

Where's the money coming from,
Coming from, coming from,
   What shall I do?

Sell father's feather bed,
Feather bed, feather bed,
   Please mother, do.

Where shall the father sleep?
Sleep in the servants' bed.
Where shall the servants sleep?
Sleep in the pig-sty.
Where shall the pig sleep?
Sleep in the washing-tub.
What shall I wash in?
Wash in a thimble.

The shirts won't go in.
Wash by the river side.
Supposing if I fall in ?
Good job too !
—Hartley Wintney, Winchfield, Hants (H. S. May).

XII.   Mother, buy the milk-pail, mother, dear mother of mine.
Where's the money to come from, children, dear chil-
       dren of mine ?
Sell father's feather bed, mother, dear mother of mine.
Where's your father to sleep in ?
Father can sleep in the servant's bed.
Where's the servant to sleep in ?
Servant can sleep in the pig-sty.
Where's the pig to sleep in ?
The pig can sleep in the wash-tub.
Where shall we wash our clothes ?
Wash our clothes at the sea-side.
If our clothes should swim away ?
Then take a boat and go after them.
O what should we do if the boat should sink ?
O then we should all of us be at an end.
                    —Swaffham, Norfolk (Miss Matthews).

XIII. We want to buy a wash-pan, wash-pan, wash-pan,
       We want to buy a wash-pan, early in the morning.

Where will you get the money from, money from, money
       from ?
We'll sell my father's feather bed, feather bed, feather
       bed.
Where will your father sleep ?
Father'll sleep in the boys' bed.
Where will the boys sleep ?
Boys will sleep in the girls' bed.
Where will the girls sleep ?
Girls will sleep in the pig-sty.
Where will the pigs sleep ?
Pigs will sleep in the washing-pan.
                    —Cowes, Isle of Wight (Miss E. Smith)

XIV.　Mother, may I buy some male-scales, mother, mother ?

　　　Mother, may I buy some male-scales, gentle mother of
　　　　mine ?

　　　Where will the money come from, daughter, daughter ?

　　　Sell my father's feather bed, mother, mother.

　　　Where will your father lie, daughter, daughter ?

　　　Lie in the boys' bed, mother, mother.

　　　Where will the boys lie, daughter, daughter ?

　　　Lie in the servants' bed, mother, mother.

　　　Where will the servants lie, daughter, daughter ?

　　　Lie in the pig-sty, mother, mother.

　　　Where will the pigs lie, daughter, daughter ?

　　　Lie in the washing-tub, mother, mother.

　　　Where will we wash our clothes, daughter, daughter ?

　　　Wash them at the sea-side, mother, mother.

　　　Suppose the clothes should float away, daughter,
　　　　daughter ?

　　　Take a boat and bring them in, mother, mother.

　　　Suppose the boat would go too slow, daughter, daughter?

　　　Take a steamboat and bring them in, mother, mother.

　　　Suppose the steamboat would go too fast, daughter,
　　　　daughter ?

　　　Then take a rope and hang yourself, mother, mother.

　　　　　　　　　　　　—South Shields (Miss Blair, aged 9).

(*b*) One child stands apart and personates the Mother. The
other children form a line, holding hands and facing the
Mother. They advance and retire singing the first, third, and
alternate verses, while the Mother, in response, sings the
second and alternate verses. While the last verse is being
sung the children all run off; the Mother runs after them,
catches them, and beats them. Either the first or last caught
becomes Mother in next game. In the Shropshire game the
Mother should carry a stick. In the Norfolk version the
Mother sits on a form or bank, the other children advancing
and retiring as they sing. After the last verse is sung the
children try to seat themselves on the form or bank where the
Mother has been sitting. If they can thus get home without
the Mother catching them they are safe. The Kentish game is

played with two lines of children advancing and retiring. This was also the way in which the London version (A. B. Gomme) was played. In the version sent by Mr. H. S. May a ring is formed by the children joining hands. One child stands in the centre—she represents the Mother. The ring of children say the first, third, and every alternate verse. The child in the centre says the second, fourth, and alternate verses, and the game is played as above, except that when the Mother has said the last verse the children call out, "Good job, too," and run off, the Mother chasing them as above. The game does not appear to be sung.

(c) This game is somewhat of a cumulative story, having for its finish the making angry and tormenting of a mother. All the versions point to this. One interesting point, that of milk-pails, is, it will be seen, gradually losing ground in the rhymes. Milk-pails were pails of wood suspended from a yoke worn on the milkmaid's shoulders, and these have been giving place to present-day milk-cans. Consequently we find in the rhymes only four versions in which milk-pails are used. In two versions even the sense of milking-can has been lost, and the South Shields version, sent me by little Miss Blair, has degenerated into "male-scales," a thoroughly meaningless phrase. The Cowes version (Miss Smith) has arrived at "wash-pan." The "burden" of the Chirbury version is "a rea, a ria, a roses," and the Sheffield is also remarkable: the "I, O, OM" refers, probably, to something now forgotten, or it may be the "Hi, Ho, Ham!" familiar in many nursery rhymes. The game seems to point to a period some time back, when milking was an important phase of the daily life, or perhaps to the time when it was customary for the maids and women of a village to go to the hilly districts with the cows (summer shealings) for a certain period of time. The references to domestic life are interesting. The scarcity of beds, the best or feather bed, and the children's bed, seeming to be all those available. The feather bed is still a valued piece of household furniture, and is considered somewhat of the nature of a heir-loom, feather beds often descending from mother to daughter for some generations. I have been told instances of this. Gregor, in *Folk-lore of East of Scotland,* p. 52, describes the Scottish box-bed. The "truckle bed" and "footman's bed" probably refers to the small bed under a large one, which was only pulled out at night for use, and pushed under during the day. Illustrations of these beds and the children's bed are given in old tales. The proximity of the pig - sty to the house is manifest. The mention of washing-tubs calls to mind the large wooden tubs formerly always used for the family wash. Before the era of laundresses washing-tubs must have constituted an important part of the family plenishing. Washing in the rivers and streams was also a thing of frequent occurrence, hot water for the purpose of cleansing clothes not being considered necessary, or in many cases desirable. Chambers gives a version of the game (*Popular Rhymes,* p. 36) and also Newell (*Games,* p. 166). Another version from Buckingham is given by Thomas Baker in the *Midland Garner,* 1st ser., ii. 32, in which the mother desires the daughter to "milk in the washing-tub," and the words also appear very curiously tacked on to the "Three Dukes a-riding" game from Berkshire (*Antiquary,* xxvii. 195), where they are very much out of place.

Mineral, Animal, and Vegetable

A ball is thrown by one player to any one of the others. The thrower calls out at the same time either "mineral," "animal," or "vegetable," and counts from one to ten rather quickly. If the player who is touched by the ball does not name something belonging to that kingdom called before the number ten is reached, a forfeit has to be paid.—London (A. B. Gomme).

This is more usually called "Animal, Vegetable, and Mineral." See "Air, Fire, and Water."

Minister's Cat

The first player begins by saying, "The minister's cat is an ambitious cat," the next player "an artful cat," and so on, until they have all named an adjective beginning with A. The next time of going round the adjectives must begin with B, the next time C, and so on, until the whole of the alphabet has been gone through.—Forest of Dean, Gloucestershire (Miss Matthews); Anderby, Lincolnshire (Miss Peacock).

This is apparently the same game as the well-known "I love my love with an A because she is amiable." In this game every player has to repeat the same sentence, but using a different adjective, which adjective must begin with the letter A. Various sentences follow. At the next round the adjectives all begin with B; the next C, until a small story has been built up. Forfeits were exacted for every failure or mistake. The formula usually was—

I love my love with an A because she is (   ).   I hate her with an A because she is (   ).   I took her to the sign of the (   ), and treated her to (   ).   The result was (   ).

Mollish's Land

Cornish name for "Tom Tiddler's Ground."—*Folk-lore Journal*, v. 57.

Monday, Tuesday

A game played with a ball. There are seven players, who each take a name from one of the days of the week. One (Sunday) begins by throwing the ball against a wall, calling out at the same time the name of one of the days, who has to run and catch it before it falls. If this one fails to catch the ball, the first player picks up the ball and tries to hit one of the six with it, who all endeavour to escape being hit. If the player succeeds, he again throws the ball against the wall, calling out another day of the week to catch it. If a player gets hit three times, he is out. The winner is he who has either not been hit at all or the fewest times, or who has been able to stay in the longest. The same game is played with twelve children, who are named after the twelve months of the year.—London and Barnes (A. B. Gomme); *Strand Magazine*, ii. 519 (F. H. Low).

This game belongs apparently to the ball games used for purposes of divination. Mr. Newell (*Games*, p. 181) describes a similar game to this, in which the player whose name is called drops the ball; he must pick it up as quickly as possible while the rest scatter. He then calls "Stand!"

upon which the players halt, and he flings it at whom he pleases. If he misses his aim, he must place himself in a bent position with his hands against a wall until every player has taken a shot at him. The idea of naming children after the days of the week occurs also in the games of "Gipsy," "Witch," and "Mother, Mother, the Pot boils over."

See "Ball," "Burly Whush," "Keppy Ball."

Moolie Pudding

The game of "Deadelie;" one has to run with the hands locked and "taen" the others.—Mactaggart's *Gallovidian Encyclopædia*.

See "Chickidy Hand," "Deadelie," "Hunt the Staigie," "Whiddy."

More Sacks to the Mill

A very rough game, mentioned in Dean Miles' MS., p. 180 (Halliwell's *Dictionary*). Lowsley (*Berkshire Glossary*) says this is "a favourite game with children at Christmas-time, when wishing for one of a romping character," but he does not describe it further. Northall (*English Folk Rhymes*, p. 354) says that in Warwickshire and Staffordshire boys torture an unfortunate victim by throwing him on the ground and falling atop of him, yelling out the formula, "Bags to [on] the mill." This summons calls up other lads, and they add their weight.

Mother, may I go out to Play?

I.　Mother, may I go out to play?
　　No, my child, it's such a wet day.
　　Look how the sun shines, mother.
　　Well, make three round curtseys and be off away.
　　　[Child goes, returns, knocks at door. Mother says,
　　　　"Come in."]
　　What have you been doing all this time?
　　Brushing Jenny's hair and combing Jenny's hair.
　　What did her mother give you for your trouble?
　　A silver penny.
　　Where's my share of it?
　　Cat ran away with it.

Where's the cat?
In the wood.
Where's the wood?
Fire burnt it.
Where's the fire?
Moo-cow drank it.
Where's the moo-cow?
Butcher killed it.
Where's the butcher?
Eating nuts behind the door, and you may have the
      nutshells.

　　　　　—London (Miss Dendy, from a maid-servant).

II.   Please, mother, may I go a-maying?
      Why, daughter, why?
      Because it is my sister's birthday.
      Make three pretty curtseys and walk away.
      Where is your may?
      I met puss, and puss met me, and puss took all my
            may away.
      Where is puss?
      Run up the wood.
      Where is the wood?
      Fire burnt it.
      Where is the fire?
      Water quenched it.
      Where is the water?
      Ducks have drunk it.
      Where are the ducks?
      Butcher killed them.
      Where is the butcher?
      Behind the churchyard, cracking nuts, and leaving
            you the shells. —Sporle, Norfolk (Miss Matthews).

III. Please, mother, may we go out to play?
      Yes, if you don't frighten the chickens.
      No, mother, we won't frighten the chickens.
         [They all go out and say, "Hush! hush!" to
            pretended chickens.]

Where have you been ?
To grandmother's.
What for ?
To go on an errand.
What did you get ?
Some plums.
What did you do with them ?
Made a plum-pudding.
What did she give you ?
A penny.
What did you do with it ?
Bought a calf.
What did you do with it ?
Sold it.
What did you do with the money ?
Gave it to the butcher, and he gave me a penny back, and I bought some nuts with it.
What did you do with them ?
Gave them to the butcher, and he's behind the church-yard cracking them, and leaving you the shells.

—Sporle, Norfolk (Miss Matthews).

IV.   Mother, mother, may I go to play ?
No, daughter, no ! for fear you should stay.
Only as far as the garden gate, to gather flowers for my wedding day.
Make a fine curtsey and go your way.
[They all curtsey and scamper off, and proceed to plan some mischief.   Then they return.]
Now where have you been ?
Up to Uncle John's.
What for ?
Half a loaf, half a cheese, and half a pound of butter.
Where's my share ?
Up in cupboard.
'Tisn't there, then !
Then the cat eat it.

And where's the cat ?
Up on the wood [*i.e.*, the faggots].
And where's the wood ?
Fire burnt it.
Where's the fire ?
Water douted it [*i.e.*, put it out].
Where's the water ?
Ox drank it.
Where's the ox ?
Butcher killed it.
And where's the butcher ?
Behind the door cracking nuts, and you may eat
    the shells of them if you like.
    —Dorsetshire (*Folk-lore Journal*, vii. 219).

V.   Please may I go out to play ?
     How long will you stay ?
     Three hours in a day.
     Will you come when I call you ?
     No.
     Will you come when I fetch you ?
     Yes.
     Make then your curtseys and be off.
The girls then scamper off as before, and as they run about
the field keep calling out, " I won't go home till seven o'clock,
I won't go home till seven o'clock." After they have been
running about for some five or ten minutes the Mother calls
Alice (or whatever the name may be) to come home, when the
one addressed will run all the faster, crying louder than before,
" I won't go home till seven o'clock." Then the Mother commences to chase them until she catches them, and when she
gets them to any particular place in the field where the others
are playing, she says—
     Where have you been ?
     Up to grandmother's.
     What have you done that you have been away so long ?
     I have cleaned the grate and dusted the room.
     What did she give you ?

A piece of bread and cheese so big as a house, and a
   piece of plum cake so big as a mouse.
Where's my share?
Up in higher cupboard.
It's not there.
Up in lower cupboard.
It's not there.
Then the cat have eat it.
Where's the cat?
Up in heath.
Where's the heath?
The fire burnt it.
[The rest is the same as in the last version, p. 393.]
                —Dorsetshire (*Folk-lore Journal*, vii. 221–222).

VI.   Mother, mother, may I (or we) go out to play?
      No, child! no, child! not for the day.
      Why, mother? why, mother? I won't stay long.
      Make three pretty courtesies, and away begone.
      One for mammy, one for daddy, one for Uncle John.
      Where, child! where, child! have you been all the day?
      Up to granny's.
      What have you been doing there?

[The answer to this is often, "Washing doll's clothes," but
anything may be mentioned.]

      What did she give you?

[The reply is again left to the child's fancy.]

      Where's my share?
      The cat ate it [or, In the cat's belly]. What's in that
         box, mother?
      Twopence, my child.
      What for, mother?
      To buy a stick to beat you, and a rope to hang you, my
         child.   —Cornwall (*Folk-lore Journal*, v. 55, 56).

VII. Grandmother, grandmother grey,
      May I go out to play?
      No, no, no, it is a very wet day.

Grandmother, grandmother grey,
May I go out to play?
Yes, yes, yes, if you don't frighten the geese away.
Children, I call you.
I can't hear you.
Where are your manners?
In my shoe.
Who do you care for?
Not for you.   —Earls Heaton, Yorks. (H. Hardy).

VIII. Pray, mother, pray,
May I go out to play?
No, daughter, no, daughter,
Not every fine day.
Why, mother, why?
I shan't be gone long.
Make a fine curtsey
And glad git you gone.—
Wait for your sister.
                —Hurstmonceux, Sussex (Miss Chase).

IX.   Please, mother, please, mother, may I go out to play?
No, child, no, child, 'tis such a cold day.
Why, mother, why, mother, I won't stay long.
Make three pretty curtseys and off you run.
                —Northants (Rev. W. D. Sweeting).

(b) One girl is chosen to act as "Mother," the rest of the players pretend to be her children, and stand in front of her, not in a line, but in a group. One of them, very frequently all the children ask her the first question, and the Mother answers. When she gives permission for the children to go out they all curtsey three times, and run off and pretend to play. They then return, and the rest of the dialogue is said, the Mother asking the questions and the children replying. At the end of the dialogue the Mother chases and catches them, one after the other, pretending to beat and punish them. In the Northants and Hurstmonceux games there appears to be no chasing. In the London version (Miss Dendy) only two children are ·mentioned as playing. When the Mother is chasing the girl she keeps asking, "Where's my share of the silver penny?" to which the girl replies, "You may have the nut-shells." In the Cornish version, when the Mother has caught one of the children, she beats her and puts her hands round the child's throat as if she were going to hang her.

(c) Miss Courtney, in *Folk-lore Journal*, v. 55, says: "I thought this game was a thing of the past, but I came across some children playing it in the streets of Penzance in 1883." It belongs to the cumulative group of games, and is similar in this respect to "Milking Pails," "Mother, Mother, the Pot boils over," &c. There seems to be no other object in the game as now played except the pleasures of teasing and showing defiance to a mother's commands, and trying to escape the consequences of disobedience by flight, in order that the mother may chase them. The idea may be that, if she is "out of breath," she cannot chastise so much. Mr. Newell (*Games*, p. 172) gives versions of a similar game.

Mother Mop

All the players, except one, stand two by two in front of each other, the inner ones forming an arch with their hands united —this is called the "oven." The odd child is "Mother Mop." She busies herself with a pretended mop, peel, &c., after the manner of old-fashioned bakers, making much ado in the valley between the rows of children. The oven soon gets demolished, and the last child vanquished becomes "Mother Mop" the next time.—Bitterne, Hants (Mrs. Byford).

It seems probable that the inner rows of children should kneel or stoop down in order that "Mother Mop" should have as much trouble as possible with her oven. The game may have lost some of its details in other directions, as there is no apparent reason why the oven is demolished or broken down.

See "Jack, Jack, the Bread's a-burning."

Mother, Mother, the Pot Boils over

A number of girls choose one of their number to represent a witch, and another to be a mother. The Witch stands near the corner of a wall, so that she can peep round. Then the

Mother counts the children by the seven days of the week, "Monday," "Tuesday," &c., and appoints another girl to act as guardian over them.   She then pretends to go out washing, removing to a short distance so as to be within ear-shot of the other children.   As soon as the Mother has gone, the old Witch comes and says, "Please, can I light my pipe?"   Then the children say, "Yes, if you won't spit on t' hearth."   She pretends to light her pipe, but spits on the hearth, and runs away with the girl called Sunday.   Then the Guardian, among the confusion, pretends to rush down stairs, and, failing to find Sunday, calls out, "Mother, mother, t' pot boils over."   The Mother replies, "Put your head in;" the Guardian says, "It's all over hairs;" the Mother says, "Put the dish-clout in;" the Guardian says, "It's greasy;" the Mother says, "Get a fork;" the Guardian says, "It's rusty;" the Mother says, "I'll come mysen."   She comes, and begins to count the children, Monday, Tuesday, up to Saturday, and missing Sunday, asks, "Where's Sunday?" the Guardian says, "T' old Witch has fetched her."   The Mother answers, "Where was you?" "Up stairs."   The Mother says, "What doing?"   "Making t' beds." "Why didn't you come down?"   "Because I had no shoes." "Why didn't you borrow a pair?"   "Because nobody would lend me a pair."   "Why didn't you steal a pair."   "Do you want me to get hung?"   Then the Mother runs after her, and if she can catch her thrashes her for letting Sunday go.   Then the Mother pretends to go out washing again, and the Witch fetches the other days of the week one by one, when the same dialogue is rehearsed.—Dronfield, Derbyshire (S. O. Addy).

This game was also played in London.   The *dramatis personæ* were a mother, an eldest daughter, the younger children, a witch, and a pot was represented by another child. The Mother names the children after the days of the week. She tells her eldest daughter that she is going to wash, and that she expects her to take great care of her sisters, and to be sure and not let the old witch take them.   She is also to look after the dinner, and be sure and not let the pot boil over. The Mother then departs, and stays at a little distance from the others.   The eldest daughter pretends to be very busy putting the house to rights, sweeps the floor, and makes everything tidy; the younger children pretend to play, and get in the elder sister's way. She gets angry with them, and pretends to beat them. Now, the girl who personates the Witch comes and raps with her knuckles on a supposed door. The Witch stooped when walking, and had a stick to help her along.

Come in, says the eldest sister. What do you want?

Let me light my pipe at your fire? My fire's out.

Yes! if you'll not dirty the hearth.

No, certainly; I'll be careful.

While the eldest sister pretends to look on the shelf for something, the Witch "dirties" the hearth, catches hold of Monday and runs off with her; and at this moment the pot boils over. The child who is the pot makes a "hissing and fizzing" noise. The daughter calls out—

Mother, mother, the pot boils over.

Take the spoon and skim it.

Can't find it.

Look on the shelf.

Can't reach it.

Take the stool.

The leg's broke.

Take the chair.

Chair 's gone to be mended.

I suppose I must come myself?

The Mother here wrings her hands out of the water in the washing-tub and comes in. She looks about and misses Monday.

Where's Monday?

Oh, please, Mother, please, I couldn't help it; but some one came to beg a light for her pipe, and when I went for it she took Monday off.

Why, that's the witch!

The Mother pretends to beat the eldest daughter, tells her to be more careful another time, and to be sure and not let the pot boil over. The eldest daughter cries, and promises to be more careful, and the Mother goes again to the wash-tub.

The same thing occurs again. The Witch comes and asks—
Please, will you lend me your tinder-box ?   My fire's out.
Yes, certainly, if you'll bring it back directly.
You shall have it in half-an-hour.
While the tinder-box is being looked for she runs off with
Tuesday.   Then the pot boils over, and the same dialogue is
repeated.   The Mother comes and finds Tuesday gone.   This
is repeated for all the seven children in turn, different articles,
gridiron, poker, &c., being borrowed each time.   Finally, the
eldest daughter is taken off too.   There is no one now to watch
the pot, so it boils over, and makes so much noise that the
Mother hears it and comes to see why it is.   Finding her
eldest daughter gone too, she goes after her children to the
Witch's house.   A dialogue ensues between the Witch and
the Mother.   The Mother asks—
    Is this the way to the Witch's house ?
    There's a red bull that way !
    I'll go this way.
    There's a mad cow that way !
    I'll go this way.
    There's a mad dog that way !
She then insists on entering the house to look for her children.   The Witch will not admit her, and says—
    Your boots are too dirty.
    I'll take my boots off.
    Your stockings are too dirty.
    I'll take them off.
    Your feet are dirty.
    I'll cut them off.
    The blood will run over the threshold.
    I'll wrap them up in a blanket.
    The blood will run through.
This enrages the Mother, and she pushes her way into the
supposed house, and looks about, and calls her children.   She
goes to one and says—
    This tastes like my Monday.
The Witch tells her it's a barrel of pork.
    No, no, this is my Monday ; run away home.

Upon this Monday jumps up from her crouching or kneeling posture [the children were generally put by the Witch behind some chairs all close together in one corner of the room], and runs off, followed by all the others and their Mother. The Witch tries to catch one, and if successful that child becomes Witch next time.—A. B. Gomme.

A probable explanation of this game is that it illustrates some of the practices and customs connected with fire-worship and the worship of the hearth, and that the pot is a magical one, and would only boil over when something wrong had occurred and the Mother's presence was necessary. The pot boils over directly a child is taken away, and appears to cease doing this when the Mother comes in. It is remarkable, too, that the Witch should want to borrow a light from the fire; the objection to the giving of fire out of the house is a well-known and widely-diffused superstition, the possession of a brand from the house-fire giving power to the possessor over the inmates of a house. The mention of the spitting on the hearth in the Sheffield version, and dirtying the hearth in the London version, give confirmation to the theory that the desecration of the fire or hearth is the cause of the pot boiling over, and that the spirit of the hearth or fire is offended at the sacrilege. The Witch, too, may be unable to get possession of a child until she has something belonging to the house. The journey of the Mother to the Witch's house in search of her children, the obstacles put in her path, and the mention of the spilling of blood on the threshold, are incidents which have great significance. Why the "keeling" or skimming of the contents of the pot should be so difficult a task for the eldest daughter that the Mother is obliged to come herself, is not so clear; the skimming is of course to prevent the pot boiling over, and the pot may be supposed to take the place of the Mother or Guardian of the hearth, and tell when misfortune or trouble is at hand. Or the "boiling over" (which, if continued, would extinguish the fire and sully the stone) may be an offence to the hearth spirit, who ceases then to protect the inmates of the house. Fairies are said to have power over the inmates of a house when the threshold and kitchen utensils are left dirty and uncared for.   Thus on the theories accompanying the ancient house ritual, this extraordinary game assumes a rational aspect, and it is not too much to suggest that this explanation is the correct one.

In the game of "Witch" practically the same incidents occur, and nearly the same dialogue, but the significant elements of pot-boiling and fire-protection do not appear in that game.   It is not certain whether we have two independent games, or whether "The Witch" is this game, the incidents of pot-boiling and the fire-protection having been lost in its transmission to more modern notions.   Although so closely allied, these games are not one at the present day, and are therefore treated separately.   Newell (*Games*, p. 218) gives some versions of "Witch" which show a connection between that game and this.   See "Keeling the Pot," "Witch."

Mount the Tin

One child throws a tin (any kind of tin will do) to some distance, and then walks towards it without looking round. The other children, in the meantime, hide somewhere near. The child who threw the tin has to guard it, and at the same time try to find those who are hiding.   If he sees one he must call the name, and run to strike the tin with his foot.   He does this until each one has been discovered.   As they are seen they must stand out.   The one who was first found has to guard the tin next time.   Should one of the players be able to strike the tin while the keeper is absent, that player calls out, "Hide again."   They can then all hide until the same keeper discovers them again.—Beddgelert (Mrs. Williams).

See "New Squat."

Mouse and the Cobbler

One girl stands up and personates a mother, another pretends to be a mouse, and crouches behind a chair in a corner.   The mother says to another player—

Go and get your father's shirt.

This player goes to the chair to look for the shirt, and is tickled or touched by the one hiding.   She rushes back and calls out—   Mother, there's a mouse.

Go and get your father's coat.
There's a mouse.
Go and get your father's watch and chain.
There's a mouse.

The Mother then goes to see herself. The second time she is scratched and chased. When caught she takes the Mouse's place.—Deptford, Kent (Miss Chase).

This is evidently the same game as "Ghost in the Garden" and "Ghost in the Copper," in a decaying stage. There is no *raison d'etre* for either mouse or cobbler. Probably these words are a corruption of the older "Ghost in the Copper."

Muffin Man

—Earls Heaton (H. Hardy).

—Congleton Workhouse (Miss A. E. Twemlow).

I. Have you seen the muffin man, the muffin man, the
        muffin man,
    Have you seen the muffin man that lives in Drury
        Lane O ?
    Yes, I've seen the muffin man, the muffin man, the
        muffin man ;
    Yes, I've seen the muffin man who lives in Drury
        Lane O.   —Earls Heaton, Yorks. (H. Hardy).

II. O, have you seen the muffin man,
     The muffin man, the muffin man ;
     O, have you seen the muffin man
     Who lives in Drury Lane O ?
                —N.-W. Lincolnshire (Rev. — Roberts).

III.   Have you seen the muffin girl,
  The muffin girl, the muffin girl?
  O have you seen the muffin girl
  Down in yonder lane?
   —Congleton Workhouse School (Miss A. E. Twemlow).

IV.   Don't you know the muffin man?
  Don't you know his name?
  Don't you know the muffin man
  That lives in our lane?
  All around the Butter Cross,
  Up by St. Giles's,
  Up and down the Gullet Street,
  And call at Molly Miles's!
   —Burne's *Shropshire Folk-lore*, p. 571.

V.   Have you seen the nutting girl,
  The nutting girl, the nutting girl?
  Have you seen the nutting girl,
   Down in yonder lane O?
    —Holmfirth (H. Hardy).

(*b*) A ring is formed by the players joining hands; one child, who is blindfolded and holds a stick, stands in the centre. The ring dance round, singing the verse. They then stand still, and the centre child holds out the stick and touches one of the ring. This player must take hold of the stick. Then the Muffin Man asks this player any questions he pleases, "Is the morn shining?" "Is ink white?" &c. The child who holds the stick answers "Yes" or "No" in a disguised voice, and the Muffin Man then guesses who it is. He is allowed three tries. If he guesses right he joins the ring, and the child who was touched takes his place in the centre. In the Yorkshire versions no questions are asked; the blindfolded child goes to any one he can touch, and tries to guess his or her name. The other version, sent by Mr. Hardy, is played in the same way, and sung to the same tune. In the Congleton version (Miss Twemlow), the blindfolded child tries to catch one of those in the ring, when the verse is sung. The lines, with an additional four from *Shropshire Folk-lore*, are given by Miss Burne among nursery rhymes and riddles.

See " Buff with a Stick," " Dinah."

Mulberry Bush

—Miss Harrison.

Here we go round the mulberry bush,
The mulberry bush, the mulberry bush,
Here we go round the mulberry bush,
On a cold and frosty morning.

This is the way we wash our hands,
Wash our hands, wash our hands,
This is the way we wash our hands,
On a cold and frosty morning.

Here we go round the mulberry bush,
The mulberry bush, the mulberry bush,
Here we go round the mulberry bush,
On a cold and frosty morning.

This is the way we wash our clothes,
Wash our clothes, wash our clothes,
This is the way we wash our clothes,
On a cold and frosty morning.

Here we go round the mulberry bush,
The mulberry bush, the mulberry bush,
Here we go round the mulberry bush,
On a cold and frosty morning.

This is the way we go to school,
We go to school, we go to school,
This is the way we go to school,
On a cold and frosty morning.

Here we go round the mulberry bush,
The mulberry bush, the mulberry bush,
Here we go round the mulberry bush,
On a cold and frosty morning.

—Liphook, Hants (Miss Fowler).

(*b*) The children form a ring, all joining hands and dancing round while singing the first verse. When singing the last line they unclasp their hands, and each one turns rapidly round. They then sing the next verse, suiting their actions to the words they sing, again turning round singly at the last line. This is done with every alternate verse, the first verse being always sung as a chorus or dance in between the different action-verses. The verses may be varied or added to at pleasure. The actions generally consist of washing and dressing oneself, combing hair, washing clothes, baking bread, sweeping the floor, going to and returning from school, learning to read, cleaning boots, and lacing stays. When "going to school," the children walk two by two in an orderly manner; when "coming home from school," jumping and running is the style adopted; "lacing stays," the hands are put behind and moved first one and then the other, as if lacing; "this is the way the ladies walk," holding up skirts and walking primly; "gentlemen walk," walking with long strides and sticks. The dressing process and cleaning boots preceded "school."

(*c*) This game is well known, and played in almost all parts of England. It is always played in the same way. There is so little variety in the different versions that it appears unnecessary to give more than one here. In the many versions sent the only variants are: In Sporle, Norfolk, Miss Matthews says the game is sometimes called "*Ivy* Bush," or "*Ivory* Bush;" and Mr. C. C. Bell, of Epworth, sends a version, "Here we go round the Mulberry *Tree*." In Notts it is called "Holly Bush" (Miss Winfield). A version given in the *Folk-lore Record*, iv. 174, is called the "*Gooseberry* Bush," and Halliwell (*Popular Nursery Rhymes*, p. 224) records a game, the "Bramble Bush." "The bush," he says, "is often imaginative, but is sometimes represented by a child in the centre." Chambers (*Popular Rhymes*, pp. 134, 135) gives the game as a form of the "Merry-

ma-tanzie "—a kind of dance. They sing while moving round
to the tune of "Nancy Dawson," and stopping short with
courtesy at the conclusion.

> Here we go round the mulberry bush,
> The mulberry bush, the mulberry bush,
> Here we go round the mulberry bush,
> And round the merry-ma-tanzie.

Disjoining hands, they then begin, with skirts held daintily
up behind, to walk singly along, singing—

> This is the way the ladies walk,
> The ladies walk, the ladies walk;
> This is the way the ladies walk,
> And round the merry-ma-tanzie.

At the last line they reunite, and again wheel round in a ring,
singing as before—

> Here we go round the mulberry bush, &c.

After which, they perhaps simulate the walk of gentlemen, the
chief feature of which is length of stride, concluding with the
ring dance as before. Probably the next movement may be—

> This is the way they wash the clothes,
> Wash the clothes, wash the clothes;
> This is the way they wash the clothes,
> And round the merry-ma-tanzie.

After which there is, as usual, the ring dance. They then
represent washing, ironing clothes, baking bread, washing the
house, and a number of other familiar proceedings.

Chambers quotes a fragment of this "little ballet," as practised
at Kilbarchan, in Renfrewshire, which contains the following
lines similar to those in this game :—

> She synes the dishes three times a day,
> Three times a day, three times a day;
> She synes the dishes three times a day,
> Come alang wi' the merry-ma-tanzie.

> She bakes the scones three times a day,
> Three times a day, three times a day;
> She bakes the scones three times a day,
> Come alang wi' the merry-ma-tanzie.

She ranges the stules three times a day,
Three times a day, three times a day ;
She ranges the stules three times a day,
Come alang wi' the merry-ma-tanzie.

This game originated, no doubt, as a marriage dance round
a sacred tree or bush. As it now exists it appears to have
no other character than the performance of duties such as
those enumerated in the description. In no version that I
am acquainted with do the elements of love and marriage
or kissing occur, otherwise the resemblance it bears to the
Scotch "Merry-ma-tanzie" would suggest that it is a portion of that game. This game possesses the centre tree,
which is not preserved in "Merry-ma-tansa." Trees were
formerly sacred to dancing at the marriage festival, as at
Polwarth in Berwickshire, where the custom once prevailed,
which is not unworthy of notice. "In the midst of the
village are two thorn trees near to each other; round these
every newly-married pair were expected to dance with all
their friends; from hence arose the old song, 'Polwarth on
the Green'" (*New Statistical Account of Scotland, Polwarth,
Berwickshire*, ii. 234). Holland (*Cheshire Glossary*), under
"Kissing Bush," says, "A bush of holly, ivy, or other ever-
greens, which is hung up in farm kitchens at Christmas, and
serves the purpose of mistletoe. The kissing bushes are usually
prepared by the farm lads on Christmas Eve, and they are
often tastefully decorated with apples, oranges, and bits of
gay-coloured ribbon. I have occasionally seen them made
upon a framework of hoop iron something in the form of a
crown, with a socket at the bottom to hold a lighted candle."
Brand (ii. 15) also describes how in Ireland men and women
dance round about a bush in a large ring on the Patron Day.
Newell (*Games*, p. 86), gives this game, and also mentions
one in which "barberry bush" is named. The tune in all
versions is the same. See " Merry-ma-tansa," " Nettles."

Munshets or Munshits

Is played by two boys as follows :—One of the boys remains
"at home," and the other goes out to a prescribed distance.

The boy who remains "at home" makes a small hole in the ground, and holds in his hand a stick about three feet long to strike with. The boy who is out at field throws a stick in the direction of this hole, at which the other strikes. If he hits it, he has to run to a prescribed mark and back to the hole without being caught or touched with the smaller stick by his play-fellow. If he is caught, he is "out," and has to go to field. And if the boy at field can throw his stick so near to the hole as to be within the length or measure of that stick, the boy at home has to go out to field. A number of boys often play together; for any even number can play. I am told that the game was common fifty years ago. In principle it resembles cricket, and looks like the rude beginning of the game.—Addy's *Sheffield Glossary*.

See "Cat," "Cudgel," "Kit-cat," "Tip-cat."

Musical Chairs

A line of chairs is placed in a row down a room (one chair less than the number of children who are playing) in such a way that every alternate chair only is available on either side for the players to seat themselves. The children walk or dance round the, chairs, keeping quite close to them. The piano or other musical instrument is played while they are dancing round. The music is continued for any length of time the player pleases, the children running round the chairs as long as the music goes on. The player stops the music suddenly, when all the children endeavour to take seats. One will be unable to find a seat, and this player remains "out." A chair is then taken away, and the music and dancing round begins again. There should always be one chair less than the number of players.—A. B. Gomme.

In Ellesmere, Miss Burne says, "Snap-tongs," called in other circles "Magic Music" or "Musical Chairs," is thus played. Five players take part; four chairs are set in the middle, and one of the players, who holds a pair of tongs, desires the others to dance round them till the clock strikes a certain hour, which is done by snapping the tongs together so many times. While they dance, a chair is taken away, and the player who cannot find a seat has to become the "snap-tongs" next time.—*Shropshire Folk-lore*, p. 525.

Nacks

A game in which pegs of wood play a similar part to the well-known object "Aunt Sally."—Robinson's *Mid Yorkshire Glossary*.

Namers and Guessers

Any number of players can play this game. Two are chosen, the one to be Namer, and the other Guesser or Witch. The rest of the players range themselves in a row. The Guesser retires out of sight or to a distance. The Namer then gives each player a secret name. When names have been given to all the players, the Namer calls on the Guesser to come, by saying—

> Witchie, witchie, yer bannocks are burnin',
> An' ready for turnin'.

Whereupon he approaches, and the Namer says—

> Come, chois me out, come, chois me in, to ——

(naming one by the assumed name). The players all shout, "Tack me, tack me," repeatedly. The Witch points to one. If the guess is correct the player goes to the Witch's side, but if it is incorrect he goes to the Namer's side. This goes on till all the players are ranged on the one side or the other. The two parties then come to a tug, with the Namer and Guesser as leaders. The gaining party then ranges itself in two lines with a space between the lines, each boy holding in his hand his cap or his handkerchief tightly plaited. The boys of the conquered side have then to run between the two lines, and are pelted by the victors. This is called, "Throuw the Muir o' Hecklepin."—Keith (Rev. W. Gregor).

This game is practically the same as "Fool, Fool, come to School," but the secret naming may indicate that this belongs to an earlier form.

See "Fool, Fool," "Hecklebirnie."

Neighbour

There is a game called "Neighbour, I torment thee," played in Staffordshire, "with two hands, and two feet, and a bob, and a nod as I do."—Halliwell's *Dictionary*.

Neiveie-nick-nack

A fireside game. A person puts a little trifle, such as a button, into one hand, shuts it close, the other hand is also shut; then they are both whirled round and round one another as fast as they can, before the nose of the one who intends to guess what hand the prize is in; and if the guesser be so fortunate as to guess the hand the prize is in, it becomes his property; the whirling of the fists is attended with the following rhyme—

> Neiveie, neiveie, nick nack,
> What ane will ye tak,
> The right or the wrang?
> Guess or it be lang,
> Plot awa' and plan,
> I'll cheat ye gif I can.
> —Mactaggart's *Gallovidian Encyclopædia.*

The Rev. W. Gregor says at Keith this game is played at Christmas, and by two. The stakes are commonly pins. One player conceals a pin, or more if agreed on, in one of his (her) hands. He then closes both hands and twirls them over each other, in front of the other player, and repeats the words—

> Nivvie, nivvie-neek-nack,
> Filk (which) (or filk han') 'ill ye tack?
> Tack the richt, tack the left,
> An' a'll deceave ye gehn (if) I can.

The other player chooses. If he chooses the hand having the stake, he gains it. If he does not, he forfeits the stake. Another form of words is—

> Nivvie, nivvie-neek-nack
> Filk (which) will ye tick-tack?
> Tack ane, tack twa,
> Tack the best amo' them a'.

And—

> Nivvie, nivvie-nick-nack,
> Which han' will ye tack?
> Tack ane, tack twa,
> Tack the best amo' them a'.

Dickinson's *Cumberland Glossary* describes this as a boyish mode of casting lots.   The boy says—

> Neevy, neevy-nack,
> Whether hand will ta tack,
> T' topmer or t' lowmer ?

Mr. W. H. Patterson (*Antrim and Down Glossary*) gives the rhyme as—

> Nievy, navy, nick nack,
> Which han' will ye tak',
> The right or the wrang ?
> I'll beguile ye if I can.

Chambers (*Popular Rhymes*, p. 117) gives the rhyme the same as that given by Mr. Patterson.   In *Notes and Queries*, 6th Series, vii. 235, a North Yorkshire version is given as—

> Nievie, nievie, nack,
> Whether hand wilta tak,
> Under or aboon,
> For a singal half-crown ?
> Nievie, nievie, nick, nack,
> Whilk han' will thou tak ?
> Tak the richt or tak the wrang,
> I'll beguile thee if I can.

Jamieson (*Supp.*, *sub voce*) adds : " The first part of the word seems to be from neive, the fist being employed in the game."   A writer in *Notes and Queries*, iii. 180, says : " The neive, though employed in the game, is not the object addressed. It is held out to him who is to guess—the conjuror—*and it is he who is addressed*, and under a conjuring name.   In short (to hazard a wide conjecture, it may be) he is invoked in the person of Nic Neville (Neivi Nic), a sorcerer in the days of James VI., who was burnt at St. Andrews in 1569.   If I am right, a curious testimony is furnished to his quondam popularity among the common people."   It will be remembered that this game is mentioned by Scott in *St. Ronan's Well*—" Na, na, said the boy, he is a queer old cull. . . . He gave me half-a-crown yince, and forbade me to play it awa' at pitch and toss." " And you disobeyed him, of course ? "   " Na, I didna disobey him—I played it awa' at ' Nievie, nievie, nick-nack.' "

See " Handy-dandy."

Nettles

Nettles grow in an angry bush,
An angry bush, an angry bush;
Nettles grow in an angry bush,
   With my high, ho, ham!

This is the way the lady goes,
The lady goes, the lady goes;
This is the way the lady goes,
   With my hi, ho, ham!

Nettles grow in an angry bush, &c.

This is the way the gentleman goes, &c.

Nettles grow in an angry bush, &c.

This is the way the tailor goes.
                                —Halliwell's *Nursery Rhymes*, 227.

(*b*) The children dance round, singing the first three lines, turning round and clapping hands for the fourth line. They curtsey while saying, "This is the way the lady goes," and again turn round and clap hands for the last line. The same process is followed in every verse, only varying what they act —thus, in the third verse, they bow for the gentleman—and so the amusement is protracted *ad libitum*, with shoemaking, washing clothes, ironing, churning, milking, making up butter, &c., &c.

(*c*) This game is practically the same as the "Mulberry Bush." The action is carried on in the same way, except that the children clap their hands at the fourth line, instead of each turning themselves round, as in "Mulberry Bush." The "High, ho, ham!" termination may be the same as the "I, O, OM" of Mr. Addy's version of "Milking Pails."

See "Mulberry Bush," "When I was a Young Girl."

New Squat

A ring is made by marking the ground, and a tin placed in the middle of it. One boy acts as keeper of the tin, the other players also stand outside the ring. One of these kicks the tin out of the ring, the others then all run to hide or squat out of sight. The keeper has to replace the tin before looking for the boys. If, after that, he can spy a boy, that boy must come out and stand by the ring. When another boy is spied, he endeavours to reach the ring before the keeper does so, and kick out the tin. If he is successful, any one of the boys who is standing by, having been previously spied, is released from the keeper, and again hides. The object of the keeper is to successfully spy all the boys. When this is accomplished the last boy becomes the keeper. — Earls Heaton, Yorks. (Herbert Hardy).

See "Mount the Tin."

Nine Holes

Nine round holes are made in the ground, and a ball aimed at them from a certain distance; or the holes are made in a board with a number over each, through one of which the ball has to pass.—Forby's *Vocabulary*.

"A rural game," says Nares, "played by making nine holes in the ground, in the angles and sides of a square, and placing stones and other things upon, according to certain rules." Moor (*Suffolk Words and Phrases*) says: "This is, I believe, accurate as far as it goes, of our Suffolk game. A hole in the middle is necessary." In Norfolk, Holloway (*Dict. Prov.*) says that nine round holes are made in the ground, and a ball aimed at them from a certain distance. A second game is played with a board having nine holes, through one of which the ball must pass. Nares quotes several authors to show the antiquity of the game. He shows that the "Nine Men's Morris" of our ancestors was but another name for "Nine Holes." Nine, a favourite and mysterious number everywhere, prevails in games.

Strutt (*Sports*, p. 384) also describes the game as played in two ways—a game with bowling marbles at a wooden bridge; and another game, also with marbles, in which four, five, or six holes, and sometimes more, are made in the ground at a distance from each other, and the business of every one of the players is to bowl a marble, by a regular succession, into all the holes, and he who completes in the fewest bowls obtains

the victory.   In Northamptonshire a game called "Nine Holes,"
or "Trunks," is played with a long piece of wood or bridge
with nine arches cut in it, each arch being marked with a
figure over it, from one to nine, in the following rotation—
VII., V., III., I., IX., II., IIII., VI., VIII.   Each player has
two flattened balls which he aims to bowl edgeways under the
arches ; he scores the number marked over the arch he bowls
through, and he that attains to forty-five first wins the game
(Baker's *Northamptonshire Glossary*).   In *Arch. Journ.*, xlix.
320, in a paper by Mr. J. T. Micklethwaite, this game is
described, and diagrams of the game given which had been
found by him cut in a stone bench in the church of Ardeley,
Hertfordshire, and elsewhere.   He has also seen the game
played in London.   It is evidently the same game as described
by Nares and Moor above.

See "Bridgeboard," "Nine Men's Morris."

Nine Men's Morris

In the East Riding this game is played thus : A flat piece of
wood about eight inches square is taken, and on it twenty-four
holes are bored by means of a hot skewer or piece of hot iron.

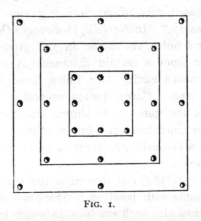

FIG. 1.

Each of the two players has nine wooden pegs, which are either
coloured or shaped differently, and the object of each player is
to get three of his own pegs in a straight line (fig. 1).   It is
called "Merrils."—Sheffield (S. O. Addy).

Cotgrave's *Dictionarie*, 1632, says: "*Merelles*, le jeu de merelles, the boyish game called merrils, or fiue-pennie morris. Played here most commonly with stones, but in France with pawns or men made of purpose, and termed merelles." Strutt (*Sports*, p. 317) says: "This was why the game received this name. It was formerly called 'Nine Men's Morris' and 'Five-penny Morris,' and is a game of some antiquity. It was certainly much used by the shepherds formerly, and continues to be used by them and other rustics to the present hour." An illustration of the form of the merelle table and the lines upon it, as it appeared in the fourteenth century, is given by him, and he observes that the lines have not been varied. The black spots at every angle and intersection of the lines are the places for the men to be laid upon. The men are different in form and colour for distinction's sake, and from the moving these men backwards and forwards, as though they were dancing a morris, I suppose the pastime received the name of "Nine Men's Morris," but why it should have been called "Five-penny Morris" I do not know. The manner of playing is briefly thus:—Two persons, having each of them nine pieces or men, lay them down alternately, one by one, upon the spots, and the business of either party is to prevent his antagonist from placing three of his pieces so as to form a row of three without the intervention of an opponent piece. If a row be formed, he that made it is at liberty to take up one of his competitor's pieces from any part he thinks most to his own advantage, excepting he has made a row, which must not be touched, if he have another piece upon the board that is not a component part of that row. When all the pieces are laid down they are played backwards and forwards in any direction that the lines run, but can only move from one spot to another at one time. He that takes off all his antagonist's pieces is the conqueror. The rustics, when they have not materials at hand to make a table, cut the lines in the same form upon the ground and make a small hole for every dot. They then collect stones of different forms or colours for the pieces, and play the game by depositing them in the holes in the same manner that they are set

over the dots on the table. Hence Shakespeare, describing the
effects of a wet and stormy season, says—

> " The folds stand empty in the drowned field,
> And crows are fatted with the murrain flock—
> The Nine Men's Morris is filled up with mud."
>
> —*Midsummer Night's Dream*, act ii. sc. 2.

Miss Baker (*Northamptonshire Glossary*), in describing
" Merell" or " Morris," says :—" On the inclosing of open
fields this game was transferred to a board, and continues a
fireside recreation of the agricultural labourer.   It is often
called by the name of ' Mill ' or ' Shepherd's Mill.' "   She says
the mode of playing now observed is this.   Each of the players
has nine pieces, or men, differing in colour, or material, from
his adversary, for distinction's sake ; which they lay down on
the spots alternately, one by one, each endeavouring to prevent
his opponent from placing three of his pieces in a line, as
whichever does so is entitled to take off any one of his antagonist's men where he pleases, without breaking a row of three,
which must not be done whilst there is another man on the
board.   After all the pieces are placed on the board, they are
moved alternately backwards and forwards along the lines ;
and as often as either of the players succeeds in accomplishing
a row of three, he claims one of his antagonist's men, which is
placed in the pound (the centre), and he who takes the most
pieces wins the game.   It is played on a board whereon are
marked three squares, one being denominated the pound.   It
is sometimes played with pegs, bits of paper, or wood, or
stone.   It is called " Peg Morris " by Clare, the Northamptonshire poet.

The ancient game of " Nine Men's Morris " is yet played by
the boys of Dorset.   The boys of a cottage, near Dorchester,
had a while ago carved a " Marrel " pound on a block of stone
by the house.   Some years ago a clergyman of one of the
upper counties wrote that in the pulling down of a wall in his
church, built in the thirteenth century, the workmen came to a
block of stone with a " Marrel's " pound cut on it.   " Merrels "
the game was called by a mason.—Barnes' *Additional Glossary ;
Folk-lore Journal,* vii. 233.

"'Nine Men's Morris,' in Gloucestershire called 'Ninepenny Morris,' was," says a correspondent in the *Midland Garner*, "largely practised by boys and even older people over thirty years ago, but is now, as far as I know, entirely disused. Two persons play. Each must have twelve pegs, or twelve pieces of anything which can be distinguished. The Morris was usually marked on a board or stone with chalk, and consists of twenty-four points. The pegs are put down one at a time alternately upon any point upon the Morris, and the first person who makes a consecutive row of three impounds one of his opponent's pegs. The pegs must only be moved on the lines. The game is continued until one or other of the players has only two pegs left, when the game is won" (1st ser., i. 20). Another correspondent in the same journal (ii. 2) says, "The game was very generally played in the midland counties under the name of 'Merrilpeg' or 'Merelles.' The twelve pieces I have never seen used, though I have often played with nine. We generally used marbles or draught pieces, and not pegs."

The following are the accounts of this game given by the commentators on Shakespeare :—

"In that part of Warwickshire where Shakespeare was educated, and the neighbouring parts of Northamptonshire, the shepherds and other boys dig up the turf with their knives to represent a sort of imperfect chess-board. It consists of a square, sometimes only a foot diameter, sometimes three or four yards. Within this is another square, every side of which is parallel to the external square; and these squares are joined by lines drawn from each corner of both squares, and the middle of each line. One party, or player, has wooden pegs, the other stones, which they move in such a manner as to take up each other's men, as they are called, and the area of the inner square is called the pound, in which the men taken up are impounded. These figures are by the country people called *nine men's morris*, or *merrils;* and are so called because each party has nine men. These figures are always cut upon the green turf, or leys as they are called, or upon the grass at the end of ploughed lands, and in rainy seasons never fail to be choked up with mud" (Farmer). "*Nine men's morris* is a game still played by the shepherds, cow-keepers, &c., in the midland counties, as follows:—A figure (of squares one within another) is made on the ground by cutting out the turf; and two persons take each nine stones, which they place by turns in the angles, and afterwards move alternately, as at chess or draughts. He who can play three in a straight line may then take off any one of his adversary's, where he pleases, till one, having lost all his men, loses the game" (Alchorne).

The following is the account of this game given by Mr. Douce in the *Illustrations of Shakespeare and of Ancient Manners*, 1807, i. 184:—"This game was sometimes called the *nine men's merrils* from *merelles*, or *mereaux*, an ancient French word for the jettons, or counters, with which it was played. The other term, *morris*, is probably a corruption suggested by the sort of dance which, in the progress of the game, the counters performed. In the French *merelles* each party had three counters only, which were to be placed in a line in order to win the game. It appears to have been the *tremerel* mentioned in an old fabliau. See *Le Grand, Fabliaux et Contes*, ii. 208. Dr. Hyde thinks the morris, or merrils, was known during the time that the Normans continued in possession of England, and that the name was afterwards corrupted into *three men's morals*, or *nine men's morals*. If this be true,

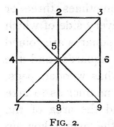

FIG. 2.

the conversion of *morrals* into *morris*, a term so very familiar to the country people, was extremely natural. The Doctor adds, that it was likewise called *nine-penny* or *nine-pin miracle, three-penny morris, five-penny morris, nine-penny morris*, or *three-pin, five-pin*, and *nine-pin morris*, all corruptions of *three-pin*, &c., *merels*" (Hyde's *Hist. Nederluddi*, p. 202). Nares says the simpler plan here represented (fig. 2), which he had also seen cut on small boards, is more like the game than the one referred to in the variorem notes of Shakespeare.

Forby has, "*Morris*, an ancient game, in very common

modern use. In Shakespeare it is called 'nine men's *morris*,' from its being played with nine men, as they were then, and still are called. We call it simply *morris*. Probably it took the name from a fancied resemblance to a dance, in the motions of the men. Dr. Johnson professes that he knew no more of it than that it was some rustic game. Another commentator speaks of it as common among shepherds' boys in some parts of Warwickshire. It cannot well be more common there than here, and it is not particularly rustic. Shepherds' boys and other clowns play it on the green turf, or on the bare ground; cutting or scratching the lines, on the one or the other. In either case it is soon filled up with mud in wet weather. In towns, porters and other labourers play it, at their leisure hours, on the flat pavement, tracing the figure with chalk. It is also a domestic game; and the figure is to be found on the back of some draught-boards. But to compare *morris* with that game, or with chess, seems absurd; as it has a very distant resemblance, if any at all, to either, in the lines, or in the rules of playing. On the ground, the men are pebbles, broken tiles, shells, or potsherds; on a table, the same as are used at draughts or backgammon. In Nares it is said to be the same as nine-holes. With us it is certainly different." Cope (*Hampshire Glossary*) says that "Nine Men's Morrice" is a game played with counters. He does not describe it further. Atkinson (*Glossary of Cleveland Dialect*) says under "Merls," the game of "Merelles," or "Nine Men's Morris." Toone (*Etymological Dictionary*) describes it as a game played on the green sward, holes being cut thereon, into which stones were placed by the players. Stead's *Holderness Glossary* calls it "Merrils," and describes it as a game played on a square board with eighteen pegs, nine on each side, called in many parts "Nine Men's Morrice." See also *Sussex Arch. Collections*, xxv. 234, and a paper by Mr. J. T. Micklethwaite (*Arch. Journ.*, xlix. 322), where diagrams of this game are given which have been found cut in several places on the benches of the cloisters at Gloucester, Salisbury, and elsewhere.

See "Noughts and Crosses."

Nip-srat-and-bite

A children's game, in which nuts, pence, gingerbread, &c., are squandered.—Addy's *Sheffield Glossary*.

Nitch, Notch, No-Notch

Children cut a number of slices from an apple, extending from the eye to the tail, broader on the outside than on the inner, which reaches nearly to the core; one piece has a part cut out, making a notch—this is called "Notch;" another is not cut at all—this is called "No-Notch;" while a third has an incision made on it, but not cut out—this is called "Nitch." The pieces when thus marked are replaced, and the game consists in one child holding the apple, and pointing to one of the pieces, asking another child which he will have, "Nitch, Notch, or No-Notch;" if he guesses right, he has it and eats it; if wrong, the other eats it.—Sussex (Holloway's *Dict. of Provincialisms*).

Not

A game where the parties, ranged on opposite sides, with each a bat in their hands, endeavour to strike a ball to opposite goals. The game is called "Not," from the ball being made of a knotty piece of wood.—Gloucestershire (Holloway's *Dict. of Provincialisms*).

See "Hawkey."

Noughts and Crosses

This game is played on slates by school-children. The accompanying diagram is drawn on the slate, and a certain

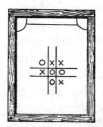

figure (generally twenty) is agreed upon as "game." There are two players, one takes noughts [o], the other crosses [×]. The three places drawn on the slate above the diagram are for the players each to put down marks or numbers for the games they win, the centre place being for "Old Nick," or "Old Tom." The object of the game is for each player to occupy three contiguous places in a row or line with either noughts or crosses, and to prevent his opponent from doing so. The diagram is of course empty when play begins. One player commences by putting his mark into either of the vacant places he prefers, the other player then places his in another, wherever he thinks he has the best opportunity to prevent his opponent getting a "three," and at the same time to get a three himself; then the first player plays again, and so on alternately until all the squares are occupied, or until one of the players has a "three" in line. If neither player gets a "three," the game is won by "Old Nick," and one is scored to his name. In the diagram the result of the game is shown when won by "Old Nick." Whichever player first wins a game adds "Old Nick's" score to his own. In some games "Old Nick" keeps all he wins for himself, and then most frequently wins the game.—London (A. B. Gomme).

See "Corsicrown," "Kit-Cat-Cannio," "Nine Men's Morris."

Nur and Spel

A boys' game in Lincolnshire, somewhat similar to "Trap Ball." It is played with a "kibble," a "nur," and a "spell." By striking the end of the spell with the kibble, the nur, of course, rises into the air, and the art of the game is to strike it with the kibble before it reaches the ground. He who drives it the greatest distance wins the game.—Halliwell's *Dictionary*.

Strutt (*Sports and Pastimes*, p. 109) describes this game as "Northern-spell," played with a trap, and the ball is stricken with a bat or bludgeon. The contest between the players is simply who shall strike the ball to the greatest distance in a given number of strokes. The length of each stroke is measured before the ball is returned, by means of a cord made fast at one end near the trap, the other being stretched into the field by a person stationed there for that purpose, who adjusts it to the ball wherever it may lie.

In a work entitled the *Costumes of Yorkshire* this game is described and represented as "Nor and Spell." The little wooden ball used in this game is in Yorkshire called the "Nor," and the receptacle in which it is placed the "Spell." Peacock

(*Manley and Corringham Glossary*) gives "knur," (1) a hard wooden ball, (2) the head. Addy (*Sheffield Glossary*) says "knur" is a small round ball, less than a billiard ball. It is put into a cup fixed on a spring which, being touched, causes the ball to rise into the air, when it is struck by a trip-stick, a slender stick made broad and flat at one end. The "knur" is struck by the broad part. The game is played on Shrove Tuesday. Brogden (*Provincial Words of Lincolnshire*) gives it under "Bandy." It is called "Knur, Spell, and Kibble" in S.-W. Lincolnshire.—Cole's *Glossary*.

The following letter relating to this game is extracted from the *Worcestershire Chronicle*, September 1847, in Ellis's edition of Brand :—"Before the commons were taken in, the children of the poor had ample space wherein to recreate themselves at cricket, *nurr*, or any other diversion ; but now they are driven from every green spot, and in Bromsgrove here, the nailor boys, from the force of circumstances, have taken possession of the turnpike road to play the before-mentioned games, to the serious inconvenience of the passengers, one of whom, a woman, was yesterday knocked down by a *nurr* which struck her in the head."

Brockett says of this game, as played in Durham: It is called "Spell and Ore," Teut. "spel," a play or sport; and Germ. "knorr," a knot of wood or ore. The recreation is also called "Buckstick, Spell, and Ore," the buckstick with which the ore is struck being broad at one end like the butt of a gun (*North Country Words*). In Yorkshire it is "Spell and Nurr," or "Knur," the ore or wooden ball having been, perhaps, originally the knurl or knot of a tree. The *Whitby Glossary* also gives this as "Spell and Knor," and says it is known in the South as "Dab and Stick." The author adds, "May not 'tribbit,' or 'trevit,' be a corruption of 'three feet,' the required length of the stick for pliable adaptation ? "

Robinson (*Mid-Yorkshire Glossary*), under "Spell and Nur," says: "A game played with a wooden ball and a stick fitted at the striking end with a club-shaped piece of wood. The 'spell' made to receive and spring the ball for the blow at a touch, is a simple contrivance of wood an inch or so in breadth and a few inches long. . . . The players, who usually go in and out by turns each time, after a preliminary series of tippings of the spell with the stick in one hand, and catches of the ball with the other, in the process of calculating the momentum necessary for reach of hand, are also allowed two trial 'rises' in a striking attitude, and distance is reckoned by scores of yards. The long pliable stick, with a loose club end, used in the game, is called the 'tribit' or 'trivit' stick. . . . The trevit is, in fact, the trap itself, and the trevit-stick the stick with which the trap is struck." The tribbit-stick is elsewhere called "primstick," "gelstick," "buckstick," "trippit," and "trevit." Atkinson says that "spell" is O.N., "spill" meaning a play or game, and the probability is that the game is a lineal descendant from the Ball-play of the Old Danes, or Northmen, and Icelanders. "Spell and knor" is a corruption of "spell a' knor," the play at ball. Nurspel is simply ball-play, therefore which name, taken in connection with the fact that the game is elsewhere called "Spell and Knor," and not "Knor and Spell," is significant. There is one day in the year, Shrove Tuesday, when the play is customarily practised, though not quite exclusively.—Atkinson's *Cleveland Glossary.*

Easther (*Almondbury Glossary*) describes it as played with a wooden ball, a spel, and a pommel. Two may play, or two sides. When a player goes in he drives the knor for, say, 100 yards, *i.e.*, five score, and he reckons five. Each person has the same number of strokes previously agreed upon, but generally only one innings. The "spell" is a kind of stage with three or four feet, to drive it into the ground. On the top of this stage is a spring made of steel, containing a cup to receive the "knor," which is about one or two inches in diameter, and is made of holly or box. The spring is kept down by a sneck, which is tapped by the pommel when the knor is intended to be struck. The pommel is thus formed—the driving part is frequently of ash-root or owler, in shape like half a sugar-loaf split lengthwise, but only three or four inches long, and the handle is of ash, wrapped with a wax band where held, which is in one hand only.

See "Kibel and Nerspel," "Trap Ball," "Trippit and Coit."

Nuts in May

—Shropshire (Miss Burne).

I.   Here we come gathering nuts in May,
Nuts in May, nuts in May,
Here we come gathering nuts in May,
On a fine summer morning.

Whom will you have for nuts in May, .
Nuts in May, nuts in May?
Whom will you have for nuts in May,
On a fine summer morning?

We'll have —— for nuts in May,
Nuts in May, nuts in May,
We'll have -—— for nuts in May,
On a fine summer morning.

Who will you send to fetch her [*or* him] away,
To fetch her away, to fetch her away?
Who will you send to fetch her away,
On a fine summer morning?

We'll send —— to fetch her away,
Fetch her away, fetch her away,
We'll send —— to fetch her away,
On a fine summer morning.
        —Liphook and Winterton, Hants (Miss Fowler).

II.   Here we come gathering nuts and May
[Nuts and May, nuts and May],
Here we come gathering nuts and May,
On a cold and frosty morning.

Pray who will you gather for nuts and May,
Pray who will you gather for nuts and May,
On a cold and frosty morning?

We'll gather —— for nuts and May,
We'll gather —— for nuts and May,
On a cold and frosty morning.

Pray who will you send to take her away,
Pray who will you send to take her away,
On a cold and frosty morning?

We'll send —— to take her away,
We'll send —— to take her away,
On a cold and frosty morning.

—Penzance (Mrs. Mabbott).

III. Here we come gathering nuts in May,
    Nuts in May, nuts in May,
    Here we come gathering nuts in May,
      May, May, May.

Who will you have for nuts in May,
Nuts in May, nuts in May?
Who will you have for nuts in May,
  May, May, May?

[Bessie Stewart] for nuts in May,
Nuts in May, nuts in May,
[Bessie Stewart] for nuts in May,
  May, May, May.

Very well, very well, so you may,
So you may, so you may,
Very well, very well, so you may,
  May, may, may.

Whom will you have to take her away,
Take her away, take her away?
Whom will you have to take her away,
  Way, way, way?

—— —— to take her away,
Take her away, take her away,
—— —— to take her away,
  Way, way, way.   —Belfast (W. H. Patterson).

IV.   Here we come gathering nuts in May,
      Nuts in May, nuts in May,
      Here we come gathering nuts in May,
      On a cold and frosty morning.

      Where do you gather your nuts in May?
      On Galloway Hill we gather our nuts.
      Who will you gather for nuts in May?
      We'll gather —— for nuts in May.
      Who will you send to fetch her away?
      We'll send —— to fetch her away.
               —Bocking, Essex (*Folk-lore Record*, iii. 169).

V.   Here we go gathering nuts away,
      Nuts away, nuts away,
      Here we go gathering nuts away,
      On a cold and frosty morning.

[Then follow verses beginning—]

      Whose nuts shall we gather away?
      We'll gather [Minnie Brown's] nuts away.
      Whom shall we send to fetch them away?

[And the final verse is—]

      We'll send [Johnny Cope] to fetch them away,
      Fetch them away, fetch them away,
      We'll send [Johnny Cope] to fetch them away,
      On a cold and frosty morning.
               —Newbury, Berks (Mrs. S. Batson).

VI.   Who will go gathering nuts in May,
      Nuts in May, nuts in May?
      Who will go gathering nuts in May,
      At five o'clock in the morning?
               —N.-W. Lincolnshire (Rev. — Roberts).

VII.   Here we come gathering nuts in May,
      Nuts in May, nuts in May,
      Here we come gathering nuts in May,
      On a cold and frosty morning.

Who will you have for your nuts in May,
Nuts in May, nuts in May?
Who will you have for your nuts in May,
On a cold and frosty morning?

We will have a girl for nuts in May,
Nuts in May, nuts in May,
We will have a girl for nuts in May,
On a cold and frosty morning.
—Earls Heaton, Yorks. (Herbert Hardy).

VIII. Here we come gathering nuts in May,
Nuts in May, nuts in May,
Here we come gathering nuts in May,
This cold frosty morning.

Who will you have for your nuts in May,
Nuts in May, nuts in May?
Who will you have for your nuts in May,
This cold frosty morning?

We will have —— for our nuts in May,
Nuts in May, nuts in May,
We will have —— for our nuts in May,
This cold frosty morning.

Who will you have to pull her away,
Pull her away, pull her away?
Who will you have to pull her away,
This cold frosty morning?

We will have —— to pull her away,
Pull her away, pull her away,
We will have —— to pull her away,
This cold frosty morning.
—Settle, Yorks. (Rev. W. S. Sykes).

IX. Here we come gathering nuts to-day,
Nuts to-day, nuts to-day,
Here we come gathering nuts to-day,
So early in the morning.

Pray, whose nuts will you gather away,
Gather away, gather away?
Pray, whose nuts will you gather away,
So early in the morning?

We'll gather Miss A——'s nuts away,
Nuts away, nuts away,
We'll gather Miss A——'s nuts away,
So early in the morning.

Pray, who will you send to take them away,
To take them away, take them away?
Pray, who will you send to take them away,
So early in the morning?

We'll send Miss B—— to take them away,
To take them away, take them away,
We'll send Miss B—— to take them away,
So early in the morning.

—Symondsbury, Dorsetshire (*Folk-lore Journal*,
vii. 226–7).

(*b*) The children form in two lines of equal length, facing one another, with sufficient space between the lines to admit of their walking in line backwards and forwards towards and away from each other, as each line sings the verses allotted to it (fig. 1). The first line sings the first, third, and fifth verses, and the opposite line the second and fourth. At the end of the fifth verse

Fig 1   Fig 2

a handkerchief or other mark is laid on the ground, and the two children (whose names have been mentioned, and who are as evenly matched as possible), take each other's right hand and endeavour to pull each other over the handkerchief to their own side (fig. 2). The child who is pulled over the handkerchief becomes the "captured nut," and joins the side of her capturers. Then the game begins again by the second line singing the first, third, and fifth verses, while advancing to gather or capture the "nuts," the first line responding with the second and fourth verses, and the same finish as before. Then the first line begins the game, and so on until all the children are in this way matched one against the other.

(c) Other versions have been sent me, with slight variations: NUTS IN MAY, with the verses ending, "On a fine summer morning," from Lincoln and Nottinghamshire (Miss M. Peacock); "So early in the morning," Sporle, Norfolk (Miss Matthews); "Six o'clock in the morning," Nottingham (Miss Wenfield); "On a cold and frosty morning," East Kirkby, Lincolnshire (Miss K. Maughan); Barnes (A. B. Gomme), Colchester (Miss G. M. Frances). NUTS AND MAY: "On a bright and sunny morning" (Mr. C. C. Bell); "On a cold and frosty morning," Forest of Dean (Miss Matthews); "Every night and morning," Gainford, Durham (Miss Edleston); "We've picked [Sally Gray] for nuts in May," "All on a summer's morning," Sheffield (Mr. S. O. Addy). A version by Miss Kimber (Newbury, Berks, and Marlborough, Wilts) ends each verse, "Nuts and May." In other respects these variants are practically the same. Printed versions not given above are Hersham, Surrey (*Folk-lore Record*, v. 85); Burne's *Shropshire Folk-lore*, p. 516; Sulhampstead, Berks (*Antiquary*, vol. xxvii., Miss E. E. Thoyts); and Dorsetshire, "Gathering nuts away" (*Folk-lore Journal*, vii. 225). From Longcot, Berks, a version sent me by Miss I. Barclay has no fourth line to the verses.

(d) This game is probably, unless we except "Mulberry Bush," the most popular and the most widely played of any singing game. It might almost be called universal. This is shown by the fact that there are few counties where it is not known, and also that important variants, either in the words or in the method of playing, are rarely met with. In all the versions which have been sent there are only the following variations in the words, and these are principally in the refrain, or last line of each verse: "On a cold and frosty morning" ends by far the greater number of versions; "On a fine summer's morning," "So early in the morning," "All on a summer's morning," "Five o'clock in the morning," "On a cold and sunny morning," coming next in number. The Belfast version ends, "May! May! May!" and a Newbury and Marlborough fourth line is simply a repetition of the second, "Nuts in May, nuts in May."

In the first line of the verse the only important variant seems to be the Symondsbury "Gathering nuts away" and "Gathering nuts to-day." "Gathering nuts away" also occurs in one version from Newbury (Berks), "Nuts and May" appearing in the larger number after the more usual "Nuts in May." In only one version is a specific place mentioned for the gathering. This is in the Bocking version, where Galloway Hill is named, in reply to the unusual question, "Where do you gather your nuts in May?" A player is usually gathered for "Nuts in May." In three or four cases only is this altered to gathering a player's "nuts away," which is obviously an alteration to try and make the action coincide exactly with the words. The game is always played in "lines," and the principal incidents running throughout all the versions are the same, *i.e.*, one player is selected by one line of players from their opponents' party. The "selected" one is refused by her party unless some one from the opposite side can effect her capture by a contest of strength. In all versions but two or three this contest takes place between the two; in one or two all the players join in the trial of strength. In another instance there appears to be no contest, but the selected player crosses over to the opposite side. Two important incidents occur in the Bocking and Symondsbury versions. In the Bocking game the side which is victorious has the right to begin the next game first: this also occurs in the Barnes version. In Symondsbury, when one child is drawn over the boundary line by one from the opposite side she has to be "crowned" immediately. This is done by the conqueror putting her hand on the captured one's head. If this is not done at once the captured one is at liberty to return to her own side. In some versions (Shropshire and London) the player who is selected for "Nuts" is always captured by the one sent to fetch her. Some Barnes children also say that this is the proper way to play. When boys and girls play the boys are always sent to "fetch away" the girls. In Sheffield (a version collected by Mr. S. O. Addy) a boy is chosen to fetch the girl away; and in the Earls Heaton version the line runs, "We'll have a girl for nuts in May."

(e) There is some analogy in the game to marriage by capture, and to the marriage customs practised at May Day festivals and gatherings. For the evidence for marriage by capture in the game there is no element of love or courtship, though there is the obtaining possession of a member of an opposing party. But it differs from ordinary contest-games in the fact that one party does not wage war against another party for possession of a particular piece of ground, but individual against individual for the possession of an individual. That the player sent to fetch the selected girl is expected to conquer seems to be implied—first, by a choice of a certain player being made to effect the capture; secondly, by the one sent "to fetch" being always successful; and thirdly, the "crowning" in the Symondsbury game. Through all the games I have seen played this idea seems to run, and it exactly accords with the conception of marriage by capture. For examples of the actual survivals in English, Scottish, Welsh, and Irish customs of marriage by capture see Gomme's *Folk-lore Relics of Early Village Life*, pp. 204–210.

The question is, How does this theory of the origin of the game fit in with the term "Nuts in May"? I attribute this to the gathering by parties of young men of bunches of May at the May festivals and dances, to decorate not only the May-pole, May "kissing-bush," but the doors of houses. "Knots of May" is a term used by children, meaning bunches of May. Thus, a note by Miss Fowler in the MS. of the games she had collected says, "In Bucks the children speak of 'knots of May,' meaning each little bunch of hawthorn blossom." The gathering of bunches of May by parties of young men and maidens to make the May-bush round which the May Day games were held, and dancing and courting, is mentioned by Wilde (*Irish Popular Superstitions*, p. 52), the game being "Dance in the

Ring." Holland (*Cheshire Glossary*) says, "May birches were branches of different kinds of trees fastened over doors of houses and on the chimney on the eve of May Day. They were fastened up by parties of young men who went round for the purpose, and were intended to be symbolical of the character of the inmates." I remember one May Day in London, when the "May girls" came with a garland and short sticks decorated with green and bunches of flowers, they sang—

> Knots of May we've brought you,
> Before your door it stands;
> It is but a sprout, but it's well budded out
> By the work of the Lord's hands,

and a Miss Spencer, who lived near Hampton (Middlesex), told me that she well remembered the May girls singing the first verse of this carol, using "knots" instead of the more usual word "branch" or "bunch," and that she knew the small bunch of May blossom by the name of "knots" of May, "bringing in knots of May" being a usual expression of children.

The association of May—whether the month, or the flower, or both—with the game is very strong, the refrain "cold and frosty morning," "all on a summer's morning," "bright summer's morning," "so early in the morning," also being characteristic of the early days of May and spring, and suggests that the whole day from early hours is given up to holiday. The familiar nursery rhyme given by Halliwell—

> Here we come a-piping,
> First in spring and then in May,

no doubt also refers to house-to-house visiting of May.

The connection between the May festival and survival in custom of marriage by capture is well illustrated by a passage from Stubbe's *Anatomie of Abuses*, p. 148. He says: "Against May Day, Whitsonday, or other time, euery Parishe, Towne and Village assemble themselves together, bothe men women and children, olde and yong, . . . and either goyng all together or diuidyng themselues into companies, they goe some to the Woodes and groves where they spend all the night in plesant pastimes; and in the morning they return bringing with them birch and branches of trees to deck their assemblies withall . . . and then they fall to daunce about it like as the heathen people did. . . . I have heard it credibly reported (and that *viva voce*) by men of great grauitie and reputation, that of fortie, threescore or a hundred maides going to the wood ouer night, there haue scaresly the third part of them returned home againe undefiled." Herrick's *Hesperides* also describes the festival, and the custom of courting and marriage at the same time.

The tune sung to this game appears to be the same in every version.

END OF VOL. I.

Volume
2

A DICTIONARY

OF

BRITISH FOLK-LORE

EDITED BY

G. LAURENCE GOMME, Esq., F.S.A.
VICE-PRESIDENT OF THE FOLK-LORE SOCIETY, ETC.

PART I.

TRADITIONAL GAMES

VOL. II.

VOL. I.

ACCROSHAY—NUTS IN MAY

Medium 8vo, xix.–424 pp. With numerous Diagrams and
Illustrations. Cloth uncut. 12s. 6d. nett.

Some Press Notices

Notes and Queries.—"A work of supreme importance . . .
a scholarly, valuable, and delightful work."

Spectator.—"Interesting and useful to the antiquarian, his-
torian, and philologist, as well as to the student of manners
and customs."

Saturday Review.—"Thorough and conscientious."

Critic (New York).—"A mine of riches to the student of
folk-lore, anthropology, and comparative religion."

Antiquary.—"The work of collection and comparison has
been done with obvious care, and at the same time with a *con
amore* enthusiasm."

Zeitschrift für vergl. Literaturgeschichte.—"In jeder Bezie-
hung erschöpfend und mustergiltig."

Zeitschrift für Pädagogie.—"Von hoher wissenschaftlicher
Bedeutung."

THE

TRADITIONAL GAMES

Of England, Scotland, and Ireland

WITH

TUNES, SINGING-RHYMES, AND METHODS OF PLAYING
ACCORDING TO THE VARIANTS EXTANT AND
RECORDED IN DIFFERENT PARTS
OF THE KINGDOM

COLLECTED AND ANNOTATED BY

ALICE BERTHA GOMME

VOL. II.

OATS AND BEANS—WOULD YOU KNOW
TOGETHER WITH A MEMOIR ON THE STUDY
OF CHILDREN'S GAMES

LONDON
DAVID NUTT, 270-71 STRAND
1898

PREFACE

THE completion of the second volume of my Dictionary has been delayed from several unforeseen circumstances, the most important being the death of my most kind and learned friend the Rev. Dr. Gregor. The loss which folk-lore students as a body sustained by this lamented scholar's death, was in my own case accentuated, not only by many years of kindly communication, but by the very special help which he generously gave me for this collection.

The second volume completes the collection of games on the lines already laid down. It has taken much more space than I originally intended, and I was compelled to add some important variants to the first volume, sent to me during the compilation of the second. I have explained in the memoir that the two volumes practically contain all that is to be collected, all, that is to say, of real importance.

The memoir seeks to show what important evidence is to be derived from separate study of the Traditional Games of England. That games of all classes are shown to contain evidence of ancient custom and belief is remarkable testimony to the anthropological methods of studying folk-lore, which I have followed. The memoir fills a considerable space, although it contains only the analytical portion of what was to have been a comprehensive study of both the analytical and comparative sides of the questions. Dr. Gregor had kindly promised to help me with the study of foreign parallels to British Games, but before his death it became apparent that this branch of the subject would almost need a separate treatise, and his death decided me to leave it untouched. I do not underrate its importance, but I am disposed to think that the survey I have given of the British evidence will not be materially shaken by the study of the comparative evidence, which will now be made the easier.

I ought perhaps to add, that the " Memoir " at the end of this volume was read as a paper at the evening meeting of the Folk Lore Society, on March 16th, 1898.

I have again to thank my many kind correspondents for their help in collecting the different versions of the games.

A. B. G.

24 DORSET SQUARE, N.W.

LIST OF AUTHORITIES

ADDENDUM TO VOL. I.

ENGLAND.

BEDFORDSHIRE—
 Bedford . . . . . Mrs. Haddon.
BERKSHIRE—
 Welford . . . . . Mrs. S. Batson.
BUCKINGHAMSHIRE—
 Buckingham . . . . *Midland Garner*.
CAMBRIDGESHIRE . . . Halliwell's *Nursery Rhymes*.
 Barrington, Girton . . Dr. A. C. Haddon.
 Cambridge . . . . Mrs. Haddon.
CORNWALL . . . . . Miss I. Barclay.
DERBYSHIRE . . . . Miss Youngman, *Long Ago*, vol. i.
DEVONSHIRE . . . . Miss Chase.
 Chudleigh Knighton . . { Henderson's *Folk-lore of the Northern Coun-
 ties of England*.
DORSETSHIRE—
 Broadwinsor . . . . *Folk-lore Journal*, vol. vii.
GLOUCESTERSHIRE . . . Northall's *English Folk Rhymes*.
HAMPSHIRE—
 Gambledown . . . . Mrs. Pinsent.
HERTFORDSHIRE—
 Harpenden, Stevenage . . Mrs. Lloyd.
HUNTINGDONSHIRE—
 St. Neots . . . . Miss Lumley.
KENT . . . . . . Miss L. Broadwood.
LANCASHIRE—
 Manchester . . . . Miss Dendy.
 Liverpool . . . . Mrs. Harley.
LEICESTERSHIRE . . . *Leicestershire County Folk-lore*.
LINCOLNSHIRE—
 Brigg . . . . . Miss J. Barker.
 Spilsby . . . . . Rev. R. Cracroft.
LONDON . . . . . Dr. Haddon, A. Nutt, Mrs. Gomme.
 Blackheath . . . . Mr. M. L. Rouse.
 Hoxton . . . . . Rev. S. D. Headlam.
 Marylebone . . . . Mrs. Gomme.
MIDDLESEX . . . . . Mrs. Pocklington Coltman.

NORFOLK	.	.	.	.	Mrs. Haddon.
Hemsby.	.	.	.	.	Mrs. Haddon.
NORTHUMBERLAND	.	.	.	.	Hon. J. Abercromby.
OXFORDSHIRE	.	.	.	.	Miss L. Broadwood.
STAFFORDSHIRE	.	.	.	.	Halliwell's *Nursery Rhymes*.
Wolstanton	.	.	.	.	Miss Bush.
SUFFOLK	.	.	.	.	Mrs. Haddon.
Woolpit, near Haughley	.				Mr. M. L. Rouse.
SURREY—					
Ash	.	.	.	.	Mrs. Gomme.
SUSSEX—					
Lewes	.	.	.	.	Miss Kimber.
WORCESTERSHIRE—					
Upton on Severn	.	.	.		Miss. L. Broadwood.
YORKSHIRE	.	.	.	.	Miss E. Cadman.

SCOTLAND.

Notes and Queries. Pennant's *Voyage to the Hebrides.*

ABERDEENSHIRE—					
Aberdeen	.	.	.	.	Mr. M. L. Rouse.
Aberdeen Training College	.				Rev. Dr. Gregor.
Corgarff, Fraserburgh, Meiklefolla, Rosehearty, Tyrie	.				Rev. Dr. Gregor.
ARGYLLSHIRE—					
Connell Ferry, near Oban				.	Miss Harrison.
BANFFSHIRE—					
Cullen, Macduff	.	.	.		Rev. Dr. Gregor.
BERWICKSHIRE	.	.	.		A. M. Bell (*Antiquary*, vol. xxx.).
ELGIN AND NAIRN—				,	
Dyke	.	.	.	.	Rev. Dr. Gregor.
Strichen	.	.	.	.	
FORFARSHIRE—					
Forfar	.	.	.	.	Rev. Dr. Gregor.
KINCARDINESHIRE—					
Banchory	.	.	.		Rev. Dr. Gregor.
KIRCUDBRIGHTSHIRE—					
Auchencairn	.	.	.		Miss M. Haddon. Dr. A. C. Haddon.
Crossmichael	.	.	.		Rev. Dr. Gregor.
Galloway	.	.	.		Mr. J. G. Carter.
Dalry	.	.	.	.	
Kirkcudbright	.	.	.		Mr. J. Lawson.
Laurieston	.	.	.	.	
New Galloway	.	.	.		Rev. Dr. Gregor.
LINLITHGOWSHIRE—					
Linlithgow	.	.	.	.	Mrs. Jamieson.
PERTHSHIRE—					
Auchterarder	.	.	.	.	Miss E. S. Haldane.
Perth	.	.	.	.	Rev. Dr. Gregor.

Ross-shire .　.　.　.　. Rev. Dr. Gregor.
Wigtonshire—
　Port William School　.　. Rev. Dr. Gregor.

IRELAND.

Carleton's *Stories of Irish Peasantry.*

Cork—
　Cork　.　.　.　.　. Mr. I. J. Dennachy.
Down—
　St. Andrews .　.　.　. Miss H. E. Harvey.
Dublin—
　Dublin .　.　.　.　. Mrs. Coffey.
　Howth .　.　.　.　. Miss H. E. Harvey.
Kerry—
　Kerry　.　.　.　.　. I. J. Dennachy.
　Waterville　.　.　.　. Mrs. B. B. Green.
Leitrim—
　Kiltubbrid　.　.　.　. Mr. L. L. Duncan.
Waterford—
　Waterford　.　.　.　. Miss H. E. Harvey.

WALES.

Roberts' *Cambrian Popular Antiquities.*

LIST OF GAMES

Oats and Beans and Barley.
Obadiah.
Odd or Even.
Odd-man.
Old Dame.
Old Roger is Dead.
Old Soldier.
Oliver, Oliver, follow the King.
One Catch-all.
Oranges and Lemons.
'Otmillo.
Over Clover.

Paddy from Home.
Paip.
Pallall.
Pally Ully.
Pat-ball.
Pay-swad.
Pednameny.
Peesie Weet.
Peg and Stick.
Peg-fiched.
Peggy Nut.
Peg-in-the-Ring.
Peg-top.
Penny Cast.
Penny Hop.
Penny Prick.
Penny Stanes.
Phœbe.
Pick and Hotch.
Pi-cow.
Pigeon Walk.
Pig-ring.
Pillie-Winkie.
Pinch.
Pinny Show.
Pins.

Pirley Pease-weep.
Pitch.
Pitch and Hustle.
Pitch and Toss.
Pit-counter.
Pits.
Pize Ball.
Plum Pudding.
Plum Pudding and Roast Beef.
Pointing out a Point.
Poncake.
Poor and Rich.
Poor Mary sits a-weeping.
Poor Widow.
Pop Goes the Weasel.
Pop-the-Bonnet.
Poppet-Show.
Port the Helm.
Pots, or Potts.
Pray, Pretty Miss.
Pretty Little Girl of Mine.
Pretty Miss Pink.
Prick at the Loop.
Prickey Sockey.
Prickie and Jockie.
Priest-Cat (1).
Priest-Cat (2).
Priest of the Parish.
Prisoner's Base.
Puff-the-Dart.
Pun o' mair Weight.
Punch Bowl.
Purposes.
Push in the Wash Tub.
Push Pin.
Push the Business On.
Puss in the Corner.
Pussy's Ground.
Pyramid.

Widow
Wiggle-Waggle.
Wild Boar.
Wild Birds.
Willie, Willie Wastell.
Wind up the Bush Faggot.
Wind, The.

Wink-egg.
Witch, The.
Witte-Witte-Way.
Wolf.
Wolf and the Lamb.
Would you know how doth the
 Peasant.

ADDENDA

A' THE BIRDIES.
All the Boys.
American Post.
As I was Walking.
Auld Grannie.

BALL.
Bannockburn.
Black Doggie.
Bonnet Ridgie.
Button.

CANLIE.
Carry my Lady to London.
Cat and Dog Hole.
Catch the Salmond.
Chicken come Clock.
Chippings, or Cheapings.
Chucks.
Churning.
Codham, or Codhams.
Colley Ball.

DAN'L my Man.
Deil amo' the Dishes.
Dig for Silver.
Dillsee Dollsie Dee.
Doagan.
Down in Yonder Meadow.
Draw a Pail of Water.
Drop Handkerchief.
Dumb Crambo.
Dump.

EENDY, Beendy.

FARMER'S Den.
Fire on the Mountains.

Fool, Fool, come to School.
French Jackie.

GALLOPING, Galloping.
Gallant Ship.
Galley, Galley Ship.
Glasgow Ships.
Granny's Needle.
Green Gravel.
Green Grass.
Green Grass (2).

HEAP the Cairn.
Hear all !
Hen and Chickens.
High Windows.
Hot Cockles.

ISABELLA.

JENNY Jones.
Jockie Rover.
Jolly Lads.
Jolly Miller.

KEYS of Heaven.
Kick the Block.

LADY of the Land.
Leap-Frog.
London Bridge.
Lubin, Looby Loo.

MAGICIAN.
Mannie on the Pavement.
Merry-ma-Tanza.
Milking Pails.
My Delight's in Tansies.

ANALYSIS OF "MEMOIR"

Children's games, a definite branch of folk-lore—Nature of material for the study—Games fall into one of two sections—Classification of the games—Under customs contained in them—Under implements of play—Skill and chance games —Importance of classification—Early custom contained in skill and chance games—In diagram games—Tabu in game of "Touch"—Methods of playing the games—Characteristics of line form—Of circle forms—Of individual form— Of the arch forms—Of winding-up form—Contest games—War-cry used in contest games—Early marriage customs in games of line form—Marriage by capture—By purchase—Without love or courtship—Games formerly played at weddings—Disguising the bride—Hiring servants game—Marriage customs in circle games—Courtship precedes marriage—Marriage connected with water custom—"Crying for a young man" announcing a want—Marriage formula— Approval of friends necessary—Housewifely duties mentioned—Eating of food by bride and bridegroom necessary—Young man's necessity for a wife—Kiss in the ring—Harvest customs in games—Occupations in games—Funeral customs in games—Use of rushes in games—Sneezing action in game—Connection of spirit of dead person with trees—Perambulation of boundaries—Animals repre- sented—Ballads sung to a dance—Individual form games—Hearth worship— Objection to giving light from a fire—Child-stealing by witch—Obstacles in path when pursuing witch—Contest between animals—Ghosts in games—Arch form of game—Contest between leaders of parties—Foundation sacrifice in games— Encircling a church—Well worship in games—Tug-of-war games—Alarm bell ringing—Passing under a yoke—Creeping through holed stones in games—Under earth sods—Customs in "winding up" games—Tree worship in games—Awaking the earth spirit—Serpentine dances—Burial of maiden—Guessing, a primitive element in games—Dramatic classification—Controlling force which has preserved custom in games—Dramatic faculty in mankind—Child's faculty for dramatic action—Observation of detail—Children's games formerly an amusement of adults —Dramatic power in savages—Dramatic dances among the savage and semi- civilised—Summary and conclusion.

CHILDREN'S GAMES

Oats and Beans and Barley

—Madeley, Shropshire (Miss Burne).

—*Northants Notes and Queries*, ii. 161 (R. S. Baker).

—Sporle, Norfolk (Miss Matthews).

I. Oats and beans and barley grow !
Oats and beans and barley grow !
Do you or I or any one know
How oats and beans and barley grow ?
First the farmer *sows* his seed,
Then he *stands* and takes his ease,
Stamps his foot, and *claps* his hands,
Then *turns round* to view the land.
       Waiting for a partner, waiting for a partner !
Open the ring and take one in !

Now you are married you must obey,
You must be true to all you say,

You must be kind, you must be good,
And help your wife to chop the wood!
—Much Wenlock (Burne's *Shropshire Folklore*, p. 508).

II.   Oats and beans and barley grow!
Does you or I or any one know
Where oats and beans and barley grow?

So the farmer sows his seed;
So he stands and takes his ease;
Stamps his foot and claps his hands,
And turns him round to view the lands.
        Waiting for a partner! waiting for a partner!

Now young couple you must obey,
You must be true in all you say,
You must be wise and very good,
And help your wife to chop the wood.
                —Monton, Lancashire (Miss Dendy).

III. Does you or I, or anie one knowe
Where oates and beanes and barlie growe?
     Where oates and beanes and barlie growe?
The farmer comes and sowes ye seede,
Then he standes and takes hys ease,
Stamps hys foote, and slappes hys hand,
And turnes hym rounde to viewe ye land.
        Waiting for a partner,
        Waiting for a partner,
Open the ringe and take mee in,
Make haste and choose youre partner.

Now you're married you must obey,
Must bee true to alle you saye,
Must bee kinde and verie goode,
And helpe your wyfe to choppe ye woode.
        —Raunds (*Northants Notes and Queries*, i. 163).

IV.   Oats and beans and barley grows,
You or I or any one knows,
You or I or any one knows,
Where oats and beans and barley grows.

Thus the farmer sows his seed,
Stamps his feet and claps his hands,
And turns around to view the land.
    Waiting for a partner,
    Waiting for a partner,

Now you are married, &c.
[same as Much Wenlock.]
        —East Kirkby, Lincolnshire (Miss K. Maughan).

V.   Oats, beans, and barley grows,
     You or I or any one knows.
     Thus the farmer sows his seed,
     Thus he stands and takes his ease,
     Stamps his feet and folds his hands,
     And turns him round to view the lands.
         Oh! waitin' for a partner,
         Waitin' for a partner.

Now you're married, &c.
[same as Much Wenlock.]
                    —Winterton (Miss Fowler).

VI. Oats and wheat and barley grows,
     You and I and every one knows
     Where oats and wheat and barley grows.
     As the farmer sows his seed,
     Folds his arms and takes his ease,
     Stamps his feet and claps his hands,
     And turns him round to view the land.
         Waiting for a partner,
         Waiting for a partner,
         Waiting for a partner,
         To open the ring
         And take one in.

Now you're married, &c.
[same as Much Wenlock.]
                —Tean, North Staffs. (Miss Keary).

VII. Oats and beans and barley grow,
You and I and every one know;
You and I and every one know
That oats and beans and barley grow.

Thus the farmer sows his seed,
Thus he stands and takes his ease,
Stamps his foot and claps his hands,
And turns him round to view the land.
        Waiting for a partner,
        Waiting for a partner.

Now you're married you must obey, &c.
    [same as Much Wenlock.]
        —Brigg, Lincolnshire (Miss Barker).

VIII. Oats and beans and barley-corns, you or I or any one
      else,
You or I or any one else, oats or beans or barley-corns;
Thus the farmer sows his seed,
Thus he stands and takes his ease,
Stamps his foot, and claps his hands,
And turns him round to view the land.
Waiting for a partner, waiting for a partner;
Open the ring and take one in,
Waiting for a partner.
Now you're married, &c.
    [same as Much Wenlock.]
        —Nottingham (Miss E. A. Winfield).

IX. Oats and beans, barley and groats,
Oats and beans, barley and groats;
You, nor I, nor anybody knows
How oats and beans and barley grows.
Thus the farmer sows his seed,
Thus he stands and takes his feed,
Stamps his foot and claps his hand,
And turns around to view the land.
Waiting for a partner, waiting for a partner.
Slip the ring, and take one in,
And kiss her when you get her in;

Now that you're married you must agree,
You must be kind to all you see;
You must be kind, you must be good,
And help your man [wife] to chop the wood.
—Isle of Man (A. W. Moore).

X.   Wuts and beäns and barley graws,
As you and I and every one knaws.

Waätin' for a pardner.

Fust the farmer saws his seäds,
Then he stands and taäke his eäse,
Stomps his feät and clops his hands,
And turns him round to view his lands.
Waätin' for a pardner.

Now you're married you must obaäy;
Must be trewe to all you saäy;
Must be kind and must be good,
And help your wife to chop the wood.
Waätin' for a pardner.
—Spilsby, N. Lincs. (Rev. R. Cracroft).

XI.   Oats and beans and barley corn,
Oats and beans and barley corn;
You and I and nobody else,
But oats and beans and barley corn.
As the farmer sows his seed,
As he stands to take us in,
Stamps his feet and claps his hands,
Turns around to field and lands.
Waiting for a partner,
Waiting for a partner,
Open the gate and let her come out,
And see the one you love the best.

Now we're merry and wish you joy,
First the girl, and then the boy,
Seven years after, seven years past,
Kiss one another and go to your class.
—Hampshire (Miss Mendham).

XII.   Where the wheat and barley grows,
       You and I and nobody knows,
       Where the wheat and barley grows,
       You and I and nobody knows.
       As the farmer sows his seed,
       As he stands and takes his ease,
       Stamps his foot and claps his hand,
       Turns around to view the land.
       Waiting for a partner,
       Waiting for a partner.
       Open the ring, take her in,
       Kiss her when you get her in.
       Now you're married you must be good,
       To make your husband chop the wood.
                    —Cowes, Isle of Wight (Miss E. Smith).

XIII. Oats and beans and barley corns,
       You nor I nor any one knows ;
       You nor I nor any one knows
       How oats and beans and barley grows.
       As the sower sows his seed,
       As he stands he takes his ease,
       Stamps his foot and claps his hands,
       And turns him round to view the land.
       Waiting for a partner,
       Open the ring and take one in.
       Now you're married, &c.
       [same as Much Wenlock.]
               —Long Eaton, Nottinghamshire (Miss Youngman).

XIV.   Hop or beans or barley corn,
       You or I or any one all :
       First the farmer sows his seed,
       Then he stands and takes his ease ;
       He stamped his foot and he clapped his hand,
       And turned around the bugle land,
               Waiting for a partner, a partner, a partner,
               He opened the ring and called one in,
               And now he's got a partner.

Now you're married we wish you good joy,
First the girl and then the boy;
Love one another like sister and brother,
And pray each couple to kiss together.
                    —Sporle, Norfolk (Miss Matthews).

XV.   See the farmer sow his seed,
      See he stands and takes them in,
      Stamps his foot and claps his hand,
      And turns him round to view the land.
          O! waiting for a partner,
          O! waiting for a partner,
          Open the ring and take one in.

Now you're married, &c.
[same as Much Wenlock.]
                    —Earls Heaton, Yorks. (H. Hardy).

XVI. A waitin' fur a pardner,
      A waitin' fur a pardner,
          You an' I an' ev'ry one knows
          How whoats an' beans an' barley grows.
      Fost tha farmer saws 'is seeds,
      Then he stans' an' teks 'is ease,
      Stamps 'is feet an' claps 'is 'ands,
      And turns him round to view tha lands.
          A waitin' fur a pardner,
          A waitin' fur a pardner,
          You an' I an' iv'ry one knows
          How whoats an' beans an' barley grows.

Now you're married, &c.
[same as Much Wenlock.]
                    —Boston, Lincs. (*Notes and Queries*,
                            7th series, xii. 493).

XVII. Oats and beans and barley grows
       Not so fine as the farmer sows,
       You nor I nor nobody knows
       Oats and beans and barley grows.
       This is the way the farmer sows,
       The farmer sows, the farmer sows,

This is the way the farmer sows.
Here he stands and takes his ease,
Stamps his foot and claps his hands,
And turns around to view the land,
Waiting for a partner, waiting for a partner,
Open the ring and take one in,
And kiss him (or her) as he (or she) enters.
                    —Aberdeen Training College (Rev. W. Gregor).

XVIII.   Waitin' for a partner,
         Waitin' for a partner,
         Open the ring and take one in,
         And now you've got your partner.

         Now you're married, &c.
         [same as Much Wenlock.]
                        —Wakefield, Yorks. (Miss Fowler).

(*c*) The players form a ring by joining hands, with one child, usually a boy, standing in the centre. The ring walks round, singing the first four lines. At the fifth line the ring stands still, and each child suits her actions to the words sung. At "the farmer sows his seed," each player pretends to scatter seed, then they all fold their arms and "stand at ease," "stamp their feet," and "clap their hands" together in order, and finally each child turns herself round. Then they again clasp hands and move round the centre child, who at the words "open the ring and take one in" chooses and takes into the ring with him one player from it. These two stand together while the ring sings the marriage formula. At the end the child first in the centre joins the ring; the second child remaining in the centre, and in her turn choosing another from the ring.

This is the (Much Wenlock) way of playing. Among the variants there are some slight differences. In the Wakefield version (Miss Fowler), a little boy is placed in the centre of the ring first, he chooses a girl out of the ring at the singing of the third line and kisses her. They stand hand in hand while the others sing the next verse. In the Tean version (Miss Keary), the children turn round with their backs to the one in the centre, and stand still when singing "Waiting for a partner." In the Hampshire (Miss Mendham), Brigg (Miss Barker), and Winterton (Miss Peacock) versions, the children dance round instead of walking. The Rev. Mr. Roberts, in a version from Kirkby-on-the-Bain (N.W. Lincolnshire), says: "There is no proper commencement of this song. The children begin with 'A waitin' fur a pardner,' or 'Oats and beans,' just as the spirit moves them, but I think 'A waitin'' is the usual beginning here." In a Sheffield version sent by Mr. S. O. Addy, four young men stand in the middle of the ring with their hands joined. These four dance round singing the first lines. After "views his lands" these four choose sweethearts, or partners, from the ring. The eight join hands and sing the remaining four lines. The four young men then join the larger ring, and the four girls remain in the centre and choose partners next time. The words of this version are almost identical with those of Shropshire. In the Isle of Man version (A. W. Moore), when the kiss is given all the children forming the ring clap their hands. There is no kissing in the Shropshire and many other versions of this game, and the centre child does not in all cases sing the words.

(*d*) Other versions have been sent from Winterton, Leadenham, and Lincoln, by Miss Peacock, and from Brigg, while the *Northamptonshire Notes and Queries*, ii. 161, gives another by Mr. R. S. Baker. The words are practically the same as the versions printed above from Lincolnshire and Northants. The words of the Madeley version are the same as the Much Wenlock (No. 1). The Nottingham tune (Miss Youngman), and three others sent with the words, are the same as the Madeley tune printed above.

(*e*) This interesting game is essentially of rural origin, and probably it is for this reason that Mr. Newell did not obtain any version from England for his *Games and Songs of American Children*, but his note that it " seems, strangely enough, to be unknown in Great Britain" (p. 80), is effectually disproved by the examples I have collected. There is no need in this case for an analysis of the rhymes. The variants fall into three categories: (1) the questioning form of the words, (2) the affirming form, and (3) the indiscriminate form, as in Nos. xvi. to xviii., and of these I am disposed to consider the first to represent the earliest idea of the game.

If the crops mentioned in the verses be considered, it will be found that the following table represents the different localities :—

	Northants.	Lancashire.	Lincolnshire.	Shropshire.	Staffordshire.	Nottingham.	Isle of Man.	Hants.	Isle of Wight.	Norfolk.
Oats . .	+	+	+	+	+	+	+	+	...	...
Beans .	+	+	+	+	...	+	+	+	...	+
Barley .	+	+	+	+	+	+	+	+	+	+
Wheat .	...	...	...	...	+	...	...	...	+	...
Groats .	...	...	...	...	...	...	...	...	...	...
Hop .	...	...	...	...	...	...	+	...	...	+

The first three are the more constant words, but it is curious that Norfolk, not a hop county, should have adopted that grain into the game. Hops are grown there on rare occasions, and it is probable that the game may have been introduced from a hop county.

In *Northants Notes and Queries*, i. 163–164, Mr. R. S. Baker gives a most interesting account of the game (No. iii.) as follows :—" Having been recently invited to join the Annual Christmas Entertainment of the Raunds Church Choir, I noticed that a very favourite pastime of the evening was one which I shall call 'Choosing Partners.' The game is played thus: The young men and maidens join hands indiscriminately, and form a ring; within the ring stand a lad and a lass; then they all step round the way the sun goes, to a plain tune. During the singing of the two last lines [of the first part] they all disjoin hands, stop and stamp their feet and clap their hands and turn right round . . . then join hands [while singing the second verse]. The two in the middle at ['Open the ring'] choose each of them a partner of the opposite sex, which they do by pointing to the one chosen; then they continue round, to the words [sang in next verse], the two pairs of partners crossing hands, first right and then left, and revolving opposite ways alternately. The march round is temporarily suspended for choosing partners. The partners salute [at 'Now you're married'], or, rather, each lad kisses his chosen lass; the first two partners go out, the game continues as before, and every one in the ring has chosen and been chosen, and every lad has saluted every lass. The antiquity of the pastime is evidenced by its not mentioning wheat; wheat was in remote times an exceptional crop—the village people lived on oatmeal and barley bread. It also points, possibly, to a period when most of the land lay in grass. Portions of the open fields were cultivated, and after a few years of merciless cropping were laid down again to recuperate. 'Helping to chop the wood' recalls the time when coal was not known as fuel. I am indebted for the correct words of the above to a Raunds maiden, Miss B. Finding, a native of the village, who kindly wrote them down for me." Mr. Baker does not say how Miss Finding got the peculiar spelling of this version. It would be interesting to know whether this form of spelling was used as indicative of the pronunciation of the children, or of the supposed antiquity of the game. The Rev. W. D. Sweeting, also writes at the same reference, "The same game is played at the school feast at Maxey; but the words, as I have taken them down, vary from those given above. We have no mention of any crop except barley, which is largely grown in the district; and the refrain, repeated after the second and sixth lines, is 'waiting for the harvest.' A lady suggested to me that the two first lines of the conclusion are addressed to the bride of the game, and the two last, which in our version run, 'You must be kind and very good,' apply to the happy swain."

This interesting note not only suggests, as Mr. Baker and Mr. Sweeting say, the antiquity of the game and its connection with harvest at a time when the farms were all laid in open fields, but it points further to the custom of courtship and marriage being the outcome of village festivals and dances held after spring sowing and harvest gatherings. It seems in Northamptonshire not to have quite reached the stage of the pure children's game before it was taken note of by

Mr. Baker, and this is an important illustration of the descent
of children's games from customs.   As soon as it has become
a child's game, however, the process of decadence sets in.
Thus, besides verbal alterations, the lines relating to farming
have dropped out of the Wakefield version.   It is abundantly
clear from the more perfect game-rhymes that the waiting for
a partner is an episode in the harvest customs, as if, when the
outdoor business of the season was finished, the domestic
element becomes the next important transaction in the year's
proceedings.   The curious four-lined formula applicable to the
duties of married life may indeed be a relic of those rhythmical
formulæ which are found throughout all early legal ceremonies.
A reference to Mr. Ralston's section on marriage songs, in his
Songs of the Russian People, makes it clear that marriages
in Russia were contracted at the gatherings called Besyedas
(p. 264), which were social gatherings held during October
after the completion of the harvest; and the practice is, of
course, not confined to Russia.

It is also probable that this game may have preserved the
tradition of a formula sung at the sowing of grain, in order to
propitiate the earth goddess to promote and quicken the growth
of the crops. Turning around or bowing to fields and lands and
pantomimic actions in imitation of those actually required, are
very general in the history of sympathetic magic among primitive peoples, as reference to Mr. Frazer's *Golden Bough* will
prove; and taking the rhyming formula together with the
imitative action, I am inclined to believe that in this game we
may have the last relics of a very ancient agricultural rite.

Obadiah

The players stand in a row.   The child at the head of the
row says, " My son Obadiah is going to be married, twiddle your
thumbs," suiting the action to the word by clasping the fingers
of both hands together, and rapidly " twiddling " the thumbs.
The next child repeats both words and actions, and so on all
along the row, all the players continuing the "twiddling."
The top child repeats the words, adding (very gravely), " Fall
on one knee," the whole row follows suit as before (still

twiddling their thumbs). The top child repeats from the beginning, adding, " Do as you see me," and the rest of the children follow suit, as before. Just as the last child repeats the words, the top child falls on the child next to her, and all go down like a row of ninepins. The whole is said in a sing-song way. This game was, so far as I can ascertain, truly East Anglian. I have never been able to hear of it in other parts of England or Wales.—Bexley Heath (Miss Morris). Also played in London.

See " Solomon."

Odd or Even

A boys' game, played with buttons, marbles, and halfpence. Peacock's *Manley and Corringham Glossary;* also mentioned in Brogden's *Provincial Words (Lincolnshire).* Mr. Patterson says (*Antrim and Down Glossary*)—A boy shuts up a few small objects, such as marbles, in one hand, and asks his opponent to guess if the number is odd or even. He then either pays or receives one, according as the guess is right or wrong. Strutt describes this game in the same way, and says it was played in ancient Greece and Rome. Newell (*Games*, p. 147) also mentions it.

See " Prickie and Jockie."

Odd-man

A game played with coins. Brogden's *Provincial Words, Lincolnshire.*

Old Dame

I.   I'll away to t' beck to wash my neck,
      When I get there, I'll ask t' ould dame what o'clock it is ?
      It's one, and you'll be hanged at two.

      I'll away to t' beck to wash my neck,
      When I get there, I'll ask t' ould dame what o'clock it is ?
      It's two, and you'll be hanged at three.

[This is repeated until the old woman says, " It's eleven, and you'll be hanged at twelve."]

—Yorkshire (Miss E. Cadman).

II. To Beccles, to Beccles,
       To buy a bunch of nettles,
       Pray, old dame, what's o'clock ?
          One, going for two.

          To Beccles, to Beccles,
          To buy a bunch of nettles,
          Pray, old dame, what's o'clock ?
             Two, going for three, &c.

[And so on until "eleven going for twelve" is said, then the
following :—]

             Where have you been ?
             To the wood.
             What for ?
             To pick up sticks.
             What for ?
             To light my fire.
             What for ?
             To boil my kettle.
             What for ?
             To cook some of your chickens.
                    —Halliwell, *Nursery Rhymes*, p. 229.

(*b*) One child sits upon a little stool. The others march
round her in single file, taking hold of each other's frocks.
They say in a sing-song manner the first two lines, and the old
woman answers by telling them the hour. The questions and
answers are repeated until the old woman says, "It's eleven,
and you'll be hanged at twelve." Then the children all run
off in different directions and the old woman runs after them.
Whoever she catches becomes old woman, and the game is
continued.—Yorkshire (Miss E. Cadman). In the version
given from Halliwell there is a further dialogue, it will be
seen, before the old woman chases.

(*c*) The use of the Yorkshire word "beck" ("stream") in
the first variant suggests that this may be the original version
from which the "Beccles" version has been adapted, a particular place being substituted for the general. The game somewhat resembles "Fox and Goose."

Old Roger is Dead

—Earls Heaton (H. Hardy).

—Sporle, Norfolk (Miss Matthews).

—Bath, (A. B. Gomme).

I.   Old Rogers is dead and is laid in his grave,
Laid in his grave,
Laid in his grave;
Old Rogers is dead and is laid in his grave,
He, hi! laid in his grave.

There grew an old apple tree over his head,
Over his head,
Over his head;
There grew an old apple tree over his head,
He, hi! over his head.

The apples grew ripe, and they all fell off,
They all fell off,
They all fell off;
The apples grew ripe, and they all fell off,
He, hi! they all fell off.

There came an old woman a-picking them up,
Picking them up,
Picking them up;
There came an old woman a-picking them up,
He, hi! picking them up.

Old Rogers jumps up and he gives her a knock,
    Gives her a knock,
    Gives her a knock ;
Old Rogers jumps up and he gives her a knock,
    He, hi ! gives her a knock.

He makes the old woman go hipperty hop,
    Hipperty hop,
    Hipperty hop ;
He makes the old woman go hipperty hop,
    He, hi ! hipperty hop.
           —Earls Heaton, Yorks. (Herbert Hardy).

II. Old Roger is dead, and lies in his grave, um, ah ! lies in
     his grave ;
    There grew an old apple tree over his head, um, ah !
     over his head.
    The apples are ripe and ready to drop, um, ah ! ready
     to drop ;
    There came an old woman, picking them up.
           —Hanbury, Staffs. (Miss Edith Hollis).

III. Sir Roger is dead and is low in his grave,
    Is low in his grave, is low in his grave ;
    Sir Roger is dead and is low in his grave,
    Hey hie ! is low in his grave.

They planted an apple tree over his head,
Over his head, over his head ;
They planted an apple tree over his head,
Hey hie ! over his head.

When they grew ripe they all fell off,
All fell off, all fell off ;
When they grew ripe they all fell off,
Hey hie ! all fell off.

There came an old woman and gathered them up,
Gathered them up, gathered them up ;
There came an old woman and gathered them up,
Hey hie ! gathered them up.

Sir Roger got up and gave her a nudge,
Gave her a nudge, gave her a nudge ;
Sir Roger got up and gave her a nudge,
Hey hie! gave her a nudge.

Which made her go off with a skip and a hop,
With a skip and a hop, with a skip and a hop ;
Which made her go off with a skip and a hop,
Hey hie! with a skip and a hop.

—Ordsall, Nottinghamshire (Miss Matthews).

IV.   Sir Roger is dead and he's laid in his grave,
Laid in his grave, laid in his grave ;
Sir Roger is dead and he's laid in his grave,
Heigh-ho! laid in his grave.

There grew a fine apple tree over his head,
Over his head, over his head ;
There grew a fine apple tree over his head,
Heigh-ho! over his head.

The apples were ripe and they all fell off,
All fell off, all fell off ;
The apples were ripe and they all fell off,
Heigh-ho! all fell off.

There came an old woman and picked them all up,
Picked them all up, picked them all up ;
There came an old woman and picked them all up,
Heigh-ho! picked them all up.

Sir Roger jumped up and he gave her a push,
Gave her a push, gave her a push ;
Sir Roger jumped up and he gave her a push,
Heigh-ho! gave her a push.

Which made the old woman go hickety-hock,
Hickety-hock, hickety-hock ;
Which made the old woman go hickety-hock,
Heigh-ho! hickety-hock.

—Brigg, Lincolnshire (Miss J. Barker).

V.   Sir Roger is dead and laid in his grave,
          Hee, haw! laid in his grave.
     They planted an apple tree over his head,
          Hee, haw! over his head.
     The apples are ripe and ready to fall,
          Hee, haw! ready to fall.
     There came a high wind and blew them all off,
          Hee, haw! blew them all off.
     There came an old woman to pick them all up,
          Hee, haw! pick them all up.
     There came a little bird and gave her a tap,
          Hee, haw! gave her a tap.
     Which made the old woman go hipperty hop,
          Hee, haw! hipperty hop.
                    —Tong, Shropshire (Miss Burne).

VI. Poor Johnnie is dead and he lies in his grave,
     Lies in his grave, lies in his grave;
     Poor Johnnie is dead and he lies in his grave,
     He-ho! lies in his grave.

     They planted an apple tree over his head,
     Over his head, over his head;
     They planted an apple tree over his head,
     He-ho! over his head.

     The apples got ripe and they all fell off,
     All fell off, all fell off;
     The apples got ripe and they all fell off,
     He-ho! all fell off.

     Here comes an old woman a-picking them up,
     A-picking them up, a-picking them up;
     Here comes an old woman a-picking them up,
     He-ho! a-picking them up.

     Poor Johnnie got up and gave her a thump,
     And gave her a thump, and gave her a thump;
     Poor Johnnie got up and gave her a thump,
     He-ho! gave her a thump.

He made the old woman go hippity-hop,
Hippity-hop, hippity-hop!
He made the old woman go hippity-hop,
He-ho! hippity-hop!

—Sporle, Norfolk (Miss Matthews).

VII. Cock Robin is dead and has gone to his grave;
There grew on old apple tree over his head;
The apples were ripe and ready to drop,
　　O my, flippity flop!

There came an old woman to pick them all up,
Cock Robin rose up and gave her a knock,
And made the old woman go flippity flop!
　　O my, flippity flop!

—Deptford, Kent (Miss Chase).

VIII. Old Roger is dead and gone to his grave,
H'm ha! gone to his grave.

They planted an apple tree over his head,
H'm ha! over his head.

The apples were ripe and ready to fall,
H'm ha! ready to fall.

There came an old woman and picked them all up,
H'm ha! picked them all up.

Old Roger jumped up and gave her a knock,
H'm ha! gave her a knock.

Which made the old woman go hippity hop,
H'm ha! hippity hop!

—Bath, from a Nursemaid (A. B. Gomme).

IX. Cock Robin is dead and lies in his grave,
Hum-ha! lies in his grave.
Place an old apple tree over his head,
Hum-ha! over his head.
When they were ripe and ready to fall,
Hum-ha! ready to fall.

There comes an old woman a-picking them up,
Hum-ha! a-picking them up.
Cock Robin jumps up and gives her a good knock,
Hum-ha! gives her a good knock.

—Derbyshire (*Folk-lore Journal*, i. 385).

X. Poor Roger is dead and lies low in his grave,
Low in his grave, low in his grave,
E. I. low in his grave.

There grew an old apple tree over his head,
Over his head, over his head,
E. I. over his head.

When the apples were ripe they all fell off,
All fell off, all fell off,
E. I. all fell off.

There was an old woman came picking them up,
Picking them up, picking them up,
E. I. picking them up.

Poor Roger jumped up and gave her a nudge,
Gave her a nudge, gave her a nudge,
E. I. gave her a nudge.

Which made the old woman go lippety lop,
Lippety lop, lippety lop,
E. I. lippety lop.

—Newark, Nottinghamshire (S. O. Addy).

XI. Poor Toby is dead and he lies in his grave,
He lies in his grave, he lies in his grave;
They planted an apple tree over his head,
Over his head, over his head.

The apples grew ripe and beginning to fall,
Beginning to fall, beginning to fall;
The apples grew ripe and beginning to fall,
Beginning to fall, beginning to fall.

There came an old woman picking them up,
Picking them up, picking them up;
Poor Toby rose up and he gave her a kick,
Gave her a kick, gave her a kick.

And the poor old woman went hipperty hop,
Hipperty hop, hipperty hop ;
And the poor old woman went hipperty hop,
Hipperty hop along.

—Belfast (W. H. Patterson).

XII.   There was an old woman we buried her here,
Buried her here, buried her here ;
There was an old woman we buried her here,
He—ho ! buried her here.

—Sporle, Norfolk (Miss Matthews).

(*b*) A ring is formed by children joining hands; one child, who represents Sir Roger, lays down on the ground in the centre of the ring with his head covered with a handkerchief. The ring stands still and sings the verses. When the second verse is begun, a child from the ring goes into the centre and stands by Sir Roger, to represent the apple tree. At the fourth verse another child goes into the ring, and pretends to pick up the fallen apples. Then the child personating Sir Roger jumps up and knocks the child personating the old woman, beating her out of the ring. She goes off hobbling on one foot, and pretending to be hurt. In the Ordsall game the children dance round when singing the verses instead of standing still, the action of the game being the same. In the Tong version, the action seems to be done by the ring. Miss Burne says the children go through various movements, finally all limping round. The Newark (Notts), and Bath versions are played as first described, Poor Roger being covered with a cloak, or an apron, and laying down in the middle of the ring. A Southampton version has additional features—the ring of children keep their arms crossed, and lay their hands on their chests, bending their heads and bodies backwards and forwards, in a mourning attitude, while they sing; in addition to which, in the Bath version, the child who personates the apple tree during the singing of the third verse raises her arms above her head, and then lets them drop to her sides to show the falling apples.

(*c*) Various as the game-rhymes are in word detail, they

are practically the same in incident. One remarkable feature stands out particularly, namely, the planting a tree over the head of the dead, and the spirit-connection which this tree has with the dead. The robbery of the fruit brings back the dead Sir Roger to protect it, and this must be his ghost or spirit. In popular superstition this incident is not uncommon. Thus Aubrey in his *Remains of Gentilisme,* notes that "in the parish of Ockley some graves have rose trees planted at the head and feet," and then proceeds to say, " They planted a tree or a flower on the grave of their friend, and they thought the soule of the party deceased went into the tree or plant " (p. 155). In Scotland a branch falling from an oak, the Edgewell tree, standing near Dalhousie Castle, portended mortality to the family (Dalyell, *Darker Superstitions,* p. 504). Compare with this a similar superstition noted in Carew's *History of Corn-wall,* p. 325, and Mr. Keary's treatment of this cult in his *Outlines of Primitive Belief,* pp. 66–67. In folk-tales this incident also appears ; the spirit of the dead enters the tree and resents robbery of its fruit, possession of which gives power over the soul or spirit of the dead.

The game is, therefore, not merely the acting of a funeral, but more particularly shows the belief that a dead person is cognisant of actions done by the living, and capable of re-senting personal wrongs and desecration of the grave.   It shows clearly the sacredness of the grave ; but what, perhaps to us, is the most interesting feature, is the way in which the game is played.   This clearly shows a survival of the method of portraying old plays.   The ring of children act the part of " chorus," and relate the incidents of the play.   The three actors say nothing, only act their several parts in dumb show. The raising and lowering of the arms on the part of the child who plays "apple tree," the quiet of " Old Roger" until he has to jump up, certainly show the early method of actors when details were presented by action instead of words. Children see no absurdity in being a " tree," or a " wall," " apple," or animal.   They simply *are* these things if the game demands it, and they think nothing of incongruities.

I do not, of course, suggest that children have preserved in this game an old play, but I consider that in this and similar games they have preserved methods of acting and detail (now styled traditional), as given in an early or childish period of the drama, as for example in the mumming plays.   Traditional methods of acting are discussed by Mr. Ordish, *Folk-lore*, ii. 334.

Old Soldier

One player personates an old soldier, and begs of all the other players in turn for left-off garments, or anything else he chooses.   The formula still used at Barnes by children is, " Here comes an old soldier from the wars [or from town], pray what can you give him ? "   Another version is—

Here comes an old soldier from Botany Bay,
Have you got anything to give him to-day.
                              —Liverpool (C. C. Bell).

The questioned child replying must be careful to avoid using the words, Yes ! No ! Nay ! and Black, White, or Grey.   These words are tabooed, and a forfeit is exacted every time one or other is used.   The old soldier walks lame, and carries a stick. He is allowed to ask as many questions, talk as much as he pleases, and to account for his destitute condition.

(*c*) Some years ago when colours were more limited in number, it was difficult to promise garments for a man's wear which were neither of these colours tabooed.   Miss Burne (*Shropshire Folk-lore*, p. 526), in describing this game says, " The words Red or Blue are sometimes forbidden, as well as Yes or No," and adds that " This favourite old game gives scope for great ingenuity on the part of the beggar, and ' it seems not improbable ' (to use a time-honoured antiquarian phrase !) that the expression ' To come the old soldier over a person' may allude to it."   Halliwell (*Nursery Rhymes*, p. 224) describes the game as above.

Oliver, Oliver, follow the King !

Oliver, Oliver, follow the King !
Oliver, Oliver, last in the ring !
Jim Burguin wants a wife, and a wife he shall have,
Nelly he kissed at the back-cellar door,
Nelly made a pudding, she made it over sweet,

She never stuck a knife in till he came home at night,
So next Monday morning is our wedding-day,
The bells they shall ring, and the music shall play!
Oliver, Oliver, follow the King! (*da capo*).
—Berrington (Burne's *Shropshire Folk-lore*, p. 508).

(*b*) The children form a ring and move round, singing the first two lines. Then they curtsey, or "douk down," all together; the one who is last has to tell her sweetheart's name. The other lines are then sung and the game is continued. The children's names are mentioned as each one names his or her sweetheart.

This is apparently the game of which "All the Boys," "Down in the Valley," and "Mary Mixed a Pudding up," are also portions.

One Catch-all

The words "Cowardy, cowardy custard" are repeated by children playing at this game when they advance towards the one who is selected to catch them, and dare or provoke her to capture them. Ray, *Localisms*, gives Costard, the head; a kind of opprobrious word used by way of contempt. Bailey gives Costead-head, a blockhead; thus elucidating this exclamation which may be interpreted, "You cowardly blockhead, catch me if you dare" (Baker's *Northamptonshire Glossary*).

The words used were, as far as I remember,
Cowardy, cowardy custard, eat your father's mustard,
Catch me if you can.

To compel a person to "eat" something disagreeable is a well-known form of expressing contempt. The rhyme was supposed to be very efficacious in rousing an indifferent or lazy player when playing "touch" (A. B. Gomme).

Oranges and Lemons

An older and more general version of the last five bars (the tail piece) is as follows:—

Here comes a   Here comes a ⎱ last · · · · · last man's head.
light, &c.   chopper, &c. ⎰

—London (A. B. Gomme).

—Yorkshire (H. Hardy).

—Sporle, Norfolk (Miss Matthews).

I. Oranges and lemons,
   Say the bells of St. Clement's;
   You owe me five farthings,
   Say the bells of St. Martin's;
   When will you pay me,
   Say the bells of Old Bailey;
   When I grow rich,
   Say the bells of Shoreditch;
   When will that be?
   Say the bells of Stepney;
   I'm sure I don't know,
   Says the Great Bell of Bow.
Here comes a light to light you to bed;
Here comes a chopper to chop off your head;
The last, last, last, last man's head.

—London (A. B. Gomme).

II. Oranges and lemons,
   Say the bells of St. Clement's;
   You owe me four farthings,
   Say the bells of St. Martin's;
   When will you pay me?
   Say the bells of Old Bailey;
   When I grow rich,
   Say the bells of Shoreditch;
   When will that be?
   Say the bells of Stepney;
   I'm sure I don't know,
   Says the Great Bell of Bow.
Here comes a candle to light you to bed;
Here comes a chopper to chop off your head;
Last, last, last, last, last man's head.

—Winterton and Leadenham, Lincolnshire; also
Nottinghamshire (Miss M. Peacock).

III. Oranges and lemons,
   Says the bells of S. Clemen's.
Brickdust and tiles,
   Says the bells of S. Giles.

You owe me five farthings,
　　Says the bells of S. Martin's.
I do not know you,
　　Says the bells of S. Bow.
When will you pay me?
　　Says the bells of Old Bailey.
When I get rich,
　　Says the bells of Shoreditch.
Here comes a candle to light you to bed,
Here comes a chopper to chop off your head.
　　　　　　　—Derbyshire (*Folk-lore Journal*, i. 386).

IV.　Oranges and lemons,
　　　　The bells of St. Clemen's;
　　You owe me five farthings,
　　　　The bells of St. Martin's;
　　When will you pay me?
　　　　Say the bells of Old Bailey;
　　When I grow rich,
　　　　Say the bells of Shoreditch;
　　When will that be?
　　　　Say the bells of Shorlea;
　　I don't know,
　　　　Says the Great Bell Bow.
　　Here comes the candle to light you to bed,
　　Here comes the chop to chop off your head.
　　Chop, chop, chop, &c.
　　　　　　　—Middlesex (Miss Winfield).

V.　Orange or lemon,
　　The bells of St. Clement's [or the bells are a
　　　　clemming].
　　I owe you five farthings,
　　And when shall I pay you,
　　To-day or to-morrow?
　　To-morrow will do.
　　Here come some great candles
　　To light you to bed,
　　Here come some great choppers
　　To chop off your head.

Come under, come under,
Come run as you ought;
Come under, come under,
Until you are caught;
Then stand just behind us
And pull either way;
Which side pulls the strongest
That side wins the day.

—Sporle, Norfolk (Miss Matthews).

VI. Oranges and lemons,
The bells of St. Clement's.
I owe you three farthings,
When shall I pay you?
When I get rich.
Here comes a candle to light you to bed,
Here comes a hatchet to chop off your head.

—Brigg (from a Lincolnshire friend of Miss Barker).

VII. Oranges and lemons,
Say the bells of St. Clemen's.
I owe you five farthins,
Say the bells of St. Martin's.
When shall I pay you?
Monday, Tuesday, Wednesday,
Thursday, Friday, Saturday,
Or Sunday?

—Symondsbury, Dorset (*Folk-lore Journal*, vii. 216).

VIII. I owe you five farthings.
When will you pay me,
To-day or to-morrow?
Here comes a candle to light you to bed,
Here comes a chopper to chop off your head.

—Broadwinsor, Dorset (*Folk-lore Journal*, vii. 217.

IX. Oranges and lemons, the bells of St. Clement's [or St. Helen's].
I owe you five farthings. And when will you pay me?
I'm sure I don't know.

Here comes a candle to light you to bed,
Here comes a chop'n bill to chop off your head—
  Chop—chop—chop—chop.
[Or Here comes a chop'n bill to chop off the last man's head.]
      —Earls Heaton, Yorks. (Herbert Hardy).

X. Lend me five shillings,
  Said the bells of St. Helen's.

 When will you pay me ?
  Said the bells of St. Philip's.

 I do not know,
  Said the Great Bell of Bold.

 Ring a ding, ding,
 Ring a ding, ding,
 Ring a ding, ding, ding, ding.
   —Earls Heaton (Herbert Hardy, as told him by A. K.).

XI. Oranges and lemons, say the bells of St. Clement's ;
 You owe me five farthings, and when will you pay
  me ?
 Say the bells of Old Bailey.
 When I grow rich, say the bells of Shoreditch.
 And the last one that comes shall be chop, chop.
    Hersham, Surrey (*Folk-lore Record*, v. 86).

XII. Orange and lemon,
  Say the bells of St. Martin (or the bells of
   Sweet Lemon) ;
  I owe you five farthings,
  But when shall I pay you ?

  Here comes a candle
  To light you to bed,
  Here comes a hatchet
  To chop off your head.
    —Eckington, Derbyshire (S. O. Addy).

XIII.   Oranges and lemons,
The bells of St. Clement's ;
I owe you five farthings,
And when will you pay me ?
Oh, that I can't tell you ;
Sim, Bim, bim, bow, bay.
—Settle, Yorks. (Rev. W. E. Sykes).

XIV.   Oranges or lemons,
The bells of St. Clement's ;
You owe me five farthings,
Pray, when will you pay me ?
Here come the clappers to knock you down
backwards, carwoo !
—Suffolk (Mrs. Haddon).

XV. Oranges and lemons, say the bells of St. Clement's ;
Brick dust and tiles, say the bells of St. Giles ;
You owe me three farthings, say the bells of St.
Martin's ;
When will you pay me ? say the bells of Old Bailey ;
When I grow rich, say the bells of Shoreditch ;
When will that be ? say the bells of Stepney ;
I'm sure I don't know, says the Great Bell of Bow.
—Perth (Rev. W. Gregor).

XVI.   Pancakes and fritters,
Says the bells of St. Peter's ;
Where must we fry 'em ?
Says the bells of Cold Higham ;
In yonder land thurrow (furrow),
Says the bells of Wellingborough ;
You owe me a shilling,
Says the bells of Great Billing ;
When will you pay me ?
Says the bells of Widdleton Cheney ;
When I am able,
Say the bells at Dunstable ;
That will never be,

Says the bells at Coventry;
Oh, yes, it will,
Says Northampton Great Bell;
White bread and sop,
Says the bells at Kingsthorp;
Trundle a lantern,
Says the bells at Northampton.
—Northamptonshire (Baker's *Words and Phrases*).

(*c*) This game is generally played as follows :—

Two of the taller children stand facing each other, holding up their clasped hands. One is named Orange and the other Lemon. The other players, grasping one another's dresses, run underneath the raised arms and round Orange, and then

Fig 1

Fig. 2

Fig. 3

under the arms again and round Lemon, while singing the verses. The three concluding lines are sung by "Orange" and "Lemon" in a slow emphatic manner, and at the word "head" they drop their arms over one of the children passing between them, and ask her secretly whether she will be *orange* or *lemon*. The captive chooses her side, and stands behind whichever leader she selects, placing her arms round her waist. The game continues till every one engaged in it has ranged herself behind one or other of the chiefs. When the two parties are ranged a "tug of war" takes place until one of the parties breaks down, or is pulled over a given mark.

In the Middlesex version (Miss Winfield) the children form
a ring and go round singing the verses, and apparently there
is neither catching the "last man" nor the "tug." Mr.
Emslie says he has seen and played the game in Middlesex,
and it always terminated with the cutting off the last man's
head. In the Symondsbury version the players drop their
hands when they say "Sunday." No tug is mentioned in
the first Earls Heaton version of the game (Mr. Hardy). In
the second version he says bells are represented by children.
They should have in their hands, bells, or some article to represent them. All stand in a row. First, second, and third bells
stand out in turn to sing. All rush for bells to sing chorus.
Miss Barclay writes: The children of the Fernham and Longcot choir, playing on Christmas Eve, 1891, pulled across a
handkerchief. In Monton, Lancashire, Miss Dendy says the
game is played as elsewhere, but without words. In a Swaffham
version (Miss Matthews), the girls sometimes call themselves
"Plum pudding and roast beef," or whatever fancy may suggest, instead of oranges and lemons. They join hands high
enough for the others to pass under, which they do to a call
of "Ducky, Ducky," presently the hands come down and catch
one, who is asked in *confidence* which she likes best. The game
then proceeds in the usual way, one side trying to pull the
other over a marked line. Oranges and lemons at Bocking,
Essex, is an abbreviated variant of the rhyme printed by
Halliwell (*Folk-lore Record*, iii., part II., 171). In Nottinghamshire, Miss Peacock says it is sometimes called "Tarts and
Cheesecakes." Moor (*Suffolk Words*) mentions "Oranges and
Lemons" as played by both girls and boys, and adds, "I
believe it is nearly the same as 'Plum Pudding and Roast
Beef.'" In the Suffolk version sent by Mrs. Haddon a new
word is introduced, "carwoo." This is the signal for one of the
line to be caught. Miss Eddleston, Gainford, Durham, says
this game is called—

> Through and through the shally go,
> The last shall be taken.

Mr. Halliwell (*Nursery Rhymes*, No. cclxxxi.) adopts the
verses entitled, "The Merry Bells of London," from Gammer

Gurton's *Garland*, 1783, as the origin of this game.   In Aberdeen, Mr. M. L. Rouse tells me he has heard Scotch children apparently playing the same game, " Oranges and Lemons, ask, Which would you have, 'A sack of corn or a sack of coals ? ' "

(*d*) This game indicates a contest between two opposing parties, and a punishment, and although in the game the sequence of events is not at all clear, the contest taking place after the supposed execution, these two events stand out very clearly as the chief factors.   In the endeavour to ascertain who the contending parties were, one cannot but be struck with the significance of the bells having different saint's names.   Now the only places where it would be probable for bells to be associated with more than one saint's name within the circuit of a small area are the old parish units of cities and boroughs. Bells were rung on occasions when it was necessary or advisable to call the people together.   At the ringing of the " alarm bell " the market places were quickly filled by crowds of citizens ; and by turning to the customs of these places in England, it will be found that contest games between parishes, and between the wards of parishes, were very frequent (see Gomme's *Village Community*, pp. 241–243).   These contests were generally conducted by the aid of the football, and in one or two cases, such as at Ludlow, the contest was with a rope, and, in the case of Derby, it is specially stated that the victors were announced by the joyful ringing of their parish bells.   Indeed, Halliwell has preserved the " song on the bells of Derby on football morning " (No. clxix.) as follows :—

> Pancake and fritters,
> Say All Saints and St. Peter's ;
> When will the *ball* come,
> Say the bells of St. Alkmun ;
> At two they will throw,
> Says Saint Werabo ;
> O ! very well,
> Says little Michel.

This custom is quite sufficient to have originated the game, and the parallel which it supplies is evidence of the connection between the two.   Oranges and lemons were, in all probability, originally intended to mean the *colours* of the two contesting parties, and not *fruits* of those names. In contests between the people of a town and the authority of baron or earl, the adherents of each side ranged themselves under and wore the colours of their chiefs, as is now done by political partizans.

The rhymes are probably corrupted, but whether from some early cries or calls of the different parishes, or from sentences which the bells were supposed to have said or sung when tolled, it is impossible to say. The "clemming" of the bells in the Norfolk version (No. 5) may have originated "St. Clements," and the other saints have been added at different times. On the other hand, the general similarity of the rhymes indicates the influence of some particular place, and, judging by the parish names, London seems to be that place. If this is so, the main incident of the rhymes may perhaps be due to the too frequent distribution of a traitor's head and limbs among different towns who had taken up his cause. The exhibitions of this nature at London were more frequent than at any other place. The procession of a criminal to execution was generally accompanied by the tolling of bells, and by torches. It is not unlikely that the monotonous chant of the last lines, "Here comes a light to light you to bed," &c., indicates this.

'Otmillo

A boy (A) kneels with his face in another's (B) lap; the other player's standing in the background. They step forward one by one at a signal from B, who says to each in turn—

'Otmillo, 'Otmillo,
Where is this poor man to go?

A then designates a place for each one. When all are despatched A removes his face from B's knees, and standing up exclaims, "Hot! Hot! Hot!" The others then run to him, and the laggard is blinded instead of A.—Warwickshire (Northall's *Folk Rhymes*, p. 402).

This is probably the same game as "Hot Cockles," although it apparently lacks the hitting or buffeting the blinded wizard.

Over Clover

The name for the game of "Warner" in Oxfordshire. They have a song used in the game commencing—

> Over clover,
> Nine times over.   —Halliwell's *Dictionary*.

See "Stag Warning."

Paddy from Home

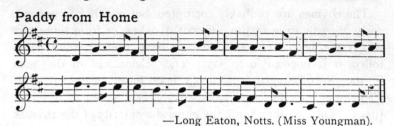

—Long Eaton, Notts. (Miss Youngman).

Paddy from home has never been,
A railway train he's never seen,
He longs to see the great machine
That travels along the railway.

> —Long Eaton, Nottinghamshire and Derbyshire
> borders (Miss Youngman).

(*c*) The children form a ring, and hold in their hands a string tied at the ends, and on which a ring is strung. They pass the ring from one to another, backwards and forwards. One child stands in the centre, who tries to find the holder of the ring. Whoever is discovered holding it takes the place of the child in the centre.

(*d*) This game is similar to "Find the Ring." The verse is, no doubt, modern, though the action and the string and ring are borrowed from an older game. Another verse used for the same game at Earl's Heaton (Mr. Hardy) is—

> The ring it is going;
> Oh where? oh where?
> I don't care where,
> I can't tell where.

Paip

Three cherry stones are placed together, and another above them. These are all called a castle. The player takes aim with a cherry stone, and when he overturns the castle he claims the spoil.—Jamieson. See "Cob Nut."

Pallall

A Scottish name for "Hop Scotch."—Jamieson.

Pally Ully

See "Hop Scotch."

Pat-ball

A child's name for the simple game of throwing a ball from one to another.—Lowsley's *Berkshire Glossary*.

Pay-swad

A boys' game, somewhat similar to "Duckstone." Each boy, when he threw his stone, had to say "Pay-swad," or he had to go down himself.—Holland's *Cheshire Glossary*.

See "Duckstone."

Pednameny

A game played with pins: also called "Pinny Ninny," "Pedna-a mean," "Heads and Tails," a game of pins.—Courtenay's *West Cornwall Glossary*.

Peesie Weet

The game of "Hide and Seek." When the object is hidden the word "Peesie-weet" is called out.—Fraserburgh, Aberdeenshire (Rev. W. Gregor).

See "Hide and Seek (2)."

Peg and Stick

The players provide themselves with short, stout sticks, and a peg (a piece of wood sharpened at one or both ends). A ring is made, and the peg is placed on the ground so as to balance. One boy then strikes it with his stick to make it spring or bounce up into the air; while in the air he strikes it with his stick, and sends it as far as he possibly can. His opponent declares the number of leaps in which the striker is to cover the distance the peg has gone. If successful, he counts the number of leaps to his score. If he fails, his opponent leaps, and, if successful, the number of leaps count to his score. He strikes the next time, and the same process is gone through.—Earls Heaton, Yorks. (Herbert Hardy).

See "Tip-cat."

Peg-fiched

A west country game. The performers in this game are each furnished with a sharp-pointed stake. One of them then strikes it into the ground, and the others, throwing their sticks across it, endeavour to dislodge it. When a stick falls, the owner has to run to a prescribed distance and back, while the rest, placing the stick upright, endeavour to beat it into the ground up to the very top.—Halliwell's *Dictionary*.

Peggy Nut

A boyish game with nuts.—Dickinson's *Cumberland Glossary*.

Peg-in-the-Ring

A game of "Peg-top." The object of this game is to spin the top within a certain circle marked out, in which the top is to exhaust itself without once overstepping the bounds prescribed (Halliwell's *Dict. Provincialisms*). Holloway (*Dictionary*) says, "When boys play at 'Peg-top,' a ring is formed on the ground, within which each boy is to spin his top. If the top, when it has ceased spinning, does not roll without the circle, it must remain in the ring to be pegged at by the other boys, or he redeems it by putting in an inferior one, which is called a 'Mull.' When the top does not roll out, it is said to be 'mulled.'" Mr. Emslie writes: "When the top fell within the ring the boys cried, 'One a penny!' When two had fallen within the ring it was, 'Two a penny!' When three, 'Three a penny, good as any!' The aim of each spinner was to do what was called 'drawing,' *i.e.*, bring his top down into the ring, and at the same time draw the string so as to make the top spin within the ring, and yet come towards the player and out of the ring so as to fall without."

See "Tops."

Peg-top

One of the players, chosen by lot, spins his top. The other players endeavour to strike this top with the pegs of their own tops as they fling them down to spin. If any one fails to spin his top in due form, he has to lay his top on the ground for the others to strike at when spinning. The object of each spinner is to split the top which is being aimed at, so as to release the peg, and the boy whose top has succeeded in splitting the other top obtains the peg as his trophy of victory. It is a matter of ambition to obtain as many pegs in this manner as possible.—London (G. L. Gomme).

See " Peg-in-the-Ring," " Tops."

Penny Cast

A game played with round flat stones, about four or six inches across, being similar to the game of quoits ; sometimes played with pennies when the hobs are a deal higher.   It was not played with pennies in 1810.— Easther's *Almondbury Glossary*. In an article in *Blackwood's Magazine*, August 1821, p. 35, dealing with children's games, the writer says, Pennystanes are played much in the same manner as the quoits or discus of the ancient Romans, to which warlike people the idle tradesmen of Edinburgh probably owe this favourite game.

See " Penny Prick."

Penny Hop

A rude dance, which formerly took place in the common taverns of Sheffield, usually held after the bull-baiting.— Wilson's Notes to *Mather's Songs*, p. 74, cited by Addy, *Sheffield Glossary*.

Penny Prick

"A game consisting of casting oblong pieces of iron at a mark."—Hunter's *Hallamsh. Gloss.*, p. 71.   Grose explains it, " Throwing at halfpence placed on sticks which are called hobs."

> Their idle houres, I meane all houres beside
> Their houres to eate, to drinke, drab, sleepe, and ride,
> They spend at shove-boord, or at pennie-pricke.
> —Scots' *Philomythie*, 1616.

Halliwell gives these references in his *Dictionary ;* Addy, *Sheffield Glossary*, describes it as above ; adding, " An old game once played by people of fashion."

See " Penny Cast."

Penny Stanes

See " Penny Cast."

Phœbe

The name of a dance mentioned in an old nursery rhyme
A correspondent gave Halliwell the following lines of a very
old song, the only ones he recollected :—

> Cannot you dance the Phœbe ?
> Don't you see what pains I take ;
> Don't you see how my shoulders shake ?
> Cannot you dance the Phœbe ?
>
> —Halliwell's *Dictionary*.

These words are somewhat of the same character as those
of " Auntie Loomie," and are evidently the accompaniment of
an old dance.

See " Lubin."

Pick and Hotch

The game of " Pitch and Toss."—Brogden's *Provincial
Words*, Lincolnshire. It is called Pickenhotch in Peacock's
Manley and Corringham Glossary.

Pi-cow

A game in which one half of the players are supposed to
keep a castle, while the others go out as a foraging or maraud-
ing party. When the latter are all gone out, one of them
cries *Pee-ku*, which is a signal to those within to be on the
alert. Then those who are without attempt to get in. If
any one of them gets in without being seized by the holders
of the castle, he cries to his companions, *The hole's won ;* and
those who are within must yield the fortress. If one of the
assailants be taken before getting in he is obliged to change
sides and to guard the castle. Sometimes the guards are
successful in making prisoners of all the assailants. Also the
name given to the game of Hide and Seek.—Jamieson.

Pigeon Walk

A boy's game [undescribed].—Patterson's *Antrim and Down
Glossary*.

Pig-ring

A game at marbles where a ring is made about four feet
in diameter, and boys " shoot " in turn from any point in the

circumference, keeping such marbles as they may knock out of the ring, but loosing their own "taw" if it should stop within.—Lowsley's *Berkshire Glossary*.   See "Ring Taw."

Pillie-Winkie

A sport among children in Fife.   An egg, an unfledged bird, or a whole nest is placed on a convenient spot.   He who has what is called the first *pill*, retires a few paces, and being provided with a cowt or rung, is blindfolded, or gives his promise to wink hard (whence he is called *Winkie*), and moves forward in the direction of the object, as he supposes, striking the ground with the stick all the way.   He must not shuffle the stick along the ground, but always strike perpendicularly.   If he touches the nest without destroying it, or the egg without breaking it, he looses his vice or turn. The same mode is observed by those who succeed him.   When one of the party breaks an egg he is entitled to all the rest as his property, or to some other reward that has been previously agreed on.   Every art is employed, without removing the nest or egg, to mislead the blindfolded player, who is also called the Pinkie.—Jamieson.   See "Blind Man's Stan."

Pinch

The game of "Pitch-Halfpenny," or "Pitch and Hustle."— Halliwell's *Dictionary*.   Addy (*Sheffield Glossary*) says this game consists of pitching halfpence at a mark.

See "Penny Cast," "Penny Prick."

Pinny Show

A child's peep-show.   The charge for a peep is a pin, and, under extraordinary circumstances of novelty, two pins.

I remember well being shown how to make a peep or poppet-show.   It was made by arranging combinations of colours from flowers under a piece of glass, and then framing it with paper in such a way that a cover was left over the front, which could be raised when any one paid a pin to peep.   The following words were said, or rather sung, in a sing-song manner:—

> A pin to see the poppet-show,
> All manner of colours oh !
> See the ladies all below.   —(A. B. Gomme).

Pansies or other flowers are pressed beneath a piece of glass, which is laid upon a piece of paper, a hole or opening, which can be shut at pleasure, being cut in the paper. The charge for looking at the show is a pin. The children say, " A pin to look at a pippy-show." They also say—

> A pinnet a piece to look at a show,
> All the fine ladies sat in a row.
> Blackbirds with blue feet
> Walking up a new street ;
> One behind and one before,
> And one beknocking at t' barber's door.

> —Addy's *Sheffield Glossary.*

In Perth (Rev. W. Gregor) the rhyme is—

> A pin to see a poppy show,
> A pin to see a die,
> A pin to see an old man
> Sitting in the sky.

Described also in Holland's *Cheshire Glossary*, and Lowsley's *Berkshire Glossary.* Atkinson's *Cleveland Glossary* describes it as having coloured pictures pasted inside, and an eye-hole at one of the ends. The *Leed's Glossary* gives the rhyme as—

> A pin to look in,
> A very fine thing.

Northall (*English Folk-rhymes*, p. 357), also gives a rhyme.

Pins

On the 1st of January the children beg for some pins, using the words, " Please pay Nab's New Year's gift." They then play " a very childish game," but I have not succeeded in getting a description of it.—Yorkshire.

See " Prickie and Jockie."

Pirley Pease-weep

A game played by boys, " and the name demonstrates that it is a native one, for it would require a page of close writing to make it intelligible to an Englishman." The rhyme used at this play is—

> Scotsman, Scotsman, lo !
> Where shall this poor Scotsman go ?

Send him east, or send him west,
Send him to the craw's nest.
—*Blackwood's Magazine*, August 1821, p. 37.

The rhyme suggests comparison with the game of "Hot Cockles."

Pitch

A game played with pennies, or other round discs. The object is to pitch the penny into a hole in the ground from a certain point.—Elworthy, *West Somerset Words*.

Probably "Pick and Hotch," mentioned in an article in *Blackwood's Mag.*, Aug. 1821, p. 35. Common in London streets.

Pitch and Hustle

"Chuck-Farthing." The game of "Pitch and Toss" is very common, being merely the throwing up of halfpence, the result depending on a guess of heads or tails.—Halliwell's *Dictionary*.

Pitch and Toss

This game was played by two or more players with "pitchers" —the stakes being buttons. The ordinary bone button, or "scroggy," being the unit of value. The "pitcher" was made of lead, circular in form, from one and a half inch to two inches in diameter, and about a quarter of an inch thick, with an "H" to stand for "Heads" cut on one side, and a "T" for "Tails" on the other side. An old-fashioned penny was sometimes used, and an old "two-penny" piece I have by me bears the marks of much service in the same cause. A mark having been set up—generally a stone—and the order of play having been fixed, the first player, A, threw his "pitcher" to the mark, from a point six or seven yards distant. If he thought he lay sufficiently near the mark to make it probable that he would be the nearest after the others had thrown, he said he would "lie." The effect of that was that the players who followed had to lie also, whatever the character of their throw. If A's throw was a poor one he took up his "pitcher." B then threw, if he threw well he "lay," if not he took up his pitcher, in hope of making a better throw, as A had done. C then played in the same manner. D followed and "lay." E played his pitcher,

and had no choice but to lie. F followed in the same way.
These being all the players, A threw again, and though his
second might have been worse than his first, he has to lie like
the others. B and C followed. All the pitchers have been
thrown, and are lying round the mark, in the following order
of proximity—for that regulates the subsequent play—B's is
nearest, then D's follows, in order by A, C, F, E. B takes the
pitchers, and piles them up one above the other, and tosses
them into the air. Three (let us say) fall head up, D's, A's,
and F's. These three B keeps in his hand. D, who was next
nearest the mark, takes the three remaining pitchers, and in
the same manner tosses them into the air. B's and C's fall
head up, and are retained by D. A, who comes third, takes
the remaining pitcher, E's, and throws it up. If it falls a
head he keeps it, and the game is finished except the reckoning; if it falls a tail it passes on to the next player, C, who
throws it up. If it fall a head he keeps it, if a tail, it is passed
on to F, and from him to E, and on to B, till it turns up a head.
Let us suppose that happens when F throws it up. The game
is now finished, and the reckoning takes place—

> B has three pitchers, D's, A's, and F's.
> D „ two „ B's and C's.
> F „ one „ E's.

A, C, and E have none.

Strictly speaking, D, A, and F should each pay a button to
B. B and C should each pay one to D. E should pay one to
F. But in practice it was simpler, F holding one pitcher had,
in the language of the game, "freed himself." D had "freed
himself," and was in addition one to the good. B had "freed
himself," and was two to the good. A, C, and E, not having
"freed themselves," were liable for the one D had won and the
two B had won, and settled with D and B, without regard to
the actual hand that held the respective pitchers. It simpli-
fied the reckoning, though theoretically the reckoning should
have followed the more roundabout method. Afterwards the
game was begun *de novo*. E, who was last, having first pitch
—the advantage of that place being meant to compensate him

in a measure for his ill luck in the former game. The stakes were the plain horn or bone buttons—buttons with nicks were more valuable—a plain one being valued at two "scroggies," or "scrogs," the fancy ones, and especially livery buttons, commanding a higher price.—Rev. W. Gregor. See "Buttons."

Pit-counter

A game played by boys, who roll counters in a small hole. The exact description I have not been able to get.—Halliwell's *Dictionary*.

Pits

A game at marbles. The favourite recreation with the young fishermen in West Cornwall. Forty years ago "Pits" and "Towns" were the common games, but the latter only is now played. Boys who hit their nails are looked on with great contempt, and are said "to fire Kibby." When two are partners, and one in playing accidentally hits the other's marble, he cries out, "No custance," meaning that he has a right to put back the marble struck; should he fail to do so, he would be considered "out."—*Folk-lore Journal*, v. 60. There is no description of the method of playing. It may be the same as "Cherry Pits," played with marbles instead of cherry stones (vol. i. p. 66). Mr. Newell, *Games and Songs of American Children*, p. 187, says "The pits are thrown over the palm; they must fall so far apart that the fingers can be passed between them. Then with a fillip of the thumb the player makes his pit strike the enemy's and wins both."

Pize Ball

Sides are picked; as, for example, six on one side and six on the other, and three or four marks or tuts are fixed in a field. Six go out to field, as in cricket, and one of these throws the ball to one of those who remain "at home," and the one "at home" strikes or pizes it with his hand. After pizing it he runs to one of the "tuts," but if before he can get to the "tut" he is struck with the ball by one of those in the field, he is said to be *burnt*, or out. In that case the other side go out to field.—Addy's *Sheffield Glossary*.

See "Rounders."

Plum Pudding

A game at marbles of two or more boys. Each puts an equal number of marbles in a row close together, a mark is made at some little distance called taw; the distance is varied according to the number of marbles in a row. The first boy tosses at the row in such a way as to pitch just on the marbles, and so strike as many as he can out of the line; all that he strikes out he takes; the rest are put close together again, and two other players take their turn in the same manner, till all the marbles are struck out of the line, when they all stake afresh and the game begins again.—Baker's *Northamptonshire Glossary*.

Plum Pudding and Roast Beef

Mentioned by Moor, *Suffolk Words and Phrases*, as the name of a game. Undescribed, but nearly the same as French and English.

Pointing out a Point

A small mark is made on the wall. The one to point out the point, who must not know what is intended, is blindfolded, and is then sent to put the finger on the point or mark. Another player has taken a place in front of the point, and bites the finger of the blindfolded pointer.—Fraserburgh, Aberdeenshire (Rev. W. Gregor).

Poncake

Name of a girl's game the same as Cheeses.—Holland's *Cheshire Glossary*. See "Turn Cheeses, Turn."

Poor and Rich

An old game mentioned in Taylor's *Motto*, sig. D, iv. London, 1622.

Poor Mary sits a-weeping

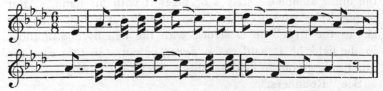

—Barnes (A. B. Gomme).

I. Poor Mary sits a-weepin',
    A-weepin', a-weepin';
    Poor Mary sits a-weepin'
    On a bright summer's day.

"Poor Mary sits a-weeping."

Pray, Mary, what're you weepin' for,
A-weepin' for, a-weepin' for?
Pray, Mary, what're you weepin' for?
On a bright summer's day.

I'm weepin' for a sweetheart,
A sweetheart, a sweetheart;
I'm weepin' for a sweetheart,
On a bright summer's day.

Pray, Mary, choose your lover,
Your lover, your lover;
Pray, Mary, choose your lover
On a bright summer's day.

Now you're married, I wish you joy;
First a girl, and then a boy;
Seven years after, son and daughter;
Pray, young couple, come kiss together.

Kiss her once, kiss her twice,
Kiss her three times over.
—Barnes, Surrey (A. B. Gomme).

II.   Poor Mary is weeping, is weeping, is weeping,
Poor Mary is weeping on a bright summer's day.

Pray tell me what you're weeping for, weeping for, weeping for,
Pray tell me what you're weeping for, on a bright summer's day?

I'm weeping for my true love, my true love, my true love,
I'm weeping for my true love, on a bright summer's day.

Stand up and choose your lover, your lover, your lover,
Stand up and choose your lover, on a bright summer's day.

Go to church with your lover, your lover, your lover,
Go to church with your lover, on a bright summer's day.

Be happy in a ring, love; a ring, love; a ring, love.
Kiss both together, love, on this bright summer's day.
—Upton-on-Severn, Worcestershire (Miss Broadwood).

III.   Pray, Sally, what are you weeping for—
Weeping for—weeping for?
Pray, Sally, what are you weeping for,
On a bright shiny day?

I am weeping for a sweetheart—
A sweetheart—a sweetheart;
I am weeping for a sweetheart,
On a bright shiny day.

Pray, Sally, go and get one—
Go and get one—get one ;
Pray, Sally, go and get one,
On a bright shiny day.

Pray, Sally, now you've got one—
You've got one—got one ;
Pray, Sally, now you've got one,
On a bright sunny day.

One kiss will never part you—
Never part you—part you ;
One kiss will never part you,
On a bright sunny day.

—Dorsetshire (*Folk-lore Journal*, vii. 209).

IV.   Poor ——— sat a-weeping,
A-weeping, a-weeping ;
Poor ——— sat a-weeping,
On a bright summer's day.

I'm weeping for a sweetheart,
A sweetheart, a sweetheart ;
I'm weeping for a sweetheart,
On a bright summer's day.

Oh, pray get up and choose one,
And choose one, and choose one ;
Oh, pray get up and choose one,
On a bright summer's day.

Now you're married, you must obey ;
You must be true to all you say.
You must be kind, you must be good,
And help your wife to chop the wood.

—Sporle, Norfolk (Miss Matthews).

V. Poor Mary sat a-weeping, a-weeping, a-weeping,
Poor Mary sat a-weeping, down by the sea-side.

By the side of the river, by the side of the river,
She sat down and cried.

Oh, pray get up and choose one, and choose one, and choose one,
Oh, pray get up and choose one, down by the sea-side.

> Now you're married, I wish you joy;
> Father and mother you must obey;
> Love one another like sister and brother,
> And pray, young couple, come kiss one another.

—Colchester (Miss G. M. Frances).

VI.   Poor Mary is a-weeping, a-weeping, a-weeping,
Poor Mary is a-weeping on a fine summer's day.

What is she weeping for, weeping for, weeping for,
What is she weeping for on a fine summer's day?

She's weeping for her sweetheart, her sweetheart, her sweetheart,
She's weeping for her sweetheart on a fine summer's day.

Pray get up and choose one, choose one, choose one,
Pray get up and choose one on a fine summer's day.

Pray go to church, love; church, love; church, love;
Pray go to church, love, on a fine summer's day.

Pray put the ring on, ring on, ring on,
Pray put the ring on, on a fine summer's day.

Pray come back, love; back, love; back, love;
Pray come back, love, on a fine summer's day.

> Now you're married, we wish you joy;
> Your father and mother you must obey;
> Love one another like sister and brother;
> And now it's time to go away.

—(*Suffolk County Folk-lore*, pp. 66, 67.)

VII.   Poor Mary sits a-weeping, a-weeping, a-weeping,
Poor Mary sits a-weeping on a bright summer's day.

Pray tell me what you are weeping for, weeping for, weeping for,
Pray tell me what you are weeping for on a bright summer's day?

I'm weeping for a sweetheart, a sweetheart, a sweetheart,
I'm weeping for a sweetheart on a bright summer's day.

Poor Mary's got a shepherd's cross, a shepherd's cross,
a shepherd's cross,
Poor Mary's got a shepherd's cross on a bright summer's
day.
—Berkshire (Miss Thoyts, *Antiquary*, xxvii. 254).

VIII. Mary sits a-weeping, a-weeping, a-weeping,
Mary sits a-weeping, close by the sea-side.

Mary, what are you weeping for, weeping for, weeping
for,
Mary, what are you weeping for, close by the sea-side ?

I'm a-weeping for my sweetheart, my sweetheart, my
sweetheart,
I'm a-weeping for my sweetheart, close by the sea-side.

Pray get up and choose one, and choose one, and
choose one,
Pray get up and choose one, close by the sea-side.
—Winterton and Lincoln (Miss M. Peacock).

IX. Poor Mary sits a-weeping, a-weeping,
Poor Mary sits a-weeping, on a bright summer's day.

She is weeping for her lover, her lover,
She is weeping for her lover on a bright summer's day.

Stand up and choose your lover, your lover,
Stand up and choose your lover, on a bright summer's
day.

And now she's got a lover, a lover,
And now she's got a lover, on a bright summer's day.
—Hanbury, Staffs. (Miss E. Hollis).

X. Oh, what is Nellie weeping for,
A-weeping for, a-weeping for ?
Oh, what is Nellie weeping for,
On a cold and sunshine day ?

I'm weeping for my sweetheart,
My sweetheart, my sweetheart;
I'm weeping for my sweetheart
On a cold and sunshine day.

So now stand up and choose the one,
And choose the one, and choose the one;
So now stand up and choose the one,
On a cold and sunshine day.

— Forest of Dean, Gloucestershire (Miss Matthews).

XI.   Poor Mary sits a-weeping, a-weeping, a-weeping,
Poor Mary sits a-weeping, on a bright summer's day.

Pray what are you a-weeping for, a-weeping for, a-
weeping for,
Pray what are you a-weeping for on a bright summer's
day ?

She's weeping for a lover, a lover, a lover,
She's weeping for a lover, this bright summer's day.

Rise up and choose your lover, your lover, your lover,
Rise up and choose your lover, this bright summer's day.

Now Mary she is married, is married, is married,
Now Mary she is married this bright summer's day.

— Enborne School, Newbury, Berks. (Miss M. Kimber).

XII.   Poor Sarah's a-weeping,
A-weeping, a-weeping;
Oh, what is she a-weeping for,
A-weeping for, a-weeping for ?

I'm weeping for a sweetheart,
A sweetheart, a sweetheart;
I'm weeping for a sweetheart
This bright summer day.

Oh, she shall have a sweetheart,
A sweetheart, a sweetheart;
Oh, she shall have a sweetheart
This bright summer day.

Go to church, loves,
Go to church, loves.
Say your prayers, loves,
Say your prayers, loves.
Kiss your lovers,
Kiss your lovers;
Rise up and choose your love.

—Liphook, Hants. (Miss Fowler).

XIII. Poor Mary sits weeping, weeping, weeping,
Poor Mary sits weeping on a bright summer's day;
On the carpet she must kneel till the grass grows on
the field.

Stand up straight upon your feet,
And show me the one you love so sweet.

Now you're married, I wish you joy;
First a girl, and second a boy;
If one don't kiss, the other must,
So kiss, kiss, kiss.

—Cambridge (Mrs. Haddon).

XIV. Poor Mary is a-weeping, a-weeping, a-weeping,
Poor Mary is a-weeping on a bright summer's day;
Pray what is she a-weeping for, a-weeping for, a-weep-
ing for,
Pray what is she a-weeping for, on a bright summer's
day?

I'm weeping for my true love, my true love, my true
love,
I'm weeping for my true love, on a bright summer's day.

Stand up and choose your true love, your true love,
your true love,
Stand up and choose your true love, on a bright
summer's day.

Ring a ring o' roses, o' roses, o' roses,
Ring a ring o' roses; a pocketful of posies.

—Ogbourne, Wilts. (H. S. May).

XV.   Poor Sally is a-weeping, a-weeping, a-weeping,
Poor Sally is a-weeping, down by the sea-side.
Pray tell me what you're weeping for, you're weeping
for, you're weeping for,
Pray tell me what you're weeping for, down by the
sea-side ?

I'm weeping for my sweetheart, my sweetheart, my
sweetheart,
I'm weeping for my sweetheart, down by the sea-side.

    A ring o' roses,
    A pocketful of posies ;
    Isham ! Isham !
    We all tumble down.
              —Manton, Marlborough, Wilts. (H. S. May).

XVI.   Poor Mary is a-weeping, a-weeping, a-weeping,
On a fine summer's day;
What is she weeping for, weeping for, weeping for ?

She is weeping for her lover, her lover, her lover ;
And who is her love, who is her lover ?

Johnny Baxter is her lover, Johnny Baxter is her lover ;
And where is her lover, where is her lover ?

Her lover is a-sleeping, her lover is a-sleeping,
Is a-sleeping at the bottom of the sea.
        —South Devon (*Notes and Queries*, 8th Series,
              i. 249, Miss R. H. Busk).

XVII.   Poor Mary, what are you weeping for ?
            You weeping for ?
            You weeping for ?
    Poor Mary, what are you weeping for,
      On a bright summer's day ?

    Pray tell us what you are weeping for ?
           You are weeping for ?
           You are weeping for ?

Pray tell us what you are weeping for,
    On a bright summer's day.

My father he is dead, sir ;
    Is dead, sir ;
    Is dead, sir.
My father he is dead, sir,
    On a bright summer's day.
            —Earls Heaton (Herbert Hardy).

XVIII.   Poor Mary is a-weeping, a-weeping, a-weeping,
    Poor Mary is a-weeping, on a fine summer's day.
    Pray tell me what you're weeping for ? &c.

Because my father's dead and gone, is dead and gone,
    is dead and gone ;
Because my father's dead and gone, on a fine
    summer's day.

She is kneeling by her father's grave, her father's
    grave, her father's grave ;
She is kneeling by her father's grave, on a fine
    summer's day.

Stand up and choose your love, choose your love,
    choose your love ;
Stand up and choose your love, on a bright summer's
    day.
            —(Rev. W. Gregor).

XIX.   Oh, what is Jennie weeping for,
    A-weeping for, a-weeping for ?
Oh, what is Jennie weeping for,
    All on this summer's day ?

I'm weeping for my own true love,
    My own true love, my own true love ;
I'm weeping for my own true love,
    All on this summer's day.

No.	Barnes.	Enborne.	Dorsetshire.	Upton.	Sporle.	Colchester.	Winterton.	Forest of Dean.
1.	Poor Mary sits a-weeping.	Poor Mary sits a-weeping.	—	Poor Mary is weeping.	Poor [ ] a-weeping.	Poor Mary sat a-weeping.	Mary sits a-weeping.	—
2.	Pray, Mary, what are you weeping for?	Pray, what are you a-weeping for?	Pray, Sally, what are you weeping for?	Pray, tell me what you're weeping for.	—	—	Mary, what are you weeping for?	Oh! what is Nellie weeping for?
3.	—	—	—	—	—	—	—	—
4.	I'm weeping for a sweetheart.	She's weeping for a lover.	I'm weeping for a sweetheart.	I am weeping for my true love.	I'm weeping for a sweetheart.	—	I'm weeping for a sweetheart.	I'm weeping for my sweetheart.
5.	On a bright summer's day.	This bright summer's day.	On a bright shiny day.	On a bright summer's day.	On a bright summer's day.	—	—	—
6.	—	—	—	—	—	By the side of the river.	—	—
7.	—	—	—	—	—	She sat down and cried.	Close by the sea side.	—
8.	—	—	—	—	—	—	—	On a cold and sunshine day.
9.	—	—	—	—	—	—	—	—
10.	Pray, Mary, choose your lover.	Rise up and choose your lover.	—	Stand up and choose your lover.	Pray, get up and choose one.	Pray, get up and choose one.	Pray, get up and choose one.	Now stand up and choose one.
11.	—	—	Pray, Sally, go and get one.	—	—	—	—	—
12.	—	—	—	—	—	—	—	—
13.	—	—	—	—	—	—	—	—
14.	Now you're married, I wish you joy,	Now Mary she is married.	—	—	—	Now you're married, I wish you joy.	—	—
15.	First a girl, then a boy.	—	—	—	—	—	—	—
16.	Seven years after, son and daughter.	—	—	—	—	—	—	—

Pray, Sally, now you've got one.

Now you're married you must obey. You must be true to all you say. You must be kind and good. Help wife to chop wood.

Father and mother you must obey. Love one another like sister and brother. Pray, young couple, come kiss together.

One kiss will never part you.

Go to church with your lover. Be happy in a ring, love. Kiss both together, love.

Pray, young couple, come kiss together.

Kiss her once, twice, kiss three times over.

17. 18. 19. 20. 21. 22. 23. 24. 25. 26. 27. 28. 29. 30 to 43.

No.	Liphook.	Earls Heaton.	Suffolk.	Berkshire.	Staffordshire.	Newbury.	South Devon.
1.	Poor Sarah's a-weeping.	—	Poor Mary sits a-weeping.	Poor Mary sits a-weeping.	Poor Mary sits a-weeping.	Poor Mary sits a-weeping.	Poor Mary is a-weeping.
2.	Oh, what is she a-weeping for?	Poor Mary, what are you weeping for.	What is she weeping for?	—	—	Pray what are you weeping for?	What is she weeping for?
3.	—	Pray tell us what you are weeping for?	—	Pray tell me what she is weeping for?	—	—	—
4.	I'm weeping for a sweetheart.	—	She's weeping for a sweetheart.	I'm weeping for a sweetheart.	She's weeping for her lover.	She's weeping for a lover.	She's weeping for her lover.
5.	This bright summer's day.	On a bright summer's day.	On a fine summer's day.	On a bright summer's day.	On a bright summer's day.	This bright summer's day.	On a fine summer's day.
6.	—	—	—	—	—	—	—
7.	—	—	—	—	—	—	[See No. 41.]
8.	—	—	—	—	—	—	—
9.	Rise up and choose your lover.	—	Pray get up and choose one.	—	Stand up and choose your lover.	Rise up and choose your lover.	—
10.	—	—	—	—	—	—	—
11, 12.	She shall have a sweetheart.	—	—	—	—	—	—
13.	—	—	Now you're married, we wish you joy.	—	—	Now Mary she is married.	—
14.	—	—	—	—	—	—	—
15, 16.	—	—	—	—	—	—	—
17, 18.	—	—	—	—	—	—	—
19.	—	—	—	—	—	—	—
20.	—	—	—	—	—	—	—

Who is her lover?
I. O. is her lover.
Where is her lover?
Her lover is sleeping.
At the bottom of the sea.

Now she's got a lover.

Mary's got a shepherd's cross.

Father and mother
you must obey
Love one another
like brother and
sister.

Pray go to church,
love.

Pray put the ring
on.
Pray come back,
love.
Now it's time to go
away.

My father he is
dead, sir.

Go to church, love.

Say your prayers,
love.
Kiss your lovers.

21.
22.
23.
24.
25.
26.
27.
28.
29.
30.
31.
32.
33.
34.
35.
36.
37.
38.
39.
40.
41.
42.
43.

No.	Cambridge.	Ogbourne.	Manton.	Berwickshire.	Scotland.
1.	Poor Mary is a-weeping.	Poor Mary is a-weeping.	Poor Sally is a-weeping.	What is Jennie weeping for?	Poor Mary is a-weeping.
2.	—	Pray what is she weeping for?	Pray tell me what you're weeping for.	—	Pray tell me what you're weeping for.
3.	—	—	—	—	—
4.	—	I'm weeping for my true love.	I'm weeping for my sweetheart.	I'm weeping for my own true love.	—
5.	—	On a bright summer's day.	—	All on this summer's day.	On a fine summer's day.
6.	—	—	—	—	—
7.	—	—	—	—	—
8.	—	—	Down by the seaside.	—	—
9.	—	—	—	—	—
10.	Stand up upon your feet and show the one you love so sweet.	Stand up and choose your true love.	—	—	Stand up and choose your love.
11.	—	.	—	—	—
12.	—	—	—	Rise up and choose another love.	—
13.	On the carpet she shall kneel till the grass grows on the field.	—	—	—	—
14.	Now you're married I wish you joy.	—	—	—	—
15.	First a girl and second a boy.	—	—	—	—
16.	—	—	—	—	—
17.	—	—	—	—	—
18.	—	—	—	—	—
19.	—	—	—	—	—
20.	—	—	—	—	—
21.	—	—	—	—	—
22.	—	—	—	—	—
23.	—	—	—	—	—
24.	—	—	—	—	—
25.	—	—	—	—	—
26.	—	—	—	—	—
27.	—	—	—	—	—
28.	—	—	—	—	—
29.	If one don't kiss, the other must.	—	—	—	—
30.	—	—	—	—	Because my father's dead and gone.
31.	—	—	—	—	She's kneeling by her father's grave.
32. to 41.	⎫⎬⎭ —	—	—	—	—
42.	—	Ring a ring o' roses a pocketful of posies.	A ring of roses a pocketful of posies.	—	—
43.	—	—	We all tumble down.	—	—

Rise up and choose another love,
Another love, another love ;
Rise up and choose another love,
All on this summer's day.
—Berwickshire (A. M. Bell, *Antiquary*, xxx. 16).

(*b*) A ring is formed by the children joining hands. One child kneels in the centre, covering her face with her hands. The ring dances round, and sings the first two verses. The kneeling child then takes her hands from her face and sings the next verse, still kneeling. While the ring sings the next verse, she rises and chooses one child out of the ring. They stand together, holding hands while the others sing the marriage formula, and kiss each other at the command. The ring of children dance round quickly while singing this. When finished the first " Mary " takes a place in the ring, and the other child kneels down (Barnes and other places). At Enborne school, Newbury (Miss Kimber), this game is played by boys and girls. All the children in the ring sing the first two verses. Then the boys alone in the ring sing the next verse; all the ring singing the fourth. While singing this the kneeling child rises and holds out her hand to any boy she prefers, who goes into the ring with her. When he is left in the ring at the commencement of the game again, a boy's name is substituted for that of " Mary." There appears to be no kissing. In the Liphook version (Miss Fowler), after the girl has chosen her sweetheart the ring breaks, and the two walk out and then kneel down, returning to the ring and kissing each other. A version identical with that of Barnes is played by the girls of Clapham High School. All tunes sent me were similar to that given.

(*c*) The analysis of the game rhymes is on pp. 56–60.

This analysis shows that the incidents expressed by the rhymes are practically the same in all the versions. In the majority of the cases the weeping is depicted as part of a ceremony, by which it is known that a girl desires a lover ; she is enabled then to choose one, and to be married. The marriage formula is the usual one in the Barnes' version, but follows another set of words in three other versions. In the cases where the marriage is neither expressed by a formula, nor implied by other means (Winterton and Forest of Dean), the versions are evidently fragments only, and probably at one time ended, as in the other cases, with marriage. But in three other cases the ending is not with marriage. The Earls Heaton and Scottish versions represent the cause of weeping as the death of a father, the Berkshire version introduces the apparently unmeaning incident of Mary bearing a shepherd's cross, and the South Devon version represents the cause of weeping the death of a lover at sea. It is obvious that at places where sailors abound, the incident of weeping for a sailor-lover who is dead would get inserted, and the fact of this change only occurring once in the versions I have collected, tells all the more strongly in favour of the original version having represented marriage and love, and not death, but it does not follow that the marriage formula belongs to the oldest or original form of the game. I am inclined to think this has been added since marriage was thought to be the natural and proper result of choosing a sweetheart.

(*d*) The change in some of the verses, as in the Cambridge version, is due to corruption and the marked decadence now occurring in these games. No. 13 in the analysis is from the game "Pretty little girl of mine," and Nos. 42-3 "Ring o' Roses."

Poor Widow

    I.   Here's an old widow who lies alone,
               Lies alone, lies alone,
        Here's an old widow who lies alone,
        She wants a man and can't get one.
        Choose one, choose two, choose the fairest.
        The fairest one that I can see
        Is [Mary Hamilton], come unto me.
        Now she is married and tied to a bag,
        She has got a man with a wooden leg.
               —Belfast (W. H. Patterson).

   II. There was an old soldier he came from the war,
          His age it was sixty and three.
      Go you, old soldier, and choose a wife,
        Choose a good one or else choose none.

Here's a poor widow she lives her lone,
 She hasn't a daughter to marry but one.
Come choose to the east, choose to the west,
 And choose the very one you love best.

Here's a couple married in joy,
 First a girl and then a boy,
Seven years after, and seven years come,
 Pree * young couple kiss and have done.
—Belfast (W. H. Patterson).

III. There was a poor widow left alone,
 And all her children dead and gone.
 Come, choose you east,
 Come, choose you west,
 Take the man you love best.
 Now they're married,
 I wish them joy,
 Every year a girl or a boy,
 I hope this couple may kiss each other.
—Nairn (Rev. W. Gregor).

(*b*) One child is chosen to act the part of the widow. The players join hands and form a circle. The widow takes her stand in the centre of the circle in a posture indicating sorrow. The girls in the circle trip round and round, and sing the first five lines. The widow then chooses one of the ring. The ring then sings the marriage formula, the two kiss each other, and the game is continued, the one chosen to be the mate of the first widow becoming the widow in turn (Nairn).

(*c*) This game is probably the same as "Silly Old Man." Two separate versions may have arisen by girls playing by themselves without boys.

Pop Goes the Weasel

Half a pound of tup'ny rice,
Half a pound of treacle ;
Mix it up and make it nice,
Pop goes the weasel.

—Earls Heaton (Herbert Hardy).

* Sometimes "pray," but "pree" seems to be the Scotch for taste :—"pree her moo "=taste her mouth=to kiss.

(*b*) Children stand in two rows facing each other, they sing while moving backwards and forwards. At the close one from each side selects a partner, and then, all having partners, they whirl round and round.

(*c*) An additional verse is sometimes sung with or in place of the above in London.

> Up and down the City Road;
> In and out the Eagle;
> That's the way the money goes,
> Pop goes the weasel.
>
> —(A. Nutt).

Mr. Nutt writes: "The Eagle was (and may be still) a well-known tavern and dancing saloon."

Pop-the-Bonnet

A game in which two, each putting down a pin on the crown of a hat or bonnet, alternately pop on the bonnet till one of the pins crosses the other; then he at whose pop or tap this takes place, lifts the stakes.—Teviotdale (Jamieson). The same game is now played by boys with steel pens or nibs.

See "Hattie."

Poppet-Show

See "Pinny Show."

Port the Helm

This is a boys' game. Any number may join in it. The players join hands and stand in line. The leader, generally a bigger boy, begins to bend round, at first slowly, then with more speed, drawing the whole line after him. The circular motion is communicated to the whole line, and, unless the boys at the end farthest from the leader run very quickly, the momentum throws them off their feet with a dash if they do not drop their hold.—Keith, Nairn (Rev. W. Gregor).

Pots, or Potts

Throwing a ball against a wall, letting it bounce and catching it, accompanied by the following movements:—

1. Simply three times each.
2. Throw, twist hands, and catch.
3. Clap hands in front, behind, in front.

4. Turn round.

5. Beat down ball on ground three times, and catch.

6. Again on ground and catch (once) at end of first " pot,"
and twice for second " pot."
—Hexham (Miss J. Barker).

Pray, Pretty Miss

I. Priperty Miss, will you come out,
Will you come out, will you come out ?
Priperty Miss, will you come out
To help us with our dancing ?

No !

The naughty girl, she won't come out,
She won't come out, she won't come out ;
The naughty girl, she won't come out
To help us with our dancing.

Priperty Miss, will you come out,
Will you come out, will you come out ?
Priperty Miss, will you come out
To help us with our dancing ?

Yes !

Now we've got another girl,
Another girl, another girl ;
Now we've got another girl
To help us with our dancing.
—Fochabers (Rev. W. Gregor).

II. Pray, pretty Miss, will you come out,
Will you come out, will you come out ?
Pray, pretty Miss, will you come out
To help me in my dancing ?

No !

Then you are a naughty Miss !
Then you are a naughty Miss !
Then you are a naughty Miss !
Won't help me in my dancing.

Pray, pretty Miss, will you come out,
Will you come out, will you come out ?

> Pray, pretty Miss, will you come out
> To help me in my dancing?
> Yes!
> Now you are a good Miss!
> Now you are a good Miss!
> Now you are a good Miss!
> To help me in my dancing.
>
> —Cornwall (*Folk-lore Journal*, v. 47, 48).

III.　Pray, pretty Miss, will you come out to help us in our
　　　dancing?
　　No!
　　Oh, then you are a naughty Miss, won't help us with
　　　our dancing.
　　Pray, pretty Miss, will you come out to help us in our
　　　dancing?
　　Yes!
　　Now we've got our jolly old lass to help us with our
　　　dancing.　—Sheffield, Yorks. (*Folk-lore Record*, v. 87).

IV.　Oh, will you come and dance with me,
　　　Oh, will you come and dance with me?
　　　No!

[They say as above to the next girl, who says "Yes."]

　　　Now we've got our bonny bunch
　　　To help us with our dancing.

　　　　　　—Hurstmonceaux, Sussex (Miss Chase).

(*b*) The Scottish version of this game is played as follows:—
All the players stand in a line except two, who stand facing
them. These two join hands crosswise, and then advancing
and retiring, sing to the child at the end of the line the first
four lines. The first child refuses, and they then dance round,
singing the second verse. They sing the first verse again,
and on her compliance she joins the two, and all three dance
round together, singing the last verse. The three then advance and retire, singing the first verse to another child.

The Cornish version is played differently: a ring is formed,
boy and girl standing alternately in the centre. The child in

the middle holds a white handkerchief by two of its corners;
if a boy he would single out one of the girls, dance backwards
and forwards opposite to her, and sing the first verse. If
the answer were "No!" spoken with averted head over the
left shoulder, he sang the second verse. Occasionally three
or four in turn refused. When the request was granted the
words were changed to the fourth verse. The handkerchief
was then carefully spread on the floor; the couple knelt on
it and kissed: the child formerly in the middle joined the
ring, and the other took his place, or if he preferred it remained in the centre; in that case the children clasped hands
and sang together the first verse over again, the last to enter
the ring having the privilege of selecting the next partner.

(c) Miss Courtney says (*Folk-lore Journal*, v. 47), that this
game is quite a thing of the past. Of the Hurstmonceaux
version, Miss Chase says, "This game is not fully remembered.
It was played about 1850." The words indicate an invitation
to the dance similar to those in "Cushion Dance," "Green
Grass."

Pretty Little Girl of Mine

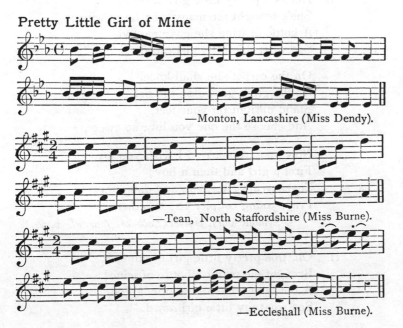

—Monton, Lancashire (Miss Dendy).

—Tean, North Staffordshire (Miss Burne).

—Eccleshall (Miss Burne).

—Nottingham (Miss Youngman).

—Hanbury, Staffordshire (Edith Hollis).

I.   Here's a pretty little girl of mine,
         She's brought me many a bottle of wine;
         A bottle of wine she gave me too—
         See what this little girl can do.

         On the carpet she shall kneel
         As the grass grows on the fiel';
         Stand upright on your feet,
         And choose the one you love so sweet.

         Now you are married I wish you joy,
         First a girl and then a boy;
         Seven years after, son and daughter;
         Pray, young couple, kiss together.
               —Symondsbury, Dorset (*Folk-lore Journal*, vii. 207).

II.   Oh, this pretty little girl of mine,
         Brought me many a bottle of wine;
         A bottle of wine and a guinea, too,
         See what my little girl *can* do.

Down on the carpet she shall kneel,
As the grass grows in the field ;
Stand upright on your feet,
And choose the one you love so sweet.

Now I'm married and wish you joy,
First a girl and then a boy ;
Seven years after, seven years past,
Kiss one another and go to your class.
— Hampshire (Miss Mendham).

III.   Here's a pretty little girl of mine,
Who's brought her bottle and glass of wine ;
A glass of wine and a biscuit too,
See what my pretty girl will do.

On the carpet she shall kneel,
While the grass grows in the field ;
Stand upright upon your feet,
Choose the one you love so sweet.

When you're married I wish you joy,
First a girl and second a boy,
Seven years after, son and daughter,
Now, young couple, kiss together.
— Gambledown, Hants (Mrs. Pinsent).

IV.   Oh ! this pretty little girl of mine,
Has cost me many a bottle of wine ;
A bottle of wine and a guinea or two,
So see what my little girl can do.

Down on the carpet she shall kneel,
While the grass grows on her field ;
Stand upright upon your feet,
And choose the one you love so sweet.

Now you are married you must obey,
Must be true in all you say ;
You must be kind and very good,
And help your wife to chop the wood.
— Maxey (*Northants Notes and Queries*, i. 214).

V.. Here's a pretty little girl of mine,
She's cost me many a bottle of wine ;
A bottle of wine and a guinea too,
See what my little girl can do.

Down on the carpet she must kneel,
As the grass grows in the field ;
Stand upright upon her feet,
And choose the one she loves so sweet.

Now you're married I wish you joy,
Father and mother you must obey ;
Love one another like sister and brother,
And pray, young couple, come kiss one another.
—Colchester (Miss G. M. Frances).

VI.   Oh ! this pretty little girl of mine,
She bought me many a bottle of wine,
A bottle of wine she gave me too,
So see what my little girl could do.

Stand up, stand up upon your feet,
And choose the one you love so sweet.
—Liphook, Hants (Miss Fowler).

VII.   See what a pretty little girl have I,
She brings me many a bottle of wi' ;
A bottle of wine and a biscuit too,
See what a little girl can do.
On the carpet she shall kneel,
As the grass grows in the fiel' ;
Stand upright upon your feet,
And choose the one you love so sweet.

Now you're married we wish you joy,
First a girl and then a boy,
Seven years after, son and daughter,
May you couple kiss together.
—South Devon (*Notes and Queries*, 8th series, i. 249 ;
Miss R. H. Busk).

VIII.   See what a pretty little girl I am,
She gave me many a bottle of wine,

Many a bottle of wine, and a biscuit too,
See what a pretty little girl can do.
On the carpet you shall kneel,
Stand up straight all in the field,
Choose the one that you love best.

Now we are married and hope we enjoy,
First a girl and then a boy,
Seven years after and seven years to come,
May young company kiss have done.
                —Holywood, Co. Down (Miss C. M. Patterson).

IX.   See what a pretty little girl I am!
      Brought me many a bottle o' wine!
      Bottle o' wine to make me shine!
      See what a pretty little girl I am!

      Upon the carpets we shall kneel,
      As the grass grows in yonder field;
      Stand up lightly on your feet,
      And choose the one you love so sweet.

      Now these two are going to die,
      First a girl, and then a boy;
      Seven years at afterwards, seven years ago,
      And now they are parted with a kiss and a go.
                —Monton, Lancashire (Miss Dendy).

X.   See this pretty little maid of mine!
      She's brought me many a bottle of wine;
      A bottle of wine, a good thing, too;
      See what this pretty maid can do!

      Down on the carpet she must kneel
      Till the grass grows on her feet;
      Stand up straight upon thy feet,
      Choose the very one that you love sweet.

      Take her by her lily-white hand,
        Lean across the water;
      Give a kiss,—one, two, three,—
        To Mrs. ———'s daughter.
                —Suffolk (Mrs. Haddon).

XI.   See what a pretty little girl I am!
They brought me many a bottle of wine—
Bottle of wine to make me shine;
See what a pretty little girl I am!

On the carpets we must kneel,
As the grass grows in yonder field;
Rise up lightly on your feet,
And kiss the one you love so sweet.

My sister's going to get married,
My sister's going to get married,
My sister's going to get married,
       Ee! Ii! Oh!

Open your gates as wide as high,
And let the pretty girls come by,
And let the $\left\{\begin{array}{l}\text{jolly}\\\text{bonny}\end{array}\right\}$ matrons * by.
       One in a bush,
       Two in a bush,
       Ee! Ii! Oh!
          —Colleyhurst, Manchester (Miss Dendy).

XII.   On the carpet you shall kneel
Where the grass grows fresh and $\left\{\begin{array}{l}\text{green;}\\\text{clean;}\end{array}\right.$
Stand up, stand up on your pretty feet,
And show me the one you love so sweet.
Now Sally's got married, we wish her good joy,
First a girl, and then a boy;
Seven years arter, a son and darter,
So, young couple, kiss together.

Or,

      Seven years now, and seven to come,
      Take her and kiss her and send her off home.
          —Eccleshall, Staffs. (Miss Burne).

XIII.   On the carpet you shall kneel,
As the grass grows on the field;

* Matron is *not* a word in common use among Lancashire people.

> Stand up straight upon your feet,
> And tell me the one you love so sweet.
>
> —————— is married with a good child,
> First with a girl and then with a boy ;
> Seven years after son and daughter,
> Play with a couple and kiss together.
> > Tean, North Staffs. (from a Monitor in the
> > National School).

XIV. On the carpet you shall kneel,
As the grass grows in the field ;
Stand up, stand up upon your feet,
And tell me whom you love so sweet.

Now you're married I wish you joy,
First a girl, and then a boy ;
Seven years after son and daughter,
Come, young couple, come kiss together.
> —Middlesex (Miss Winfield).

XV. On the carpet you shall kneel,
As the grass grows in the field ;
Stand up, stand up on your feet,
Show the girl you love so sweet.

Now you're married I hope you'll enjoy
A son and a daughter, so
Kiss and good-bye.
> Long Eaton, Nottinghamshire (Miss Youngman).

XVI. Down on the carpet you shall kneel,
While the grass grows on your field ; *
Stand up straight upon your feet,
And choose the one you love so sweet.
Marry couple, married in joy,
First a girl and then a boy ;
Seven years after, seven years come,
Please,† young couple, kiss and have done.
> —Belfast (W. H. Patterson).

* *d* not sounded.
† Another version has "pree," which means in Scotch, *taste*, hence *kiss*.

XVII.   On the carpet you shall kneel,
         While the grass grows fresh and green ;
         Stand up straight upon your feet,
         And kiss the one you love so sweet.

         Now they're married, love and joy,
         First a girl and then a boy ;
         Seven years after, seven years ago,
         Now's the time to kiss and go.
                 —Liverpool and neighbourhood (Mrs. Harley).

XVIII.   On the carpet you shall kneel,
         As the grass grows in the field ;
         Stand up, stand up on your feet,
         And shew me the girl you love so sweet.
         Now Sally's married I hope she'll enjoy,
         First with a girl and then with a boy ;
         Seven years old and seven years young,
         Pray, young lady, walk out of your ring.
                 —Derbyshire (*Folk-lore Journal*, i. 385).

XIX.   On the carpet you shall kneel,
         Where the grass grows fresh and green ;
         Stand up, stand up on your pretty feet,
         And show me the one you love so sweet.
            —Berrington (Burne's *Shropshire Folk-lore*, p. 509).
         [Same ending as Eccleshall version.]

XX.   On the carpitt you shall kneel,
         While the grass grows in the field ;
         Stand up, stand up on your feet,
         Pick the one you love so sweet.
                 —Wakefield, Yorks. (Miss Fowler).

XXI.   King William was King David's son,
         And all the royal race is run ;
         Choose from the east, choose from the west,
         Choose the one you love the best.*

---

* At Earls Heaton two verses or lines are added, viz. :—
         " If she is not here to take her part,
         Choose another with all your heart."

Down on this carpet you shall kneel,
While the grass grows in yond field;
Salute your bride and kiss her sweet,
    Rise again upon your feet.
        —Hanging Heaton, Yorks. (Herbert Hardy).

XXII.   On the carpet you shall kneel, while the grass grows
        at your feet ;
Stand up straight upon your feet, and choose the one
    you love so sweet.
Now Sally is married, life and joy, first a girl and
    then a boy ;
Seven years after, seven years ago, three on the
    carpet, kiss and go.
        —Hanbury, Staffordshire (Miss Edith Hollis).

XXIII.   I had a bonnet trimmed wi' blue.
    Why dosn't wëare it ? Zo I do ;
    I'd wëare it where I con,
    To tëake a walk wi' my young mon.
    My young mon is a-gone to sea,
    When he'd come back he'll marry me.
    Zee what a purty zister is mine,
    Doan't 'e think she's ter'ble fine ?
    She's a most ter'ble cunnèn too,
    Just zee what my zister can do.
    On the carpet she can kneel,
    As the grass grow in the fiel'.
    Stand upright upon thy feet,
    And choose the prettiest you like, sweet.
—Hazelbury Bryan, Dorset (*Folk-lore Journal*, vii. 208).

XXIV.   Kneel down on the carpets, we shall kneel ;
The grass grows away in yonder fiel',
Stand up, stand up upon your feet,
And show me the one you love so sweet.

Now they get married, I wish they may joy
Every year a girl or a boy ;

Loving together like sister and brother,
Now they are coupled to kiss together.
—Galloway, N.B. (J. G. Carter).

(*c*) This game is played in the same way in all the different variants I have given, except a slight addition in the Suffolk (Mrs. Haddon). A ring is formed by the children joining hands—one child stands in the centre. The ring dances or moves slowly round, singing the verses. The child in the centre kneels down when the words are sung, rises and chooses a partner from the ring, kisses her when so commanded, and then takes a place in the ring, leaving the other child in the centre. In those cases where the marriage formula is not given, the kissing would probably be omitted.

(*d*) Of the twenty-four versions given there are not two alike, and this game is distinguished from all others by the singular diversity of its variants; although the original structure of the verses has been preserved to some extent, they seem to have been the sport of the inventive faculty of each different set of players. Lines have been added, left out, and altered in every direction, and in the example from Hazelbury Bryan, in Dorsetshire (No. xxiii.), a portion of an old song or ballad has been added to the game rhyme. These alterations occur not only in different counties, but in the same counties, as may be seen by the Dorset, Hants, Staffordshire, and Northants examples. Mr. Carter says of the Galloway game that the kissing match sometimes degenerates into a spitting match, according to the temper of the parties concerned. In the Suffolk version (Mrs. Haddon), at the words " Lean across the water," the two in the centre lean over the arms of those forming the ring. These words and action are probably an addition. They belong to the "Rosy Apple, Lemon and Pear" game.

These peculiar characteristics of the game do not permit of much investigation into the original words of the game-rhyme, but they serve to illustrate, in a very forcible manner, the exactly opposite characteristics of nearly all the other games, which preserve, in almost stereotyped fashion, the words of the rhymes. It appears most probable that the verses belonged originally to some independent game like "Sally, Sally Water," and that, when divorced from their original context, they lent themselves to the various changes which have been made. The minute application of modern ideas is seen in the version from Gambledown, where "A bottle of wine and a guinea, too," becomes "A bottle of wine and a biscuit, too;" and at West Haddon, in Northamptonshire, a variant of the marriage formula is given in *Northants Notes and Queries*, ii. 106, as—

> Now you're married, we wish you joy,
> First a girl and then a boy;
> Cups and saucers, sons and daughters,
> Now join hands and kiss one another.

Another version from Long Itchington, given in *Notes and Queries*, 7th series, x. 450, concludes with—

> Up the kitchen and down the hall,
> Choose the fairest of them all;
> Seven years now and seven years then,
> Kiss poor Sally and part again.

Pretty Miss Pink

> Pretty Miss Pink, will you come out,
> Will you come out, will you come out?
> Pretty Miss Pink, will you come out,
> To see the ladies dancing?
> No, I won't.
> Pretty Miss Pink, she won't come out,
> Won't come out, won't come out, &c.
> She will come out.
> Pretty Miss Pink, she has come out, &c.

> —Winterton Lincs and Nottinghamshire
> (Miss M. Peacock.)

(*b*) The children place themselves in a row. They each choose a colour to represent them. One player must be *pink*. Another player stands facing them, and dances to and fro, singing the first four lines. The dancer then sings the next two lines, and Miss Pink having answered rushes forward, catches hold of the dancer's hand, and sings the next verse. Each colour is then taken in turn, but Miss Pink must always be first.

(c) This is clearly a variant of " Pray, Pretty Miss," colours being used perhaps from a local custom at fairs and May meetings, where girls were called by the colours of the ribbons they wore.

Prick at the Loop

A cheating game, played with a strap and skewer at fairs, &c., by persons of the thimble-rig class, probably the same as the game called " Fast and Loose."

Prickey Sockey

Christmas morning is ushered in by the little maidens play-ing at the game of " Prickey Sockey," as they call it. They are dressed up in their best, with their wrists adorned with rows of pins, and run about from house to house inquiring who will play at the game. The door is opened and one cries out—

Prickey sockey for a pin,
I car not whether I loss or win.

The game is played by the one holding between her two forefingers and thumbs a pin, which she clasps tightly to pre-vent her antagonist seeing either part of it, while her opponent guesses. The head of the pin is " sockey," and the point is "prickey," and when the other guesses she touches the end she guesses at, saying, " this for prickey," or " this for sockey," At night the other delivers her two pins. Thus the game is played, and when the clock strikes twelve it is declared up; that is, no one can play after that time.—*Mirror*, 1828, vol. x. p. 443.

See " Headicks and Pinticks."

Prickie and Jockie

A childish game, played with pins, and similar to " Odds or Evens,"—Teviotdale (Jamieson), but it is more probable that this is the game of " Prickey Sockey," which Jamieson did not see played.

Priest-Cat (1)

See " Jack's Alive."

Priest-Cat (2)

A peat clod is put into the shell of the crook by one person, who then shuts his eyes. Some one steals it. The other then goes round the circle trying to discover the thief, and addressing particular individuals in a rhyme—

> Ye're fair and leal,
> Ye canna steal;
> Ye're black and fat,
> Ye're the thief of my priest-cat!

If he guesses wrong he is in a wadd, if right he has found the thief.—Chambers' *Popular Rhymes*, p. 128.

This is an entirely different game to the "Priest-Cat" given by Mactaggart (see "Jack's Alive"), and seems to have originated in the discovery of stolen articles by divination.

Priest of the Parish

William Carleton describes this game as follows:—"One of the boys gets a wig upon himself, goes out on the floor, places the boys in a row, calls on his man Jack, and says to each, 'What will you be?' One answers, 'I'll be Black Cap,' another, 'Red Cap,' and so on. He then says, 'The priest of the parish has lost his considering-cap. Some says this, and some says that, but I say my man Jack.' Man Jack then, to put it off himself, says, 'Is it me, sir?' 'Yes you, sir.' 'You lie, sir.' 'Who then, sir?' 'Black Cap.' If Black Cap then doesn't say, 'Is it me, sir?' before the priest has time to call him he must put his hand on his ham and get a pelt of the brogue. A boy must be supple with the tongue in it."—*Traits and Stories of the Irish Peasantry*, p. 106 (Tegg's reprint).

This game is no doubt the original form of the game imperfectly played under the name of "King Plaster Palacey" (see *ante*, i. 301).

Prisoner's Base or Bars

The game of "The Country Base" is mentioned by Shakespeare in "Cymbeline"—

> "He, with two striplings (lads more like to run
> The country base, than to commit such slaughter),
> Made good the passage."—Act v., sc. 3.

Also in the tragedy of Hoffman, 1632—

> " I'll run a little course
> At *base*, or barley-brake."

Again, in the Antipodes, 1638—

> " My men can runne at *base*."

Also, in the thirtieth song of Drayton's " Polyolbion "—

> " At hood-wink, barley-brake, at tick, or *prison-base*."

Again, in Spenser's " Faerie Queen," v. 8—

> " So ran they all as they had been at *bace*."

Strutt (*Sports and Pastimes*, p. 78), says, " This game was much practised in former times. The first mention of this sport that I have met with occurs in the Proclamations at the head of the Parliamentary proceedings, early in the reign of Edward III., where it is spoken of as a childish amusement ; and prohibited to be played in the avenues of the palace at Westminster during the Sessions of Parliament, because of the interruption it occasioned to the members and others in passing to and fro. . . . The performance of this pastime requires two parties of equal number, each of them having a base or home, as it is usually called to themselves, at the distance of about twenty or thirty yards. The players then on either side taking hold of hands extend themselves in length and opposite to each other, as far as they conveniently can, always remembering that one of them must touch the base ; when any one of them quits the hand of his fellow and runs into the field, which is called giving the chase, he is im-mediately followed by a second from the former side, and he by a second opponent ; and so on alternately, until as many are out as choose to run, every one pursuing the man he first followed and no other ; and if he overtake him near enough to touch him, his party claims one toward their game, and both return home. Then they run forth again and again in like manner, until the number is completed that decides the victory ; this number is optional. It is to be observed that every person on either side who touches another during the chase, claims one for his party."

Strutt describes the game in Essex as follows :—" They play

this game with the addition of two prisons, which are stakes
driven into the ground, parallel with the home boundaries,
and about thirty yards from them ; and every person who is
touched on either side in the chase is sent to one or other of
these prisons, where he must remain till the conclusion of the
game, if not delivered previously by one of his associates, and
this can only be accomplished by touching him, which is a
difficult task, requiring the performance of the most skilful
players, because the prison belonging to either party is always
much nearer to the base of their opponents than to their own ;
and if the person sent to relieve his confederate be touched
by an antagonist before he reaches him, he also becomes a
prisoner, and stands in equal need of deliverance."—*Sports and
Pastimes*, p. 80.

But this is not quite the same as it is played in London.
There the school ground is divided in the following manner :—
The boys being divided into equal
sides, with a captain for each, one
party takes up its quarters in A, the
other in B.   Lots are chosen as to
which side commences.   Then one
member of the side so chosen (say A)
starts off for the middle of the playground and cries out "Chevy, Chevy
Chase, one, two, three ; " thereupon
it becomes the object of the side B
to touch him before reaching home

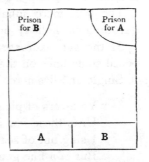

again.   If unsuccessful one from side B goes to the middle,
and so on until a prisoner is secured from one of the sides.
Then the struggle commences in earnest, after the fashion
described by Strutt as above.   If a boy succeeds in getting
to the prison of his side without being touched by an opponent,
he releases a prisoner, and brings him back home again to help
in the struggle.   The object of the respective sides is to place
all their opponents in prison, and when that is accomplished
they rush over to the empty home and take possession of it.
The game then begins again from opposite sides, the winning
side counting one towards the victory.—London (G. L. Gomme).

This was once a favourite game among young men in North Shropshire (and Cheshire). It was played yearly at Norton-in-Hales Wakes, and the winning party were decorated with ribbons. Men-servants, in the last century, were wont to ask a day's holiday to join or witness a game of " Prison-bars," arranged beforehand as a cricket-match might be (see *Bye-gones*, 2nd May 1883). A form of the game still survives there among the school-children, under the name of " Prison Birds." The Birds arrange themselves in pairs behind each other, facing a large stone or stump placed at some little distance. Before them, also facing the stone, stands one player, called the Keeper. When he calls, " Last pair out ! " the couple next behind him run to the stone and touch hands over it. If they can do so without being touched by the Keeper, they are free, and return to a position behind the other birds ; but any one whom he touches must remain behind the stone " in prison."— Ellesmere (Burne's *Shropshire Folk-lore*, p. 524).

The Ellesmere inhabitants were formerly accustomed to devote their holiday occasions to the game, and in the year 1764 the poet laureate of the town (Mr. David Studley) composed some lines on the game as it was played by the Married *v.* Single at Ellesmere. They are as follows :—

"Ye lovers of pleasure, give ear and attend,
    Unto these few lines which here I have penned,
    I sing not of sea fights, of battles nor wars,
    But of a fine game, which is called ' Prison Bars.'

This game was admired by men of renown,
    And played by the natives of fair Ellesmere town ;
    On the eighth day of August in the year sixty-four,
    These nimble heel'd fellows approached on the moor.

Twenty-two were the number appear'd on the green,
    For swiftness and courage none like them were seen ;
    Eleven were married to females so fair,
    The other young gallants bachelors were.

Jacob Hitchen the weaver commands the whole round,
    Looks this way, and that way, all over the ground,

Gives proper directions, and sets out his men,
So far go, my lads, and return back again.

Proper stations being fixed, each party advance,
And lead one another a many fine dance.
There's Gleaves after Ellis, and Platt after he,
Such running before I never did see.

Huzza! for the young men, the fair maids did say,
May heaven protect you to conquer this day,
Now, my brave boys, you're not to blame,
Take courage, my lads, nine and eight is the game.

Now behold the Breeches makers, master and man,
Saddlers, Slaters, and Joiners, do all they can;
The Tailor so nimble, he brings up the rear,
Cheer up, my brave boys, you need not to fear.

Alas! poor old Jacob, thy hopes are in vain,
Dick Chidley is artful, and spoils all thy schemes.
The Barber is taken, the Currier is down,
The Sawyer is tired, and so is the Clown."

The moor referred to in the last line of the second verse was the Pitchmoor. The Clown was a nickname for one of the players, who, on hearing the song repeated in the presence of the author, became so exasperated, that, to appease him, the words "the game is our'n" were substituted for the words "so is the Clown" in the last line of the concluding verse.

Puff-the-Dart

A game played with a long needle inserted in some worsted, and blown at a target through a tin tube.—Halliwell's *Dictionary*. This game is also mentioned in Baker's *Northamptonshire Glossary*.

Pun o' mair Weight

A rough play among boys, adding their weight one upon another, and all upon the one at the bottom.—Dickinson's *Cumberland Glossary*.

Punch Bowl

    I.   Round about the punch bowl,—
           One, two, three;
      If anybody wants a bonnie lassie,
           Just take me.

Another form of words is—
      The fillan o' the punch bowl,
           That wearies me;
      The fillan o't up, an' the drinkan' o't doon,
      An' the kissan o' a bonnie lass,
           That cheeries me.
                    —Fochabers (Rev. W. Gregor).

    II.   Round about the punch bowl,
           Punch bowl, punch bowl;
    Round about the punch bowl, one, two, three.

    First time never to fall,
           Never to fall, never to fall;
    First time never to fall, one, two, three.

    Second time, the catching time,
           Catching time, catching time;
    Second time, the catching time, one, two, three.

    Third time, the kissing time,
           Kissing time, kissing time,
    Third time, the kissing time, one, two, three.
                    —Belfast (W. H. Patterson).

    III.   Round about the punch bowl,—one, two, three;
    Open the gates and let the bride through.

    Half-a-crown to know his name, to know his name, to
      know his name,
    Half-a-crown to know his name,
    On a cold and frosty morning.

    Ah! (Michael Matthews) is his name, is his name, is
      his name;
    (Michael Matthews) is his name,
    On a cold and frosty morning.

Half-a-crown to know her name, to know her name, to
    know her name,
Half-a-crown to know her name,
On a cold and frosty morning.

(Annie Keenan) is her name, is her name, is her name,
(Annie Keenan) is her name,
On a cold and frosty morning.

They'll be married in the morning,
Round about the punch bowl, I [? Hi!].
          —Annaverna, Ravensdale, Co. Louth, Ireland
          (Miss R. Stephen).

(*b*) The Fochabers' game is played by girls only. The
players join hands and form a ring. They dance briskly
round, singing the verse. The last word, "me," is pronounced
with strong emphasis, and all the girls jump, and if one falls
she has to leave the ring. The game is carried on until all
the players fall. In the Belfast game, at the words "one,
two, three," the players drop down in a crouching position
for a few seconds. In the Louth (Ireland) game the players all
curtsey after the first line, and the one who rises last is the bride.
She is led outside the ring by another, and asked to whom she
is engaged. She tells without letting those in the ring hear,
and the two return to the ring saying the second line. Then
all the ring sing the next three lines, and then the girl who
has been told the name tells it to the ring, who thereupon
sing or say the remaining lines of the verse.

(*c*) The Louth version has more detail in its movements,
and probably represents the oldest form. At all events, it
supplies the reason for the words and movements, which are
not quite so obvious in the other versions. Many ancient
monoliths are known as "Punch Bowls," and it may be that
this game is the relic of an old marriage ceremony, "at the
stones."

Purposes

A kind of game. "The prettie game which we call purposes" (Cotgrave in *v.* "Opinion").—Halliwell's *Dictionary*.

Push in the Wash Tub

A ring of girls is formed. Two go in opposite directions outside the ring, and try to get back first to the starting-point; the one succeeding stops there, rejoining the ring, the other girl *pushes* another girl into the ring, or *wash tub*, with whom the race is renewed.—Crockham Hill, Kent (Miss Chase).

Push-pin, or Put-pin

A child's play, in which pins are pushed with an endeavour to cross them.   So explained by Ash, but it would seem, from Beaumont and Fletcher, vii. 25, that the game was played by aiming pins at some object.—Halliwell's *Dictionary.*

> " To see the sonne you would admire,
> Goe play at push-pin with his sire."
> —*Men's Miracles*, 1656, p. 15.

> " Love and myselfe, beleeve me on a day,
> At childish push-pin for our sport did play."
> —Herrick's *Works*, i. 22.

There is an allusion to it under the name of put-pin in Nash's *Apologie,* 1593—

> " That can lay down maidens bedds,
> And that can hold ther sickly heds ;
> That can play at put-pin,
> Blow poynte and near lin."

Two pins are laid upon a table, and the object of each player is to push his pin across his opponent's pin.—Addy's *Sheffield Glossary.*

See " Hattie," " Pop the Bonnet."

Push the Business On

I.   I hired a horse and borrowed a gig,
And all the world shall have a jig ;
And I'll do all 'at ever I can
To push the business on.

To push the business on,
To push the business on ;
And I'll do all 'at ever I can
To push the business on.
—North Kelsey, Anderby, and near the Trent,
Nottinghamshire (Miss M. Peacock).

II.   Beeswax and turpentine make the best of plaster,
    The more you try to pull it off, it's sure to stick the faster.
    I'll buy a horse and hire a gig,
    And all the world shall have a jig;
    And you and I'll do all we can
        To push the business on,
        To push the business on;
    And we'll do all that ever we can
        To push the business on.
               —Brigg, Lincolnshire (Miss Barker, from a
                    Lincolnshire friend).

III.   I'll buy a horse and steal a gig,
    And all the world shall have a jig;
    And I'll do all that ever I can
    To pass the business on.
        To pass the business on,
        To pass the business on;
    And I'll do all that ever I can
        To pass the business on.
    —Wolstanton, North Staffs. (Miss Bush, Schoolmistress)

IV.   We'll borrow a horse and steal a gig,
    And round the world we'll have a jig;
    And I'll do all that ever I can
    To push the business on.
               —Earls Heaton (Herbert Hardy).

V.   I'll hire a horse and steal a gig,
    And all the world shall have a jig;
    And I'll do all that éver I can
    To push the business on,
        To push the business on, to push the business on,
        And I'll do all that ever I can to push the business on.
              —Settle, Yorkshire (Rev. W. S. Sykes).

(*b*) The players stand in a circle, boy and girl alternately, and sing the lines. At the fourth line they all clap their hands, keeping time with the song. When singing the seventh line each boy takes the girl on his left hand,—dances round with her and places her on his right hand. This is done till each girl has been all round the circle, and has been turned or danced with by each boy. In the Wolstanton version (Miss Bush), after singing the first four lines, the children fall behind one another, march round, clapping their hands and singing; at the seventh line they all join in couples and galop round very quickly to the end. When they finish, the girls stand at the side of the boys in couples, and change places every time they go round until each girl has partnered each boy. At Hexham there is rather more of the regular dance about the game at the beginning. At the fourth line they set to partners and swing round, the girls changing places at the end, and continuing until they have been all round each time with a different partner.

(*c*) This game seems of kin to the old-fashioned country dances. Miss Bush writes that this game was introduced into the school playground from Derbyshire a few years ago, and is sung to a simple tune.

Puss in the Corner

The children stand at fixed points: one stands in the middle and chants, "Poor puss wants a corner." The others beckon with the fore - finger, and call-ing, "Puss, puss," run from point to point. Puss runs also to one of the vacant spaces. The one left out becomes puss.—Monton, Lancashire (Miss Dendy).

The players place themselves each in some "coign of van-tage," as the play place allows; one player in the middle is "out." Those in the corners change places with each other at choice, calling, "Puss, puss, puss," to attract each other's attention. The one who is out watches his opportunity to slip into a vacant corner, and oblige some one else to be "out." A favourite game *in the streets* of Market Drayton.—Burne's *Shropshire Folk-lore*, p. 523.

When we played this game, the child who was to be " Puss "
was invariably decided upon by a counting-out rhyme. He or
she being the last of the five players " not he." The words we
used when wishful to change corners were, " Puss, puss, give me
a drop of milk." The players in the corners beckoned with the
finger to an opposite player in another corner (A. B. Gomme).

The game in Scotland is called " Moosie in the Corner,"
and is played by boys or girls, or by both together, either
outside or in a room. Each player takes a corner, and one
stands in the middle. On a given signal, usually by calling
out the word " Change," a rush is made from the corners.
The aim of the one standing in the middle is to reach a
vacant corner. If the game is played in a room, as many
chairs, or other seats, are placed as there are players, less
one. Each takes a seat, and one is left standing. On the
word " Change " being called out, each jumps from the seat
and makes for another. The one standing strives to get a
seat in the course of the change.—Nairn and Macduff (Rev.
W. Gregor).

Pussy's Ground

Name for Tom Tiddler's Ground in Norfolk.
See " Tom Tiddler's Ground."

Pyramid

A circle of about two feet in diameter is made on the ground,
in the centre of which a pyramid is formed by several marbles.
Nine are placed as the base, then six, then four, and then one
on the top. The keeper of the pyramid then desires the other
players to shoot. Each player gives the keeper one marble for
leave to shoot at the pyramid, and all that the players can
strike out of the circle belong to them.—London streets (A. B.
Gomme), and *Book of Sports*.
See " Castles."

Quaker

Men and women stand alternately in a circle, and one man
begins by placing his left hand on his left knee, and saying,
" There was an old Quaker and he went so." This is repeated
all round the circle; the first man then says the same thing

again, but this time he places his *right* hand on his *right* knee. Then he places his hand on the girl's shoulder, then round her neck, and on her far shoulder, then looks into her face, and, lastly, kisses her.—Sharleston, Yorks (Miss Fowler).

Quaker's Wedding

> Hast thou ever been to a Quaker's wedding?
>   Nay, friend, nay.
> Do as I do; twiddle thy thumbs and follow me.

The leader walks round chanting these lines, with her eyes fixed on the ground. Each new comer goes behind till a long train is formed, then they kneel side by side as close together as possible. The leader then gives a vigorous push to the one at the end of the line [next herself, and that one to the next], and the whole line tumble over.—Berkshire (Miss Thoyts in the *Antiquary*, xxvii. 194).

See "Obadiah," "Solomon."

Queen Anne

> I.   Lady Queen Ann she sits in her stand,
>   And a pair of green gloves upon her hand,
>   As white as a lily, as fair as a swan,
>   The fairest lady in a' the land;
>   Come smell my lily, come smell my rose,
>   Which of my maidens do you choose?
>   I choose you one, and I choose you all,
>   And I pray, Miss (   ), yield up the ball.
>   The ball is mine, and none of yours,
>   Go to the woods and gather flowers.
>   Cats and kittens bide within,
>   But we young ladies walk out and in.
>   —Chambers' *Pop. Rhymes*, p. 136.

> II. Queen Anne, Queen Anne, who sits on her throne,
>   As fair as a lily, as white as a swan;
>   The king sends you three letters,
>   And begs you'll read one.

>   I cannot read one unless I read all,
>   So pray (   ) deliver the ball.

The ball is mine and none of thine,
So you, proud Queen, may sit on your throne,
While we, your messengers, go and come.

(Or sometimes)—

The ball is mine, and none of thine,
You are the fair lady to sit on;
And we're the black gipsies to go and come.

—Halliwell's *Pop. Rhymes*, p. 230.

III. Queen Anne, Queen Anne, you sit in the sun,
As fair as a lily, as white as a wand,
'I send you three letters, and pray read one.
You must read one, if you can't read all,
So pray, Miss or Master, throw up the ball.

—Halliwell's *Pop. Rhymes*, p. 64.

IV. Here we come a-piping,
First in spring and then in May.
The Queen she sits upon the sand,
Fair as a lily, white as a wand:
King John has sent you letters three,
And begs you'll read them unto me.
We can't read one without them all,
So pray, Miss Bridget, deliver the ball.

—Halliwell's *Pop. Rhymes*, p. 73.

V. Queen Anne, Queen Anne,
She sot in the sun;
So fair as a lily,
So white as a nun;
She had a white glove on,
She drew it off, she drew it on.

Turn, ladies, turn.

The more we turn, the more we may,
Queen Anne was born on Midsummer Day;
We have brought dree letters from the Queen,
Wone of these only by thee must be seen.
We can't rëade wone, we must rëade all,
Please (   ) deliver the ball.

—Dorsetshire (*Folk-lore Journal*, vii. 229).

VI.   Here come we to Lady Queen Anne,
With a pair of white gloves to cover our hand;
As white as a lily, as fair as the rose,
But not so fair as you may suppose.

Turn, ladies, turn.

The more we turn the more we may,
Queen Anne was born on Midsummer Day.

The king sent me three letters, I never read them all,
So pray, Miss ————, deliver the ball.

The ball is yours, and not ours,
You must go to the garden and gather the flowers.

The ball is ours, and not yours,
We go out and gather the flowers.
—Cornwall (*Folk-lore Journal*, v. 52–53).

VII.   Queen Anne, Queen Anne, she sits in the sun,
As fair as a lily, so white and wan;
A pair of kid gloves she holds in her hand,
There's no such a lady in all the fair land.

Turn all.

The more we turn the better we are,
For we've got the ball between us.
—North Kelsey, Lincolnshire (Miss M. Peacock).

VIII.   Lady Queen Anne she sits on a stand [sedan],
She is fair as a lily, she is white as a swan;
A pair of green gloves all over her hand,
She is the fairest lady in all the land.
Come taste my lily, come smell my rose,
Which of my babes do you choose?
I choose not one, but I choose them all,
So please, Miss Nell, give up the ball.

The ball is ours, it is not yours,
We will go to the woods and gather flowers;
We will get pins to pin our clothes,
You will get nails to nail your toes.
—Belfast (W. H. Patterson).

IX.   Queen Anne, Queen Anne, she sits in the sun,
      As fair as a lily, as brown as a bun ;
      We've brought you three letters, pray can you read
          one ?
      I can't read one without I read all,
      So pray ———— deliver the ball.

      You old gipsy, sit in the sun,
      And we fair ladies go and come ;
      The ball is mine, and none o' thine,
      And so good-morning, Valentine.
               —Swaffham, Norfolk (Miss Matthews).

X.   Queen Anne, Queen Anne, she sits in the sun,
      As fair as a lily, as brown as a bun.

      Turn, fair ladies, turn.

      We bring you three letters, and pray you read one.
      I cannot read one without I read all,
      So please (   ) give up the ball.

[If the wrong guess is made the girls say—]
      The ball is ours, and none of yours,
      And we've the right to keep it.

[If the right child is named, they say—]
      The ball is yours, and is not ours,
      And you've the right to take it.

[Some of the children said this rhyme should be—]
      The ball is ours, and none of yours,
      So you, black gipsies, sit in the sun,
      While we the fair ladies go as we come.
                —London (A. B. Gomme).

XI.   Queen Anne, Queen Anne, she sits in the sun,
      As fair as a lily, as white as a swan ;
      I bring you three letters, so pray you choose one,
      I cannot read one without I read all,
      So pray ———— give up the ball.

[If the wrong girl is asked, they say—]
      The ball is ours, it is not yours,
      And we've the right to keep it.

[When the right one is guessed—]
> The ball is yours, it is not ours,
> And you've the right to keep it.
> > —Barnes, Surrey (A. B. Gomme).

XII. The lady Queen Anne she sat in a tan (sedan),
> As fair as a lily, as white as a swan;
> The Queen of Morocco she sent you a letter,
> So please to read one.

> I won't read one except them all,
> So please, Miss ———, deliver the ball.
> > —Hersham, Surrey (*Folk-lore Record*, v. 87).

XIII. Queen Ann, Queen Ann,
> She sits in the sun,
> As fair as a lily, and bright as one;
> King George has sent you three letters,
> And desires you to read one.

> > I cannot read one
> > Without I read all,
> > So pray, Miss ( ),
> > Deliver the ball.

[Rhyme when right is seldom in use, and the one when wrong forgotten.]

> The ball is ours, and none of yours,
> So, black gipsies, sit in the sun,
> And we, fair ladies, go as we come.
> > —Sussex, about 1850 (Miss Chase).

XIV. Queen Ann, Queen Ann,
> She sat in the sun;
> A pair of white gloves to cover her hands,
> As white as a lily, as red as a rose,
> To which young lady do you propose?
> > —Devon (Miss Chase).

XV. Here come seven sisters,
> And seven milken daughters,
> And with the ladies of the land,
> And please will you grant us.

I grant you once, I grant you twice,
I grant you three times over;
A for all, and B for ball,
And please [   ] deliver the ball.
       —Bocking, Essex (*Folk-lore Journal*, vi. 211).

(*b*) Sides are chosen, and two lines are formed; the words are said by each line alternately. One line, in which is the Queen, standing still or sitting down, the other line advancing and retiring while singing the words. The latter line gives one of their number a ball or some other small object to hold in the hand in such a manner that it cannot be perceived. All the players on this side then assume the same position— either all put their hands behind them or fold their arms, put

their hands under their armpits, or under their skirts or pinafores. The object of the other side is to guess which child in the line has the ball. The line which has the ball commences the game by advancing singing or saying the first three or four lines. Queen Anne answers, and then names one of the girls on the opposite side whom she suspects to have the ball, and if she be right in her guess the lines change sides. If she be wrong, the line retires in triumph, the girl who possesses the ball holding it up to show the Queen she is wrong. The children all curtsey when leaving the Queen's presence. Another girl of the line then takes the ball and the game continues till the right holder of the ball is named. When the Queen tells the line of players to "turn," they all spin round, coming back to face the Queen, and then stand still again. In the North Kelsey version (Miss Peacock) there is only one player on Queen Anne's side, the rest form the line. This is also the case with the Cornish game.

(*c*) The analysis of the game-rhymes is as follows:—

No.	Scotland (Chambers).	Halliwell (1).	Halliwell (2).	Halliwell (3).	Dorsetshire.	Cornwall.	North Kelsey.
1.	—	—	—	Here we come a-piping.	—	—	—
2.	—	—	—	First in Spring, then in May.	—	—	—
3.	Lady Q. Anne.	Q. Anne, Anne.	Queen Anne.	Queen.	Queen Anne.	Lady Queen Anne.	Queen Anne.
4.	Sits in her stand.	Sits on her throne.		Sits upon the sand.			
5.			Sits in the sun.		Sot in the sun.		Sits in the sun.
6.					White glove on.		
7.	Pair of green gloves on her hand.					Pair of white gloves to cover our hand.	Pair of kid gloves in her hand.
8.						White as lily, fair as rose.	
9.	White as a lily, fair as a swan.	Fair as lily, white as swan.	Fair as lily, white as wand.	Fair as lily, white as wand.	Fair as lily, white as nun.		Fair as lily, white and wan.
10.							No such lady in the land.
11.	Fairest lady in the land.						
12.						Not so fair as you may suppose.	
13.	Smell my lily, smell my rose.						
14.	Which of my maidens do you choose?						
15.					Turn, ladies.	Turn, ladies.	Turn all.
16.			I send you three letters.		More we turn, more we may.	More we turn, more we may.	More we turn, better we are.
17.			Pray read one.		Queen Anne was born on midsummer day.	Q. Anne was born on midsummer day.	
18.	King sends three letters.	King sends three letters.		King John has sent three letters.	We've brought three letters.	King sent me three letters.	
19.	Begs you'll read one.	Begs you'll read one.		Begs you'll read them unto me.			
20.					One of these only by you must be seen.		

21. Choose you one and choose you all.	Cannot read one unless I read all.	You must read one, if you can't all.	We can't read one without all.	We can't read one, must read all.	I never read them all.	—
22. —	—	—	—	—	—	—
23. Pray, Miss, yield up the ball.	Pray [ ] deliver the ball.	Pray, Miss [ ], throw up the ball.	Pray, Miss [ ], deliver the ball.	Please [ ] deliver the ball.	Pray, Miss [ ], deliver the ball.	—
24. —	—	—	—	—	—	We've got the ball between us.
25. The ball is mine, and none of yours.	The ball is mine, and none of thine. You, proud Queen, may sit on your throne.	—	—	—	The ball is yours, and not ours.	—
26. —		—	—	—	—	—
27. —	While we, your messengers, go and come.	—	—	—	—	—
28. Go to the woods and gather flowers.	—	—	—	—	Go to the garden and gather flowers.	—
29. —	—	—	—	—	—	—
30. —	The ball is mine, and none of thine. You are the fair lady to sit on.	—	—	—	The ball is ours, and none of yours.	—
31. —		—	—	—	—	—
32. —	And we're black gipsies to go and come.	—	—	—	—	—
33. —	—	—	—	—	We must go to the garden and gather flowers.	—
34. —	—	—	—	—	—	—
35. Cats and kittens, bide within.	—	—	—	—	—	—
36. We young ladies walk out and in.	—	—	—	—	—	—
37. —	—	—	—	—	—	—
38. —	—	—	—	—	—	—
39. —	—	—	—	—	—	—

No.	Belfast.	Swaffham.	London.	Barnes.	Hersham.	Sussex.	Devon.
1.	—	—	—	—	—	—	—
2.	Lady Queen Anne.	Queen Anne.	Queen Anne.	Queen Anne.	Lady Queen Anne.	Queen Ann.	Queen Ann.
3.	Sits on a stand.	—	—	—	Sits in a tan.	—	—
4.	—	—	—	—	—	—	—
5.	—	Sits in the sun.	Sits in the sun.	Sits in the sun.	—	Sits in the sun.	Sat in the sun.
6.	—	—	—	—	—	—	—
7.	Pair of green gloves all over her hand.	—	—	—	—	—	Pair of white gloves to cover her hand.
8.		—	—	—	—	—	
9.	Fair as lily, white as swan	Fair as lily, brown as bun.	Fair as lily, brown as bun.	Fair as lily, white as swan,	Fair as lily, white as swan.	Fair as lily, bright as one.	White as lily, red as rose,
10.	—						
11.	Fairest lady in the land.	—	—	—	—	—	—
12.	—	—	—	—	—	—	—
13.	Taste my lily, smell my rose.	—	—	—	—	—	—
14.	Which of my babes do you chose?	—	—	—	—	—	To which young lady do you propose?
15.	—	—	—	—	—	—	—
16.	—	—	—	—	—	—	—
17.	—	—	—	—	—	—	—
18.	We've brought three letters.	We've brought three letters.	We bring you three letters.	I bring you three letters.	Queen of Morocco sent you a letter.	King Geo. has sent you three letters.	—
19.	Pray can you read one.	Pray can you read one.	Pray you read one.	Pray you choose one.	Please to read one.	Desires you to read one.	—

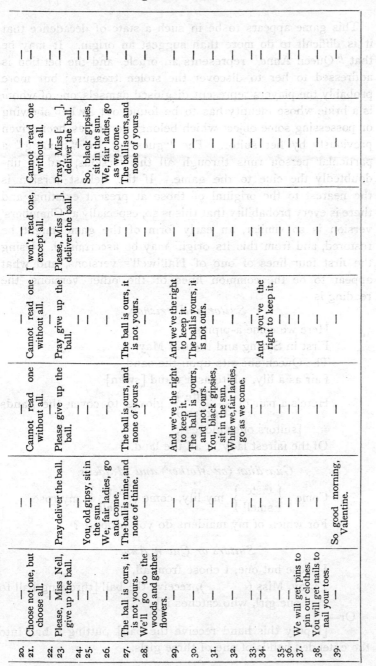

No.						
20. 21.	Cannot read one without all.	I won't read one, except all.	Cannot read one without all.	Cannot read one without all.	—	Choose not one, but choose all.
22. 23.	Pray, Miss [ ], deliver the ball.	Please, Miss [ ], deliver the ball.	Pray give up the ball.	Please give up the ball.	Pray deliver the ball.	Please, Miss Nell, give up the ball.
24. 25. 26.	So, black gipsies, sit in the sun. We, fair ladies, go as we come.	—	—	—	You, old gipsy, sit in the sun. We, fair ladies, go and come.	—
27. 28.	The ball is ours, and none of yours.	—	The ball is ours, it is not yours.	The ball is ours, and none of yours.	The ball is mine, and none of thine.	The ball is ours, it is not yours. We'll go to the woods and gather flowers.
29. 30. 31. 32.	—	—	And we've the right to keep it. The ball is yours, it is not ours.	And we've the right to keep it. The ball is yours, and not ours. You, black gipsies, sit in the sun. While we, fair ladies, go as we come.	—	—
33. 34.	—	—	And you've the right to keep it.	—	—	—
35. 36. 37. 38.	—	—	—	—	—	We will get pins to pin our clothes. You will get nails to nail your toes.
39.	—	—	—	—	So good morning, Valentine.	—

This game appears to be in such a state of decadence that it is difficult to do more than suggest an origin. It may be that "Queen Anne" represents an oracle, and the petition is addressed to her to discover the stolen treasure; but more probably the players represent disguised damsels, one of whom is a bride whose identity has to be found out by her showing or possessing some object which belongs to or has been given previously by her suitor. The "guessing" or "naming" a particular person runs through all the versions, and is undoubtedly the clue to the game. If the Belfast version is the nearest to the original of those at present existing, and there is every probability that this is so, especially as Chambers' version is so similar, an early form of the game might be restored, and from this its origin may be ascertained. Using the first four lines of one of Halliwell's versions, and what appear to be the common lines of the other versions, the reading is—

Suitor and Friends.

Here we come a-piping,
First in Spring and then in May.
The Queen she sits upon the sand,
Fair as a lily, white as a wand [swan].

Here's a pair of $\left\{\begin{matrix}\text{white}\\\text{green}\end{matrix}\right\}$ gloves to cover the hands [suitors offer gloves],
Of the fairest lady in all the land.

Guardian (or Mother) and Maidens.

Come $\left\{\begin{matrix}\text{taste}\\\text{smell}\end{matrix}\right\}$ my lily, come $\left\{\begin{matrix}\text{taste}\\\text{smell}\end{matrix}\right\}$ my rose,
For which of my maidens do you propose?

Suitors or Queen Anne.

I chose but one, I chose from all,
I pray, Miss (　　　), receive the ball [throwing ball to one girl, who catches it].

Or—

[I pray this hand receive the ball], putting a ball into the extended hands of one of three girls.

Guardian then disguises three girls (one with the ball) with veils or other coverings, so that they precisely resemble each other, and returns with the girls to the suitors, saying to the girls—

Turn, ladies, turn; turn, ladies, turn;

and to the suitors—

Come choose your own, come choose from all.
I've brought you three letters, pray can you read one?

Suitor

(touching one of the disguised girls).

I cannot read one without I read all.
I pray, Miss (   ), yield up the ball.]

Disguised Maiden

(one who did not receive the ball).

The ball is mine, and none of thine,
And so, good morning, Valentine.

Chorus of Maidens (curtseying).

We will go to the wood and gather flowers,
We will get pins to pin our clothes,
You will get nails to nail your toes.
Cats and kittens bide within,
But we, young maidens, come out and in.

The inference being that the chosen maiden is still free until the suitor can try again, and is fortunate enough to indicate the right maiden.

If this conjectural restoration of the verses be accepted on the evidence, it would suggest that this game originated from one of the not uncommon customs practised at weddings or betrothals—when the suitor has to discriminate between several girls all dressed precisely alike and distinguish his bride by some token. (See "King William.") This incident of actual primitive custom also obtains in folk tales, thus showing its strong hold upon popular tradition, and hence increasing the probability that it would reappear in games. It must be remembered that the giving of gloves was a significant fact in betrothals.

This game is said by some to have its origin in the use of the sedan chair. A version taken from a newspaper cutting (unfortunately I had not recorded the name and date, but think it was probably the *Leeds Mercury* some years ago) gives the following rhyme. The writer does not say whether he knows it as a game—

> Lady Lucan she sits in a sedan,
> As fair as a lily, as white as a swan;
> A pair of green gloves to doff and to don.
> My mistress desires you will read one,
> I can't read one without them all,
> So I pray this hand decline the ball.

In this version there is still the puzzle to solve, or riddle to read.

Queen Mary

—Hexham (Miss J. Barker).

I. Queen Mary, Queen Mary, my age is sixteen,
   My father's a farmer on yonder green;
   He has plenty of money to dress me in silk—
   Come away, my sweet laddie, and take me a walk.

One morning I rose and I looked in the glass,
I thought to myself what a handsome young lass;
My hands by my side, and a gentle ha, ha,
Come away, my sweet lassie, and take me a walk.

Father, mother, may I go, may I go, may I go;
Father, mother, may I go, to buy a bunch of roses?
Oh yes, you may go, you may go, you may go;
Oh yes, you may go, buy a bunch of roses!

Pick up her tail and away she goes, away she goes,
    away she goes;
Pick up her tail and away she goes, to buy a bunch
    of roses.
—Sang by the children of Hexham Workhouse
(Miss J. Barker).

II. Queen Mary, Queen Mary, my age is sixteen,
My father's a farmer on yonder green;
He has plenty of money to keep me sae braw,
Yet nae bonnie laddie will tak' me awa'.

The morning so early I looked in the glass,
And I said to myself what a handsome young lass;
My hands by my side, and I gave a ha, ha,
Come awa', bonnie laddie, and tak' me awa'.
—Berwickshire, A. M. Bell, *Antiquary*, xxx. 17.

III. My name is Queen Mary,
My age is sixteen,
My father's a farmer in Old Aberdeen;
He has plenty of money to dress me in black—
There's nae [no] bonnie laddie 'ill tack me awa'.
Next mornin' I wakened and looked in the glass,
I said to myself, what a handsome young lass;
Put your hands to your haunches and give a ha, ha,
For there's nae bonnie laddie will tack ye awa'.
—N. E. Scotland (Rev. W. Gregor).

IV. My name is Queen Mary,
My age is sixteen,
My father's a farmer in yonder green;

He's plenty of money to dress in silk [fu' braw'],
For there's nae bonnie laddie can tack me awa'.
One morning I rose and I looked in the glass,
Says I to myself, I'm a handsome young lass;
My hands by my edges, and I give a ha, ha,
For there's nae bonnie laddie t' tack me awa'.
                                        —Cullen (Rev. W. Gregor).

(*b*) The Scottish game is played by girls. The players join hands, form a circle with one in the centre, and dance round singing. At the words "'ill tack me awa'," the centre player chooses another one, and the two wheel round. Then the singing proceeds. At the exclamation "ha! ha!" the players suit the action to the words of the line. In the Cullen game the girls stand in a row with one in front, who sings the verses and chooses another player from the line. The two then join hands and go round and round, singing the remaining verses.

Queen of Sheba

Two rows of people sit on chairs face to face on each side of a door, leaving just sufficient space between the lines for a player to pass. At the end of the rows furthest from the door sits the "Queen of Sheba," with a veil or shawl over her head. A player, hitherto unacquainted with the game, is brought to the door, shown the Queen, and told to go up between the rows, after being blindfolded, to kiss her, taking care, meanwhile, to avoid treading on the toes of the people on each side the alley leading to the lady. While his mind is diverted by these instructions, and by the process of blindfolding, the Queen gives up her seat to "the King," who has been lurking in the background. He assumes the veil and receives the kiss, to the amusement of every one but the uninitiated player.
                      —Anderby, Lincolnshire, and near the Trent,
                       Nottinghamshire (Miss M. Peacock).

Ragman

An ancient game, at which persons drew by chance poetical descriptions of their characters, the amusement consisting—as at modern games of a similar kind—in the peculiar application or misapplication of the verses so selected at hazard by the drawers.—Halliwell's *Dictionary*. Halliwell goes on to

say that the meaning of this term was first developed by
Mr. Wright in his *Anecdota Literaria*, 1844, where he has
printed two collections of ancient verses used in the game of
" Ragman." Mr. Wright conjectures that the stanzas were
written one after another on a roll of parchment; that to each
stanza a string was attached at the side, with a seal or piece of
metal or wood at the end ; and that when used the parchment
was rolled up with all the strings and their seals hanging
together, so that the drawer had no reason for choosing one
more than another, but drew one of the strings by mere chance,
and which he opened to see on what stanza he had fallen. If
such were the form of the game, we can very easily imagine
why the name was applied to a charter with an unusual
number of seals attached to it, which, when rolled up, would
present exactly the same appearance. Mr. Wright is borne
out in his opinion by an English poem, termed " Ragmane
roelle," printed from MS., Fairfax, 16 :—

> " My ladyes and my maistresses echone,
> Lyke hit unto your humbyble wommanhede,
> Resave in gré of my sympill persone
> This rolle, which, withouten any drede,
> Kynge Ragman me bad me sowe in brede,
> And cristyned yt the merour of your chaunce ;
> Drawith a strynge, and that shal streight yow leyde
> Unto the verry path of your governaunce."

That the verses were generally written in a roll may perhaps
be gathered from a passage in Douglas's Virgil :—

> " With that he raucht me ane roll : to rede I begane,
> The royetest ane ragment with mony ratt rime."

Halliwell also quotes the following :—

> "Venus, whiche stant withoute lawe,
> In non certeyne, but as men drawe
> Of Ragemon upon the chaunce,
> Sche leyeth no peys in the balaunce."
> —Gower, MS. *Society of Antiquaries*, 134, 244.

The term rageman is applied to the devil in " Piers Ploughman," 335.

Rag-stag

See "Stag Warning."

Rakes and Roans

A boys' game, in which the younger ones are chased by the larger boys, and when caught carried home pick-a-back.— Halliwell's *Dictionary*.

Moor (*Suffolk Words and Phrases*) says this game is often called "Rakes" only, and is the same, probably, that is thus alluded to: "To play Reaks, to domineer, to show mad pranks." The jest of it is to be carried home a pig-back, by the less swift wight who you may catch.

Rakkeps

A game among boys [undescribed].—Dickinson's *Cumberland Glossary*.

Range the Bus

Sides are chosen, and a line made across the playground. One of the sides goes up and the other goes down, and throws their bonnets on the ground. Then one side tries to get one of the opposite side across the line and crown him, and one of the opposite side tries to crown him back. If another boy can catch this player before he gets near him, he is crowned also. All the time the one side is trying to take the bonnets.— Old Aberdeen (Rev. W. Gregor).

See "French and English," "Scotch and English."

Rax, or Raxie-boxie, King of Scotland

The players, except one, take their stand at one side, and one stands at the other side in front of them. When all are ready, the one in front calls out "Cock," or "Caron," when all rush across to the other side, and he tries to catch one of them in crossing. The one caught helps to catch the others as they run back. Each time the players run from the one side to the other the word "Cock," or "Caron," is called out, and the change is continued till all are caught—each one as caught becoming a catcher. In Tyrie the game is called "Dyke King" when played by boys, and "Queen" when played by girls.

The word "King," or "Queen," is called out before each run, according as the game is played by boys or girls.—Ballindalloch (Rev. W. Gregor).

This game is called "Red Rover" in Liverpool (Mr. C. C. Bell). "Red Rover" is shouted out by the catcher when players are ready to rush across.

See "King Cæsar."

Relievo

This game is played by one child trying to catch the rest. The first prisoner taken joins hands with the captor and helps in the pursuit, and so on till all the playmates have been taken. —Anderby, Lincs. (Miss M. Peacock).

This game is the same as "Chickiddy Hand," "Stag Warning."

Religious Church

The children stand in a line. One child on the opposite side, facing them, says—

> Have you been to a religious church?

Row of children answer—

> No!
> Have I asked you?
> No!
> Put your fingers on your lips and follow me.

All the row follow behind her to some other part of the ground, where she stands with her back to them, and they form a new row. One child out of the row now steps forward, and standing behind the first girl says—

> Guess who stands behind you?

If the first girl guesses right she keeps her old place, and they begin again. If she is wrong the child who has come from the row takes her place, and a new game is begun. Of course the child who asks the last question alters its voice as much as possible, so as not to be recognised.—Liphook, Hants. (Miss Fowler).

Rigs

A game of children in Aberdeenshire, said to be the same as Scotch and English, and also called Rockety Row.—Jamieson's *Dictionary*.

Ring

See " Ring-taw."

Ring a Ring o' Roses

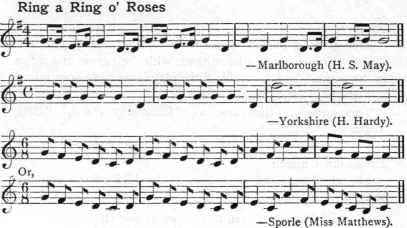

—Marlborough (H. S. May).

—Yorkshire (H. Hardy).

Or,

—Sporle (Miss Matthews).

I. Ring a ring o' roses,
   A pocket-full o' posies ;
   One for me, and one for you,
   And one for little Moses—
   Hasher, Hasher, Hasher, all fall down.
   —Winterton, Lincoln, and Leadenham
   (Miss M. Peacock).

II. A ring, a ring o' roses,
   A pocket-full o' posies ;
   One for Jack, and one for Jim, and one for little
      Moses—
   A-tisha ! a-tisha ! a-tisha !
   —Shropshire (Burne's *Shropshire Folk-lore*, p. 511).

III. A ring, a ring o' roses,
   A pocket-full o' posies ;
   A curchey in, and a curchey out,
   And a curchey all together.
   —Egmond (Burne's *Shropshire Folk-lore*, p. 571).

IV.   Ring, a ring o' roses,
A pocket full o' posies ;
Up-stairs and down-stairs,
In my lady's chamber—
Husher! Husher! Cuckoo!
        —Wakefield, Yorks. (Miss Fowler).

V.   Ring, a ring of roses,
Basket full of posies—
Tisha! Tisha! all fall down.
        —Penzance, Cornwall (Mrs. Mabbott).

VI.   Ring, a ring a roses,
A pocketful of posies ;
Hush, oh! hush, oh!
All fall down !
        —Colchester, Essex (Miss G. M. Frances).

VII.   Ring, a ring a rosy,
A pocket full of posies ;
One for you, and one for me,
And one for little Moses—
Atishm! Atishm!
        —Beddgelert (Mrs. Williams).

VIII.   A ring, a ring of roses,
A pocket full of posies—
Hist! hush! last down dead!
        —Gainford, Durham (Miss A. Eddleston).

IX.   Ring, a ring a row-o,
See the children go-o,
Sit below the goose-berry bush ;
Hark! they all cry Hush! hush! hush!
Sitty down, sit down.

Duzzy, duzzy gander,
Sugar, milk, and candy ;
Hatch-u, hatch-u, all fall down together.
        —South Shields (Miss Blair, aged 9).

X.   Ringey, ringey rosies,
        A pocketful of posies—
        Hach-ho, hach-ho, all fall down.

Another version—

        Hash-ho! Tzhu-ho! all fall down.
                                —Sporle, Norfolk (Miss Matthews).

XI. Windy, windy weather,
        Cold and frosty weather,
        When the wind blows
        We all blow together.
        I saw Peter!
        When did you meet him?
        Merrily, cherrily [so pronounced]
        All fall down.

        A ring, a ring of roses,
        A pocketful of posies—
        Ashem, ashem, all fall down.
                                —Sheffield (S. O. Addy).

(*b*) A ring is formed by the children joining hands. They
all dance round, singing the lines. At the word "Hasher" or
"Atcha" they all raise their hands [still clasped] up and down,
and at "all fall down" they sit suddenly down on the ground.
In Lancashire (Morton) they pause and curtsey deeply. The
imitation of sneezing is common to all. Miss Peacock says, in
Nottinghamshire they say "Hashem! Hashem!" and shake
their heads. In the Sheffield version the children sing the
first eight lines going round, and all fall down when the
eighth is sang. They then form a ring by holding hands, and
move round singing the next three lines, and then they all fall
either on their knees or flat on their faces.

(*c*) Versions of this game, identical with the Winterton one,
have been sent me by Miss Winfield, Nottingham; others, almost
identical with the second Norfolk version, from Monton, Lancashire (Miss Dendy), North Staffs. Potteries, Norbury, Staffs.,
(Miss A. Keary), Earls Heaton, Yorks. (H. Hardy). Addy,
Sheffield Glossary, gives a version almost identical with the
last Sporle version.

Addy, *Sheffield Glossary*, compares the old stories about rose-laughing in Grimm's *Teut. Myth.* iii. 1101. "Gifted children of fortune have the power to laugh roses, as Treyja wept gold. Probably in the first instance they were Pagan beings of light, who spread their brightness in the sky over the earth —'rose children,' 'sun children.'" This seems to me to be a very apposite explanation of the game, the rhymes of which are fairly well preserved, though showing in some of the variants that decay towards a practical interpretation which will soon abolish all traces of the mythical origin of game-rhyme. It may, however, simply be the making, or "ringing," a ring or circle of roses or other flowers and bowing to this. Mr. Addy's suggestion does not account for the imitation of sneezing, evidently an important incident, which runs through all versions. Sneezing has always been regarded as an important or supernatural event in every-day life, and many superstitious beliefs and practices are connected with it both in savage and civilised life. Newell (*Games and Songs of American Children*, p. 127) describes "Ring around the Rosie," apparently this game, but the imitation of sneezing has been lost.

Ring by Ring

> Here we go round by ring, by ring,
>   As ladies do in Yorkshire;
> A curtsey here, a curtsey there,
> A curtsey to the ground, sir.
>   —Hersham, Surrey (*Folk-lore Record*, v. 86).

There is no description of the way this game is played, but it is evidently a similar game to "Ring-a-Ring o' Roses."

Ringie, Ringie, Red Belt

Take a small splint of wood, kindle it, and when it is burning turn it rapidly round in a circle, repeating the words—

> Ringie, ringie, Red Belt, rides wi' the king,
> Nae a penny in's purse t' buy a gold ring.
> Bow—ow—ow, fat dog art thou,
> Tam Tinker's dog, bow—ow—ow.
>   —Corgarff (Rev. W. Gregor).

This goes by the name of "Willie Wogie" at Keith, but no words are repeated as the splint is whirled.

See "Jack's Alive."

Ring-me-rary

    I.   Ring me (1), ring me (2), ring me rary (3),
         As I go round (4) ring by ring (5),
         A virgin (6) goes a-maying (7);
         Here's a flower (8), and there's a flower (9),
         Growing in my lady's garden (10).
         If you set your foot awry (11),
         Gentle John will make you cry (12);
         If you set your foot amiss (13),
         Gentle John (14) will give you a kiss.

         This [lady or gentleman] is none of ours,
         Has put [him or her] self in [child's name] power;
         So clap all hands and ring all bells, and make the
             wedding o'er.
                    —Halliwell's *Nursery Rhymes*, p. 67.

    II.   As I go round ring by ring,
         A maiden goes a-maying;
         And here's a flower, and there's a flower,
         As red as any daisy.
         If you set your foot amiss,
         Gentle John will give you a kiss.
                    —Halliwell's *Nursery Rhymes*, p. 125.

(*b*) A number of boys and girls stand round one in the middle, who repeats the lines, counting the children until one is counted out by the end of the verse. The child upon whom (14) falls is then taken out and forced to select one of the other sex. The middle child then proceeds to say the three last lines. All the children clap hands during the saying (or singing) of the last line. If the child taken by lot joins in the clapping, the selected child is rejected, and, I believe, takes the middle place. Otherwise, I think there is a salute.—Halliwell.

(*c*) This game is recorded by no authority except Halliwell, and no version has reached me, so that I suppose it is now obsolete. It is a very good example of the oldest kind of game, choosing partners or lovers by the "lot," and may be a relic of the May-day festival, when the worship of Flora was accompanied by rites of marriage not in accord with later ideas.

Ring-taw

A rough ring is made on the ground, and the players each place in it an equal share in "stonies," or alleys. They each bowl to the ring with another marble from a distance. The boy whose marble is nearest has the first chance to "taw;" if he misses a shot the second boy, whose marble was next nearest to the ring, follows, and if he misses, the next, and so on. If one player knocks out a marble, he is entitled to "taw" at the rest in the ring until he misses; and if a sure "tawer" not one of the others may have the chance to taw. Any one's "taw" staying within the ring after being tawn at the "shots," is said to be "fat," and the owner of the "taw" must then replace any marbles he has knocked out in the ring. — Earls Heaton, Yorks. (Herbert Hardy). Halliwell (*Dictionary*) describes this game very much as above, except that a fine is imposed on those who leave the taw in the ring. Ross and Stead (*Holderness Glossary*) give this game as follows: — "Two boys place an equal number of marbles in the form of a circle, which are then shot at alternately, each boy pocketing the marbles he hits." Addy (*Sheffield Glossary*) says, "Ring - taw" is a marble marked with a red ring used in the game of marbles. This is commonly called "ring" for short. Evans (*Leicestershire Glossary*) describes the game much the same as above, but adds some further details of interest. "If the game be knuckle-up the player stands and shoots in that position. If the game be knuckle-down he must stoop and shoot with the knuckle of the first finger touching the ground at taw. In both cases, however, the player's toe must be on taw. The line was thus called taw as marking the place for the toe of the player, and the marble a taw as being the one shot from the taw-line, in contradistinction to those placed passively in the ring-'line' in the one case, and 'marble' in the other being dropped as superfluous."—Strutt (*Sports and Pastimes*, p. 384) alludes to the game.

In Ireland this game is also called "Ring," and is played with marbles and buttons. A ring is marked out on a level hard place, and every boy puts down a button. The buttons are lightly struck in the centre of the ring, and all play their marbles to the buttons. The nearest to them play first. The line from which they play is generally about eight feet away, and everybody does his best to strike the buttons. Any put out are kept by the boy putting them out, and if a boy strikes a button, or buttons, out, he can play on until he misses.— Waterville, Cos. Kerry and Cork, T. J. Dennachy (through Mrs. B. B. Green of Dublin).

Rin-im-o'er

A game among children, in which one stands in the middle of a street, road, or lane, while others run across it within a certain given distance from the person so placed, and whose business it is to catch one in passing, when he is released, and the captive takes his place.—Teviotdale (Jamieson's *Dictionary*).

It nearly resembles "Willie Wastle."

Robbing the Parson's Hen-Roost

This game is played by every player, except one (the questioner), choosing a word, and introducing it into his phrase whenever he gives an answer. For example, X, Y, and Z have chosen the words elephant, key-hole, and mouse-trap.

Questioner. "What did you steal from the parson's hen-roost?"

X. "An elephant."

Q. "How did you get into the hen-roost?"

Y. "Through the key-hole."

Q. "Where did you put what was stolen?"

Z. "Into a mouse-trap."

And so on with the other players.—Lincoln [generally known] (Miss M. Peacock).

The players choose a name, and another player asks them questions, beginning with, "The Parson's hen-roost was robbed last night, were you there?" To all questions each player must answer by repeating his own name only: if he forgets and says, "Yes" or "No," he has to take the questioner's place.—Haxey, Lincolnshire (Mr. C. C. Bell).

Rockety Row

A play in which two persons stand with their backs to each other, one passing his arms under the shoulders of the other, they alternately lift each other from the ground.—Jamieson's *Dictionary*.

See "Bag o' Malt," "Weigh the Butter."

Roll up Tobacco

See "Bulliheisle," "Eller Tree," "Wind up the Bush Faggot."

Roly-poly

A game played with a certain number of pins and a ball, resembling half a cricket ball. One pin is placed in the centre, the rest (with the exception of one called the Jack) are placed in a circle round it; the Jack is placed about a foot or so from the circle, in a line with the one in the circle and the one in the centre. The centre one is called the King, the  one between that and the Jack, the Queen. The King counts for three, the Queen two, and each of the other pins for one each, except Jack. The art of the game lies in bowling down all the pins except Jack, for if Jack is bowled down, the player has just so many deducted from his former score as would have been added if he had not struck the Jack (Holloway's *Dict. Provincialisms*). This game was formerly called "Half-bowl," and was prohibited by a statute of Edward IV. (Halliwell's *Dictionary*). Brockett (*North Country Words and*

Phrases) says it is a game played at fairs and races. It is, under the name of "Kayles," well described and illustrated by Strutt (*Sports and Pastimes*, p. 270, 271), which is reproduced here. It will be seen that Jamieson describes it as played with a pole or cudgel. He says this game no doubt gave origin to the modern one of "Nine-pins;" though primitively the Kayle-pins do not appear to have been confined to any certain number nor shape. . . . The Kayle-pins appear to have been placed in one row only. He also says that "Half-bowl," played in Hertfordshire, was called "Roly-poly."

Jamieson (*Dictionary*) gives this as "Rollie-poly," a game of nine-pins, called also *Kayles*. The name "Rollie-poly" was given to it because it was played with a pole, or cudgel, by which the pins were knocked over. In the West of Scotland, where this game was in great repute in olden times, it formed one of the chief sports of Fastern's-e'en, and was a favourite amusement at fairs and races. The awards for successful throwing were generally in the form of small cakes of ginger-bread, which were powerful incentives to the game, and never failed to attract players in response to the cry, "Wha'll try the lucky Kayles?"

Ronin the Bee

A rude game. A cazzie, or cassie, is unexpectedly thrown over the head of a person. When thus blindfolded he is pressed down, and buckets of water are thrown upon the cassie till the victim is thoroughly saturated.—Jamieson's *Dictionary*.

See "Carrying the Queen a Letter," "Ezzeka."

Rosy Apple, Lemon and Pear

—Sporle, Norfolk (Miss Matthews).

I. Rosy apple, lemon, or pear,
Bunch of roses she shall wear;
Gold and silver by her side,
I know who will be the bride.
  Take her by her lily-white hand,
  Lead her to the altar;
  Give her kisses,—one, two, three,—
  Mrs. (child's name) daughter.
          —Hersham, Surrey (*Folk-lore Record*, v. 58).

II. Rosy apple, lemon, and pear,
A bunch of roses she shall wear;
Gold and silver by her side,
Choose the one shall be her bride.
  Take her by her lily-white hand,
  Lead her to the altar;
  Give her kisses,—one, two, three,—
  To old mother's runaway daughter.
—Symondsbury, Dorsetshire (*Folk-lore Journal*, vii. 210).

III. Rosy apple, lemon, and a pear,
A bunch of ribbons she shall wear;
Gold and silver by her side,
I know who will be her bride.

Take her by the lily-white hand,
Lead her over the water;
Give her kisses,—one, two, three,—
For Mrs. ——— daughter.
            —Maxey, Northants. (Rev. W. D. Sweeting).

IV.   Rosy apple, lemon, and a pear,
      Bunch of roses you shall wear;
      Gold and silver by your side,
      I know who shall be a bride.
        Take her by the lily-white hand,
        Lead her 'cross the water;
        Give her kisses,—one, two, three,—
        For Mrs. (So-and-so's) daughter.
                      —Deptford, Kent (Miss Chase).

V.   Rosie had an apple and a pear,
      A bunch of roses she shall wear;
      Gold and silver by her side,
      I knows who shall be her bride.
        Take her by the lily-white hand,
        Lead her across the water;
        Give her a kiss, and one, two, three,
        Old Mother Sack-a-biddy's daughter!
                      —Ogbourne, Wilts. (H. S. May).

VI.   Rosy apples, mellow pears,
      Bunch of roses she shall wear;
      Gold and silver by her side,
      Tell me who shall be her bride.
        Take her by her lily-white hand,
        Lead her across the ocean;
        Give her a kiss, and one, two, three,
        Mrs. ——— daughter.
                      —Sporle, Norfolk (Miss Matthews).

VII. A rosy apple, lemon, and a pear,
      A bunch of roses she shall wear;
      Gold and silver by your side,
      Choose the one to be your bride.

Take her by her lily-white hand,
Lead her to the altar;
Give her a kiss by one, two, three,
Mrs. ——— daughter.
                —Cowes, I. of Wight (Miss E. Smith).

VIII. Roses up, and roses down,
Roses in the garden;
I wadna gie ye a bunch o' flowers
For tenpence halfpenny farden.
  Take her by the lily-white hand,
  Lead her across the water;
  Gie her a kiss, and one, two, three,
  For she's a lady's daughter.
                —Berwickshire (A. M. Bell) *Antiquary*, xxx. 16.

IX. Maggie Littlejohn, fresh and fair,
A bunch of roses in her hair;
Gold and silver by her side,
I know who is her bride.
  Take her by the lily-white hand,
  Lead her over the water;
  Give her kisses,—one, two, three,—
  For she's a lady's daughter.
  Roses up, and roses down,
  And roses in the garden;
  I widna give a bunch of roses
  For twopence ha'penny farthing.
                —Rev. W. Gregor.

X. Roses up, and roses down,
And roses in the garden;
I widna gie a bunch o' roses
For tippence ha'penny farden.
So and so, fresh and fair,
A bunch o' roses she shall wear;
Gold and silver by her side,
Crying out, " Cheese and bride " (bread).

Take her by the lily-white hand,
Lead her on the water;
Give her kisses,—one, two, three,—
For she's her mother's daughter.

—Fraserburgh (Rev. W. Gregor).

XI.   Roses up, and roses down,
And roses in the garden;
I wadna gie a bunch o' roses
For twopence ha'penny farthin'.
———, fresh and fair,
A bunch of roses she shall wear;
Gold and silver by her side,
I know who's her bride.
Take her by the lily-white hand,
And lead her o'er the water;
And give her kisses,—one, two, three,—
For she's the princess' daughter.

—Cullen (Rev. W. Gregor).

XII.   Maggie Black, fresh and fair,
A bunch of roses she shall wear;
I know who I'll take.
Give her kisses,—one, two, three,—
For she's a lady's daughter.
Roses in, and roses out,
Roses in a garden;
I would not give a bunch of roses
For twopence halfpenny " farden."

—Nairn (Rev. W. Gregor).

(c) The players form a ring, one child stands in the centre,
who chooses a sweetheart from the ring when the fifth line
is sung; the two kiss, the first child takes her place in the
ring, the second child remains in the centre, and the game
begins again. This is the method adopted in most of the
versions. The Symondsbury game is slightly different; the
first part is the same, but when the last line is sung the child
who was first in the middle must run away and take a place
in the ring as soon as she can. The second one remains in

the centre.   The Maxey (Northants.) version is altogether different.   All the children but one stand in a row.   The one
stands in front of them and sings the lines by herself; at
the last line she selects one from the line by naming her.
These two then sing the lines, "swinging round," so described
by Mr. Sweeting's informant.   They then select a third when
singing the last line, and the three then swing round.   This
is repeated till all the children from the line come into the
ring.

In the Scotch versions the players all stand in a line, with
one in front, and sing.   At the end of the fourth line the one
in front chooses one from the line, and all again sing, mentioning the name of the one chosen (Fraserburgh).   At Cullen,
one child stands out of the line and goes backwards and
forwards singing, then chooses her partner, and the two go
round the line singing.

(d) A version which I collected in Barnes is not so perfect
as those given here, only the four first lines being sung.   A
Kentish version sent me by Miss Broadwood is almost identical with the Deptford game.   Miss Broadwood's version
commences—

Rosy apple, miller, miller, pear.

An Ipswich version is almost identical with that of Hersham,
Surrey (Lady C. Gurdon's *Suffolk County Folk-lore*, p. 64),
except that it begins "Golden apple" and ends with the
marriage formula—

Now you're married, I wish you joy,
Father and mother you must obey;
Love one another like sister and brother,
And now's the time to kiss away.

(e) This game is probably derived from the mode of dressing
the bride in the marriage ceremony, and is not very ancient.
The line "Lead her to the altar" probably indicates the earliest
version, corrupted later into "Lead her across the water," and
this would prove a comparatively modern origin.   If, however,
the "altar" version is a corruption of the "water" version, the
game may go back to the pre-Christian marriage ceremony, but
of this there is little evidence.

Roundabout, or Cheshire Round

This is danced by two only, one of each sex; after leading off into the middle of an imaginary circle, and dancing a short time opposite to each other, the one strives by celerity of steps in the circumference of the circle to overtake and chase the other round it; the other in the meantime endeavouring to maintain an opposite situation by equal celerity in receding.— Roberts' *Cambrian Popular Antiquities*, p. 46.

Halliwell gives Round, a kind of dance. " The round dance, or the dancing of the rounds."—*Nomenclator*, 1585, p. 299. There was a sort of song or ballad also so called.—*Dict. Provincialisms*.

Round and Round the Village

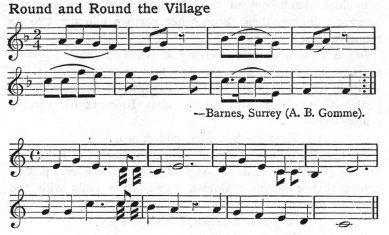

—Barnes, Surrey (A. B. Gomme).

—Hanbury, Staff. (Edith Hollis).

I.   Round and round the village,
      Round and round the village;
      Round and round the village,
      As we have done before.

      In and out the windows,
      In and out the windows;
      In and out the windows,
      As we have done before.

Stand and face your lover,
Stand and face your lover;
Stand and face your lover,
As we have done before.

Follow her to London,
Follow her to London;
Follow her to London,
As we have done before.

Kiss her before you leave her,
Kiss her before you leave her;
Kiss her before you leave her,
As we have done before.

—Barnes, Surrey (taken down from children
of village school—A. B. Gomme).

II. Round and round the village,
Round and round the village;
Round and round the village,
As you have done before.

In and out the window,
In and out the window;
In and out the window,
As you have done before.

Stand and face your lover,
Stand and face your lover;
Stand and face your lover,
As you have done before.

—Deptford, Kent (Miss Chase).

III. Round and round the village,
In and out of the window;
Stand and face your lover,
As you have done before.

Stand and face your lover,
Stand and face your lover;
Oh, stand and face your lover,
As you have done before.

Follow me to London,
Follow me to London;
Oh, follow me to London,
As you have done before.
—Wakefield, Yorks. (Miss Fowler).

IV. Round and round the village,
In and out of the window;
Stand and face your lover,
As you have done before;
Oh, stand and face your lover,
As you have done before, O.

Follow me to London,
Follow me to London;
Follow me to London,
As you have done before.
—Winterton and Bottesford, Lincolnshire
(Miss M. Peacock).

V. Round and round the village,
Round and round the village;
Round and round the village,
As you have done before.

In and out the windows,
In and out the windows;
In and out the windows,
As you have done before.

Stand and face your lover,
Stand and face your lover;
Stand and face your lover,
As you have done before.

Shake hands with your lover,
Shake hands with your lover;
Shake hands with your lover,
As you have done before.
—From girls of Clapham High School
(Miss F. D. Richardson).

VI. Out and in the villages,
    Out and in the villages ;
    Out and in the villages,
    As you have done before.
    Out and in the windows,
    Out and in the windows ;
    Out and in the windows,
    As you have done before.
    Stand before your lover,
    Stand before your lover ;
    Stand before your lover,
    As you have done before.
             —Cullen (Rev. W. Gregor).

VII. Go round and round the village,
    Go round and round the village,
      As we have done before.

    Go in and out the window,
    Go in and out the window,
      As we have done before.

    Come in and face your lover,
    Come in and face your lover,
      As we have done before.

    I measure my love to show you,
    I measure my love to show you,
      As we have done before.

    I kneel because I love you,
    I kneel because I love you,
      As we have done before.

    Follow me to London,
    Follow me to London,
      As we have done before.

    Back again to Westerham,
    Back again to Westerham,
      As we have done before.
         —Crockham Hill, Kent (Miss Chase).

VIII. Walking round the village,
       Walking round the village;
       Walking round the village,
           As we have done before.

       In and out the windows,
       In and out the windows;
       In and out the windows,
           As you have done before.

       Stand and face your lover,
       Stand and face your lover;
       Stand and face your lover,
           As you have done before.

       Now they go off courting,
       Now they go off courting;
       Now they go off courting,
           As they have done before.

       Chase her back to Scotland,
       Chase her back to Scotland;
       Chase her back to Scotland,
           As you have done before.
                   —Penzance, Cornwall (Mrs. Mabbott).

IX.   Round about the village,
      Round about the village;
      Round about the village,
      As you have done before.

      In and out of the windows,
      In and out of the windows;
      In and out of the windows,
      As you have done before.

      I stand before my lover,
      I stand before my lover;
      I stand before my lover,
      As I have done before.

Follow me to London,
Follow me to London;
Follow me to London,
As you have done before.

Dance away to Fairyland,
Dance away to Fairyland;
Dance away to Fairyland,
As we have done before.
　　—Stevenage, Herts. (Mrs. Lloyd, taught to a
　　friend's children by a nurse from Stevenage).

X. All round the village,
All round the village;
All round the village,
As we have done before.

In and out of the window,
In and out of the window;
In and out of the window,
As we have done before.

Stand and face your lover,
Stand and face your lover;
Stand and face your lover,
As we have done before.

Kiss her if you love her,
Kiss her if you love her;
Kiss her if you love her,
As we have done before.

Take her off to London,
Take her off to London;
Take her off to London,
As we have done before.
　　　—Earls Heaton, Yorks. (Herbert Hardy).

XI. All round the village,
All round the village;
All round the village,
As you have done before.

In and out the windows,
In and out the windows ;
In and out the windows,
As you have done before.

Stand and face your lover,
Stand and face your lover;
Stand and face your lover,
As you have done before.

Follow her to London,
Follow her to London ;
Follow her to London,
As you have done before.

—Tean, North Staffs. (from a Monitor in
the School).

XII.   Round and round the village, &c.,
As you have done before.

In and out the windows, as you have done before.

Stand and face your lover, &c.

Follow me to London, &c.

—Roxton, St. Neots (Miss E. Lumley).

XIII.   Out and in the windows,
Out and in the windows ;
Out and in the windows,
As you have done before.

Stand before your lover,
Stand before your lover;
Stand before your lover,
As you have done before.

Follow her to London,
Follow her to London ;
Follow her to London,
Before the break of day.

—Fraserburgh (Rev. W. Gregor).

XIV.   In and out of the window,
       In and out of the window;
       In and out of the window,
          As you have done before.

       Stand and face your lover,
       Stand and face your lover;
       Stand and face your lover,
          As you have done before.

       Give me a kiss, my darling,
       Give me a kiss, my darling;
       Give me a kiss, my darling,
          As you have done before.

       Follow me to London,
       Follow me to London;
       Follow me to London,
          As you have done before.
              —Hanbury, Staffordshire (Miss E. Hollis).

XV.   Marching round the ladies,
Marching round the ladies, as you have done before.
In and out the windows,
In and out the windows, as you have done before.
Stand and face your lover,
Stand and face your lover, as you have done before.
Follow me to London,
Follow me to London, as you have done before.
Bring me back to Belfast,
Bring me back to Belfast, as you have done before.
              —Belfast, Ireland (W. R. Patterson).

XVI.   Come gather again on the old village green,
Come young and come old, who once children have been.
Such frolics and games as ne'er before were seen,
We join in riots and play [? riotous].
Take her off to London,
Take her off to London,
Take her off to London.

In and out the windows,
In and out the windows ;
In and out the windows,
As you have gone before.

Round about the village,
Round about the village ;
Round about the village,
As you have gone before.

Soon we will get married,
Soon we will get married ;
Soon we will get married,
And never more depart.

—Sporle, Norfolk (Miss Matthews).

XVII.   Three jolly sailor boys
Lately come ashore,
Spend their time in drinking lager wine,
As they have done before.

We go round, and round, and round,
As we have done before ;
And this is a girl, and a very pretty girl,
A kiss for kneeling there.

Go in and out the window,
Go in and out the window ;
Go in and out the window,
   As we have done before.

Follow me to London,
Follow me to London ;
Follow me to London,
   As we have done before.

Go back and face your lover,
Go back and face your lover ;
Go back and face your lover,
   As we have done before.

—Brigg (from a Lincolnshire friend of Miss J. Barker).

XVIII. Up and down the valley,
       Up and down the valley ;
       Up and down the valley,
          As I have done before.

       In and out the window,
       In and out the window;
       In and out the window,
          As I have done before.

       Stand and face your lover,
       Stand and face your lover ;
       Stand and face your lover,
          As I have done before.

       Follow me to London,
       Follow me to London ;
       Follow me to London,
          As I have done before.
             —Settle, Yorks. (Rev. W. S. Sykes).

XIX. In and out the willows,
       In and out the willows ;
       In and out the willows,
          As you have done before.

       Stand and face your lover,
       Stand and face your lover ;
       Stand and face your lover,
          As you have done before.

       Follow me to London,
       Follow me to London ;
       Follow me to London,
          As you have done before.
      —West Grinstead, Sussex (*Notes and Queries*,
           8th Series, i. 249, Miss Busk).

(*c*) The children join hands and form a ring with one child standing outside. The ring stands perfectly still throughout this game and sings the verses, the action being confined to at first one child, and then to two together. During the singing of the first verse the outside child dances round the ring on the outside. When the ring commences to sing the second verse the children hold up their arms to form arches, and the child who has been running round outside runs into the ring under one pair of joined hands, and out again under the next pair of arms, continuing this "in and out" movement until the third verse is commenced. The child should try and run in and

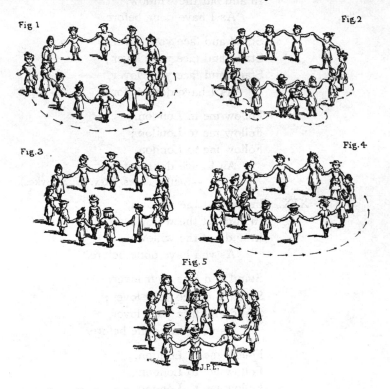

out under all the joined hands. At the third verse the child stops in the ring and stands facing one, whom she chooses for her lover, until the end of the verse ; the chosen child then leaves the ring, followed by the first child, and they walk round the ring, or they walk away a little distance, returning at the commencement of next verse. In the first three versions the second child is chased back and caught by the first child. In the Clapham version the two shake hands in the last verse.

The Barnes version has kissing for its finale. The Hanbury also has kissing, but it precedes the following to London. In the Brigg, Lincolnshire (Miss Barker), a child stands in the middle and points with her finger to each one she passes ; finally selects one, who leaves the ring and kneels in front of the girl in the middle. At the end of the second verse the kneeling child gets up and the first child goes in and out under the arms of the players, followed by the other. At the fourth they reverse and go back under the arms in the opposite direction, finally stopping in the middle of the ring, when another child is chosen and the first one in goes out. In the Winterton and Bottesford versions (Miss Peacock), at the words "Stand and face your lover," the child who has been going "in and out" stands before the one she chooses, beckons to her, and sings the next verse. Then the chosen one chases her until she can catch her. In the Crockham Hill version (Miss Chase) the love is measured out with a handker-chief three times, and after kneeling in the road, the chosen partner follows round the ring and reverses for the return.

(d) The analysis of the game-rhymes is on pp. 134–39. This shows that we are dealing with a game which repre-sents a village, and also the houses in it. The village only disappears in six out of the twenty versions. In three of these (Hanbury, Fraserburgh, and West Grinstead) the line has gone altogether. In the fourth (Lincolnshire) it becomes "Round and round and round," no mention being made of the village. In the fifth (Belfast) the line has become "Marching round the ladies." In the sixth (Settle) it has become "Up and down the valley," which also occurs in another imperfect version, of which a note was sent me by Miss Matthews from the Forest of Dean, where the line has become "Round and round the valley." The substitution of "ladies" for "village" is very significant as evidence that the game, like all its compeers, is in a declining stage, and is, therefore, not the invention of modern times. The idea of a circle of children representing a village would necessarily be the first to die out if the game was no longer supported by the influence of any custom it might represent. The line of decadence

No.	Cornwall, Penzance.	Kent, Crockham Hill.	Herts, Stevenage.	Yorks, Earls Heaton.	N. Staffordshire, Tean.	Surrey, Clapham.	Lincolnshire.
1.	—	—	—	—	—	—	Three jolly sailor boys.
2.	Walking round the village.	Go round and round the village.	Round about the village.	All round the village	All round the village.	Round and round the village.	—
3.	—	—	—	—	—	—	—
4.	—	—	—	—	—	—	We go round and round and round.
5.	—	—	—	—	—	—	
6.	—	—	—	—	—	—	—
7.	As we have done before.	As we have done before. —	As you have done before.	As we have done before. —	As you have done before.	As you have done before.	As we have done before.
8.	—	—	—	—	—	—	And this a girl and a very pretty girl.
9.	—	—	—	—	—	—	A kiss for kneeling here.
10.	In and out the windows. —	Go in and out the windows.	In and out of the windows.	In and out of the window.	In and out the window.	In and out the window.	Go in and out the window.
11.		—	—				
12.	As you have done before.	As we have done before.	As you have done before.	As we have done before. —	As you have done before.	As you have done before.	As we have done before. —
13.	Stand and face your lover.	—	Stand before my lover.	Stand and face your lover.	Stand and face your lover.	Stand and face your lover.	—
14.	—	Come in and face your lover.	—	—	—	—	—
15.	—	—	—	—	—	—	Go back and face your lover.
16.	As you have done before.	As we have done before.	As I have done before.	As we have done before.	As you have done before.	As you have done before.	As we have done before.

No.							
17.	Now they go off courting.						
18.		I measure my love to show you.					
19.				Kiss her if you love her.		Shake hands with your lover.	
20.							
21.							
22.							
23.	As they have done before.	As we have done before.		As we have done before.		As you have done before.	
24.		I kneel because I love you.					
25.		As we have done before.					
26.	Chase her back to Scotland.						
27.		Follow me to London.	Follow me to London.		Follow her to London.		Follow me to London.
28.				Take her off to London.			
29.	As you have done before.	As we have done before.	As you have done before.	As we have done before.	As you had done before.		
30.							
31.		Back again to Westerham.					
32.			Dance away to fairyland.				
33.							
34.		As we have done before.	As we have done before.				As we have done before.

No.	Surrey, Barnes.	Norfolk, Sporle.	Staffordshire, Hanbury.	Belfast.	Wakefield	Lincolnshire, Winterton.	Deptford.
1.	—	Come gather again on the old village green.	—	—	—	—	—
2.	Round and round the village.	Round about the village.	—	—	Round and round the village,	Round and round the village.	Round and round the village.
3.	—	—	—	—	—	—	—
4.	—	—	—	—	—	—	—
5.	—	—	—	—	—	—	—
6.	—	—	—	Marching round the ladies,	—	—	—
7.	As we have done before.	As you have done before.	—	As you have done before.	—	—	As you have done before.
8.	—	—	—	—	—	—	—
9.	—	—	—	—	—	—	—
10.	In and out the windows,	In and out the windows,	In and out of the windows,	In and out windows,	In and out of the window.	In and out of the window,	In and out the windows.
11.	—	—	—	—	—	—	—
12.	As we have done before,	As you have done before,	As you have done before.	As you have done before.	—	—	As you have done before.
13.	Stand and face your lover.	—	Stand and face your lover.	Stand and face your lover.	Stand and face your lover.	Stand and face your lover.	Stand and face your lover.
14.	—	—	—	—	—	—	—
15.	—	—	—	—	—	—	—
16.	As we have done before.	—	As you have done before.	As you have done before.	As you have done before,	As you have done before.	As you have done before.

Follow me to London.
As you have done before.

Follow me to London,
As you have done before.

Follow me to London, ...
As you have done before.
Bring me back to Belfast.
As you have done before.

Give me a kiss, my darling,
As you have done before.
Follow me to London.
As you have done before.

Soon we will get married.
Take her off to London.

17.
18.
19. Kiss her before you leave her.
20.
21.
22.
23. As we have done before.
24.
25.
26.
27. Follow her to London.
28.
29. As we have done before.
30.
31.
32.
33.
34.

No.	Cullen.	Roxton.	Fraserburgh.	Settle.	West Grinstead.
1.	—	—	—	—	—
2.	—	Round and round the village.	·	—	—
3.	Out and in the villages.	—	—	Up and down the valley.	—
4.	—	—	—	—	—
5.	—	—	—	—	—
6.	—	—	—	—	—
7.	As you have done before.	As you have done before.	—	As I have done before.	—
8.	—	—	—	—	—
9.	—	—	—	—	—
10.	Out and in the windows.	In and out the windows.	Out and in the windows.	In and out the window.	In and out the windows.
11.	—	—	—	—	—
12.	As you have done before.	As you have done before.	As you have done before.	As I have done before.	As you have done before.
13.	Stand before your lover.	Stand and face your lover.	Stand before your lover.	Stand and face your lover.	Stand and face your lover.
14.	—	—	—	—	—
15.	—	—	—	—	—
16.	—	—	As you have done before.	As I have done before.	As you have done before.

Follow me to London.

As you have done before.

Follow me to London.

As I have done before.

Follow her to London.

Before the break of day.

Follow me to London.

17. 18. 19. 20. 21. 22. 23. 24. 25. 26. 27. 28. 29. 30. 31. 32. 33. 34.

becomes in this way an important argument for the discovery of the original form.

The next incident, No. 10 of the analysis, goes through all the games except one (West Grinstead), where the very obvious corruption of "willows" for "windows" occurs. This incident takes us to the houses of the village; and thus the two lines show us a procession, first, going round outside the boundary of the village, and, secondly, proceeding in serpentine fashion through the houses. Incident 13 has a few variations which do not point to anything more than verbal alteration, due to the changes which have occurred in the conception of the game. Incidents 17 to 22 are not constant to all the versions, and their variations are of an unimportant character. Incident 27 is an important element in the game. The prevalence of London as the place of assignation is probably due to the influence of that city in the popular mind; but the real significance seems to be that the lover-husband follows his bride to her own village. In only two versions is this incident varied (No. 28) to indicate that the husband took his wife with him, and only three versions have dropped out the incident altogether.

Abnormal incidents occur in only seven versions, and they are not of great significance. The Lincolnshire and Sporle versions have a line of general introduction (No. 1) before the game proper begins. Incidents 8 and 9 occur only in the Lincolnshire version, and do not disturb the general movement beyond indicating that the game has become, or is becoming, an indoor game. Incident 21 is obviously a modern line. Nos. 26 and 31 suggest a chase after a fugitive pair which, as they do not occur in other versions, must be considered as later introductions, belonging, however, to the period when runaway marriages were more frequent than they are now, and thus taking us back to, at least, the beginning of this century; while the significant and pretty variant No. 32 shows that the game has lost touch with the actual life of the people. No. 30 in the Fraserburgh version has a suspicious likeness to a line in the American song "I'm off to Charlestown," but as it occurs only in this one version it cannot count as an important element in the history of the game.

(*e*) Miss Matthews notes a Forest of Dean version. The children form a ring, singing, " Round and round the valley, where we have been before," while one child walks round the outside. Then they stand with uplifted hands, joined together, and sing, " In and out of the windows, as we have done before," while the child threads her way in and out of the ring. Then they sing, " Stand and face your lover, as we have done before ; " the child then stands in the centre of the ring and faces some one, whom she afterwards touches, and who succeeds her. A version from North Derbyshire (Mr. S. O. Addy) is practically the same as the Tean, North Staffs. version, except that the third verse is " Run to meet your lover," instead of " Stand and face your lover." The first child, during the singing of the third verse, walks round outside the ring, and touches one she chooses, who then runs away. While the fourth verse is being sung she is chased and caught, and the game begins again with the second child walking round the village. So far as Lancashire is concerned, Miss Dendy says, " I have no good evidence as yet that it is a Lancashire play. I think it has been imported here by board-school mistresses from other counties."

(*f*) The burden of this game-rhyme is undoubtedly the oldest part that has been preserved to modern times. It runs through all the versions without exception, though variations in the other lines is shown by the analysis to occur. The words of the line, " As we have done before," convey the idea of a recurring event, and inasmuch as that event is undoubtedly marriage, it seems possible to suggest that we have here a survival of the periodical village festival at which marriages took place. If the incidents in the game compare closely with incidents in village custom, the necessary proof will be supplied, and we will first examine how far the words of the rhyme and the action of the game supply us with incidents ; and, secondly, how far these incidents have been kept up in the village custom.

There is nothing in the words to suggest that the incidents which the game depicts belong to a fixed time, but it is an important fact that they are alluded to as having previously taken place. If, then, we have eventually to compare the game with a fixed periodical custom, we can at least say that the rhymes, though not suggesting this, do not oppose it.

This game belongs to the group of "custom games." The first characteristic which suggests this is that the children, who join hands and form a circle, are always stationary, and do not move about as in dance games. To the minds of the children who play the game, each child in the circle represents something other than human beings, and this "something" is indicated in the first and second verses, which speak of the "windows," of houses, and a journey round "a village." In this game, too, the children, who thus represent a village, also act as "chorus," for they describe in the words they sing the various actions of those who are performing their parts, as in the game of "Old Roger."

With this evidence from the game itself, without reference to anything outside, it is possible to turn to custom to ascertain if there is anything still extant which might explain the origin of the game. Children copy the manners and customs of their elders. If they saw a custom periodically and often practised with some degree of ceremonial and importance, they would in their own way act in play what their elders do seriously.

Such a custom is the perambulation of boundaries, often associated with festive dances, courtship, and marriage. More particularly indicative of the origin of the game is the Helston Furry Dance—"About the middle of the day the people collect together to dance hand-in-hand round the streets, to the sound of the fiddler playing a particular tune, which they continue to do till it is dark. This is called a 'Faddy.' In the afternoon the gentility go to some farmhouse in the neighbourhood to drink tea, syllabab, &c., and return in a morrice-dance to the town, where they form a Faddy and dance through the streets till it is dark, claiming a right of going through any person's house, in at one door and out at the other."—*Gent. Mag. Lib. Manners and Customs*, p. 217. "In one, if not more, of the villages," says Mr. Gregor (*Folk-lore N.E. Scotland*, p. 98), "when the marriage takes place in the home of the bride the whole of the marriage party makes the circuit of the village."

In South-Eastern Russia, on the eve of marriage the bride goes the round of the village, throwing herself on her knees before the head of each house. In an Indian custom the bride and bridegroom are conveyed in a particular "car" around the village.—Gomme, *Folk-lore Relics*, pp. 214, 215. According to Valle, a sixteenth century traveller, "At night the married couples passed by, and, according to their mode, went round about the city with a numerous company.—Valle's *Travels in India* (Hakluyt Soc.), p. 31.*

In these marriage customs there is ample evidence to suggest that the Indo-European marriage-rite contained just such features as are represented in this game, and the changes from rite to popular custom, from popular custom to children's game, do much to suggest consideration of the evidence that folk-lore supplies.

This game is not mentioned by Halliwell or Chambers, nor, so far as I am aware, has it been previously printed or recorded in collections of English games. It appears in America as "Go round and round the Valley" (Newell, *Games*, p. 128).

See "Thread the Needle."

Round and Round went the Gallant Ship

I. Round and round went the gallant, gallant ship,
    And round and round went she;
    Round and round went the gallant, gallant ship,
    Till she sank to the bottom of the sea, the sea, the sea,
    Till she sank to the bottom of the sea.
All go down as the ship sinks.   —Cullen (Rev. W. Gregor).

II. Three times round goes our gallant ship,
    And three times round went she;
    Three times round went our gallant ship,
    Then she sank to the bottom of the sea.
As the players all "bob" down they cry out "the sea, the sea, the sea."   —Aberdeen Training College
    (Rev. W. Gregor).

---

* Among the Ovahereri tribe, at the end of the festive time, the newly-married pair take a walk to visit all the houses of the "Werst." The husband goes first and the wife closely follows him.—*South African Folk-lore Journal*, i. 50.

Round Tag

A large ring is formed, two deep, with wide right and left hand intervals between each couple, and one child stands in the ring and another outside. When the play begins the child in the middle runs and places herself in front of one of the groups of two, thus forming a group of three. Thereupon the third child, that is, the one standing on the outer ring, has to run and try to get a place in front of another two before the one outside the ring can catch her. Then she who is at the back of this newly-formed three must be on the alert not to be caught, and must try in her turn to gain

a front place. The one catching has all along to keep outside the ring, but those trying to escape her may run in and out and anywhere; whoever is caught has to take the catcher's place.—Sporle, Norfolk (Miss Matthews).

This game, called "Short Terrace" at East Kirkby, is played in the same way as that described from Sporle, with the exception that three players stand together instead of one in the centre to start the game. The player who stands immediately outside the circle is called the "clapper;" it is his object to *hit* the player who stands behind two others.—East Kirkby, Lincolnshire (Miss K. Maughan).

"Twos and Threes" is the name by which this game is

known in Hampshire, Monton in Lancashire (Miss Dendy), and other places. It is played in precisely the same manner as at Sporle.

Halliwell's *Dictionary* says of this game as played in Devon, "A round game, in which they all stand in a ring."

See "Tag."

Rounders

This is a boys' game. A round area is marked out by boundary sticks, and at a chosen point of the boundary the base is fixed. This is marked out independently of the boundary, but inside it. Sides are then chosen. One side are the "ins," and strike the ball; the other side are the "outs," and deliver the ball, scout, and endeavour to get their opponents, the "ins," out as soon as possible. The ball (an indiarubber one) is delivered by the "feeder," by pitching it to a player, who stands inside the base armed with a short stick. The player endeavours to strike the ball as far away as possible from the fielders or scouts. As soon as the ball is struck away he runs from the base to the first boundary stick, then to the second, and so on. His opponents in the meantime secure the ball and endeavour to hit him with it as he is running from stage to stage. If he succeeds in running completely round the boundary before the ball is returned it counts as one rounder. If he is hit he is out of the game. He can stay at any stage in the boundary as soon as the ball is in hand, getting home again when the next player of his own side has in turn hit the ball away. When a ball is returned the feeder can bounce it within the base, and the player cannot then run to any new stage of the boundary until after the ball has again been hit away by another player. If a player misses a ball when endeavouring to strike at it he has two more chances, but at the third failure he is bound to run to the first boundary stick and take his chance of being hit with the ball. If a ball is caught the whole side is out at once; otherwise, the side keeps in until either all the players have been hit out with the ball or until the base is crowned. This can be done by bouncing the ball in the base whenever there is no player there to receive the delivery from the feeder.

When a complete rounder is obtained, the player has the privilege either of counting the rounder to the credit of his side, or of ransoming one of the players who have been hit out, who then takes his part in the game as before. When all but one of the players are "out," this last player in hitting the ball must hit it away so as to be able to make a rounder, and return to the base before his opponents get back the ball to crown the base.

An elaborate form of this game has become the national game of the United States.

Rounds
See "Roundabout."

Row-chow-Tobacco
See "Bulliheisle," "Eller Tree," "Snail Creep," "Wind up the Bush Faggot."

Rowland-Ho
A Christmas game.—Halliwell's *Dictionary*.

Rumps
A game with marbles [undescribed].—Dickinson's *Cumberland Glossary*.

Rusty
A boys' game, exactly the same as "Ships."—Addy's *Sheffield Glossary*.

Sacks
A number of children place their closed fists on top of one another in a pile. The leader asks, pointing to the topmost fist, "What's in that sack?" Answer, Potatoes, or anything the child chooses. The leader tips it off with her finger, saying, "Knock it away," and so to the very undermost fist, when she asks, "What's in this sack?" The answer must be, "Bread and cheese;" and then the following dialogue takes place:—

> Where's my share?
> The mouse eat it.
> Where's the mouse?
> The cat killed it.

> Where's the cat ?
> The dog worried it.
> Where's the dog ?
> The cow tossed it.
> Where's the cow ?
> The butcher killed it.
> Where's the butcher ?
> Behind the door.

And who ever speaks the first word shall get a sound round box on the ear.—Co. Cork (Mrs. B. B. Green).

Saddle the Nag

An equal number of players is chosen on each side. Two chiefs are chosen by lot. One of the chiefs takes his stand by a wall, and all his party bend their backs, joined in a line. One of the opposite side leaps on the back of the one farthest from the one standing at the wall, and tries to make his way over the backs of all the stooping boys, up to the one standing. Those stooping move and wriggle to cast him off, and if they succeed in doing so, he stands aside till all his side have tried. When all have tried and none succeed in crowning the one standing, the sides change. If one or more succeed, then each such has a second chance before the sides change. Each side commonly has six chances. The side that succeeds in oftenest touching the chief's head wins the game.—Dyke (Rev. W. Gregor).

See "Skin the Goatie."

Saggy

A game with marbles [undescribed].—Dickinson's *Cumberland Glossary*.

Sailor Lad

> A sailor lad and a tailor lad,
> And they were baith for me ;
> I wid raither tack the sailor lad,
> And lat the tailor be.

What can a tailor laddie dee
 Bit sit and sew a cloot,
When the bonnie sailor laddie
 Can turn the ship aboot.

He can turn her east, and he can turn her west,
 He can turn her far awa';
He aye tells me t' keep up my hairt
 For the time that he's awa'.

I saw 'im lower his anchor,
 I saw 'im as he sailed;
I saw 'im cast his jacket
 To try and catch a whale.

He skips upon the planestanes,
 He sails upon the sea;
A fancy man wi' a curly pow
 Is aye the boy for me,
 Is aye the boy for me;
A fancy man wi' a curly pow
 Is aye the boy for me.

He daurna brack a biscuit,
 He daurna smoke a pipe;
He daurna kiss a bonnie lass
 At ten o'clock at night.

I can wash a sailor's shirt,
 And I can wash it clean;
I can wash a sailor's shirt,
 And bleach it on the green.
  Come a-rinkle-tinkle, fal-a-la, fal-a-la,
  Aboun a man-o'-war.
      —Rosehearty (Rev. W. Gregor).

A circle is formed by joining hands. They dance round
and sing. Sometimes at Rosehearty two play the game by
the one taking hold of the other's left hand with her right.

Sally go Round the Moon

> Sally go round the moon,
> Sally go round the stars;
> Sally go round the moon
> On a Sunday afternoon.

—Deptford, Kent (Miss E. Chase).

Three or more girls take hold of hands, forming a ring; as they spin round they sing the lines. They then reverse and run round in the other direction with an *O!* or repeat over again.

This game is mentioned in the *Church Reformer*, by the Rev. S. D. Headlam, as one being played at Hoxton, but no account of how the game is played is given.

Sally Water

—Yorkshire (Mr. H. Hardy).

—Lancashire (Miss Dendy).

—Enborne (Miss Kimber).

Welford (Mrs. Stephen Batson).

—Liverpool (Mr. C. C. Bell).

Biddgelert, Wales (Mrs. Williams).

—Nottingham (Miss Youngman).

I. Sally, Sally Water,
   Sprinkle in the pan ;
   Rise, Sally, rise, Sally,
   And choose a young man.
   Choose [or bow] to the east,
   Choose [or bow] to the west,
   And choose [or bow to] the pretty girl [or young man]
   That you love best.

[Another version has :

             Choose for the best one,
             Choose for the worst one,
             Choose for the pretty girl
             That you love best.]

   And now you're married I wish you joy ;
   First a girl and then a boy ;
   Seven years after son and daughter ;
   And now, young people, jump over the water."
                    —Symondsbury, Dorsetshire (*Folk-lore
                                   Journal*, vii. 207).

II.   Sally, Sally Walker, sprinkle water in the pan ;
Rise, Sally, rise, Sally, and seek your young man ;
Turn to the east and turn to the west,
And choose the one that you love best.

Now you're married we wish you joy,
First a girl and then a boy,
Seven years after a son and a daughter,
So young lovers kiss together.
> —Chudleigh Knighton, Devon (Henderson's *Folk-lore
> of the Northern Counties*, p. 27).

III.   Sally, Sally Water,
Sprinkle in the pan ;
Hi ! Sally ; Ho ! Sally,
Choose a young man ;
Choose for the best,
Choose for the worst,
Choose for the very one you love best.

Now you're married we wish you joy,
First a girl and then a boy,
Seven years after sister and brother ;
Kiss each other and come out of the water.
> —Somersetshire, *Notes and Queries*, 8th series,
> i. 249 (Miss R. H. Busk).

IV.   Sally Waters, Sally Waters, come sprinkle in the pan ;
Rise, Sally ; rise, Sally, for a young man !
Choose for the best, choose for the worst,
Choose for the very one you love the best.

Now you are married, we wish you joy ;
First a girl and then a boy,
Seven years afterwards son and daughter ;
Pray, young couple, kiss together.
> —London version (Miss Dendy).

V.   Sally, Sally Walker,
Sprinkling in a pan ;
Rise, Sally ; rise, Sally,
For a young man.

Come, choose from the east,
 Come, choose from the west,
Come, choose out the very one
 That you love best.

Now there's a couple
 Married in joy;
First a girl,
 And then a boy.

Now you're married;
 You must obey
Every word
 Your husband says.

Take a kiss
 And walk away,
And remember the promise
 You've made to-day.
      —Fochabers (Rev. W. M'Gregor).

VI. Sally, Sally Waters,
  Sprinkled in the pan;
  Rise, Sally, rise, Sally,
  For a young man,
  Choose the best and choose the worst,
  And choose the prettiest you love best.
     —Welford, Berks (Mrs. Stephen Batson).

VII. Sally, Sally Wallflower,
  Sprinkled in the pan, &c.,
  Now you're married, &c.,
  On the carpet you shall kneel, &c.
    —*Notes and Queries*, 5th series, iii.

VIII. Sallie, Sallie Waters,
  Sprinkled in a pan;
  Rise, Sallie, rise, Sally,
  Choose a young man.
  Choose the best, and
  Choose the worst, and
  Choose the one that you love best.

Now that you are married,
I'm sure we wish you joy,
First a girl, then a boy ;
Seven years after,
Son and daughter,
Pray, young couple, come kiss together.

        —Enborne, Berks ; Marlborough, Wilts ;
          Lewes, Sussex (Miss Kimber).

IX.   Sally, Sally Waters,
      Sprinkle in a pan ;
      Cry, Sally, cry, Sally,
      For a young man.
      Come choose the worst,
      Come choose the best,
      Come choose the young man
      That you like the best.

      And now you're married
      I wish yer good joy,
      Every year a girl and a boy.
      Come love one another
      Like sister and brother,
      And kiss together for joy.

      Clash the bells,
      Clash the bells.

  —Maxey, Northants ; and Suffolk (Rev. W. D. Sweeting).

X.   Sally, Sally Water, sprinkle in the pan ;
      Rise, Sally, rise, Sally, for a young man.
      Pick and choose, but choose not me,
      Choose the fairest you can see.

      Now Sally is married, we wish her much joy,
      First a girl and then a boy ;
      Seven years after a son and a daughter,
      Please to come and kiss together.

        —Summertown, Oxford (A. H. Franklin in
          Midland Garner, N. S. ii. 32).

XI.   Sally, Sally Waters, sprinkle in the pan;
      Rise, Sally, rise, Sally, for a young man.
      Choose for the worst, choose for the best,[1]
      Choose for the prettiest that you loves best.
      Now you are married, &c.
                —Longcot, Berkshire, (Miss J. Barclay).

XII.   Sally, Sally Waters,
      Sprinkle in a pan;
      Cry, Sally, cry, Sally,
      For a young man.

      Rise up, Sally,
      Dry your tears;
      Choose the one you love the best,
      Sally, my dear.
                —Earls Heaton, Yorks. (Herbert Hardy).

XIII.   Sally, Sally Water, sprinkle in the pan,
      Is not —— a nice young man? and
      Is not (girl's name) as good as he?
      They shall be married if they can agree.
      I went to her house and I dropped a pin,
      I asked if Mrs. —— was in.
      She is not within, she is not without,
      She is up in the garret walking about.
      Down she comes as white as milk,
      With a rose in her bosom as soft as silk.
      She off with her glove and showed me her ring,
      To-morrow, to-morrow the wedding begins.
                —Surrey (*Folk-lore Record*, v. 88).

XIV.   Sally, Sally Walker, come sprinkle your pan,
      For down in the meadows there's a nice young man;
      Rise up, Sally, don't look sad,
      For you shall have a husband, good or bad.

[1] Redruth version—

      Fly for the east, fly for the west,
      Fly for the very one you love best.

On the carpet you shall kneel
Till the grass grows round your feet;
Stand up straightly on your feet,
And choose the one you love so sweet.

Now Sally's married, we wish her joy,
First a girl, then a boy;
If it's a boy, we'll buy him a cap,
If it's a girl, we will buy her a hat.
If one won't do, will buy you two,
If two won't do, will buy you three,
If three won't do, will get you four,
If four won't do, will get no more,
So kiss and shake hands, and come out.
　　　　　　　—Tong, Shropshire (Miss C. F. Keary).

XV.　Sally, Sally Water, come sprinkle your pan (*or* plants),
For down in the meadows there lies a young man.
Rise, Sally, rise, and don't you look sad,
For you shall have a husband, good or bad.
Choose you one, choose you two,
Choose the fairest you can see!

　　The fairest one as I can see,
　　Is *Jenny Wood*, pray come to me!

Now you are married, I wish you good joy,
First a girl and then a boy;
Seven years now, and seven to come,
Take her and kiss her, and send her off home.
　　　　　　　—*Shropshire Folk-lore*, p. 509.

XVI.　Sally, Sally Water (or Slauter),
Come sprinkle in your can,
Why do you get married
To a foolish young man?
Pick the worst, and pick the best,
And pick the one that you love best.

To a nice young man

.   .   .   .

So kiss and say good-bye.
[My informant forgets the rest.]
—Nottinghamshire (Miss M. Peacock).

XVII. Sally Water, Sally Water,
Come sprinkle your can,
Why don't you rise, Sally,
And choose a young man ?
Come choose of the wisest,
Come choose of the best,
Come choose of the young man
That lies in your breast.
—Gloucestershire and Warwickshire (Northall, 378).

XVIII. Sally Water, Sally Water,
Come, sprinkle your can ;
Who do you lie mourning,
All for a young man ?
Come, choose of the wisest,
Come, choose of the best,
Come, choose of the young men
The one you love best.   —Addy's *Sheffield Glossary.*

XIX. Sally, Sally Salter,
Sprinkle in some water ;
Knock it in a mortar,
And send it in a silver saucer
To —— —— door.
—Stixwould, Lincolnshire, seventy years ago
(Miss M. Peacock).

XX. Sally Water, Sally Water,
Springin' in a pan ;
Cry, Sally, cry, Sally,
For a young man ;
Choose for the worst 'un,
Choose for the best 'un,
Choose the little gell 'at you love the best.

Now you're married
I wish you joy;
First a girl, and then a boy;
Seven years after
Son and daughter.
Pray, young couple, come kiss together.
—Wakefield, Yorkshire (Miss Fowler).

XXI. Sally, Sally Water,
Come, water your can,
Such a young lady before a young man;
Rise, Sally Water,
Don't look so sad,
For you shall have a husband, good or bad.

Now you're married we wish you joy;
Father and mother, you need not cry;
Kiss and kiss each other again;
Now we're happy, let's part again.
—Long Itchington, Warwickshire (*Northamptonshire
Notes and Queries*, ii. 105).

XXII. Sally, Sally Slarter,
Sitting by the water,
Crying out and weeping
For a young man.
Rise, Sally, rise,
Dry up your eyes;
Turn to the east,
Turn to the west,
Turn to the young man
That you love the best.
So now you've got married
I hope you'll enjoy
Your sons and your daughters,
So kiss and good-bye.   —Addy's *Sheffield Glossary*.

XXIII. Sally, Sally Walker, sprinkled in a pan;
What did she sprinkle for? for a young man;
Sprinkle, sprinkle, daughter, and you shall have a cow;
I cannot sprinkle, mother, because I don't know how.

Sprinkle, sprinkle, daughter, and you shall have a
    man;
I cannot sprinkle, mother, but I'll do the best I can.
Pick and choose, but don't you pick me;
Pick the fairest you can see.
The fairest one that I can see is ——.   Come to me.
Now you're married I wish you much joy;
Your father and mother you must obey;
Seven long years a girl and a boy;
So hush, a bush, bush, get out of the way.
                        —Buckingham (Thos. Baker in *Midland Garner*,
                                New Series, ii. 31).

XXIV.   Little Sally Walker sitting in a sigh,
        Weeping and waiting for a young man.
        Come choose you east, come choose you west,
        The very one that you love best.
                        —Nairn (Rev. W. Gregor).

XXV.   Little Sally Walker sitting on the sand,
        Crying and weeping for a young man.
        Rise, Sally, rise, Sally, wipe away your tears,
        Try for the east, and try for the west,
        Try for the (little) very one you love best.

        Now they're married I wish them joy,
        Every year a girl and boy,
        Loving each other like sister and brother,
        I hope to see them meet again.
                        —Fraserburgh (Rev. W. Gregor).

XXVI.   Little Sally Sander
        Sitting in the sander,
        Weeping and crying for her young man.
        Rise, Sally, rise
        And wipe away your tears;
        Choose to the east,
        Choose to the west,
        And choose to the very one that you love best.

Now you're married we wish you joy,
First a girl and then a boy;
Twelve months after son and daughter,
All join hands and kiss together.

—Penzance, Cornwall (Mrs. Mabbott).

XXVII.   Sally, Sally Walker, tinkle in a can;
Rise up, Sally, and choose a young man.
Look to the east, and look to the west,
Choose the one that you love the best.

Settle, Yorkshire (Rev. W. S. Sykes).

XXVIII.   Sally Water, Sally Water,
Come sprinkle your fan;
Sally, Sally Waters, sprinkle in a pan;
Rise, Sally, rise, Sally, for a young man.
Choose to the east, and choose to the west,
And choose thc dearest one that you love best.

Now you're married, we wish you joy,
First a girl and then a boy;
Love one another like sister and brother,
And never lose time by kissing one another.

—West Haddon (*Northamptonshire Notes
and Queries*, ii. 104).

XXIX.   Little Sally Waters, sitting in the sun,
Crying and weeping for her young man.
Rise, Sally, rise, wipe up your tears,
Fly to the east, fly to the west,
Fly to the one that you love the best.

—Brigg, Lincolnshire (Miss Barker).

XXX.   Hie Sally Walker, hie Sally Ken,
Hie Sally Walker, follow young men.
Choose to the east, and choose to the west,
Choose to the very one you love best.

Marriage comfort and marriage joy,
First a girl and then a boy.
Seven years after, seven years to come,
Fire on the mountain, kiss and run.

—Belfast, Ireland (W. H. Patterson).

XXXI.   Little Alice Sander
        Sat upon a cinder,
        Weeping and crying for her young man.
        Rise up, Alice, dry your tears,
        Choose the one that you love best,
        Alice my dear.

        Now they have got married
        I hope they will joy,
        Seven years afterwards, seven years ago,
        Now is the time to kiss and go.
                    —Earls Heaton, Yorks. (Herbert Hardy).

XXXII. Rise, Sally Walker,
        Rise if you can,
        Rise, Sally Walker, and follow your good man ;
        Choose to the east, and choose to the west,
        Choose to the one you love best.
        There is a couple married in joy,
        Past a girl and then a boy,
        Seven years after, seven years to come,
        Kiss you couple, kiss and be done.
        A' the many hours to us a happy life,
        Except —— and he wants a wife.
        A wife shall he have,
        And a widower shall he be,
        Except —— that sits on his knee,
        A guid fauld hoose and a blacket fireside,
        Draw up your gartens and show all your bride.
                            —(Rev. W. Gregor).

XXXIII. Arise, Sally Walker, arise, if you can,
        Arise, Sally Walker, and follow your good man ;
        Come choose to the east, come choose to the west,
        Come choose to the very one you love best.

        This is a couple married with joy ;
        First a girl and then a boy,
        Seven years after and seven years to come,
        This young couple married and begun.

[The Christian name of a girl] made a pudding so
    nice and sweet,
[Boy's Christian name] took a knife and tasted it.
Taste love, taste love, don't say No,
The next Sunday morning
To church we shall go.
Clean the brazen candlesticks,
And clean the fireside,
 Draw back the curtains,
And lat's see the bride.
A' the men in oor toon leads a happy life,
Except [a boy's full name], and he wants a wife.
A wife shall he hae, and a widow she shall be;
For look at [a girl's full name] diddling on's knee.
He paints her cheeks and he curls her hair,
And he kisses the lass at the foot o' the stair.
                —Tyrie (Rev. W. Gregor).

[The form of words at Cullen is the same for the first seven
lines, and then the words are :—]

XXXIV.   This young couple be married and be done,
          A' the men in oor toon leads a happy life,
          Except —— and he wants a wife.
          A wife he shall have, and a widow she shall be,
          Except [a girl's name] that sits on his knee,
          Painting her face and curling her hair,
          Kissing [a girl's name] at the foot o' the stair.
                —Cullen (Rev. W. Gregor).

XXXV.   Rise, Sally Walker, rise if you can,
          Rise, Sally Walker, follow your gudeman.
          Come choose to the east, come choose to the
              west,
          Come choose to the very one that you love best.

          Now they're married I wish them joy,
          Every year a girl or boy,
          Loving each other like sister and brother,
          And so they may be kissed together.

Cheese and bread for gentlemen,
And corn and hay for horses,
A cup of tea for a' good wives,
And bonnie lads and lassies.
When are we to meet again ?
And when are we to marry ?
Raffles up, and raffles down, and raffles a' a
    dancin',
The bonniest lassie that ever I saw,
Was [child in the centre] dancin'.
        —Aberdeen Training College (Rev. W. Gregor.)

XXXVI.   Sally, Sally Walker, sitting in the sun,
      Weeping and wailing for a young man,
    Rise, Sally, rise, and wipe away your tears,
      Fly to the east, fly to the west,
    And fly to the very one that you love best.

    Uncle John is very sick,
      He goes a courting night and day ;
    Sword and pistol by his side,
      Little Sally is his bride.
    He takes her by the lily white hand,
      He leads her over the water ;
    Now they kiss and now they clap,
      Mrs. Molly's daughter.
        —Nairn, Perth, Forfar (Rev. W. Gregor).

XXXVII.   Sally, Sally Waters, why are you so sad ?
    You shall have a husband, either good or bad ;
    Then rise, Sally Waters, and sprinkle your pan,
    For you're just the young woman to get a nice
      man.
    Now you're married, we wish you joy,
    Father and mother and little boy,
    Love one another like sister and brother,
    And now, good people, kiss each other.
        —Halliwell, *Popular Rhymer*, p. 229.

XXXVIII. Rise, Sally Walker,
         Rise if you can (Northumberland),
         Sprinkle in the pan (Yorks. and Midlands),
         Rise, Sally Walker,
         For a young man.
         Choose to the east,
         Choose to the west,

         Choose to the $\begin{cases} \text{very one (Northumberland),} \\ \text{pretty girl (Yorks., \&c.).} \end{cases}$
         You love best.

         Now you're married,
         I wish you joy,
         First a girl,
         And then a boy.

         Seven years after,
         Seven years over, $\Big\}$ (Northumberland).
         Now's the time to
         Kiss and give over.

         Five years after
         A son and daughter, $\Big\}$ (Yorks., &c.)
         Pray, young couple,
         Kiss away.
                    —Hexham (Miss J. Barker).

XXXIX.   Sally Waters, Sally Waters, come rise if you can,
         Come rise in the morning, all for a young man;
         Come choose, come choose, come choose if you can,
         Come choose a good one or let it alone.
              —Monton, Lancashire (Miss Dendy).

XL.   Sally Waters, Sally Waters,
         Come rise if you can,
         Come rise in the morning,
         All for a young man.
         First to the east, then to the west,
         Then to the bonny lass that you love best.

Now, Sally, you are married,
I hope you'll agree,
Seven years at afterwards, seven years ago,
And now they are parted with a kiss and a blow.
—Monton, Lancashire (Miss Dendy).

The last two lines were supplied by a girl in a very poor district of Manchester (note by Miss Dendy).

XLI. Rise, Sally Walker, rise, if you can,
Rise, Sally Walker, and follow your gueedman,
Choose to the east, and choose to the west,
Choose to the one that you love best.
There is a couple married in joy,
First a girl and then a boy,
Seven years after, seven years to come.
—Rosehearty (Rev. W. Gregor).

XLII. Little Polly Sanders sits on the sand,
Weeping and crying for her young man;
Rise up, Polly, wipe your tears,
Pick the one you love so sweet.
Now Polly's got married, we hope she'll have joy,
For ever and ever a girl or a boy.
If one won't do, she must have two,
So I pray you, young damsels, to kiss two and two.
—Liverpool (C. C. Bell).

XLIII. Here sits poor Sally on the ground,
Sighing and sobbing for her young man.
Arise, Sally, rise, and wipe your weeping eyes,
And turn to the east, and turn to the west,
And show the little boys that you love best.

A bogie in, a bogie out,
A bogie in the garden,
I wouldn't part with my young man
For fourpence ha'penny farthing.
—Long Eaton, Nottingham (Miss Youngman).

[In London the above is :]—

XLIV.   A beau in front and a beau behind,
        And a bogie in the garden oh !
        I wouldn't part with my sweetheart
        For tuppence (two) ha'penny farthing.
                              —London (Mrs. Merck).

XLV.   Sally Walker, Sally Walker,
        Come spring time and love,
        She's lamenting, she's lamenting,
        All for her young man.
        Come choose to the east, come choose to the west,
        Come choose the one that you love best.

        Here's a couple got married together,
        Father and mother they must agree,
        Love each other like sister and brother,
        I pray this couple to kiss together.
                              —Morpeth (Henderson's *Folk-lore of
                              Northern Counties*, p. 26).

XLVI.   Rise, Sally Walker, rise if you can,
        Rise, Sally Walker, and choose your good man,
        Choose to the east, and choose to the west,
        And choose the very one you love best.
        Now they're married, wish them joy,
        First a girl, and then a boy,
        Seven years after, seven years to come,
        Now's the time to kiss and be done.
                              —Gainford, Durham (Miss A. Edleston).

XLVII. Little Alexander sitting on the sand,
        Weeping and crying for a young man ;
        Rise up, Sally, and wipe your tears,
        Pick the very one that you like best.
        Now, Sally, now married, I hope she'll (or you'll) enjoy,
        For ever and ever with that little boy
        (or with her or your young boy).
                              —Beddgelert, Wales (Mrs. Williams).

XLVIII. Rice, Sally Water, rice if you can,
　　　 Rice, Sally Water, and choose your young man;
　　　 Choose to the east, choose to the west,
　　　 Choose to the prettiest that you love.

　　　 Now you're married, we wish you good joy,
　　　 First a little girl, and then a little boy;
　　　 Seven years after, seven years to come,
　　　 Seven years of plenty, and kiss when you done.
　　　　　　　　　　　　—Norfolk (Mrs. Haddon).

(c) A ring is formed by the children joining hands. One girl kneels or sits down in the centre, and covers her face with her hands as if weeping. The ring dances round and sings the words. The child in the centre rises when the command is given, and chooses a boy or girl from the ring, who goes into the centre with her. These two kiss together when the words are said. The child who was first in the centre then joins the ring, the second remaining in the centre, and the game continues.

All versions of this game are played in the same way, except slight variations in a few instances. Kissing does not prevail in all the versions. In the Earls Heaton game, the child who kneels in the centre also pretends to weep and dries her tears before choosing a partner. Miss Burne, in *Shropshire Folk-lore*, says the girl kneels disconsolately in the middle of the ring. In the Strixould version, the child stands in the centre holding in her hands something resembling a saucer; she then pretends to "knock it in a mortar," and gives the saucer to the one whom she chooses. This one exchanges places with her. In the Northants version, at the words "clash the bells," the children dash down their joined hands to imitate ringing bells. Addy, *Sheffield Glossary*, says one girl sits in the middle weeping. When the girl has chosen, the young man remains in the centre, and the word "Sally" is changed to "Billy," or some other name, and "man" to "girl." In the Beddgelert version, the centre child wipes her eyes with a handkerchief in the beginning of the game. Several other versions have been sent me, all being the same as those printed here, or varying so slightly, it is unnecessary to repeat them.

(d) The analysis of the game-rhymes is as follows:—

No.	Dorsetshire.	Devonshire.	Somersetshire.	London.	Fochabers.	Berkshire.	Crockham Hill, Kent.	Wiltshire.
1.	Sally Water.	Sally Walker.	Sally Water.	Sally Waters.	Sally Walker.	Sally Waters.	Sally Wall-flowers.	Sally Waters.
2.	—	—	—	—	—	—	—	—
3.	—	—	—	—	—	—	—	—
4.	—	—	—	—	—	—	—	—
5.	—	—	—	—	—	—	—	—
6.	Sprinkle in pan.	Sprinkle water in the pan.	Sprinkle in the pan.	Sprinkle in the pan.	Sprinkling in a pan.	Sprinkled in the pan.	Sprinkled in the pan.	Sprinkled in a pan.
7.	—	—	—	—	—	—	—	—
8.	—	—	—	—	—	—	—	—
9.	—	—	—	—	—	—	—	—
10.	—	—	—	—	—	—	—	—
11.	—	—	—	—	—	—	—	—
12.	—	—	—	—	—	—	—	—
13.	Rise and choose a young man.	Rise and seek a young man.	Hi, choose a young man.	Rise for a young man.	Rise for a young man.	Rise for a young man.	—	Rise and choose a young man.
14.	—	—	—	—	—	—	—	—
15.	—	—	—	—	—	—	—	—
16.	—	—	—	—	—	—	—	—
17.	—	—	—	—	—	—	—	—
18.	Choose east, west.	Turn east, west.	Choose best, worst.	Choose best, worst.	Choose east, west.	Choose best, worst.	—	Choose best worst.
19.	—	—	—	—	—	—	—	—
20.	Choose the best loved.	Choose the best loved.	Choose the best loved.	Choose the best loved.	Choose the best loved.	Choose the best loved.	—	Choose the best loved.
21.	—	—	—	—	—	—	—	—
22.	Now you're married, &c.	Now you're married, &c.	Now you're married, &c.	Now you're married, &c.	—	—	—	Now you're married, &c.
23.	—	—	—	—	You must obey, &c.	—	—	—
24.	—	—	—	—	—	—	—	—
25.	—	—	—	—	—	—	—	—
26.	—	—	—	—	—	—	—	—
27.	—	—	—	—	—	—	—	—

No.	Northants.	Oxford.	Yorkshire.	Surrey.	Shropshire (1).	Shropshire (2).	Notts.
1.	Sally Waters.	Sally Water.	Sally Waters,	Sally Water.	Sally Walker.	Sally Water.	Sally Water.
2.	—	—	—	—	—	—	—
3.	—	—	—	—	—	—	—
4.	—	—	—	—	—	—	—
5.	—	—	—	—	—	—	—
6.	Sprinkle in a pan.	Sprinkle in the pan.	Sprinkle in a pan.	Sprinkle in the pan.	Sprinkle in your pan.	Sprinkle in your pan.	Sprinkle in your can.
7.	—	—	—	—	—	—	—
8.	—	—	—	—	—	—	—
9.	—	—	—	—	—	—	—
10.	—	—	—	—	—	—	—
11.	—	—	—	—	—	—	—
12.	—	—	—	—	—	—	—
13.	—	Rise for a young man.	—	—	—	Rise, for you shall have a husband.	—
14.	Cry for a young man.	—	Cry for a young man.	—	—	—	—
15.	—	—	—	Is not — a nice young man.	Down in the meadow there's a nice young man.	—	Why do you marry a foolish young man.
16.	—	—	—	—	—	—	—
17.	—	—	—	—	—	—	—
18.	—	—	—	—	—	—	Pick worst, best.
19.	Choose best, worst.	Choose fairest.	—	—	—	Choose fairest.	—
20.	Choose the best loved.	—	Choose the best loved.	—	—	—	Choose the best loved.
21.	—	—	—	—	—	—	—
22.	Now you're married, &c.	Now she's married, &c.	—	—	—	Now your married, &c.	—
23.	—	—	—	They shall be married if they agree, &c.	—	—	—
24.	—	—	—	—	—	—	—
25.	—	—	—	—	On the carpet she shall kneel, &c.	—	—
26.	—	—	—	—	—	—	—
27.	—	—	—	—	—	—	—

No.	Gloucestershire.	Sheffield.	Lincolnshire.	Wakefield.	Warwickshire.	Sheffield.	Bucks.
1.	Sally Water.	Sally Water.	—	Sally Water.	Sally Water.	—	—
2.	—	—	—	—	—	—	Sally Walker.
3.	—	—	Sally Salter.	—	—	Sally Slarter.	—
4.	—	—	—	—	—	—	—
5.	—	—	—	—	—	—	—
6.	Sprinkle your can.	Sprinkle your can.	—	—	—	—	Sprinkled in a pan.
7.	—	—	Sprinkle in some water.	—	Water your can.	Sitting by the water.	—
8.	—	—	—	Springin' in a pan.	—	—	—
9.	—	—	—	—	—	—	—
10.	—	—	—	—	—	—	—
11.	—	—	—	—	—	—	—
12.	—	—	—	—	Rise for a husband.	—	—
13.	Why don't you rise for a young man.	Who do you lie mourning for a young man.	—	—	—	—	—
14.	—	—	—	Cry for a young man.	—	Crying for a young man.	—
15.	—	—	Send it in a silver saucer to [ ].	—	—	—	—
16.	—	—		—	—	—	—
17.	—	—	—	—	—	Turn east, west.	Sprinkle for a young man.
18.	—	—	—	Choose worst, best.	—	—	—
19.	Choose wisest, best.	Choose wisest, best.	—	—	—	—	—
20.	—	—	—	—	—	—	Choose fairest.
21.	Choose the one that lies in your breast.	Choose the best loved.	—	Choose the best loved.	—	Choose the best loved.	—
22.	—	—	—	Now you're married, &c.	Now you're married, &c.	Now you're married, &c.	Now you're married, &c.
23.	—	—	—	—	—	—	—
24.	—	—	—	—	—	—	—
25.	—	—	—	—	—	—	—
26.	—	—	—	—	—	—	—
27.	—	—	—	—	—	—	—

No.	Nairn.	Fraserburgh.	Cornwall.	Settle.	Northants.	Brigg.	Belfast.
1.	Sally Walker.		—				
2.	—	Sally Walker.		Sally Walker.	Sally Water.	Sally Waters.	Sally Walker.
3.	—	—	—	—	—	—	—
4.	—	—	—	—	—	—	—
5.	—	—	Sally Sander.	—	—	—	—
6.	—	—	—	—	Sprinkle in a pan.	—	—
7.	—	—	—	—	—	—	—
8.	—	—	—	—	—	—	—
9.	Sitting in a sigh.	—	—	—	—	—	—
10.	—	Sitting on the sand.	Sitting in the sander.	—	—	—	—
11.	—	—	—	Tinkle in a can.	—	—	—
12.	—	—	—		—	Sitting in the sun.	—
13.	—	—	—	Rise and choose a young man.	Rise for a young man.	Crying for a young man.	Hi for a young man.
14.	Weeping for a young man,	Weeping for a young man,	Weeping for a young man.	—	—		—
15.	—	—	—	—	—	—	—
16.	—	—	—	—	—	—	—
17.	—	—	—	Look east, west.	—	Fly east, west.	—
18.	Choose east, west.	Try east, west.	Choose east, west.		Choose east, west.		Choose east, west.
19.	—						
20.	—	—	—	—	—	—	—
21.	Choose the best loved.	Choose the best loved.	Choose the best loved.	Choose the best loved.	Choose the best loved.	Choose the best loved.	Choose the best loved.
22.	—	Now they're married, &c.	Now you're married, &c.		Now you're married, &c.		Married, &c.
23.	—	—	—	—	—	—	—
24.	—	—	—	—	—	—	—
25.	—		—	—			
26.	—	—	—	—	—	—	—
27.	—	—	—	—	—	—	—

No.	Earls Heaton.	Scotland.	Tyrie.	Aberdeen.	Nairn.	Halliwell.	Hexham.
1.		Sally Walker.	Sally Walker.	Sally Walker.	Sally Walker.	Sally Water.	Sally Walker.
2.							
3.	Alice Sander.						
4.							
5.							Sprinkle in the pan.
6.							
7.							
8.	Sat upon a cinder.						
9.							
10.							
11.							
12.					Sitting in the sun.		
13.		Rise for a young man.	Rise for a young man.	Rise for a young man.			Rise for a young man.
14.	Weeping for a young man.				Weeping for a young man.		
15.							
16.							
17.						Sprinkle for a young man.	
18.		Choose east, west.	Choose east, west.	Choose east, west.	Fly east, west.		Choose east, west.
19.							
20.							
21.	Choose the best loved.	Choose the best loved.	Choose the best loved.	Choose the best loved.	Fly to the best loved.		Choose the best loved.
22.	Now they're married, &c.	Now they are married, &c.	Now they're married, &c.	Now they're married, &c.		Now you're married, &c.	Now you're married, &c.
23.							
24.							
25.							
26.							
27.					Goes courting, &c.		

No.	Lancashire.	Rosehearty.	Notts.	Morpeth.	Gainford.	Norfolk.	Beddgelert.
1.	Sally Waters.	Sally Walker.	Sallie [ ].	Sally Walker.	Sally Walker.	Sallie [ ]	Sallie [ ].
2.	—	—	—	—	—	—	—
3.	—	—	—	—	—	—	—
4.	—	—	—	—	—	—	—
5.	—	—	—	—	—	—	—
6.	—	—	—	—	—	—	—
7.	—	—	—	—	—	—	—
8.	—	—	—	—	—	—	—
9.	—	—	—	—	—	—	—
10.	—	—	Sitting on the ground.	—	—	—	Sitting in sand.
11.	—	—	—	—	—	—	—
12.	—	—	—	—	—	—	—
13.	Rise for a young man.	Rise for a good man.	—	—	Rise and choose your good man.	Rise and choose.	—
14.	—	—	Sobbing for a young man.	Lamenting for a young man.	—	—	Crying for a young man.
15.	—	—	—	—	—	—	—
16.	—	—	—	—	—	—	—
17.	—	—	—	—	—	—	—
18.	First east, west.	Choose east, west.	Turn east, west.	Choose east, west.	Choose east, west.	Choose east, west.	—
19.	—	—	—	—	—	—	—
20.	—	—	—	—	—	—	—
21.	Then to the best loved.	—	Turn to the best loved.	Choose the best loved.	Choose the best loved.	Choose the prettiest.	Pick the one you like best.
22.	Now you're married, &c.	There's a couple, &c.	—	Here's a couple, &c.	Now they're married, &c.	Now your married, &c.	Now you're married, &c.
23.	—	—	—	—	—	—	—
24.	—	—	—	—	—	—	—
25.	—	—	—	—	—	—	—
26.	—	—	—	—	—	—	—
27.	—	—	A bogie in, &c.	—	—	—	—

The first thing to note from this analysis are the words Sally and Water. In twenty-three versions they are Sally Water or Waters, in seventeen versions it is Sally Walker, in six versions it is another name altogether, while in two versions it is Sallie only. The most constant name, therefore, points to Sally Water as the oldest version; and it is noticeable that in the Lincolnshire and Sheffield versions, where the name is not Sally Water, the word water is introduced later on in the line which directs the action of sprinkling water. Is it possible, then, that Sally Water may be a corruption from an earlier form where Sally is some other word, not the name of a girl, as it is usually supposed to be, and the word water is connected, not with the name of the maiden, but with the action of sprinkling which she is called upon to perform? If we could surmise that the early form was "Sallie, Sallie, water sprinkle in the pan," the accusative being placed before the verb, the problem would be solved in this manner; but there is no warrant for this poetical licence in popular verses, and I prefer to suggest that "water" got attached as a surname by simple transposition, such as the Norfolk and Beddgelert versions allow as evidence. It follows from this that Walker and other names appear as degraded forms of the original, and do not enter into the question of origins, a point which may readily be conceded, considering that the general evidence of all these singing games is, that no special names are ever used, but that names change to suit the players. The next incident in the analysis is the ceremony of "sprinkling the water," which is constant in twenty-one versions, while the Wakefield "Springin' in the pan," the Settle "Tinkle in a can," Halliwell's "Sprinkle for a young man," and the eight versions in which this incident is wholly absent in any form, are evident corruptions. The tendency of the corruption is shown by this to be that the "sprinkling of water" came to be omitted from the verse, and therefore the other variants—

Sitting by the water (Sheffield),
Water your can (Warwickshire),
Sitting in a sigh (Nairn),
Sitting on the sand (Fraserburgh and Beddgelert).

  Sitting in the sander (Cornwall),
  Sitting in the sun (Brigg. and Nairn),
  Sat upon a cinder (Earls Heaton),
  Sitting on the ground (Notts.),

are but the steps through which the entire omission of the
water incident was finally attained. The third incident is
"Rise and choose" a young man, the alternative being "Crying for a young man." The first indicates a kneeling and
reverential attitude before the water, and occurs in twenty-
one versions, while the second only occurs in fourteen versions.

  The expression "crying" is really to "announce a want,"
as "wants" were formerly cried by the official "crier" of
every township, and indeed as children still in games "cry"
the forfeits; but losing this meaning, the expression came to
mean crying in the sense of "weeping," and appearing to the
minds of children as a natural way of expressing a want, would
therefore succeed in ousting any more archaic notion. The
incident of crying for a lover appears in other singing games,
as, for instance, in "Poor Mary." Especially may this be considered the process which has been going on when it is seen
that "choosing" is an actual incident of the game, even in
those cases where "crying" has replaced the kneeling. The
choosing incident also assumes two forms, namely, with respect
to "east and west" in twenty-two versions, and "best and
worst" in nine versions. Now, the expression, "for better for
worse," is an old marriage formula preserved in the vernacular
portion of the ancient English marriage service (see Palgrave,
English Commonwealth, ii., p. cxxxvi.); and I cannot but think
that we have the same formula in this game, especially as the
final admonition· in nearly all the versions is to choose "the
one loved best." Following upon this comes the very general
marriage formula noted so frequently in these games. It is
slightly varied in some versions, and is replaced by a different
formula, but one that also appears in other games, in two or
three versions. One feature is very noticeable in the less
common versions of this game, viz., the assumption of the
marriage being connected with the birth of children, and the

indulgences of the lovers, as in the Tong and Scottish versions
xxxii., xxxiii., and xxxiv.

(e) In considering the probable origin of the game, the
first thing will be to ascertain as far as possible what ideas
the words are intended to convey. Taking note of the
results of the analysis, so far as they show the corruptions
which have taken place in the words, it seems clear that though
it is not possible to restore the original words, their original
meaning is still preserved. This is, that they accompanied the
performance of a marriage ceremony, and that a chief feature of
this ceremony was connected with some form of water-worship,
or some rite in which water played a chief part. Now it has
been noted before that the games of children have preserved,
by adaptation, the marriage ceremony of ancient times (e.g.,
"Merry ma Tansa," "Nuts in May," "Poor Mary," " Round and
Round the Village "); but this is the first instance where such
an important particularisation as that implied by water-worship
qualifies the marriage ceremony. It is therefore necessary to see
what this exactly means. Mr. Hartland, in his *Perseus* (i. 167–9),
draws attention to the general significance of the water ceremonial in marriage customs, and Mr. F. B. Jevons, in his introduction to Plutarch's *Romane Questions*, and in the *Transactions
of the Folk-lore Congress*, 1891, deals with the subject in reference to the origin of custom obtaining among both Aryan and
non-Aryan speaking people. In this connection an important
consideration arises. The Esthonian brides, on the morning
after the wedding, are taken to make offerings to the water
spirit, and they throw offerings into the spring (or a vessel of
water), overturn a vessel of water in the house, and sprinkle
their bridegrooms with water. The Hindoo offerings of the bride
were cast into a water vessel, and the bride sprinkles the court of
the new house with water by way of exorcism, and also sprinkles
the bridegroom (Jevons, *loc. cit.*, p. 345). Here the parallel between the non-Aryan Esthonian custom and the Aryan Hindoo
custom is very close, and it is a part of Mr. Jevons' argument
that, among the Teutons, with whom alone of Aryan speaking
peoples the Esthonians came into contact, the custom was limited
to the bride simply stepping over a vessel of water. There is

certainly something a great deal more than the parallel to the
Teutonic custom in the game of " Sally, Sally Water," and as it
equates more nearly to Hindoo and Esthonian custom, the question is, Does it help Mr. Jevons in the important point he raises ?
I think it does. A custom is very low down among the strata of
survivals when it is only to be recognised as part of a children's
singing game, and the proposition it suggests is that children
have preserved more of the old custom than was preserved by
the people who adopted a portion of it into their marriage
ceremony. A custom so treated must be older than the
marriage ceremony with which it thus came into contact, and
if this is a true conclusion, we have in this children's game a
relic of the pre-Celtic peoples of these islands—a relic therefore
going back many centuries for its origin, and which is of inesti-
mable service in discussing some important problems of the
ethnic significance of folk-lore. These conclusions are entirely
derived from the significant position which this game occupies
in relation to Esthonian (non-Aryan) and to Teutonic (Aryan)
marriage customs respectively, and therefore it is of considerable importance to note that it entirely fits in with the conclusion which my husband has drawn as to the non-Aryan origin of
water-worship (see Gomme's *Ethnology of Folk-lore*, pp. 79–105).

There is, however, something further which seems to bring
this game into line with non-Aryan marriage customs. The
marriage signified by the game is acknowledged and sanctioned
by the presence of witnesses; is made between two people
who choose each other without any form of compulsion; is
accompanied by blessings upon the young couple and prognostications of the birth of children. These points show that the
marriage ceremony belongs to a time when the object of the
union was to have children, and when its duration was not
necessarily for life. It is curious to note that water worship is
distinctly connected with the desire to have children (*Proc.
Roy. Irish Acad.*, 3rd ser., ii. 9); and that the idea of the
temporary character of the marriage status of the lower classes
of the people is still extant I have certain evidence of. Early
in November of 1895, a man tried for bigamy gave as his
defence that he thought his marriage was ended with his first

wife, as he had been away seven years. It is a frequently told story. A year and a day and seven years are the two periods for which the popular mind regards marriage binding. "I was faithful to him for seven years, and had more than my two children," a woman said to me once, as if two children were the required or expected number to be born in that period. If there is a popular belief of this kind, it is strangely borne out by this game-rhyme. "First a girl, and then a boy," may also be shown to be a result to be desired and prayed for, in the popular belief that a man's cycle of life is not complete until he is the father of a daughter, who, in her turn, shall have a son. Miss Hawkins Dempster obtained evidence of such a belief from the lips of a man who considered he was entitled to marry another woman, as his wife had only borne him sons, and therefore his life was not (like hers) complete.

The free choice of both woman and man is opposed to the theory of our present marriage ceremony, where permission or authority to marry is only necessary for the woman, the man being able to do as he pleases. This is now regarded as a sign of women's early subjection to the authority of men and their subordinate place in the household. But it does not follow that this was the relative position of men and women when a ceremony was first found needful and instituted. I am inclined to think it must have been, rather, the importance attached to the woman's act of ratification, in the presence of witnesses, of her formal promise to bear children to a particular man. Marriage would then consist of contracts between two parties for the purpose of, and which actually resulted in, the birth of children; of concubinage, or the wife consenting to children being born to her husband by another woman in her stead, if she herself failed in this respect (such children being hers and her husband's jointly); of marriage without ceremony or set purpose, resulting from young people being thrown together at feast times, gathering in of harvests, &c., which might or might not result in the birth of children. These conditions of the marriage rite are at variance with what we know of the Aryan marriage generally and its results; and that they flow from the customs preserved in the game under consideration is further proof of the origin of the game from a marriage rite of the pre-Celtic people of these islands. The "kissing together" of the married couple is the token to the witnesses of their mutual consent to the contract.

Attention has already been directed to the fact that parts of the formula preserved in this game are also found in other games, and it may possibly be assumed therefrom that the same origin must be given to these games as to "Sally Water." The objection to such a conclusion is mainly that it is impossible to decide to which game the popular marriage formula originally belonged, and from which it has been borrowed by the other games. Seeing how exactly it fits the circumstances of "Sally Water," it might not be too much to suggest that it rightly belongs to this game. Another point to be noted is that the tune to which the words of the marriage formula are sung is always the same, irrespective of that to which the previous verses are sung, and this rule obtains in all those games in which this formula appears—a further proof of the antiquity of the formula as an outcome of the early marriage ceremony.

Sally Sober

A game among girls [undescribed].—Dickinson's *Cumberland Glossary* (*Supplement*).

Salmon Fishers

  I. Cam' ye by the salmon fishers,
    Cam' ye by the roperee ?
    Saw ye a sailor laddie
    Sailing on the raging sea ?
    Oh, dear ——, are ye going to marry ?
    Yes, indeed, and that I am.
    Tell to me your own true lover,
    Tell to me your lover's name ?
    He's a bonnie lad, *he's* a bonnie fellow,
    Oh, he's a bonnie lad,
    Wi' ribbons blue and yellow,
    Stockings of blue silk ;
    Shoes of patent leather,
    Points to tie them up.

A gold ring on his finger.
Did you see the ship he came in ?
Did you see it comin' in ?
Every lassie wi' her laddie,
Every widow wi' her son.
Mother, struck eight o'clock,
Mother, may I get out ?
For my love is waiting
For to get me out.
First he gave me apples,
Then he gave me pears,
Then he gave me a sixpence
To kiss him on the stairs.
Oh, dear me, I wish I had my tea,
To write a letter to my love
To come back and marry me.
                    —Rosehearty (Rev. W. Gregor).

II.   Cam' ye by the salmon fishers ?
      Cam' ye by the roperee ?
      Saw ye a sailor laddie
      Waiting on the coast for me ?
      I ken fahr I'm gyain,
      I ken fahs gyain wi' me ;
      I ha'e a lad o' my ain,
      Ye daurna tack 'im fae me.
      Stockings of blue silk,
      Shoes of patent leather,
      Kid to tie them up,
      And gold rings on his finger.
      Oh for six o'clock !
      Oh for seven I weary !
      Oh for eight o'clock !
      And then I'll see my dearie.
                    —Fochabers (Rev. W. Gregor).

III. Come ye by the salmon fishers ?
      Come ye by the roperee ?
      Saw ye my dear sailor laddie
      Sailing on the raging sea ?

Tip for gold and tip for silver,
Tip for the bonnie laddie I do adore;
My delight 's for a sailor laddie,
And shall be for evermore.
Sit you down, my lovely Elsie,
Take your baby on your knee;
Drink your health for a jolly sailor,
He will come back and marry you.
He will give you beads and ear-rings,
He will give you diamonds free;
Sailors they are bonnie laddies,
Oh, but they are neat and clean!
They can kiss a bonnie lassie
In the dark, and A, B, C;
When the sailors come home at evening
They take off their tarry clothes,
They put on their light blue jackets,
That is the way the sailors go.

—Rev. W. Gregor.

A circle is formed, and the children dance round singing. Before beginning they agree which of the players is to be named in the fifth line of the Rosehearty version.

Jamieson's *Dictionary* (*sub voce*), "Schamon's Dance," says, "Some particular kind of dance anciently used in Scotland."

Blaw up the bagpyp than,
The schamon's dance I mon begin,
I trow it sall not pane.

—"Peblis to the Play," *Chronicles of Scottish Poetry*, i. 135.

Pinkerton defines salmon as "probably *show-man, shaw-man.*"

See "Shame Reel, or Shamit Dance."

Salt Eel

This is something like "Hide and Find." The name of Salt Eel may have been given it from one of the points of the game, which is to baste the runaway individual, whom you may overtake, all the way home with your handkerchief, twisted hard for that purpose. Salt Eel implies on board ship a rope's ending, and on shore an equivalent process.—Moor's *Suffolk Words and Phrases.*

Save All

Two sides are chosen in this game. An even number of boys, say eight on each side. Half of these run out of the line, and are chased by half of the boys from the other side. If two out of four get "home" to door or lamp-post, they *save all* the prisoners which have been made; if two out of four are caught before the others get "home," the side catching them beats.—Deptford (Miss Chase).

Say Girl

A game undescribed, recorded by the Rev. S. D. Headlam as played by some Hoxton school children.—*Church Reformer*, 1894.

Scat

A paper-knife, or thin slip of wood, is placed by one player on his open palm. Another takes it up quickly, and tries to "scat" his opponent's hand before he can draw it away. Sometimes a feint of taking the paper-knife is made three or four times before it is really done. When the "scat" is given, the "scatter" in his turn rests the knife on his palm. Scat is the Cornish for "slap."—*Folk-lore Journal*, v. 50.

Scop-peril, or Scoperel

Name for teetotum ordinarily manufactured by sticking a pointed peg through a bone button.—Easther's *Almondbury Glossary;* also in SW. Lincolnshire, Cole's *Glossary.*

See "Totum."

Scotch-hoppers

In *Poor Robin's Almanack* for 1677, in the verses to the reader, on the back of the title-page, concerning the chief matters in the volume, among many other articles of intelligence, the author professes to show—

"The time when school boys should play at *Scotch-hoppers.*"

Another allusion occurs in the same periodical for 1707—
"Lawyers and Physitians have little to do this month, and therefore they may (if they will) play at *Scotch-hoppers.* Some

men put their hands into peoples' pockets open, and extract
it clutch'd, of that beware. But counsel without a cure, is a
body without a soul." And again, in 1740—"The fifth house
tells ye whether whores be sound or not; when it is good
to eat tripes, bloat herrings, fry'd frogs, rotten eggs, and
monkey's tails butter'd, or an ox liver well stuck with fish
hooks; when it is the most convenient time for an old man
to play at *Scotch-hoppers* amongst the boys. In it also is
found plainly, that the best armour of proof against the fleas,
is to go drunk to bed."

See "Hopscotch," "Tray-Trip."

Scots and English

Boys first choose sides. The two chosen leaders join both
hands, and raising them high enough to let the others pass
through below, cry—

> Brother Jack, if ye'll be mine,
> I'll gie ye claret wine;
> Claret wine is good and fine,
> Through the needle ee, boys.

Letting their arms fall they enclose a boy and ask him to
which side he will belong, and he is disposed of according
to his own decision. The parties being at length formed, are
separated by a real or imaginary line, and place at some
distance behind them, in a heap, their hats, coats, &c. They
stand opposite to each other, the object being to make a
successful incursion over the line into the enemy's country,
and bring off part of the heap of clothes. It requires both
address and swiftness of foot to do so without being taken by
the foe. The winning of the game is decided by which party
first loses all its men or its property. At Hawick, where the
legendary mimicry of old Border warfare peculiarly flourishes, the
boys are accustomed to use the following rhymes of defiance :—

> King Covenanter, come out if ye daur venture!
> Set your foot on Scots' ground, English, if ye daur!
> —Chambers' *Popular Rhymes*, p. 127.

The following version was written down in 1821 under the
name of Scotch and English :—Two parties of boys, divided

by a fixed line, endeavoured to pull one another across this line, or to seize by bodily strength or nimbleness a "wad" (the coats or hats of the players) from the little heap deposited in the different territories at a convenient distance. The person pulled across or seized in his attempt to rob the camp was made a prisoner and conducted to the enemy's station, where he remained under the denomination of "stinkard" till relieved by one of the same side, or by a general exchange of prisoners.—*Blackwood's Magazine*, August 1821, p. 25. The *Denham Tracts*, i. 150, gives a version of the game much the same as these, except that the words used by the English are, "Here's a leap into thy kingdom, dry-bellied Scot." See also Hutton's *History of Roman Wall* (1804), p. 104. Brockett's account, under the title of "Stealy Clothes, or Watch Webs," is as follows:— The players divide into two parties and draw a line as the boundary of their respective territories. At an equal distance from this line each player deposits his hat or some other article of his dress. The object of the game is to seize and convey these singly to your own store from that of the enemy, but if you are unfortunately caught in the attempt, you not only restore the plunder but become a prisoner yourself. This evidently takes its origin from the inroads of the English and Scotch; indeed, it is plainly proved from the language used on the occasion, which consists in a great measure of the terms of reproach still common among the Borderers.— Brockett's *North Country Words*.

Jamieson, also, describes the game under the title of "English and Scotch," and says the game has originated from the mutual incursions of the two nations.

See "French and English," "Prisoner's Base," "Rigs."

Scratch Cradle
The game of "Cat's Cradle."

Scrush
A game much like Shinty between two sides of boys, each with bandies (scrushes) trying to knock a roundish stone over the other's line.—Barnes' *Dorset Glossary*. See "Shinney."

Scurran-Meggy

A game much in vogue in Cumberland during the last century, and in which a peculiar form of top called a "scurran top" was used.—Halliwell's *Dictionary*.

See-Saw

—London (A. B. Gomme).

I. Titty cum tawtay,
    The ducks in the water;
Titty cum tawtay,
    The geese follow after.
           —Halliwell's *Nursery Rhymes*, p. 213.

II. See-saw, Margery Daw,
Sold her bed to lie upon straw;
Wasn't she a dirty slut
To sell her bed to lie upon dirt?
           —London (A. B. Gomme).

III. See-saw, Margery Daw,
Johnny shall have a new master;
He shan't have but a farthing a day,
Because he can't work any faster.
           —London (G. L. Gomme).

IV. See-saw, sacradown,
Which is the way to London town?
One boot up, and the other down,
And that is the way to London town.
           —Halliwell's *Nursery Rhymes*, No. cccxxx.

V. The poor man was digging,
    To and fro, to and fro;
And his spade on his shoulder,
    To and fro, to and fro.

> The poor man was digging,
> To and fro, to and fro;
> And he caught the black cross,
> To and fro, to and fro.—Isle of Man (A. W. Moore).

A common game, children sitting on either end of a plank supported on its centre, and made to rock up and down. While enjoying this recreation, they sing the verse. Addy, *Sheffield Glossary*, gives Ranty or Rantypole, a plank or pole balanced evenly, upon which children rock up and down in see-saw fashion. Jamieson, *Etymological Dictionary*, gives Coup-the-Ladle as the name for See-saw in Aberdeen. Moor, *Suffolk Words and Phrases*, describes this game, and gives the same words to be sung while playing as Halliwell's above. Grose gives "Weigh," to play at See-saw. Holloway, *Dictionary of Provincialisms*, says, in Norfolk See-saw is called Titti cum Totter; and in Gainford, Durham, Ewiggy Shog. Halliwell gives versions of Nos. II. and III. in his *Nursery Rhymes*, and also other verses with the opening words "See-saw," namely, "See-saw, Jack-a-Daw," "See-saw, Sack-a-day;" but these are not connected with the game by Halliwell, and there is nothing in the words to indicate such a connection. Mactaggart, *Gallovidian Encyclopædia*, calls the game "Coggle-te-Carry," but gives no verses, and Strutt calls it "Titter Totter."—*Sports*, p. 303. He does not give any rhymes, except to quote Gay's poem, but it is possible that the rhyme to his game may be No. I. Brogden gives "Hightte" as the game of See-saw. The Manx version has not before been published, and Mr. Moore says is now quite forgotten in the Isle. The game is called "Shuggy-shoo" in Irish, and also "Copple-thurrish," evidently "Horse and Pig," as if the two animals were balancing against each other, and alternately becoming elevated and depressed.— *Ulster Journ. Arch.*, vi. 102. The child who stands on the plank in the centre and balances it, is frequently called the "canstick" or "candlestick."

See-Sim

A children's game. If one of the party is blindfolded, it is "Blind-Sim."—Spurden's *East Anglian Glossary*.

Shame Reel, or Shamit Dance

In several counties of Scotland this was the name of the first dance after the celebration of marriages. It was performed by the bride and best man and the bridegroom and best maid. The bride's partner asked what was to be the "sham spring," and she commonly answered, "Through the world will I gang wi' the lad that lo'es me," which, on being communicated to the fiddlers, was struck up, and the dance went on somewhat punctiliously, while the guests looked on in silence, and greeted the close with applause. This dance was common in Forfarshire twenty years ago.—Jamieson's *Dictionary*.

See "Cushion Dance," "Salmon Fishers."

She Said, and She Said

This game requires two confederates; one leaves the room, and the other in the secret asks a player in the room to whisper to him whom she (or he) loved; he then calls in his companion, and the following dialogue is carried on:—

> "She said, and she said!
> And what did she say?"
> "She said that she loved."
> "And whom did she love?
> Suppose she said she loved —— ?"
> "No! she never said that, whatever she said."

An indefinite number of names are mentioned before the right one. When that came, to the surprise of the whisperer, the answer is—

> "Yes! she said that."

The secret was very simple; the name of a widow or widower known to both players was always given before that whispered. —Cornwall (*Folk-lore Journal*, v. 50).

Shepherd and Sheep

Children choose, by "counting out," or otherwise, a Shepherd and a Wolf (or Mother Sheep, and Wolf). The Wolf goes away, and the rest of the players are the Sheep (or Lambs) and stand in a row. The Shepherd counts them—Sunday, Monday, Tuesday, &c. Then—

Shepherd—"What shall I bring home for you for dinner, Sunday, I'm going to market?"

Sunday chooses something—roast veal, apple tart, or anything else that she likes.   Then Monday, Tuesday, and the rest choose also.   Shepherd goes away, saying—
> "Mind you are all good children."

The Wolf comes directly the Shepherd goes out of sight, and takes away one of the Sheep.   Shepherd comes back and begins to distribute the different things—
"Sunday, Monday,——why, where's Tuesday?" (or Wednes
> day, as the case may be.)

The Children cry in chorus—
"Old Wolf came down the chimney and took him (or her)
> away."

This formula is repeated till all the children (sheep) are stolen.

The Shepherd now goes to the Wolf's house to look for his sheep—

Shepherd—"Good morning, have you seen my sheep?"

Wolf—"Yes, they went down Red Lane."

[Shepherd looks down Red Lane.]

Shepherd—"I've been down Red Lane, and they're not there."

Wolf—"I've just seen them pass, they're gone down Green Lane,"
> &c.   These questions and answers continue as long as the
> children's fancy holds out; then the Shepherd comes back.

Shepherd—"I've looked everywhere, and can't find them.   I
> b'lieve you've got them?   I smell meat; may I go up and
> taste your soup?"

Wolf—"You can't go upstairs, your shoes are too dirty."

Shepherd—"I'll take off my shoes" (pretends to take them off).

Wolf—"Your stockings are too dirty."

Shepherd—"I'll take off my stockings" (suits the action).

Wolf—"Your feet are too dirty."

Shepherd—"I'll cut my feet off" (pretends to cut them off).
> (Milder version, "I'll wash my feet.")

Wolf—"Then the blood 'll run about."
> (Milder version, "Then they'll wet my carpet.")

Shepherd—"I'll tie up my feet."
> (Or, "I'll wipe my feet.")

Wolf—"Well, now you may go up."

Shepherd—"I smell my sheep."

The Shepherd then goes to one child, pretends to taste—using fingers of both hands as though holding a spoon and fork—on the top of the child's head, saying, "That's my sheep," "That's Tuesday," &c., till he comes to the end of the row, then they all shout out and rush home to the fold, the Wolf with them. A fresh Shepherd and Wolf are chosen, and the game starts once more.—Cornwall (Miss I. Barclay).

One player is chosen to be the Shepherd, another the Thief, and the rest the sheep, who are arranged in a long row. The Shepherd pretends to be asleep; the Thief takes away one of the sheep and hides it; he then says—

Thief—" Shepherdy, shepherdy, count your sheep!"
Shepherd—" I can't come now, I'm fast asleep."
Thief—" If you don't come now, they'll all be gone,
      So shepherdy, shepherdy, come along!"

The Shepherd counts the sheep, and missing one, asks where it is gone. The Thief says, "It is gone to get fat!" The Shepherd goes to sleep again, and the same performance is repeated till all the sheep are hidden; the Shepherd goes in search of them, and when found they join him in the pursuit of the Thief.—Oswestry (Burne's *Shropshire Folk-lore*, p. 520).

Mr. Northall (*Folk Rhymes*, p. 391) gives a version from Warwickshire, and says he believes the Shepherd's dog to be the true thief who hides his propensity in the dialogue—

      Bow, wow, wow, What's the matter now?
      A leg of a louse came over my house,
      And stole one of my fat sheep away.

The game is played as in Shropshire. The dialogue in the Cornish game is similar to that of "Witch." See "Wolf."

Shepherds

One child stands alone, facing the others in a line opposite. The single child shouts, "Shepherds, shepherds, give warning." The others reply, "Warn away! warn away!" Then she asks, "How many sheep have you got?" They answer, "More than you can carry away." She runs and catches one—they two join hands and chase the rest; each one, as caught,

joining hands with the chasers until all are caught.—Liverpool
(Mr. C. C. Bell.)   See "Stag," "Warney."

Shinney, or Shinty, or Shinnops

A writer in *Blackwood's Magazine*, August 1821, p. 36, says:
The boys attempt to drive with curved sticks a ball, or what
is more common, part of the vertebral bone of a sheep, in
opposite directions.   When the object driven along reaches the
appointed place in either termination, the cry of hail! stops
the play till it is knocked off anew by the boy who was so
fortunate as to drive it past the gog.   In the Sheffield district
it is played as described by Halliwell.   During the game the
boys call out, "Hun you, shin you." It is called Shinny in
Derbyshire.—Addy's *Sheffield Glossary*.   Halliwell's description does not materially differ from the account given above
except that when the knur is down over the line it is called a
"bye."—(*Dictionary*).   In *Notes and Queries*, 8th series, viii.
446; ix. 115 *et seq*, the game is described as played in Lincolnshire under the name of "Cabsow," which perhaps accounts for
the Barnes game of Crab-sowl.

In Perthshire it is described as a game in which bats somewhat resembling a golf club are used.   At every fair or meeting of the country people there were contests at racing,
wrestling, putting the stone, &c., and on holidays all the males
of a district, young and old, met to play at football, but oftener
at shinty.—*Perthshire Statistical Account*, v. 72; Jamieson's
description is the same.

Mactaggart's *Gallovidian Encyclopædia* says: A game described by Scotch writers by the name of Shintie; the shins,
or under parts of the legs, are in danger during the game of
being struck, hence the name from shin.—Dickinson, *Cumberland Glossary*, mentions Shinny as a boyish game, also called
Scabskew, catty; it is also the name of the crook-ended stick
used in the game.   Patterson, *Antrim and Down Glossary*,
under name Shinney, says, This game is played with shinneys,
i.e., hooked sticks, and a ball or small block of wood called the
"Golley," or "Nag."

In London this game is called Hockey.   It seems to be the
same which is designed *Not* in Gloucestershire; the name

being borrowed from the ball, which is made of a knotty piece of wood.—Grose's *Glossary*.

It has been said that Shinty and Hockey differ in this respect, that in the latter two goals are erected, each being formed by a piece of stick with both ends stuck in the ground. The players divide into two parties; to each of these the care of one of the goals belongs. The game consists in endeavouring to drive the ball through the goal of the opposite party.— *Book of Sports* (1810), pp. 11–13. But in Shinty there are also two goals, called hails; the object of each party being to drive the ball beyond their own hail, but there is no hole through which it must be driven. The ball, or knot of wood, is called Shintie.

See "Bandy," "Camp," "Chinnup," "Crab-sowl," "Doddart," "Hockey," "Scrush."

Ship

A boy's game. It is played in two ways—(1) Of a single character. One boy bends down against a wall (sometimes another stands pillow for his head), then an opponent jumps on his back, crying "Ships" simply, or "Ships a-sailing, coming on." If he slips off, he has to bend as the other; but if not, he can remain as long as he pleases, provided he does not laugh or speak. If he forgets to cry "Ships," he has to bend down. (2) Sometimes sides are chosen; then the whole side go down heads and tails, and all the boys on the other side have to jump on their backs. The game in each case is much the same. The "naming" was formerly "Ships and sailors coming on."—Easther's *Almondbury Glossary*. Mr. H. Hardy sends an account from Earls Heaton, which is practically the same as these.

Ship Sail

A game usually played with marbles. One boy puts his hand into his trousers pocket and takes out as many marbles as he feels inclined; he closes his fingers over them, and holds out his hand with the palm down to the opposite player, saying, "Ship sail, sail fast. How many men on board?" A guess is made by his opponent; if less he has to give as many marbles as will make up the true number; if more, as many as he said over. But should the guess be correct he takes them, and then in his turn says, "Ship sail," &c.—Cornwall (*Folk-lore Journal*, v. 59).

See "Handy Dandy," "Neivvie-nick-nack."

Shiver the Goose

A boys' game. Two persons are trussed somewhat like fowls; they then hop about on their "hunkers," each trying to upset the other.—Patterson's *Antrim and Down Glossary*.

See "Curcuddie."

Shoeing the Auld Mare

A dangerous kind of sport. A beam of wood is slung between two ropes, a person gets on to this and contrives to steady himself until he goes through a number of antics; if he can do this he shoes the auld mare, if he cannot do it he generally tumbles to the ground and gets hurt with the fall.—Mactaggart's *Gallovidian Encyclopædia*.

Shue-Gled-Wylie

A game in which the strongest acts as the Gled or Kite, and the next in strength as the mother of a brood of birds; for those under her protection, perhaps to the number of a dozen, keep all in a string behind her, each holding by the tail of one another. The Gled still tries to catch the last of them, while the mother cries "Shue! Shue!" spreading out her arms to keep him off. If he catch all the birds he wins the game.—Fife, Teviotdale (Jamieson).

See "Fox and Geese," "Gled-Wylie," "Hen and Chickens."

Shuttlefeather

This game is generally known as "Battledore and Shuttle-cock." The battledore is a small hand bat, formerly made of wood, then of a skin stretched over a frame, and since of catgut strings stretched over a frame. The shuttlecock consists of a small cork into which feathers of equal size are fixed at even distances. The game may be played by one, two, or more persons. If by one person, it merely consists of batting up the shuttlecock into the air for as long a time as possible; if by two persons, it consists of batting the shuttlecock from one to the other; if by more than two, sides are chosen, and a game has been invented, and known as "Badminton." This latter game is not a traditional game, and does not therefore concern us now.

Strutt (*Sports and Pastimes*, p. 303) says this is a sport of long standing, and he gives an illustration, said to be of the fourteenth century, from a MS. in the possession of Mr. F. Douce. This would probably be the earliest mention of the game. It appears to have been a fashionable pastime among grown persons in the reign of James I. In the *Two Maids of Moreclacke*, 1609, it is said, "To play at Shuttlecock methinkes is the game now," and among the anecdotes related of Prince Henry, son to James I., is the following: "His Highness playing at shittle-cocke with one farr taller than himself, and hittyng him by chance with the shittle-cock upon the forehead" (*Harl. MS.*, 6391). Among the accounts of money paid for the Earl of Northumberland while he was prisoner in the Tower for supposed complicity in the Gunpowder Plot, is an item for the purchase of shuttlecocks (*Hist. MSS. Com.*, v. p. 354).

But the popular nature of the game is not indicated by these facts. For this we have to turn to the doings of the people. In the villages of the West Riding the streets may be seen on the second Sunday in May full of grown-up men and women playing "Battledore and Shuttlefeathers" (Henderson's *Folklore of the Northern Counties*, p. 80). In Leicester the approach of Shrove Tuesday (known amongst the youngsters as "Shuttlecock Day") is signalised by the appearance in the streets of a number of children playing at the game of "Battledore and Shuttlecock." On the day itself the streets literally swarm with juveniles, and even grown men and women engage in the pastime. Passing through a by-street the other day I heard a little girl singing—

Shuttlecock, shuttlecock, tell me true
How many years have I to go through?
One, two, three, four, &c.
—*Notes and Queries*, 3rd series, iii. 87.

The occurrence of this rhyme suggests that there is some sort of divination in the oldest form of the game, and it appears to me that the origin of the game must be sought for among the ancient practices of divination. An example is found among the customs of the children of Glamorganshire during the cowslip season. The cowslip heads are strung on a piece of thread and tied into a "posty," and the play is to throw it up a tolerable height, catching it on the distended palm with a blow that sends it up again, while the player sings:—

> Pisty, posty, four and forty,
> How many years shall I live?
> One, two, three, four, &c.

Of course, if it falls to the ground uncaught, or even if caught in the clenched hand, there is an end of the player's "life." There is a good deal of emulation amongst the children as to who shall live the longest (*Notes and Queries*, 3rd ser., iii. 172). Miss Burne (*Shropshire Folk-lore*, p. 530) mentions the same custom, giving the rhyme as—

> Toss-a-ball, toss-a-ball, tell me true
> How many years I've got to go through,

and she says the cowslip is thence called a "tissy-ball." In this custom we have no artificial aids to form a game, but we have a significant form of divination from natural flowers, accompanied by a rhyming formula exactly parallel to the rhymes used in the Leicestershire game of "Shuttlecock," and I conclude therefore that we have here the true origin of the game. This conclusion is confirmed when it is found that divinatory verses generally accompany the popular form of the game.

At Wakefield the children playing "Battledore and Shuttle-cock" take it in turn, and say the following sentences, one clause to each bat, and repeated until the shuttlecock falls:—

1st. This year, next year, long time, never.

2nd. Monday, Tuesday, Wednesday, Thursday, Friday, Saturday, Sunday.

3rd. Tinker, tailor, soldier, sailor, rich man, poor man, beggar-man, thief.

4th. Silk, satin, cotton, rags.

5th. Coach, carriage, wheelbarrow, donkey-cart.—Miss Fowler

At Deptford the rhymes were—

> Grandmother, grandmother,
> Tell me the truth,
> How many years have I been to school?
>> One, two, three, &c.

> Grandmother, grandmother,
> Tell me no lie,
> How many children
> Before I die?
>> One, two, three, &c.

In the same way the following questions are put and answered:—

> How old am I?
> How long am I going to live?
> How many children shall I have?

>> Black currant,
>> Red currant,
>> Raspberry tart,
>> Tell me the name
>> Of my sweetheart.
>>> A, B, C, D, &c.

Tinker, tailor, soldier, sailor, potter's boy, flour boy, thief.
Silk, satin, cotton, muslin, rags.
Coach, carriage, wheelbarrow, dungcart.
On their buttons they say: "Bought, given, stolen," to show how acquired.—Miss Chase.

In London the rhymes were—

> One, two, buckle my shoe,
> Three, four, knock at the door,
> Five, six, pick up sticks,
> Seven, eight, lay them straight,
> Nine, ten, a good fat hen,
> Eleven, twelve, ring the bell,
> Thirteen, fourteen, maids a courting,
> Fifteen, sixteen, maids in the kitchen,
> Seventeen, eighteen, mistress waiting,
> Nineteen, twenty, my plate's empty.

> One, two, three, four,
> Mary at the cottage door,
> . Eating cherries off a plate,
> Five, six, seven, eight.

> Up the ladder, down the wall,
> A twopenny loaf to serve us all ;
> You buy milk and I'll buy flour,
> And we'll have pudding in half an hour.
> One, two three, four, five, six, &c.

This year, next year, some time, never, repeated.

A, B, C, D, E, &c., repeated for the initial letter of the future husband's name.

Tinker, tailor, soldier, sailor, apothecary, ploughboy, thief, for future husband's vocation.

Monday, Tuesday, &c., for the wedding day.

Silk, satin, cotton, rags, for the material of the wedding gown.

Coach, carriage, wheelbarrow, dungcart, for conveyance on wedding day.

Big house, little house, pigsty, barn, for future home.—(A. B. Gomme.)

It will be seen that many of these divination formulæ are used in other connections than that of "Shuttlecock," but this rather emphasises the divinatory character of the game in its original form.—See "Ball," "Teesty-tosty."

Shuvvy-Hawle

A boys' game at marbles. A small hole is made in the ground, and marbles are pushed in turn with the side of the first finger ; these are won by the player pushing them into the shuvvy-hawle.—Lowsley's *Berkshire Glossary.*

Silly Old Man

—Leicester (Miss Ellis).

—Monton, Lancashire (Miss Dendy).

I.   Silly old man, he's all alone,
He wants a wife and can't get one;
Round and round and choose a good one,
Or else choose none.

This young couple are married together,
Their fathers and mothers they must obey;
Love one another like sister and brother,
And down on their knees and kiss one another.
—Leicester (Miss Ellis).

II.   Silly old man, he walks alone,
He walks alone, he walks alone;
Silly old man, he walks alone,
He wants a wife and can't get one.

All go round and choose your own,
Choose your own, choose your own;
All go round and choose your own,
And choose a good one or else choose none.

Now young couple you're married together,
Married together, married together;
Now young couple you're married together,
Your father and mother you must obey.
So love one another like sister and brother,
And now young couple pray kiss together.
—Lancashire (*Notes and Queries*, 5th series, iv. 157).

III.   Silly old maid (*or* man), she walks alone,
She walks alone, she walks alone;
Silly old maid, she walks alone,
She wants a man (*or* wife) and she can't get one.

Go around and choose your own,
Choose your own, choose your own ;
Go around and choose your own,
And take whoever you like in.

Now these two are married together,
Married together, married together ;
Now these two are married together,
I pray love, kiss again.   —Isle of Man (A. W. Moore).

IV.   Here's a silly ould man that lies all alone,
That lies all alone, that lies all alone ;
Here's a silly ould man that lies all alone,
He wants a wife and he can get none.

Now young couple you're married together,
You're married together, you're married together ;
You must obey your father and mother,
And love one another like sister and brother.
I pray, young couple, you'll kiss together.
                    —Carleton's *Traits and Stories of the Irish
                              Peasantry*, p. 107.

V.   Silly old man, he walks alone,
Walks alone, walks alone ;
Silly old man, he walks alone,
Wants a wife and he canna get one.

All go round and choose your own,
Choose your own, choose your own ;
All go round and choose your own,
Choose a good one or let it alone.

Now he's got married and tied to a peg,
Tied to a peg, tied to a peg ;
Now he's got married and tied to a peg,
Married a wife with a wooden leg.
                    —Monton, Lancashire (Miss Dendy).

VI.   Silly old maid, she lives alone,
She lives alone, she lives alone ;
[Silly old maid, she lives alone,]
Wants a husband but can't get one.

So now go round and choose your own,
Choose your own, choose your own;
Now go round and choose your own,
Choose the very one you love best.

Now young couple, you're married for ever,
Your father and mother you must obey;
Love another like sister and brother,
And now young couple, pray kiss together.
—Dublin (Mrs. Lincoln).

(*c*) The children form a ring, joining hands. A child, usually a boy, stands in the middle. The ring dances round and sings the verses. The boy in the centre chooses a girl when bidden by the ring. These two then stand in the centre and kiss each other at the command. The boy then takes a place in the ring, and the girl remains in the centre and chooses a boy in her turn. In the Dublin and Isle of Man versions a girl is first in the centre; in the Manx version (A. W. Moore) the two children hold hands when in the centre.

(*d*) In the *Traits and Stories of the Irish Peasantry*, Mr. Carleton gives this game as one of those played by young people of both sexes at funeral wakes. It is played in the same way as the game now is; boys and girls stand alternately in a ring holding hands, choosing each other in turn, and kissing. The other versions do not differ materially from each other, except that the Lancashire version described by Miss Dendy has evidently been corrupted quite lately, because a purer form is quoted from the same county in *Notes and Queries*. The game seems to be one of the group of marriage games arising from the fact that at any gathering of people for the purpose of a ceremonial, whether a funeral or a festival, it was the custom to form matrimonial alliances. The words are used for kiss-in-the-ring games, and also in some marriage games when the last player is left without a partner.

Skin the Goatie

One boy takes his stand in an upright position at a wall. Another boy stoops with his head in the breast of the one standing upright. A third boy jumps stride-leg on his back, and tries to "crown," *i.e.*, put his hand on the head of the boy at the wall. The boy on whose back he is tries every means by shifting from side to side, and by throwing up his back, to prevent him from doing so, and to cast him off. If he succeeds in doing so, he takes his stand behind the stooping boy in the same position. Another boy then tries to do the same thing over the two stooping boys. If he succeeds in crowning the standing boy, he takes his station at the wall. If not, he takes his stand behind the two stooping boys. The game goes on till a boy "crowns" the one standing at the wall.—Banchory (Rev. W. Gregor).

See "Saddle the Nag."

Skipping

Strutt says (*Sports*, p. 383), "This amusement is probably very ancient. Boys often contend for superiority of skill in this game, and he who passes the rope about most times without interruption is the conqueror. In the hop season a hop-stem, stripped of its leaves, is used instead of a rope, and, in my opinion, it is preferable." On Good Friday on Brighton beach the fisher folk used to play at skipping, six to ten grown-up people skipping at one rope.

Apart from the ordinary, and probably later way of playing, by one child holding a rope in both hands, turning it over the head, and either stepping over it while running, or standing still and jumping until the feet catch the rope and a trip is made, skipping appears to be performed in two ways, jumping or stepping across with (1) more or less complicated movements of the rope and feet, and (2) the ordinary jumping over a turned rope while chanting rhymes, for the purpose of deciding whether the players are to be married or single, occupation of future husband, &c.

Of the first class of game there are the following variants :—

"Pepper, salt, mustard, cider, vinegar."—Two girls turn the rope slowly at first, repeating the above words, then they turn it as quickly as possible until the skipper is tired out, or trips.

" Rock the Cradle."—In this the holders of the rope do not throw it completely over, but swing it from side to side with an even motion like the swinging of the pendulum of a clock.

" Chase the Fox."—One girl is chosen as a leader, or fox. The first runs through the rope, as it is turned towards her, without skipping; the others all follow her; then she runs through from the other side as the rope is turned from her, and the others follow. Then she runs in and jumps or skips once, and the others follow suit; then she skips twice and runs out, then three times, the others all following in turn until one trips or fails. The first one to do this takes the place of one of the turners, the turner taking her place as one of the skippers.

" Visiting."—One girl turns the rope over herself, and another jumps in and faces her, while skipping in time with the girl she visits. She then runs out again without stopping the rope, and another girl runs in.

" Begging."—Two girls turn, and two others run and skip together side by side. While still skipping they change places; one says, as she passes, " Give me some bread and butter; " the other answering, " Try my next door neighbour." This is continued until one trips.

" Winding the Clock."—Two turn the rope, and the skipper counts one, two, three, up to twelve, turning round each time she jumps or skips.

" Baking Bread."—Two girls turn, and another runs in with a stone in her hand, which she puts down on the ground, and picks up again while skipping.

" The Ladder."—The girls run in to skip, first on one foot and then the other, with a stepping motion.

Two other games are as follows :—(1.) Two ropes are used, and a girl holds either end in each hand, turning them alternately; the skipper has to jump or skip over each in turn. When the rope is turned inwards, it is called " double dutch," when turned outwards, " French dutch." (2.) The skipper has a short rope which she turns over herself, while two other girls turn a longer rope over her head.

The second class of games consists of those cases where the skipping is accompanied by rhymes, and is used for the purpose

of foretelling the future destiny of the skipper.   These rhymes
are as follows (all collected by Miss Chase) :—

> Ipsey, Pipsey, tell me true
> Who shall I be married to ?
> A, B, C, &c.

Letters—initial of one to whom you'll be married.—Hurstmonceux, Sussex.

> Half pound tuppeny rice,
> Half a pound of treacle,
> Penny 'orth of spice
> To make it nice,
> Pop goes the weazle.   —Crockham Hill, Kent.

> When I was young and able,
> I sat upon the table ;
> The table broke,
> And gave me a poke,
> When I was young and able.

[The children now add that when singing

> Pass the baker,*
> Cook the tater,

is the full couplet.]—Deptford.

> Every morning at eight o'clock,
> You all may hear the postman's knock.
> 1, 2, 3, 4.   There goes " Polly."

Girl named running out, and another girl running in directly.
—Marylebone.

> Up and down the ladder wall,
> Ha'penny loaf to feed us all ;
> A bit for you, and a bit for me,
> And a bit for Punch and Judy.
>
> —Paddington Green.

As they run thus, each calls in turn, "Red, yellow, blue,
white."   Where you are tripped, the colour stopped on marks
that of your wedding gown.—Deptford.

---

* To change from left to right side, crossing a second skipper, is called " Pass
the Baker."

Each of the two girls turning the rope takes a colour, and as the line of children run through, they guess by shouting, "Red?" "Green?" When wrong nothing happens; they take the place of turner, however, if they hit upon her colour. Another way is to call it "Sweet stuff shop," or "green grocers," and guess various candies and fruits until they choose right.—Deptford.

When several girls start running in to skip, they say,
> "All in, a bottle of gin,"
and as they leave at a dash, they cry—
> "All out, a bottle of stout."

While "in" jumping, the turners time the skippers' movements by a sing song.
> Up and down the city wall,
> Ha'penny loaf to feed us all;
> I buy milk, you buy flour,
> You shall have *pepper* in half an hour.
> > —Deptford.

At pepper turn swiftly.

> Up and down the ladder wall,
> Penny loaf to feed us all;
> A bit for you, and a bit for me,
> And a bit for all the familee. —Marylebone.

> Up and down the city wall,
> In and out "The Eagle,"
> That's the way the money goes,
> Pop goes the weazel.
> > —From "A London Maid."

> Dancing Dolly had no sense,
> For to fiddle for eighteenpence;
> All the tunes that she could play,
> Were "Sally get out of the donkey's way."
> > —Deptford.

> My mother said
> That the rope must go
> Over my head. —Deptford.

Andy Pandy,
Sugardy candy,
French almond
Rock.   —Deptford.

B-L-E-S-S-I-N-G.
Roses red, roses white,
Roses in my garden ;
I would not part
With my sweetheart
For tuppence hapenny farthing.
A, B, C, &c., to X, Y, Z.—Deptford.

Knife and fork,
Lay the cloth,*
Dont forget the salt,
Mustard, vinegar,
Pepper !   —Deptford.

They sometimes make a girl skip back and forth the long
way of the rope, using this dialogue—
Girl skipping.—"Father, give me the key."
Father.—"Go to your mother."
Girl jumping in opposite direction.—"Mother, give me the
key."
Mother.—"Go to your father."

Lady, lady, drop your handkerchief,
Lady, lady, pick it up.
Suiting action to the words, still skipping.

Rhyme to time the jumps—
Cups and saucers,
Plates and dishes,
My old man wears
Calico breeches.

Skyte the Bob

This game might be played by two, three, or more. A
small stone of a squarish form, called the "bob," was placed

* In Marylebone add here, " Bring me up a leg of pork."

on a level piece of ground. On this stone each player placed an old button, for buttons were the stakes. A point was fixed several yards from the stone, and a line was drawn. Along this line, "the stance," the players took their stand, each holding in his hand a small flat stone named "the pitcher." This stone was thrown so as to strike "the bob" and make the buttons fall on "the pitcher," or nearer it than "the bob." The button or buttons that lay nearer "the pitcher" than "the bob" fell to the lot of the player. The second player did the same, but he had to guard against driving any of the buttons nearer the first player's stone. If a button was nearer his stone than "the bob," or the first player's stone, he claimed it. The third player followed the same course if all the buttons had not been won by the two players. If the buttons were not all won at the first throw, the first player had a second chance, and so on till all the buttons were won. If two played, if each won a button, they alternately began, but if one gained the two buttons, the other began. When three played, if one had two for his share he played last in the following game, and the one that had nothing played first. If the players, when three played, were experts, the one whose lot it was to play second, who was called the "poust," lost heavily, and to be "pousted" was always looked upon as a misfortune, for the reason that the first player often by the first throw gained the whole stake, and then in the following game the last player became the first, and the gainer in the foregoing game became the last. If this player carried off the whole stake, he in the next game took the last place, and the last took the first, and so between the two good players the "poust" had no chance.—Aberdeenshire (Rev. W. Gregor). —See "Buttons."

Smuggle the Gig

Mr. Ballantyne describes the game as played in his young days at Biggar as follows:—Two boys would each select his own side. "First pick" was decided by lot. A third boy took two straws, one shorter than the other, and held them between his finger and thumb in such a way that only equal lengths were visible. Each leader drew a straw. The one who drew the longest had "first pick" of all the intended players, the other leader had the next; alternate choice was then made by them until both sides were complete, and were ranged by their leaders. Then lots were again drawn as to which side should go out first. The side going out had to show the Gig; anything easily carried in the hand sufficed. The "outs" went out from the den twenty or thirty yards, some- times round the end of a house, to "smuggle the Gig"—that is, to give one of their number the Gig to carry, care being taken that the "ins" did not know who had it. During this time the leader of the ins called "out" in a loud voice—

Zimerie, twaerie, hickeri seeven,
Aucherie, daucherie, ten and eleven;
Twall ran musha dan
Tweedledum, twadledum, twenty-one. Time's up!

Outs had all to appear by " Ready " when the chase began. Boundary limits were fixed, beyond which outs could not run and ins could not stand, within a fixed distance of the den. This den was a place marked by a mark or rut in the ground, about four feet by six feet. The outs endeavoured (particularly the one carrying the Gig) to get into the den before any one could catch and "crown" him. The pursued, when caught, was held by the pursuer, his cap taken off, and the palm of the hand was placed on the crown of his head. As he did so the pursuer would say, "Deliver up the Gig." If he had it not, the pursuer went off after another player. If he had the Gig, and succeeded in getting into the den without being "crowned," outs won the game; but if the Gig was caught and "crowned," ins won.

At Fraserburgh the players are divided equally. A spot is marked off, called the Nestie. Any small object known to all is chosen as the Gig. One half of the players receive the Gig and retire, so as not to be seen distinctly by the other half that remains in and near the Nestie. The Gig is concealed on the person of one of the players that retire. When every- thing is ready those having the Gig move towards the Nestie, and those in the Nestie come to meet them. The aim is to catch the player who has the Gig before reaching the Nestie. If this is done the same players again hide the Gig, but if the Gig is discovered, the players discovering it now hide it.

At Old Aberdeen sides are chosen, then a small article (such as a knife) is made the *gig*. Then one side, determined by a toss, goes out and smuggles the gig and cries out, "Smuggle the gig." Then the other side rushes in and tries to catch the one that has the "gig." If the one that has the gig is free, the same side goes out again.—Rev. W. Gregor.

See "Gegg."

Snail Creep

In Mid-Cornwall, in the second week of June, at St. Roche, and in one or two adjacent parishes, a curious dance is performed at their annual "feasts." It enjoys the rather undignified name of "Snail Creep," but would be more properly called the "Serpent's Coil." The following is scarcely a perfect description of it :—"The young people being all assembled in a large meadow, the village band strikes up a simple but lively air and marches forward, followed by the whole assemblage, leading hand-in-hand (or more closely linked in case of engaged couples), the whole keeping time to the tune with a lively step. The band, or head of the serpent, keeps marching in an ever-narrowing circle, whilst its train of dancing followers becomes coiled around it in circle after circle. It is now that the most interesting part of the dance commences, for the band, taking a sharp turn about, begins to retrace the circle, still followed as before, and a number of young men, with long leafy branches in their hands as standards, direct this counter movement with almost military precision."—W. C. Wade (*Western Antiquary*, April 1881).

A game similar to the above dance is often played by Sunday school children in West Cornwall, at their out-of-door summer treats, called by them "Roll tobacco." They join hands in one long line, the taller children at their head. The first child stands still, whilst the others in ever-narrowing circles dance around singing until they are coiled into a tight mass. The outer coil then wheels sharply in a contrary direction, followed by the remainder, retracing their steps.— Courtney's *Cornish Feasts and Folk-lore*, p. 39. A Scottish game, "Row Chow Tobacco," described by Jamieson, is played in the same way, the boy at the extremity being called the "Pin." A clamorous noise succeeds the "winding up," the players crying out "Row Chow Tobacco" while giving and receiving the fraternal hug. The words are pronounced Rowity-chowity-bacco. The naming of this game in connection with tobacco is curious. It is undoubtedly the same as "Snail Creep." I am inclined to think that all these games are connected with an ancient form of Tree-worship, and that the analogy of tobacco-rolling is quite modern.

See "Bulliheisle," "Eller Tree," "Tuilyie-waps," "Wind up the Bush Faggot."

Snapping Tongs
See "Musical Chairs."

Snatch Apple
A game similar to "Bob Cherry," but played with an apple. —Halliwell's *Dictionary*.

Snatch Hood
An undescribed boy's game mentioned in a statute of Edward III.'s time.—Halliwell's *Dictionary*.

Soldier

I am an old soldier, I come from the war,
　　Come from the war ;
I am an old soldier, I come from the war,
　　And my age it is sixty-and-three.

I have but one son and he lies alone, lies alone,
　　I have but one son and he lies alone ;
And he's still making moan for lying alone.

Son, go choose a wife of your own,
Choose a good one or else choose none,
Or bring none home to me.

Now they're got married, they're bound to obey,
Bound to obey in every degree ;
And as you go round kiss all but me.
　　　　　　　　　—Belfast, Ireland (W. H. Patterson).

The players form a ring and sing the first three verses. Then one of the players chooses a girl from the ring. The first three verses are again sung until the whole ring is arranged in couples; then the first couple kneels in the middle, and the rest dance round them singing the marriage formula; then the second couple, and so on, each couple kissing.

Solomon

The players knelt in a line; the one at the head, in a very solemn tone, chaunted, "Solomon had a great dog;" the others answered in the same way, "Just so" (this was always the refrain). Then the first speaker made two or three more ridiculous speeches, ending with, "And at last this great dog died, and fell down," giving at the same time a violent lurch against his next neighbour, who, not expecting it, fell against his, and so on, to the end of the line.—Cornwall (*Folk-lore Journal*, v. 50).

See "Obadiah," Quaker's Wedding.

Sort'em-billyort'em

A Lancashire game, very similar to "Hot Peas and Bacon."
—Halliwell's *Dictionary*.

Sow-in-the-Kirk

A large hole is made in the ground, surrounded by smaller ones, according to the number of the players, every one of whom has a shintie, or hooked stick. The middle hole is called the kirk. He who takes the lead in the game is called the sow-driver. His object is to drive a small piece of wood or bone, called the sow, into the large hole or kirk; while that of his opponents, every one of whom keeps his shintie in one of the smaller holes, is to frustrate his exertions by driving back the sow. If he succeeds, either in knocking it into one of the small holes, while one of his antagonists is in the act of striking it back, he is released from the drudgery of being driver. In the latter case, the person whose vacancy he has occupied takes the servile station which he formerly held.—Lothian (Jamieson). This is said to be the same game with "Church and Mice" in Fife. Jamieson's description is not very lucid. It appears that each player must hold his shintie with its end in his hole, and it is only when he takes it out to prevent the sow-driver getting his sow into or towards the kirk, that the sow-driver has the chance of putting the sow into the player's hole, and so causing that player to take the place of sow-driver.

See " Kirk the Gussie."

Span Counter

A common game among boys. " You shall finde me playing at Span Counter."—Dekker's *Northward Hoe.* Toone, *Etymological Dictionary*, mentions this as a juvenile game played with counters.

> Boys shall not play
> At span counter or blow pipe.
> —Donne (*Satire* iv.).

Dr. Grosart, in noting this passage, says, " I rather think the game is still played by boys when they directly, or by rebound, endeavour to play their button or marble into a hole." Strutt briefly notes the game as being similar to " Boss Out."—*Sports*, p. 384. Halliwell (*Dictionary*) simply gives the quotation from Donne's Poems, p. 131, mentioning the game.

See " Boss Out."

Spang and Purley

A mode resorted to by boys of measuring distances, particularly at the game of marbles. It means a space and something more.—Brockett's *North Country Words*.

Spangie

A game played by boys with marbles or halfpence. A marble or halfpenny is struck against the wall. If the second player can bring his so near that of his antagonist as to include both within a *span*, he claims both as his.—Jamieson.

This is the same game as " Banger," " Boss Out." Probably the Old English game of " Span Counter," or " Span Farthing," was originally the same.—See Johnson's *Dictionary*.

Spannims

A game at marbles played in the eastern parts of England.
—Halliwell's *Dictionary*.

Spawnie

The same game as "Spangie."—Keith (Rev. W. Gregor).

Spinny-Wye

The name of a game among children at Newcastle-upon-
Tyne. I suspect this is nearly the same with "Hide and
Seek." "I spye" is the usual exclamation at a childish game
called "Hie, spy, hie."—Brand, ii. 442.

Splints

A game at marbles, in which they are dropped from the hand
in heaps.—Easther's *Almondbury Glossary*.

Spurn point

An old game (undescribed) mentioned in the play *Apollo
Shroving*, London, 1627, p. 49.

Spy-arm

A game of Hide-and-Seek, with this difference, that when
those are found who are hid the finder cries Spy-arm ; and if
the one discovered can catch the discoverer, he has a ride upon
his back to the dools.—Mactaggart's *Gallovidian Encyclopædia*.

See "Hide and Seek" (1).

Stacks

A stack in the centre of the stackyard was selected, and round
a part of one side a rut was marked in the earth usually by the
toe-bit of the ploughman's boot. This enclosure, not over
four feet wide at the broadest part, was called the den. One
of the players, selected to be the catcher, stood within this den,
and when all the players were ready turned his face to the
stack, and counted out loud the numerals from one to twenty,
the last with a great shout. During the count the players ran
round the stacks out of sight, but no hiding nor leaving the stackyard, this was "not fair." When twenty was heard one would
shout back "Ready!" Then out came the catcher. He was
not permitted to stand in or near the den, but went out among
the stacks and caught as many players as he could before they

reached the den. The great aim of those " out " was to get into the den unseen and untouched. If all the players got in, then the catcher had to try again; but when all were caught (which was seldom or ever), the last one caught was catcher for the next game. When one player was touched by the catcher he or she had to remain in the den till the rest were all in.—Biggar (Wm. Ballantyne).

Mr. Ballantyne says, "This game usually ended in a promiscuous 'catching' and 'touching' game, each lad trying to catch the lass he liked best, and some lads, for the fun of the thing, would try and get a particular girl first, her wishes and will not being considered in the matter; and it seemed to be an unwritten law among them for the lass to 'gang wi' the lad that catched her first,' yet I have known lassies take this opportunity to favour the lad they preferred. It was the correct thing for the people to visit each other's farms in rotation to play 'the stacks.'" This game was played when all the crops of grain were in the stackyard under thack and rape (? nape). Then it was customary for the servant lads and lasses of neighbours' "ferm toons" to gather together and play at this game. Mr. Ballantyne considers it was the third of three festivals formerly held at the ingathering of the crops.

See "Barley Break."

Stag

A boys' game. One boy issues forth and tries to "tig" another, previously saying this nominy, or the first two lines—

> Stag, stag arony,
> Ma' dog's bony,
> Them 'at Aw catch
> 'Ill ha' to go wi' me.

When one boy is tigged (or " tug ") the two issue forth hand in hand, and when more, all hand in hand. The other players have the privilege of breaking the chain, and if they succeed the parties forming it are liable to be ridden back to the den. At Lepton, where the game was publicly played, the boundaries were " Billy tour end, Penny Haas end, and I' Horsin step." So played in 1810, and is still.—Easther's *Almondbury Glossary*.

In the Sheffield district it is called " Rag Stag," and is

usually played in the playground, or yard, attached to a school. Any number can play. A place is chalked out in a corner or angle formed by the walls or hedges surrounding the playground. This is called the den, and a boy stands within the den. Sometimes the den is formed by chalking an area out upon a footpath, as in the game of "Bedlams." The boy in the den walks or runs out, crying, "Rag-stag, jinny I over, catching," and having said this he attempts to catch one of the boys in the playground who have agreed to play the game. Having caught him he takes him back into the den. When they have got into the den they run out hand-in-hand, one of them crying, "Rag-stag, jinny I over, touching," whilst the other immediately afterwards calls out, "Rag-stag, jinny I over, catching." They must keep hold of each other's hands, and whilst doing so the one who cried out "Touching" attempts to touch one of the boys in the playground, whilst the one who cried "Catching" attempts to catch one of such boys. If a boy is caught or touched, the two boys who came out of the den, together with their prisoner, run back as quickly as possible into the den, with their hands separated. If whilst they are running back into the den any boy in the playground can catch any one of the three who are running back, he jumps on his back and rides as far as the den, but he must take care not to ride too far, for when the boys who are already caught enter the den they can seize their riders, and pull them into the den. In this case the riders too are caught. The process is repeated until all are caught.—Addy's *Sheffield Glossary*.

Another name for the game is "Stag-out." One player is Stag, and has a place marked out for his bounds. He stands inside, and then rushes out with his hands clasped together, and endeavours to touch one of the other players, which being accomplished, he has the privilege of riding on the boy's back to his bounds again.—*Book of Sports*. In a London version the hands were held above the head, and joined by interlacing the thumbs, the fingers being outspread, the boy had to touch another while in this position.

In Shropshire it is called "Stag-warning." One boy is chosen Stag; he runs about the playground with his clasped hands held palms together in front of him, trying to tick (= touch) others. Each whom he touches joins hands with him, and they run together in an ever-lengthening chain, sweeping the playground from end to end, the boys at each end of the chain "ticking" others with their disengaged hands, till all are caught but one, who becomes the next "Stag." The Stag gives notice of his start by exclaiming—

> Stag-warning, stag-warning,
> Come out to-morrow morning!   —Shrewsbury.

> Stag a-rag a-rorning
> Very frosty morning!
> What I cannot catch to-night I'll catch to-morrow
> morning!
> —Chirbury (Burne's *Shropshire Folk-lore*, p. 523).

The game is mentioned by Mr. Patterson in his *Antrim and Down Glossary*. Northall's *English Folk Rhymes*, p. 392, gives a Warwickshire and Staffordshire version, in which the first player "ticked" or "tagged" becomes Stag when the first game is concluded, all having been caught. The words used are—

> Stag aloney,
> My long poney,
> Kick the bucket over.

Halliwell (*Dictionary*) also describes the game, and indicates its origin. The boy chosen for the game clasps his hands together, and, holding them out, threatens his companions as though pursuing them with horns, and a chase ensues in which the Stag endeavours to strike one of them, who then becomes Stag in his turn. Unfortunately, Halliwell does not, in this instance, give his authority, but if it is taken from the players themselves, it is a sufficient account of the origin of the game, apart from the evidence of the name. All this group of games is evidently to be traced to one original, though in different places the detail of the game has developed somewhat differently. It evidently comes down from the time when stags were hunted not so much for sport as for food.

See "Chickidy Hand," "Hornie," "Hunt the Stagie," "Shepherds," "Warney."

Stagging

A man's game. Two men have their ankles tied together and their wrists tied behind their backs. They then try to knock each other down.—Patterson's *Antrim Glossary*.

See "Hirtschin Hairy."

Steal the Pigs

The game represents the stealing of a woman's children and the recovery of them. The mother, before beginning to wash, disposes of her children in a safe place. She proceeds to do her washing. While she is busy a child-snatcher comes and takes away one. The others begin to cry. The mother hears them crying. She goes and asks the reason of their crying, and is told that a woman came and took away one of them. She scolds and beats them all; tells them to be more careful for the time to come, and returns to her washing. Again the children cry, and the mother goes to see what is the matter with them, and is told the same thing. She repeats her admonition and bodily correction, and returns to her work. This process is repeated till all the children are stolen. After finishing her washing, she goes to her children and finds the last one gone. She sets out in search of them, and meets a woman whom she questions if she had seen her children. She denies all knowledge of them. The mother persists, and at last discovers all her stolen children. She demands them back. The stealer refuses, and puts them behind her and stands on her defence. A tussel takes place. The mother in the long run rescues her children.—Fraserburgh (Rev. W. Gregor).

See "Mother, Mother, Pot boils over," "Witch."

Stealy Clothes

See "Scots and English."

Steik and Hide

The game of Hide and Seek.—Aberdeen (Jamieson).

Sticky-stack

A game among young people in running up the face or cut part of a hay-stack to try who can put in a stick the highest.—Brockett's *North Country Words*.

Sticky Toffey

Name of a game (undescribed) recorded by the Rev. S. D. Headlam, as played by Hoxton School children at Hoxton.— *Church Reformer*, 1894.

Stiff Police

A game (undescribed) recorded by the Rev. S. D. Headlam, as played by Hoxton School children.—*Church Reformer*, 1894.

Stik-n Snael (Stick and Snell)

Game of cat.—Elworthy, *West Somerset Words*. The short stick, pointed at both ends, is called a snell.

Stocks

A schoolboys' game. Two boys pick a side, and there is one den only, and they toss to see which side shall keep it. The side which wins the toss then goes out, and when two boys have got a good distance off they cry " Stocks." The boys who keep the den run after them to catch them. When one is caught his capturer counts ten while he holds him (in a more primitive but less refined state, spat over his head) and cries *Stocks.* This prisoner is taken into the den. If they are all caught the other side turns out. But if one of the outer side can manage to run through the den and cry "Stocks," all the prisoners are relieved, and can go out again.—Easther's *Almondbury Glossary.* See " Stacks."

Stones

A circle of stones is formed according to the number of players, generally five or seven each side. One of the out party stands in the centre of the circle, and lobs at the different stones in rotation ; each hit a player gives all his side must change stations, in some places going round to the left and in others to the right. The stones are defended by the hand or a stick, according as a ball or stick is lobbed. All the players are out if the stone is hit, or the ball or stick caught, or one of the players is hit while running. In different counties or places these games are more or less modified.—Dublin, *Folk-lore Journal*, ii. 264–265.

Mr. Kinahan, who describes this game, adds a very instructive note, which is worth quoting :—

"These games I have seen played over half a century ago, with a lob-stick, but of later years with a ball, long before a cricket club existed, in Trinity College, Dublin, and when the game was quite unknown in a great part of Ireland. At the same time, they may have been introduced by some of the earlier settlers, and afterwards degenerated into the games mentioned above ; but I would be inclined to suspect that the Irish are the primitive games, they having since been improved into cricket. At the present day these games nearly everywhere are succeeded by cricket, but often of a very primitive form, the wickets being stones set on end, or a pillar of stones ; while the ball is often wooden, and very rudely formed."

Stool-ball

The first mention of this game is by Smyth in his *Berkeley Manuscripts*. In the reign of Elizabeth, the Earl of Leicester, with an extraordinary number of attendants and multitudes of country people, and "whom my neighbours parallel to Bartholomew faire in London, came to Wotton, and thence to Michaelwood Lodge, castinge down part of the pales, which like a little park then enclosed the Lodge (for the gates were too narrow to let in his Trayne), and thence went to Wotton Hill, where hee plaid a. match at stoball."—*Gloucestershire County Folk-lore*, p. 26.

The earliest description of the game, however, is by Aubrey. He says " it is peculiar to North Wilts, North Gloucestershire, and a little part of Somerset near Bath. They smite a ball, stuffed very hard with quills and covered with soale leather, with a staffe, commonly made of withy, about three feet and a half long. Colerne down is the place so famous and so frequented for stoball playing. The turfe is very fine and the rock (freestone) is within an inch and a halfe of the surface which gives the ball so quick a rebound. A stobball ball is of about four inches diameter and as hard as a stone. I do not heare that this game is used anywhere in England but in this part of Wiltshire and Gloucestershire adjoining." (Aubrey's *Natural*

History of Wiltshire, p. 117; *Collections for North Wilts*, p. 77). It is no doubt the same game as Stool-ball, which is alluded to by Herrick in 1648 (*Hesperides*), and in Poor Robin's Almanack for 1677 (see Halliwell's *Dictionary*). D'Urfey's *Don Quixote*, written in 1694, alludes to it as follows :—

> "Down in a vale, on a summer's day,
>   All the lads and lasses met to be merry ;
> A match for kisses at stool-ball to play,
>   And for cakes and ale, and cider and perry."

> *Chorus ;*
> "Come all, great, small, short, tall—
>   Away to stool-ball."

It is also alluded to in Poor Robin's Almanack for 1740:

> "Now milkmaids pails are deckt with flowers,
> And men begin to drink in bowers,
> The mackarels come up in shoals,
> To fill the mouths of hungry souls ;
> Sweet sillabubs, and lip-lov'd tansey,
> For William is prepared by Nancy.
> Much time is wasted now away,
> At pigeon-holes, and nine-pin play,
> Whilst hob-nail Dick, and simpring Frances,
> Trip it away in country dances ;
> At *stool-ball* and at barley-break,
> Wherewith they harmless pastime make."

It is described by Strutt in *Sports and Pastimes*, p. 103, as a variety of game more commonly known as "goff" or "bandy ball," the paganica of the Romans, who also stuffed their balls with feathers. According to Dr. Johnson, the balls are driven from stool to stool, hence the name.

In spite of Aubrey's opinion as to the limited range of this game, it appears to have been pretty generally played. Thus, Roberts' *Cambrian Antiquities* says, "Stool-ball, resembling cricket, except that no bats are used and that a stool was substituted for the wicket, was in my memory also a favourite game on holydays, but it is now seldom or ever played. It generally began on Easter Eve" (p. 123). It was also an old Sussex game. Mr. Parish's account is that it was "similar in many respects to cricket, played by females. It has lately been revived in East Sussex by the establishment of stool-ball clubs in many villages. The elevens go long distances to play their matches; they practise regularly and frequently, display such perfection of fielding and wicket-keeping as would put most amateur cricketers to shame. The rules are printed and implicitly obeyed."—Parish's *Dictionary of Sussex Dialect.*

Miss Edith Mendham says of the Sussex game, it is supposed to derive its name from being played by milkmaids when they returned from milking. Their stools were (I think) used as wickets, and the rules were as follows:—

1. The wickets to be boards one foot square, mounted on a stake, which, when fixed in the ground, must be four feet nine inches from the ground.

2. The wickets to be sixteen yards apart, the bowling crease to be eight yards from the wicket.

3. The bowler to stand with one foot behind the crease, and in bowling must neither jerk nor throw the ball.

4. The ball to be of that kind known as "Best Tennis," No. 3.

5. The bats to be of wood, and made the same size and shape as battledores.

6. The striker to be out if the ball when bowled hits the wicket, or if the ball be caught in the *hands* of any of the opposing side, or if in running, preparing to run, or pretending to run, the ball be thrown or touch the wicket before the striker reaches it, and the ball in all cases must strike the face of the wicket, and in running the striker must at each run strike the wicket with her bat.

7. There should be eleven players on each side.

8. Overs to consist of eight balls.

Miss F. Hagden, in her short History of Alfriston, Sussex, says, "In the Jubilee year the game of stool-ball was revived and played in the Tye field. The rules resemble those of cricket, but the wickets are square boards on posts; the bowler stands in the centre of the pitch, the bats used are round boards with a handle. The game in Alfriston seems now to have died out again, but in many villages there are regular clubs for the girls," p. 43. It also appears to be a game among Lancashire children to this day. A stool is used as a wicket, at which it is attempted to throw the ball; a player stands near the stool, and using his or her hand as a bat, wards off the blow. If the ball hits the stool the thrower takes the place at wicket; or if the ball is caught the catcher becomes the guardian of the stool. Stool-ball, like all ball games, was usually played at Easter for tansy cakes. Mr. Newell (*Games and Songs*) says this game is recorded by the second governor of Massachusetts as being played under date of the second Christmas of the colony.

See " Bittle-battle," " Cricket," " Stool-ball."

Strik a Licht

A version of hide and seek. One player is chosen to be "it." The other players go away to a distance and "show a light," to let "it" understand they are ready. They then hide, and the first one found has to be "it" in place of the previous seeker.—Aberdeen (Rev. W. Gregor).

See " Hide and Seek."

Stroke

A game at marbles, where each player places a certain number on a line and plays in turns from a distance mark called "scratch," keeping such as he may knock off.—Lowsley's *Berkshire Glossary.*

Stroke Bias

Brome, in his *Travels over England*, 1700, p. 264, says: "The Kentish men have a peculiar exercise, especially in the eastern parts, which is nowhere else used in any other country, I believe, but their own; it is called 'Stroke Bias,' and the manner of it is thus. In the summer time one or two parishes convening make choice of twenty, and sometimes more, of the best runners which they can cull out in their precincts, who send a challenge to an equal number of racers within the liberties of two other parishes, to meet them at a set day upon some neighbouring plain; which challenge, if accepted, they repair to the place appointed, whither also the county resort in great numbers to behold the match, when having stripped themselves at the goal to their shirts and drawers, they begin the course, every one bearing in his eye a particular man at which he aims; but after several traverses and courses on both sides, that side, whose legs are the nimblest to gain the first seven strokes from their antagonists, carry the day and win the prize. Nor is this game only appropriated to the men, but in some places the maids have their set matches too, and are as vigorous and active to obtain a victory."

Sun and Moon

"A kinde of play wherein two companies of boyes holding hands all on a rowe, doe pull with hard hold one another, till one be overcome."—Quoted by Halliwell (*Dictionary*), from *Thomasii Dictionarium*, London, 1644.

Sunday Night

1. Sunday night an' Nancy, oh!
   My delight and fancy, oh!
   All the world that I should know
   If I had a Katey, oh!

   "He! ho! my Katey, oh!
   My bonny, bonny Katey, oh!
   All the world that I should keep
   If I had a Katey, oh!"
   —Liphook, Hants (Miss Fowler).

2. Sunday night and brandy, O!
   My life and saying so,
   My life and saying so,
   Call upon me Annie, O!
   I Annie, O!
      Bonnie, bonnie Annie, O!
   She's the girl that I should like
   If I had an Annie, O!
   —Earls Heaton, Yorks. (H. Hardy).

(b) The children stand in a row with backs against a wall or fence, whilst one stands out and stepping backwards and forwards to the tune sings the first verse. Then she rushes to pick out one, taking her by the hands and standing face to face with her, sings the other verse. Then the two separate their hands, and standing side by side sing the first verse over again, taking another girl from the row, and so on again.

"Monday night," or "Pimlico," is the name of a singing game mentioned by the Rev. S. D. Headlam, in *The Church Reformer*, as played by children in the schools at Hoxton, which he says was accompanied by a kind of chaunt of a very fascinating kind.

Sun Shines

The sun shines above and the sun shines below,
And a' the lasses in this school is dying in love I know,
Especially (girl's name) she's beautiful and fair;
She's awa wi' (a boy's name) for the curl o's hair.
In comes (girl's name) mother with the glass in her han',
Says—My dearest daughter, I'm glad you're gettin a man,
I'm glad you're gettin a man and a cooper to trade,
And let a' the world say he is a rovin' blade.
                    —Fraserburgh (Rev. W. Gregor).

All sing to "especially," boy chooses girl, and then the two whirl round, and all sing to the end.

Sweer Tree

Two persons sit down feet to feet and catch a stick with their hands; then whoever lifteth the other is the strongest.
—Mactaggart's *Gallovidian Encyclopædia*.

Compare "Honey pots."

Swinging

Rhymes were said or sung by children and young people when swinging. They were of the same character, and in many instances the same as those given in "See-saw" and "Shuttle-feather," and were used formerly for purposes of divination. The following extract, from the *Pall Mall Gazette* of Sept. 19th, 1895, seems to indicate an early notion connected with swinging. It is taken from one of the articles in that paper upon Jabez Balfour's diary during his residence in the Argentine Republic:—"On the 2nd November he (Balfour) mentions a curious Bolivian custom on All Souls' Day, when 'they erect high swings, and old and young swing all day long, in the hope that while they swing they may approach the spirits of their departed friends as they fly from Purgatory to Paradise.' Two days later he adds: 'I have to-day heard another explanation of the Bolivian practice of swinging on All Souls' Day. They swing as high as they can so as to reach the topmost branches of the trees, and whenever they are thereby able to pull off a branch they release a soul from Purgatory.'"—*Notes and Queries*, 8th series, vi. 345. With this may be compared one of the methods and words used while swinging which I remember playing, namely, that while swinging, either in a room or garden, the object was to endeavour to touch either a beam in the ceiling or the top branches of a tree, singing at the same time a rhyme of which I only recollect this fragment:

One to earth and one to heaven,
And *this* to carry my soul to heaven.

The last was said when the effort was made to touch the ceiling or tree with the feet.—(A. B. Gomme.)

Miss Chase has sent me the following rhymes:

I went down the garden
And there I found a farth'ng;
I gave it to my mother
To buy a little brother;
The brother was so cross
I sat him on the horse;
The horse was so bandy
I gave him a drop (*or* glass) of brandy;
The brandy was so strong
I set him on the pond;
The pond was so deep
I sent him off to sleep;
The sleep was so sound
I set him on the ground;
The ground was so flat
I set him on the cat;
The cat ran away
With the boy on his back;

And a good bounce [A great push here]
Over the high gate wall.
Said while swing stops itself :—

Die, pussy, die,
Shut your little eye,
When you wake,
Find a cake ;
Die, pussy, die.   —Deptford.

Wingy, wongy,
Days are longy,
Cuckoo and the sparrow ;
Little dog has lost his tail,
And he shall be hung to-morrow.

—Marylebone.

The Deptford version is practically the same as known in several parts of the country, and Mr. Gerish has printed a Norfolk version in *Folk-lore* (vi. 202), which agrees down to the line " sent him off to sleep," and then finishes with—

With a heigh-ho !
Over the bowling green.

When they came to the " heigh-ho " a more energetic push than usual was given to the occupant of the swing, who was then expected to vacate the swing and allow another child a turn. Thus the rhyme served as an allowance of time to each child.

An amusement of boys in Galloway is described as on the slack rope, riding and shoving one another on the curve of the rope : they recite this to the swings—

Shuggie show, druggie draw,
Haud the grip, ye canna fa' ;
Haud the grup or down ye come,
And danceth on your braid bum.

—Mactaggart's *Gallovidian Encyclopædia*.

Brockett (*North Country Words*) describes as a swing: a long rope fastened at each end, and thrown over a beam, on which young persons seat themselves and are swung backwards and forwards in the manner of a pendulum.

See " Merritot."

Tait

The Dorset game of "See-saw."—Halliwell's *Dictionary*.

Teesty-Tosty

The blossoms of cowslips collected together tied in a globular form, and used to toss to and fro for an amusement called "Teesty-Tosty," or simply sometimes "Tosty."—Somerset (Holloway's *Dict. of Provincialisms*).

A writer in *Byegones* for July 1890, p. 142, says, "Tuswball" means a bunch. He gives the following rhyme, used when tossing the ball:—

> Tuswball, tuswball, tell unto me
> What my sweetheart's name shall be.

Then repeating letters of the alphabet until the ball falls, and the letter last called will indicate the sweetheart's name.

See "Ball," "Shuttlefeather," "Trip Trout."

Teter-cum-Tawter

The East Anglian game of "See-saw."—Halliwell's *Dictionary*.

Tee-to-tum. See "Totum"

Thimble Ring

> I come with my ringle jingles
> Under my lady's apron strings.
> First comes summer, and then comes May,
> The queen's to be married on midsummer day.
> Here she sits and here she stands,
> As fair as a lily, as white as a swan;
> A pair of green gloves to draw on her hands,
> As ladies wear in Cumberland.
> I've brought you three letters, so pray you read one,
> I can't read one unless I read all,
> So pray, Miss Nancy, deliver them all.
> —Sheffield (S. O. Addy).

A number of young men and women form themselves into an oval ring, and one stands in the centre. A thimble is given to one of those who form the ring, and it is passed round from one to another, so that nobody knows who has it. Then the one who stands in the centre goes to the man at the top of the oval ring and says, " My lady's lost her gold ring. Have you got it ?" He answers " Me, sir ? no, sir." The one in the middle says, " I think you lie, sir, but tell me who has got it." Then he points out the one who has the thimble, of which he takes possession, and then says the above lines. Then the one who was found to have had the thimble takes the place of the one inside the ring, and the game is repeated.

Halliwell gives a version of this game under the name of Diamond Ring (*Nursery Rhymes*, p. 223), but the words used consist only of the following lines :—

> My lady's lost her diamond ring,
> I pitch upon you to find it.

In the two following games from Yorkshire and Lincolnshire there are no words used in rhymes or couplets.

One child stands in the centre of a ring, which is formed by each member clasping the wrist of his or her left hand neighbour with the left hand, thus leaving the right hand free. A thimble is provided, and is held by one of the players in the right hand. No circular movement is necessary, but as the tune is sung, the right hand of each member is placed alternately in that of their right and left hand neighbour, each performing the action in a swinging style, as if they had to pass the ring on, and in such a manner, that the one standing in the centre cannot detect it. The thimble may be detained or passed on just as the players think fit. The words are the following :—

> The thimble is going,
> I don't know where.

Varied with

> It's first over here,

Or

> It's over there,

as the case may be, or rather may not be, in order to throw the victim in the centre off the scent.—West Riding of Yorkshire (Miss Bush).

The players sit in a row or circle, with their hands held palm to palm in their laps.   The leader of the game takes a thimble, and going to every member of the company in turn, pretends to slip it between their fingers, or to hide it in their pinafores, saying as she does so—" I bring you my lady's thimble, you must hold it fast, and very fast indeed."   Whereon each child thus addressed should assume an air of triumph suitable to the possession of such a treasure.   After the whole party have gone through the farce of receiving the thimble, the girl who carried it round calls a player from the circle to discover who holds it.   For every wrong guess a fine must be paid.   When the searcher discovers the thimble she begins a new round of the game by taking the place of leader; and so on, till the accumulation of forfeits is sufficient to afford amusement in " loosing the tines."   The game is called " Lady's Thimble." —Lincoln, Scawby and Stixwould 76 years ago (Miss M. Peacock).

The rhyme used in the Sheffield game is that used in " Queen Anne," but it appears to have no relevance to this game.

Thing done

A game described by Ben Jonson in his play of *Cynthia's Revels* (act iv. scene 1).   The passage is as follows :—

" PHANTASTE.   Nay, we have another sport afore this, of ' A thing done, and who did it,' &c.

" PHILANTIA.   Ay, good Phantaste, let's have that : distribute the places.

" PHANTASTE.   Why, I imagine A thing done; Hedon thinks who did it; Maria, with what it was done; Anaides, where it was done; Argurion, when it was done; Amorphus, for what cause was it done; you, Philantia, what followed upon the doing of it; and this gentleman, who would have done it better. . . ."

Gifford thinks that this sport was probably the diversion of the age, and of the same stamp with our modern " Cross Purposes," " Questions," and " Commands," &c.

Thread the Needle

—Miss Dendy.

—Harpenden (Miss Lloyd).

I.   Thread my grandmother's needle!
     Thread my grandmother's needle!
     Thread my grandmother's needle!
     Open your gates as wide as high,
     And let King George and me go by.
     It is so dark I cannot see
     To thread my grandmother's needle!
          Who stole the money-box?
                              —London (Miss Dendy).

II. Open your gates as wide as I, [high ?]
     And let King George's horses by;
     For the night is dark and we cannot see,
     But thread your long needle and sew.
                              —Belfast (W. H. Patterson).

III. Thread the tailor's needle,
     The tailor's blind, so he can't see;
     So open the gates as wide as wide,
     And let King George and his lady pass by.
               —Bocking, Essex (*Folk-lore Record*, iii. 170).

IV. Thread my grandmother's needle,
     Thread my grandmother's needle;
     It is too dark we cannot see
     To thread my grandmother's needle.
                              —Harpenden (Mrs. Lloyd).

V. Thread the needle,
    Thread the needle,
    Nine, nine, nine,
    Let King George and I pass by.
                    —Liphook, Hants (Miss Fowler).

VI. Open the gates as wide as wide,
     And let King George go through with his bride;
     It is so dark, we cannot see
     To threaddle the tailor's needle.
                    —Parish *Dictionary of the Sussex Dialect*.

VII. Brother Jack, if ye were mine,
      I would give you claret wine;
      Claret wine's gude and fine—
      Through the needle-e'e, boys!
                    —*Blackwood's Magazine*, August 1821.

VIII. Through the needle-e'e, boys,
       One, two, three, boys.
                    —Ross-shire (Rev. W. Gregor).

IX. Hop my needle, burn my thread,
     Come thread my needle, Jo-hey.
                    —Lincoln (C. C. Bell).

X. Come thread a long needle, come thread,
    The eye is too little, the needle's too big.
                    —Hanbury, Staffs. (Miss Edith Hollis).

XI. Thread the needle thro' the skin,
     Sometimes out and sometimes in.
                    —Warwickshire, Northall's *Folk Rhymes*, 397.

XII. Open the gates as wide as the sky,
      And let King George and his lady go by.
                    —Ellesmere, Burne's *Shropshire Folk-lore*, p. 321.

(*b*.) The children stand in two long rows, each holding the hands of the opposite child, the two last forming an arch. They sing the lines, and while doing so the other children run under the raised arms. When all have passed under, the first two hold up their hands, and so on again and again, each pair in turn becoming the arch. Mrs. Lloyd (Harpenden version) says the two first hold up a handkerchief, and the children all run under, beginning with the last couple. In the London version (Miss Dendy) the "last line is called out in quite different tones from the rest of the rhyme. It is reported to have a most startling effect." The Warwickshire version is played differently. The players, after passing under the clasped hands, all circle or wind round one of their number, who stands still.

(c.) In some cases the verse, "How many miles to Babylon ? " is sung before the verses for "Thread the needle," and the reference made (*ante*, vol. i., p. 238) to an old version seems to suggest the origin of the game. This, at all events, goes far to prove that the central idea of the game is not connected with the sewing needle, but with an interesting dance move-ment, which is called by analogy, Thread the needle. It is, however, impossible to say whether the verses of this game are the fragments of an older and more lengthy original, which included both the words of "How many miles to Babylon" and "Thread the needle," or whether these two were indepen-dent games, which have become joined; but, on the whole, I am inclined to think that "Thread the needle," at all events, is an independent game, or the central idea of an independent game, and one of some antiquity.

This game is well illustrated by custom. At Trowbridge, in Wilts, a game, known as "Thread the needle," used to be the favourite sport with the lads and lasses on the evening of Shrove Tuesday festival. The vocal accompaniment was always the following :—

Shrove Tuesday, Shrove Tuesday, when Jack went to plough,
His mother made pancakes, she didn't know how ;
She tipped them, she tossed them, she made them so black,
She put so much pepper she poisoned poor Jack.

—*Notes and Queries*, 5th series, xi. p. 227.

At Bradford-on-Avon, as soon as the "pancake bell" rang at eleven A.M., the school children had holiday for the remainder of the day, and when the factories closed for the night, at dusk the boys and girls of the town would run through the streets in long strings playing "Thread the needle," and whooping and hallooing their best as they ran, and so collecting all they could together by seven or eight o'clock, when they would adjourn to the churchyard, where the old sexton had opened the churchyard gates for them; the children would then join hands in a long line until they encompassed the church; they then, with hands still joined, would walk round the church three times; and when dismissed by the old sexton, would return to their homes much pleased that they "Clipped the Church," and shouting similar lines to those said at Trowbridge.

At South Petherton, in South Somerset, sixty or seventy years ago, it was the practice of the young folk of both sexes to meet in or near the market-place, and there commence "Threading the needle" through the streets, collecting numbers as they went. When this method of recruiting ceased to add to their ranks, they proceeded, still threading the needle, to the church, which they tried to encircle with joined hands; and then, whether successful or not, they returned to their respective homes. Old people, who remember having taken part in the game, say that it always commenced in the afternoon or evening of Shrove Tuesday, "after having eaten of their pancakes." In *Leicestershire County Folk-lore*, p. 114, Mr. Billson records that it was formerly the custom on Shrove Tuesday for the lads and lasses to meet in the gallery of the Women's Ward in Trinity Hospital to play at "Thread the Needle" and similar games.

At Evesham the custom is still more distinctly connected with the game, as the following quotation shows:—"One custom of the town is connected with a sport called 'Thread my needle,' a game played here by the children of the town throughout the various streets at sunset upon Easter Monday, and at no other period throughout the year. The players cry while elevating their arms arch-wise—

> Open the gates as high as the sky,
> And let Victoria's troops pass by."
> —May's *History of Evesham*, p. 319.

As all these customs occur in the early spring of the year, there is reason to think that in this game we have a relic of the oldest sacred dances, and it is at least a curious point that in two versions (Bocking and Ellesmere) the Anglo-Saxon title of "Lady" is applied to the Queen.

The writer in *Blackwood's Magazine*, who quotes the rhymes as "immemorial," says: "Another game played by a number of children, with a hold of one another, or 'tickle tails,' as it is technically called in Scotland, is 'Through the needle-e'e.'" Moor (*Suffolk Words and Phrases*) mentions the game. Patterson (*Antrim and Down Glossary*) gives it as "Thread the needle and sew." Barnes (*Dorset Glossary*) calls it "Dred the wold woman's needle," in which two children join hands, and the last leads the train under the lifted arms of the first two. Holloway (*Dictionary of Provincialisms*) says the children form a ring, holding each other's hands; then one lets go and passes under the arms of two who still join hands, and the others all follow, holding either by each other's hands or by a part of their dress. "At Ellesmere," Miss Burne says, "this game was formerly called 'Crew Duck.' It now only survives among little girls, and is only played on a special day." It is alluded to in *Poor Robin's Almanack* for 1738: "The summer quarter follows spring as close as girls do one another when playing at Thread my needle; they tread upon each other's heels." Strutt calls this "Threading the Taylor's needle." Newell (*Games of American Children*) gives some verses, and describes it as played in America.

See "How many miles to Babylon," "Through the Needle 'ee."

Three Days' Holidays

Two players hold up their joined hands, the rest pass under one by one, repeating, "Three days' holidays, three days' holidays!" They pass under a second time, all repeating, "Bumping day, bumping day!" when the two leaders strike each player on the back in passing. The third time they say, "Catch, catch, catch!" and the leaders catch the last in the train between their arms. He has the choice of "strawberries or grapes," and is placed behind one of the leaders, according to his answer. When all have been "caught," the two parties pull against each other.—Berrington (Burne's *Shropshire Folklore*, p. 522).

"Holidays," says Miss Burne, "anciently consisted of three days, as at Easter and Whitsuntide, which explains the words of this game;" and the manorial work days were formerly three a week. See "Currants and Raisins."

Three Dukes

—Madeley, Shropshire (Miss Burne).

Biggar, Lanarkshire (W. Ballantyne).

Sporle, Norfolk (Miss Matthews).

—Isle of Man (A. W. Moore).

I.   Here come three dukes a-riding,
         A-riding, a-riding;
      Here come three dukes a-riding,
         With a rancy, tancy, tay!

      What is your good will, sirs?
         Will, sirs? will, sirs?
      What is your good will, sirs?
         With a rancy, tancy, tay!

      Our good will is to marry,
         To marry, to marry;
      Our good will is to marry,
         With a rancy, tancy, tay!

      Marry one of us, sirs,
         Us, sirs, us, sirs;
      Marry one of us, sirs,
         With a rancy, tancy, tay!

      You're all too black and greasy [or dirty],
         Gréasy, greasy;
      You're all too black and greasy,
         With a rancy, tancy, tay!

      We're good enough for you, sirs,
         You, sirs, you, sirs;
      We're good enough for you, sirs,
         With a rancy, tancy, tay!

      You're all as stiff as pokers,
         Pokers, pokers;
      You're all as stiff as pokers,
         With a rancy, tancy, tay!

      We can bend as much as you, sirs,
         You, sirs, you, sirs;
      We can bend as much as you, sirs,
         With a rancy, tancy, tay!

Through the kitchen and down the hall,
    I choose the fairest of you all;
The fairest one that I can see
    Is pretty Miss ——, walk with me.
                —Madeley, Salop (Miss Burne), 1891.

[Another Shropshire version has for the fourth verse—
        Which of us will you choose, sirs?
Or,
        Will you marry one of my daughters?]

II.   Here comes three dukes a-riding, a-riding,
        With a ransome dansome day!

    Pray what is your intent, sirs, intent, sirs?
        With a ransome dansome day!

    My intent is to marry, to marry!

    Will you marry one of my daughters, my daughters?

    You are as stiff as pokers, as pokers!

    We can bend like you, sir, like you, sir!

    You're all too black and too blowsy, too blowsy,
        For a dilly-dally officer!

    Good enough for *you*, sir! for *you*, sir!

    If I must have any, I will have this,
    So come along, my pretty miss!
                —Chirbury (*Shropshire Folk-lore*, p. 517).

III.   Here come three dukes a-riding,
        A-riding, a-riding;
    Here come three dukes a-riding,
        With a rancy, tancy, tee!

    Pray what is your good will, sirs?
        Will, sirs, will, sirs?
    Pray what is your good will, sirs?
        With a rancy, tancy, tee!

My will is for to marry you,
　　To marry you, to marry you;
My will is for to marry you,
　　With a rancy, tancy, tee!

You're all so black and blousey (blowsy ?),
Sitting in the sun so drowsy;
With silver chains about ye,
　　With a rancy, tancy, tee!

Or,

[With golden chains about your necks,
Which makes you look so frowsy.]

Walk through the kitchen, and through the hall,
And pick the fairest of them all.

This is the fairest I can see,
So pray, Miss ———, walk with me.
　　　　　　　　—Leicester (Miss Ellis).

IV.　Here come three dukes a-riding, a-riding, a-riding,
　　Here come three dukes riding, riding, riding;
　　　Ransam, tansam, tisum ma tea (*sic*).

Pray what is your good will, sir, will, sir, will, sir?
Pray what is your good will, sir?
　　Ransam, tansam, tisum ma tea!

My will is for to marry, to marry, to marry,
My will is for to marry;
　　Ransam, tansam, tisum ma tea!

Pray who will you marry, you marry, you marry?
Pray who will you marry?
　　Ransam, tansam, tisum ma tea!

You're all too black and too brown for me,
You're all too black and too brown for me,
　　Ransam, tansam, tisum ma tea!

We're quite as white as you, sir; as you, sir; as you, sir;
We're quite as white as you, sir;
　　Ransam, tansam, tisum ma tea!

You are all as stiff as pokers, as pokers, as pokers,
You are all, &c.,
   Ransam, tansam, tisum ma tea!

We can bend as well as you, sir; as you, sir; as you, sir;
We can bend as well as you, sir;
   Ransam, tansam, tisum ma tea!

Go through the kitchen, and through the hall,
And take the fairest of them all;

The fairest one that I can see is " ———,"
So come to me.

        Oxfordshire version, brought into Worcestershire
        (Miss Broadwood).

V. Here come three dukes a-riding, a-riding, a-riding;
    With a ransom, tansom, titty foll-la!
    With a ransom, tansom, tay!

And pray what do you want, sirs? want, sirs? want, sirs?
    With a ransom, tansom, titty foll-la!
    With a ransom, tansom, tay!

I want a handsome wife, sir; wife, sir; wife, sir;
    With a ransom, tansom, titty foll-la!
    With a ransom, tansom, tay!

I have three daughters fair, sir; fair, sir; fair, sir:
    With a ransom, tansom, titty foll-la!
    With a ransom, tansom, tay!

They are all too black and too browny,
They sit in the sun so cloudy;
    With a ransom, tansom, titty foll-la!
    With a ransom, tansom, tay!

Go through my kitchen and my hall,
And find the fairest of them all;
    With a ransom, tansom, titty foll-la!
    With a ransom, tansom, tay!

The fairest one that I can see,
Is little ——— ———, so come to me.

        —Monton, Lancashire (Miss Dendy).

VI.   Here come three dukes a-riding, a-riding, a-riding;
       Here come three dukes a-riding, with a ransom, tansom,
          te !

       Pray what is your intention, sir [repeat as above].

       My intention is to marry, &c.

       Which of us will you choose, sir, &c.

       You're all too black and too browsy, &c.

       We're good enough for you, sir, &c.

       Through the kitchen and over the wall,
       Pick the fairest of us all.

       The fairest is that I can see, pretty Miss ——, come
          to me.
                    — East Kirkby, Lincolnshire (Miss K. Maughan).

VII.   Here come three dukes a-riding,
          A-riding, a-riding;
       Here come three dukes a-riding,
          With a dusty, dusty, die !

       What do you want with us, sirs ? [repeat as above].

       We've come to choose a wife, Miss, &c.

       Which one of us will you have, sirs ? &c.

       You're all too black and too browsy,
       You sit in the sun so drowsy;
       With a golden chain about your neck,
       You're all too black and too browsy.

       Quite good enough for you, sirs, &c.

       We walk in our chamber,
       We sit in our hall,
       We choose the fairest of you all;
       The fairest one that we can see
       Is little —— ——, come to me.
                    —Wakefield, Yorks. (Miss Fowler).

VIII. Here come three dukes a-riding, a-riding, a-riding,
        Here come three dukes a-riding;
           A randy, dandy, very fine day!

        And pray what is your will, sirs? &c. [as above].

        We come for one of your daughters, &c.

        Which one will you have, sir? &c.

        They are all as black as a browsie, browsie, browsie,
          &c.
        One can knit, and one can sew,
        One can make a lily-white bow;
        One can make a bed for a king,
        Please take one of my daughters in.

        The fairest one that I can see
        Is [   ], come to me.
                —Gainford, co. Durham (Miss A. Edleston).

IX. Here comes a poor duke a-riding, a-riding,
        Here comes a poor duke a-riding;
           With the ransom, tansom, tee!

        Pray who will you have to marry, sir? &c.

        You're all so black and so dirty, &c.

        We are quite as clean as you, sir, &c.

        Through the kitchen, and through the hall,
        Pick the fairest one of all.

        The fairest one that I can see
        Is ——,
        The fairest one that I can see,
        With a ransom, tansom, tee!
                —Sporle, Norfolk (Miss Matthews).

X. Here comes one duke a-riding,
          A-riding, a-riding;
        Here comes one duke a-riding,
          With a ransom, tansom, terrimus, hey!

What is your intention, sir ? &c. [as above].

My intention is to marry, &c.

Marry one of us, sir ? &c.

You're all too black and dirty (or greasy), &c.

We're good enough for you, sir, &c.

You're all as stiff as pokers, &c.

We can bend as much as you, sir, &c.

Through the kitchen and through the hall,
I choose the fairest of you all;
The fairest one as I can see
Is pretty —— ——, come to me.

Now I've got my bonny lass,
  Bonny lass, bonny lass;
Now I've got my bonny lass
  To help us with our dancing.
                    —Barnes, Surrey (A. B. Gomme).

XI.   Here comes one duke a-riding, a-riding, a-riding;
      Here comes one duke a-riding
      On a ransom, dansom bay!

      You're all so black and dirty, &c.

      Pray which of us will you choose, sir, &c.

      Up in the kitchen, down in the hall,
      And choose the fairest one of all.
      The fairest one that I can see
      Is pretty Miss ———, so come to me.
                    —Bocking, Essex (*Folk-lore Record*, vol. iii.,
                          pt. ii., pp. 170–171).

XII.   Here comes one duke a-riding, a-riding, a-riding,
       Here comes one duke a-riding, with a ransom, tansom,
          ta!
       Pray which of us will you choose, sir ? &c.

       You're all so black and so blousey, &c.

       We're quite as white as you, sir, &c.

Up of the kitchen, down of the hall,
Pick the fairest girl of all;
The fairest one that I can see
Is —— ——, come to me. —Suffolk (Mrs. Haddon).

XIII. Here comes the Duke of Rideo,
Of Rideo, of Rideo;
Here comes the Duke of Rideo,
Of a cold and frosty morning.

My will is for to get married, &c.

Will any of my fair daughters do? &c.
[The word "do" must be said in a drawling way.]

They are all too black or too proudy,
They sit in the sun so cloudy;
With golden chains around their necks,
That makes them look so proudy.

They're good enough for you, sir! &c.

I'll walk the kitchen and the hall,
And take the fairest of them all;
The fairest one that I can see
Is Miss ——
So Miss ——, come to me.

Now we've got this pretty girl,
This pretty girl, this pretty girl;
Now we've got this pretty girl,
Of a cold and frosty morning.
—Symondsbury, Dorsetshire (*Folk-lore Journal*, vii. 222–223).

XIV. Here come three dukes a-riding, a-riding, a-riding,
Here come three dukes a-riding;
With a ransom, tansom, tisamy, tea!

What is your good will, sirs? &c.

My good will is to marry, &c.

One of my fair daughters? &c.

You're all too black and browsy, &c.

Quite as good as you, sirs, &c.

[The dukes select a girl who refuses to go to them.]

O, naughty maid ! O, naughty maid !
You won't come out to me !
You shall see a blackbird,
A blackbird and a swan ;
You should see a nice young man
Persuading you to come.
　　　　　　　—Wrotham, Kent (Miss Dora Kimball).

XV.　Here comes a duke a-riding, a-riding, a-riding ;
　　　Here comes a duke a-riding, to my nancy, pancy,
　　　　disimi, oh !

Which of us will you have, sir ? &c.

You're all so fat and greasy, &c.

We're all as clean as you, sir, &c.

Come down to my kitchen, come down to my hall,
I'll pick the finest of you all.   The fairest is that girl
I shall say, " Come to me."

I will buy a silk and satin dress, to trail a yard as we go
　　to church,
Madam, will you walk ? madam, will you talk ?
Madam, will you marry me ?

I will buy you a gold watch and chain, to hang by your
　　side as we go to church ;
Madam, will you walk ? madam, will you talk ?
Madam, will you marry me ?

I will buy you the key of the house, to enter in when
　　my son's out ;
Madam, will you walk ? madam, will you talk ?
Madam, will you marry me ?
　　　　　　　—Earls Heaton, Yorks. (H. Hardy).

XVI.　Here comes one duke a-riding,
　　　　With a rancey, tancey, tiddy boys, O !
　　　　　Rancey, tancey, tay !

Pray which will you take of us, sir? &c.

You're all as dark as gipsies, &c.

Quite good enough for you, &c.

Then we'll take this one, &c.

[After all are taken, the dukes say]—
Now we've got this bonny bunch, &c.
—Hurstmonceux, Sussex, about 1880 (Miss E. Chase).

[A Devon variant gives for the third verse—
You are all too black and ugly, and ugly, and ugly.
And—
You are all too black and *browsie*, &c.
With the additional verse—
I walked through the kitchen,
I walked through the hall,
For the prettiest and fairest
Of you all.
Ending with—
Now I have got my bonny lass, &c.
And something like—
Will you come and dance with me?
—Devon (Miss E. Chase)].

XVII.   Here comes a duke a-riding, a-riding, a-riding;
Here comes a duke a-riding to the ransy, tansy, tay!

Pray what do you come riding for? &c.

For one of your fairy [? fair] daughters, &c.

Will either one of these do? &c.

They're all too black and too dirty, &c.

They're quite as clean as you, sir, &c.

Suppose, then, I take you, Miss, &c.
—Clapham, London (Mrs. Herbertson).

[Another version is played by the duke announcing that he
wants a wife. The circle of maids and duke then reply to
each other as follows:—

Open the door and let him in.

They're all as stiff as pokers.

Quite as good as you, sir.

I suppose I must take one of them?

Not unless you like, sir.

I choose the fairest of you all,
The fairest one that I can see
Is ————, come to me.
—Clapham Middle-class Girls School (Mrs. Herbertson)].

XVIII. Here comes the duke a-riding,
With my rantum, tantum, tantum, tee!
Here comes the duke a-riding,
With my rantum, tantum, tee!

What does the duke a-riding want?
With his rantum, tantum, tantum, tee, &c.

The youngest and fairest daughter you've got, &c.
—Dublin (Mrs. Coffey).

XIX. Here comes a duke a-riding, a-riding, a-riding;
Here comes a duke a-riding, a ransom, tansom, tee!

What is your good will, sir, &c.

My will is for to marry, &c.

Will ever a one of us do? &c.

You're all so black and so browsy.
You sit in the sun and get frowsy,
With golden chains about your necks,
You're all so black and so browsy.

Quite as good as you, sir, &c.

[There is more of this, but it has been forgotten by my authority.]   —Thos. Baker, junr. (*Midland Garner*, N. S., ii. 32).

XX. Here comes a duke a-riding,
With a ransom, tansom, titta passee!
Here comes a duke a-riding,
With a ransom, tansom, tee!

Pray what is your good will, sir ?
With a ransom, tansom, titta passee !
Pray what is your good will, sir ?
With a ransom, tansom, tee !

My will is for to marry you (as above).

Pray which of us will you have, sir ? &c.

Through the gardens and through the hall,
With a ransom, tansom, titta passee !
I choose the fairest of you all,
With a ransom, tansom, tee !

     —Settle, Yorks. (Rev. W. G. Sykes).

XXI. There came three dukes a-riding, ride, ride, riding ;
   There came three dukes a-riding,
   With a tinsy, tinsy, tee !

   Come away, fair lady, there is no time to spare ;
   Let us dance, let us sing,
   Let us join the wedding ring.
     —West of Scotland (*Folk-lore Record*, iv. 174).

XXII. Here come three dukes a-riding,
   A-riding, a-riding.

   They will give you pots and pans,
   They will give you brass ;
   They will give you pots and pans
   For a pretty lass.
     —Penzance, Cornwall (Mrs. Mabbott).

XXIII. Here come four dukes a-riding,
   Ring a me, ding a me, ding.

   What is your good will, sirs ?
   Ring a me, ding a me, ding.

   Our good will's to marry, &c.

   Marry one of us then, &c.

   You're too poor and shabby, &c.

   We're quite as good as you are, &c.

Suppose we have one of you then, &c.

Which one will you have, &c.

We'll have —— to marry, &c.

Who will you send to fetch her, &c.

We'll send —— to fetch her.
—Roxton, St. Neots (Miss E. Lumley).

XXIV. Here come three dukes a-riding,
  With me rancy, tansy, tissimy tee,
  Here come three dukes a-riding,
  With a ransom, tansom, tissimy tee.
  Here come three dukes a-riding,
  With a ransom, tansom, tissimy tee.

  Pray which of us will you have, sir (repeat as
   above).

  I think I will have this one (repeat).

   .   .   .   .   .

[Forgotten, but the girls evidently decline to part with one
of their number.]
  You are all too black and too blousy (repeat).
  We're far too good for you, sir (repeat).
    —Isle of Man (A. W. Moore).
    Played at a Manx Vicarage
   nearly sixty years ago (Rev. T. G. Brown).

XXV. Here comes a Jew a riding,
  With the ransom, tansom, tissimi, O !

  And pray what is your will, sir ? (as above).

  Then pray take one of my daughters, &c.

  They are all too black and too browsy, &c.

  They are good enough for you, sir, &c.

  My house is lined with silver, &c.

  But ours is lined with gold, sir, &c.

  Then I'll take one of your daughters, &c.
   —Forest of Dean, Gloucester (Miss Matthews).

XXVI.   The Campsie dukes a-riding, a-riding, a-riding ;
The Campsie dukes a riding, come a rincey,
dincey, dee.   —Biggar (Wm. Ballantyne).

XXVII.   Five dukes comes here a-ridin',
A-ridin' fast one day ;
Five dukes comes here a-riding,
With a hansom, dansom day.

What do you want with us, sirs,
With us, sirs, &c.

We want some wives to marry us,
To marry us, to marry us, &c.

Will you marry us, Miss Nancy,
Miss Nancy, Miss Nancy, &c.

We won't marry you to-day, sirs, &c.

Will you marry us to-day, Miss ? &c. (to another girl).

We will marry you to-day, sirs, &c.
—London, Regent's Park (A. B. Gomme).

XXVIII.   There's three dukes a-riding, a-riding,
There's three dukes a-riding,
Come a ransin, tansin, my gude wife.

Come a ransin, tansin te-dee,
Before I take my evening walk,
I'll have a handsome lady,
The fairest one that I do see.
—Rosehearty, Pitsligo (Rev. W. Gregor).

XXIX.   One duck comes a-ridin', sir, a-ridin', sir,
A-ridin' to marry you.

And what do you want with me, sir ?

I come to marry you two.

There's some of us ready to dance, sir ;
Ready to dance and sing ;
There's some of us ready to dance, sir,
And ready to marry you.

Then come to me, my darlin', my darlin', darlin' day,
With a ransom, tansom, tansom, tansom tay.
—London, Regent's Park (A. B. Gomme).

XXX.   There's a young man that wants a sweetheart—
Wants a sweetheart—wants a sweetheart—
There's a young man that wants a sweetheart,
To the ransom tansom tidi-de-o.

Let him come out and choose his own,
Choose his own, choose his own ;
Let him come out and choose his own,
To the ransom tansom tidi-de-o.

Will any of my fine daughters do, &c.

They are all too black and brawny,
They sit in the sun uncloudy,
With golden chains around their necks,
They are too black and brawny.

Quite good enough for you, sir ! &c.

I'll walk in the kitchen, and walk in the hall,
I'll take the fairest among you all ;
The fairest of all that I can see,
Is pretty Miss Watts, come out to me.
Will you come out ?

Oh, no ! oh, no !

Naughty Miss Watts she won't come out,
She won't come out, she won't come out ;
Naughty Miss Watts she won't come out,
To help us in our dancing.
Won't you come out ?

Oh, yes ! oh, yes !
—Dorsetshire (*Folk-lore Journal*, vii. 223–224).

(*c.*) Three children, generally boys, are chosen to represent the three dukes. The rest of the players represent maidens. The three dukes stand in line facing the maidens, who hold hands, and also stand in line. Sufficient space is left between the two lines to admit of each line in turn advancing and retiring. The three dukes commence by singing the first verse, advancing and retiring in line while doing so. The line of maidens then advances singing the second verse. The alternate verses demanding and answering are thus sung. The maidens make curtseys and look coquettishly at the dukes when singing the fourth verse, and draw themselves up stiffly and indignantly when singing the sixth, bending and bowing lowly at the eighth. The dukes look contemptuously and criticisingly at the girls while singing the fifth and seventh verses; at the ninth or last verse they "name" one of the girls, who then crosses over and joins hands with them. The game then continues by all four singing "Here come four dukes a-riding," and goes on until all the maidens are ranged on the dukes' side.

This method of playing obtains in most versions of the game, though there are variations and additions in some places. In the Bocking, Barnes, Dublin, Hurstmonceux, Settle, Symondsbury, Sporle, Earls Heaton, and Clapham versions, where the verses begin with "Here comes one Duke a-riding," one boy stands facing the girls, and sings the first verse advancing and retiring with a dancing step, or with a step to imitate riding. In some instances the "three Dukes" advance in this way. In the Barnes version, when the chosen girl has walked over to the duke, he takes her hands and dances round with her, while singing the tenth verse. In the Symondsbury (Dorset) version the players stand in a group, the duke standing opposite, and when singing the sixth verse, advances to choose the girl. When there is only one player left on the maidens' side the dukes all sing the seventh verse; they then come forward and claim the last girl, and embrace her as soon as they get her over to their side. In the Hurstmonceux version, when the girls are all on the dukes' side, they sing the last verse. Miss Chase does not say whether this is accompanied by dancing round, but it probably would be. In the Dublin version, after the third verse, the duke tries to carry off the youngest girl, and her side try to save her. In the Wrotham version, after the girls' retort, "Quite as good as you, sir," the dukes select a girl, who refuses to go to them: they then sing the last six lines when the girl goes over. In the second Dorset version (which appeared in the *Yarmouth Register*, Mass., 1874) the players consisted of a dozen boys standing in line in the usual way, and a dozen girls on the opposite side facing them. The boys sing the first two verses alternately; the girl at first refuses and then consents to go. Dancing round probably accompanies this, but there is no mention of it. In Roxton, St. Neots, after the verses are sung, the duke and the selected girl clasp hands, and he pulls her across to the opposite side, as in "Nuts in May." In Settle (Yorks.) the game is called "The Dukes of York and Lancaster." The first duke advances with a dancing step. The game is then played in the usual way until all the players are ranged on the dukes' side; then the two original dukes, one of whom is "red" and the other "white," join hands, and the other players pass under their raised hands. The dukes ask each of them, in a whisper, "red?" or "white?" The player then goes behind the one he or she has chosen, clasping the duke's waist. When all the players have chosen, a tug-of-war ensues between the two sides. In the Earls Heaton version, the duke sings the verses, offering gifts to the girl when she has been selected. In the Oxfordshire version (Miss Broadwood) one player sings the words of the verse, and all join in the refrain as chorus. In the Monton (Lancashire) version the duke sings the last verse, and then takes a girl from the opposite side; and in another version from Barnes, in which the words of the last verse are the same as these, one of the dukes' side crosses over and fetches the girl. The duke bows lowly before the chosen girl in the Liphook version before she joins his side. In the East Kirkby, Lincolnshire, version, when the dukes sing the last verse, they advance towards the opposite side, who, when they see the direction in which they are coming, form two arches, by three of the players holding up their arms, the dukes' side going through one arch and returning through the other, bringing the chosen girl with them. One Clapham version is played in a totally different manner: the maidens form a circle instead of a line, and the duke stands outside this until he is admitted at the line which says, "let him in." At the conclusion of the dialogue he breaks in and carries one player off. This is an unusual form; I have only met with one other instance of it.

(*d*.) The action in many of these versions is described as very spirited : coquetry, contempt, and annoyance being all expressed in action as the words of the game demands. The dancing movement of the boys in the first verse to imitate riding, though belonging to the earlier forms, is, with the exception of two or three versions, only retained in those which are commenced by one player, partly, perhaps, because of the difficulty three or more players experience in "riding" or "prancing" while holding each other's hands in line form. I have seen the game played when the "prancing" of the dukes (in a game where there were a dozen or more players on each side at starting, as in the Dorset version) was as important a feature as the maidens' actions in the other verses. I think the oldest form of the game is that played by a fairly equal number of players on each side, boys on one side and girls on the other, rather than that of "one" or "three" players on the dukes' side, and all the others opposite. The game then began with the present words, "Here come three dukes ; " these three each chose a girl at the same time, and when these three were wived, another three "dukes" would pair with three more of the girls, and after that another three, and so on. This form would account for the modern idea that the number of dukes increases on every occasion that the verses are sung, after the first wife has been taken over, and until all the girls have been thus chosen. This idea is expressed in some versions by the change of words : "Here's a fourth [or fifth, and so on] duke come a riding" to take a wife, the chosen maiden becoming a duke as soon as she has passed over on to the dukes' side. The process of innovation may be traced by the methods of playing. Thus, in one version played at Barnes (similar in other respects to No. 10). beginning "three dukes a riding," *three* girls were chosen by the three first dukes, one by each, at the same time, and all three girls walked across with the three dukes to the boys' line, and stood next their respective partners. In two imperfect versions I have obtained in Regent's Park, London, the same principle occurs. One girl began—"One duck comes a ridin', " and two girls from the opposite side walked across ; the other

"Five dukes come here a ridin'" was played by five players on each side, and this was continued throughout. When the verses were said, each of the five dukes took a player from the opposite side and danced round with her. Again, in those versions (Symondsbury and Barnes), where when one player is left on the maidens' side without a partner, and all the dukes are mated, the additional verse is sung, and this player is taken over too. Beyond these versions are the large number beginning with three or more children singing the formula of "three dukes," and choosing one girl at a time, until all are taken over on to the dukes' side. Finally, there are the versions, more in accord with modern ideas, which commence with one duke coming for a wife, and continue by the girls taken over counting as dukes, the formula changing into two dukes, and so on.

If this correctly represents the line of decadence in this game, those versions in which additional verses appear are, I think, instances of the tacking on of verses from the "invitation to the dance" or "May" games; particularly in the cases in which the words "Now I've got my bonny lass" appear. The Earls Heaton version is curious, in that it has several verses which remind us of the old and practically obsolete "Keys of Canterbury" (Halliwell, 96). It may well be that a remembered fragment of that old ballad, which was probably once danced as a dramatic round, has been tacked on to this game. The expression "walk with me," or "walk abroad with me," is significant of an engaged or betrothed couple. "I'm walking or walking out with so and so" is still an expression used by young men and young women to indicate an engagement. "She did ought to be married now; she've walked wi' him mor'n'er a year now." Some of the versions show still more marked signs of decadence. The altered wording, "Here comes a Jew a riding," "Here comes the Duke of Rideo," "A duck comes a ridin'," and the Scotch "Campsie Dukes a riding;" a Berkshire version, collected by Miss Thoyts (*Antiquary*, xxvii. p. 195), similar to the Shropshire game, but with a portion of the verse of "Milking Pails" added to it, and the refrain of "Ransome, tansome, tismatee;" together

with the disappearance of some of the verses, are all evidently
the results of the words being learnt orally, and imperfectly
understood, or not understood at all.

In this game, said in Lancashire to be the "oldest play
of all," judging both by the words and method of playing, we
have, I believe, a distinct survival or remembrance of the
tribal marriage—marriage at a period when it was the custom
for men of a clan to seek wives from the girls of another clan,
both clans belonging to one tribe. The game is a purely
marriage game, and marriage in a matter-of-fact way. Young
men of a clan or village arrive at the abode of another clan
for the purpose of seeking wives, probably at a feast or fair
time. The maidens are apparently ready and expecting their
arrival. They are as willing to become wives as the dukes are
to become husbands. It is not marriage by force or capture,
though the triumphant carrying off of a wife appears in some
versions. It is exogamous marriage custom, after the tribe
had settled down and arranged their system of marriage in lieu
of a former more rude system of capture. The suggested
depreciation of the girls, and their saucy rejoinders, may be
looked upon as so much good-humoured chaff and banter
exchanged between the two parties to enhance each other's
value, and to display their wit. While it does not follow that
the respective parties were complete strangers to one another,
these lines may indicate that each individual wished "to have
as good a look round as possible" before accepting the offer
made. It will be seen that there is no mention of "love" in
the game, nor is there any individual courtship between boy
and girl. The marriage formula does not appear, nor is there
any sign that a "ceremony" or "sanction" to conclude the
marriage was necessary, nor does kissing occur in the game.

There is evidence of the tribal marriage system in the
survivals of exogamy and marriage by capture occasionally
to be noted in traditional local custom. Thus the custom
recorded by Chambers (*Book of Days*, i. 722) of the East
Anglians (Suffolk), where whole parishes have intermarried
to such an extent that almost everybody is related to or connected with everybody else, is distinctly a case in point, the

intermarrying of "parishes" for a long series of years necessarily resulting in close inter-relationship.   One curious effect
of this is that no one is counted as a "relation" beyond first
cousins; for if " relationship" went further than that it might
"almost as well include the whole parish."   The old proverb
(also from East Anglia):

"To change the name, and not the letter,

Is a change for the worse, and not for the better;"

that is, it is unlucky for a woman to marry a man whose
surname begins with the same letter as her own, also indicates
a survival of the necessity of marrying into another clan or
tribal family.

Another interesting point in the game is the refrain, "With
a rancy, tancy, tay," which with variations accompanies all
versions, and separates this game from some otherwise akin
to it.   There is little doubt that this refrain represents an old
tribal war cry, from which "slogans" or family "cries" were
derived.   These cries were not only used in times of warfare,
tribes were assembled by them, each leader of a clan or party
having a distinguishing cry and blast of a horn peculiar to
himself, and the sounding of this particular blast or cry would
be recognised by men of the same party, who would go to each
other's assistance if need were.   The refrain is sung by all
the players in Oxfordshire and Lancashire, and in some versions the players in this game put their hands to their mouths
as if imitating a blast from a horn, and a Lancashire version
(about 1820–1830), quoted by Miss Burne, has for the refrain,
"With a rancy, tancy, terry boys horn, with a rancy, tancy,
tee."   "The burden," says Miss Burne, "evidently represented
a flourish of trumpets."   The Barnes version, "With a rancy,
tancy, terrimus hey!" and many others confirm this.

An interesting article by Dr. Karl Blind (*Antiquary*, ix.
63–72), on the Hawick riding song, "Teribus ye Teri Odin,"
points out that this slogan, which occurs in the "Hawick
Common-Riding Song," a song used at the annual Riding of
the Marches of the Common, is an ancient Germanic war-cry.
Dr. Blind, quoting from a pamphlet, *Flodden Field and New
Version of the Common Riding Song*, says, "It is most likely

that the inspiring strains of 'Terribus' would be the marching
tune of our ancestors when on their way for Flodden Field and
other border battles, feuds, and frays. The words of the
common-riding song have been changed at various periods,
according to the taste and capacity of poets and minstrels, but
the refrain has remained little altered. . . . The origin of the
ancient and, at one time, imperative ceremony of the common-
riding is lost in antiquity, and this old, no longer understood,
exclamation, 'Teribus ye Teri Odin,' has (says Dr. Blind) all
through ages in the meanwhile clung to that ceremony."

If we can fairly claim that the words of this game have
preserved an old slogan or tribal cry, an additional piece of
evidence is supplied to the suggestion that the game is a
reflection of the tribal marriage—a reflection preserved by
children of to-day by means of oral tradition from the children
of a thousand years ago or more, who played at games in
imitation of the serious and ordinary actions of their elders.

Three Flowers

> My mistress sent me unto thine,
> Wi' three young flowers baith fair and fine—
> The Pink, the Rose, and the Gilliflower:
> And as they here do stand,
> Whilk will ye sink, whilk will ye swim,
> And whilk bring hame to land?

A group of lads and lasses being assembled round the fire,
two leave the party and consult apart as to the names of three
others, young men or girls, whom they designate Red Rose,
the Pink, and the Gilliflower. If lads are first pitched upon,
the two return to the fireside circle, and having selected a lass,
they say the above verse to her. The maiden must choose one
of the flowers named, on which she passes some approving
epithet, adding, at the same time, a disapproving rejection of
the other two; for instance, I will sink the Pink, swim the
Rose, and bring home the Gilliflower to land. The two young
men then disclose the names of the parties upon whom they
had fixed those appellations respectively, when of course it
may chance that she has slighted the person she is understood

to be most attached to, or chosen him whom she is believed to regard with aversion; either of which events is sure to throw the company into a state of outrageous merriment.—Chambers' *Popular Rhymes*, p. 127. Mr. W. Ballantyne has given me a description of this game as played at Biggar when he was a boy, which is practically the same as this.

Three Holes

Three holes were made in the ground by the players driving the heels of their boots into the earth, and then pirouetting. The game was played with the large marbles (about the size

B

Taw   O   A   O   O

1   2   3

of racket balls) known as "bouncers," sometimes as "bucks." The first boy stood at "taw," and bowled his marble along the ground into 1. (It was bad form to make the holes too large; they were then "wash-hand basins," and made the game too easy.) Taking the marble in his hand, and placing his foot against 1, he bowled the marble into 2. He was now "going up for his firsts." Starting at 2, he bowled the marble into 3, and had now "taken off his firsts," and was "coming down for his seconds." He then bowled the marble back again into 2, and afterwards into 1. He then "went up for his thirds," bowling the marble into 2, and afterwards into 3, and had then won the game. When he won in this fashion, he was said to have "taken off the game." But he didn't often do this. In going up for his firsts, perhaps his marble, instead of going into 2, stopped at A; then the second boy started from taw, and, having sent his marble into 1, bowled at A; if he hit the marble, he started for 2, from where his marble stopped; if he missed, or didn't gain the hole he was making for, or knocked his antagonist's marble into a hole, the first boy played again, hitting the other marble, if it brought him nearer to the hole he was making for, or else going on. In such a case as I have supposed, it would be the player's aim to knock A on to B, or some place between 2 and 3, so as to enter 2, and then strike again so as to near 3, enter 3, and strike on his way down for his seconds, and near 2 again.   These were the chances of the game; but if the boy who started went through the game without his antagonist having a chance, he was said "to take off the game."—London (J. P. Emslie).

Three Jolly Welshmen

One child is supposed to be taking care of others, who take hold of her or of each other.   Three children personate the Welshmen.   These try to rob the mother or caretaker of her children.   They each try to capture as many as they can, and I think the one who gets most is to be mother next time.— Beddgelert (Mrs. Williams).

See "Gipsy," "Mother, Mother," "Shepherd and Sheep," "Witch."

Three Knights from Spain

I.   Here come two dukes all out of Spain,
A courting to your daughter Jane.

My daughter Jane, she is so young,
She can't abide your flattering tongue.

Let her be young, or let her be old,
It is the price, she must be sold,
Either for silver or for gold.
So fare you well, my lady gay,
For I must turn another way.

Turn back, turn back, you Spanish knight,
And rub your spurs till they be bright.

My spurs they are of a costliest wrought,
And in this town they were not bought,
Nor in this town they won't be sold,
Neither for silver, nor for gold.
So fare you well, my lady gay,
For I must turn another way.

Through the kitchen, and through the hall,
And take the fairest of them all;
The fairest is, as I can see,
Pretty Jane—come here to me.

Now I've got my pretty fair maid,
Now I've got my pretty fair maid,
To dance along with me,
To dance along with me !
    —Eccleshall, Halliwell's *Nursery Rhymes*, p. 222.

II.   Here comes three lords dressed all in green,
       For the sake of your daughter Jane.

My daughter Jane, she is so young,
She learns to talk with a flattering tongue.

Let her be young, or let her be old,
For her beauty she must be sold.

My mead's not made, my cake's not baked,
And you cannot have my daughter Jane.
    —Cambridgeshire, Halliwell's *Nursery Rhymes*, p. 222.

III.   We are three brethren out of Spain,
       Come to court your daughter Jane.

My daughter Jane, she is too young,
And has not learned her mother tongue.

Be she young, or be she old,
For her beauty she must be sold.
So fare you well, my lady gay,
We'll call again another day.

Turn back, turn back, thou scornful knight,
And rub thy spurs till they be bright.

Of my spurs take you no thought,
For in this town they were not bought.
So fare you well, my lady gay,
We'll call again another day.

Turn back, turn back, thou scornful knight,
And take the fairest in your sight.
The fairest maid that I can see,
Is pretty Nancy—come to me.

Here comes your daughter, safe and sound,
Every pocket with a thousand pound,
Every finger with a gay gold ring,
Please to take your daughter in.
—Halliwell's *Nursery Rhymes*, cccxxxiii.

IV.   We are three brethren come from Spain,
        All in French garlands;
      We are come to court your daughter Jean,
        And adieu to you, my darlings.

      My daughter Jean, she is too young,
        All in French garlands;
      She cannot bide your flattering tongue,
        And adieu to you, my darlings.

      Be she young, or be she old,
        All in French garlands;
      It's for a bride she must be sold,
        And adieu to you, my darlings.

      A bride, a bride, she shall not be,
        All in French garlands;
      Till she go through this world with me,
        And adieu to you, my darlings.

[There is here a hiatus, the reply of the lovers being
wanting.]
        Come back, come back, you courteous knights,
          All in French garlands;
        Clear up your spurs, and make them bright,
          And adieu to you, my darlings.

[Another hiatus.]
        Smell my lilies, smell my roses,
          All in French garlands;
        Which of my maidens do you choose?
          And adieu to you, my darlings.

      Are all your daughters safe and sound?
        All in French garlands;
      Are all your daughters safe and sound?
        And adieu to you, my darlings.

In every pocket a thousand pounds,
   All in French garlands;
On every finger a gay gold ring,
   And adieu to you, my darlings.
           —Chambers's *Popular Rhymes*, 143.

V.   Here come three Spaniards out of Spain,
     A courting to your daughter Jane.

Our daughter Jane, she is too young,
She hath not learnt the Spanish tongue.

Whether she be young, or whether she be old,
It's for her beauty she must be sold.

Turn back, turn back, ye Spanish knight,
And rub your spurs till they be bright.

Our spurs are bright and richly wrought,
For in this town they were not bought;
And in this town they shan't be sold,
Neither for silver nor for gold.

Pass through the kitchen, and through the hall,
And pick the fairest of them all.

This is the fairest I can see,
So pray, young lady, walk with me.
           —Leicester (Miss Ellis).

VI.   Here come three Spaniards out of Spain,
     A courting of your daughter Jane.

My daughter Jane, she is too young,
She has not learned the Spanish tongue.

Whether she be young or old,
She must have a gift of gold;
So fare you well, my lady gay,
We'll turn our heads another way.

Come back, come back, thou Spanish knight,
And pick the fairest in this night.
           —Addy's *Sheffield Glossary*.

VII. There were three lords they came from Spain,
They came to court my daughter Jane;

My daughter Jane, she is too young
To hear your false and flattering tongue.

So fare thee well, your daughter Jane,
I'll call again, another day, another year.

Turn back, turn back, and choose
The fairest one that you can see.

The fairest one that I can see,
Is pretty Jane, will you come with me.

[Jane says No.]

The proud little girl, she won't come out, she won't
    come out, to help us with our dancing;
So fare you well, I'll come again another day.

Turn back, turn back, and choose
The fairest one that you can see.

The fairest one that I can see,
Is pretty Sarah, will you come with me?

[Yes.]

Now we have got the pretty fair maid
To help us with our dancing,
Dance round the ring.   —Belfast (W. H. Patterson).

VIII. There was one lord came out of Spain,
He came to court our daughter Jane.

Our daughter Jane, she is too young,
To be controlled by flattering tongue.

Oh! fare thee well. Oh! fare thee well,
I'll go and court some other girl.

Come back, come back, your coat is wide,
And choose the fairest on our side.

The fairest one that I can see,
Come unto me, come unto me.
                    —Belfast (W. H. Patterson).

IX.　There were three lords came out of Spain,
　　　They came to court my daughter Jane ;

　　　My daughter Jane, she is too young
　　　To bear your false and flattering tongue.

　　　So fare you well, so fare you well,
　　　I'll go and court some other girl.

　　　Come back, come back, your coat is white,
　　　And choose the fairest in your sight,

　　　The fairest one that I can see,
　　　Is [　　　　　　　] come unto me.
　　　　　　　　　　　　—Belfast (W. H. Patterson).

X.　Here come three dukes dressed all in green,
　　　They come to court your daughter Jane.

　　　My daughter Jane, she is too young
　　　To understand your flattering tongue.

　　　Let her be young, or let her be old,
　　　It is for her beauty she must be sold.

　　　Eighteenpence would buy such a wench,
　　　As either you or your daughter Jane.*
　　　　　　　　　　　—Middlesex (from Mrs. Pocklington-
　　　　　　　　　　　　　　　Coltman's maid).

XI.　There came a king from Spain,
　　　To court your daughter Jane.

　　　My daughter Jane, she's yet too young
　　　To be deluded by a flattering tongue.

　　　Whether she's old, or whether she's young,
　　　It's for her beauty she must come.

　　　Then turn about, her coat is thin,
　　　And seek the fairest of your right.

　　　The fairest one that I can see
　　　Is fair and lovely Jan-ie.

* Incomplete, there is more of the game, but the maid could not remember it.

Then here's my daughter safe and sound,
And in her pocket three hundred pound,
And on her finger a gay gold ring,
She's fit to walk with any king.

—Annaverna, Ravensdale, Co. Louth
(Miss R. Stephens).

XII. There came three dukes a-riding, riding, riding;
Oh! we be come all out of Spain,
All for to court your daughter Jane.

My daughter Jane, she is too young,
She has not learned her mother-tongue.

Let her be young, or let her be old,
The fate of beauty's to be sold.

Here's my daughter safe and sound,
And in her pocket a thousand pound,
And on her finger a gay gold ring.

Here's your daughter not safe nor sound,
And in her pocket no thousand pound,
And on her finger no gay gold ring;
Open your door and take her in.

—London (Miss Dendy).

XIII. There came three dukes all out of Spain,
All for to court your daughter Jane.

My daughter Jane, she is too young,
She has not learned her mother-tongue.

Let her be young, let her be old,
The fate of beauty's to be sold.

Walk through the parlour, walk through the hall,
And choose the fairest one of all.

The fairest one that I can see
Is little ———, so come to me.   No

Will you come?   No!

Naughty one, naughty one, you won't come out
   To join us in our dancing!
      Will you come?   Yes!

Now we've got a pretty fair one
To join us in our dancing.
              —Colleyhurst, Manchester (Miss Dendy).

XIV. Two poor gentlemen are come out of Spain,
     Come to court your daughter Jane.

My daughter Jane, is yet too young
To understand your flattering tongue.

Let her be young, or let her be old,
She must be sold for Spanish gold.

Turn back, turn back, you haughty knight,
And take the fairest in your sight.

This is the fairest I can see,
So (   ) must come to me.
              —Bexley Heath (Miss Morris).

XV. Here come three lords all dressed in green,
     All for the sake of your daughter Jane.

My daughter Jane, she is so young,
She doesn't know her mother-tongue.   [Or,

My cake ain't baked, my ban [*qy.* beer or barm] ain't
    brewed,
And yew can't hev my daughter Jane.]

Fie upon you and your daughter Jane; [scornfully,]
Eighteenpence will buy a good wench,
As well as you and your daughter Jane.
             —Swaffham, Norfolk (Miss Matthews).

XVI. Here come three lords all dressed in green,
      Here come three lords all come from Spain,
      All for the sake of your daughter Jane.

My daughter Jane, she is so young,
She hath no knowledge in her tongue.
               Kent (Miss Fowler).

XVII. I am a gentleman come from Spain ;
      I've come to court your daughter Jane.

My daughter Jane, is yet too young
To understand your flattering tongue.

Let her be young, or let her be old,
She must be sold for Spanish gold.
So fare thee well, my lady gay,
I'll call upon you another day.

Turn back, turn back, you saucy lad,*
And choose the fairest you can spy !

The fairest one that I can see
Is pretty Miss ———. Come to me !

I've brought your daughter home safe and sound,
With money in her pocket here, a thousand pound :
Take your saucy girl back again.
      —Bocking, Essex (*Folk-lore Record*, iii. pt. ii. 171).

XVIII. Here comes three knights all out of Spain,
      A-courting of your daughter Jane.

My daughter Jane, she is too young,
She can't abide your flattering tongue.

If she be young, or she be old,
She for her beauty must be sold.

Go back, go back, you Spanish knight,
And rub your spurs till they are bright:

My spurs are bright and richly wrought,
And in this town they were not bought,
And in this town they shan't be sold,
Neither for silver nor for gold. .

Walk up the kitchen and down the hall,
And choose the fairest of us all.

* Probably once " boy," pronounced " by " in Essex.

Madams, to you I bow and bend,
I take you for my dearest friend;
You are two beauties, I declare,
So come along with me, my dear.
—Wenlock, Condover, Ellesmere, Market Drayton
(*Shropshire Folk-lore*, p. 516).

XIX. Here come three dukes all out of Spain,
In mourning for your daughter Jane.

My daughter Jane, is yet too young
To cast her eyes on such a one.

Let her be young, or let her be old,
'Tis for her beauty she must be sold.
So fare thee well, my lady gay,
I'll call on you another day.

Turn back, turn back, you saucy Jack,
Up through the kitchen and through the hall,
And pick the fairest of them all.

The fairest one that I can see.
So please, Miss ——, come with me.
—Pembrokeshire, Wales (*Folk-lore Record*, v. 89).

XX. Here's two brothers come from Spain,
For to court your daughter Jane.

My daughter Jane, she is too young,
She has not learned her mother tongue.

Be she young, or be she old,
For her beauty she must be sold.

But fare thee well, my lady gay,
And I'll call back some other day.

Come back! come back! take the fairest you see.

The fairest one that I can see
Is bonnie Jeanie [or Maggie, &c.], so come to me.

Here's your daughter, safe and sound,
In every pocket a thousand pound,
On every finger a gay gold ring,
So, pray, take your daughter back again.
                    —*People's Friend*, quoted in review of
                         "Arbroath : Past and Present."

XXI. We are three suitors come from Spain,
      Come to court your daughter Jane.

      My daughter Jane she is too young
      To be beguiled by flattering tongue.

      Let her be young, or let her be old,
      For her beauty she must be sold.

      Return, return, your coat is white,
      And take the fairest in your sight.

      Here's your daughter safe and sound,
      And in her pocket five hundred pound,
      On her finger a gay gold ring,
      Fit to walk with any king.
                    —Dublin (Mrs. Lincoln).

XXII. Here comes a poor duke out of Spain,
      He comes to court your daughter Jane.

      My daughter Jane is yet too young,
      She has a false and flattering tongue.

      Let her be young, or let her be old,
      Her beauty is gone, she must be sold.

      Fare thee well, my lady gay,
      I'll call again another day.

      Turn back, turn back, you ugly wight,
      And clean your spurs till they shine bright.

      My spurs they shine as bright as snow,
      And fit for any king to show;
      So fare thee well, my lady gay,
      I'll call again another day.

Turn back, turn back, you ugly wight,
And choose the fairest one you like.

The fairest one that I can see,
Is you, dear ——, so come with me.
—*Notes and Queries* (1852), vol. vi. 242.

XXIII.   Here comes three knights all out of Spain,
We have come to court your daughter Jane.

Our daughter Jane she is too young,
She has not learned the Spanish tongue.

Whether she be young or old,
'Tis for her beauty she must be sold.

Turn back, turn back, ye Spanish knights,
And rub your spurs till they are bright.

Our spurs are bright and richly wrought,
For in this town they were not bought;
And in this town they shan't be sold,
Neither for silver nor for gold.

Turn back, turn back, ye Spanish knights,
And brush your buckles till they are bright.

Our buckles are bright and richly wrought,
For in this town they were not bought;
And in this town they shan't be sold,
Neither for silver nor for gold.
—Yorkshire (Miss E. Cadman).

XXIV.   There was one lord that came from Spain,
He came to court my daughter Jane;

My daughter Jane, she is too young
To be controlled by a flattering tongue.

Will you ?   No.
Will you ?   Yes.

[This second one then joins hands with the "lord," and they
dance round together, saying—]
You dirty wee scut, you wouldn't come out
To help us with our dancing.
—Ballymiscaw school, co. Down (Miss C. N. Patterson).

XXV. There were one lord came out of Spain,
Who came to court your daughter Jane.

Your daughter Jane, she is too young
To be controlled by flattering tongue.

Oh! fare thee well; oh! fare thee well;
I'll go and court some other girl.

Come back, come back, your coat is white,
And choose the fairest in your sight.

The fairest one that I can see, is ———, come to me.
—Holywood, co. Down (Miss C. N. Patterson).

XXVI. Here's two dukes come out from Spain,
For to court your daughter Jane;

My daughter Jane is far too young,
She cannot hear your flattering tongue.

Be she young, or be she old,
Her beauty must be sold,
Either for silver or for gold;
So fare you well, my lady fair,
I'll call again some other day.
—Galloway (J. G. Carter).

XXVII. Here's one old Jew, just come from Spain,
To ask alone your daughter Jane.

Our daughter Jane is far too young
To understand your Spanish tongue.

Go away, Coat-green.

My name is *not* Coat-green,
I *step* my foot, and away I go.

Come back, come back, your coat is green,
And choose the fairest one you see.

The fairest one that I can see
Is pretty Alice.   Come to me.

I will not come.

Naughty girl, she won't come out,
  She won't come out, she won't come out;
Naughty girl, she won't come out,
  To see the ladies dancing.

    I will come.

Pretty girl, she has come out,
  She has come out, she has come out;
Pretty girl, she has come out,
  To see the ladies dancing.
     —Berwickshire (A. M. Bell, *Antiquary*, vol. xxx. p. 15).

XXVIII.   Here come two Jews, just come from Spain,
      To take away your daughter Jane.

      My daughter Jane is far too young,
      She cannot bear your chattering tongue.

      Farewell! farewell! we must not stay;
      We'll call again another day.

      Come back, come back, your choice is free,
      And choose the fairest one you see.

      The fairest one that I can see
      Is A——— F———. Come to me.
         —Cowes, Isle of Wight (Miss E. Smith).

XXIX.   There came three dukes a-riding, a-riding, a-riding,
     There came three dukes a-riding,
     To court my daughter Jane.

     My daughter Jane is far too young, far too young,
     My daughter Jane is far too young,
     She hath a flattering tongue.

     They're all as red as roses, as roses, as roses,
     They're all as red as roses with sitting in the sun.
         —Perth (Rev. W. Gregor).

XXX.   Here comes a duke a-riding,
     To court your daughter Jane.

My daughter Jane is far too young
To listen to your saucy tongue;
Go back, go back, you saucy Jack,
And clean your spurs and . . . . . .

My spurs are bright as bright can be,
With a tissima, tissima, tissima tee.

Go through the house, go through the hall,
And choose the fairest of them all.

The fairest one that I can see
Is ———.   Come to me.
                    —Clapham School (Mrs. Herbertson).

XXXI.   Here comes three dukes a-riding, a-riding,
         Here comes three dukes a-riding, to court your
              daughter Jane.

My daughter Jane is yet too young
To bear your silly, flattering tongue.

Be she young, or be she old,
She for beauty must and shall be sold.
So fare thee well, my lady gay,
We'll take our horse and ride away,
And call again another day.

Come back, come back! you Spanish knight,
And clean your spurs, they are not bright.

My spurs are bright as "rickety rock" [and richly
    wrought],
And in this town they were not bought,
And in this town they shan't be sold,
Neither for silver, copper, nor gold.
    So fare thee well, &c.

Come back! come back! you Spanish Jack [or cox-
    comb].

Spanish Jack [or coxcomb] is not my name,
I'll stamp my foot [stamps] and say the same.
    So fare thee well, &c.

Come back! come back! you Spanish knight,
And choose the fairest in your sight.

This is the fairest I can see,
So pray, young damsel, walk with me.

We've brought your daughter, safe and sound,
And in her pocket a thousand pound,
And on her finger a gay gold ring,
We hope you won't refuse to take her in.

I'll take her in with all my heart,
For she and "me" were loth to part.
—Cornwall (*Folk-lore Journal*, v. 46, 47).

XXXII.   Here comes three dukes all out of Spain,
For to court your daughter Jane.

My daughter Jane, she is too young,
She cannot bear your flattering tongue.

Be she young, or be she old,
For her beauty she must be sold.

So fare thee well, my lady gay,
We'll call again another day.

Turn back, turn back, you Spanish knight,
And take the fairest in your sight.

Well through the kitchen and through the hall,
I take the fairest of you all.

The fairest one that I can see
Is pretty ——, come to me.
—Gloucestershire (Northall's *Rhymes*, p. 385).

XXXIII.   Two poor sailors dressed in blue,
Two poor sailors dressed in blue,
Two poor sailors dressed in blue,
We come for the sake of your daughter Loo.

My daughter Loo, she is too young,
She cannot bear your flattering tongue.

Whether she be young, or whether she be old,
It is our duty, she must be sold.

Take her, take her, the coach is free,
The fairest one that you can see.

The fairest one that we can see,
Is bonnie [   ].   Come to me.

Here's all your daughters safe and sound,
In every pocket a thousand pound,
On every finger a guinea gold ring,
So please, take one of your daughters in.
            —Fochabers, N.E. Scotland (Rev. W. Gregor).

XXXIV.   Two poor sailors dressed in blue, dressed in blue,
                dressed in blue,
          Two poor sailors dressed in blue, come for the sake
                of your daughter Loo.

          My daughter Loo, she is too young, she is too
                young, she is too young,
          She cannot bear your flattering tongue.

          Let her be young, or yet too old, yet too old, yet
                too old,
          But for her beauty she must be sold.

          The haughty thing, she won't come out, she won't
                come out, she won't come out ;
          The haughty thing, she won't come out,
          To help us with our dancing.

          Now we have got a beautiful maid, a beautiful
                maid, a beautiful maid ;
          Now we have got a beautiful maid,
          To help us with our dancing.
                        —Nairn (Mrs. Jamieson, through
                              Rev. W. Gregor).

XXXV.   One poor sailor dressed in blue, dressed in blue,
                dressed in blue,
          One poor sailor dressed in blue,
          Has come for the sake of your daughter Sue.

          My daughter Sue, she is too young,
          She cannot bear your flattering tongue.

Whether she be young, or whether she be old,
For her beauty she must be sold.

Take her, take her, the coach is free.

The fairest one that I can see is bonny (   ),
    come with we.
    [No !]

The dirty sclipe, she won't come out, she won't
    come out, she won't come out ;
The dirty sclipe, she won't come out to dance
    along with me.

Now, I have got another poor maid, &c.,
To come along with me.
                —Cullen (Rev. W. Gregor).

XXXVI.   Here comes two ladies down from Spain,
        A len (?) [all in] French garland.
     I've come to court your daughter Jane,
        And adieu to you, my darling.
       —Scotland (*Notes and Queries*, 3rd series, v. 393).

XXXVII. Here are just three tribes come down from Spain,
      To call upon my sister Jane.

My sister Jane, she is far too young ;
I cannot bear her chattering tongue.

The fairest lily that I can see,
Is pretty little Lizzie, will ye come to me ?
    [No !]

The dirty thing, she won't come out, she won't
    come out, she won't come out ;
The dirty thing, she won't come out, to help us
    with the dancing.
    [Yes !]

Now we've got a pretty maid, a pretty maid, a
    pretty maid ;
Now we've got a pretty maid, to help us with the
    dancing.   —Waterford (Miss H. E. Harvey).

(*b*) The players stand in two lines, facing one another, three boys on one side and the girls (any number) on the other. The boys advance and retire dancing, and saying the first two lines. The girls stand still, one who personates a mother answers with the next two lines. The boys then advance and reply. When they are retiring the mother says the next lines and the boys reply; they then choose a girl and take her over to their side. The dialogue is generally spoken, not sung. The boys turn their toes outwards to show their spurs. The number of players on the girls' side is generally an uneven one, the odd one is the mother and says the dialogue. This is the most general way of playing, but there are interesting variations. Chambers says two parties play, one representing a dame and her daughters, the other the suitors. The suitors move backwards and forwards with their arms entwined. The mother offers her daughters when she says "Smell my lilies," and the game ends by some little childish trick, but unfortunately, he does not describe this. Miss Ellis (Leicester) says if the number of players suited, probably all the boys, instead of three, would be on one side and the girls on the other, but there is no hard and fast line. They turn out their toes to show their spurs: when they sing or say, "Pass through the kitchen," &c., the girls stretch out their arms, still keeping hold of hand, and the boys, forming a long tail, wind in and out under their arms as they stand. Having previously decided among themselves which girl they shall seize, they go up and down the lines several times, until the period of suspense and expectation is supposed to have lasted long enough. Then the last boy in the line puts his arms round the chosen girl's waist and carries her off. This goes on until there is only one girl left, who recommences the game on her part by singing the first lines, choosing first a boy, who then becomes a Spaniard. In the first version from Belfast, the first girl who is asked to go refuses, and another is asked, who consents. In the Manchester version (Miss Dendy), the girl refuses twice, then accepts. The "mother" is seated in state with her "daughters" round her in the Bexley Heath (Miss Morris) version. The two "gentlemen" advance to her and

turn haughtily away when refused. Then they choose a girl
and take her over to their side. In the Shropshire (Edgmond)
version, two girls, one from each end of the line of "daughters,"
goes over to the knights' side, who also "bow" and "bend"
when saying the lines, and the game is repeated saying five,
seven, &c., knights. Here, also, the last player left on the girls'
side takes the knight's part in the next game. Miss Burne
adds, at other places the knights call only one girl by name each
time. Both lines in the Shropshire game advance and retire.
In the Dublin game (Mrs. Lincoln), three young boys are
chosen for the suitors, one girl is the mother, and any number
from three to six personate the daughters. The first boy only
speaks the lines. At "Return, return, your coat is white,"
he, with the other two "suitors," takes the girl, brings her
back, and says the last verse. They then sit down, and the
second suitor does the same thing, then the third one. Then
the game is begun again [with three other boys] until all the
daughters have been taken. In the version quoted from *Notes
and Queries*, two children, mother and daughter, stand on one
side, the other players opposite to them, and advance and
retire. The contributor says they chant the words to a
pleasing old melody. The Yorkshire version (Miss E. Cadman)
is played in the usual way, both sides advancing and retiring
in turn, and at the end one of the "knights" tries to catch
one of the girls. They cross the room to each other's places.
In Co. Down, at Ballymiscaw, Miss Patterson says one player
refuses when asked, and another consents, this one and the
"lord" then join hands and dance round together, saying the
last words. The Annaverna version is sung by one on each
side—"king and the mother." The Berwickshire game was
played by six children, one on one side, five on the other.
The first lines are sung on both sides; then the rest is dialogue
until the girl refuses, when the "Jew" dances round by himself, singing the words; she then consents, and the two dance
round with joined hands as in a reel, singing the last verse.
The dialogue is spoken with animation, and the "Jew steps
his foot" and prances away when saying these words. Twelve
children in the Perth version stand in a row, another stands a

little in advance, who is called "daughter Jane," another is the "mother." Three more stand in front of the twelve and are the "Dukes." These dance forwards and backwards before "Jane and her mother," singing the first lines. The mother answers. When they sing the last line the "Dukes" choose one of the twelve, and sing the words over again until all the twelve are on the "Dukes'" side. Then they try to carry off "Jane" and the "mother," and run until they are caught. In the Clapham school version (Mrs. Herbertson), the "Duke" tries to drag by force the chosen girl across a handkerchief or other boundary, if successful she goes on his side. In the Cornwall version the "Dukes" retire and consult before choosing a girl, then select one. When all have been taken they bring them back in the same order to the "mother," saying the last verse, and the "mother" replies in the last two lines. In the London version, the "Dukes" take the girl and rob her, then bring her back. In the Fochabers version (Rev. W. Gregor), the two "sailors" join hands crosswise, walk backwards and forwards, and sing the words. The girl crosses over to them when chosen. When all are chosen the "sailors" bring all the girls before the mother, singing the last verse. The mother searches the daughters one after the other, finding neither money nor ring. She then chases the sailors, and the one caught becomes mother next game.

(c) This game has been said by previous collectors, and at first sight may be thought to be merely a variant of "Three Dukes," but it will on investigation, I think, prove to be more than this. In the first place, the obvious borrowing from the "Three Dukes" of a few words, as in versions Nos. 29, 30, and 31, tells against the theory of identity of the two games. Then the form of marriage custom is different, though it is still marriage under primitive conditions of society. The personal element, entirely absent from the "Three Dukes," is here one of the principal characteristics. The marriage is still one without previous courtship or love between two individuals, but the parental element is present here, or at anyrate that of some authority, and a sanction is given, although there is no trace of any actual ceremony. The young men, or suitors, apparently desire a particular person in marriage, and although there is no wooing of that person a demand is made for her. These suitors are, I think, making the demand on the part of another rather than for themselves. They are the ambassadors or friends of the would-be bridegrooms, and are soliciting for a marriage in which purchase money or dowry is to be paid. The mention of "gold and silver" in many versions, and the line, "she must be sold," is important.

All these indications of purchase refer to a time when the custom of offering gold, money, or other valuables for a bride was in vogue. While, therefore, the game has traces of carrying off the bride, this carrying off is in strict accord with the conditions prevalent when marriage by purchase had succeeded to marriage by capture. The bargaining spirit is not much "en evidence" in this game, not, that is to say, in the same sense as is shown in "Three Sailors," p. 282, but there is sufficient evidence of a mercantile spirit to prove that women and girls were too valuable to be parted with by their own tribe or family without something deemed equivalent being given in return. There is a desire shown to possess the girl for her beauty; and that a choice of a suitor could or would be made is shown by the remarks that she is too young and does not know the language and customs of this suitor.

The mention of the spurs conveys the suggestion that the suitors or ambassadors are men of quality and renown. To win their spurs was an object greatly desired by all young men. Their reply to the taunt that their spurs are "dull" may mean that they are not bright from use, and may also show the idea that these men have come on a journey from some distance for a bride or brides, and this only is responsible for their spurs not being as bright as usual. Again, being "richly wrought" is probably an indication of wealth or consequence. Mention must be made of the mead not being made nor the cake yet baked, which occurs in two versions. If these two versions can be considered old ones, this would tend to show evidence of the ceremony of the eating together of particular food, which forms the most important element in primitive marriage ceremonies.

There occurs in some versions the incident of asking the girl to come, and the dancing round when she consents, mostly in connection with the incident of invitation to dance.   This may not therefore belong, and I do not think it does, to the early forms of this game; but we must remember that dancing formed a part of the marriage ceremonies down to quite a late date, and it is therefore not surprising it should be found in many versions.

It has been suggested that this game has for its origin an historical event in the reign of Edward III., whose daughter Jane married a prince of Spain.   There is some possibility in this, as doubtless the marriage was conducted by ambassadors first of all with pomp and ceremonial, but I think the game really dates from a much earlier period, and if there are any grounds for connecting it with this particular royal marriage, it may merely have altered and fixed some of the words, such as " daughter Jane," " Lords from Spain," " Spanish gold," in people's minds, and in this way tended to preserve the game in its modern form.

Mr. Addy, in his *Sheffield Glossary*, considers that the mention of the three knights and gifts of gold is a fragment of some old pageant of the Three Kings of Cologne, who, according to ancient legend, brought gifts to the infant Jesus, but I can see no evidence of this.

It is somewhat curious that this game is very rarely sung to a tune, nor have I succeeded in obtaining one.   It is usually said to a sort of sing-song chant, or else it is spoken in dialogue, and that with a good deal of animation.

Mr. Newell gives versions, as played in America, similar to many here given, and Mr. Northall (*Folk Rhymes*, p. 385) gives one from Gloucestershire and Warwickshire.

Three Little Ships

—London (A. B. Gomme).

—Rimbault's *Nursery Rhymes.*

I. Three little ships come sailing by,
 Sailing by, sailing by ;
 Three little ships come sailing by,
 New Year's day in the morning.

Who do you think was in the ships,
 In the ships, in the ships ;
 Who do you think was in the ships,
 New Year's day in the morning ?

Three pretty girls were in the ships,
 In the ships, in the ships ;
 Three pretty girls were in the ships,
 New Year's day in the morning.

One could whistle, and one could sing,
 One could play on the violin ;
 One could whistle, and one could sing,
 New Year's day in the morning.

—London (A. B. Gomme).

II. I saw three ships come sailing by,
 Come sailing by, come sailing by ;
 I saw three ships come sailing by
 On New Year's day in the morning.

And what do you think was in them then,
 In them then, in them then ;
 And what do you think was in them then,
 On New Year's day in the morning ?

Three pretty girls were in them then, &c.

One could whistle, and one could sing,
 The other could play on the violin ;
 Such joy was there at my wedding,
 On New Year's day in the morning.

—Rimbault's *Nursery Rhymes.*

III. As I sat on a sunny bank,
   A sunny bank, a sunny bank ;
   As I sat on a sunny bank
   On Christmas day in the morning.

   I saw three ships come sailing by,
   Come sailing by, come sailing by ;
   I saw three ships come sailing by
   On Christmas day in the morning.

   And who do you think was in those ships ? &c.
   But Joseph and his lady.

   And he did whistle, and she did sing,
   And all the bells on earth did ring
   For joy our Saviour he was born
   On Christmas day in the morning.
                    —Burne's *Shropshire Folk-lore*, p. 564.

[The above verses, except the last one, are sung at Oswestry
with these additional ones :—]
   Pray, whither sailed those ships all three ? &c.
   Oh ! they sailed unto Bethlehem, &c.
   They combed his hair with an ivory comb, &c.
   They washed his face in a golden cup, &c.
   They wiped his face with a lily-white cloth, &c.
   They brushed his shoes with a hairy brush, &c.
                    —Burne's *Shropshire Folk-lore*, p. 564.

(*c*) In the London version, which I obtained from a maid-
servant—two lines of children stand, hand in hand, facing one
another.   They advance and retire in line, with dancing steps,
alternately.   The children sing the lines.   When the last verse
is sung a girl from the end of each line advances, and the two
dance round together.   This is continued until all have danced
in turn in the space between the lines.

(*d*) It will be seen that there is a probability of the version I
collected as a dance game and Rimbault's nursery song being
derived from the Christmas carol, a variant of which I reprint
from Miss Burne's *Shropshire Folk-lore*. A version of this
carol from Kent is given in *Notes and Queries*, 3rd series, iii. 7.

Mr. A. H. Bullen, in *Carols and Poems*, gives an older version of the same. In this version there is no mention of whistling, singing, or playing the violin; but in the Kent version, the third verse is the same as the fourth of that collected by Miss Burne, and the dance collected by myself. In the *Revue Celtique*, vol. iv., Mr. Fitzgerald considers this carol to have been the original from which the pretty words and dance, "Duck Dance," were derived, see *ante*, vol. i. p. 113. If these words and dance owe their origin to the carol, they may both show connection with an older form, when the carol was danced as a dramatic round.

Three Old Bachelors

<blockquote>
Here come three old bachelors,
Walking in a row,
Seeking wives, and can't find 'em;
So open the ring, and take one in.
Now you're married, you must obey;
You must be true to all you say;
You must be kind, you must be good,
And help your wife to chop the wood.
</blockquote>

—Earls Heaton, Yorks. (Herbert Hardy).

Mr. Hardy suggests that this is a variant of "See the Farmer Sow his Seed," but it more nearly resembles "Silly Old Man," although the marriage formula is that of "Oats and Beans."

Three Sailors

Two last verses only.

—London (A. B. Gomme).

I. Here come three sailors, three by three,
To court your daughter, a fair lady (pronounced ladee) ;
[*Or*, And down by your door they bend their knee].
Can we have a lodging here, here, here ?
Can we have a lodging here ?

Sleep, sleep, daughter, do not wake,
Here are three sailors we can't take ;
You cannot have a lodging here, here, here,
You cannot have a lodging here.

Here come three soldiers, three by three,
To court your daughter, a fair lady ;
Can we have a lodging here, here, here ?
Can we have a lodging here ?

Sleep, sleep, daughter, do not wake,
Here are three soldiers we can't take ;
You cannot have a lodging here, here, here,
You cannot have a lodging here.

Here come three kings, three by three,
To court your daughter, a fair lady ;
Can we have a lodging here, here, here ?
Can we have a lodging here ?

Wake, wake, daughter, do not sleep,
Here come three kings that we can take ;
You can have a lodging here, here, here,
You can have a lodging here.

Here's my daughter, safe and sound,
And in her pocket one hundred pound,
And on her finger a gay gold ring,
And she is fit to walk with a king.

Here's your daughter, not safe nor sound,
Nor in her pocket one hundred pound,
On her finger no gay gold ring,
I'm sure she's not fit to walk with a king.
—Barnes, Surrey, and London (A. B. Gomme).

II.　Here come three tinkers, three by three,
　　　To court your daughter, fair lady;
　　　Oh! have you any lodgings here, oh, here?
　　　Oh! have you any lodgings here?

Sleep, sleep, daughter, do not wake,
Here come three tinkers we cannot take;
We haven't any lodgings here, oh, here,
We haven't any lodgings here.

Here come three soldiers, three by three,
To court your daughter, fair lady;
Oh! have you any lodgings here, oh, here?
Oh! have you any lodgings here?

Sleep, sleep, daughter, do not wake,
Here come three soldiers we cannot take;
We haven't any lodgings here, oh, here,
We haven't any lodgings here.

Here come three kings, three by three,
To court your daughter, fair lady;
Oh! have you any lodgings here, oh, here?
Oh! have you any lodgings here?

Wake, wake, daughter, do not sleep,
Here come three kings that we can take;
We have some lodgings here, oh, here,
We have some lodgings here.

Here's my daughter, safe and sound,
And in her pocket five hundred pounds,
And on her finger a five guinea gold ring,
And she is fit to walk with a king.

Here's your daughter, nor safe nor sound,
And in her pocket no five hundred pound,
And on her finger no five guinea gold ring,
And she's not fit to walk with the king.

—Sporle, Norfolk (Miss Matthews).

III. Here's three sweeps, three by three,
      And down by the door they bend their knee;
      Oh! shall we have lodgings here, oh, here?
      Oh! shall we have lodgings here?

      Sleep, dear daughter, do not wake,
      For here's three sweeps coming to take;
      Lodgings here they shall not have,
      So sleep, dear daughter, sleep.

      Here's three bakers, three by three,
      And down by the door they bend their knee;
      Oh! shall we have lodgings here, oh, here?
      Oh! shall we have lodgings here?

      Sleep, dear daughter, do not wake, &c. (as above).

      Here's three kings, three by three, &c. (as above).

      Wake, dear daughter, do not sleep,
      For here's three kings coming to take;
      Lodgings here they all may have,
      So wake, dear daughter, wake.

      Here's my daughter, safe and sound,
      And on her finger a guinea gold ring,
      And in her pocket a thousand pounds,
      So she is fit to marry a king.

      Here's your daughter, safe and sound,
      And on her finger no guinea gold ring,
      And in her pocket no thousand pounds,
      So she's not fit to marry a king.
                    —Aberdeen Training College (Rev. W. Gregor).

IV. Here come three tailors, three by three,
     To court your daughter, fair and fair;
     Have you got a lodger here, oh, here?
     Have you got a lodger here?

     Sleep, daughter, sleep, sleep,
     Here come three tailors we can't take;
     We haven't got a lodger here, oh, here,
     We haven't got a lodger here.

[The verses are repeated for "sailors," "blacksmiths," &c.,

and then "kings," and ends in the same way as the preceding
version.]　　　　　　　　　—Swaffham, Norfolk (Miss Matthews).

　　V.　Here come three sailors, three by three,
　　　　　A courting your daughter, Caroline Mee;
　　　　　[Some would sing it " Because your daughter "]
　　　　　Can we have a lodging here to-night ?

　　　　　Sleep, daughter, do not wake,
　　　　　Here's three sailors we can't take;
　　　　　You cannot have a lodging here to-night.

　　　　　Here come three soldiers, three by three,
　　　　　A courting your daughter, Caroline Mee;
　　　　　Can we have a lodging here to-night ?

　　　　　Sleep, daughter, do not wake,
　　　　　Here's three soldiers we can't take;
　　　　　You cannot have a lodging here to-night.

[This is repeated for "kings," and the game ends as in the
previous versions. "Three" hundred pounds being substituted
for "five."]　　　　　　　　　—Deptford, Kent (Miss Chase).

　　VI.　Here come some travellers three by three,
　　　　　And down by a door they bend their knee.
　　　　　" Can we get lodgings here ? "
　　　　　The fairest one that I can see
　　　　　Is pretty little ———, come to me,
　　　　　And you'll get lodgings here—
　　　　　" Will you come ? "　" Yes," or " No ! "
　　　　　　　　　　　　Isle of Man (A. W. Moore).

(c) The players form in two lines, and stand facing one another.
One line consists of a mother and daughters.　The other of the
suitors.　The mother stands a little in advance of her daughters.
They remain stationary during the game, the mother alone
singing the words on her side.　The suitors advance and retire
in line while singing their verses.　The mother turns partly
round when singing the two first lines of her verses addressing
her daughters, and then faces the suitors when singing to them
the remaining two lines.　When she accepts the "kings" she

brings one of her daughters forward, presents her to the suitors, and shows them the money in her pocket, and the ring on her finger. The daughter goes with the kings, who take her a little way apart, pretend to rob her of her ring, money, and clothes, and then bring her back to her mother, and sing the last verse. They then run off in all directions, and the mother and daughters chase and catch them, and they change sides. Sometimes all the daughters are taken by the suitors before they are robbed and brought back. The game is also played by five players only; three representing the sailors or suitors, and two the mother and daughter. The mother then chases the suitors, and whoever she catches becomes the daughter the next game. These are the usual methods of playing. In the Norfolk version the middle one of the three suitors takes the girl, robs her, and all three bring her back and sing the verses. In the Isle of Man version one player sits down, the others join hands, advance and retire singing the lines. The girl who is chosen joins the one sitting down.

(d) This game points to that period of tribal society, when the youths of one tribe sought to obtain their wives from the maidens of another tribe according to the laws of exogamy, but a definite person is here selected for the wife, and it is to the relatives or persons having authority (as in "Three Knights") that the demand for the bride is made, and not to the girl personally, as in "Three Dukes."

The game, while not so interesting a one to us as "Three Dukes," and "Three Knights," has its particular or peculiar features. It is probably later, and shows more clearly that position and wealth were of importance to a man in the obtaining of a wife. Individually he has not (apparently) courted the girl before, but he comes for that purpose now. He may be announcing himself under the various ranks or professions mentioned, before stating his real position; or, this may show that the girl having many suitors, and those of all degrees, the "mother" or relatives are actuated by purely mercenary motives, and wish to select the best and richest suitor for her. We must remember that it was accounted great honour to a girl to have many suitors and amongst these men distinguished by the performance of brave deeds, which had gained them renown and pre-eminence, or wealth. The fact that the rejection or acceptance of the suitors is made known to the girl by the "mother," or person having authority, shows that "sanction" or permission is necessary, and that "rejection" or "acceptance" is signified to the suitors in the words, you "may not," or, you "may" have a lodging here, signifies admission into the family. This is a most interesting feature. The girl is to "wake up," that would be to rouse up, be merry, dress in bridal array and prepare for the coming festival. She is also given to the suitors with "in her pocket one hundred pounds," and "on her finger a gay gold ring." This, it will be seen, is given her by her "mother" or person having authority, and probably refers to the property the girl brings with her to her new abode for her proper maintenance there; the ring shows likewise her station and degree in her former abode, and is the token that she is fit bride for a king, and must be treated accordingly. Curious, too, is "Here's my daughter safe and sound," which looks like a warrant or guarantee of the girl's fitness to be a bride. The expression "walk with," meaning "to marry," again occurs in this game as in "Three Dukes." The line occurring in two versions, "And down by the door they bend their knee," is suggestive of courtesy shown to the bride and her family at the threshold of the house.

The incident of the three kings becoming robbers is not easily understood. Robbery was common of course, particularly when money and valuables were known to be carried on the person; but I do not think this is sufficient in itself to account for the incident. It may be a reflection of the later fact that a man always took possession of his wife's personal property after marriage, and considered it his own to do as he pleased with. When this idea became codified in written law, the idea might readily get reflected in the game, when *kings* would not be understood as apparently taking things that did not belong to them, unless they were bandits in disguise. This last verse and the robbery may be a later addition to the game, when robbery was of everyday occurrence. There may have been (although there is nothing now in any version to warrant the idea) some similar action on the part of the kings, such as a further arraying of the bride, and presenting her to their party or house, which has been misunderstood. Mr. Newell suggests that children having forgotten the original happy finish, and not understanding the "haggling" over the suitors, turned the kings into bandits. Children think it such a natural thing to wish to marry kings, princes, and princesses, and are so sincere in thinking it a matter of course to refuse a sailor or soldier for a king, when it is only a question of marriage, and not of choosing the one you like the best, that this reason does not to me seem to apply to a game of this kind.

Through the Needle Eye, Boys

Two leaders each choose a name such as " Golden Apple " and " Golden Pear." The remaining children all hold each other's waists in a long string, the " Golden Apple" and " Golden Pear" holding hands aloft like an arch. The string of children then runs under the arch. The last child that passes under is detained by the " Golden Apple" and " Golden Pear " (they having dropped hands previously). The detained child is asked in a whisper which she prefers, " Golden Apple," " Golden Pear ; " she chooses, and then stands at the back of the " Golden Apple" or " Golden Pear." When all the children have passed through, the " Golden Apple" and " Golden Pear" hold each other's hands and stand with the others behind them and pull like a " Tug of War." There should be a line drawn between the " Golden Apple" and the " Golden Pear," and whichever side pulls the other over the line, wins the game.—Northumberland (from a lady friend of Hon. J. Abercromby).

The formula sung in Fraserburgh when the players are running under the raised arms is—

> Clink, clink, through the needle ee, boys,
> One, two, three,
> If you want a bonnie lassie,
> Just tak me.

After the tug of war the victors call out " Rotten eggs, rotten eggs " (Rev. W. Gregor).

The words used in Galloway are—

> Through the needle e'e, boys,
> Through the needle e'e !
> If 'twasna for your granny's sake,
> I wadna let 'e through.
>
> —Galloway (J. G. Carter).

Jamieson describes this game in the south of Scotland as follows: "Two children form an arch with both hands. The rest, who hold each other by the skirts following in a line, attempt to pass under the arch. The first, who is called the king, is sometimes laid hold of by those who form the arch, each letting fall one of his arms like a portcullis for enclosing the passenger. But more generally the king is suffered to pass, the attempt being reserved for the last; whoever is seized is called the prisoner. As soon as he is made captive he takes the place of one of those who formed the arch, and who afterwards stand by his side."

It is differently played in Mearns, Aberdeen, and some other counties. A number of boys stand with joined hands in a semicircle, and the boy at one end of the link addresses the boy at the other end of the line:

> A—— B——, if ye were mine,
> I wad feed you with claret wine ;
> Claret wine is gude and fine,
> Through the needle-ee, boys.

The boy to whom this is addressed makes room between himself and his next neighbour, as they raise and extend their arms to allow the opposite boy to run through the opening followed by all the other boys still linked to each other. If in running through the link should be broken, the two boys who are the cause suffer some punishment.—Ed. Jamieson's Dictionary.

The Northumberland game resembles "Oranges and Lemons." The other versions are nearer the "Thread the Needle" and "How many Miles to Babylon" games. Both games may be derived from the same custom.

See "How many Miles to Babylon," "Thread the Needle."

Thun'er Spell

A thin lath of wood, about six inches long and three or four inches broad, is taken and rounded at one end. A hole is bored in that end, and in the hole is tied a piece of cord between two and three yards long. It is then rapidly swung round, so as to produce a buzzing sound. The more rapidly it is swung, the louder is the noise. It was believed that the use of this instrument during a thunder-storm saved one from being struck with "the thun'er bolt." I have used it with this intention (Keith). In other places it is used merely to make a noise. It is commonly deeply notched all round the edges to increase the noise.

Some years ago a herd boy was observed making one in a farm-kitchen (Udny). It was discovered that when he was sent to bring the cows from the fields to the farmyard to be milked, he used it to frighten them, and they ran frantically to their stalls. The noise made the animals dread the bot-fly or "cleg." This torment makes them throw their tails up, and rush with fury through the fields or to the byres to shelter themselves from its attacks. A formula to effect the same purpose, and which I have many and many a time used when herding, was: Cock tail! cock tail! cock tail! Bizz-zz-zz! Bizz-zz-zz. —Keith (Rev. W. Gregor).

Dr. Gregor secured one of these that was in use in Pitsligo, and sent it to the Pitt-Rivers Museum at Oxford, where it now lies. Professor Haddon has made a collection of these toys, and has written on their connection with the Australian boomerang.

They are still occasionally to be met with in country districts, but are used simply for the purpose of making a noise.

See "Bummers."

Tick

A game mentioned by Drayton, and still played in Warwickshire.—Halliwell's *Dictionary*. The same game as "Touch."

Tickle me Quickly

An old game (undescribed) mentioned in Taylor's *Motto*, 1622, sig. D, iv.

Ticky Touchwood.

Ticky, ticky Touchwood, my black hen,
She lays eggs for gentlemen ;
Sometimes nine and sometimes ten,
Ticky, ticky Touchwood, my black hen.
—Sporle, Norfolk (Miss Matthews).

Addy (*Sheffield Glossary*, under "Tiggy Touchwood") says, "One player who is called Tiggy stands out, and each of the others takes hold of or touches a piece of wood, such as a door, or rail, &c.   One then leaves his 'wood' and runs across the playground, and if whilst doing so Tiggy can touch him he must stand out or take Tiggy's place."

One child is chosen to be "Ticky," *i.e.*, to be on the *qui vive* to lay hold of or touch any one who is not touching wood.   If played out of doors it must be clearly defined *what is wood*, trees and all growing wood being forbidden.   The fun consists in the bold ventures of those who tempt "Ticky" to run after them, and contrive to touch "wood" just before he touches them.   When one is caught he is "Ticky" in turn.—Swaffham, Norfolk (Miss Matthews).

Played within a given boundary, in which were wooden buildings or fences.   When one of the players was being pursued by the tigger, if he touched wood he could not be made prisoner, but he was not allowed to remain long in that position, and directly his hand left wood he was liable to instant capture.   If when pursued he called out "a barla!" he was again exempt from capture, but he could not move from the position or place where he or she was when they called out, a barla!   When wishing to move he had to call out "Ma barla oot!"   No den in this game, but constant running.—Biggar (Wm. Ballantyne).

Lowsley (*Berkshire Glossary*) says, "Boys have games called Touch-wood and Touch-iron, where any one not touching either of the substances named is liable to be caught by the one standing out."

Ross and Stead (*Holderness Glossary*) give this game as Tiggy Touchwood, a game similar to Tig, but in which the player must touch wood.   It is called Ticky, Ticky Touchwood by Brogden (*Lincolnshire Provincial Words*), and Tiggy in Addy's *Sheffield Glossary*.

Also played in another way. One tree or piece of wood was selected for " Home," and the players darted out from this saying, " Ticky, Ticky Touchwood," then running back to the tree and touching it before Ticky caught them. " Parley " or " fainits " were the words called out when exempt.—London (A. B. Gomme).

It is also described in Patterson's *Antrim and Down Glossary*.

Tig.

A game in which one player touches another, then runs off to be pursued and touched in turn.

Mr. Addy says, " Children *tig* each other when they leave school, and there is a rivalry among them to get the last tig. After a boy has said *tig-poison*, he is not to be 'tigged' again." Brockett says: " Tig, a slight touch (as a mode of salutation), a play among children on separating for the night, in which every one endeavours to get the last touch; called also Last Bat."—Brockett's *North Country Words*, and consult Dickinson (*Cumberland Glossary*), also Jamieson. A boys' game, in which the player scores by touching one who runs before him. —Stead's *Holderness Glossary*. A play among children when separating for the night.—Willan's *Dialect Words of West Riding of Yorks*. Called also " Touch " and " Tigga Tiggy," in East and West Cornwall; (Courtney and Couch), also Patterson's *Antrim and Down Glossary*.

See " Canlie," " Cross Tig."

Time.

The players stand in a line. Two are chosen, who stand apart, and fix on any hour, as one, two, three, &c., or any half-hour. A nestie is marked off at some distance from the row of players. One of the two goes in front of the line of players, and beginning at one end asks each the hour. This is done till the hour fixed on between the two is guessed. The one that makes the right guess runs to catch the other of the two that fixed the hour, and she makes off to the " nestie." If she is caught she goes to the line of players, and the one that caught her takes her place. If she reaches the "nestie" without being caught, she has still to run to the line of players; if she does this without being caught she holds her place as one of the time-fixers, but if caught she takes her stand in the line, and the one that caught her becomes time-fixer.—Fraserburgh (Rev. W. Gregor).

Tip it.

This is played by six players, divided into two sides of three each, with one captain to each side. A ring or other small object is taken by the side which wins the toss, and then both sides sit down to a small table. The in-side puts their hands under the table, and the ring is given to one of the three players. At a given signal they all bring up their closed hands on to the table, and the other side has to guess in which closed fist the ring is. The guesser has the privilege of ordering "off" the hands which he thinks are empty. If he succeeds in getting the empty hands off, he says "tip it" to the remaining one. If he guesses right the ring changes sides. The game is to keep the ring or other object on one side as long as possible.—London (Alfred Nutt).

Tip-Cat.

Strutt says this is so denominated from the piece of wood called a cat, about six inches in length, and an inch and a half or two inches in diameter, diminished from the middle to both ends. When the cat is on the ground the player strikes it smartly, when it rises with a rotatory motion high enough for him to hit it again before it falls, in the same manner as a ball. He says there are various methods of playing the game, and describes the two following: A large ring is made in the ground; in the middle of this the striker takes his station; his business then is to hit the cat over the ring. If he fails in doing so he is out, and another player takes his place; if successful, he judges with his eye the distance the cat is driven from the centre of the ring, and calls for a number at pleasure to be scored towards his game: if the number demanded be found upon measurement to exceed the same number of lengths of the bludgeon, he is out; on the contrary, if it does not, he obtains his call.

The second way of playing is to make four, six, or eight holes in the ground in a circular direction, and at equal distances from each other, at every hole is placed a player with his bludgeon: one of the opposite party who stand in the field tosses the cat to the batsman who is nearest him, and every time the cat is struck the players are obliged to change their situations, and run once from one hole to another in succession ; if the cat be driven to any great distance they continue to run in the same order, and claim a score towards their game every time they quit one hole and run to another; but if the cat be stopped by their opponents and thrown across between any two of the holes before the player who has quitted one of them can reach the other, he is out.

Mr. Kinahan says there is among old Irish games one some-times called cat, played with three or more players on each side, two stones or holes as stations, and a lobber, but the regular cat is played with a stick four inches long, bevelled at each end, called the cat.   This bevelled stick is laid on the ground, and one end hit with a stick to make it rise in the air, when it is hit by the player, who runs to a mark and back to his station. The game is made by a number of runs; while the hitter is out if he fails three times to hit the cat, or if he is hit by the cat while running.—(*Folk-lore Journal,* ii. 264.)   The common game of " tip-cat " was called *cat-and-kitten* by Dorset children. The long stick represented the " cat " and the small pieces the " kitten."—(*Folk-lore Journal,* vii. 234.)   Elworthy (*West Somerset Words*) calls it Stick and Snell. Brogden (*Provincial Words, Lincolnshire*) gives it as tip-cat, as does Lowsley (*Berkshire Glossary*), also Trippit and Coit, and Trippit and Rack in some parts of the North.—Brockett's *North Country Words.*   Once commonly played in London streets, now forbidden.

See " Cudgel," " Waggles."

Tip-tap-toe.

A square is drawn having nine smaller squares or houses within it.   Two persons play.   They alternately make the one a square and the other a cross in any one of the

houses. He that first gets three in a line wins the game.
—Peacock's *Manley and Corringham Glossary*. Brogden
(*Provincial Words, Lincolnshire*) calls it Tit-tat-toe, also Low-
sley (*Berkshire Glossary*).

Northall says called Tick-tack-toe in Warwickshire and
Staffordshire; the rhyme is " Tick-tack-toe, I've caught you."

This game is called " Noughts and Crosses," in London,
probably from those marks being used in the game.

See " Kit-Cat-Cannio," " Noughts and Crosses."

Tiring Irons.

An old game with iron rods and rings.—Holland's *Cheshire
Glossary*.

Tisty Tosty

See " Shuttlefeather," " Teesty Tosty."

Titter-totter

The game of see-saw.—Halliwell's *Dictionary*.

Tit-tat-toe.

A game played by school children on slates. A round is
drawn, which is divided into as many divisions as is thought
necessary, sixteen being generally the least. These divisions
are each numbered, the centre containing a higher figure
than any in the divisions, usually 25, 50, or 100. Several
children can play. They each have a place or square allotted
to them on the slate in which to record the numbers they
obtain. A space is allotted to " Old Nick " or the " Old Man."
The players alternately take a pencil in their right hand (holding it point downwards on 1, and tapping on each number
with it), and shutting their eyes move round and round the
diagram saying—

> " Tit, tat, toe, my first go,
> Three jolly butcher boys all in a row
> Stick one up, stick one down,
> Stick one in the old man's ground,"

stopping and keeping the pencil in an upright position when
the last word is said. The player then opens his eyes, and
registers in his square the number at which the pencil stopped.

This number is then scratched through on the diagram, to signify that it is taken, the other players proceed in the same manner as the first; then the first one begins again. This is continued till all the numbers are scratched out, or till one of the players puts his pencil into the centre, and thus wins the game. If all the figures are taken before the centre is touched, the game goes to the " Old man " or " Old Nick." Also, if one player puts his pencil in a division already taken, he records nothing and loses that turn; this is also the case if, after the

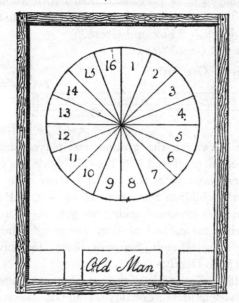

verse is repeated, the pencil is found to be on a division or boundary line or outside the round.—London (A. B. Gomme).

I was taught by a maid servant to play this game on the ground. This girl drew the round and divisions and figures on the gravel path or mould in the garden, and sharpened a piece of stick at one end for the pointer. She did not know the game as one played on slates, but always played it on the ground in this way.

This game appears to indicate a lottery, and might originally have had something to do with allotting pieces of land or other property to prospective owners under the ancient common field system. The places when taken by one player not being available for another, and the fact of it being known as played on the ground, and not on slates, are both significant indications of the suggested origin. The method of allotting lands by lottery is described in Gomme's *Village Community*. Mr. Newell, *Games*, p. 140, records a similar game called "Wheel of Fortune."

Tods and Lambs

A game played on a perforated board with wooden pins.— Jamieson. The Editor adds that the game is materially the same as the English "Fox and Geese."

See "Fox and Geese" (2).

Tom Tiddler's Ground

D.C. ad lib.

—Liverpool (Mrs. Harley).

A line is drawn on the ground, one player stands behind it. The piece so protected is "Tom Tiddler's ground." The other players stand in a row on the other side. The row breaks and the children run over, calling out, "Here we are on Tom Tiddler's ground, picking up gold and silver." Tom Tiddler catches them, and as they are caught they stand on one side. The last out becomes Tom Tiddler.—Monton, Lancashire (Miss Dendy).

Tom Tiddler's Ground is played at Chirbury under the name of "Boney" = Bonaparte! one boy taking possession of a certain area, and the others trespassing on it, saying, "I am on Boney's ground." If they are caught there, they are put "in prison" till released by a touch from a comrade.—Chirbury (*Shropshire Folk-lore*, p. 523–524).

> I'm on Tom Tinker's ground,
> I'm on Tom Tinker's ground,
> I'm on Tom Tinker's ground,
> Picking up gold and silver.
> —Derbyshire (*Folk-lore Journal*, i. 386).

Northall (*Folk Rhymes*) gives the following lines, and describes it as played as above, except that Tom Tinder is

provided with a knotted handkerchief, with which he buffets
any one caught on his property :—

>Here we are on Tom Tinder's ground,
>Picking up gold and silver ;
>You pick weeds, and I'll pick seeds,
>And we'll all pick carraway comfits.

In the Liverpool district the game is called "Old Daddy
Bunchey" (Mrs. Harley), and in Norfolk "Pussey's Ground"
(Miss Matthews).

It is also mentioned by Lowsley (*Berkshire Glossary*).

Tops

The special games now played with tops are mentioned
under their respective titles, but the general allusions to the
ancient whipping-tops are important enough to note.

Strutt says the top was known with us as early at least as
the fourteenth century, when its form was the same as now,
and the manner of using it can admit of but little if any
difference. Representations of boys whipping tops occur in
the marginal paintings of the MSS. written at this period ; and
in a work of the thirteenth century, "Le Miracle de Saint
Loys," the whipping top (Sabot) is mentioned. The top was
probably in use as a toy long before. Strutt records the following anecdote of Prince Henry, son of James I., which he met
with in a MS. at the Museum, the author of which speaks
of it as perfectly genuine. His words are—"The first tyme
that he, the prince, went to the towne of Sterling to meete
the king, seeing a little without the gate of the towne a stack
of corne in proportion not unlike to a topp wherewith he used
to play ; he said to some that were with him, 'Loe there is a
goodly topp ;' whereupon one of them saying, 'Why doe you
not play with it, then ?' he answered, 'Set you it up for me,
and I will play with it.'"—*Sports*, p. 385.

Northbroke, in his Treatise against Dicing, 1579, p. 86,
says : "Cato giveth counsell to all youth, saying, ' *Trocho* lude,
aleas fuge, *playe with the toppe*, and flee dice-playing.'"

In the English translation of Levinus Lemnius, 1658,
p. 369 : "Young youth do merrily exercise themselves in

whipping-top, and to make it run swiftly about, that it cannot
be seen, and will deceive the sight."

Cornelius Scriblerus, in his Instructions concerning the
Plays and Playthings to be used by his son Martin, says: "I
would not have Martin as yet to scourge a top, till I am better
informed whether the trochus which was recommended by Cato
be really our present top, or rather the hoop which the boys
drive with a stick."—*Pope's Works*, vi. 115.

Among well-known classical allusions may be noted the
following mention of whipping the top, in Persius's third
Satire:

> "Neu quis callidior buxum torquere flagello."

Thus translated by Dryden:

> "The whirling top they whip,
> And drive her giddy till she fall asleep."

Thus also in Virgil's *Æneid*, vii. 378:

> "Ceu quondam torto volitans sub verbere turbo,
> Quem pueri magno in gyro vacua atria circum
> Intenti ludo exercent.   Ille actus habenâ
> Curvatis fertur spatiis: stupet inscia supra,
> Impubesque manus, mirata volubile buxum:
> Dant animos plagæ."

Thus translated by Dryden:

> "As young striplings whip the top for sport,
> On the smooth pavement of an empty court;
> The wooden engine whirls and flies about,
> Admired with clamours of the beardless rout,
> They lash aloud, each other they provoke,
> And lend their little souls at ev'ry stroke."

And so Ovid, Trist. l. iii. Eleg. 12:

> "Otia nunc istic: junctisque ex ordine ludis
>   Cedunt verbosi garrula bella fori.
> Usus equi nunc est, levibus nunc luditur armis:
> Nunc pila, *nunc celeri volvitur orbe trochus.*"

Passing from these general allusions to the top as a form of amusement, we enter on more significant ground when we take into consideration the various passages in the early dramatists and other writers (collected together in Nares' *Glossary*), which show that tops were at one time owned by the parish or village.

"He's a coward and a coystril that will not drink to my niece, till his brains turn like a parish-top."—Shakespeare, *Twelfth Night*, i. 3.

> "A merry Greek, and cants in Latin comely,
>   Spins like the parish-top."
>   —Ben Jonson, *New Inn*, ii. 5.

>   "I'll hazard
> My life upon it, that a boy of twelve
> Should scourge him hither like a parish-top,
> And make him dance before you."
>   —Beaumont and Fletcher, *Thierry and Theod.*, ii. 1.

"And dances like a town top, and reels and hobbles."
        —Ibid., *Night Walker*, i. 1.

Every night I dream I am a town-top, and that I am whipt up and down with the scourge stick of love.—"Grim, the Collier of Croydon," ap. *Dodsley*, xi. 206.

In the Fifteen Comforts of Marriage, p. 143, we read: "Another tells 'em of a project he has to make town tops spin without an eel-skin, as if he bore malice to the school-boys."

Poor Robin, in his Almanack for 1677, tells us, in the Fanatick's Chronology, it was then "1804 years since the first invention of town-tops."

These passages seem to refer to a custom of keeping tops by a township or parish, and they are confirmed by Evelyn, who, speaking of the uses of willow wood, among other things made of it, mentions great "town-topps" (*Sylva*, xx. 29). The latest writers who give positive information on the subject are Black-stone, who, in his note on Shakespeare, asserts that to "sleep like a town top" was proverbial, and Hazlitt, who, in his col-lection of *English Proverbs*, has "like a parish-top." (See also Brand, ii. 448.)

Steevens, in his notes on Shakespeare, makes the positive assertion that "this is one of the customs now laid aside: a large top was formerly kept in every village, to be whipt in frosty weather, that the peasants might be kept warm by exercise, and out of mischief, while they could not work."

This passage is repeated in Ellis's edition of Brand, so that there is only one authority for the two statements. The question is whether Steevens was stating his own independent knowledge, or whether he based his information upon the passage in Shakespeare which he was illustrating. I think there can be no doubt that the custom existed, in whatever way we accept Steevens' statement, and the question is one of considerable interest.

"Tops" is one of those games which are strictly limited to particular seasons of the year, and any infringement of those seasons is strictly tabooed by the boys. Hone (*Every Day Book*, i. 127), records the following rhyme:—

> Tops are in, spin 'em agin ;
> Tops are out, smuggin' about,

but does not mention the season. It is, however, the early spring. This rhyme is still in use, and may occasionally be heard in the streets of London in the top season. Smugging is legitimate stealing when boys play out of season. "Marbles furst, then comes tops, then comes kites and hoops," said a London boy who had acquired some tops by "smuggin;" but these rules are fast becoming obsolete, as is also the use of a dried eel skin as the favourite whip or thong used.

The keeping of a top by the parish in its corporate capacity is not likely to have arisen for the sake of supplying people with amusement, and we must look to a far more ancient origin for this singular custom. Hone mentions a doubtful story of a top being used in the ritual of one of the churches at Paris. (The burial of Alleluia. The top was whipped by a choir-boy from one end of the choir to the other: *Every Day Book*, i. 100), and if this can be confirmed it would be a link in the chain of evidence. But the whole subject requires much more evidence than it is now possible to go into here, though even, as far as we can now go, I am tempted to suggest that this well-known toy takes us back to the serious rites of ancient religions.

Brady's *Clavis Calendaria*, i. 209, mentions the discontinued custom of whipping tops on Shrove Tuesday as originating in the Popish Carnival as types of the rigour of Church discipline.

It is not improbable that the tee-totum is the earliest form of top, and as its use is for gambling, it is probable that this and the top were formerly used for purposes of divination.

See "Gully," "Hoatie," "Hoges," "Peg Top," "Peg in the Ring," "Scurran-Meggy," "Totum."

The Totum, or Tee-to-tum

The Totum is really only a top to spin by hand. It is made of a square piece of wood or bone, the four sides being each marked with a letter, and the peg is put through a hole in the centre. Sometimes the totum is shaped to a point on the under side, and a pin fixed in the upper part, by which it is twirled round.

The game played is one of chance; it may be played by two or more, either boys or girls, and is played only at Christmas. In Keith the letters are A, N, D, T. In playing the stake is one pin, and each plays in turn. If the side with A on it falls uppermost the player wins the whole stake—"A, tack a'." If N turns up the player gets nothing—"N, nikil (nihil), nothing." If T turns up one pin falls to the player—"T, tack ane." If D comes uppermost the player has to lay down a pin—"D, dossie doon." At times the game was played by paying a stake to all the letters except A, and the words used were—"D, dip it," "T, tip it," and "N, nip it."—Keith (Rev. W. Gregor).

We played the game when children usually at Christmas time. The players sat round a table. A pool was made, each player putting in the same amount of stakes, either pins, counters, nuts, or money. One player collected the pool and then spun the tee-totum by his fingers. Whichever letter was uppermost when it stopped, the player had to obey.

T, was take all (the contents of the pool).

H, half the contents.

N, nothing.

P, to put into the pool the same amount as the stakes were at first.

When this was done the next player spun the totum in his turn. When one player got T a fresh pool had to be collected. —London (A. B. Gomme).

Jamieson's *Dictionary* says children lay up stores of pins to play at this game at Christmas time.

William Dunbar, the Scottish poet (James IV.), seems to refer to this game in the poem, *Schir, ʒit remembir as of befoir*, in the words—

"He playis with *totum*, and I with *nichell*" (l. 74).

Strutt (*Sports and Pastimes*, page 385) says the four sides were marked with letters, and describes the game as we now play it in London.

All tee-totums or whirligigs seem to have some reference to tops, except that the tee-totum is used principally for gambling.

Some have numbers on their sides like dice instead of letters, and some are of octagonal shape.

See "Lang Larence," "Scop-peril," "Tops."

Touch

One player is chosen " he." He then runs amidst the other players and tries to touch one, who then becomes "Tig" or "Touch" in turn.

See "Ticky Touchwood, "Tig."

Tower of London

The Tower is formed by a circle of children, two of whom constitute the gate. These two join hands, and raise or lower their arm to open or shut the gate. The Tower is summoned to open its gates to admit "King George and all his merry men," how represented I can't remember; but I know that at one point there is a chase, and the prisoner is caught and brought before the king, when there ensues a scrap of dialogue in song (Mrs. Harley).

See "How many miles to Babylon," "King of the Barbarie."

Town Lovers

There is a girl of our town,
She often wears a flowered gown;

Tommy loves her night and day,
And Richard when he may,
And Johnny when he can ;
I think Sam will be the man !

Halliwell's *Nursery Rhymes*, pp. 217–218.

A girl is placed in the middle of a ring and says the lines, the names being altered to suit the players. She points to each one named, and at the last line the one selected immediately runs away ; if the girl catches him he pays a forfeit, or the game is commenced again, the boy being placed in the middle.

Trades

Sides are chosen. These stand apart from each other, inside the line of their den. One side chooses amongst themselves a trade, and then walk over to the other side, imitating the actions pertaining to different parts of that trade, and giving the initial letter. If the trade is guessed by the opposite side, that side chooses the next trade, and performs the actions. If the trade is not guessed, the side is at liberty to choose another, and continue until one is guessed.—Forest of Dean, Gloucestershire (Miss Matthews).

The players that are to act the dumb tradesmen agree among themselves what trades are to be imitated. When this point is settled they present themselves before those that are to guess the trade, and proclaim three poor tradesmen wanting a trade —dumb. They then begin the work of imitation. The onlooker that first discovers the trade calls it out, and he becomes the dumb tradesman during the next round.—Fraserburgh (Rev. W. Gregor).

Some of the players form a line, while three others come up and say—

"Here are three men from Botany Bay,
Got any work to give us to-day."

The others ask, "What can you do ? " To which they reply, "Anything." And the others retort, "Set to work, then."

The three then do some imaginary work, while those in the line have to guess what it is.—Ogbourne, Wilts (H. S. May).

"Two broken tradesmen newly come over,
    The one from France and Scotland, the other from Dover."
"What's your trade?"

Two boys privately arrange that the pass-word shall be some implement of a particular trade. The trade is announced after the above dialogue, and carpenters, nailors, sailors, smiths, tinkers, or any other is answered; and on guessing the instrument, "Plane him," "Hammer him," "Rasp him," or "Solder him," is called out; then the fun is that the unfortunate wight who guesses the "tool" is beaten with the caps of his fellows till he reaches a fixed goal, after which he goes out in turn.—Halliwell's *Nursery Rhymes*, cccxvi. In his *Dictionary* it is called "Trades, and Dumb Motions."

Northall (*English Folk Rhymes*) records this game as being played in Warwickshire. The method is practically the same as the Forest of Dean, except that the "tradesmen" are beaten if their trade is easily guessed by the others. They may also be beaten if they show their teeth during the operations.

Trap, Bat, and Ball

A game played with a trap, a ball, and a small bat. The trap is of wood made like a slipper, with a hollow at the heel end for the ball, and a kind of wooden spoon moving on a pivot, in the bowl of which the ball is placed. Two sides play—one side bats, the other fields. One of the batsmen strikes the end or handle of the spoon, the ball then rises into the air, and the art of the game is for the batsman to strike it as far as possible with the bat before it reaches the ground. The other side who are "fielding," try either to catch the ball before it falls to the ground, or to bowl it from where it falls to hit the trap. If they succeed in catching the ball all the "ins" are out, and their side goes in to strike the ball, and the previous batsmen to field; if the trap is hit the batsman is out and another player of his side takes his place. The batsman is also out if he allows the ball to touch the trap when in the act of hitting it.—(A. B. Gomme.)

Halliwell (*Dictionary*) says, "Nurspell" in Lincolnshire is somewhat similar to "Trap Ball." It is played with a kibble, a nur and a spell. By striking the end of the spell with the kibble the nur rises into the air, and the game is to strike it with the kibble before it reaches the ground. He who drives it the greatest distance is the winner. Miss Burne (*Shropshire Folk-lore*, p. 527) says, " Trib and Knurr," otherwise " Dog Stick," are local names for " Knur and Spell," a superior form of " Trap Ball." The " knurr " is a hard wooden ball, the " trib " is the trap or receptacle, the " Dog Stick " the sort of club with which it is struck. The game is played as described by Halliwell. She adds it was formerly the favourite pastime of young men on Shrove Tuesday.

At Bury St. Edmonds, on Shrove Tuesday, Easter Monday, and Whitsuntide festivals, twelve old women side off for a game at " Trap and Ball," which is kept up with the greatest spirit and vigour until sunset.—*Suffolk County Folk-lore*, p. 56. See also Chambers's *Book of Days*, i. p. 428, for a similar custom among women at Chester.

See " Nur and Spel," " Tribet," " Trippit and Coit."

Tray-Trip

Grose says this was an ancient game, like Scotch-hop, played on a pavement marked out with chalk into different compartments. According to Halliwell (*Dictionary*), it was a game at dice.

See " Hop-scotch," " Scotch Hop."

Tres-acre

A game in which generally six are engaged—one taking a station before two about 12 yards behind him, three 12 yards behind these two. One is the catch-pole. Never more than two can remain; the supernumerary one must always shift and seek a new station. If the catch-pole can get in before the person who changes his station, he has the right to take his place, and the other becomes pursuer.—Jamieson.

This is not very descriptive, but the game is evidently the same as " Round Tag " and " Twos and Threes," played with a small number.

Tribet

A common children's game played in Lancashire; which, perhaps, may be the primitive form of " Trap." It is played with a "pum," a piece of wood about a foot long and two inches in diameter, and a "tribet," a small piece of hard wood.—Halliwell's *Dictionary*.

See "Trap, Bat, and Ball."

Trippit and Coit

A game formerly known under the appellation of "Trippets," Newcastle. It is the same as "Trip-cat" in some southern counties. The trippet is a small piece of wood obtusely pointed —something like a shoe—hollow at one end, and having a tail a little elevated at the other, which is struck with a buckstick. It is also called "Buckstick, Spell-and-Ore."—Brockett's *North Country Words*. See also Dickinson's *Cumberland Glossary*. Halliwell's *Dictionary* says—The game is almost peculiar to the North of England. There is a poem called "The Trip Match" in *Mather's Songs*.

See "Nur and Spel," "Trap, Bat, and Ball."

Trip and Go

> Trip and go, heave and hoe,
> Up and down, to and fro ;
> From the town to the grove,
> Two and two let us rove ;
> A-maying, a-playing,
> Love hath no gainsaying ;
> So merrily trip and go,
> So merrily trip and go.
> —Halliwell's *Nursery Rhymes*, cccxlviii.

A game rhyme, but undescribed.

Trip-trout

A game in which a common ball is used instead of the cork and feathers in "Shuttlecock."—(Kinross) Jamieson.

See "Shuttlefeather," "Teesty Tosty."

Troap

A game played by two persons, with bandies or sticks hooked at the end, and a bit of wood called a nacket. At each end of the ground occupied a line is drawn. He who strikes off the nacket from the one line, tries to drive it as near the other as possible. The antagonist who stands between him and the goal tries to throw back with his hand the nacket to the line from which the other has struck it. If he does this he takes the place of the other. If not, the distance is measured between the striking point and the nacket with one of the sticks used in striking, and for every length of the stick one is counted against the caster.—(Angus) Jamieson. The editor of Jamieson adds that the name must have been originally the same as the English Trap, although in this game a ball is used instead of a nacket, and it is struck off as in cricket.

Troco, Trucks

This was an old English game formerly known as "trucks." Strutt, p. 270, 299 (who gives an illustration of it), considers this game to be the original of billiards. Professor Attwell says, *Notes and Queries*, 7th series, xii. 137, "This game was played at Nassau House School, Barnes, for twenty years. It is played on a lawn with balls, cues, and rings."

Troule-in-Madame

In the Benefit of the Auncient Bathes of Buckstones, compiled by John Jones at the King's Mede, nigh Darby, 1572, 4to. p. 12, we read: "The ladyes, gentle woomen, wyves, and maydes, maye in one of the galleries walke; and if the weather bee not aggreeable too theire expectacion, they may haue in the ende of a benche eleuen holes made, intoo the which to trowle pummetes, or bowles of leade, bigge, little, or meane, or also of copper, tynne, woode, eyther vyolent or softe, after their owne discretion; the pastyme *troule-in-madame* is termed." Probably similar to "Nine Holes."

Trounce-Hole

A game at ball resembling trap, but having a hole in the ground for the trap, a flat piece of bone for a trigger, and a cudgel for a bat.—Norfolk, Holloway's *Dictionary of Provincialisms*.

See "Trunket."

Troy Town

A game in which a plan of a labyrinth is drawn on a slate and presented as a puzzle by boys to their schoolfellows for them to find a way into the central citadel. It appears to owe its origin to the mediæval mazes or labyrinths called " Troy Towns," or " Troy Walls," many of which existed in different parts of England and Wales. It appears that games connected with the midsummer festivals were held in these labyrinths. This may, perhaps, account for the origin of this puzzle being considered a game. For accounts of labyrinths or mazes called "Troy Towns," see *Notes and Queries*, 1st series, xi. 132, 193 ; 2nd series, v. 211–213 ; 8th series, iv. 96, 97 ; in which many references are given ; *Tran. Cymmrodorion Soc.*, 1822, i. 67–69 ; Roberts' *Cambrian Antiquities* (in which is a plan), 212, 213 ; and *Folk-lore Journal*, v. 45.

Truncher

A game requiring dexterity. A young man lies flat, resting only on his toes at a certain mark at one extremity and on a trencher in each hand at the other. He then tries to reach out the trenchers as far as possible, and if not held at the right angle and edgewise, down they go and he is defeated.—Dickinson's *Cumberland Glossary*.

Trunket

A game at ball played with short sticks, and having a hole in the ground in lieu of stumps or wickets as in "Cricket"; and with these exceptions, and the ball being " cop'd," instead of bowled or trickled on the ground, it is played in the same way ; the person striking the ball must be caught out, or the ball must be deposited in the hole before the stick or cudgel can be placed there.—Halliwell's *Dictionary*.

See "Cudgel," "Trounce Hole."

Truss

A boy's game like " Leap-Frog."—Halliwell's *Dictionary*.

Tuilyie-wap

A childish amusement in Teviotdale, in which a number of boys take hold of each other's hands and wrap themselves round the one who is at the head; clasping themselves as firmly together as possible, and every one pushing till the mass falls over.—Jamieson.

See "Bulliheisle," "Eller Tree," "Snail-Creep," "Wind the Bush Faggot."

Turn, Cheeses, Turn

> Green cheeses, yellow laces,
> Up and down the market places ;
> First a penny and then a groat,
> Turn, cheeses, turn.   —Leicester (Miss Ellis).

> Green cheeses, yellow laces,
> Up and down the market places,
> Turn, cheeses, turn !
> —Halliwell's *Nursery Rhymes*, cccx.

This is acted by two or more girls who walk or dance up and down, turning, when they say "Turn, cheeses, turn." —Halliwell.

I remember playing this game, but my remembrance is very imperfect. As far as I remember, there were two lines or rows of children. They danced forwards and backwards, crossing to the opposite side, and turning round. At the words, "Turn, cheeses, turn," the cheeses all turned round rapidly and then sank on the ground. The players tried to inflate their dresses as much as possible, and then stooped down to the ground, so that the dress remained inflated; only the head and shoulders surrounded by a ball-like skirt then appeared, intended to represent a cheese. All joined hands and danced round at the end. The lines sang were the same as the Leicester except the third, which was—"Some a penny, some a groat, turn, cheeses, turn." It was necessary for skirts to be very "full" to make good cheeses—as wide at the waist as at the bottom of the skirt.—(A. B. Gomme.)

Holland (*Cheshire Glossary*) says, a frequent amusement of girls is making cheeses. They turn round and round till their dresses fly out at the bottom; then suddenly squatting down, the air confined under the dress causes the skirt to bulge out like a balloon. When skilfully done the appearance is that of a girl's head and shoulders peeping out of an immense cushion. Evans' *Leicestershire Glossary* mentions this game. He says, "The performers sing a song of which the refrain is 'Turn, cheeses, turn,' but I do not remember to have heard the example cited by Mr. Halliwell-Phillips."—*Percy Soc.*, iv. p. 122.

I always understood that the green cheeses were sage cheeses—cheeses containing sage. Halliwell says, "Green cheeses, I am informed, are made with sage and potato tops. Two girls are said to be 'cheese and cheese.'"

Turn Spit Jack

A game at country balls, &c., in which young men compete by singing for their partners in the next dance.—Patterson's *Antrim and Down Glossary*.

Turn the Ship

This is commonly a girls' game. Two join hands and trip along, with hands crossed, turning from one side to the other, and crossing their arms over their heads without letting go their hold of each other, singing at the same time—

> Tip, tip, toe, London, lo!
> Turn, Mary Ann, and away you go.

Or—

> Tip, tip, toe, leerie, lo!
> Turn the ship and away you go;
> A penny to you, and a penny to me,
> And a penny to turn the basket.

> Fochabers (Rev. W. Gregor).

Turn the Trencher, or, My Lady's Toilet

An indoor game played at Christmas time by children and adults. All the players in the room must be seated. They are then asked by the leader of the game to choose some article of a lady's toilet, which article they will personally represent, such as diamond ring, bracelet, comb, brush, jug, basin, powder, hair-dye, dress, mantle, &c.—any article, in fact, belonging to the toilet.

The leader then goes to the centre of the room with a

small trencher, round card tray, plate, or saucer in her hand. She spins this (the trencher) round as quickly as possible, saying, " My lady's going out and needs her ' dress,' " or any other article she chooses to name. The player who has taken the name of " dress " must get up from her seat and catch the trencher before it falls. If successful this player then spins the trencher, calling out the name of another article of the toilet. If the player fails to catch it, a forfeit is demanded by the leader. Occasionally the spinner will say, " My lady's going to a ball (or elsewhere), and needs the whole of her toilet." When this is said, every player has to get up and take another place before the trencher falls; the last one to get a place has to take the trencher, and if it is down, to pay a forfeit. At the end of the game the forfeits are " cried " in the usual way.—(A. B. Gomme.)

This (called " Truckle the Trencher ") used to be a standard game for winter evenings. A circle was formed, and each one was seated on the floor, every player taking the name of a flower. This game was entered into with the greatest vivacity by staid and portly individuals as well as by their juniors.—Dorsetshire (*Folk-lore Journal*, vii. 238).

A trencher, saucer, or plate is used. The players sit in a circle, and one twirls the trencher, at the same time calling out the name of one of the players. He or she jumps up and tries to catch the whirling trencher before it falls. If it fall or is knocked over, a forfeit is lodged, and the player who lodged the forfeit now becomes the twirler. If the trencher is caught, it is handed back and twirled again, and another name called out. The game continues till all or, at least, most of the players have lodged forfeits. It is called " Turn the Plettie.— Macduff (Rev. W. Gregor).

This game is played in the same way in Ireland. It is called " Twirl the Trencher," and the players take names of towns or beasts.—(Miss Keane.)

Brogden (*Provincial Words, Lincolnshire*) and Halliwell (*Dictionary*) mention it as " Turn Trencher," a game played at Christmas time. Moor (*Suffolk Words and Phrases*) calls it " Move all."

Turvey

Turvey, turvey, clothed in black,
With silver buttons upon your back ;
One by one, and two by two,
Turn about, and that will do.

—Haverfordwest (*Notes and Queries,* 3rd series, v. 394).

The children marched two and two, in a measured step to a given distance, then turned and marched back again.

See "Alligoshee."

Tutt-ball

"Tut-ball," * as played at a young ladies' school at Shiffnal fifty years ago. The players stood together in their "den," behind a line marked on the ground, all except one, who was "out," and who stood at a distance and threw the ball to them. One of the players in the den then hit back the ball with the palm of the hand, and immediately ran to one of three brickbats, called "tuts," which were set up at equal distances on the ground, in such positions that a player running past them all would describe a complete circle by the time she returned to the den.' The player who was "out" tried to catch the ball, and to hit the runner with it while passing from one "tut" to another. If she succeeded in doing so, she took her place in the den, and the other went "out" in her stead. This game is very nearly identical with "rounders."—*Shropshire Folklore,* p. 524.

A game at ball, now only played by boys, but half a century ago by adults on Ash Wednesday, believing that unless they did so they would fall sick in harvest time. This is a very ancient game, and was elsewhere called "Stool-ball," indulged in by the clergy as well as laity to avert misfortune.—Ross and Stead's *Holderness Glossary.* The game is not described.

Addy (*Sheffield Glossary*) says this game is the same as "Pize-ball." Halliwell (*Dictionary*) says it is a sort of "Stob-ball Play."

See "Cat and Dog," "Rounders," "Stool Ball."

---

* *Tut,* a prominence, from A. S. *tótian,* whence also E. *tout,* q. v.—W. W. S.

Twelve Days of Christmas

Repeat from *.   —Rimbault's *Nursery Rhymes*.

I. The first day of Christmas, my true love sent to me
A partridge in a pear-tree.

The second day of Xmas, my true love sent to me
Two turtle doves and a partridge in a pear-tree.

The third day of Xmas, my true love sent to me
Three French hens and two turtle doves and
A partridge in a pear-tree.

The fourth day of Xmas, my true love sent to me
Four colly birds, three French hens, two turtle doves, and
A partridge in a pear-tree.

The fifth day of Xmas, my true love sent to me
Five gold rings, four colly birds, three French hens,
Two turtle doves, and a partridge in a pear-tree.

The sixth day of Xmas, my true love sent to me
Six geese a-laying, five gold rings,
Four colly birds, three French hens,
Two turtle doves, and a partridge in a pear-tree.

The seventh day of Xmas, my true love sent to me
Seven swans a-swimming,
Six geese a-laying, five gold rings,
Four colly birds, three French hens,
Two turtle doves, and a partridge in a pear-tree.

The eighth day of Xmas, my true love sent to me
Eight maids a-milking, seven swans a-swimming,
Six geese a-laying, five gold rings,
Four colly birds, three French hens, two turtle doves, and
A partridge in a pear-tree.

The ninth day of Xmas, my true love sent to me
Nine drummers drumming, eight maids a-milking,
Seven swans a-swimming, six geese a-laying,
Five gold rings, four colly birds, three French hens,
Two turtle doves, and
A partridge in a pear-tree.

The tenth day of Xmas, my true love sent to me
Ten pipers piping, nine drummers drumming,
Eight maids a-milking, seven swans a-swimming,
Six geese a-laying, five gold rings,
Four colly birds, three French hens,
Two turtle doves, and
A partridge in a pear-tree.

The eleventh day of Xmas, my true love sent to me
Eleven ladies dancing, ten pipers piping,
Nine drummers drumming, eight maids a-milking,
Seven swans a-swimming, six geese a-laying,
Five gold rings, four colly birds,
Three French hens, two turtle doves, and
A partridge in a pear-tree.

The twelfth day of Xmas, my true love sent to me
Twelve lords a-leaping, eleven ladies dancing,
Ten pipers piping, nine drummers drumming,
Eight maids a-milking, seven swans a-swimming,
Six geese a-laying, five gold rings,
Four colly birds, three French hens,
Two turtle doves, and
A partridge in a pear-tree.

—Halliwell's Nursery Rhymes, cccxlvi.

II. The king sent his lady on the first Yule day,
A papingo-aye [a peacock];
Wha learns my carol and carries it away?

The king sent his lady on the second Yule day,
Three partridges, a papingo-aye ;
Wha learns my carol and carries it away ?

The king sent his lady on the third Yule day,
Three plovers, three partridges, a papingo-aye ;
Wha learns my carol and carries it away ?

The king sent his lady on the fourth Yule day,
A goose that was grey,
Three plovers, three partridges, a papingo-aye ;
Wha learns my carol and carries it away ?

The king sent his lady on the fifth Yule day,
Three starlings, a goose that was grey,
Three plovers, three partridges, and a papingo-aye ;
Wha learns my carol and carries it away ?

The king sent his lady on the sixth Yule day,
Three goldspinks, three starlings, a goose that was grey,
Three plovers, three partridges, and a papingo-aye ;
Wha learns my carol and carries it away ?

The king sent his lady on the seventh Yule day,
A bull that was brown, three goldspinks, three starlings,
A goose that was grey,
Three plovers, three partridges, and a papingo-aye ;
Wha learns my carol and carries it away ?

The king sent his lady on the eighth Yule day,
Three ducks a-merry laying, a bull that was brown—
                              [The rest to follow as before.]

The king sent his lady on the ninth Yule day,
Three swans a-merry swimming—   [As before.]

The king sent his lady on the tenth Yule day,
An Arabian baboon—   [As before.]

The king sent his lady on the eleventh Yule day,
Three hinds a-merry hunting—   [As before.]

The king sent his lady on the twelfth Yule day,
Three maids a-merry dancing—   [As before.]

The king sent.his lady on the thirteenth Yule day,
Three stalks o' merry corn, three maids a-merry dancing,
Three hinds a-merry hunting, an Arabian baboon,
Three swans a-merry swimming,
Three ducks a-merry laying, a bull that was brown,
Three goldspinks, three starlings, a goose that was grey,
Three plovers, three partridges, a papingo-aye ;
Wha learns my carol and carries it away ?
—Chambers's *Pop. Rhymes*, p. 42.

III.   My lady's lap dog,
    Two plump partridges and my lady's lap dog ;
    Three grey elephants, two plump partridges and my
        lady's lap dog ;
    Four Persian cherry trees, three grey elephants, &c. ;
    Five Limerick oysters, four Persian cherry trees, &c. ;
    Six bottles of frontignac, &c. ;
    Seven swans a-swimming, &c.,
    Eight flip flap, floating fly boats, &c. ;
    Nine merchants going to Bagdad, &c. ;
    Ten Italian dancing-masters going to teach ten Arabian
        magpies how to dance, &c. ;
    Eleven guests going to celebrate the marriage of the
        Princess Baldroulbadour with the Prince of Terra-
        del-Fuego, &c. ;
    Twelve triumphant trumpeters triumphantly trumpeting
        the tragical tradition of Telemachus.
—London (A. B. Gomme).

IV.   Twelve huntsmen with horns and hounds,
    Hunting over other men's grounds !
    Eleven ships sailing o'er the main,
    Some bound for France and some for Spain ;
    I wish them all safe home again.
    Ten comets in the sky,
    Some low and some high ;
    Nine peacocks in the air,
    I wonder how they all come there,
    I do not know and I do not care.

Eight joiners in a joiners' hall,
Working with the tools and all;
Seven lobsters in a dish,
As fresh as any heart could wish;
Six beetles against the wall,
Close by an old woman's apple stall;
Five puppies of our dog Ball,
Who daily for their breakfast call;
Four horses stuck in a bog,
Three monkeys tied to a clog;
Two pudding ends would choke a dog,
With a gaping wide-mouthed waddling frog.
                    —Halliwell's *Nursery Rhymes*, cclxxx., cvi.

(*c*) "The Twelve Days" was a Christmas game. It was a customary thing in a friend's house to play "The Twelve Days," or "My Lady's Lap Dog," every Twelfth Day night. The party was usually a mixed gathering of juveniles and adults, mostly relatives, and before supper—that is, before eating mince pies and twelfth cake—this game and the cushion dance were played, and the forfeits consequent upon them always cried. The company were all seated round the room. The leader of the game commenced by saying the first line. Generally the version used was similar to No. I. In later years the shorter version, No. III., was said. The lines for the "first day" of Christmas was said by each of the company in turn; then the first "day" was repeated, with the addition of the "second" by the leader, and then this was said all round the circle in turn. This was continued until the lines for the "twelve days" were said by every player. For every mistake a forfeit—a small article belonging to the person—had to be given up. These forfeits were afterwards "cried" in the usual way, and were not returned to the owner until they had been redeemed by the penalty inflicted being performed.

In version No. IV., the game began by the leader saying to the player sitting next to her, "Take this!" holding the hands as if giving something. The neighbour answered, "What's this?" The leader answered, "A gaping, wide-mouthed, waddling frog." The second player then turned to the third and repeated, " A gaping, wide-mouthed, waddling frog," and so on all round the room. The leader then said, " Two pudding-ends would choke a dog," continuing in the same way until twelve was reached. Chambers does not describe the way the game given by him was played, but it was probably much in the same manner. Rimbault's *Nursery Rhymes* gives the tune to which words of the song were repeated. The words given are almost identical with No. I., but the tune, copied here, is the only recorded one I have found.

(*d*) It seems probable that we have in these rhymes a remnant of a practice of singing or chanting carols or rhymes relating to the custom of sending gifts to friends and relatives during the twelve days of Christmas. The festival of the twelve days was an important one. The great mid-winter feast of Yule consisted of twelve days, and from the events occurring during those days it is probable that events of the future twelve months were foretold.—On the festival of the twelve days consult Keary's *Outlines of Primitive Belief*, p. 381. Miss Burne records that the twelve days rule the year's weather; as the weather is on each day of the twelve, so will it be in the corresponding month, and for every mince-pie eaten in friends' houses during these days a happy month is promised. In the games usually played at this season, viz., those in which forfeits are incurred, and the redemption of these by penances inflicted on the unhappy perpetrators of mistakes, we may perhaps see a relic of the observance of certain customs and ceremonies, and the penalties likely to be incurred by those persons who omitted to religiously carry them out. It is considered unlucky in the North of England and Scotland to enter a neighbour's house empty-handed. Christmas bounties, and the practice of giving presents of food and corn and meal on St. Thomas's Day, 21st December, to the poorer people, when they used to go round to the farmers' houses to collect food to prepare for this festival, may have had its origin in the idea that nothing could be prepared or cooked during the festival of the twelve days. It was a very general practice for work of all kinds to be put entirely aside before Christmas and not resumed until after Twelfth Day. Dr. Gregor records that no bread should be baked nor washing done during this period, nor work left unfinished. Jamieson, in a note on Yule, says that the *gifts* now generally conferred at the New Year seem to have originally belonged to Yule. Among the northern nations it was customary for subjects at this season to present gifts to their sovereign,—these were called Jolagiafir, *i.e.* Yule gifts. The custom in Scotland of presenting what we vulgarly call a sweetie-skon, or a loaf enriched with raisins and currants, has an analogy to this.

It is difficult, with the scanty evidence at command, to do more than make the simple suggestions above. The game is evidently in a process of very rapid decadence, and we have probably only poor specimens of what was originally the form of verses sung in the two versions from Halliwell and Chambers. The London version, No. III., is only recognisable as belonging to this game from the fact that it was known as playing at the "twelve days," was always played on Twelfth Day, and it was not considered proper nor polite for the guests to depart until this had been played. This fact has induced me to add the fourth version from Halliwell, because it appears to me that it may belong to the final form which this game is taking, or has taken, namely, a mere collection of alliterative nursery words, or rhymes, to puzzle the speaker under a rapid repetition, and to exact forfeits for the mistakes made.

See "Forfeits."

Twelve Holes

A game similar to "Nine Holes," mentioned in Florio ed., 1611, p. 20.—Halliwell's *Dictionary*.

Uncle John is Ill in Bed

Uncle John is ill in bed,
    What shall I send him?
Three good wishes, and three good kisses,
    And a race of ginger.
Who shall I send it by?
    By the carrier's daughter;

Catch her by the lily-white hand
 And carry her over the water.
Sally goes a-courting night and day,
Histal, whistal, by her side,
Johnny Everall by her side.
   —Shrewsbury, Chirbury (Burne's *Shropshire
     Folk-lore*, p. 511).

Uncle Tom is very sick,
What shall we send him?
A piece of cake, a piece of bread,
A piece of apple dumpling.
Who shall we send it with?
Mrs. So and So's daughter.
She is neither without,
She is neither within,
She is up in the parlour romping about.
She came downstairs dressed in silk,
A rose in her breast as white as milk.
She pulled off her glove,
She showed me her ring,
To-morrow, to-morrow the wedding shall begin.
   —Nairn (Rev. W. Gregor).

(*b*) The Shropshire version is played by the children forming a ring by joining hands. After the eighth line is sung all
the children stoop down—the last to do so has to tell her
sweetheart's name. In the Scotch version the players stand
in a row. They sing the first five lines, then one player is
chosen (who chooses another); the other lines are sung, and the
two shake hands. Another version from Scotland (Laurieston
School, Kirkcudbright, Mr. J. Lawson), is very similar to the
one from Nairn.

Mr. Newell (p. 72) gives versions of this game which are
fuller and more complete than those given here. He thinks
it bears traces of ancient origin, and may be the last echo
of a mediæval song, in which an imprisoned knight is saved
from approaching death by the daughter of the king, or soldan,
who keeps him in confinement.

Up the Streets

—Liverpool (C. C. Bell).

I. Up the streets and down the streets,
    The windows made of glass;
    Is not [naming one of the children] a nice
            young lass?
    She can dance, she can sing,
    She can show her wedding-ring.
    Fie, for shame! fie, for shame!
    Turn your back behind you.
                        —Liverpool (C. C. Bell).

II. Up streets, down streets,
    Windows made of glass;
    Isn't "Jenny Jenkins" a handsome young lass?
    Isn't "Johnny Johnson" as handsome as she?
    They shall be married,
    When they can agree.
            —Monton, Lancashire, Collyhurst, Manchester
                    (Miss Dendy).

III. Up street and down street,
     Each window's made of glass;
     If you go to Tommy Tickler's house
     You'll find a pretty lass.
                —Halliwell's *Nursery Rhymes*, cccclxxx.

(*b*) In the Liverpool version the children stand in a ring and
sing the words. At "Fie, for shame," the child named ceases
to sing, and the others address her particularly. When the

verse is ended she turns her back to the inside of the ring.   All
do this in turn.   The Monton game is played the same as
"kiss-in-the-ring" games.

(*c*) Northall (*English Popular Rhymes*, p. 549), gives a version almost the same as the Monton version.   He also quotes
some verses from a paper by Miss Tennant in the *English
Illustrated Magazine*, June 1885, which she gives as a song of
the slums of London.   In *Gammer Gurton's Garland* (1783,
reprint 1810, p. 34), is a verse which is the same as Halliwell's,
with two additional lines—

> Hug her, and kiss her, and take her on your knee,
> And whisper very close, Darling girl, do you love me?

Wadds and the Wears (1)

Mactaggart, in describing this, says it is one of the most
celebrated amusements of the Ingle ring.   To begin it, one
in the ring speaks as follows:—

> I hae been awa at the wadds and the wears
> These seven lang years;
> And come hame a puir broken ploughman,
> What will ye gie me to help me to my trade?

He may either say he's a "puir broken ploughman" or any
other trade, but since he has chosen that trade some of the
articles belonging to it must always be given or offered to recruit
it.   But the article he most wants he privately tells one of the
party, who is not allowed to offer him anything, as he knows
the thing, which will throw the offerer in a wadd, and must be
avoided as much as possible, for to be in a wadd is a very
serious matter.   Now, the one on the left hand of the "poor
ploughman" makes the first offer by way of answer to what
above was said—"Ill gie ye the coulter to help ye to your trade."
The ploughman answers, "I don't thank ye for the coulter; I
hae ane already."   Then another offers him another article
belonging to the ploughman's business, such as the moolbred,
but this also is refused: another gives the sock, another the
stilts, another the spattle, another the naigs, and so on until
one gives the soam, which was the article he most wanted, and
was the thing secretly told to the one player.   This throws the

giver into a wadd, out of which he is relieved in the following manner :—

The ploughman says to the one in the wadd, "Whether will ye hae three questions and two commands, or three commands and two questions to answer, or gang on wi', sae that ye may win out o' the wadd ?" For the one so fixed has always the choice which of these to take. Suppose he takes the first, two commands and three questions, then a specimen of these may be—" I command ye to kiss the crook," says the ploughman, which must be completely obeyed by the one in the wadd; his naked lips must kiss the sooty implement. Secondly, says the ploughman, I command ye to stand up in that neuk and say—

> " Here stan' I, as stiff 's a stake,
> Wha 'ill kiss me for pity's sake ? "

which must also be done; in a corner of the house must he stand and repeat this couplet, until some tender-hearted lass relieves him. Then the questions are asked, such as—"Suppose you were in a bed with Maggie Lowden and Jennie Logan, your twa great sweethearts, what ane o'm wad ye ding owre the bedside, and what ane wad ye turn to and clap and cuddle ?" He has to choose one, perhaps to the great mirth of the company. Secondly, "Suppose ye were stannin' stark naked on the tap o' Cairnhattie, whether wad ye cry on Peggie Kirtle or Nell o' Killimingie to come wi' your claise ?" He has again to choose. Lastly, "Suppose ye were in a boat wi' Tibbie Tait, Mary Kairnie, Sally Snadrap, and Kate o' Minnieive, and it was to coup wi' ye, what ane o' 'em wad ye sink ? what ane wad ye soom ? wha wad ye bring to lan' ? and wha wad ye marry ?" Then he has again to choose between the girls named.

Chambers gives the following versions of the " Wadds " :—

The wadds was played by a group seated round the hearth fire, the lasses being on one side and the lads on the other. The questions are asked and answers given alternately. A lad first chants—

> O it's hame, and it's hame, and it's hame, hame, hame,
> I think this night I maun gae hame.

One of the opposite party then says—

Ye had better light, and bide a' night,
And I'll choose you a bonny ane.

O wha will ye choose, an' I wi' you abide?
The fairest and rarest in a' the country side.

At the same time presenting an unmarried female by name.
If the choice give satisfaction—

I'll set her up on the bonny pear-tree;
It's straught and tall, and sae is she;
I wad wake a' night her love to be.

If the choice do not give satisfaction, from the age of the party—

I'll set her up i' the bank dike;
She'll be rotten ere I be ripe;
The corbies her auld banes wadna pike.

If from supposed want of temper—

I'll set her up on the high crab-tree;
It's sour and dour, and sae is she;
She may gang to the mools unkissed by me.

A civil mode of declining is to say—

She's for another, and no for me;
I thank you for your courtesie.

The same ritual is gone through with respect to one of the other sex; in which case such rhymes as the following are used :—

I'll put him on a riddle, and blaw him owre the sea,
Wha'll buy [Johnie Paterson] for me?
I'll put him on my big lum head,
And blaw him up wi' pouther and lead.

Or, when the proposed party is agreeable—

I'll set him on my table head,
And feed him up wi' milk and bread.

A refusal must be atoned for by a wadd or forfeit. A piece of money, a knife, or any little thing which the owner prizes, will serve. When a sufficient number of persons have made forfeits, the business of redeeming them is commenced, and generally it is then that the amusement is greatest. The duty of kissing some person, or some part of the room, is usually

assigned as a means of redeeming one's wadds.   Often for this
purpose a lad has to kiss the very lips he formerly rejected ;
or, it may be, he has to kneel to the prettiest, bow to the
wittiest, and kiss the one he loves best before the forfeit is
redeemed.—The substance of the above is from a note in
Cromek's *Remains of Nithsdale and Galloway Song*, p. 114,
who says—In this game formerly young men and women
arranged themselves on each side of the fire, and alternately
bestowed husbands and wives on each other.   Carleton's
Traits and Stories of the Irish Peasantry, p. 106, also describes the game without any material difference.

Another form of this game, practised in Dumfriesshire in
the last century, and perhaps still, was more common.   The
party are first fitted each with some ridiculous name, not very
easy to be remembered, such as *Swatter-in-the-Sweet-Milk*,
Butter-Milk-and-Brose, the Gray Gled o' Glenwhargan Craig,
&c.   Then all being seated, one comes up, repeating the
following rhymes—

I never stealt Rob's dog, nor never intend to do,
But weel I ken wha stealt him, and dern'd him in a cleugh,
And pykit his banes bare, bare, bare eneugh !
    Wha but——wha but——

The object is to burst out suddenly with one of the fictitious
names, and thus take the party bearing it by surprise.   If the
individual mentioned, not immediately recollecting the name
he bore, failed, on the instant, to say "No me," by way of
denying the accusation respecting the dog, he was ·subjected
to a forfeit; and this equally happened if he cried "No me."
when it was the name of another person which was mentioned.
The forfeits were disposed of as in the former case.—*Popular
Rhymes*, pp. 125–126.

It will be seen that the first version of Chambers more
nearly resembles "Hey Wullie Wine" (vol. i. p. 207), and that
the latter part of the version given by Mactaggart is similar to
"Three Flowers" (ante, p. 255, and the first part to "Trades,"
p. 305).   Mr. W. Ballantyne sent me a version from Biggar as
played when he was a boy.   It is similar to Mactaggart's.

This game may indicate an earlier form of playing at forfeits

than the "Old Soldier," "Turn the Trencher," and kindred
English games. Mactaggart does not state that any article
belonging to the person who perpetrates the offence was
given up and afterwards redeemed by the owner performing
a penalty. In Chambers' versions this is done. It may be
that, in Mactaggart's case, each offending person paid his or
her penalty immediately after committing the blunder or
offence instead of a leader collecting the forfeits from all
offenders first, and then "crying" all together afterwards.
Whether the game originated in the practice of "tabu," or
was an outcome of the custom of restitution, or ransom, legally
made for the commission of crimes, such as that called wergeld,
the penalty or price to be paid to the relatives of a slain man,
or of punishment for certain offences then being in the hands
of a certain class of people, we cannot now decide; but it
was customary for penalties to be attached to the commission
of minor offences, and the punishment enforced without appeal
to any legally constituted authority. The object of most of the
present forfeit games seems to have been to make the offenders
ridiculous, or, in the case of the above form of games, to
find out the person loved or hated. In Shropshire "Crying
the Weds" is the name given to the game of playing at
forfeits. Wadd means a pledge. Jamieson says "Wears"
signifies the "Wars." "At the wars" is a common mode
still retained of describing the life of a soldier. Ihre supposes that the early term wadd or wed is derived from wadd-
cloth, from this kind of merchandise being anciently given and
received instead of money; when at any time a pledge was
left, a piece of cloth was used for this purpose, and hence a
pledge in general would be called wadd.

In Waldron's description of the Isle of Man (ante, vol. i.
p. 139) is an account of a Twelfth Day custom which throws
light on the game as described by Chambers.

See "Forfeits," "Hey Wullie Wine," "Three Flowers,"
"Trades."

Wadds and the Wears (2)

Jamieson describes the game differently. He says—The

players being equally divided, and a certain space being marked out between them, each lays down one or more wadds, or pledges, at that extremity where the party to which he belongs choose their station. A boundary being fixed, the object is to carry off the wadds from the one of these to the other. The two parties advancing to the boundary seize the first opportunity of crossing it, by making inroads on the territories of the other. If one who crosses the line is seized by the opposite party before he has touched any of their wadds, he is set down beside them as a prisoner, and receives the name of a "stinker"; nor can he be released until one of his own party can touch him without being intercepted by any of the others, in which case he is free. If any one is caught in the act of carrying off a wadd, it is taken from him; but he cannot be detained as a prisoner, in consequence of his having touched it. If he can cross the intermediate line with it, the pursuit is at an end. When one party has carried off to their ground all the wadds of the other the game is finished.

Waggles

A game of tip-cat. Four boys stand at the corners of a large paving-stone; two have sticks, the other two are feeders, and throw the piece of wood called a "cat." The batters act much in the same way as in cricket, except that the cat must be hit whilst in the air. The batter hits it as far away as possible, and whilst the feeder is fetching it, gets, if possible, a run, which counts to his side. If either of the cats fall to the ground both batters go out, and the feeders take their place. A game called "Whacks" is played in a similar way.—London Streets (F. H. Low, *Strand Magazine*, Nov. 1891).

See "Tip-cat."

Wallflowers

—Nottingham (Miss Youngman).

—Connell Ferry, near Oban (Miss Harrison).

—Beddgelert (Mrs. Williams).

—Ogbourne, Wilts. (H. S. May).

Longcot choir girls, Berks. (Miss I. Barclay).

I. Wallflowers, wallflowers, growing up so high,
All of you young ladies are sure to die.
Excepting ——, she's the best of all.
She can hop, and she can skip,
And she can turn a candlestick.
Oh my, fie for shame, turn your face to the wall again.
—Fernham and Longcot (Miss I. Barclay).

II. Wallflowers, wallflowers,
    Growing up so high,
    All you young ladies
    Are meant to die.
    Excepting little ——,
    She is the best of all.
    She can skip, and she can dance,
    She can turn the candlestick.
    O my, fie for shame,
    Turn your back to the wall again.
            —From London maidservant (Miss E. Chase).

III. Willy, willy wallflower,
     Growin' up so high,
     We are all maidens,

We shall all die.
Excepting ——,
She's the youngest daughter,
    She can hop,
    She can skip,
She can turn the candlestick.
    Fee, fie, shame, shame,
Turn your backs together again :—
——, your sweetheart is dead,
He's sent you a letter to turn back your head.
            —Wakefield, Yorks (Miss Fowler).

IV. Wallflowers, wallflowers,
    Growing up so high,
    We young ladies, we shall die.
    Except 'tis ——,
    She's the youngest daughter.
    She can hop, and she can skip,
    She can play the wire,
    Oh for shame, fie for shame,
    Turn your back and have a game.
          —Hampshire (Miss E. Mendham).

V. Wally, wally wallflower,
    Growing up so high—
    All ye young ladies
    You must all die.
    Excepting ——,
    She's the best of all—
    She can hop, and she can skip,
    She can turn the mangle,
    Oh my, fie for shame,
    Turn your back to the wall again.
          —Barnes, Surrey (A. B. Gomme).

VI. Wall flowers, wall flowers, growing up so high,
We are all children, and we shall all die.
Excepting ——, she's the youngest child,
She can hop, she can skip,
She can turn the wedding ring,
Fie, fie, fie for shame,
Turn your face to the wall again.
          —Nottingham (Miss Youngman).

VII. Wally, wally wall-flower,
    A-growen up so high,
    All we children be sure to die.
    Excepting [naming the youngest]
    'Cause she's the youngest,
    Oh! fie! for shame! fie! for shame!
    Turn your back to the wall again.
    —Symondsbury, Dorset (*Folk-lore Journal*, vii. 215).

VIII.   Wall-flowers, wall-flowers, growing up so high,
        We are all living, and we shall all die.
        Except the youngest here [naming her].
        Turn your back to overshed. (?)
(This last line is repeated three times.)
                        —Symondsbury, Dorset (*Folk-lore Journal*, vii. 215).

IX.   Wall-flowers, wall-flowers, growing up so high!
        We shall all be maidens, [and so] we shall all die! *
        Excepting *Alice Gittins*, she is the youngest flower,
        She can hop, and she can skip, and she can play the
            hour!
        Three and four, and four and five,
        Turn your back to the wall-side!
Or,
        She can dance and she can sing,
        She can play on the tambourine!
        Fie, fie! fie, for shame!
        Turn your back upon the game!
                        —Ellesmere, Berrington, Wenlock (*Shropshire
                            Folk-lore*, p. 513).

X.   Willie, willie wall-flowers, growing up so high!
        We are all fair maids, we shall all die!
        Excepting little ——, and she's the youngest here,
        Turn your head towards the south, and she's the one
            to bear,
        The willie, willie wallflowers.
Or,
        Oh! for shame, fie, for shame, turn yourself to the wall
            again—   —Sprole, Norfolk (Miss Matthews).

XI.   Wall-flowers, wall-flowers, growing up so high!
        We are all ladies, we must all die!
        Excepting ——, who is the prettiest child.
        Fie, for shame, fie, for shame, turn your back to the
            wall again.
                        —Nottinghamshire and Lincolnshire (Miss Winfield)

* At Wenlock they add to the chorus :
    O *Alice!* your true love will send you a letter to turn round your head !
    And she can turn the handlestick.

XII.   Wall-flowers, wall-flowers, growing up so high!
       We're all ladies, and we shall all die!
       Excepting [naming smallest child in ring],
       She can hop, and she can skip, and she can play the
           organ!
       Oh! for shame, fie, for shame,
       Turn your back upon our game.
                           —Enbourne School, Berks. (Miss M. Kimber).

XIII. Wall-flowers, wall-flowers, growing up so high!
       We are all pretty maidens, we all have to die!
       Except ——, she's the youngest girl,
       Ah! for shame, ah! for shame,
       Turn your back to us again.
       I'll wash you in milk,
       I'll dress you in silk,
       I'll write down your name,
       With a gold pen and ink.
                           —Earls Heaton (Herbert Hardy).

XIV.   Oh flower, oh flower, growing up so high!
       We are all children, we have all to die!
       Except ——, she the youngest gay,
       Oh! for shame, fie, for shame,
       Turn your back against the wall.
                           —Beddgelert (Mrs. Williams).

XV.   Wall-flowers, wall-flowers, growing up so high!
       We are all little, and we've got to die!
       Excepting ——, and she's the only one,
       Oh! for shame, fie, for shame,
       Turn your back to the wall again.
                           —Cowes, Isle of Wight (Miss E. Smith).

XVI.   Little Molly white-flower, we are all maidens,
       And we shall all die, except Polly Pegg,
       She's the best of all,
       She can hop, and she can skip, and she can turn the
           candlestick!
       Oh! fie, for shame,
       Turn your back to the wall.
                           —Hanbury, Staffordshire (Miss Edith Hollis).

XVII.   Wall-flowers, wall-flowers, growing up so high!
We are all playmates, we shall all die!
Excepting ——, for she's the youngest flower,
Cry shame, cry shame,
And turn your face to the wall again.
—Sheffield (S. O. Addy).

XVIII.   Wall-flower, wall-flower, growing up so high!
All the pretty maidens shall not die!
Excepting ——, she is the youngest child,
Oh! for shame, fie, for shame!
Turn your back to the wall again.
—Dean, near Salisbury (Mrs. C. Brough).

XIX.   Water, water wall-flower, growing up so high,
We are all maidens, we must all die,
Except ——, the youngest of us all.
She can laugh, and she can dance, and she can play
at ball;
Fie! fie! fie for shame! turn your face to the wall
again.   —Connell Ferry, near Oban (Miss Harrison).

XX.   Water, water wall-flower, growing up so high,
We are all maidens, we must all die.
Except ——, she's the youngest of them all;
She can dance, she can sing,
And she can dance the wedding ring (or "Hieland fling")
Fie! fie! fie for shame!
Turn your back to the wall again.
—Galloway (J. G. Carter).

XXI.   Wall-flowers, wall-flowers,
Growing up so high;
All ye young maidens
Are all fit to die.
Excepting ——, and she's the worst of all,
She can hop, and she can skip,
And she can turn the candlestick.
Fye! fie! for shame,
Turn your face to the wall again.
—(*Suffolk County Folk-lore*, p. 67.)

XXII.　Wall-flowers, wall-flowers, growing up so high,
All you young ladies will soon have to die ;
Excepting ——, and she's the best of all.
She can dance, she can skip, she can turn the
mangle quick ;
Hi, ho ! fie for shame ! turn your back to the wall
again.　　　　　　　—Cambridge (Mrs. Haddon).

XXIII.　Wally, wally wall-flower, growing up so high,
We are all maidens, and we shall die ;
All except the youngest one, and that is [child's
name].
Choose for the best, choose for the worst,
Choose the one that you love best.

Now you're married, I wish you joy,
First a girl and then a boy,
Seven years after son and daughter,
Now, young couple, kiss together.
　　　　　—Hersham, Surrey (*Folk-lore Record*, v. 84).

XXIV.　Wally, wally wall-flowers,
Growing up so high ;
We're all ladies,
We shall all die.
Excepting little ——,
She's the only one ;
She can hop, she can skip,
She can play the herald,
Fie ! fie ! fie for shame !
Turn your back to the wall again.
　　　　　　　—Deptford, Kent (Miss Chase).

XXV.　Water, water wall-flower,
Growing up so high ;
We are all maidens,
And we must all die.
—— is the youngest,
She must kick,
And she must fling,

And she must turn the sofa;
Fie! fie! fie, for shame!
Turn your back to the wall again.

XXVI.   Except ——, and she's the youngest one,
        She can hop, and she can skip,
        She can turn the sofa;
        Oh fie! fie! fie, for shame!
        Turn your back to the wall again.
                        —Cullen and Nairn (Rev. W. Gregor).

XXVII. She can skip, she can dance,
        She can ding us all o'er.
                        —Aberdeen (Rev. W. Gregor).

XXVIII. Green, green grovers, growing up so high,
        We are all maidens,
        And we must all die;
        Except ——, the youngest of us all,
        She can dance, and she can sing,
        She can dance the Hieland fling;
        Fie! fie! fie, for shame!
        Turn your back to us again.
                        —Nairn (Rev. W. Gregor).

XXIX.   Water, water, well stones,
        Growing up so high,
        We are all maidens,
        And we must all die.
        Except ——,
        She's the youngest of us all,
        She can dance, she can sing,
        She can dance the " Hielan' Fling," *
        Oh fie, fie, for shame,
        Turn your back to us again.
                        —Dyke (Rev. W. Gregor).

* Another version from Forfarshire gives " Green, green, grivers," and " Pull
the cradle string" for " Dance the Hielan' Fling," and one from Nairn is " Turn
your back to the wall again."

XXX.   Here's a pot of wall-flowers,
Growing up so high ;
We're all maidens, and we shall die.
Excepting [girl's name],
She can hop, and she can skip,
And she can play the organ.
Turn your back, you saucy Jack,
You tore your mother's gown.
—Northants (Rev. W. Sweeting).

XXXI.   Wall-flowers, wall-flowers, growin' up so high,
Neither me nor my baby shall ever wish to die,
Especially [girl's name], she's the prettiest flower.
She can dance, and she can sing, and she can tell the
hour,
With her wee-waw, wy-waw, turn her face to the wall.
—Howth, Dublin (Miss H. E. Harvey).

Or,   Turn your back to all the game.
—Bonmahon, Waterford (Miss H. E. Harvey).

XXXII.   Sally, Sally, wall-flower [or Waters],
Springing up so high,
We're all fair maids,
And we shall all die.
Excepting [girl's name],
She's the fairest daughter,
She can hop, and she can skip,
She can turn the organ.
Turn your face toward the wall,
And tell me who your sweetheart's called.

Mr Moffit is a very good man,
He came to the door with his hat in his hand,
He pulled up his cloak, and showed me the ring ;
To-morrow, to-morrow, the wedding begins.
First he bought the frying-pan,
Then he bought the cradle,
And then one day the baby was born,
Rock, rock the cradle.
—Hurstmonceux, Sussex (Miss Chase).

XXXIII.   Water, water, wild flowers,
      Growing up so high,
      We are all maidens,
      And we shall all die,
      Excepting [Eva Irving],
      And she's the youngest of us all,
      And she can hop, and she can skip,
      And she can turn the candlestick,
      [Or " She can play the organ."]
      Piper shame ! piper shame !
      Turn your back to the wall again.
      I pick up a pin,
      I knock at the door,
      I ask for ——,
      She's neither in,
      She's neither out,
      She's up the garden skipping about.
      Down come ——, as white as snow,
      Soft in her bosom as soft as glow.
      She pulled off her glove,
      And showed us her ring,
      To-morrow, to-morrow,
      The bells shall ring.
                  —Ogbourne, Wilts. (H. S. May).

XXXIV.   Water, water, wall-flowers, growing up so high,
      We are all maidens, and we must all die,
      Except ——, she's the only one,
      She can dance, she can sing, she can play the organ,
      Fie, fie, fie for shame, turn your face to the wall
        again.
      Green grevel, green grevel, the grass is so green,
      The fairest young lady that ever was seen.
      O ——, O ——, your true love is dead,
      He'll send you a letter to turn back your head.
        — Laurieston School, Kirkcudbright (J. Lawson).

XXXV. [Mary Kelly's] stole away, stole away, stole away,
      [Mary Kelly's] stole away,
      And lost her lily-white flowers.

It's well seen by her pale face, her pale face, her pale face,
It's well seen by her pale face,
She may turn her face to the wall.

—Belfast (W. H. Patterson).

(c) The children form a ring by joining hands. They all dance slowly round, singing the words. When the one child is named by the ring she turns round, so that her face is turned to the outside of the ring and her back inside. She still clasps hands with those on either side of her, and dances or walks round with them. This is continued until all the players have turned and are facing outwards.

This concludes the game in many places, but in others the game is continued by altering the last line of the verses, and the children alternately turning round when named until they all face inside again. In some of the versions the first child to turn her face to the wall is the youngest, and it is then continued by the next youngest, until the eldest is named. This obtains in Hampshire (Miss Mendham), Nottingham, Symondsbury, Shropshire, Beddgelert, Sheffield, Connell Ferry, Oban, Hersham, Surrey, Dyke. In the London (Miss Chase) and Sheffield versions the child named leaves the ring and turns with her face to a wall. In the Wakefield version Miss Fowler says a child stands in the middle, and at the fifth line all the children say their own name. At the end of the verse they all unclasp hands, and turn with their faces outside the circle; the verse is repeated, when they all turn again facing inwards, and so on over again. In the Nairn version, after all the players have turned their faces outside the ring, they all throw their arms over their heads, and turn so as to face inwards if possible without disjoining hands. The children at Ogbourne, Wilts, clap hands when singing the last two lines of the verses. At Enbourne School it is the tallest child who is first named, and who turns her back; presumably the next tallest is then chosen. In the Suffolk game one child stands outside the ring; the ring sings the first four lines, and the child outside sings the rest. At Wenlock Miss Burne says each child is summoned in turn by name to turn their heads when the last line is said. At Hurstmonceux a girl chooses a boy after her face is turned to the wall.

(*d*) The most interesting point about this game is that it appears to refer to a custom or observance which particularly concerns young girls. We cannot say what the custom or observance was originally, but the words point to something in which a young maiden played the principal part. "We are all maidens" and "she's the youngest here" runs through most of the versions. A death seems to be indicated, and it may be that this game was originally one where the death of the betrothed of the youngest maiden was announced. This would account for the "turning the face to the wall," which is indicative of mourning and great sorrow and loss. The mention of the girl's accomplishments may mean that being so young and accomplished she would quickly get another suitor, and this might also account for the "fie for shame!"—shame to be thinking of another lover so soon; or, on the other hand, the other maidens may regret that by the loss of her lover and betrothed this young maiden's talents will be lost in "old maidenhood," as she will not now be married, and this will be "a shame." She will be, in fact, "on the shelf" or "out of sight" for the rest of her life, and through no fault of her own. The "we are all maidens" might refer to the old custom of maidens carrying the corpse of one of their number to the grave, and the words may have originally been the lament over her death.

With reference to the words "turn the candlestick," which occurs in six versions, "M. H. P.," in *Notes and Queries* (7th ser., xi. 256), says: "*Turning the Candlestick.*—A candlestick in the game of 'See-saw' is the Yorkshire name for the child who stands in the centre of the plank, and assists the motion by swaying from side to side." Toone (*Etymological Dictionary*) says—Before the introduction of the modern candlestick, the custom was to have the candle held by a person appointed for that purpose, called a candle-holder, and hence the term became proverbial to signify an idle spectator.

"I'll be a candle-holder and look on."—*Romeo and Juliet.*

"A candle-holder sees most of the game."—Ray's *Proverbs.*

If this should be the meaning of the phrase in these rhymes, "she can turn the candlestick" may have originally meant that now this maiden can be nothing but a "looker on" or "candle-holder" in the world. The meaning has evidently been forgotten for a long time, as other expressions, such as "she can turn the organ," have had to be adopted to "make sense" of the words.

Aubrey (*Remaines of Judaisme*, p. 45) mentions the sport called "Dancing the Candlerush," played by young girls; in Oxford called "Leap Candle," which consisted of placing a candle in the middle of the room and "dancing over the candle back and forth" saying a rhyme. This may be the "dance" referred to in the rhymes.

The tune of most versions is the same. It is pretty and plaintive, and accords with the idea of mourning and grief. The Rev. W. D. Sweeting says the tune in Northants seems to be lost. The game is sung to a sort of monotone.

Northall gives a version from Warwickshire similar to several given here, and Mr. Newell (*Games and Songs of American Children*) gives a version and tune which is similar to that of Hurstmonceux, Surrey.

See "Green Grass."

Warney

I'm the wee mouse in the hole in the wa',
I'm come out to catch you a'.

One of the players starts with clasped hands to catch another. When this is done they join hands—each one, on being caught, going into the number to form a chain. If the chain breaks no one can be caught.—Laurieston School, Kirkcudbright (J. Lawson).

See "Stag," "Whiddy."

Way-Zaltin

A sort of horse-game, in which two boys stand back to back with their arms interlaced; each then alternately bends forward, and so raises the other on his back with his legs in the air. This term, too, is sometimes used for see-sawing.—Elworthy's *West Somerset Words*. Barnes (*Dorset Glossary*) calls this game "Wayzalt." Holloway (*Dict. Prov.*) says, in Hants the game is called "Weighing."

See "Weigh the Butter."

We are the Rovers

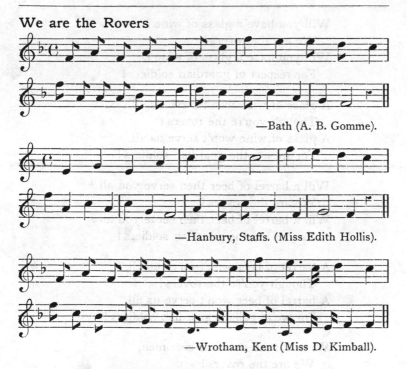

—Bath (A. B. Gomme).

—Hanbury, Staffs. (Miss Edith Hollis).

—Wrotham, Kent (Miss D. Kimball).

I. We are coming to take your land,
   We are the rovers!
   We are coming to take your land,
   [Though you] are the guardian soldiers!

   We don't care for your men nor you,
   [Though you] are the rovers!
   We don't care for your men nor you,
   For we are the guardian soldiers!

   We will send our dogs to bite,
   We are the rovers!
   We will send our dogs to bite,
   Though you are the guardian soldiers!

   We don't care for your dogs nor you,
   Though you're the rovers!
   We don't care for your dogs nor you,
   For we are the guardian soldiers!

Will you have a glass of wine ?
  We are the rovers !
Will you have a glass of wine ?
  For respect of guardian soldiers !

A glass of wine won't serve us all,
  Though you're the rovers !
A glass of wine won't serve us all,
  For we are the guardian soldiers !

Will a barrel of beer then serve you all ?
  We are the rovers !
Will a barrel of beer then serve you all ?
  As you are the guardian soldiers !

A barrel of beer won't serve us all,
  Though you're the rovers !
A barrel of beer won't serve us all,
  For we're gallant guardian soldiers !

We will send our blue-coat men,
  We are the rovers !
We will send our blue-coat men,
  Though you are the guardian soldiers !

We don't fear your blue-coat men,
  Though you're the rovers !
We don't fear your blue-coat men,
  For we are the guardian soldiers !

We will send our red-coat men,
  We are the rovers !
We will send our red-coat men,
  Though you are the guardian soldiers !

We don't mind your red-coat men,
  Though you're the rovers !
We don't mind your red-coat men,
  For we are the guardian soldiers !

Are you ready for a fight ?
  We are the rovers !
Are you ready for a fight ?
  Though you are the guardian soldiers !

Yes, we are ready for a fight,
  Though you're the rovers !
Yes, we are ready for a fight,
  For we are the guardian soldiers !
          —Ellesmere (*Shropshire Folk-lore*, p. 518),

II. We have come for a glass of wine,
    We are the Romans !
We have come for a glass of wine,
    We are King William's soldiers !

We won't serve you with the wine,
    We are the Romans !
We won't serve you with the wine,
    We are King William's soldiers !

We will set our dogs to watch,
    We are the Romans !
We will set our dogs to watch,
    We are King William's soldiers !

We don't care for you and your dogs,
    We are the Romans !
We don't care for you and your dogs,
    We are King William's soldiers !

We will set our police to watch,
    We are the Romans !
We will set our police to watch,
    We are King William's soldiers !

We don't care for you and your police,
    We are the Romans !
We don't care for you and your police,
    We are King William's soldiers !

Are you ready for a fight?
We are the Romans!
Are you ready for a fight?
We are King William's soldiers!

We are ready for a fight,
We are the Romans!
We are ready for a fight,
We are King William's soldiers!
—Wrotham, Kent (Miss D. Kimball).

III. Will you have a gill of ale?
We are the Romans!
Will you have a gill of ale?
For we are the Roman soldiers!

A gill of ale won't serve us all,
We are the English!
A gill of ale won't, &c.,
For we are the English soldiers!

Take a pint and go your way,
We are, &c.   [As above.]

A pint of ale won't serve us all,
We are, &c.

Take a quart and go your way,
We are, &c.

A quart of ale won't serve us all,
We are, &c.

Take a gallon and go your way,
We are, &c.

A gallon of ale won't serve us all,
We are, &c.

Take a barrel and go your way,
We are, &c.

A barrel of ale will serve us all,
We are, &c.
—Lancashire : Liverpool and its neighbourhood
(Mrs. Harley).

IV.   Have you any bread and wine,
          For we are the Romans!
      Have you any bread and wine,
          We are the Roman soldiers!

      Yes, we have some bread and wine,
          For we are the English!
      Yes, we have some bread and wine,
          We are the English soldiers!

      Will you give us a glass of it?
          For we are, &c.   [As above.]

      Yes, we'll give you a glass of it,
          For we are, &c.

      A glass of it won't serve us so,
          For we are, &c.

      Then you shan't have any at all,
          For we are, &c.

      Then we will break all your glasses,
          For we are, &c.

      Then we will go to the magistrates,
          For we are, &c.

      Then you may go to the magistrates,
          For we are, &c.

      Then let us join our happy ring,
          For we are, &c.
              —Hartley Witney, Winchfield, Hants. (H. S. May).

V.   Have you any cake and wine?
          For we are the English!
      Have you any cake and wine?
          For we're the English soldiers!

      Yes, we have some cake and wine,
          For we are the Romans!
      Yes, we have some cake and wine,
          For we're the Roman soldiers!

Will you give us cake and wine? &c.

No, we won't give you cake and wine, &c.

Then we'll tell our magistrates, &c.

We don't care for your magistrates, &c.

Then we'll tell our highest men, &c.

We don't care for your highest men, &c.

Turn up your sleeves and have a fight,
    For we are the Romans [English]! &c.
        —Enbourne School, Berks. (Miss M. Kimber).

VI.   Have you any bread and wine?
      We are the Romans!
    Have you any bread and wine?
      For we're the government soldiers!

Yes! we have some bread and wine, &c.

Will you give us a glass of it? &c.

We will give you a glass of it, &c.

A glass of it won't serve us all, &c.

We will give you a gallon of it, &c.

We will break all your glasses, &c.

We will tell the magistrates, &c.

What care we for the magistrates, &c.

Are you ready for a fight? &c.

Yes, we're ready for a fight, &c.

Tuck up your sleeves up to your arms, &c.
    Present! Shoot! Bang! Fire!!
      —Maxey, Northamptonshire (Rev. W. D. Sweeting).

VII.   Have you any bread and wine?
      We are the English!
    Have you any bread and wine?
      We are the English soldiers!

No, we have no bread and wine,
  We are the Romans!
No, we have no bread and wine,
  We are the Roman soldiers!

A quart of ale won't serve us all, &c.

Take a gallon and go your way, &c.

A gallon of ale won't serve us all, &c.

We will fetch the magistrate, &c.

We don't care for the magistrate, &c.

We will fetch the p'liceman, &c.

We don't care for the p'liceman, &c.

Are you ready for a fight? &c.

Yes, we're ready for a fight, &c.
                    —Hanbury, Staffs. (Miss Edith Hollis).

VIII. Have you any bread and wine, bread and wine, bread
         and wine,
     Have you any bread and wine,
       For we are English soldiers!

     Yes, we have some bread and wine, bread and wine,
         bread and wine,
     For we are French soldiers!

     Will you give us a quarter of it? &c.

     No, we won't give you a quarter of it, &c.

     Then we will send the magistrate, &c.

     What do we care for the magistrate, &c.

     What do we care for the convent dogs, &c.

     Are you ready for a fight, &c.

     Yes, we are ready for a fight, &c.
                    —Hurstmonceux, Sussex (Miss E. Chase, 1892).

IX.   Have you any bread and wine,
      Bread and wine, bread and wine ?
      Have you any bread and wine,
          My Theerie and my Thorie ?

      Yes, we have some bread and wine, bread and wine, &c.

      We shall have one glass of it, one glass of it, &c.

      Take one glass and go your way, go your way, &c.

      We shall have two glasses of it, two glasses of it, &c.

      Take two glasses and go your way, go your way, &c.

[Repeat for three, four, and five glasses of it, then—]

      We shall have a bottle of it, a bottle of it, &c.

      A bottle of it ye *shall not* have, ye shall not have, &c.

      We will break your glasses all, your glasses all, &c.

      We will send for the magistrates, the magistrates, &c.

      What care we for the magistrates, the magistrates ? &c.

      We will send for the policemen, the policemen, &c.

      What care we for the policemen, the policemen ? &c.

      We will send for the red coat men, the red coat men, &c.

      What care we for the red coat men, the red coat men? &c.

      What kind of men are ye at all, are ye at all ? &c.

      We are all Prince Charlie's men, Prince Charlie's men, &c.

      But what kind of men are *ye* at all, are *ye* at all ? &c.

      We are all King George's men, King George's men, &c.

      Are ye for a battle of it, a battle of it ? &c.

      Yes, we're for a battle of it,
      A battle of it, a battle of it,
      Yes, we're for a battle of it,
          My Theerie and my Thorie.
                              —Perthshire (Rev. W. Gregor).

X. What men are ye of?
    What men are ye of?
    What men are ye of?
        Metherie and Metharie.

    We are of King George's men,
    King George's men, King George's men,
    We are of King George's men,
        Metherie and Metharie.

    We will send for the policemen, &c.

    What care we for the policemen? &c.

    We will have a bottle of wine, &c.

    You shall not have, &c.

    We will have three bottles of wine, &c.

    You shall not have, &c.

    We will send for Cripple Dick, &c.

    What care we for Cripple Dick, &c.

    We finish off with a battle three, &c.

                —Northumberland (from a lady friend of
                    Hon. J. Abercromby).

XI. We shall have a glass of wine,
    A glass of wine, a glass of wine,
    We shall have a glass of wine,
        Methery I methory.

    You shall not have a glass of wine,
    A glass of wine, a glass of wine,
    ·You shall not have a glass of wine,
        Methery I methory.

    Then we'll break your dishes, then, &c.

    Then we'll send for the blue coat men, &c.

    What care I for the blue coat men, &c.

    Then we'll send for the red coat men, &c.

What care we for the red coat men, &c.

We are all King George's men, &c.

We are all King William's men, &c.
          —Auchencairn, Kirkcudbright (Prof. A. C. Haddon).

XII.   Have you any bread and wine, bread and
          wine, bread and wine ?
       Have you any bread and wine ?
          Come a theiry, come a thory.

Yes, we have some bread and wine, &c.

Will you give us a glass of it ? &c.

Yes, we'll give you a glass of it, &c.

Will you give us two glasses of it ? &c.

Yes, we'll give you two glasses of it, &c.

Will you give us a pint of it ? &c.

A pint of it you shall not get, &c.

We will break your window pane, &c.

We will tell the policemen, &c.

What care we for the policemen, &c.

We will tell the red coat men, &c.

What care we for the red coat men, &c.

We will tell the magistrate, &c.

What care we for the magistrate, &c.

Will you try a fight with us ? &c.

Yes, we'll try a fight with you, &c.

Are you ready for it now ? &c.

Yes, we're ready for it now, &c.
          —Perth (Rev. W. Gregor).

XIII.   Have you got any bread and wine, bread
          and wine, bread and wine ?
        Have you got any bread and wine ?
          Come a theory, oary mathorie.

Yes, we have some bread and wine, &c.

We shall have one glass of it, &c.

You shall not have one glass of it, &c.

To what men do you belong? &c.

We are all King George's men, &c.

To what men do you belong, &c.

We are all King William's men, &c.

We shall have a fight, then, &c.

       —Perth (Rev. W. Gregor).

XIV. Have you any bread and wine,
   Ye o' the boatmen?
  Have you any bread and wine,
   Ye the drunk and sober?

Yes, we have some bread and wine, &c.

Will you give us of your wine, &c.

Take one quart and go your way, &c.

One quart is not enough for us, &c.

Take two quarts and go your way, &c.

[Continue up to six quarts, then—]

Pray, what sort of men are you? &c.

We are all King George's men, &c.

Are you ready for a fight? &c.

Yes, we're ready for a fight, &c.

      —Forest of Dean (Miss Matthews).

XV. I will fetch you a pint of beer,
     He I over;
  I will fetch you a pint of beer,
   Whether we are drunk or sober.

  I will fetch you a quart of beer,
     He I over;
  I will fetch you a quart of beer,
   Whether we are drunk or sober.

I will fetch you two quarts of beer, &c.

I will fetch you three quarts of beer, &c.

I will fetch you a gallon of beer, &c.

I will fetch you a barrel of beer, &c.

I will fetch the old police, &c.

Are you ready for a fight, &c.

—Earls Heaton (H. Hardy)

[Another variant from Earls Heaton is :—]

> Have you got a bottle of gin ?
>> He I over ;
> Have you got a bottle of gin,
>> As in that golden story ? —(H. Hardy).

XVI. Have you any bread and wine,
   Bread and wine, bread and wine ?
  Have you any bread and wine ?
   Cam a teerie, arrie ma torry.

Yes, we have some bread and wine,
  Bread and wine, bread and wine ;
Yes, we have some bread and wine,
  Cam a teerie, arrie ma torry.

We shall have one glass of it, &c.

One glass of it you shall not get, &c.

We are King George's loyal men,
  Loyal men, loyal men ;
We are King George's loyal men,
  Cam a teerie, arrie ma torry.

What care we for King George's men,
  King George's men, King George's men ;
What care we for King George's men,
  Cam a teerie, arrie ma torry.

—People's Friend, quoted in a review of
" Arbroath : Past and Present," by J. M. M'Bain.

XVII.   We shall have one glass of wine,
      We are the robbers;
  We shall have one glass of wine,
      For we are the gallant soldiers.

  You shall have no glass of wine,
      We are the robbers;
  You shall have no glass of wine,
      For we are the gallant soldiers.

  We shall have two glasses of it, &c.

  You shall have no glass of it, &c.

  We will break your tumblers, then, &c.

  We shall send for the policeman, &c.

  What care we for the policeman, &c.

  We shall send for the red coat men, &c.

  What care we for the red coat men, &c.

  We shall send for the blue coat men, &c.

  What care we for the blue coat men, &c.

  We shall send for the magistrate, &c.

  What care we for the magistrate, &c.

  We shall send for Cripple Dick, &c.

  What care we for Cripple Dick, &c.

  We shall have a battle then, &c.

  Yonder is a battle field, &c.
        —Laurieston School, Kirkcudbright (J. Lawson).

XVIII.   Here comes three dukes a-riding, a-riding, a-riding;
  Here comes three dukes a-riding, a-riding, a-riding;
    My fair ladies.

  Have you any bread and wine, bread and wine,
    bread and wine?
  Have you any bread and wine, bread and wine,
    bread and wine,
      My fair ladies?

How do you sell your bread and wine, &c.

I sell it by a gallon, sir, &c.

A gallon is too much, fair ladies, &c.

Sell it by a gallon, my fair ladies, &c.

Then we'll have none at all, &c.

Are you ready for a fight, &c.

Yes, we are ready for a fight, &c.
　　My dear sirs.
　　　　　　　　—Sporle, Norfolk (Miss Matthews).

(*c*) The players divide into two sides of about equal numbers, and form lines. The lines walk forwards and backwards in turn, each side singing their respective verses alternately. When the last verse is sung both lines prepare for a fight.

This is the usual way of playing, and there is but little variation in the methods of the different versions. In some versions (Enbourne, Berks.; Maxey, Northants., and Bath) sleeves are tucked up previous to the pretended fight, and in one or two places sticks and stones are used; again in the Northamptonshire and Bath games, at " Present! Shoot! Bang! Fire!!" imitations are given of firing of guns before the actual fight takes place. In the Hants (H. S. May) and Lancashire (Mrs. Harley) versions, when the last verse is reached the players all join hands, form a ring, and dance round while they sing the last verse. In several versions too, when they sing " We don't care for the magistrates," or other persons of authority, the players all stamp their feet on the ground. In the Hurstmonceux version the children double their fists before preparing to fight. Some pretend to have swords to fight with, but the greater number use their fists. In most of the versions the players on both sides join in the refrain or chorus.

(*d*) This game represents an attacking or invading party and the defenders. It probably owes its origin to the border warfare which prevailed for so long a period between Highlanders and Lowlanders of Scotland, the Scotch and English of the northern border counties, and in the country called the marches between Wales and England. Contests between different nationalities living in one town or place, as at Southampton and Nottingham, would also tend to produce this game. That the game represents this kind of conflict rather than an ordinary battle between independent countries is shown by several significant points. These are, the dialogue between the opposing parties before the fight begins, the mention of bread, ale, or other food, and more particularly the threat to appeal to the civil authorities, called in the different versions, magistrates, blue coat men, red coat men, highest men, policemen, and Cripple Dick. Such an appeal is only applicable where the opposing parties were, theoretically at all events, subordinate to a superior authority. The derision, too, with which the threat is received by the assailants is in strict accord with the facts of Border society. Scott in *Waverley* and the *Black Dwarf* describes such a raid, and the suggestion to appeal to the civil authority in lieu of a raid is met with the cry of such an act being useless. The passage from the *Black Dwarf* is: "'We maun tak the law wi' us in thae days, Simon,' answered the more prudent elder. 'And besides,' said another old man, 'I dinna believe there's ane now living that kens the lawful mode of following a fray across the Border. Tam o' Whittram kend a' about it; but he died in the hard winter.' 'Hout,' exclaimed another of these discording counsellors, 'there's nae great skill needed; just put a lighted peat on the end of a spear, a hayfork, or siclike, and blaw a horn and cry the gathering word, and then it's lawful to follow gear into England and recover it by the strong hand, or to take gear frae some other Englishmen, providing ye lift nae mair than's been lifted frae you. That's the auld Border law made at Dundrennan in the days of the Black Douglas.'" In *Waverley* the hero suggests "to send to the nearest garrison for a party of soldiers and a magistrate's warrant," but is told that "he did not understand the state of the country and of the political parties which divided it" (chap. xv.). The position of this part of the country is best understood from the evidence of legal records, showing how slowly the king's record ran in these parts. Thus Mr. Clifford (*Hist. of Private Legislation*)

quotes from Hodgson's *Hist. of Northumberland* (vol. iii.
pt. 2, p. 171), a paper, in the Cotton MS., on "The bounds
and means of the 'batable land belonging to England and
Scotland." It was written in 1550 by Sir Robert Bowes, a
Northumbrian, at the request of the Marquis of Dorset, then
Warden General of the Marches, and gives a graphic picture
of Border life at that time. The writer describes Cassope
bridge as "a common passage for the thieves of Tyndalle, in
England, and for the thieves of Liddesdalle, in Scotland, with
the stolen goods from one realm to the other." The head of
Tyndalle is a place "where few true men have list to lodge."
North Tyndall "is more plenished with wild and misdemeaned
people" than even South Tyndall. The people there "stand
most by four surnames," the Charltons, Robsons, Dodds, and
Milbornes. "Of every surname there be sundry families, or
graves, as they call them, of every of which there be certain
headsmen that leadeth and answereth for all the rest. There
be some among them that have never stolen themselves, which
they call true men. And yet such will have rascals to steal
either on horseback or foot, whom they do reset, and will
receive part of the stolen goods. There be very few able men
in all that country of North Tyndalle, but either they have
used to steal in England or Scotland. And if any true man
of England get knowledge of the theft or thieves that steal his
goods in Tyndalle or Ryddesdale, he had much rather take a
part of his goods again in composition than pursue the extremity by law against the thief. For if the thief be of any
great surname or kindred, and be lawfully executed by order
of justice, the rest of his kin or surname bear as much malice,
which they call deadly feade (feud), against such as follow the
law against their cousin the thief, as though he had unlawfully
killed him with a sword; and will by all means they can seek
revenge thereupon." At sundry times the dalesmen "have
broken out of all order, and have then, like rebels or outlaws,
committed very great and heinous attempts, as burning and
spoiling of whole townships and murdering of gentlemen and
others whom they have had grief or malice unto, so that for
defence of them there have been great garrisons laid, and raids

and incourses both against them and by them, even as it were
between England and Scotland in time of war. And even at
such times they have done more harm than they have received."
A number of the Tyndaller's houses are set together, so that
they may give each other succour in frays, and they join
together in any quarrel against a true man, so that for dread
of them "almost no man dare follow his goods stolen or spoiled
into that country."

The sides in the game are under the different names or leader-
ship of Romans and English, King William's men, rovers and
guardian soldiers, Prince Charlie's men, King George's men, &c.
These names have probably been given in memory of some local
rising, or from some well-known event which stamped itself upon
the recollection of the people. It is very curious that in four or
five versions a refrain, which may well be a survival of some
of the slogans or family "cries" (see "Three Dukes"), should
occur instead of the "Roman" and "English" soldiers, &c.
These refrains are, "My theerie and my thorie," "Metherie and
metharie," "Methory I methory," "Come a theeiry, come a
thory," "Come a theory, oary mathorie," "Cam a teerie, arrie
ma torry," and the three which apparently are still further de-
gradations of these, "Ye o' the boatmen," "Drunk and sober,"
"He I over." That "slogans" or "war cries" were used in
this species of tribal war there is little doubt. In the Northumberland and Laurieston versions the name is "Cripple
Dick," these words, now considered as the name of a powerful
and feared leader, may also indicate the same origin. The
versions with these refrains come from Perthshire (three
versions), Authencairn, and Northumberland; Yorkshire has
He I over; while the Romans and English, King George's
men, King William's men, guardian soldiers, rovers, &c., are
found in Shropshire, Staffordshire, Gloucester, Kent, Hants,
Bath, Berks, Northamptonshire, Sussex, some of which are
Border counties to Wales, and others have sea-coasts where
at different times invasions have been expected. In Sussex,
Miss Chase says the game is said to date from the alarm of
Napoleon's threatened landing on the coast; this is also said
in Kent and Hampshire. Miss Burne considers the game in

Shropshire to have certainly originated from the old Border warfare. She also considers that the bread and wine, barrels of ale, &c., are indications of attempts made to bribe the beleagured garrison and their willingness to accept it; but I think it more probably refers to the fact that some food, cattle, and goods were oftentime given to the raiders by the owners of the lands as blackmail, to prevent the carrying off of all their property, and to avoid fighting if possible. It will be noticed that fighting ensues as the result of a sufficient quantity of food and drink being refused. Scott alludes to the practice of blackmail, having to be paid to a Highland leader in *Waverley*, in the raid upon the cattle of the baron of Bradwardine (see chap. xv.). The farms were scattered, and before the defenders could combine to offer resistance, cattle and goods would be carried off, and the ground laid waste, if resistance were offered.

The tune of the Northants game (Rev. W. Sweeting) and Hants (H. S. May) are so nearly like the Bath tune that it seemed unnecessary to print them. The tune of the Surrey game is that of "Nuts in May." The words of the Bath version collected by me are nearly identical with the Shropshire, except that "We are the Romans" is said instead of "We are the Rovers." They are not therefore printed here, but I have used this version in my *Children's Singing Games*, series I., *illustrated*. The tune of the Hants version (H. S. May) is similar to that of Wrotham, Kent (Miss D. Kimball).

Weary

> Weary, weary, I'm waiting on you,
> I can wait no longer on you;
> Three times I've whistled on you—
> Lovey, are you coming out?
>
> I'll tell mamma when I go home,
> The boys won't let my curls alone;
> They tore my hair, and broke my comb—
> And that's the way all boys get on.
> —Aberdeen Training College (Rev. W. Gregor).

The girls stand in a row, and one goes backwards and forwards singing the first four lines. She then takes one out of the row, and they swing round and round while they all sing the other four lines.

Weave the Diaper

Weave the diaper tick-a-tick tick,
Weave the diaper tick ;
Come this way, come that,
As close as a mat,
Athwart and across, up and down, round about,
And forwards and backwards and inside and out ;
Weave the diaper thick-a-thick thick,
Weave the diaper thick.

—Halliwell's *Nursery Rhymes*, p. 65.

(*b*) This game should be accompanied by a kind of pantomimic dance, in which the motions of the body and arms express the process of weaving, the motion of the shuttle, &c.

(*c*) Mr. Newell (*Games and Songs of American Children*, p. 80) mentions a dance called " Virginia Reel," which he says is an imitation of weaving. The first movement represents the shooting of the shuttle from side to side and the passage of the woof over and under the threads of the warp ; the last movements indicate the tightening of the threads and bringing together of the cloth. He also says that an acquaintance told him that in New York the men and girls stand in rows by sevens, an arrangement which may imitate the different colours of strands. Mr. Newell does not say whether any words are sung during the dancing of the reel. Halliwell gives another rhyme (p. 121), which may have belonged to this weaving game. It is extremely probable that in these fragments described by him we have remains of one of the old trade dances and songs.

Weigh the Butter

Two children stand back to back, with their arms locked. One stoops as low as he can, supporting the other on his back, and says, "Weigh the butter ;" he rises, and the second stoops in his turn with "Weigh the cheese." The first repeats with

"Weigh the old woman:" and it ends by the second with "Down to her knees."—*Folk-lore Journal*, v. 58.

The players turn their backs to each other, and link their arms together behind. One player then bends forward, and lifts the other off his [her] feet. He rises up, and the other bends forward and lifts him up. Thus the two go on bending and rising, and lifting each other alternately, and keep repeating—

> Weigh butter, weigh cheese,
> Weigh a pun (pound) o' can'le grease.
> —Keith (Rev. W. Gregor).

Mr. Northall (*English Folk Rhymes*) gives this game with the words as—

> A bag o' malt, a bag o' salt,
> Ten tens a hundred.

This game is described as played in the same way in Antrim and Down (Patterson's *Glossary*), and also by Jamieson in Roxburgh.

See "Way-Zaltin."

When I was a Young Girl

—Platt School, nr. Wrotham, Kent (Miss Burne).

—Hanbury, Staffs. (Miss Edith Hollis).

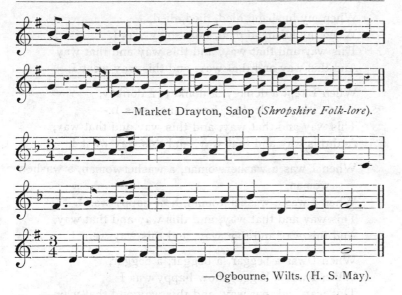

—Market Drayton, Salop (*Shropshire Folk-lore*).

—Ogbourne, Wilts. (H. S. May).

I.   When I was a young girl, a young girl, a young girl,
When I was a young girl, how happy was I.
This way and that way, and this way and that way,
And this way and that way, and this way went I.

When I had a sweetheart, a sweetheart, a sweetheart,
When I had a sweetheart, how happy was I.
This way and that way, and this way and that way,
And this way and that way, and this way went I.

When I got married, got married, got married,
When I got married, how happy was I.
This way and that way, and this way and that way,
And this way and that way, and this way went I.

When I had a baby, a baby, a baby,
When I had a baby, how happy was I.
This way and that way, and this way and that way,
And this way and that way, and this way went I.

When my baby died, died, died,
When my baby died, how sorry was I.
This way and that way, and this way and that way,
And this way and that way, and this way went I.

When my husband died, died, died,
When my husband died, how sorry was I.
This way and that way, and this way and that way,
And this way and that way, and this way went I.

When I kept a donkey, a donkey, a donkey,
When I kept a donkey, how happy was I.
This way and that way, and this way and that way,
And this way and that way, and this way went I.

When I was a washerwoman, a washerwoman, a washer-
woman,
When I was a washerwoman, how happy was I.
This way and that way, and this way and that way,
And this way and that way, and this way went I.

When I was a beggar, a beggar, a beggar,
When I was a beggar, how happy was I.
This way and that way, and this way and that way,
And this way and that way, and this way went I.

—Platt School, near Wrotham, Kent (Miss Burne).

II.   When I was a young girl, a young girl, a young girl,
When I was I young girl, how happy was I.
And this way and that way, and this way and that way,
and this way and that way, and this way went I.

When I was a school-girl, a school-girl, a school-girl,
When I was a school-girl, oh, this way went I.
And this way and that way, and this way and that way,
and this way and that way, and this way went I.

When I was a teacher, a teacher, a teacher,
When I was a teacher, oh, this way went I.
And this way and that way, and this way and that way,
and this way and that way, and this way went I.

When I had a sweetheart, a sweetheart, a sweetheart,
When I had a sweetheart, oh, this way went I.
And this way and that way, and this way and that way,
and this way and that way, and this way went I.

When I had a husband, a husband, a husband,
When I had a husband, oh! this way went I.
And this way and that way, and this way and that way,
 and this way and that way, and this way went I.

When I had a baby, a baby, a baby,
When I had a baby, how happy was I.
And this way and that way, and this way and that way,
 and this way and that way, and this way went I.

When my baby died, oh, died, oh, died,
When my baby died, how sorry was I.
And this way and that way, and this way and that way,
 and this way and that way, and this way went I.

When I took in washing, oh, washing, oh, washing,
When I took in washing, oh, this way went I.
And this way and that way, and this way and that way,
 and this way and that way, and this way went I.

When I went out scrubbing, oh, scrubbing, oh, scrubbing,
When I went out scrubbing, oh, this way went I.
And this way and that way, and this way and that way,
 and this way and that way, and this way went I.

When my husband did beat me, did beat me, did beat me,
When my husband did beat me, oh, this way went I.
And this way and that way, and this way and that way,
 and this way and that way, and this way went I.

When my husband died, oh, died, oh, died,
When my husband died, how happy was I.
And this way and that way, and this way and that way,
 and this way and that way, and this way went I.

      Hurrah!
    —Barnes, Surrey (A. B. Gomme).

III. When I was a young gell, a young gell, a young gell,
 When I was a young gell, i' this a way went I.
 An' i' this a way, an' i' that a way, an' i' this a way went I.

 When I wanted a sweetheart, a sweetheart, a sweetheart,
 When I wanted a sweetheart, i' this a way went I.
 An' i' this a way, an' i' this a way, an' i' this a way went I.

When I went a-courting, a-courtin', a-courtin',
When I went a-courtin', i' this a way went I.
An' i' this a way, an' i' this a way, an' i' this a way went I.

When I did get married, get married, get married,
When I did get married, i' this a way went I.
An' i' this a way, an' i' this a way, an' i' this a way went I.

When I had a baby, &c.

When I went to church, &c.

My husband was a drunkard, &c.

When I was a washerwoman, &c.

When I did peggy, &c.

My baby fell sick, &c.

My baby did die, &c.

My husband did die, &c.

—Liphook, Wakefield (Miss Fowler).

IV. When I wore my flounces, my flounces, my flounces,
When I wore my flounces, this a-way went I.

When I was a lady, a lady, a lady,
When I was a lady, this a-way went I.

When I was a gentleman, a gentleman, a gentleman,
When I was a gentleman, this a-way went I.

When I was a washerwoman, &c.

When I was a schoolgirl, &c.

When I had a baby, &c.

When I was a cobbler, &c.

When I was a shoeblack, &c.

When my husband beat me, &c.

When my baby died, &c.

When my husband died, &c.

When I was a parson, &c.

—Hanbury, Staffs. (Miss Edith Hollis).

V. When I was a lady, a lady, a lady,
When I was a lady, a lady was I.
'Twas this way and that way, and this way and that.

When I was a gentleman, a gentleman, a gentleman,
When I was a gentleman, a gentleman was I.
'Twas this way and that way, and this way and that.

When I was a schoolgirl, a schoolgirl, a schoolgirl,
When I was a schoolgirl, a schoolgirl was I, &c.

When I was a schoolboy, a schoolboy, a schoolboy, &c.

When I was a schoolmaster, a schoolmaster, a schoolmaster, &c.

When I was a schoolmistress, a schoolmistress, a schoolmistress, &c.

When I was a donkey, a donkey, a donkey, &c.

When I was a shoeblack, a shoeblack, a shoeblack, &c.
—Ogbourne, Wilts. (H. S. May).

VI. When I was a naughty girl, a naughty girl, a naughty girl,
When I was a naughty girl, a-this a-way went I !
    And a-this a-way, and a-that a-way,
    And a-this a-way, and a-that a-way,
    And a-this a-way, and a-that a-way,
        And a-this a-way went I !

When I was a good girl, &c., a-this a-way went I ! &c.

When I was a naughty girl, &c.

When I went courting, &c.

When I got married, &c.

When I had a baby, &c.

When the baby cried, &c.

When the baby died, &c.
—Berrington (*Shropshire Folk-lore*, p. 514).

VII. When I was a naughty girl, &c. [as above]

When I went to school, &c.

When I went a-courting, &c.

When I got married, &c.

When I had a baby, &c..

When the baby fell sick, &c.

When my baby did die, &c.

When my husband fell sick, &c.

When my husband did die, &c.

When I was a widow, &c.

Then I took in washing, &c.

Then my age was a hundred and four, &c.

—Market Drayton (*Shropshire Folk-lore*, p. 515).

VIII. First I was a school-maid, a school-maid, how happy was I !

And a-this a-way, and a-that a-way went I !

And then I got married, how happy was I ! &c.

And then I had a baby, how happy was I ! &c.

And then my husband died, how sorry was I ! &c.

And then I married a cobbler, how happy was I ! &c.

And then the baby died, how sorry was I ! &c.

And then I married a soldier, how happy was I ! &c.

And then he bought me a donkey, how happy was I ! &c.

And then the donkey throwed me, how sorry was I ! &c.

And then I was a washing-maid, how happy was I ! &c.

And then my life was ended, how sorry was I !

—Chirbury (*Shropshire Folk-lore*, p. 515).

IX. When first we went to school—to school—to school—
How happy was I !
'Twas this way and that way,
How happy was I !

Next I went to service—to service—to service—
How happy was I !
'Twas this way, and that way,
How happy was I ! &c.

Next I had a sweetheart—a sweetheart—a sweetheart—
How happy was I ! &c.

Next I got married—got married—got married—
How happy was I ! &c.

Next I had a baby—a baby—a baby—
How happy was I ! &c.

Next my husband died—he died—he died—
How sorry was I ! &c.

Next my baby died—she died—she died—
How sorry was I ! &c.

> —Dorsetshire (*Folk-lore Journal*, vii. pp. 218-219).

X.   Oh ! when I was a soldier, I did this way, this way.

Oh ! when I was a mower, I did this way, this way.

Oh ! when I was a hedge cutter, I did this way, this way.

Oh ! when I was a boot cleaner, I did this way, this way.

Oh ! when I was a teacher, I did this way, this way.

Oh ! when I was a governess, I did this way, this way.

Oh ! when I had a baby, I did this way, this way.

Oh ! when my baby died, I did this way, this way.

> —Fernham and Longcot Choir Girls, Berks.
> (Miss I. Barclay).

XI.   When I was a school-boy, a school-boy, a school-boy,
When I was a school-boy, this way went I.

When I was a school-girl, &c.

When I was a-courting, &c.

When I got married, &c.

When I had a baby, &c.

When my baby died, &c.

When my husband was ill, &c.

When I was a shoe-black, &c.

When I was a washerwoman, &c.

When I was a soldier, &c.

When I was a sailor, &c.

—Frodingham and Nottinghamshire
(Miss M. Peacock).

XII.   When I was a school girl, a school girl, a school girl,
When I was a school girl, a this way went I.

When I was a teacher, a teacher, a teacher,
When I was a teacher, a this way went I.

[Verses follow for courtin'—
married woman,
having a baby,
death of baby.]

—Earls Heaton (H. Hardy).

XIII.   When I went a courting, I went just so.
When next I went a courting, I went just so;
When next I went a courting, I went just so;
When next I went a courting, I went just so.

—Haxey, Lincolnshire (C. C. Bell).

(c) The children join hands and form a ring. They all dance or walk round singing the words of the first two lines of each verse. Then all standing still, they unclasp hands, and continue singing the next two lines, and while doing so each child performs some action which illustrates the events, work, condition, or profession mentioned in the first line of the verse they are singing; then rejoining hands they all dance round in a circle again. The actions used to illustrate the different events are: In the versions from Platt school, for "young girl," each child holds out her dress and dances a step first to the right, then to the left, two or three times, finishing by turning herself quite round; for a "sweetheart," the children turn their heads and kiss their hands to the child behind them; for "got married," they all walk round in ring form, two by two, arm in arm; for having a baby, they each "rock" and "hush" a pretended baby; when the baby dies, each pretends to cry; when the husband dies, they throw their aprons or handkerchiefs over their heads and faces; for "keeping a donkey," each child pretends to beat and drive the child immediately in front of her; for "washerwoman," each pretends to wash or wring clothes; for a "beggar," each drops curtseys, and holds out her hand as if asking alms, putting on an imploring countenance. The Barnes' version is played in the same way, with the addition of holding the hands together to represent a book, as if learning lessons, for "schoolgirl"; pretending to hold a cane, and holding up fingers for silence, when a "teacher"; when "my husband did beat me," each pretends to fight; and for "my husband died," each child walks round joyfully, waving her handkerchief, and all calling out Hurrah! at the end; the other verses being acted the same as at Platt. The Liphook version is much the same: the children beckon with their fingers when "wanting a sweetheart"; kneel down and pretend to pray when "at church"; prod pretended "clothes" in a wash-tub with a "dolly" stick when "I did peggy" is said; and mourn for the "husband's" death. In the Hanbury game, the children dance round or shake themselves for "flounces"; hold up dresses and walk nicely for "lady"; bow to each other for "gentlemen"; pretend to mend shoes when "cobblers"; brush shoes for "shoeblack"; clap hands when the "husband" dies; and kneel when they are "parsons." In the Ogbourne game, the children "hold up their dresses as ladies do" in the first verse; take off their hats repeatedly when "gentlemen"; pretend to cry when "schoolgirls"; walking round, swinging their arms, and looking as cocky as possible, when "schoolboys"; patting each other's backs when "schoolmasters"; clapping hands for "schoolmistresses"; stooping down and walking on all fours for a "donkey"; and brushing shoes for "shoeblack." In the Shropshire games at Berrington, each child "walks demurely" for a good girl; puts finger on lip for "naughty girl"; walks two and two, arm in arm, for "courting"; holds on to her dress for "married"; whips the "baby," and cries when it dies. In the Market Drayton game, each pretends to tear her clothes for "naughty girl"; pretends to carry a bag for "school-girl"; walk in pairs side by side for "courting"; the same, arm in arm, for "married"; "hushes" for a baby, pretends to pat on the back for sick baby; covers her face with handkerchief when baby dies; pats her chest when husband is sick, cries and "makes dreadful work" when he dies; puts on handkerchief for a widow's veil for a widow; hobbles along, and finally falls down when "a hundred and four." In the Dorset game, when at "service," an imitation of scrubbing and sweeping is given; walk in couples for sweethearts, and married; the remaining verses the same as the Platt version. In the Fernham game the children shoot out their arms alternately for a soldier; for a mower, they stand sideways and pretend to cut grass; for hedge-cutter, they pretend to cut with a downward movement, as with a belt [*qy.* bill] hook, the other action similar to the Platt and Barnes games. In the Frodingham game they stamp and pretend to drill for "school-boys," pretend to sew as "schoolgirls," kiss for "courting," put on a ring for "getting married," run for a doctor when "husband" is ill, punch and push each other for "soldiers," and haul ropes for "sailors." In other versions, in which carpenters, blacksmiths, farmers, bakers appear, actions showing something of those trades are performed.

(*d*) It will be seen, from the description of the way this game is played, that it consists of imitative actions of different events in life, or of actions imitating trades and occupations. It was probably at one time played by both girls and boys, young men and young women. It is now but seldom played by boys, and therefore those verses containing lines describing male occupations are not nearly so frequently met with as those describing girls' or womens' life only. Young girl, sweetheart, or going courtin', marriage, birth of children, loss of baby and husband, widowhood, and the occupations of washing and cleaning, exactly sum up the principal and important events in many working womens' lives—comprising, in fact, the whole. This was truer many years ago than now, and the mention in many versions of school girl, teacher, governess, indicate in

those versions the influence which education, first in the shape
of dame or village schools, Sunday schools, and latterly Board
schools, has had upon the minds and playtime of the children.
These lines may certainly be looked upon as introductions by
the children of comparatively modern times, and doubtless have
taken the place of some older custom or habit. This game is
exactly one of those to which additions and alterations of this
kind can be made without destroying or materially altering, or
affecting, its sense. It can live as a simple game in an almost
complete state long after its original wording has been lost or
forgotten, and as long as occupations continue and events
occur which lend themselves to dumb action. The origin of
the game I consider to be those dances and songs performed
in imitation of the serious avocations of life, when such ceremonies were considered necessary to their proper performance,
and acceptable to the deities presiding over such functions,
arising from belief in sympathetic magic.

At harvest homes it was customary for the men engaged in
the work of the farm to go through a series of performances
depicting their various occupations with song and dance, from
their engagement as labourers until the harvest was completed,
and at some fairs the young men and women of the village, in
song and dance, would go through in pantomimic representation, the several events of the year, such as courting, marriage,
&c., and their several occupations.

Perhaps the most singular instance of imitative action being
used in a semi-religious purpose, is that recorded by Giraldus
Cambrensis in the twelfth century, who, speaking of the church
of St. Almedha, near Brecknock, says a solemn feast is held
annually in the beginning of August: "You may see men and
girls, now in the church, now in the churchyard, now in the
dance, which is led round the churchyard with a song, on a
sudden falling on the ground as in a trance, then jumping up
as in a frenzy, and representing with their hands and feet
before the people whatever work they have unlawfully done on
feast days; you may see one man put his hands to the plough,
and another, as it were, goad on the oxen, one man imitating a
shoemaker, another a tanner. Now you may see a girl with a

distaff drawing out the thread and winding it again on the spindle; another walking and arranging the threads for the spindle; another throwing the shuttle and seeming to weave" (*Itinerary of Wales*, chap. ii.).

For the significance of some of the pantomimic actions used, I may mention that in Cheshire for a couple to walk "arm-in-arm" is significant of a betrothed or engaged couple.

Other versions have been sent me, but so similar to those given that it is unnecessary to give them here. The tunes vary more. In some places the game is sung to that of "Nuts in May." In Barnes the tune used was sometimes that of "Isabella," vol. i. p. 247, and sometimes the first one printed here.

The game is mentioned by Newell (*Games*, p. 88).

Whiddy

> Whiddy, whiddy, way,
> If you don't come, I won't play.

The players, except one, stand in a den or home. One player clasps his hands together, with the two forefingers extended, He sings out the above, and the boys who are "home" then cry—

> Warning once, warning twice,
> Warning three times over;
> When the cock crows out come I,
> Whiddy, whiddy, wake-cock. Warning!

This is called "Saying their prayers." The boy who begins must touch another boy, keeping his hands clasped as above. These two then join hands, and pursue the others; those whom they catch also joining hands, till they form a long line. If the players who are in the home run out before saying their prayers, the other boys have the right to pummel them, or ride home on their backs.—London (J. P. Emslie, A. B. Gomme).

See "Chickidy Hand," "Hunt the Staigie," "Stag," "Warney."

Whigmeleerie

A game occasionally played in Angus. A pin was stuck in the centre of a circle, from which there were as many radii as there were persons in the company, with two names of each person at the radius opposite to him.   On the pin an index was placed, and moved round by every one in turn, and at whatsoever person's radius it stopped, he was obliged to drink off his glass.—Jamieson.

A species of chance game, played apparently with a kind of totum.

Whip

A boy's game, called in the South "Hoop or Hoop Hide." This is a curious instance of corruption, for the name hoop is pronounced in the local manner as hooip, whence whip.—Easther's *Almondbury Glossary*.

Whishin Dance

An old-fashioned dance, in which a cushion is used to kneel upon.—Dickinson's *Cumberland Glossary*.

See " Cushion Dance."

Who goes round my Stone Wall

I.   Who's going round my stone wall ?
  Nobody, only little Jacky Lingo.
  Pray don't steal none of my fat sheep,
  Unless I take one by one, two by two, three by three,
  Follow me.
  Have you seen anything of my black sheep ?
  Yes ! I gave them a lot of bread and butter and sent
    them up there [pointing to left or right].
  Then what have you got behind you ?
  Only a few poor black sheep.
  Well ! let me see.
[The child immediately behind Johnny Lingo shows its foot between her feet, and on seeing it the centre child says]
  Here's my black sheep.
—Winterton, Anderby, Nottinghamshire
(Miss M. Peacock).

II.   Who's that going round my stony walk ?
  It's only Bobby Bingo.
  Have you stolen any of my sheep ?
  Yes ! I stole one last night and one the night before.
—Enbourne School, Berks (Miss M. Kimber).

III.   Who goes round this stoney wa'?
       Nane but Johnnie Lingo.
       Tak care and no steal ony o' my fat sheep away!
       Nane but ane.   —Galloway (J. G. Carter).

IV.   Who goes round my pinfold wall?
       Little Johnny Ringo.
       Don't steal all my fat sheep!
       No more I will, no more I may,
       Until I've stol'n 'em all away,
       Nip, Johnny Ringo.   —Addy's *Sheffield Glossary*.

V.   Who's that walking round my sandy path?
       Only Jack and Jingle.
       Don't you steal none of my fat geese!
       Yes, I will, or No, I won't.   I'll take them one by one,
           and two by two, and call them Jack and Jingle.
                              —Barnes, Surrey (A. B. Gomme).

VI.   Who runs round my pen pound?
       No one but old King Sailor.
       Don't you steal all my sheep away, while I'm a wailer!
       Steal them all away one by one, and leave none but
           old King Sailor.
                    —Raunds (*Northants Notes and Queries*, i. p. 232).

VII.   Who's that walking round my walk?
     Only Jackie Jingle.
     Don't you steal of my fat sheep;
     The more I will, the more I won't,
     Unless I take them one by one,
     And that is Jackie Jingle.
               —Hersham, Surrey (*Folk-lore Record*, v. 85).

VIII.   Who's going round my sunny wall to night?
     Only little Jacky Lingo.
     Don't steal any of my fat chicks.
     I stole one last night
     And gave it a little hay,
     There came a little blackbird,
     And carried it away.
               —Bocking, Essex (*Folk-lore Record*, iii. 170).

IX.   Who's that round my stable door [or stony wall]?
     Only little Jack and Jingo.
     Don't you steal any of my fat pigs!
     I stole one last night and the night before,
     Chick, chick, come along with me.
               —Deptford, Kent (Miss Chase).

X.   Who's this walking round my stony gravel path?
     Only little Jacky Jingle.
     Last night he stole one of my sheep,
     Put him in the fold,
     Along came a blackbird, and pecked off his nose.
               —Hampshire (Miss Mendham).

XI.   Who is going round my fine stony house?
     Only Daddy Dingo.
     Don't take any of my fine chicks.
     Only this one, O!
               —Ellesmere (Burne's *Shropshire Folk-lore*, p. 520).

XII.   Who is that walking round my stone-wall?
     Only little Johnnie Nero.
     Well, don't you steal any of my fat sheep!
     I stole one last night and gave it a lock of hay,
     Here come I to take another away.
               —Sporle, Norfolk (Miss Matthews).

XIII. Who's that going round my pretty garden?
Only Jacky Jingo.
Don't you steal any of my fat sheep!
Oh, no I won't; oh, yes I will; and if I do I'll take
    them one by one, so out comes Jacky Jingo.
—Ogbourne, Wilts. (H. S. May).

XIV. Who's going round my sheepfold?
Only poor Jack Lingo.
Don't steal any of my black sheep!
No, I won't, only buy one.
—Roxton, St. Neots (Miss E. Lumley).

XV. Who goes round my house this night?
None but Limping Tom.
Do you want any of my chickens this night?
None but this poor one.   —Macduff (Rev. W. Gregor).

XVI. Who goes round my house this night?
Who but Bloody Tom!
Who stole all my chickens away?
None but this poor one.
—Chambers's *Pop. Rhymes*, 122.

XVII. Who goes round the house at night?
None but Bloody Tom.
Tack care an' tack nane o' my chickens awa'!
None but this poor one.   —Keith (Rev. W. Gregor.

XVIII. Johnny, Johnny Ringo,
Don't steal all my faun sheep.
Nob but one by one,
Whaul they're all done.
—Easther's *Almondbury Glossary*.

XIX. Who's going round my stone wall?
Only an old witch.
Don't take any of my bad chickens!
No, only this one.   —Hanbury, Staffs. (Miss E. Hollis).

(*b*) The players stand in a circle, but they do not necessarily hold hands, nor do they move round. One player
kneels or stands in the centre, and another walks round out-

side the circle. The child in the centre asks the questions, and the child outside (Johnny Lingo) replies. When the last answer is given, the outside player, or Johnny Lingo, touches one of the circle on the back; this player, without speaking, then follows Johnny Lingo and stands behind her holding her by her dress, or round the waist. The dialogue is then repeated, and another child taken. This is continued until all the circle are behind Johnny Lingo. Then the child in the centre tries to catch one of them, and Johnny Lingo tries to prevent it; as soon as one player is caught she stands aside, and when all are caught the game is over.

This is the usual way of playing. The variations are: in Galloway, Enbourne, Keith, and Hanbury, the centre player shuts her eyes, or is blindfolded. In the Almondbury version, when the centre child gets up to look for his sheep, and finds them (they do not stand behind Johnny Ringo, but hide), they run about "baaing;" when he catches them he pretends to cut their heads off. In Chambers's description of the game, all the players except two sit upon the ground in a circle (sitting or lying down also obtains at Barnes), one of the two stands inside, and the other personates "Bloody Tom." Bloody Tom tries to carry off a player after the dialogue has been said, and the centre child tries to prevent this one from being taken, and the rest of the circle "cower more closely round him." In the Macduff version, when all the players have been taken, the centre child runs about crying, "Where are all my chickens?" Some of the "chickens," on hearing this, try to run away from "Limping Tom" to her, and he tries to prevent them. He puts them all behind him in single file, and the centre child then tries to catch them; when she catches them all she becomes Limping Tom, and he the shepherd or hen. Dr. Gregor says (Keith)—The game is generally played by boys; the keeper kneels or sits in the middle of the circle; when all the sheep are gone, and he gets no answers to his questions, he crawls away still blindfolded, and searches for the lost sheep. The first player he finds becomes keeper, and he becomes Bloody Tom. In the Winterton version (No. I.) there is a further dialogue. The game is played in the usual way at the beginning. When Jacko Lingo says, "Follow me" (he had previously, when saying one by one and two by two, &c., touched three children on their back in turn), the third one touched leaves the ring, and stands behind him holding his clothes or waist. This is done until all the children forming the circle are holding on behind him. The child in the centre then asks the next question. When she says, "Here's my black sheep," she tries to dodge behind Jacky Lingo, and catch the child behind him. When she has done this she begins again at "Have you seen anything of my black sheep," until she has caught all the children behind Jacky Lingo. In two versions, Deptford and Bocking, there is no mention of a player being in the centre, but this is an obvious necessity unless the second player stands also outside the circle. In the Raunds version the ring moves slowly round. In the Hants version (Miss Mendham) the children sit in a line. The thief takes one at a time and hides them, and the shepherd pulls them out of their hiding-places. In the Shropshire game, the chickens crouch down behind their mother, holding her gown, and the fox walks round them.

(c) This game appears to represent a village (by the players standing still in circle form), and from the dialogue the children not only represent the village, but sheep or chickens belonging to it. The other two players are—one a watchman or shepherd, and the other a wolf, fox, or other depredatory animal. The sheep may possibly be supposed to be in the pound or fold; the thief comes over the boundaries from a neighbouring village or forest to steal the sheep at night; the watchman or shepherd, although at first apparently deceived by the wolf, discovers the loss, and a fight ensues, in which the thief gets the worse, and some of the animals, if not all, are supposed to be recovered. The names used in the game,—pen pound, pinfold, fold, stone wall, sunny wall, sandy path, gravel path, sheep fold, garden, house, are all indications that a village and its surroundings is intended to be represented, and this game differs in that respect from the ordinary Fox and Geese and Hen and Chickens games, in which no mention is made of these.

Halliwell records two versions (*Nursery Rhymes*, pp. 61, 68). The words and method of playing are the same as some of those recorded above. There is also a version in *Suffolk County Folk-lore*, pp. 65, 66, which beginning with "Who's going round my little stony wall?" after the sheep are all stolen, continues with a dialogue, which forms a part of the game of "Witch." The Rev. W. S. Sykes sends one from Settle, Yorkshire, the words of which are the same as No. XIV., except that the last line has "just one" instead of "buy one." Mr. Newell gives a version played by American children.

Widow

   I. One poor widder all left alone,
      Only one daughter to marry at home,
      Chews [choose] for the worst, and chews for the best,
      And chews the one that yew [you] love best.

      Now you're married, I wish ye good joy,
      Ivery year a gal or a boy!
      If one 'ont dew, ye must hev tew,
      So pray, young couple, kiss te'gither.
                     —Swaffham, Norfolk (Miss Matthews).

  II. Here is a poor widow who is left alone,
      And all her children married and gone;
      Come choose the east, come choose the west,
      Come choose the one you love the best.

      Now since you've got married, I wish you joy,
      Every year a girl and boy;
      Love one another like sister and brother,
      I pray you couple come kiss together.
                     —Perth (Rev. W. Gregor).

 III. One poor widow was left alone,
      Daughter, daughter, marry at home;
      Choose the worst, or choose the best,
      Choose the young gentleman you love best.

      Now you are married, I wish you joy,
      Father and mother, you must obey,

Love one another like sister and brother,
And now, young couple, come kiss together.
                    —Bexley Heath (Miss Morris.)

IV.   One poor widow is left all alone, all alone, all alone,
      Choose the worst, and choose the best,
      And choose the one that you like best.

      Now she's married I wish her joy,
      Her father and mother she must obey,
      Love one another like sisters and brothers,
      And now it's time to go away.
                    —-Suffolk County Folk-lore, p. 67.

V.   One poor widow was left alone,
      She had but one daughter to marry alone ;
      Come choose the worst, come choose the best,
      Come choose the young girl that you like best.
                    —Maxey, Northants (Rev. W. D. Sweeting).

VI.   Here's a poor widow she's left alone,
      She has got nothing to marry upon ;
      Come choose to the east, come choose to the west,
      Come choose the one that you love best.

      Now they're married, we wish them joy,
      Every year a girl and a boy ;
      Seven years old, seven years to come,
      Now kiss the couple, and that's well done.
                    —Auchterarder, N.B. (Miss E. S. Haldane).

(*b*) The children form a ring by joining hands. One player
stands in the centre. The ring dance round singing the first
verse ; the widow then chooses one player from the ring, who
goes into the centre with her, and the ring dances round
singing the second part. The one first in the centre then
joins the ring, and the second player becomes the widow and
chooses in her turn.

This belongs to the marriage group of Kiss in the Ring
games.   Northall (*English Folk Rhymes*, p. 374), gives a
version similar to the above.

See "Kiss in the Ring," "Poor Widow," "Sally Water,"
"Silly Young Man."

Wiggle-Waggle

The players sit round a table under the presidency òf a " Buck." Each person has his fingers clenched, and the thumb extended. Buck from time to time calls out as suits his fancy : " Buck says, Thumbs up ! " or, " Buck says, Thumbs down ! " or, " Wiggle-waggle ! " If he says " Thumbs up ! " he places both hands on the table, with the thumbs sticking straight up. If " Thumbs down ! " he rests his thumbs on the table with his hands up. If " Wiggle-waggle ! " he places his hands as in " Thumbs up ! " but wags his thumbs nimbly. Everybody at the table has to follow the word of command on the instant, and any who fail to do so are liable to a forfeit.—Evan's *Leicestershire Words*.

See " Horns."

Wild Boar

" Shoeing the Wild Boar," a game in which the player sits cross-legged on a beam or pole, each of the extremities of which is placed or swung in the eyes of a rope suspended from the back tree of an outhouse. The person uses a switch, as if in the act of whipping up a horse; when being thus unsteadily mounted, he is most apt to lose his balance. If he retains it, he is victor over those who fail.—Teviotdale (Jamieson).

Wild Birds

" All the Wild Birds in the Air," the name of a game in which one acts the dam of a number of birds, who gives distinct names of birds, such as are generally known to all that are engaged in the sport. The person who opposes tries to guess the name of each individual. When he errs he is subject to a stroke on the back. When he guesses right he carries away on his back that bird, which is subjected to a blow from each of the rest. When he has discovered and carried off the whole, he has gained the game.—Jamieson. Jamieson adds that this sport seems only to be retained in Abernethy, Perthshire; and it is probable, from the antiquity of the place, that it is very ancient.

See " All the Birds in the Air," " Fool, Fool."

Willie, Willie Wastell

> Willie, Willie Wastell,
> I am on your castle,
> A' the dogs in the toun
> Winna pu' Willie doun.
>
> Like Willie, Willie Wastel,
> I am in my castel
> A' the dogs in the toun
> Dare not ding me doun.—Jamieson.

A writer in the *Gentlemen's Magazine* for 1822, Part I. p. 401, says that the old distich—

> "Willy, Willy Waeshale!
> Keep off my castle,"

used in the North in the game of limbo, contains the true etymon of the adjective "Willy."

The same game as "Tom Tiddler's Ground." It is played in the same way. Jamieson says the second rhyme given shows that the rhyme was formerly repeated by the player holding the castle, and not, as now, by the opposing players.

See "King of the Castle," "Tom Tiddler's Ground."

Wind up the Bush Faggot

Andante, with determined deliberation.

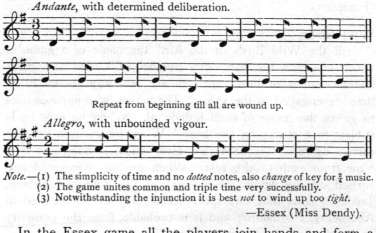

Repeat from beginning till all are wound up.

Allegro, with unbounded vigour.

Note.—(1) The simplicity of time and no *dotted* notes, also *change* of key for $\frac{2}{4}$ music.
(2) The game unites common and triple time very successfully.
(3) Notwithstanding the injunction it is best *not* to wind up too *tight*.

—Essex (Miss Dendy).

In the Essex game all the players join hands and form a long line. They should stand in sizes, the tallest should be

the first, and should stand quite still.   All the rest walk round
this tallest one, singing—

Wind up the bush faggot, and wind it up tight,
Wind it all day and again at night,

to the first part of the tune given—that in three-eight time.
This is to be repeated until all the players are wound round
the centre or tallest player, in a tight coil.   Then they all
sing—

Stir up the dumplings, the pot boils over,

to the second part of the tune in 2-4 time.   This is repeated,
all jumping simultaneously to the changed time, until there
is a general scrimmage, with shrieking and laughter, and a
break up.   The players should look somewhat like a watch
spircng. As soon as the last one is wound up, no
matter in what part of the 3-8 time music they may be, they
leave off and begin to jump up and down, and sing to the
2-4 music.—Essex (Miss Dendy).

This game is called "Wind up the Watch" in Wolstanton,
North Staffordshire Potteries, and is played in the same manner.
The words are only, "Wind up the Watch," and are said.
When all the players are wound up they begin to unwind,
saying, "Unwind the Watch."—Miss Bush.   Called "Wind
up Jack" in Shropshire.   It is the closing game of any playtime, and was played before "breaking-up" at a boys' school
at Shrewsbury, 1850–56.   The players form a line hand in
hand, the tallest at one end, who stands still; the rest walk
round and round him or her, saying, "Wind up Jack!   Wind
up Jack!" (or at Ellesmere, "Roll up the tobacco-box"), till
"Jack" is completely imprisoned.   They then "jog up and
down," crying, "A bundle o' rags, a bundle o' rags!"—Berrington, Ellesmere (*Shropshire Folk-lore*, p. 521).

In Scotland the game is known as "Row-chow-Tobacco;"
a long chain of boys hold each other by the hands: they have
one standing steadily at one of the extremities, who is called
the *Pin*.   Round him the rest coil like a watch chain round
the cylinder, till the act of winding is completed.   A clamorous

noise succeeds, in which the cry Row-chow-Tobacco prevails; after giving and receiving the *fraternal hug*, they disperse, and afterwards renew the process. In West of Scotland, it is Rowity-chow-o'-Tobacco, pronounced, *rowity-chowity-bacco*, and as the first syllable of each word is shouted, another hug or squeeze is given. The game is not so common as formerly. The same game is played in West Cornwall by Sunday-school children at their out-of-door treats, and is called "Roll Tobacco."

It is known as "The Old Oak Tree" in Lincoln, Kelsey, and Winterton, and is played in the same manner. When coiling round, the children sing—

> Round and round the old oak tree :
> I love the girls and the girls love me.

When they have twisted into a closely-packed crowd they dance up and down, tumbling on each other, crying—

> A bottle of rags, a bottle of rags.

In the Anderby and Nottinghamshire version of the game the children often sing—

> The old oak tree grows thicker and thicker every Monday
> morning.   —Miss M. Peacock.

In Mid-Cornwall, in the second week in June, at St. Roche, and in one or two adjacent parishes, a curious dance is performed at the annual "feasts." It enjoys the rather undignified name of "Snails Creep," but would be more properly called the "Serpent's Coil." The following is scarcely a perfect description of it :—"The young people being all assembled in a large meadow, the village band strikes up a simple but lively air and marches forward, followed by the whole assemblage, leading hand-in-hand (or more closely linked in case of engaged couples), the whole keeping time to the tune with a lively step. The band, or head of the serpent, keeps marching in an ever-narrowing circle, whilst its train of dancing followers becomes coiled round it in circle after circle. It is now that the most interesting part of the dance commences, for the band, taking a sharp turn about, begins to retrace the circle, still followed as before, and a number of young men, with long leafy branches in their hands as standards, direct this counter movement with almost military precision."—W. C. Wade (*Western Antiquary*, April 1881).

From this description of the "Snail Creep," it is not difficult to arrive at an origin for the game. It has evidently arisen from a custom of performing some religious observance, such as encircling sacred trees or stones, accompanied by song and dance. "On May Day, in Ireland, all the young men and maidens hold hands and dance in a circle round a tree hung with ribbons and garlands, or round a bonfire, moving in curves from right to left, as if imitating the windings of a serpent."— Wilde (*Ancient Cures, Charms, and Usages of Ireland*, 106).

It is easy to conjecture how the idea of "winding up a watch," or "rolling tobacco," would come in, and be thought the origin of the game from the similarity of action; but it is, I think, evident that this is not the case, from the words "a bundle o' rags," the mention of trees, and the "jogging" up and down, to say nothing of the existence of customs in Ireland and Wales similar to that of "Snail Creep." It is noticeable, too, that some of these games should be connected with trees, and that, in the "Snail Creep" dance the young men should carry branches of trees with them.

See "Bulliheisle," "Eller Tree."

Wind, The

I. The wind, the wind, the wind blows high,
The rain comes pouring from the sky;
Miss So-and-So says she'd die
For the sake of the old man's eye.
She is handsome, she is pretty,
She is the lass of the golden city;
She goes courting one, two, three,
Please to tell me who they be.
A. B. says he loves her,
All the boys are fighting for her,
Let the boys say what they will
A. B. has got her still.
—Forest of Dean, Gloucestershire (Miss Matthews).

II. The wind, wind blows, and the rain, rain goes,
And the clouds come gathering from the sky!

Annie Dingley's very, very pretty,
She is a girl of a noble city ;
She's the girl of one, two, three,
Pray come tell me whose she'll be.

Johnny Tildersley says he loves her,
All the boys are fighting for her,
All the girls think nothing of her.
Let the boys say what they will,
Johnny Tildersley's got her still.

He takes her by the lily-white hand
   And leads her over the water,
Gives her kisses one, two, three,
   Mrs. *Dingley's* daughter !
—Berrington, Eccleshall (*Shropshire Folk-lore*, p. 510).

III.   When the wind blows high,
When the wind blows high,
The rain comes peltering from the sky.
She is handsome, she is pretty,
She is the girl in all the city.
She [He ?] comes courting one, two, three,
Pray you tell me who she be.
I love her, I love her,
All the boys are fighting for her.
Let them all say what they will,
I shall love her always still.
She pulled off her gloves to show me her ring,
To-morrow, to-morrow, the wedding bells ring.
     —Cowes, Isle of Wight (Miss E. Smith).

IV.   The wind, the wind, the wind blows high,
The rain comes falling from the sky.
She is handsome, she is pretty,
She is the girl of London city.
She goes a courting one, two, three,
Please will you tell me who is he ?
[Boy's name] says he loves her.
All the boys are fighting for her.
Let the boys do what they will,

[Boy's name] has got her still.
He knocks at the knocker and he rings at the bell,
Please, Mrs. ——, is your daughter in ?
She's neither ways in, she's neither ways out,
She's in the back parlour walking about.
Out she came as white as snow,
With a rose in her breast as soft as silk.
Please, my dear, will you have a drop of this ?
No, my dear, I'd rather have a kiss.

       —Settle, Yorks. (Rev. W. G. Sykes).

V. The wind, the wind, the wind blows high,
The rain comes sparkling from the sky,
[A girl's name] says she'll die
For a lad with a rolling eye.
She is handsome, she is pretty,
She is the flower of the golden city.
She's got lovers one, two, three.
Come, pray, and tell me who they be.
[A boy's name] says he'll have her,
Some one else is waiting for her.
Lash the whip and away we go
To see Newcastle races, oh.

       —Tyrie (Rev. W. Gregor).

[Another version after—
   —— says he'll have her,
is—
   In his bosom he will clap her.]
[Another one after—
   She has got lovers one, two, three.
continues—
   Wait till [a boy's name] grows some bigger,
   He will ride her in his giggie.
   Lash your whip and away you go
   To see Newcastle races, O !]

       —Pittulie (Rev. W. Gregor).

[And another version gives—
   —— says she'll die
   For the want of the golden eye.]

       —Fochabers (Rev. W. Gregor).

VI. The wind blows high, and the wind blows low,
The snow comes scattering down below.
Is not —— very very pretty ?
She is the flower of one, two, three.
Please to tell me who is he.
—— says he loves her,
All the boys are fighting for her.
Let the boys say what they will,
—— loves her still.   —Perth (Rev. W. Gregor).

A ring is formed by the children joining hands, one player standing in the centre. When asked, "Please tell me who they be," the girl in the middle gives the name or initials of a boy in the ring (or *vice versa*). The ring then sings the rest of the words, and the boy who was named goes into the centre. This is the Forest of Dean way of playing. In the Shropshire game, at the end of the first verse the girl in the centre beckons one from the ring, or one volunteers to go into the centre ; the ring continues singing, and at the end the two children kiss ; the first one joins the ring, and the other chooses in his turn. The other versions are played in the same way.

Northall (*English Folk-Rhymes*, p. 380) gives a version from Warwickshire very similar.

Wink-egg

Elworthy (*West Somerset Words*) says—When a nest is found boys shout, "Let's play 'Wink-egg.'" An egg is placed on the ground, and a boy goes back three paces from it, holding a stick in his hand ; he then shuts his eyes, and takes two paces towards the egg and strikes a blow on the ground with the stick—the object being to break the egg. If he misses, another tries, and so on until all the eggs are smashed. In Cornwall it is called "Winky-eye," and is played in the spring. An egg taken from a bird's nest is placed on the ground, at some distance off—the number of paces having been previously fixed. Blindfolded, one after the other, the players attempt with a stick to hit and break it.—*Folk-lore Journal*, v. 61.

See "Blind Man's Stan."

Witch, The

This game is played by nine children. One is chosen as Mother, seven are chosen for her children, and the other is a Witch. The Mother and Witch stand opposite the seven children. The *Mother* advances and names the children by the days of the week, saying—

> Sunday, take care of Monday,
> Monday, take care of Tuesday,
> Tuesday, take care of Wednesday,
> Wednesday, take care of Thursday,
> Thursday, take care of Friday,
> Friday, take care of Saturday.

Take care the Old Witch does not catch you, and I'll bring you something nice.

The Mother then goes away, and the Witch advances saying—

Sunday, your mother sent me for your best bonnet, she wants to get one like it for Monday. It is up in the top long drawer, fetch it quick.

Sunday goes away, and the Witch then seizes Saturday and runs off with her.

The Mother re-enters, and names the children again, Sunday, Monday, Tuesday, Wednesday, Thursday, Friday, misses Saturday, and says—

> Where's Saturday ?

The children all cry and say—

> The Old Witch has got her.

This part is then repeated until the Witch has taken all the children and put them in a corner one by one, and stands in front to guard them. The Mother sets out to find the children, she sees the Old Witch, and says to her—

Have you seen my children ?

Witch. Yes, I saw them walking down High Street.

Mother then goes away, does not find them, and comes back asking—

Have you seen my children ?

W. Yes, I saw them going to school.

Mother then goes away, does not find them, and comes back asking—

Have you seen my children?

W. Yes, they are gone to church.

Mother again goes away, does not find them, and comes back asking—

Have you seen my children?

W. They are having dinner—you can't see them.

Mother again goes away, does not find them, and comes back asking—

Have you seen my children?

W. They are in bed.

M. Can't I go up and see them?

W. Your shoes are too dirty.

M. Can't I take them off?

W. Your stockings are too dirty.

M. Can't I take them off?

W. Your feet are too dirty.

M. Can't I cut them off?

W. The blood would run on the floor.

M. Can't I wrap them up in a blanket?

W. The fleas would hop out.

M. Can't I wrap them up in a sheet?

W. The sheet is too white.

M. Can't I ride up in a carriage?

W. You would break the stairs down.

The children then burst out from behind the Witch and they and the Mother run after her, crying out, "Burn the Old Witch." They continue chasing the Witch till she is caught, and the child who succeeds in catching her, takes the part of the Witch in the next game.—Dartmouth (Miss Kimber).

The children choose from their party an Old Witch (who is supposed to hide herself) and a Mother. The other players are the daughters, and are called by the names of the week. The Mother says that she is going to market, and will bring home for each the thing that she most wishes for. Upon this they all name something. Then, after telling them upon no account to allow any one to come into the house, she gives her children in charge of her eldest daughter, Sunday, and goes away. In a moment, the Witch makes her appearance, and asks to borrow some trifle.

Sunday at first refuses, but, after a short parley, goes into the next room to fetch the required article. In her absence the Witch steals the youngest of the children (Saturday), and runs off with her. Sunday, on her return, seeing that the Witch has left, thinks there must be something wrong, and counts the children, saying, "Monday, Tuesday," &c., until she comes to Saturday, who is missing. She then pretends to cry, wrings her hands, and sobs out—"Mother will beat me when she comes home."

On the Mother's return, she, too, counts the children, and finding Saturday gone, asks Sunday where she is. Sunday answers, "Oh, mother! an Old Witch called, and asked to borrow ——, and, whilst I was fetching it, she ran off with Saturday." The Mother scolds and beats her, tells her to be more careful in the future, and again sets off for the market. This is repeated until all the children but Sunday have been stolen. Then the Mother and Sunday, hand in hand, go off to search for them. They meet the Old Witch, who has them all crouching down in a line behind her.

Mother. Have you seen my children?

Old Witch. Yes! I think by Eastgate.

The Mother and Sunday retire, as if to go there, but, not finding them, again return to the Witch, who this time sends them to Westgate, then to Southgate and Northgate. At last one of the children pops her head up over the Witch's shoulder, and cries out, "Here we are, Mother." Then follows this dialogue :—

M. I see my children, may I go in?

O. W. No! your boots are too dirty.

M. I will take them off.

O. W. Your stockings are too dirty.

M. I will take them off.

O. W. Your feet are too dirty.

M. I will cut them off.

O. W. Then the blood will stream over the floor.

The Mother at this loses patience, and pushes her way in, the Witch trying in vain to keep her out. She, with all her children, then chase the Witch until they catch her; when they pretend to bind her hand and foot, put her on a pile, and burn her, the children fanning the imaginary flames with their pinafores. Sometimes the dialogue after "Here we are, mother," is omitted, and the Witch is at once chased.—Cornwall (*Folklore Journal*, v. 53–54).

One child represents an old woman who is blind, and has eight children. She says she is going to market, and bids her eldest daughter let no one into the house in her absence. The eldest daughter promises. Then a second old woman knocks, and bribes the daughter, by the promise of a gay ribbon, to give her a light. Whilst the daughter is getting the light, the Witch steals a child and carries it off.

The daughter comes back, and makes all the other children promise not to tell their Mother. The Mother returns and says: "Are all the children safe?"

The daughter says, "Yes." "Then let me count them." The children stand in a row, and the Mother counts by placing her hands alternately on their heads. The eldest daughter runs round to the bottom of the row, and so is counted twice.

This is repeated until all the children are gone. At the end the eldest daughter runs away, and the Mother finds all her children gone. Then the Witch asks the old woman to dinner, and the children, who have covered their faces, are served up as beef, mutton, lamb, &c. Finally they throw off their coverings and a general scrimmage takes place.—London (Miss Dendy).

At Deptford the game is played in the same way, and the dialogue is similar to the Cornish version, then follows—

> I'll ride in a pan.
> That will do.

The Mother gets inside to her children and says to them in turn, "Poke out your tongue, you're one of mine," then they run away home.—Deptford (Miss Chase).

In another Deptford version the children are named for days of the week, the Mother goes out, and the Witch calls and asks—

> Please you, give me a match.

The minder goes upstairs, and the Witch carries a child off.
The Mother comes home, misses child, and asks—

>Where's Monday?
>She's gone to her grandma.

Mother pretends to look for her, and says—

>She ain't there.
>She's gone to her aunt's.

Children own at last—

>The bonny Old Witch has took her!

The Mother beats the Daughter who has been so careless,
goes to Witch, and says—

>Have you any blocks of wood?
>No.
>Can I come in and see?
>No, your boots are too dirty, &c.
>[Same as previous versions.]

A number of girls stand in a line. Three girls out of the
number represent Mother, Jack, and Daughter. The Mother
leaves her children in charge of her Daughter, counts them,
and says the following:—

>I am going into the garden to gather some rue,
>And mind old Jack-daw don't get you,
>Especially you my daughter Sue,
>I'll beat you till you're black and blue.

While the Mother is gone Jack comes and asks for a match;
he takes a child and hides her up. The Mother comes back,
counts her children, and finds one missing. Then she asks
where she is, and the Daughter says that Jack has got her.
The Mother beats the Daughter, and leaves them again, saying
the same words as before, until all the children have gone.—
Ipswich (*Suffolk Folk-lore*, p. 62).

>I'll charge my children every one
>To keep good house till I come home,
>Especially you my daughter Sue,
>Or else I'll beat you black and blue.
>>—Hersham, Surrey (*Folk-lore Record*, v. 88).

Halliwell gives a version of this which he calls the game of
the "Gipsy." He gives no dialogue, but his game begins by

the Mother saying some lines to the eldest daughter, which are almost identical with those given from Hersham, Surrey. Mr. Newell gives some interesting American versions.

This game appears in the versions given above to be a child-stealing game, and it may originate from this being a common practice some years ago, but it will be found on comparison to be so much like "Mother, mother, the pot boils over" (vol. i. p. 396) that it is more probable that this is the same game, having lost the important element of the "giving of fire," or a "light from the fire" out of the house, so soon as the idea that doing this put the inhabitants of the house into the power of the receiver or some evil spirit had become lost as a popular belief. "Matches" being asked for and a "light" confirms this. It will be seen that a Witch or evilly-disposed person is dreaded by the Mother, the eldest Daughter being specially charged to keep a good look-out. The naming of the children after the days of the week, the counting of them by the Mother, and the artifice of the eldest Daughter, in the London version, who gets counted twice, are archaic points. The discovery by tasting of the children by their Mother, and their suggested revival; the catching and "burning" of the Witch in the Dartmouth and Cornish games, are incidents familiar to us from nursery tales and from the trials of people condemned for witchcraft. Of the Cornish version it is said that "it has descended from generation to generation."

Mr. Newell's versions tend, I think, to strengthen my suggestion in "Mother, the pot boils over," that the "fire" custom alluded to is the origin of that game and this. The fire incident has been forgotten, and the game therefore developed into a child-stealing or gipsy game.

See "Mother, Mother."

Witte-Witte-Way

A game among boys, which I do not remember in the South.—Brockett's *North Country Words*. Probably the same as "Whiddy," which see.

Wolf

I.   Sheep, sheep, come home !
    We dare not.

What are you frightened of?
The wolf.
The wolf has gone home for seven days,
Sheep, sheep, come home.

—Settle, Yorks. (Rev. W. S. Sykes).

II. Sheep, sheep, come home!
I'm afraid.
What of?
The wolf.
The wolf's gone into Derbyshire,
And won't be back till six o'clock.
Sheep, sheep, come home.

—Hanbury, Staffordshire (Miss Edith Hollis).

III. Sheep, sheep, go out!
I'm afraid.
What you're 'fraid of?
Wolf.
Wolf has gone to Devonshire;
Won't be back for seven year.
Sheep, sheep, go out!

—Hurstmonceux, Sussex, as played about forty
years ago (M ss E. Chase).

IV. Sheep, sheep, come home!
I'm afraid.
What of?
The wolf.
The wolf's gone to Devonshire,
And won't be back for seven year.
Sheep, sheep, come home.

Anderby (Miss M. Peacock), Barnes (A. B. Gomme).

V., VI. Won't be back for eleven year.

Nottinghamshire (Miss M. Peacock).
Marlborough, Wilts (H. S. May).

(*b*) One player acts as Shepherd, and stands at one side of the playground or field; another acts as Wolf. He crouches in one corner, or behind a post or tree. The other players are sheep, and stand close together on the opposite side of the ground to the Shepherd. The Shepherd advances and calls the sheep.

At the end of the dialogue the sheep run across to the Shepherd
and the Wolf pounces out, chases, and tries to catch them.
Whoever he catches has to stand aside until all are caught.
The game is played in this way in all versions sent me except
Hurstmonceux, where there is the following addition:—The
Wolf chases until he has caught all the sheep, and put them in
his den.   He then pretends to taste them, and sets them aside
as needing more salt.   The Shepherd or Mother comes after
them, and the sheep cover their heads with their aprons.   The
Mother guesses the name of each child, saying, "This is my
daughter ——.   Run away home!" until she has freed them all.

Versions of this game, almost identical with the Anderby
version, have been collected from Sporle, Norfolk (Miss Matthews); Crockham Hill, Kent (Miss E. Chase); Hersham,
Surrey (*Folk-lore Record*, v. p. 88); Marlborough, Wilts (H. S.
May); Ash and Barnes, Surrey (A. B. Gomme).   In Nottinghamshire, Derbyshire is the place the wolf is said to have gone
to.   Mr M. L. Rouse sends the following fuller description of
the game as played at Woolpit, near Haughley, Suffolk, which
gives, I think, the clue to the earlier idea of the game:—

The game was played out of doors in a meadow.   Two long
parallel lines were drawn about fifty yards apart, forming bases
behind them.   Two boys stood some distance apart between
the bases, and the rest of the players all stood within one base.
One of the two boys in the centre acting as decoy cried "Sheep,
sheep, come home!"   The sheep represented by the boys in
the base cried back, "We can't, we're afraid of the Wolf."   The
decoy then said—

> The wolf's gone to Devonshire,
> And won't be back for seven year.
> Sheep, sheep, come home.

The sheep then made rushes from different points, and tried
to get across to the other base.   The other player in the centre
tried to catch the sheep as they ran.   Those caught joined
the side of the wolf, and caught others in their turn.

It appears clear that the "Decoy" is the correct character
in this game instead of a "shepherd" or "master," as now given.

The decoy is evidently assuming the character and voice of the shepherd, or shepherd's dog, to induce the sheep to leave the fold where they are protected, in order to pounce upon them as they endeavour to go in the direction the voice calls them.   The game owes its origin to times and places, when wolves were prowling about at night, and sheep were penned and protected against them by shepherds and watch-dogs.

Wolf and the Lamb, The

Two are chosen—one to represent the wolf and the other the lamb.   The other players join hands and form a circle round the lamb.   The wolf tries to break through the circle, and carry off the lamb.   Those in the circle do all they can to prevent the wolf from entering within the circle.   If he manages to enter the circle and seize the lamb, then other two are chosen, and the same process is gone through till all have got a chance of being the lamb and wolf.   This game evidently represents a lamb enclosed in a fold, and the attempts of a wolf to break through and carry it off.

—Fraserburgh, Aberdeen, *April* 14, 1892 (Rev. W. Gregor).

Would you know how doth the Peasant

—Monton, Lancashire (Miss Dendy).

I.   Would you know how doth the peasant ?
Would you know how doth the peasant ?
Would you know how doth the peasant
Sow his barley and wheat !

· And it's so, so, doth the peasant,
And it's so, so, doth the peasant,
And it's so, so, doth the peasant
Sow his barley and wheat !

Would you know how doth the peasant, &c.,
Reap his barley and wheat ?

It is so, so, doth the peasant, &c.,
Reap his barley and wheat!

Would you know how doth the peasant, &c.,
Thresh his barley and wheat?

It is so, so, doth the peasant, &c.,
Thresh his barley and wheat!

Would you know how doth the peasant, &c.,
When the seed time is o'er?

It is so, so, doth the peasant, &c.,
When the seed time is o'er!

Would you know how doth the peasant, &c.,
When his labour is done?

It is so, so, doth the peasant, &c.,
When his labour is done!

And it's so, so, doth the peasant,
And it's so, so, doth the peasant,
And it's so, so, doth the peasant,
When his labour is o'er.

—Monton, Lancashire (Miss Dendy).

II. It is so, so, does the peasant [or, farmer],
It is so, so, does the peasant,
It is so, so, does the peasant,
When sowing times come.

It is so, so, does the peasant, &c.,
When reaping time comes.
It is so, so does the peasant, &c.,
When his threshing times comes.

It is so, so, does the peasant, &c.,
When the hunting's begun.
It is so, so does the peasant, &c.,
When the day's work is done.

—Frodingham, Lincoln and Notts (Miss M. Peacock).

(c) The leader of this game stands in the middle, the players stand in a ring round him ; when there are a sufficient number of players, several rings are formed one within the other, the smallest children in the inner ring. The different rings move in alternate directions when dancing round. All the children sing the words of each verse and dance round. They unclasp hands at the end of each alternate verse, and suit their actions to the words sung. At the end of the first verse they stand still, crook their arms as if holding a basket, and imitate action of sowing while they sing the second verse; they then all dance round while they sing the third, then stand still again and imitate reaping while they sing the fourth time. Then again dance and sing, stand still and imitate "thrashing" of barley and wheat; after "seed time is o'er," they drop on one knee and lift one hand as if in prayer, again dancing round and singing. Then they kneel on one knee, put their hands together, lay their left cheek on them, and close their eyes as if asleep; while singing, "when his labour is o'er," at the last verse, they all march round, clapping hands in time.

This is the Monton game. The Frodingham game is played in the same way, except that the children walk round in a circle, one behind another, when they sing and imitate the actions they mention. "When the hunting's begun" they all run about as if on horseback; "when the day's work is done," they all kneel on one knee and rest their heads on their hands.

This game is evidently a survival of the custom of dancing, and of imitating the actions necessary for the sowing and reaping of grain which were customary at one time. Miss Dendy says—"It is an undoubtedly old Lancashire game. It is sometimes played by as many as a hundred players, and is then very pretty. The method of playing varies slightly, but it is generally as described above." The fact that this game was played by such a large number of young people together, points conclusively to a time when it was a customary thing for all the people in one village to play this game as a kind of religious observance, to bring a blessing on the work of the season, believing that by doing so, they caused the crops to grow better and produce grain in abundance.

See "Oats and Beans and Barley."

ADDENDA

A' the Birdies. [See "All the Birds," vol. i. p. 2; "Oranges and Lemons," vol. ii. pp. 25–35.]

> A' the birdies i' the air
> Tick tae to my tail.

A contest game of the oranges and lemons class. Two players, who hold hands and form the arch, call out the formula, and the other players, who are running about indifferently, go one by one to them and decide, when asked, which side they will favour, and stand behind one or the other.

After the tug the side which has lost is called "Rotten eggs, rotten eggs."—Aberdeen (Rev. Dr. Gregor).

All the Boys. [Vol. i. pp. 2–6.]

Two versions of this game, one from Howth and another from St. Andrews, sent me by Miss H. E. Harvey, do not differ sufficiently from the versions i. and ii. printed as above to be given here in full.

The St. Andrews game, after the line,

> "I love you, and you love me"

(as printed in vol. i. version ii.), continues—

> When we get married, I hope you will agree,
> I'll buy the chest of drawers, you'll buy the cradle.
> Rock, rock, bubbly-jock,
> Send her upstairs, lay her in her bed,
> Send for the doctor before she is dead.
> In comes the doctor and out goes the clerk,
> In comes the mannie with the sugarally hat.
> Oh, says the doctor, what's the matter here?
> Oh, says Johnny, I'm like to lose my dear.
> Oh, says the doctor, nae fear o' that.

American Post.

One player of a party acts as post and leaves the room. When he is outside he knocks at the door. Another player, who is the doorkeeper (inside), calls out, "Who's there?" The reply is, "American post." "What with?" "A letter." "For whom?" The name of one of the players in the room is given by the post. The one named then must go outside, and kiss the post, and in turn becomes post.—Fraserburgh (Rev. Dr. Gregor).

This, sometimes called "Postman," is now more generally played as a penalty when forfeits are being performed. The player whose penalty it is, is the first one to be "post." Postage is demanded, the amount being paid by kisses.

As I was Walking.

The players, usually girls, stand in line up to a wall. One in front sings, going backwards and forwards.

As I was walking down a hill, down a hill, down a hill,
As I was walking down a hill,
Upon a frosty morning.
Who do you think I met coming down, coming down, &c.,
Who do you think I met, &c.

She then chooses one from the line and both sing:—

I met my true love coming down, &c.
He gave me kisses, one, two, three (clap hands),
Upon a frosty morning.

—Cullen (Rev. Dr. Gregor).

Auld Grannie. [A version of "Hen and Chickens," vol. i. pp. 201, 202.]

Here a variation of dialogue occurs. The game is played as previous Hen and Chicken games. The Hen says—

What are ye scrapin' for?

Auld grannie says—

A darning needle?
What are ye going to do with the darning needle?
Mak a poke.
What to do with the poke?

To gang to the peat moss to get some peats.
What for?
To make a fire, to make some tea, to pour over your wee
    chickens.

Auld grannie rushes at them, and pretends to throw the water
over them. When she has caught some players, and the sides
are about equal in strength, the game ends in a tug of war.—
Dalry, Galloway (J. G. Carter.)

Another, called "Grannie's Needle," has a slightly different
parley.

What are you looking for, granny?
My granny's needle.
What are you going to do with the needle, granny?
To make a bag.
And what are you going to do with the bag, granny?
To gather sand.
What are you going to do with the sand, granny?
To sharpen knives.
And what are you going to do with the knives, granny?
To cut off your chickens' heads.
                              —Belfast (W. H. Patterson).

Ball. [Pots, vol. ii. p. 64.]

1. Throw the ball up against a wall three times and catch it.
2. Throw it up and clap hands three times before catching it.
3. Throw it up and put your hands round in a circle.
4. Throw it up and clap your hands before and behind.
5. Throw it up and clap and touch your shoulder.
6. Throw it up and clap and touch your other shoulder.
7. Throw it up three times with your right hand and catch
it with your right.
8. Throw it up with your left and catch it with your left.
9. Throw it up with your right and catch it with your right,
dog snack fashion (*i.e.* as a dog snacks, knuckles up).
10. Throw it up with your left and catch it with your left
(dog snack).
11. Throw it up and clap and touch your knee.
12. Throw it up and clap and touch your other knee.

13. Throw it up and turn round.

These actions should each be performed three times.—
Laurieston School, Kircudbrightshire (J. Lawson).

This is a more complete version of " Pots."

Another game is—

One girl takes a ball, strikes it on the ground, and keeps
pushing it down with her hand. While she is doing this, the
other players stand beside her, and keeping unison with the
ball, repeat—

> Game, game, ba' ba',
> Twenty lasses in a raw,
> Nae a lad amon them a'
> Bits game, game, ba', ba'.

If the girl keeps the ball dancing up and down—"stottin'"
during the time the words are being repeated, it counts one
game gained. She goes on "stottin'" the ball, and the others
go on repeating the words till she allows the ball to escape
from her control.—Fraserburgh (Rev. Dr. Gregor); Dalry, Galloway (J. G. Carter).

Another rhyme for a ball game is—

> Little wee laddie, foo's yer daidie ?
> New come oot o' a basket shadie.
> A basket shadie's ower full,
> New come oot o' a roarin' bull.
> A roarin bull's ower fat,
> New come oot o' a gentleman's hat.
> A gentleman's hat's ower fine,
> New come oot o' a bottle o' wine.
> A bottle o' wine is ower reid,
> New come oot o' a crust o' breid.
> A crust o' breid is ower broon,
> New come oot o' a half-a-croon.
> A half-a-croon is ower little,
> New come oot o' a weaver's shuttle.
> A weaver's shuttle's ower holey,
> New come oot o' a paint pottie,
> Game, game, game, game, game !
>
> —Rev. Dr. Gregor.

Bannockburn [See Fool, Fool, come to school, vol. i. p. 132.]

Played as "Fool" with these differences. The namer cries to the fool in the same formula as the Sussex version (vol. i. p. 133). The fool, called here "Bannockburn," says, "Are ye it?" to each player pointing to them in turn. When she points at the correct one that player runs off. Bannockburn runs after and tries to catch her. If the first runner can get back into the row untouched she gets renamed, if caught she has to take Bannockburn's place.

During the naming, Bannockburn tries to overhear the names given. But when noticed coming near, those being named, cry "Bannockburn away dune the sea."—Dalry, Galloway (J. G. Carter).

Black Doggie [see Drop Handkerchief, vol. i. 109-112.]

A form of Drop Handkerchief differing from those versions previously given.

The players join hands, form a circle and stretch out as far as each one's arms will allow. One player is outside the ring. When she sees they can stretch no further she cries out "Break," when they all loose hands and stand as far apart as possible. The player outside then goes round the ring singing, "I have a black doggie, but it winna' bite you, nor you, nor you," until she comes to one whom she chooses; she then throws the handkerchief down on the ground behind this one quietly. If this player does not notice the handkerchief, not one in the circle must tell her, or they are "out." The player who dropped the handkerchief walks round until she comes again to the one behind whom she dropped it. She picks it up and tells her she is "burnt." Then this player has to stoop down on her knees and is out of the game. Should the selected player notice the handkerchief, she picks it up and pursues the other round and through the ring, following wherever the first one leads until she catches her; they then change places; should she not follow the exact way the first player went, she too is out and must go down on her knees.—Rosehearty (Rev. Dr. Gregor).

Another version from Fraserburgh says that the players may

either join hands in a ring or sit upon the ground on their knees. The outside player goes round the circle three times, first saying "Black Doggie winna tack you, nor you." Then she goes round again and drops the handkerchief behind any one she pleases. She then runs and is pursued until caught, the other child following Black Doggie in and out wherever she goes.

Bonnet Ridgie. ["Scots and English," vol. ii. pp. 183–184.]

Players are chosen alternately by two chiefs. The line is drawn between the two sides, and the caps of each side are placed on the ground at each of the ends. When the two sides are ranged, the players try to catch and pull each other across the line. If one is pulled across he is called a "slink," and must stand till he is set at liberty by one of his own side crossing the line and touching him. If this one manages to touch him before he is crowned, *i.e.*, has the crown of his head touched by one of his opponents, and if he is able to regain his own side before the same operation takes place, both are free. Each player watches an opportunity to gather up the caps of the opposing side. If one is clever and swift enough to reach the caps and gather them all before he is crowned, his side wins.—Dyke School (Rev. Dr. Gregor.)

Button, The. ["Diamond Ring," vol. i. p. 96 ; "Forfeits," p. 137 ; "Wads and the Wears," vol. i. pp. 327–8.]

Played as "Diamond Ring," except that all sit round the fire, one man takes a button, puts it between his two hands, and goes round to each of the other players, who have their two hands held out, palms together, saying, "Don't tell what you got," and quietly dropping the button into one player's hands. He then asks the first man, saying, "Who has the button?" One player is named. The master of the game says then "What forfeit will you give me that he has it?" The player gives a forfeit. So on all round, every one guessing and giving a forfeit (including he who holds the button, who, of course, keeps his secret). When all the forfeits are in the master says, "Button, button, show, and let all fools know;" then those who

have guessed right receive back their forfeits. The holder of
the button then kneels down to deliver sentences on the others.
The master takes a forfeit and holds it over the kneeler's
head, saying, "Fine, fine, superfine, what's the owner of this
fine thing of [gentleman's or lady's] wear to do?" The man
kneeling gives a sentence, such as—to take the broom, ride
it three times round the room, and each time kiss the crook
hanging in the chimney—and so on.

If a man refuses to perform his sentence he is made to kneel
down, and everything that can be got hold of is piled on his
back.—Kiltubbrid, Co. Leitrim (L. L. Duncan).

Canlie. [See "Tom Tiddler's Ground," vol. ii. p. 298.]
Name for "Friar's Ground," in Co. Cork. "Canlie" is
the Friar. The game is played as at Chirbury.—Co. Cork
(Mrs. B. B. Greene).

Carry my Lady to London. [Vol. i. p. 59.]

> Carry a lady to London town,
> London town, London town ;
> London town's a bonny place,
> It's a' covered o'er in gold and lace.

Or—

> Carry a lady to London town,
> London town, London town ;
> Carry a lady to London town
> Upon a summer's day.

Another rhyme for "Carry my Lady to London," and played
in the same way.—Galloway, N. B. (J. G. Carter).

Cat and Dog Hole. [Vol. i. p. 63 ; "Tip-cat," vol. ii. p. 294.]
Two versions of this, differing somewhat from those given
previously.

(1.) Played by two players. A hole is dug in the ground,
and one player with a "catch-brod" stands in a stooping
attitude in front of it, about a foot and a-half away, placing
one end of the "catch-brod" on the ground. The other player
goes to a distance of some yards, to a fixed point called "the

stance." From here he throws a ball, intending to land it in the hole. The other player's object is to prevent this by hitting it away with his "catch-brod." If the bowler succeeds they change places.

(2.) This also is played by two players, and in the same way, except that a stone is substituted for the hole, and the bowler's object is to strike the stone with the ball. Sometimes it is played with three players, then running is allowed. When the ball is hit the batter tries to run to the "stance" and back, the bowler or the third player then tries to hit the "stance" with the ball while the batter is away making the run. If the third player can catch the ball before it touches the ground he tries to hit the stone with it, thus sending the batter out.—Keith (Rev. Dr. Gregor).

Catch the Salmond.

Two boys take each the end of a piece of rope, and give chase to a third till they contrive to get the rope round him. They then pull him hither and thither in all directions. —Banchory (Rev. Dr. Gregor).

Evidently an imitation of net-fishing.

Chicken come Clock [See "Fox and Goose," "Hen and Chicken," vol. i. pp. 139–141, 201; vol. ii. p. 404.]

The children, boys and girls, squat down and take hold of hands, going round, and saying—

> Chicken come clock around the rock,
> Looram, lorram, lumber lock.
> Five mile and one o'clock,
> Now the thief is coming.
> In comes Tod with his long rod,
> And vanishes all from victim vad.
> It is, it was, it must be done,
> Tiddlum, toddlum, twenty-one.
> Johnny, my dear, will you give me the loan of your spear,
> Till I fight for one of those Kildares,
> With a hickety, pickety pie.

At these words one lad, who has been hiding behind a tree, runs in to catch one of the chickens. As the rhyme is finished, they all run, and the fox tries to catch one, another player, the old hen, trying to stop him, the chickens all taking hold of her by the tail.

The fox has to keep on his hands and feet, and the old hen has to keep "clocking" on her "hunkers."

Some of the children substitute these words for the latter part of the above :—

> The crow's awake, the kite's asleep,
> It's time for my poor chickens
> To get a bit of something to eat—
> What time is it, old granny ?
> —Kiltubbrid, Co. Leitrim (L. L. Duncan).

Mr. Duncan says this game has almost died out, and the people were rather hazy about the words they used to say.

Chippings, or Cheapings. [See "Tops," vol. ii. pp. 229–303.]

A game with peg tops played by two or more boys. A large button, from which the shank has been removed, or a round piece of lead about the size of a penny, is placed on the ground between two agreed goals. The players divide into sides, each side tries to send the button to different goals, the tops are spun in the usual way, and then taken up on the hand while spinning, and allowed to revolve once round the palm of the hand, and then thrown on the ground on the button in such a way that the button is projected some distance along the ground. Then a boy on the opposite side spins his top and tries to hit the button in the opposite direction. This is continued alternately until one or other side succeeds in getting the button to the goal.—London Streets (A. B. Gomme).

Chucks. [Vol. i. p. 69 ; also "Five-stones," pp. 122–129, "Huckle-bones," pp. 239–240.]

A rhyme repeated while playing at "Chucks" with five small stones, lifting one each time.

> Sweep the floor, lift a chair,
> Sweep below it, and lay it down.

> Cream the milk, cream the milk,
> Quick, quick, quick,
> Spread a piece and butter on it thick, thick, thick.
> —Perth (Rev. Dr. Gregor).

Churning.

> Churn the butter-milk, quick, quick, quick,
> I owe my mother a pint of milk.

This game used to be played on the shore, just as the tide went out, when the feet sank easily into the sand. The children turned half-way round as they repeated the words.—Isle of Man (A. W. Moore).

Codham, or Cobhams. ["Tip it," vol. ii. p. 292.]

A game resembling "Tip it," and a better form of the game. The parties are decided by a toss up. The object is passed from hand to hand under the table, until the leader of the opposite side calls out "up" or "rise." When all the closed hands are on the table, the leader orders any hands off which he thinks do not contain the object. If the last hand left on the table contains the object the sides change places, if not the same sides repeat, twelve successful guesses making "game," each failure counting one to the opposite side. The game is called "Up Jenkins" in the North of Scotland. The words have to be called out when the hands are called to show. Another name is "Cudlums;" this word was called out when the leader pointed to the hand which he believed held the object.—Bedford (Mrs. A. C. Haddon).

Colley Ball. ["Monday," vol. i. p. 389.]

The same game as "Monday," with this difference. The player who first throws the ball against the wall calls out the name of the child he wishes to catch it, saying "A—— B——, no rakes, no better ball." If the ball goes on the ground the one called has to snatch the ball up and throw it at one of the retreating children. — Hemsby, Norfolk (Mrs. A. C. Haddon).

Also sent me from Isle of Man (A. W. Moore), where it is called "Hommer-the-let."

Dan'l my Man. ["Jack's Alive," vol. i. p. 257.]

A little slip of wood or straw is lit and blown out, and while it is red it is passed round from one to another, each man repeating as fast as he can—

> Dan'l, my man,
> If ye die in my han',
> The straddle and mat is sure to go on.

The man in whose hand the spark dies has to go down on his knees. A chair, or some other article, is held over him, and he has to guess what it is, the others crying out—

> Trum,[1] trum, what's over your head?

If he is wrong it is left on him and another article brought, and so on.—Kiltubbrid, Co. Leitrim (L. L. Duncan).

Deil amo' the Dishes, The. ["Ghost at the Well," vol. i. p. 149.]

One player acts as mother, and sends off one of the other players (her daughters) to take a message. She comes back, pretends to be frightened, and says she can't go, as there's something "chap, chap, chappin'." The mother sends another daughter with her this time, telling them "It's only your father's breeks, drap, drap, drappin'." These two return in the same way, saying again "There's something chap, chap, chappin'." Another daughter is now sent with the other two, the mother saying "Its only the ducks, quack, quack, quackin'." They all come back again more frightened saying the same thing. Then the mother and all the others go together to see what the matter is. They come upon another player who has been sitting apart making a noise with a stone. They all cry out "The deil's amo' the dishes," and there is a great chase.— Aberdeen (Rev. Dr. Gregor).

Dig for Silver.

> Dig for silver, dig for gold,
> Dig for the land that I was told.
> As I went down by the water side
> I met my lad with a tartan plaid.

---

[1] "Trum" is for the Irish "trom," = heavy.

My wee lad is a jolly sailor,
And shall be for evermore.
(Name of boy) took the notion
To go and sail on the ocean.
He took poor (name of girl) on his knee,
And sailed across Kilmarnock sea.
Stop your weeping, my dear ——,
He'll come back and marry you.
He will buy you beads and earrings,
He will buy you a diamond stone,
He will buy a horse to ride on,
When your true love is dead and gone.
What care I for the beads and earrings,
What care I for the diamond stone,
What care I for the horse to ride on,
When my true love is dead and gone.
—Laurieston School, Kircudbrightshire (J. Lawson).

Another version is—

Billy Johnston took a notion
For to go and sail the sea;
He has left his own true love
Weeping on the Greenock quay.
I will buy you beads and earrings,
I will buy you diamonds three,
I will buy you beads and earrings,
Bonny lassie, if you marry me.
What care I for beads and earrings,
What care I for diamonds three,
What care I for beads and earrings,
When my own true love is far from me.
—Perth (Rev. Dr. Gregor).

Compare with this "Keys of Heaven," p. 437, and "Paper of Pins," p. 450.

Dilsee Dollsie Dee. [See "Here's a Soldier," vol. i. p. 206, and "Three Dukes," vol. ii. pp. 233-255].

A ring is formed, one child standing in the middle, all sing the words—

Which of us all do you love best, do you love best, do you
    love best,
Which of us all do you love best, my dilsee dollsie dee.
Which of us all do you love best, my dilsee dollsie dofficer.
The child in the centre says—
You're all too black and ugly (three times), my dilsee
    dollsie dee,
You're all too black and ugly, my dilsee dollsie dofficer.
The first verse is repeated, and the child in the centre points
to one in the ring and says—
This is the one that I love best, that I love best, that I
    love best,
This is the one that I love best, my dilsee dollsie dee.
This is the one I love the best, my dilsee dollsie dofficer.
The centre child takes the one selected by the hand, and
they stand together in the centre, while the ring dances round
and sings—
Open the gates to let the bride out, to let the bride out, to
    let the bride out,
Open the gates to let the bride out, my dilsee dollsie dee.
Open the gates to let the bride out, my dilsee dollsie
    dofficer.
The children then unclasp hands, and the two children walk
out. Another child goes in the centre and the game is begun
again, and continued until the ring is too small for dancing
round. Sometimes, instead of this, the two children return
to the ring singing, "Open the gates and let the bride in," and
then they take places in the circle, while another goes in the
centre.—(Dr. A. C. Haddon.)

Doagan. An extraordinary game, which was played by
Manx children sixty years ago. A rude wooden representation
of the human form was fastened on a cross, and sticks were
thrown at it, just after the fashion of the modern "Aunt Sally."
But it is quite possible that this game, taken in connection with
the following very curious words which the children repeated
when throwing the sticks, is a survival of a more serious
function—

Shoh dhyt y Doagan.
"This to thee, the Doagan."
Cre dooyrt y Doagan ?
"What says the Doagan ?"
Dar y chrosh, dar y chron,
"Upon the cross, upon the block,"
Dar y maidjey beg, jeeragh ny cam,
"Upon the little staff, straight or crooked,"
Ayns y cheylley veg shid hoal,
"In the little wood over yonder."
My verrys oo yn kione jeh'n Doagan,
"If thou wilt give the head of the Doagan,"
Verym y kione jeeds er y hon.[1]
"I will give thy head for it."

Mr. Moore writes that Kelly, who gives these words in his Dictionary, says that Doagan was a play, and that it refers to the head of Dagon being broken off. Does he mean the Philistine god of that name ? As he is capable of seeing a reference to the god, Baal, in the Manx word for May-day, Boaldyv, it is quite possible that his imagination may lead him so far !—Isle of Man (A. W. Moore).

Down in Yonder Meadow. [Vol. i. p. 99; ii. p. 323; "All the Boys," i. 2–6.]

Down in yonder meadow where the green grass grows,
Where (name of girl) she bleaches her clothes ;
She sang, she sang, she sang so sweet,
She sang (name of boy) across the street.
He kissed her, he kissed her, he bought her a gown,
He bought her a gown and a guinea gold ring,
A guinea, a guinea, a guinea gold ring,
A feather for the church and a pea-brown hat.
Up the streets and down the streets the windows made of glass,
Oh, isn't (name of girl) a braw young lass.
But isn't (name of boy) as nice as she,
And when they get married I hope they will agree.

[1] Manx Society, vol. xiii. p. 63.

Agree, agree, I hope they will agree,
And when they get married I hope they will agree.
—Laurieston School, Kircudbrightshire (J. Lawson).

Down in yonder meadow where the green grass grows,
Where so and so (a girl's name) she bleaches her clothes ;
She sang, and she sang, and she sang so sweet,
Come over (a boy's name), come over, come over the street.
So and so (same girl's Christian name) made a pudding
    so nice and sweet,
So and so (same boy's Christian name) took a knife and
    tasted it.
Taste, love ; taste, love ; don't say no,
For the next Sabbath morning to church we must go.
Clean sheets and pillowslips, and blankets an' a',
A little baby on your knee, and that's the best of a'.
Heepie tarrie, heepie barrie, bo barrie grounds,
Bo barrie ground and a guinea gold ring,
A guinea gold ring and a peacock hat,
A cherry for the church and a feather at the back.
She paints her cheeks and she curls her hair,
And she kisses (boy's name) at the foot o' the stair.
—Fraserburgh (Rev. Dr. Gregor).

The above are played in the same way as previously described.

Another version, from Perth, says, after the line, " She sang, and she sang " (as above).

Come over the water, come over the street,
She baked him a dumpling, she baked it so sweet
That bonny (Billie Sanders) was fain for to eat, &c.

Down in the meadows where the green grass grows,
There's where my Nannie she sound her horn ;
She sound, she sound, she sound so sweet ;

Nannie made the puddin' so nice and so sweet,
Johnny took a knife and he taste a bit ;
Love, taste ; love, taste, and don't say nay,
For next Sunday mornin' is our weddin'-day.

Off wid the thimble and on wid the ring;
A weddin', a weddin', is goin' to begin.
O Nannie, O Nannie, O Nannie my joy,
Never be ashamed for to marry a boy!
For I am but a boy, and I'll soon be a man,
And I'll earn for my Nannie as soon as I can.
And every evenin' when he comes home,
He takes her for a walk on the Circular Road.
And every little girl that he sees passin' by,
He thinks 'tis his Nannie he has in his eye.
—Howth, Dublin (Miss H. G. Harvey).

Draw a Pail of Water. [Vol. i. pp. 100–107].
A lump of sugar,
Grind your mother's flour,
Three sacks an hour,
One in a rush, two in a crush,
Pray, old lady, creep under the bush (all jump round).
—Girton village, Cambridgeshire (Dr. A. C. Haddon).

Drop Handkerchief. [Vol. i. pp. 109–112; "Black Doggie," vol. ii. p. 407.]
As played at Fochabers the game varies slightly in the way it is played from those previously described. The words are—
"I dropt it, I dropt it, a king's copper next,
I sent a letter to my love, and on the way I dropt it."
The players forming the ring are forbidden to look round. The one having the handkerchief endeavours to drop it at some one's back without his or her knowledge, and then to get *three* times round the ring without being struck by the handkerchief. If the player does not manage this she has to sit in the centre of the ring as "old maid;" the object in this version evidently is not to let the player upon whom the handkerchief is dropped be aware of it.—Fochabers, N.E. Scotland (Rev. Dr. Gregor).

Dumb Crambo. [See "Hiss and Clap," vol. i. p. 215.]
The players divide into two sides: one side goes outside the room, the other remains in the room, and decides on some

verb to be guessed and acted by the other. The outside party is told that the chosen verb "rhymes with ———." The outside party decide on some verb, and come in and act this word in dumb show, whilst the inside party sit and look on, hissing if the guess is wrong, and clapping if the acting shows the right word is chosen. No word must pass on either side.—Bedford, and generally known (Mrs. A. C. Haddon).

Dump. [Vol. i. p. 117.]

A version of this game played by three children. The three sit close together, close their hands and place them over each other, the first one on the knee of one of them. One then asks, "Faht's that cockin' up there?" "Cock a pistol; cock it aff," replies another. The same process is gone through till only one hand is left on the knee. Then the one whose hand was uppermost at the beginning of the game says—

> Faht's in there?
> Gold and money (is the answer).
> Fahr's my share o't?
> The moosie ran awa' wi't.
> Fahr's the moosie?
> In her hoosie.
> Fahr's her hoosie?
> In the wood.
> Fahr's the wood?
> The fire brunt it.
> Fahr's the fire?
> The water quencht it.
> Fahr's the water?
> The broon bull drank it.
> Fahr's the broon bull?
> At the back a (of) Burnie's hill.
> Fahr's the back a Burnie's hill?
> A' claid wi' snaw.
> Fahr's the snaw?
> The sun meltit it.
> Fahr's the sun?
> Heigh, heigh up i' the air."

He who speaks first, or laughs first, or lats (lets) their teeth be seen, gets nine nips, nine nobs, an' nine double douncornes, an' a gueed blow on the back o' the head.—Corgarff (Rev. Dr. Gregor).

Eendy, Beendy.

> Eendy, Beendy, baniba, roe,
> Caught a chicken by the toe;
> To the east, to the west,
> To the old crow's nest,
> Hopping in the garden, swimming in the sea,
> If you want a pretty girl, please take me.
>
>   —N. Scotland, locality forgotten (Rev. Dr. Gregor).

One girl dances forward from a line of children singing the words. Another from a line opposite responds, and they dance together. They look first to the east and then to the west by turning their heads in those directions alternately.

Farmer's Den, The.

All players but one form a ring, this one stands in the centre. The ring dances round singing the words—

> The farmer in his den, the farmer in his den,
> For it's oh, my dearie, the farmer's in his den.
> For the farmer takes a wife,
> For the farmer takes a wife;
> For it's oh, my dearie, the farmer takes a wife.

The child in centre then chooses one from the circle, who goes in the middle, and the ring dances round again singing—

> For the wife takes a child, &c. (as above).

And choosing another child from the ring, then—

> For the child takes a nurse, &c. (as above),
> For the nurse takes a dog, &c. (as above).

Then all the players join in singing—

> For we all clap the dog,
> For we all clap the dog.
> For it's oh! my dearie, we all clap the dog.

While singing this all the players pat the one who was chosen as "dog" on his or her back.—Auchencairn, N.B. (Mary Haddon).

Fire on the Mountains. [See "Round Tag," vol. ii. pp. 144–145.]

The players arrange themselves into a double circle with a space between each pair. The one at the back stands and the inside players kneel. Another player stands in the centre and cries out, "Fire on the mountain; run, boys, run!" Those players who are standing in the outer circle begin to run round, those kneeling remaining in that position. They continue running until the centre player cries "Stop!" They all then (including the centre player) make a rush to get a stand behind one of the kneeling players, the one who is left out going into the centre. — Auchterarder, N.B. (Miss E. S. Haldane).

This game may possibly suggest an origin for "Round tag," although the incident of "catching" or "touching" a runner does not appear, and the inner circle of players apparently are always stationary.

Fool, Fool, come to School. [Vol. i. p. 132.]

Played in the usual way with the following difference in the formula. The leader says, "Fool, foolie, come to your schoolie." When the fool comes, the leader says, "What have you been doing to-day?" Fool says, "Cursin' and swearin'." Fool is then chased off, recalled, and again questioned. Fool answers, "Suppin' my porridge and readin' my Bible." She is then welcome, and asked in the usual way to point out one from the school.—Aberdeen (Rev. Dr. Gregor).

Another formula sent me by Mr. C. C. Bell is to say, when the fool is sent back, "Fool, fool, go back to school, and learn more wit."

French Jackie, name for "Round Tag" and "Two and Threes," in Tyrie (Rev. Dr. Gregor).

Galloping.

> Galloping, galloping to the fair,
> Courting the girls with the *red* petticoats;
> Galloping, galloping all day long,
> Courting the girls with the *speckled* petticoats.

Girls sing this resting one knee on the ground, striking the other knee with their right hand as they say each word. The length of the song depends upon the ingenuity of the players in finding new colours for the petticoats each time.—Isle of Man (A. W. Moore).

The game is not known now.

Gallant Ship. [See "Round and Round the Gallant Ship," vol. ii. p. 143.]

Up spoke a boy of our gallant ship,
And a well-spoken boy was he—
I have a mother in London town,
This night she'll be looking for me.

She may look, she may sigh, with the tear in her eye,
She may look to the bottom of the sea.
Three times round went our gallant ship,
And three times round went she!
And three times round went our gallant ship,
Till she came to the bottom of the sea!

The players form a ring and dance round, getting quicker as they sing "Three times round," &c. When the last line is sung they let go hands and sink to the ground. The player who sinks down first is taken away by the others and asked whom he or she loves best. The ring is then reformed, and the child who has given her sweetheart's name is placed in the centre. The ring then dances round singing out the name of the sweetheart.

Mrs. Brown is new comed hame,
A coach and four to carry hame.
—Galloway (J. G. Carter).

Galley, Galley Ship. [See "Merry-ma-tansa," vol. i. pp. 369–376; ii. p. 443.]

Three times round goes the galley, galley ship,
And three times round goes she;
Three times round goes the galley, galley ship,
And she sank to the bottom of the sea.

Choose your neighbours one or two,
One or two, one or two;

Choose your neighbours one or two,
Around about Mary Matanzie.

A treacle scone to tell her name,
To tell her name, to tell her name ;
A treacle scone to tell her name,
Around about Mary Matanzie.

A guinea gold watch to tell his name,
To tell his name, to tell his name ;
A guinea gold watch to tell his name,
Around about Mary Matanzie.

(Name of boy) is his name,
Is his name, is his name,
—— is his name,
Around about Mary Matanzie.
                    —Laurieston School, Kircudbrightshire (J. Lawson).

A version of " Merry-ma-tansa incomplete.   [See vol. i.
p. 375.]
Another is—
        Three times around goes our gallant ship,
        And three times around goes she, she, she ;
        And three times around goes our gallant ship,
        And she sinks to the bottom of the sea.
Played in ring form with one child in centre.   All sink down
on the ground when the above lines are sung, and the last to
rise must tell the name of her sweetheart.   Then the circle
forms around her, and all sing—
        Here's the bride just new come in,
        Just new come in, just new come in ;
        Here's the bride just new come in,
        Around the merry guid tanzy.

        Guess wha's her guid lad,
        Her guid lad, her guid lad ;
        Guess wha's her guid lad,
        Around the merry guid tanzy.

(Willie Broon) is his name,
Is his name, is his name,
(Willie Broon) is his name,
Around the merry guid tanzy.
                —St. Andrews and Howth (Miss H. E. Harvey).

Miss Harvey writes: I believe "tanzy" is the name of a kind of dance.

Glasgow Ships.

Glasgow ships come sailing in,
Come sailing in, come sailing in ;
Glasgow ships come sailing in,
On a fine summer morning.

You daurna set your foot upon,
Your foot upon, your foot upon ;
You daurna set your foot upon,
Or gentle George will kiss you.

Three times kiss you, four times bless you,
Five times butter and bread
Upon a silver salver.

Who shall we send it to,
Send it to, send it to?
Who shall we send it to ?
To Mrs. ——'s daughter.
Take her by the lily-white hand,
Lead her over the water ;
Give her kisses, one, two, three.
She is the favourite daughter.
                        —Perth (Rev. Dr. Gregor).

Glasgow ships come sailing in, &c. (three times)
Three times bless you, three times kiss you,
Three times butter and bread upon a silver saucer.
Whom shall I send it to, I send it to, I send it to ?
To Captain Gordon's daughter.
                        —Rosehearty (Rev. Dr. Gregor).

The Glasgow ships come sailing in, &c. (as first version).
Three times down and then we fall, then we fall, then
    we fall,
Three times down and then we fall, in a fine summer
    morning.
Three times butter and bread, butter and bread, butter
    and bread,
Three times butter and bread upon a silver saucer.
Come, choose you east, come choose you west,
Come, choose you east, come choose you west,
To the very one that you love best.
                                        —Nairn (Rev. Dr. Gregor).

Glasgow ships come sailing in, &c. (as first version)
She daurna set a foot upon, &c.
Or gentle John will kiss her.
Three times round the ring, three times bless her,
I sent a slice of bread and butter upon a silver saucer.
Whom shall we send it to ? &c.
To Captain ——'s daughter.
Her love's dead and gone, dead and gone, dead and
    gone,
She turns her back to the wa's again.
She washes her face, she combs her hair,
She leaves her love at the foot of the stair,
She wears on her finger a guinea gold ring,
And turns her back to the wa's again.

All join hands and form a ring. At the end of verses
the girl named turns her back, and the game is resumed.—
Fochabers (Rev. Dr. Gregor); Port William School, Wigtonshire.

In a version from Auchterarder, N. B., sent by Miss E. S.
Haldane, the words are very similar to these. After all the
children have turned their backs to the inside they have what
is called the "pigs' race," which is running swiftly round in
this position. See "Uncle John," vol. ii. pp. 321–322.

Granny's Needle.   [See "Auld Grannie."]

Green Gravel. [Vol. i. pp. 170–183.]
> Round apples, round apples, by night and by day,
> There stands a valley in yonder haze ;
> There stands poor Lizzie with a knife in her hand,
> There's no one dare touch her, or she'll go mad ;
> Her cheeks were like roses, and now they're like snow,
> Poor Lizzie! poor Lizzie! you're dying, I know,
> We'll wash you with milk, and we'll dry [or roll] you
> > with silk,
> And we'll write down your name with a gold pen
> > and ink. —New Galloway (Rev. Dr. Gregor).

Boys and girls take hands and go round saying—
> Round the green gravel
> Grass grows green,
> Many's the lady fit to be seen,
> Washed in milk and dried in silk.
> The last pops down !

The last boy or girl to pop down has to tell who he (or she) is courting.—Kiltubbrid, Co. Leitrim (L. L. Duncan).

Green Grass. [Vol. i. pp. 153–169.]

All the girls arrange themselves in a line, and one stands in front. The one in front sings—
> Dis-a-dis-a green grass,
> Dis-a-dis-a-dis ;
> Come all ye pretty fair maids,
> And walk along wi' us.
> Will ye have a duck, my dear (pointing to
> > one of the girls in the line),
> Or will ye have a drake,
> Or will ye have a young man
> To answer for your sake ?

The girl pointed to answers—
> I'll neither have a duck, my dear,
> Nor will I have a drake ;
> But I will have a young man
> To answer for my sake.

She now leaves the line and takes her stand beside the one that stands in front, and all begin to clap their hands and sing—

> The bells will ring,
> And the psalms will sing,
> And we'll all claps hands together.

The two in front then begin to sing what the one first sang, and the same goes on till all are chosen.—Peterhead; St. Andrews (Mrs. Stewart, when a girl).

> Here we go in a merry band,
> Round about the berry buss;
> Come all ye pretty fair maids,
> And dance along with us;
> We shall have a duck and drake,
> We shall have a dragon,
> We shall have a young man,
> The prince of the Saigen.
> The young man dies,
> And leaves the girl a widow.
> The birds shall sing, the bells shall ring,
> And we will all clap hands together.
> Here we go a roving,
> A roving in a band;
> I will take my pretty Mary,
> I will take her by the hand.
>   —Perth (Rev. Dr. Gregor).

Another version, very similar to that given in vol. i. pp. 161–162 from Congleton Workhouse School, and sent me by Mr. J. Lawson, Laurieston School, Kirkcudbrightshire, begins, "Will you take silver and gold?"

Another Scottish version of this game is given in *Notes and Queries*, 3rd ser., v. 393, as follows :—

> A duss, a duss of green grass,
> A duss, a duss, a duss;
> Come all you pretty maidens,
> And dance along with us;
> You shall have a duck, my dear,
> And you shall have a dragon,

And you shall have a young gudeman,
    To dance ere you're forsaken.
        The bells shall ring,
        The birds shall sing,
    And we'll all clap hands together.

Green Grass. [A game so called by Dr. Gregor, but apparently
    not belonging to the one usually known under that name.]
The girls stand in a line, and one stands in front. All sing—
    Green grass suits us,
    As my boots are lined with silver;
    E. I. O, E. I. O, my ain bonnie (a girl's Christian name).
The girl in front then chooses the girl named, and both girls
join hands and wheel round, whilst all sing—
        I kissed her once, I kissed her twice,
        I kissed her three times over.
        Hop, hop, the butcher's shop,
        I cannot stay any longer.
        If I stay my mother will say
        I played with the boys up yonder.
                    —Tyrie (Rev. Dr. Gregor).
Another version is—
    Green grass set her fair, a bunch of gold and silver,
    A white rosette upon her breast, a gold ring on her finger,
    A I O, my Jessie O; I wish I had my Jessie O.
    I kissed her once, &c., as above.

Heap the Cairn. [See "More Sacks to the Mill," vol. i. p. 390.]
One boy is thrown flat on the ground, then another is
thrown over him, and then another and another, and the bigger
boys dash the smaller ones on those that are down, while all
keep shouting—
            Heap the cyarn—
            Dirt and sharn.
                    —Keith (Rev. Dr. Gregor).

Hear all! Let me at her.
        Hear all! let me at her;
        Hear all! let me go;
        Hear all! let me at her,
            When my mammy will or no.

—— has ta'en a notion
   For to go and sail the sea ;
There he's left his own dear ——,
   Weeping on the Greenland sea.

Hold your tongue, my own dear ——,
   Take your baby on your knee.
Drink his health, my jolly sailors,
   I'll come back and marry thee.

I will buy thee beads and ear-rings,
   I will buy thee diamond stones,
I will buy thee silken ribbons,
   When thy baby's dead and gone.

—— says she'll wear the ribbons,
   —— says she'll wear them a'—
—— says she'll wear the ribbons
   When her baby's dead and gone.

A ring is formed, one player in the centre. When the verses are sung the girl in the middle chooses another to take her place.—Fochabers (Rev. Dr. Gregor.)

Hen and Chickens. [See "Auld Grannie," p. 404.]

High Windows. [See "Drop Handkerchief," vol. i. pp. 109–112; "Black Doggie," vol. ii. pp. 407–408.]
Boys hold hands and go round in ring form.
One player stands in the middle and strikes one of those in the ring with a bit of grass ; both players then run out of the ring, and the boy who was in the midst must catch the other before he goes round three times. At the third time the boys all cry "High Windows," raising their hands at the same time to let the two inside the circle.—Kiltubbrid, Co. Leitrim (L. L. Duncan).

Hot Cockles. [Vol. i. p. 229.]
A version of this game, in which a dell or goal is appointed. The players stand together, one player places his head between the knees of another, who bends down, and slaps him on the back, keeping time to the following rhyme, saying—

Skip, skip, sko,
Where shall this young man go?
To the east, or the west?
Or the young crow's nest?

The kneeling boy shouts out the name of the dell, and the other players all rush off shouting out its name. The one who gets there first wins the game.—Meiklefolla, Aberdeenshire (Rev. Dr. Gregor).

Hulla-balloo-ballee. [See "Lubin," vol. i. pp. 352–361.]
One version of Lubin Loo, from Forfar, Linlithgow, and Argyllshire, is the same as those given in vol. i. A Nairnshire version is called "Hullabaloo-ballee.

Hulla-balloo, ballee,
Hulla-balloo, ballight;
Hulla-balloo, ballee,
All on a winter's night,
Put your right foot in, &c.
Turn round about.

At "turn round about," they reverse the direction, and dance round the other way, and so on.—Rev. Dr. Gregor; and Mrs Jamieson.

Another version is—

Old Simon, the king, young Simon, the squire,
Old Simon, the king, sat round a nice warm fire;
Keep your right hand in, shove your right hand out,
Shake it a little, a little, and turn yourself about!
Keep your right foot in, shove your left foot out,
Shake it a little, a little, and turn yourself about.
Hally gallee, gallee, gallee;
Hally gallo, gallo, gallo;
Hally gallee, gallee, gallee,
Upon a Saturday night.
Keep your right hand in, &c.

—Galloway (J. G. Carter).

Several versions of this game are given by Mr. E. W. B. Nicholson in his interesting little book "Goldspie," pp. 176–184. He considers "Hilli-ballu," "Hulla-baloo," and similar

words to be the original of the English forms "Here we
dance Looby Loo," or Lubin, and all of these to be derived
from hunting cries, such as ha, là bas! loup! uttered by
huntsmen to definite musical notes, possibly introduced into
songs and afterwards adapted as lullabies because of their
resemblance to the lulling-cries ba (= bye) and lulli.

Isabella. [Vol. i. pp. 247–256.]

Two or three versions which vary slightly in method of
playing may be given. The first is played in the usual way
until the last line is said, when the player turns her back to
the circle facing outwards as in Wall-flowers.

> Isabella, Isabella, Isabella, farewell;
> There is my hand, love, there is my hand, love, farewell!
> Over the mountains, over the mountains, over the moun-
>   tains, farewell!
> Her love's dead and gone, dead and gone, dead and gone!
> Her love's dead and gone, turn your back behind her.
>   —Perth (Rev. Dr. Gregor).

Another version is—

> Isabella, fare ye wella; Isabella, fare ye wella; Isabella,
>   farewell!

One player then leaves the ring singing—

> " I'm off to the Indies," &c.

The ring all sing—

> " Over the mountains " (as above) six times, ending with—
>   " Isabella, Isabella, farewell " (as above).

The player who had previously left the ring returns singing,
" I'm come back from the Indies," &c.

A ring is formed, one player kneels in the centre, the players
in the ring fix their eyes steadily on the kneeling girl all the
time.—Fochabers, N.E. Scotland (Rev. Dr. Gregor).

In the next version the words of each verse are :—

> Isabella, farewella, &c.
> Back from London, &c.
> Go to London, &c.
> Pull the brooch off my bosom, &c.
> Pull the ring off my finger, &c.
>   —Laurieston School, Kircudbrightshire (J. Lawson).

Jenny Jones. [Vol. i. pp. 260–283.]

The versions printed here vary, it will be seen, from those printed in vol. i., principally in the words used towards the end of the game, the earlier portions being very similar. The first one is an exceedingly interesting variant, the funeral details being fuller, and the idea of the spirit of the dead or Ghost surviving also.

The first lines of each verse are as follows :—

> I've come to see Jenny Jones,
> How does she do ?
> She is washing, &c., you can't see her now.
> I've come to see Jenny Jones, &c.
> She is scrubbing, &c., you can't see her now.
> I've come to see, &c.
> She is ill, &c.
> I've come to see, &c.
> She's very ill, &c.
> I've come to see, &c.
> She's dying, &c.
> I've come to see.
> She's dead.
> We'll come in blue, blue, blue. Will that suit ?
> Blue is for sailors, &c. That won't suit.
> We'll come in red, &c.
> Red is for soldiers, &c.
> We'll come in white, &c.
> White is for weddings, &c.
> We'll come in black, &c.
> Black is for mourning, &c. That will suit.

They then take up Jenny Jones, and carry her to a little distance off, lay her on the ground, and all stand round. One child stands over the grave, and while sprinkling Jenny with dust, says—

> Ashes to ashes, dust to dust.
> If God won't have you, the devil must.

Then Jenny jumps up and runs after the other children, who try to escape. The one she catches is "Jenny" next time.— Barrington (Dr. A. C. Haddon).

In another version called "Georgina" one player selected to act as Georgina kneels down against a wall, and the others stand round to conceal her. Two go apart to act as callers, while another stands near the group as mother. The callers come forward and say—

> We came to see Georgina, &c.
> And how is she to-day?
> She's upstairs washing, &c.,
> And you can't see her to-day.
> Farewell, ladies.

They then retire, but return in a little while, and put the question as before. She is then "starching," said as above; and next time she is "ironing," the fourth time the mother's answer is, "She fell downstairs and broke her arm, and you can't see her to-day;" the fifth time, "Two doctors are at her;" the sixth, she is "worse;" and the seventh, she is "dead." The two callers remain when this reply is given. At this point Georgina makes a noise by rapping two stones together. The two at once exclaim, "Oh! mother, mother, what's that knocking?" and she answers, "The coach going by." The knocking is repeated, and the question, and she says, "The wall falling down." On the knocking being heard a third time, she tells them to "take a candle and look." They pretend to do so, and "Georgina" starts up to chase them. They all run off shouting, "The Ghost." — Strichen and Fochabers (Rev. Dr. Gregor).

> I came to see Georgina, Georgina, Georgina,
> I came to see Georgina, and how is she to-day?
> > She's upstairs ironing.
> I came to see Georgina, &c. (as above).
> > She fell downstairs and broke her muckle toe.
> I'm very sorry to hear that, &c.
> > She's dead.
> Bad news, bad news, bad news to-day.
> What shall we dress her in? &c.
> > Dress her in red.
> Red is for the soldier, and that won't do, &c.
> What shall we dress her in? &c.

Dress her in blue.
Blue is for the sailor, &c.
What shall we dress her in ? &c.
Dress her in white.
White is for the angels, that will do, &c.
Mother, mother, what's that ? &c.
A gig running past.
Mother, mother, what's that ? &c.
The boys playing at marbles.
Mother, mother, what's that ? what's that ? what's that ?
Mother, mother, what's that ?
Georgina's ghost ! !
Ending with a general stampede.

—Nairnshire (Mrs. Jamieson).

We've come to see poor Janet,
And how is she to-day ?
She's up the stairs washing,
She can't come down to-day.
Very well, we'll call another day.
We've come to see poor Janet,
And how is she to-day ?
She's up the stairs ironing, &c.
Well, we'll call, &c.
We've come to see poor Janet, &c.
She's fallen downstairs and broken her horn
toes, &c.
Poor Janet, we'll call, &c.
We've come, &c.
She's dead, &c.
What's she to be dressed in ?
Red.
That's for soldiers ; that won't do.
Blue.
That's for sailors ; that won't do.
White.
That will do.   —Rosehearty (Rev. Dr. Gregor).

Played in usual way until the end. Janet is then carried off
and laid down on the ground, but she starts up and chases them.

Many other versions have been sent me, but none with different features. The best is one from Mr. J. G. Carter, Dalry, Galloway, called "Jenny Jo," but presenting no fresh details, and where white is used for the burial. Four children stand on one side with Jenny at their back, the other players on the opposite. She is buried with great mourning. In a version from Hemsby (Mrs. Haddon) the words are the same, except: "White is the colour for weddings," and black is for funerals. Then Jenny is carried to the grave, the other children walking behind two by two; they kneel round Jenny, and have a good cry over her. Another version from Laurieston School (Mr. J. Lawson), called "Jerico," very similar to above, gives two additional verses. The first lines are, "Carry a poor soldier to the grave," and "Now the poor mother's weeping at the grave." In one version, after Jenny has been carried to her grave, the children stand round and sprinkle earth over her, and say, "Dust and dust, dust and dust," and then pretend to strew flowers. This I got in London. Another version from North Scotland begins, "I come to see *Geneva*," continues in usual way until "she is lying" instead of "ill"; then "she's dying," followed by "she's dead"; then the funeral. In another version Dr. Haddon sent me, the game is only a fragment. After "Jenny Jo's dead and gone, all the day long," they continue, "Pipes and tobacco for Jenny Jo" (repeat twice), "Pipes and tobacco for Jenny Jo, all the day long."

Jockie Rover. [See "Stag," vol. ii. pp. 212, 374.]

One is chosen to be Rover, and a place is marked off called "The Den," from which he starts, and to which he and the others caught can run for protection. He has to clasp his hands and set off in pursuit of one of the players, whom he must crown without unclasping his hands. Before he leaves the den he calls out—

> Jockie Rover,
> Three times over,
> If you do not look out,
> I'll gie you a blover.

When he catches one he unclasps his hands, and makes for

the den along with the one caught. The players close in upon
them, and beat them with their caps. The two now join hands,
and before leaving the den repeat the same words, and give
chase to catch another. When another is caught, the three
run to the den, followed by the others pelting them.

During the time they are running to catch another player,
every attempt is made by the others to break the band by
rushing on two outstretched arms, either from before or from
behind. Every time one is taken or the band broken, all
already taken rush to the den, beaten by those not taken.—
Dyke (Rev. Dr. Gregor).

A form of " Warney," " Whiddy."

Jolly Lads, Bold.   [Vol. i. pp. 294–296.]

> Here come two bold, jolly lads,
>   Just new come from the shore :
> We'll spend our time in drinking wine,
>   As we have done before.
> Then the ring dances round, singing—
>   We will have a round, and a round,
> We will have a pretty, pretty girl,
>   For to dance upon the ground.
>   Her shoes are made of morocco,
>   Her stockings lined with silk,
>   Her teeth are white as anything,
> And her skin as white as milk.
>   We shall have a round, and a round, &c.
>   —Auchterarder, N. B. (Miss E. S. Haldane).

A ring is formed by players joining hands. Two other
players dance round the ring in opposite directions, singing the
first four lines while the ring stands still. Then the ring
dances round singing the rest of the lines. The two outside
then each take a player from the ring and begin again.

The words of the dance game, " Here we go around," vol. i.
p. 205, are practically the same as the latter part of this, and
suggests that this or a similar round is its original.

Jolly Miller.   [Vol. i. pp. 289–293.]

This is played with the usual double ring, boys on the outside, girls inside, one child in centre. At the last a rush is made to obtain a vacant place.

He was a jolly miller,
He lived by himself.
As the wheel went round, he made his wealth,
One hand in his pocket, the other at his back,
As the mill went round, he made his wealth.

The girls being in the inside, turn and go the opposite way; and, while doing so, sing—

A hunting we will go,
A hunting we will go,
We'll catch a little fox, and we'll put him in a box,
And a hunting we will go.
—Auchterarder, N. B. (Miss E. S. Haldane).

In this version the "grab" appears to be lost, and the "hunting" put in before the rush for the vacant place is made.

Keys of Heaven.

I will give you a golden ring,
And jewels to hang and birds to sing,
If you'll be my true lover,
And true love of mine.

I will give you the keys of the chest,
And gold enough to dress you in church,
If you'll be my true lover,
And true love of mine.

I will give you the keys of even [heaven],
And angels to wait upon you six and seven,
If you'll be my true lover,
And true love of mine.   —Marylebone (A. B. Gomme).

Children form a ring by joining hands; they dance round. One stands in centre. She chooses another from the ring after singing the words, and the two dance round together.

This game is evidently but a fragment, the proper way of playing being forgotten. It would originally have been played in line form instead of a circle, and answers of "No" or "Yes," or other verses implying negative and then affirmative, given by the chosen or selected girl. These lines, and those given *post* (p. 450), as "Paper of pins," are interesting fragments probably of one and the same game.

Kick the Block.   [See vol. i. p. 401.]

A small circle is made, and the stone or block is put in it. A boy stands with his foot on the stone and his eyes shut until all the other players are hid.   He then tries to find them, and keep his block in its place.   If one should come out when he is away from his block it is kicked out, and all the boys that were found hide again.—Laurieston School, Kirkcudbrightshire (J. Lawson).

Another version of the same game, sent me by Mr. William P. Merrick, Shepperton, Middlesex, is called "Fly Whip."

The same game as "Mount the Tin," played somewhat differently.

Lady of the Land.   [Vol. i. pp. 315–319.]

A number of girls stand in a line.   One of them represents the widow and the other the children.   Another stands in front. All sing—

> There came a poor widow from Sunderland,
> With all her children in her hand,
> One can bake, and one can sew,
> And one can do the hilygoloo.
> Please take one out.

The player who is standing alone in front of the other players chooses one from the line.   The two then join right and left hands and wheel round in front, all singing—

> Oh there's poor (girl's name chosen),
> She has gone without a farthing in her hand,
> Nothing but a guinea gold ring,
> Good-bye (girl's name),
> Good-bye, good-bye.

The mother shakes hands with the one chosen.

—Fraserburgh (Rev. Dr. Gregor).

Another version—

> There is a poor widow from Sankelone,
> With all her children in her hand,

> One can knit, and one sew,
> And one can play the liligolor.

The widow then says—

> Please take one in,
> Please take one in.

The one in front picks out one and places her at her back, and she lays hold of her dress, then all sing—

> Now for poor (girl's name who has been chosen), she is
> gone,
> Without her father (? farthing) in her hand,
> She has lost her guinea gold ring,
> Good-bye, good-bye,
> Good-bye, good-bye.

The widow shakes hands with the girl. This is repeated till all are taken out and the widow is left by herself. She cries, and tries to take back her daughters. All run off.

—Cullen (Rev. Dr. Gregor).

Another Isle of Man version varies slightly, beginning, "We're three young mothers from Babylon," and continuing in a similar way to the one in vol. i. p. 315—

> One can wash, and one can sew,
> Another can sit by the fire and spin,
> The other can make a fine bed for the king,
> Please, ma'am, to take one in.

The queen then says—

> Come, my dearest . . . and give me your hand,
> And you shall have the nicest things in all this pleasant land.

The girls are thus gradually chosen.

—Isle of Man (A. W. Moore).

> Here's a poor widow from Babylon,
> Six poor children left alone,
> One can bake, and one can brew,
> And one can shape, and one can sew.
> One can sit by the fire and spin,
> And one can make a bed for a king;
> Come Tuesday east, come Tuesday west,
> Come choose the one that you love best.

—Galloway, N. B. (J. G. Carter).

Leap-Frog. [Vol. i. pp. 133, 327, 328.]

The chief rules of this game, obtaining in N.E. Scotland in Dr. Gregor's boyhood, were :—The boy that stooped his back was called "the bull," pronounced "bill." The bull was not to "horn," *i.e.*, throw up his back when the player placed his hands on it to leap over, or to bend his back down, and that the player was to lay his hands on the bull's back quite flat, and not to "knockle," *i.e.*, drive the knuckles into it. The best way to play was :—A line was drawn beside the bull, over which the heel of the player must not pass. All the players, the one after the other in succession, leaped over the bull. The one last over called out, "Fit it," *i.e.*, foot it, which meant that the bull had to measure from the line a breadth and a length of his foot. This done he stooped, and all the players went over as before, and another breadth and length of foot were added. This went on as long as the players thought they were able to leap over the bull. When they thought they could not do so, the last player called out, "Hip it," *i.e.*, take a hop. This done, the bull put himself into position, and each player now took a hop from the line to the bull, and then went over him. Here the same process of footing was gone through as before, as long as the players were able to go clear over the bull. Then came a step with as much footing as was considered safe, and then came a jump with so much footing. It was now with the players "hip, step, an' jump," and over the bull. Then more "fitin'," and perhaps another "hip," and so on—two hips, two steps, two jumps, and a flying leap over the bull. It was not often the game reached this point. Some one of the players had failed to pass right over the bull and caused him to fall, or had overstepped the line. When any player did either the one or the other, he had to become bull.—Keith (Rev. Dr. Gregor).

This is a fuller and more complete description than that of "Foot and Over" (vol. i. p. 133).

Another mode of playing leap-frog is: the players stand with their backs to the leapers, and only bend the head and the leaper's hands are placed between the shoulders. Instead of running a few yards in front, each player advances only a few feet, leaving just as much room as to allow the player scope to fall and spring again. This mode requires considerable agility and practice. The higher the leap, so much the greater the fun.—Keith (Rev. Dr. Gregor.)

London Bridge. [Vol. i. pp. 333–350.]

In the following versions of the game only the first lines of each verse are given, as said by each side. Descriptions of method of playing were not in all cases sent me. They are probably the same as those given under this game in vol. i., which is for two players to form an arch by holding up their joined hands, and the other players running under it.

(1.) London Bridge is falling down, &c., my fair lady.
    What will it take to build it up? &c.
    Needles and pins will build it up, &c.
    Needles and pins will not hold, &c.
    Bricks and mortar will build it up, &c.
    Bricks and mortar will wash away, &c.
    Silver and gold will build it up, &c.
    Silver and gold will be stolen away, &c.
    We will set a watchman to watch all night, &c.
    What if the watchman falls asleep, &c.
    We will set a dog to bark, &c.
    See the robbers passing by, &c.
    What have the robbers done to you? &c.
    They have broke my locks and stole my gold, &c.
    Off to prison they must go, &c.
    What will you take to set them free? &c.
                        —Perth (Rev. Dr. Gregor).

(2.) London Bridge is broken down,
    Build it up with lime and stone;
    Lime and stone will build and break;
    Set an old man to watch all night.
    Perhaps this man will run away,
    Ten times the wedding day.
                        —Tyrie (Rev. Dr. Gregor).

(3.) Broken bridges falling down, falling down, falling
      down, my fair lady.
    What will you give to mend it up ? &c.
  Those running under the arch say—
  A guinea gold ring will mend it up, &c.
  The two players say no.
  A pin I'll give to mend it up.
  No !
  A thousand pounds to mend it up ;
  This will waste away, my fair lady ;
  We'll mend it up with golden pins, my fair lady,
  For golden pins will never rust, never rust, my fair lady.
            —Fochabers, N.E. Scotland (Rev. Dr. Gregor).

(4.) The broken bridge is falling down, falling down, fall-
      ing down,
  The broken bridge is falling down, my fair lady ;
  Stones and bricks will build it up, &c.
            —Nairnshire (Rev. Dr. Gregor).

    (5.) Broken bridges falling down,
      My fair lady, which will you have ?
      Open the door for the king's soldiers.
      What king are you ?
      I am true to the very last one.
            —Isle of Man (A. W. Moore).

Versions of this game from Scotland have been sent me,
which show great similarity to those previously printed, but
the game is more or less in a state of decàdence. The best
version is that from Perth. One from St. Andrews, Peterhead,
though only consisting of the first verse, has preserved the
refrains, "Dance o'er the Lady Lee" and "With a gay lady"
of Halliwell's version. The others commence "broken bridges."
The Isle of Man version is still more incomplete. A version
sent me by Dr. Haddon from Barrington is similar to the one
given, vol. i. p. 338–9, from Enborne School, and is not therefore printed here.

Magician.

  A mirror is covered with a cover, and a girl or boy is taken
into the room. She or he is then asked what animal or thing

they would like to see. As soon as the wish is stated, the cover is raised, and the child sees his or herself.—London (A. B. Gomme).

Mannie on the Pavement.

One player has charge of the pavement. It is his duty to keep the others off. The others try how often they can touch the wall, and when the "mannie" catches one, that one becomes "mannie."—Aberdeen (Rev. Dr. Gregor).

Merry-ma-Tansa. [Vol. i. pp. 369–376; ii. 422–424.]

Here we go round by jingo ring, by jingo ring, by
    jingo ring,
Here we go round by jingo ring, in a cold and
    frosty morning.
Twice about and then we fall, and then we fall, and
    then we fall,
Twice about and then we fall, in a cold and frosty
    morning.

All bend down. The one who rises up last goes into the centre of the circle, and those in the circle sing—

Choose your maidens all around, all around, all around,
Choose your maidens all around, on a cold and frosty
    morning.

The one in the centre chooses two from the ring, and retires with them a short distance away, when the name of a boy is selected as the lover. During the time the three are standing apart, those in the ring let go each other's hands, and take hold of the sides of their dresses, and make as if they were sweeping a house, singing the while—

Swype the hoose till the bride comes hame, the bride
    comes hame, the bride comes hame,
Swype the hoose till the bride comes hame, on a cold
    and frosty morning.

When the three come back, the one that was in the centre takes up the same position, and the two she picked out join those in the circle. Then all wheel round and sing—

A golden pin to tell her name, tell her name, tell her
name,
A golden pin to tell her name, in a cold and frosty
morning.
The answer is—
—— (girl's name is given) is her name, is her name,
is her name,
—— is her name, in a cold and frosty morning.
Then comes the lover's name—
A golden watch to tell his name, tell his name, tell
his name,
A golden watch to tell his name, in a cold and frosty
morning.
The answer is—
So-and-so is his name, is his name, is his name,
So-and-so is his name, in a cold and frosty morning.
The one in the middle is then blindfolded, and all wheel
round and sing—
Blindfolded dinna catch me, dinna catch me, dinna
catch me,
Blindfolded dinna catch me, on a cold and frosty
morning.
The blindfolded tries to catch one in the ring. The ring
should not break, but it is often broken by the one that is on
the eve of being caught. The one caught takes her stand in
the centre, and the game begins anew from that point.—Dyke
(Rev. Dr. Gregor).

This is a most interesting variant of this game—blindfolding
the bridegroom in order that he must first catch his bride,
and her attempts to elude his caresses, are significant of early
custom.

Here we go round by jing-ga-ring,
Jing-ga-ring, jing-ga-ring ;
Here we go round by jing-ga-ring,
Around the merry-ma-tansy.

Three times round, and then we fall,
Then we fall, then we fall ;

> Three times round, and then we fall,
> Around the merry-ma-tansy.

> Choose your maidens all around,
> All around, &c. ;

> High gates till the bride comes in,
> The bride comes in, &c.

> A golden pin to tell her name,
> To tell her name, &c.

> (Mary Anderson) is her name,
> Is her name, &c.

> Blindfold you all around,
> All around, &c.

A ring with one child in centre, who chooses one from the circle, at the end of third verse, after whispering the bride's name together *outside* the circle, they are admitted at "high gates," when all the girls hold up their hands in arches as they dance round. All players in the ring are then blindfolded, and have to catch the child in the centre.—Nairnshire (Rev. Dr. Gregor).

Another version is—

> Here we go round by jingo-ring,
> By jingo-ring, by jingo-ring,
> Here we go round by jingo-ring,
> And round by merry matansy.
> Twice about, and then we fall,
> And then we fall, and then we fall,
> Twice about, and then we fall,
> And round by merry matansy.
> —Fochabers (Rev. Dr. Gregor).

In another version from St. Andrews and Peterhead, with same words, the players all flop down, then rise again and dance round.

Another form of words is—

> Here we go round by jingo-ring,
> Jingo-ring, jingo-ring.
> Here we go round by jingo-ring,
> In a cold and frosty morning.

> Three times round, and then we fall,
> Then we fall, then we fall,
> Three times round, and then we fall,
> In a cold and frosty morning.
> —Nairn (Rev. Dr. Gregor).

Another similar version from N. Scotland, locality not known.

> Round about the jingo-ring, &c.
> Round about the jingo-ring, &c.
> First time is catching time, &c., round, &c.
> A fine gold ring to tell her name, &c.
> (—— ——) is her name, &c.
> Third time is kissing time, &c., round, &c.
> —London (A. B. Gomme), from Scotch source.

Milking Pails. [Vol. i. pp. 376–388.]

A version sent me by Mr. M. L. Rouse, Blackheath, is similar to those previously printed, varying only at the end. After the "wash in the river," and "the stream will carry the clothes away," the children say, "Men, you may run after them." Hereupon they all run off, but the mother does not chase them. They return, and a dialogue ensues similar to a part of "Mother, may I go out to play," follows between the mother and children :—

"Where have you been all day?"

"Working for Jack, or aunt."

"What did he give you?"

"A piece of plum-pudding as big as a flea, or a piece of bread as big as a house, and a piece of cheese as big as a mouse."

The children then run off again, come quickly back with the news that they had seen a large bull in the meadow.

"Where's the butcher?"

"Behind the stable door cracking nuts, and you may have the shells." The mother then chases the children, beating all she can catch.

My Delight's in Tansies. [See "Sunday Night," vol. ii. p. 221.]

All the girls stand in a line except one who stands in front

of the others. This one walks or dances backwards and forwards. All sing the words—

> My delight's in tansies, O!
> My delight's in bransies, O!
> My delight's in a red, red rose;
> The colour o' my ——

the name of one in the line chosen by the one in front is said.
The two in front join right and left hands, and all sing—

> Hey ho, my ——, O!
> My bonnie, bonnie ——, O!
> A' the warld wid I gie,
> For a kiss o' ——, O.
> My delight's in Nancy, O!
> My delight's in tancy, O!
> My delight's in a red, red rose,
> [She chooses out a girl]
> Call her, oh! my (a girl's name), O!
> Hey, ho, my ——, O!
> My bonnie, bonnie ——, O!
> A' the warld wad I gie
> For a kiss o' ——, O!

> —Fraserburgh (Rev. Dr. Gregor).

Namer and Guesser. [Vol. i. p. 409.]

Another version of this game. It is begun in the same way.
As each player gets his name, he or she turns their back to the
namer. When all are named, and are standing with their
backs to the namer, the namer calls out, "Baker, baker, your
bread is burnin'," or "Bakerie, bakerie, your bread is burnin'."
The guesser answers, "Will you give a corner of it to me?"
or "Give me a corner of it," and takes a stand beside the
namer. The namer then says—

> Come, cheese me east,
> Come, cheese me west,
> Come, cheese me to "Rose."

The guesser points to one of the players. If the guess is
right, the player goes to the guesser's side; if wrong, to the
namer's side, when all the players except one are chosen.
This one gets two names, say "Needles" and "Preens." The

namer then says to the guesser, "Needles" or "Preens"? A guess is made. This is done three times, and each time the names are changed. If the last guess is made correctly, then the player goes to the guesser, if not, to the namer. Sometimes it is decided by "the best o' three." Then comes the "tug of war." The gaining side calls out "Rotten eggs, rotten eggs!"—Fraserburgh (Rev. Dr. Gregor).

Needle Cases.

Needle cases, needle cases, in a silver saucer.
Who shall I direct it to but Captain ——'s daughter.
What will you give to tell her name, tell her name, tell
    her name?
A hundred pounds and a glass of wine.
(The girl's name is given, and she then asks)—
What will you give to tell his name?
(The others answer)—
Two hundred pounds and a glass of wine.
(Boy's name given by girl).
As I gaed down to borrow a pan,
I saw her sitting kissing her man;
She off with the glove and on with the ring.
To-morrow, to-morrow the wedding begins.
Clean the brass candlesticks, clean the fireside,
Draw up the curtains and let's see the bride.

All the players but one stand in a circle—this one goes round with a handkerchief, singing the first lines. When the girl's name is mentioned she tells her sweetheart's name to the girl with the handkerchief, sits down in the centre, and covers her face with her hands. The one with the handkerchief goes round again, asking, "What will you give?" and the ring answers. Her name is then given, and the girl with the handkerchief again asks, "What will you give to tell *his* name?" The ring answers again, and the sweetheart's name is then given. The girl with the handkerchief goes round again and sings the last lines, the ring singing with her. Then the one in the centre joins the ring, and the game begins again.— Aberdeen (Rev. Dr. Gregor).

Nuts in May. [Vol. i. pp. 424–433.]

Many versions of this have been sent me, but none differ materially from those printed previously.

Odd Man.

A game played by two or three hundred persons who form a circle; every one places his stick in the ground before him, by way of barrier. A person called the odd man stands in the middle and delivers his bonnet to any one in the ring. This is nimbly handed round, and the owner is to recover it; and on succeeding, takes the place of the person whom he took it from, and that person takes the middle place.—Pennant's "Voyage to the Hebrides," p. 231.

Old Cranny Crow. [Vol. i. p. 201; ii. pp. 404–405.]

This game resembles "Hen and Chickens," but though of that class of game it is not, it will be seen, the usual form of "Hen and Chickens" at its conclusion. The earlier part of the game and dialogue, if any, may, however, have been similar. Mr. Rouse says: "I cannot recollect more of Old Cranny Crow than that she entices children one by one out for a walk, and steals them from their supposed mother. The mother is then invited to dine by Old Cranny Crow, and has a pie (one of her children) set before her, with pepper and salt, which she pretends to eat, and when doing so discovers it to be just like her Tommy (or other child's name). Then Cranny Crow puts another pie before her; this she discovers to be just like her Katy. She finds out all her children one by one, and they come to life again and run home.—M. L. Rouse, Blackheath. [See "Mother, mother, pot boils over," "Witch."]

Old Johanny Hairy, Crap in!

All players sit round the fire and put out their right feet. The Master of the game repeats—

> Onery, twoery, dickery dary,
> Wispy, spindey, spoke of the lindey,
> Old Johanny Hairy
>   Crap in![1]

[1] Crap—draw.

Each word is repeated to a man ; and when the leader comes to "Crap in," the man specified draws in his foot. When all have drawn in their feet but one, this one must then kneel down, and his eyes being blindfolded, the master of the game puts his elbow on his back and strikes him with his elbow or fist, saying—

> Hurley, burley, trump the trace,
> The cow ran through the market-place.
> Simon Alley hunt the buck,
> How many horns stand up ?

At the same time holding up several fingers. The man kneeling down has to guess the number. If he guesses correctly, the master of the game takes his place. If he fails to guess he is kept down, and another man goes and strikes his back, and so on.—Kiltubbrid, Co. Leitrim (L. L. Duncan.)

A version of " Hot Cockles," with interesting variations.

Mr. Duncan, when sending me the games he collected, said— "It is very possible that the people may have brought some of the games from England when returning from harvesting. This, however, does not apply to 'Old Johnny Hairy, crap in,' as it is now called in English. Crap isteach is the Irish for 'draw in,' as in Mr. O'Faharty's 'Sports of the Winter' there is a Gaelic version. This, I should imagine, makes it certain that, although well known elsewhere, the game also obtained in the West of Ireland.

Paper of Pins.

> Paper of pins to you I bring ;
> Say is my love worth anything ?
>
> Gold and silver to you I bring ;
> Say is my love worth anything ?
>
> No, I'll not have anything ;

or,

> Yes, I will have what you bring.

A ring is formed, and one player walks round outside saying the first four lines, stopping at any child she chooses who answers "Yes" or "No." If "Yes," the two go into the ring and kiss.—Marylebone, London (A. B. Gomme).

This is interesting, as a possible fragment of the old Keys of Canterbury [Halliwell's "Nursery Rhymes," No. cccclxvi.] and of the Paper of Pins, described so fully by Mr. Newell in "Games and Songs of American Children," pp. 51–55.

See "Keys of Heaven," *ante*, p. 437.

Pickie. A form of Hopscotch. [See "Hopscotch," vol. i. pp. 223–227.]

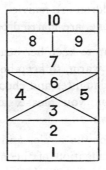

One player commences first by winning the toss. The pick (a small flat stone) is pitched into No. 1 bed. It is then moved out of this first place, backward across the front line, and not otherwise by touching or forcing it with one foot, the other foot being kept up; that is, the player must hop and use the foot on the ground to strike "pick." No line must be touched. If this happens, or if the pick, when being driven towards the pitching line, gets away otherwise than across the front line, the player is "out," and the next boy goes in. All the beds are done likewise, and all must be then done in a reverse way, beginning with No. 10. The first player who completes the game wins.—Waterville, Co. Kerry (Mrs. B. B. Green).

Poor Widow. [Vol. ii. pp. 62, 63.]

Here's a poor widow from Babylon,
All her sons and daughters are gone.
Come choose to the east, come choose to the west,
Come choose you the very one that you like best.
Now they are married I wish them joy,
Every year a girl and boy.

Loving each other like sister and brother,
A happy new couple may kiss together.
—Laurieston School, Kircudbrightshire (J. Lawson).

A circle is formed, two children in the centre, one of whom
kneels, the other walks round singing—

I am a poor widow go walking around,
Go walking around, go walking around, my own.
And all of my children are married but one,
Are married but one, are married but one, my own.

I put on a nightcap to keep her head warm,
To keep her head warm, to keep her head warm, my own.
Then rise up my daughter and choose whom you please,
And choose whom you please, and choose whom you
please, my own.

The mother then joins the circle, and the daughter becomes
poor widow. On the mention of the nightcap a white handkerchief is spread over the head, the circle walking around
slowly, and chanting the words slowly and dismally.
—Penzance (Miss Courtney).

See " Widow," *ante*, p. 381.

Rashes.

A game played by children with rushes in Derbyshire, which
is a relic of the old custom of rush-bearing. In the warm days
of May and June the village children proceed in parties to the
sedges and banks of dyke and brook, there to gather the finest
and best rushes. These are brought with childish ceremony
to some favourite spot, and then woven into various articles,
such as baskets, parasols, and umbrellas. Small arbours are
made of green bushes and strewn with rushes, inside which
the children sit and sing and play at "keeping house" with
much lordly ceremony. At these times they play at a game
which consists in joining hands in a circle, and going round a
heap of rushes singing or saying—

Mary Green and Bessy Bell,
They were two bonny lasses;

They built a house in yonder hill,
And covered it with rashes.
Rashes, rashes, rashes!

At each repetition of the word "rashes" (rushes) they loosen hands, and each picking up a lot of rushes, throw them into the air, so that they may fall on every one in the descent. Many of the articles made with rushes are hung over the chimney-piece in houses, and in children's bedrooms, as ornaments or samples of skill, and there remain until the next season, or until the general cleaning at Christmas.—Thomas Radcliffe, in "Long Ago," vol. i. p. 49 (1873).

Queen Anne. [Vol. ii. pp. 90–102.]

Lady Queen Anne, she sits in her pan,
As fair as a lilly, as white as a lamb;
Come tittle, come tattle, come tell me this tale,
Which of these ladies doth carry the ball?
My father sent me three letters, please deliver the ball.

If a correct guess is made by the opposite side, the queen and the child who had the ball say—

The ball is mine, it is not yours,
You may go to the garden and pick more flowers.
—Isle of Man (A. W. Moore).

Sally Water. [Vol. ii. pp. 150–179.]

Sally, Sally, Walker, sprinkling in a pan,
Rye, Sally; rye, Sally, for a young man,
Come, choose to the east, come, choose to the west,
And come choose to the very one that you love best.

The choice is made here, and the two stand in the centre as usual.

Now there's a couple married in joy,
First a girl and then a boy.
—— made a pudding nice and sweet,
—— took a knife and tasted it.
Taste, love; taste, love, don't say no,
Next Monday morning is our marriage day.

Seven years after, seven years to come,
This young man shall be kissed and be done.
                    —Fochabers, N. E. Scotland (Rev. Dr. Gregor).

Sally, Sally, Water, sprinkled in a pan,
Rise, Sally; rise, Sally, for a young man.
Choose the best, leave the worst,
Choose the prettiest you can.

Now you're married we wish you joy,
First a girl and then a boy,
Seven years after son and daughter,
Kiss before you go over the water.
                    —London (Dr. A. C. Haddon, from Miss E. A. Passmore).

Played in usual way.

Shuffle the Brogue. [See "Hunt the Slipper," vol. i. pp. 241, 242.]

The boys sat on their haunches in a circle. One of the players takes a small object, and hands it from one to another under the legs from behind. The players as they pass the brogue repeat the words—

Shuffle the brogue once,
Shuffle the brogue twice,
Shuffle the brogue thrice.

The object has always to be passed along in the same direction. One player who is blindfolded has to catch it as it is passing along. The one in whose hand it is found becomes the catcher.
—Crossmichael, Kirkcudbrightshire (Rev. Dr. Gregor).

Soldiers, Soldiers.

Soldiers, soldiers, march away,
Monday morning's here again;
The drums shall rattle, the pipes shall play
"Over the hills and far away."
Now you're married I wish you joy,
First a girl and then a boy;
If one don't kiss, the other must,
So kiss, kiss, kiss.
                    —Girton Village, Cambridgeshire (Dr. A. C. Haddon).

A circle is formed, and the children sing the first four lines.
One chooses a partner, and they dance round in the ring.

Three Dukes. [Vol. ii. pp. 233–255.]

In a version of the Three Dukes, collected by Dr. A. C.
Haddon, the first lines are—

> Here comes one duke a riding by, a riding by,
> A riding by (repeat).
> Rasima, Tasima, Tisima tay;
> Pray what is your will, sir?
> My will is to get married.
> Will any of my fair daughters do?
> They're all as stiff as pokers.
> We can bend as well as you, sir.

The duke goes round, chooses one, and sings—

> I go to the kitchen, I go to the hall,
> I pick the fairest one of all (as previous versions).
> —Girton Village, Cambridgeshire (Dr. A. C. Haddon).

Three Knights from Spain. (Vol. ii. pp. 257–279.]

A version of this game called "Gipsies," varies slightly from
those previously printed.

> Here comes one gipsy come from Spain,
> To call upon your daughter Jane;
>
> Our daughter Jane is far too young,
> To be controlled by flattering tongue.
>
> Oh, very well, I must away;
> I'll call again some other day.
>
> Come back, come back,
> Your tails are flag,
> And choose the fairest one you see.

The gipsy then chooses a girl from the line of players, and
asks her to come. The girl asked replies, "No." Then the
gipsy turns round and dances, saying, "Naughty girl, she
won't come out (repeat), to help me in my dancing." Again the
gipsy asks the girl, when she replies, "Yes," and goes to the
gipsy, who says, "Now we have got the flower of May, the

flower of May, &c., to help us with our dancing."—Auchencairn, N. B. (Mary Haddon).

Tug-of-War Game.

> Apples and oranges, two for a penny,
> Come all ye good scholars, buy ever so many.
> Come choose the east, come choose the west,
> Come choose the one you love the best.

Played like "Oranges and Lemons." One child is "Apple," and another "Orange."—Ross-shire (Rev. Dr. Gregor).

Played in the same way is—

> Pancakes and flitters is the wax of cantailers,[1]
> I owe you two farthings, I'll pay you to-morrow;
> Here comes a candle to light you to bed,
> Here comes a hatchet to chop off your head.
>   —Isle of Man (A. W. Moore).

We are the Rovers. [Vol. ii. pp. 343–360].

In a version sent me by Dr. Haddon, there is a slight variation. The first lines of each verse are—

> Have you any bread and wine?
> We are the Romans.
> Have you, &c.
>
> Yes, we have some bread and wine,
> We are the English.
> Yes, we have, &c.
>
> Will you give us some of it, &c.
> No; we'll give you none of it, &c.
> We will tell our magistrates, &c.
> We don't care for your magistrates, &c.
> We will tell our new-born prince, &c.
> We don't care for your new-born prince, &c.
> Are you ready for a fight?
> Yes, we're ready for a fight.
> Tuck up sleeves and have a fight.

General scrimmage follows.—Girton Village, Cambridgeshire (Dr. A. C. Haddon).

[1] Mr. Moore says he does not know the meaning of this word.

When I was a Young Girl. [Vol. ii. pp. 362–374.]
  The first lines are—
    When I was a naughty girl, &c., and this way went I
        (shrugging shoulders),
    When I was a good girl, &c. (folding arms, walking
        soberly),
    When I was a teacher (beating time or whacking,
        optional),
    When I went a-courting (walking arm in arm),
    When I had a baby (nursing apron as baby),
    When my baby died (crying),
    When my father beat me (hitting one another),
    When my father died,
        How I did laugh! (laughing).
                —Girton Village, Cambridgeshire (Dr. A. C. Haddon).

MEMOIR ON THE STUDY OF CHILDREN'S GAMES

CHILDREN'S games have not hitherto been studied in the same way as customs and superstitions and folk-tales have been studied, namely, as a definite branch of folk-lore. It is well however, to bear in mind that they form a branch by themselves, and that, as such, they contribute to the results which folk-lore is daily producing towards elucidating many unrecorded facts in the early history of civilised man.

Although games have been used by Dr. Tylor and others as anthropological evidence, these authorities have mostly confined themselves to those games of skill or chance which happen to have parallels in savage life; and the particular point of their conclusions rests rather upon the parallels, than upon the substantive evidence of the games themselves.

I will first point out the nature of the material for the study. It will be seen that the greater number of games printed in these two volumes have been collected by myself and many kind correspondents, from children in the present day—games that these children have learned from other children or from their parents, and in no case, so far as I am aware, have they been learned from a printed source. To this collection I have added all printed versions of the traditional game, that is, versions of games written down by the collector of folk-lore and dialect—in some cases unconscious collectors of folk custom—from any available source. A distinctive feature of the collection is, therefore, that I have printed all versions of each game known to me which show differences of words or methods of play. The importance of having all the principal variants from different parts of the country will be obvious when definite conclusions as to the origin and significance of traditional games are being considered.

Strutt mentions many games played by boys in his day, but his remarks are confined principally to games of skill with marbles, tops, &c., and games like " Prisoner's Base," " Scots and English," " Hot Cockles," &c. He records none of those interesting dialogue games which we know now as singing games. It may be that these games were in his day, as now, the property more of girls than of boys, and he may not have looked for or thought of recording them, for it can hardly be imagined that he was unaware of their existence. He records swinging and ball and shuttlecock playing as girls' amusements, but very little else, and it cannot even be suggested that the singing game and dialogue game have arisen since his time. Indeed, an examination of the games will, I hope, prove for them a very remote origin, showing traces of early beliefs and customs which children could not have invented, and would not have made the subjects of their play unless those beliefs and customs were as familiar to them as cabs, omnibuses, motor cars, and railways, are to the children of to-day, who use these things as factors in games which they make up.

I do not pretend to have made a complete collection of all versions of games to be found in the United Kingdom and Ireland. It will be seen from my list that some counties are entirely unrepresented ; but I think examples enough have been brought together from a sufficient number of different places to show that, even could I obtain the games of every county, I could not reasonably hope to obtain any that would be completely different from those appearing here. Versions differing, more or less, in words from these would, doubtless, appear, but I do not think an entirely different game, or any variants that would materially alter my conclusions, will now be found. All those sent me during the progress of the volumes through the press—and these are a considerable number—show no appreciable differences.

A detailed examination of each game has led me to draw

certain conclusions as to the origin of many of the games. These conclusions differ materially from those advanced by Halliwell, Strutt, or the earlier writers, when they have attempted to suggest the origin of a game. I also differ from Mr. Newell in many of the conclusions advanced in his admirable collection of American children's games, although I fully recognise the importance of his method of research. I believe, too, that hitherto no attention has been paid to the manner or method in which the game is played. It is to the "method" or "form" of play, when taken together with the words, that I wish to draw particular attention, believing it to be most important to the history of the games.

I do not, of course, claim that all the games recorded in these two volumes are traditional in their present form, or have had independent origins; many of these now known under different names have a common origin. There is, probably, not one game in the same condition, especially as regards words, as it was fifty or a hundred years ago; but I consider the "form" or "method" would remain practically the same even if the words get materially altered.

All games seem primarily to fall into one of two sections: the first, dramatic games; the second, games of skill and chance. Now the game proper, according to the general idea, must contain the element of winning or losing. Thus, the games of skill and chance are played either for the express purpose of winning property of some sort from a less fortunate or skilful player, or to attain individual distinction. Games of this kind are usually called boys' games, and are played principally by them; but beyond these generally recognised games is the important section of dramatic games, which are regarded as the property of the girls, and played principally by them.

These two sections are generally considered as the peculiar and particular property of each sex. Although this idea is borne out by a study of the traditional game, it will be found that the boys have dramatic games of their own, and the girls have special games of skill and chance. It has so happened, however, that the development in the case of the boys' dramatic games has been in the direction of increasing the rules or laws of a game, introducing thereby so much variety that it is difficult to recognise them as descendants of the dramatic originals. This has probably been the result of their use in school playgrounds, while the girls' dramatic games, not being utilised as a means of exercise, have been left alone, and are dying a natural death.

It will be convenient if, at this point, the games are classified as I shall use them in discussing the question of origin. The first necessary classification will relate to the incidents which show the customs and rites from which the games have descended; the second classification will relate to the dramatic force of the games, as it is from this that I hope to construct the ladder by which the game can be shown to have descended from a long past stage of culture.

The classification, according to incident, is as follows, the name of each game referring to the title-name in the dictionary :—

MARRIAGE GAMES.

All the Boys.	Merry-ma-tanza.
Babbity Bowster.	Nuts in May.
Cushion Dance.	Oats and Beans.
Down in the Valley.	Oliver, Oliver, follow the King.
Galley, Galley, Ship.	Pretty little Girl of Mine.
Glasgow Ships.	Queen Anne.
Hear all ! let me at her.	Rosy Apple.
Here comes a Virgin.	Round and round the Village.
Here's a Soldier left alone.	Sally Water.
Here stands a Young Man.	Silly Old Man, he walks alone.
Isabella.	Three Dukes.
Jolly Miller.	Three Knights.
King William.	Three Sailors.
Kiss in the Ring.	Widow.
Mary mixed a Pudding.	

COURTSHIP AND LOVEMAKING GAMES.

Curly Locks.	Jolly Hooper.
Dig for Silver.	Jolly Sailors.
Gallant Ship.	Knocked at the Rapper.
Here comes a Lusty Wooer.	Lady on the Mountain.
Here I sit on a Cold Green Bank.	Paper of Pins.
Hey Wullie Wine.	Pray, pretty Miss.

Queen Mary.
Ring me Rary.
Salmon Fishers.
Shame Reel.

Soldier.
Sun shines.
Three Old Bachelors.
Wind, The.

FORTRESS GAMES.

Barbarie, King of the.
Canlie (Addenda).
How many Miles to Babylon.
King of the Castle.

London Bridge.
Tower of London.
Willie Wastell.

FUNERAL GAMES.

Booman.
Green Grass.
Green Gravel.

Jenny Jones.
Old Roger.
Wallflowers.

HARVEST GAMES.

Oats and Beans and Barley.

Would you know how doth the
Peasant?

TRADE GAMES.

Dumb Motions.

Trades.

GHOST GAMES.

Deil amo' the Dishes.
Ghost at the Well.

Mouse and Cobbler.

WELL WORSHIP GAME.

Draw a Pail of Water.

RUSH-BEARING GAME.

Rashes.

TREE WORSHIP GAME.

Eller Tree.

WINDING UP GAMES.

Bulliheisle.
Port the Helm.
Snail Creep.

Tuilzie Wap.
Wind up the Bush Faggot.

TABU GAME.

Old Soldier.

DIVINATION GAMES.

Dan'l my Man.
Hot Cockles.
Jack's Alive.
Keppy Ball.
'Ot millo.

Priest Cat.
Ragman.
Ringie Red Belt.
Shuttlefeather.
Swinging.

VICTIMISING OR PENALTY GAMES.

(*Forms of Torture.*)

Block, Hammer, and Nail.
Bonnety.
Carrying the Queen a Letter.
Cat Beds.
Cobbin Match.
Cry Notchil.
Dump.
Ezzeka.
Father's Fiddle.
Heap the Cairn.
Hecklebirnie.
Hewley Puley.
Hickety Bickety.

Hiry Hag.
Hot Cockles.
Jack's Alive.
Magic Whistle.
More Sacks to the Mill.
Namers and Guessers.
Priest of the Parish.
Pun o' mair Weight.
Ronin the Bee.
Sacks.
Salt Eel.
Shoe the Auld Mare.
Wild Birds.

CHARM GAMES.

Cockeldy Bread.

Thun'er Spell.

EFFIGY GAME.

Drawing Dun out of the Mire.

IMITATION OF SPORT GAMES.

All a Row.
Cock-fight.
Hare and Hounds.

Hunting.
Knights.
Puff in the Dart.

IMITATION OF SPORTS (WITH ANIMAL) GAMES.

Badger the Bear.
Bull in the Park.
Call the Guse.
Cockertie-hooie.
Cock-fight.
Cock's-heading.
Doncaster Cherries.
Fox.

Fox in the Fold.
Fox in the Hole.
Frog in the Middle.
Garden Gate.
Hare and Hounds.
Shue-Gled-Wylie.
Wolf

WEIGHING GAMES.

Bag o' Malt.
Honey Pots.
Rockety Row.

Way Zaltin'.
Weigh the Butter.

WITCH OR CHILD STEALING GAMES.

Gipsy.
Keeling the Pot.
Mother, Mother, the Pot boils over.
Old Cranny Crow.

Steal the Pigs.
Three Jolly Welshmen.
Witch.

ANIMAL CONTEST GAMES.

Chickens, come clock.
Fox and Geese.
Gled-Wylie.
Hen and Chickens.
Letting the Buck out.

Old Dame.
Shepherds and Sheep.
Who goes round my Stone Wall?
Wolf.
Wolf and Lamb.

FISHING GAME.

Catch the Salmond.

CHURNING GAME.

Churning.

CONUNDRUM GAMES.

Cross Questions.
Thing done.

Three Flowers.

GUESSING GAMES.

All the Birds in the Air.
Bannockburn.
Bird Apprentice.
Birds, Beasts, and Fishes.
Brother Ebenezer.
Buck, Buck.
Buff.
Dumb Crambo.
Fool, Fool, come to School.
Handy Croopen.
Handy Dandy.

Hiss and Clap
Hot Cockles.
King Plaster Palacey.
Little Dog I call you.
Namers and Guessers.
Old Johnny Hairy.
Priest-Cat (2).
Religious Church.
Thimble Ring.
Trades.

CONTEST GAMES.

To take Prisoners.
  Bedlams.
  Blackthorn.
  Buckey-how.
  Canlie.
  Chickidy Hand.
  Click.
  Cock.
  Flowers.
  Hornie.
  Hunt the Staigie.
  Johnny Rover.
  King Cæsar.
  King Come-a-lay.
  King of Cantland.
  Lamploo.
  Over Clover.
  Prisoner's Base.
  Range the Bus.
  Rax.
  Relievo.
  Rin-im-over.
  Save all.
  Shepherds.
  Stacks.
  Stag.
  Stag Warning.
  Warney.

Catching and Touching for "he" or "it."
  Black Doggie.
  Blackman's Tig.
  Boggle about the Stacks.
  Canlie.
  Cross Tig.
  Cutters and Trucklers.
  Drop Handkerchief.
  Fire on the Mountains.
  Hand in and Hand out.
  High Windows.
  Jinkie.
  King o' the Castle.
  Letting the Buck out.
  Long Terrace.
  Mannie on the Pavement.
  One Catch all.
  Push in the Wash Tub.
  Puss in the Corner.
  Rakes and Roans.
  Round Tag.
  Ticky Touchwood.
  Tig.
  Time.
  Tom Tiddler's Ground.
  Touch.
  Tres-acre.
  Twos and Threes.

Prisoners and Possession of Ground.
  Barley Break.
  French and English.
  How many Miles to Babylon (2).
  Pi-cow.
  Prisoner's Base.
  Range the Bus.
  Rigs.
  Scots and English.

Tug of War.
  A' the Birdies.
  Namers and Guessers.
  Oranges and Lemons.
  Sun and Moon.
  Three Day's Holidays.
  Through the Needle 'ee.

DANCE GAMES.

(*With words and singing.*)

All the Soldiers in the Town.
Alligoshee.
Auntie loomie.
As I was walking.
Ball of Primrose.
Basket.

Bell-Horses.
Betsy Bungay.
Bingo.
Bold Jolly Lads.
Boys and Girls.
Carry my Lady to London.

Chicamy.
Click, Clock, Cluck.
Contrary, Rules of.
Dinah.
Duck Dance.
Duck under the Water.
Farmer's Den.
Frincy-francy.
Galloping.
Green Grass (Addenda).
Green grow the Leaves (2).
Green grow the Leaves.
Here we go Around.
Jenny Mac.
Jingo Ring.
Leap Candle.
Leaves are Green.
Long Duck.
Lubin.
My delight's in Tansies.
Phœbe.
Pop goes the Weasel.

Pray, pretty Miss.
Pretty Miss Pink.
Push the Business on.
Queen Mary.
Ring by Ring.
Ring o' Roses.
Round and Round went the Gallant Ship.
Sailor Lad.
Sally go round.
Sunday Night.
Three Little Ships.
Town Lovers.
Trip and Go.
Turn Cheeses.
Turn the Ship.
Turvey Turvey.
Uncle John.
Up the Streets.
Weary.
Weave the Diaper.

DANCE AND SEE-SAW GAMES.

Cobble.
Cobler's Hornpipe.
Curcuddie.
Cutch-a-Cutchoo.
Harie Hutcheon.

Hirtschin Hairy.
Huckie Buckie down the Brae.
See-saw.
Skiver the Guse.

HIDE AND SEEK GAMES.

(1.) PERSONS—
Bicky.
Cuckoo.
Gilty Galty
Hide and Seek (1).
Howly.
Kick the Block.
King by your Leave.
Mount the Tin.
Salt Eel.
Spy Arm.
Strike-a-licht.

(2). OBJECTS—
Codham.
Find the Ring.
Gigg.
Hide and Seek (2).
Kittlie-cout.
Odd-man.
Peesie Weet.
Priest Cat (2).
Shuffle the Brogue.
Smuggle the Gig.
Thimble Ring.
Tip it.

LEAP-FROG AND HOPPING GAMES.

Accroshay.
Bung the Bucket.
Cat Gallows.
Foot and Over.
Half Hammer.
Hop Frog.

Hopscotch.
Leap-frog.
Loup the Bullocks.
Saddle the Nag.
Ships.
Skin the Goatie.

CARRYING GAMES.

Betsy Bungay.
Carry my Lady to London.
King's Chair.

Knapsack.
Knights.

BLINDFOLD GAMES.

Blind Bell.
Blindman's Buff.
Blindman's Stan.
Buff.
Cock Stride.
Dinah.
French Blindman's Buff.
Giddy.

Hot Cockles.
Kick the Block.
Muffin Man.
Old Johnny Hairy, Crap in!
'Ot millo.
Pillie Winkie.
Pointing out a Point.
Queen of Sheba.

FOLLOW MY LEADER GAMES.

Follow my Gable.
Follow my Leader.
Jock and Jock's Man.
Quaker.

Quaker's Wedding.
Religious Church.
Solomon.
The Drummer Man.

FORFEIT GAMES.

American Post.
Button.
Cross Questions.
Diamond Ring.
Fire, Air, Water.
Follow my Gable.
Forfeits.
Genteel Lady.
Jack's Alive.

Malaga Raisins.
Mineral, Animal, Vegetable.
Minister's Cat.
Mr. Barnes.
Old Soldier.
Turn the Trencher.
Twelve Days of Christmas.
Wads and the Wears.

BALL, HAND.

Ball.
Ball in the Decker.
Balloon.
Balls and Bonnets.
Burly Whush.

Caiche.
Colley Ball.
Cuck-ball.
Cuckoo.
Han'-and-Hail.

Hats in Holes.
Keppy Ball.
Monday, Tuesday.
Pat-Ball.
Pize Ball.

Pots.
Stones.
Teesty-Tosty.
Trip-Trout.
Tut-ball.

BALL, FOOT.

Camp.
Football.

Hood.

BALL GAMES.

(*With bats and sticks played by rival parties.*)

Bad.
Baddin.
Bandy-ball.
Bandy-cad.
Bandy-hoshoe.
Bandy-wicket.
Bittle-battle.
Buzz and Bandy.
Cat and Dog.
Cat and Dog Hole.
Catchers.
Cat i' the Hole.
Chinnup.
Chow.
Church and Mice.
Codlings.
Common.
Crab-sowl.
Crooky.
Cuck-ball.
Cudgel.
Dab-an-Thricker.
Doddart.
Hawkey.
Hockey.

Hornie Holes.
Hummie.
Hurling.
Jowls.
Kibel and Nerspel.
Kirk the Gussie.
Kit-Cat.
Lobber.
Munshets.
Nur and Spel.
Peg and Stick.
Rounders.
Scrush.
Shinney.
Sow-in-the-Kirk.
Stones.
Stool-ball.
Tip-cat.
Trap-bat and ball.
Tribet.
Trippet and coit
Troap.
Trounce hole.
Trunket.
Waggles.

GAMES OF SKILL AND CHANCE.

AIM—*Throwing sticks or stones to hit particular object.*
  All in the Well.
  Cockly Jock.
  Cogs.
  Doagan.
  Duck at the Table.

Duckstone.
Loggats.
Mag.
Nacks.
Paip.
Pay Swad.
Peg-fiched.

Penny Cast.
Penny Prick.
Roly Poly.

BUTTONS.
Banger.
Buttons.
Cots and Twisses.
Hard Buttons.
Pitch and Toss.
Skyte the Bob.

CHANCE, or GAMBLING.
Chuck Farthing.
Cross and Pile.
Dab.
Davie Drap.
Hairry my Bossie.
Headicks and Pinticks.
Heads and Tails.
Hustle Cap.
Jingle-the-Bonnet.
Lang Larence.
Neivie-nick-nack.
Odd-man.
Odd or Even.
Pednameny.
Pick and Hotch.
Pinch.

CHERRY STONES.
Cherry Odds.
Cherry-pit.
Paip.

EGGS.
Blindman's Stan.
Cogger.
Jauping Paste-eggs.
Pillie Winkie.
Wink-egg.

MARBLES.
Boss-out.
Bridgeboard.
Bun-hole.
Capie-hole.
Castles.
Chock or Chock-hole.
Cob.
Crates.
Dumps.

Ho-go.
Hoilakes.
Holy Bang.
Hundreds.
Hynny-pynny.
Lab.
Lag.
Long-Tawl.
Marbles.
Nine Holes.
Pig-ring.
Pit-Counter.
Pits.
Plum Pudding.
Pyramids.
Ring-taw.
Ship-sail.
Shuvvy-Hawle.
Span-counter.
Spangie.
Spannims.
Splints.
Stroke.
Three Holes.

NUTS ON STRING.
Cob-nut.
Cock-battler.
Cogger.
Conkers.
Conquerors.
Jud.
Peggy Nut.

ON DIAGRAM OR PLAN.
Corsicrown.
Fipenny Morell.
Fox and Geese (2).
Hap-the-beds.
Hickety-Hackety.
Hopscotch.
Kit-cat-cannio.
London.
Nine Men's Morris.
Noughts and Crosses.
Pickie.
Tip-tap-toe.
Tit-tat-toe.
Tods-and-lambs.
Tray Trip.
Troy Town.

PENCE.
    Chuck Farthing.
    Chuck Hole.

PINS.
    Hattie.
    Pinny-Show.
    Pins.
    Pop-the-Bonnet.
    Push-pin.

SHUTTLECOCK.
    Shuttlefeather.

STONES AND DICE.
    Chance Bone.
    Checkstones.
    Chucks.
    Dalies.
    Dibbs.

    Ducks and Drakes.
    Gobs.
    Huckle-Bones.
    Jackysteauns.

TOPS.
    Chippings.
    Gully.
    Hoatie.
    Hoges.
    Peg-in-the-Ring.
    Peg Top.
    Scop-peril.
    Scurran-Meggy.
    Tops.
    Totum.
    Whigmeleerie.

WITH FINGERS AND STRING.
    Cat's-Cradle.

This leaves over a few games which do not come under either of these chief heads, and appear now to be only forms of pure amusement.   These are :—

    Blow-point.
    Bob Cherry.
    Bummers.
    Chinny-mumps.
    Cuddy among the Powks.
    Dish-a-loof.
    Dust Point.
    Handy Dandy.
    Level Coil.
    Lug and a Bite.
    Lugs.
    Magician.
    Malaga Raisins.
    Musical Chairs.
    Neighbour, I torment thee.
    Obadiah.
    Penny Hop.
    Pigeon Walk.
    Pinny Show.

    Pins.
    Pirly Peaseweep.
    Pon Cake.
    Poor and Rich.
    Prick at the Loop.
    Robbing the Parson's Hen Roost.
    Scat.
    She Said, and She Said.
    Stagging.
    Sticky-stack.
    Stroke Bias.
    Sweer Tree.
    Thing Done.
    Troco.
    Troule-in-Madame.
    Truncher.
    Turn Spit Jack.
    Wiggle Waggle.
    Wild Boar.

In order to show the importance of this classification, let me first refer to the games of skill.   These are (1) where one individual plays with some articles belonging to himself against several other players who play with corresponding articles belonging to them; (2) where one player attempts to gain articles deposited beforehand by all the players as stakes or objects to be played for. These games are played with buttons, marbles, cherry-stones, nuts, pins, and pence. In the second group, each player stakes one or more of these articles before beginning play, which stakes become the property of the winner of the game. The object of some of the games in the first group is the destruction of the article with which the opponent plays. This is the case with the games of "conkers" played with nuts on a string, and peg-top; the nuts and top are broken, if possible, by the players, to prevent their being used again, the peg of the top being retained by the winner as a trophy. The successful nut or top has the merit and glory of having destroyed previously successful nuts or tops. The victories of the one destroyed are tacked on and appropriated by each victor in succession. So we see a nut or a top which has destroyed another having a record of, say, twenty-five victories, taking these twenty-five victories of its opponent and adding them to its own score. In like manner the pegs of the tops slain in peg-top are preserved and shown as trophies. That the destruction of the implements of the game, although not adding to the immediate wealth of the winner, does materially increase his importance, is manifest, especially in the days when these articles were comparatively much more expensive than now, or when it meant, as at one time it must have done, the making of another implement.

These games are of interest to the folk-lorist, as showing connection with early custom. We know that playing at games for stakes involving life or death to the winner, or the possession of the loser's magical or valuable property or knowledge, is not only found in another branch of folk-lore, namely, folk-tales, but there is plenty of evidence of the early belief that the possession of a weapon which had, in the hands of a skilful chief, done great execution, would give additional skill and power to the person who succeeded in obtaining it. When I hear of a successful "conker" or top being preserved and handed down from father to son,[1] and exhibited with tales of its former victories, I believe we have survivals of the form of transmission of virtues from one person to another through the means of an acquired object. I do not think that the cumulative reckoning and its accompanying ideas would occur to modern boys, unless they had inherited the conception of the virtue of a conquered enemy's weapon being transferred to the conqueror's.

Other games of skill are those played by two or more players on diagrams or plans. Many of these diagrams and plans are found scratched or carved on the stone flooring or walls of old churches, cathedrals, and monastic buildings, showing that the boys and men of the Middle Ages played them as a regular amusement—probably monks were not averse to this kind of diversion in the intervals of religious exercise; plans were also made on the ground, and the games played regularly by shepherds and other people of outdoor occupation. We know this was so with the well-known "Nine Men's Morris" in Shakespeare's time, and there is no reason why this should not be the case with others, although "Nine Men's Morris" appears to have been the favourite. These diagram games are primitive in idea, and simple in form. They consist primarily of two players trying to form a row of three stones in three consecutive places on the plan; the one who first accomplishes this, wins. This is the case with "Kit-Cat-Cannio" (better known as "Noughts and Crosses") "Corsicrown" and "Nine Men's Morris."

Now, in "Noughts and Crosses" the simplest form of making a "row of three," where only two players play, and in another diagram game called "Tit-Tat-Toe," it is possible for neither player to win, and in this case the result is marked or scored to an unknown or invisible third player, who is called "Old Nick," "Old Tom," or "Old Harry." In some versions this third player is allowed to keep all the marks he registers, and to win the game if possible; in others, the next successful player takes "Old Nick's" score and adds it to his own.

[1] I know of one nut which was preserved and shown to admiring boys as a conqueror of 1000.

Here we have an element which needs explanation, and it is interesting to remind oneself of the primitive custom of assigning a certain proportion of the crops or pieces of land to the devil, or other earth spirit, which assignment was made by lot. It seems to me that a game in which an invisible player takes part must come from an era in which unknown spirits were believed to take part in people's lives, the interpretation of such part being obtained by means of divination.

Again, in the games played with ball (hand) are remains of divination, and the ball games played by two opposite parties with bats and sticks, the origin of our modern cricket and football, have been developed from those early contests which have played such an important part in parish and town politics. Even in the simple game of "Touch" or "Tig" a primitive element can be found. In this game, as in many others, it is one of the fundamental rules, now unfortunately being disregarded, that the player who is "he" or "it" must be chosen by lot; one of the "counting out" rhymes is said until all the players but one are counted out—this one is then "he." This "he" is apparently a "tabooed" person; he remains "he" until he succeeds in touching another, who becomes "tabooed" in turn, and the first is then restored to his own personality. There would be no necessity for this deciding by lot unless something of an ignominious or "evil" character had been originally associated with the "unnamed" or "tabooed" player. In some games the player who is counted out is the victim of the rough play or punishment, which is the motive of the game. It is possible that the game of "Touch" has developed from the practice of choosing a victim by lot, or from tabooing people suffering from certain diseases or subjected to some special punishment.

The "counting out" rhymes of children are in themselves an interesting and curious study. They contain the remains in distorted form of some of the early numerals. The fact of a counting-out rhyme being used in the games is of itself evidence of antiquity and old usage. For those interested in this branch of study I can refer to the valuable book on this subject by Mr. H. Carrington Bolton, which contains hundreds of these rhymes collected from various sources.

I mention these instances of possible connection between the games of skill and ancient belief and custom, to show that the anthropological significance of traditional games is not absent from what might perhaps be considered quite modern games. This is important to my argument, because when I turn to the dramatic section of children's games there is so much evidence of the survival of ancient custom and belief, that I am supported in the arguments which I shall advance by the fact that the whole province of children's play, and not particular departments, contribute to this evidence. It will be seen from the classification that many customs are dramatised or represented in a more or less imperfect form in a large number of games, and that these customs have been those which obtained a firm hold on the people, and formed an integral part of their daily life. Courtship, love, and marriage form the largest number; then the contest games for the taking of prisoners and of territory are the next in point of numbers. Funerals appear as the next most widely spread, then harvest customs, while the practice of divination, the belief in ghosts and charms, well-worship, tree-worship, and rush-bearing, witches, and child-stealing, are fully represented. Next come imitations of sports (animal), and contest games between animals, and then a number of games in which "guessing" is a principal feature, and a large number dealing with penalties or punishments inflicted for breach of rules.

A survey of the classification scheme of traditional games introduces the important fact that games contain customs; in other words, that games of skill and chance have come down from a time when practices were in vogue which had nothing originally to do with games, and that dramatic games have come down from times when the action they dramatise was the contemporary action of the people. It becomes important, therefore, to work more closely into the details of these games, to ascertain if we can what customs are preserved, to what people or period of culture they might have belonged. In many instances enough is said under each game to show the significance of the conclusions, but when brought together and compared one with another these conclusions become more significant. The fact that marriage custom is preserved in a given form becomes of immense value when it is found to have been preserved in many games. I shall not go further into the games of skill and chance, but confine myself to the important class of dramatic games.

By the dramatic game I mean a play or amusement which consists of words sung or said by the players, accompanied by certain pantomimic actions which accord with the words used, or, as I prefer to put it, of certain definite and settled actions performed by the players to indicate certain meanings, of which the words are only a further illustration.

To take the method of play first, I have found five distinct and different methods :—

(1) The line form of game, played by the children being divided into two sides of about an equal number on each side, with a space of ground of about eight or ten feet between the two lines. Each line joins hands, and advances and retires in turn while singing or saying their parts.

(2) The circle form, played by the children joining hands and forming a circle, and all walking or dancing round together when singing the words.

(3) The individual form, where the children take separate characters and act a little play.

(4) The arch form, in which two children clasp each other's hands, hold their arms high, and so form a kind of arch, beneath which all the other players run in single file.

(5) Winding-up form, in which the players, clasping hands, wind round another player until all are wedged closely together, and then unwind again, generally assuming a serpentine form in so doing.

It will be well, in the first place, to arrange the games played under each of these methods :—

GAMES PLAYED IN LINE FORM (*with singing and action*).

Babity Bowster.	Here comes a Lusty Wooer.
Green Grass.	Here comes one Virgin on her
Hark the Robbers (*one form*).	Knee.

Jenny Jones (*one form*).
Jolly Hooper (*only one line advance*).
Lady of the Land.
London Bridge (*one form*).
Mary Brown (*one form*).
Milking Pails.

Nuts in May.
Pray, pretty Miss (*one form*).
Queen Anne.
Three Dukes.
Three Knights.
Three Sailors.
We are the Rovers.

CIRCLE FORM (*singing and action subdivided into three methods*).

(1) Green Gravel.
Jolly Miller.
London Bridge (*some versions*).
Lubin.
Mulberry Bush.
Nettles.
Oats and Beans and Barley.
Ring a Ring o' Roses.
Rushes.
Wallflowers.
When I was a Young Girl.
Would You know how doth the Peasant?

(2) All the boys.
Down in the Valley.
Glasgow Ships.
Here stands a Young Man.
Isabella.
Jolly Fisherman.
Jolly Sailors.
King William.
Kiss in the Ring.
Knocked at the Rapper.

Lady on the Mountain.
Mary Brown.
Mary mixed a Pudding.
Merry-ma-tanza.
Needle Cases.
Old Widow.
Oliver, Oliver, follow the King.
Poor Mary sits a-weeping.
Poor Widow.
Pretty little Girl of Mine.
Punch Bowl.
Queen Mary.
Rosy Apple, Lemon, and Pear.
Round and Round the Gallant Ship.
Sally Water.
Silly Old Man.
Uncle John.
Wind.

(3) Booman.
Old Roger.
Round and Round the Village.
Who goes round my Stone Wall?

INDIVIDUAL FORM (*dialogue game*).

Auld Grannie.
Baste the Bear.
Fox and Goose.
Ghost at the Well.
Gipsey.
Gled-wylie.
Hen and Chickens.
Honey Pots.
Jack, Jack, the Bread's a-burnin'.
Keeling the Pot.
King of the Barbarie.
Lady on yonder Hill.

Lend Me your Key.
Mother, may I go out?
Mother Mop.
Mother, Mother, the Pot boils over.
Mouse and Cobbler.
Old Granny Crow.
Old Woman.
Shepherds and Sheep.
Steal the Pigs.
Three Jolly Welshmen.
Witch.

The arch form of game, or tug-of-war as it is usually called, subdivide into two methods :—

ARCH FORM.

(1) Draw a Pail of Water.
    Hark the Robbers (*some versions*).
    How many Miles to Babylon.
    London Bridge.
    Long Duck.
    Thread the Needle.
    Through the Needle Eye.

(2) Fool, Fool, come to School.
    Hark the Robbers (*some versions*).
    Little Dog, I call you.
    Namers and Guessers.
    Oranges and Lemons.
    Three Days' Holidays.
    Tug of War.

WINDING UP, OR SERPENT'S COIL FORM.

Bulliheisle.
Eller Tree.
Port the Helm.

Snail Creep.
Tuilzie Wap.
Winding up the Bush Faggot.

The first or line form of games is characterised by no one player being distinguished above his fellows; there are no distinct or separate characters to be played. All the players on one line say the same words and perform the same actions; all advance together and retire together. Each line stands still while the other line advances, retires, and has its "say." In this way questions are asked and answers are given. Questions and answers form an essential part of the line form of game. The one line of players imply action of a party composed of several persons who are of the same opinion, and the line on the opposite side is a party who hold different opinions, and express these in words and by actions; so that in no game played in line form do we get unanimous action of all the players, but half and half.

These line games represent in the main a contest, and there are contests of different kinds; that is, war between the people of two different locations, between parishes or border countries of different nationalities, and contests for wives, of a more or less friendly nature. That the lines or sides indicate people who come from one country or district to another country or district is shown, I think, by the fact that a line is drawn in the middle of the ground, which line separates the territory of the two sides. Players can go as far as the line on their own side, but one step over lands them in the enemy's territory. In a marriage game of the line form, the girl when unwilling is pulled across the line, and when willing she walks across to the opposite side. It is also clear that in the marriage games the party on one side represents young men, and on the other side young women.

In the second group, the circle form, all the players join hands to form a circle. They all perform the same actions and say the same words. This circle form is used in three ways.

In the first or simplest class all the players perform the same actions, sing the same words all together. There is no division into parties, and no individual action or predominance. This method is adopted when a certain recurring custom is celebrated or a special event is commemorated. The event is described in pantomimic action, and accompanied with dance and song.

In the second class the circle is formed, the players all clasp hands, dance round together, and sing the same words; but the action is confined to first one and then two players, who are taken by "choice" from those forming the circle. This class principally consists of courtship, love-making, and marriage games. The two principal parties concerned usually have no words to say, though in some "love" games the centre player does express his or her own feelings in verse. The fact that this form is used for love and marriage games accounts for the much larger number of games in this class and their greater variety.

In the third class of the circle game the players form the circle to act the part of "chorus" to the story. There are also two, three, or four players, as required, who act parts in dumb show suitable to the character personified. In this class the circle personate both animate and inanimate objects. The circle is stationary—at least the players forming it do not dance or walk round. They sometimes represent houses; a village, and animals are usually represented rather than people.

The circle games I consider to be survivals of dramatic representations of customs performed by people of one village or of one town or tribe—representations of social customs of one place or people, as distinct from the "line" form of games, which represent a custom obtaining between two rival villages or tribes. Thus I am inclined to consider the joining of hands in a circle as a sign of amity, alliance, and kinship. In the case of the line games hands are clasped by all players on each side, who are thus in alliance against those on the opposite side. When hands are joined all round so that a circle is formed, all are concerned in the performance of the same ceremony. There is no division into parties, neither is difference of opinion shown either by action or words in circle games.

In the third class of game there are several distinct characters, and the game partakes more of the nature of what we should call a play proper, and may be considered an outcome of the circle play. There are several characters, usually a mother, a witch or old woman, an elder daughter and several younger children, a ghost, and sometimes animals, such as sheep, wolves, fox, hen, and chickens. The principal characters (not more than two or three) are played by different children, and these having each a part allotted to them, have also a certain amount of dialogue to say, and corresponding actions to perform. The remaining characters, whether children or animals, merely act their part when action is required, all doing the same thing, and have no words to say. The dialogue in these games is short and to the point. It has not been learnt from written sources, but orally, and as long as the main idea and principal incidents are not departed from, the players may, according to their capacity, add to or shorten the dialogue to heighten the situation. There is no singing in these games, though there is what perhaps might be called the remains of rhyme in the dialogue.

The fourth form, that of the arch, is played in two ways. In the first, two children clasp their hands and hold them up to form an arch. Under this all the other players run as if going through an arch or gateway, and the players are generally stopped by the two who form the arch. Then a circle is formed, and all the players join hands and dance round together. In the second way, the arch is formed as above, and all the players run under. These players are then caught one by one within the arch, and have to choose one of the two leaders, behind whom they stand. A tug-of-war then ensues between the two leaders and their followers.

The first of these, that ending with the circle or dancing, indicates the celebration of an event in which all the people join, and all are of one way of thinking—differing from this group of customs celebrated by the simple circle game by each person in turn performing a ceremony, signified in games by the action of going under or through an arch.

The second way, when the "tug" follows, represents a contest, but I do not think the contest is of the same kind as that of the line form. This rather represents the leaders of two parties who are antagonistic, who call, in the words of the rhymes, upon the people of a town, or faction, to join one of the two sides. The fact that each player in the line or string is caught by the leaders, and has to choose which of them he will fight under, together with the tug or pulling of one side over a marked line, by the other side, indicates a difference in the kind of warfare from the line contests, where territory is clearly the cause of the struggle and fight. The line contest shows a fight between people of different lands; and the arch contest, a method of choosing leaders by people living in one land or town.

In the fifth form, "winding up games," the players join hands in a long line, and wind round and round one player at the end of the line, usually the tallest, who stands still until all are formed in a number of circles, something like a watch spring. They then unwind, sometimes running or dancing, in a serpentine fashion until all are again in straight line. These games probably refer to the custom of encircling trees, as an act of worship. They differ from the circle game in this way: The players in a circle game surround something or some one. In the "winding up" game they not only surround, but attachment or "hold" to the thing surrounded has to be kept.

The fact that these games lend themselves to such treatment, and the fact that I am obliged to use the terms, district, tribe, localities, obliged to speak of a state of contest between groups, of the sacred encircling of a tree, and of other significant usages, go far to suggest that these games must contain some element which belongs to the essential part of their form, and my next quest is for this element. I shall take each class of game, and endeavour to ascertain what element is present which does not necessarily belong to games, or which belongs to other and more important branches of human action; and it will depend on what this element is as to what can ultimately be said of the origin of the games.

Of the games played in "line" form, "We are the Rovers" is the best representative of pure contest between two opposing parties. If reference is made to the game (vol. ii. pp. 343–356), the words will be found to be very significant. In my account of the game (pp. 356–60), I suggest that it owes its origin to the Border warfare which existed on the Marches between England and Scotland and England and Wales, and I give my reasons, from analysing the game, why I consider it represents this particular form of contest rather than that of a fight between two independent countries. Both sides advancing and retiring in turn, while shouting their mutual defiance, and the final fight, which continues until all of one side are knocked down or captured, show that a deliberate fight was intended to be shown. I draw attention, too, to the war-cry used by each side, which is also significant of one of the old methods of rallying the men to the side of their leader—an especially necessary thing in undisciplined warfare. This game, then, contains relics of ancient social conditions. That such a contest game as this is represented by the line form combining words, singing, and action, is, I submit, good evidence of my contention that the line form of game denotes contest. This game, then, I consider a traditional type of contest game.

It is remarkable that among the ordinary, now somewhat old-fashioned, contest games played by boys there should be some which, I think, are degenerate descendants of this traditional type. There are a number of boys' games, the chief features of which are catching and taking prisoners and getting possession of an enemy's territory—as in the well-known "Prisoner's Base" and "Scots and English." "Prisoner's

Base" (ii. pp. 80–87) in its present form does not appear to have much in common with games of the type of "We are the Rovers," but on turning to Strutt we find an earlier way of playing (*ibid*. p. 80). Now, this description by Strutt gives us "Prisoner's Base" played by two lines of players, each line joining hands, their homes or bases being at a distance of twenty to thirty feet apart. That the line of players had to keep to their own ground is, I think, manifest, from it being necessary for one of the line to touch the base. There is no mention of a leader. Thus we have here an undoubted form of a contest game, where the taking of prisoners is the avowed motive, played in almost the same manner as the line dramatic game. When the dramatic representation of a contest became formulated in a definite game, the individual running out and capturing a certain player on the opposite side would soon develop and become a rule of the game, instead of all on one side trying to knock down all on the other side. It may be a point to remember, too, that in primitive warfare the object is to knock down and kill as many of the enemy as possible, rather than the capture of prisoners.

In other games of a similar kind, the well-known "Scots and English" (ii. p. 183), for example, we have the ground divided into two parts, with a real or imaginary line drawn in the middle; the players rush across the line and try to drag one of the opposite side across it, or to capture the clothes of the players.

In other boys' games—"Lamploo," "Rax," "King of Cantland," "King Cæsar," "Stag"—there are the two sides; the players are sometimes all on one side, and they have to rush across to the other, or there are some players on each side, who rush across to the opposite, trying to avoid being taken prisoner by a player who stands in the middle between the opposite goals. When this player catches a boy, that boy joins hands with him; the next prisoner taken also joins hands, and these assist in capturing others. This is continued until all the players are caught and have joined hands in a long line, practically reverting to the line form of game, and showing, according to my theory of the line

game, that all joining hands are of one side or party. If
the line gets broken the players can run back to their own
side. There are many other games which are played in a
similar way (see Contest Games), though farther removed from
the original form. In most of these we have practically the
same thing—the sides have opposite homes, and the leader,
though individual at first, becomes merged in the group when
the line is formed, and the game ends by all the players being
on one side. It must be mentioned, too, that in these boys'
games of fighting, the significant custom of "crowning," that
is, touching the head of the captured one, obtains. If this is
omitted the prisoner is at liberty to escape (see "Cock," "King
of Cantland").

Although there is no dialogue between the opposing parties
in these contest games, there are in some versions undoubted
remains of it, now reduced to a few merely formal words
called a "nominy." These "nominys" must be said before
the actual fight begins, and the remains are sufficient to
show that the nominy was originally a defiance uttered by
one side and answered by the other. For these nominys,
see "Blackthorn," "Chickidy Hand," "Hunt the Staigie,"
"Scots and English," "Johnny Rover," "Shepherds," "Stag,"
"Warney," &c.

The next most important games in line form are marriage
games. In the well-known "Nuts in May" (vol. i. p. 424–
433) there is a contest between the two parties, but the
contest here is to obtain an individual for the benefit of the
side. A line is drawn on the ground and a player is deliberately sent to "fetch" another player from the opposite side,
and that this player is expected to conquer is shown by
the fact that he is selected for this purpose, and also because
the ceremony of "crowning" prevails in some versions. The
boy, after he has pulled the girl across the line, places his hand
on her head to complete the capture and to make a prisoner.
This custom of "crowning" prevails in many games where prisoners are made, and I have already mentioned it as occurring in
the boys' contest games. If the crowning is performed, the
capture is complete; if not performed, the prisoner may escape.

The evidence of this game, I consider, points to customs which belong to the ancient form of marriage, and to what is technically known as marriage by capture.

In the game of the "Three Dukes" (vol. ii. p. 233–255), it will be noticed that the actions are very spirited. Coquetry, contempt, and annoyance are all expressed in action, and the boys imitate riding and the prancing of horses. I must draw special attention to the remarks I have made in my account of the game, and for convenience in comparing the line marriage games I will repeat shortly the principal points here.

In some versions, the three dukes each choose a wife at the same time, and when these three are "wived" or "paired" another three do the same. In another version "five" dukes each choose a wife, and all five couples dance round together. But most significant of all is the action of the dukes after selecting the girl, trying to carry her off, and her side trying to prevent it.

In this game, then, I think we have a distinct survival of or remembrance of the tribal marriage—marriage at a period when it was the custom for the men of a clan or village to seek wives from the girls of another clan—both belonging to one tribe. The game is a marriage game of the most matter-of-fact kind. Young men arrive from a place at some distance for the purpose of seeking wives. The maidens are apparently ready and expecting their arrival. They are as willing to become wives as the men are to become husbands. It is not marriage by force or capture, though the triumphant carrying off of a wife appears. It is exogamous marriage custom. The suggested depreciation of the girls, and their saucy rejoinders, are so much good-humoured chaff and banter exchanged to enhance each other's value. There is no mention of "love" in the game, nor courtship between the boy and girl. The marriage formula does not appear, nor is there any sign that a "ceremony" or "sanction" to marry is necessary, nor does "kissing" occur. Another interesting point about this game is the refrain, "With a rancy, tancy, tee," which refrain, or something similar, accompanies all verses of all versions, and separates this game from others akin to it. This refrain is doubtless a survival of an old tribal war-cry.

The game of "The Three Knights from Spain" (ii. pp. 257–279), played in the same way as "Three Dukes," may appear at first to be a variant of the "Three Dukes"; but it is significant that the form of marriage custom is different, though it is still marriage under primitive conditions of society. The personal element, entirely absent from the "Three Dukes," is here one of the principal characteristics. The marriage is still one without previous courtship or love between two individuals, but the parental element is present here, or, at any rate, if not parental, there is that of some authority, and a sanction to marry is given, although there is no trace of any actual ceremony. The young men apparently desire some particular person in marriage, and a demand is made for her. The suitors here are, I think, making a demand on the part of another rather than for themselves. They may be the ambassadors or friends of the would-be bridegroom, and are soliciting for a marriage in which purchase-money or dowry is to be paid. The mention of "gold" and "silver" and the line, "She must be sold," and the offering of presents by the "Knights," are important. These indications of purchase refer to a time when the custom of offering gold, money, and other valuables for a bride was in vogue. While, therefore, the game has traces of capturing or carrying off the bride, this carrying off is in strict accord with the conditions prevalent when marriage by purchase had succeeded to marriage by capture. There is evidence in this game of a mercantile spirit, which suggests that women and girls were too valuable to be parted with by their own tribe or family without something deemed an equivalent in return.

In another line game, "Here comes Three Sailors" (ii. pp. 282–289), there is still more evidence of the mercantile or bargaining spirit. Here the representative of the parental element or other authority selects the richest and highest in rank of the suitors, and a sum of money is given with the bride. The suitors are supposed to have performed some actions which have gained them renown and entitled them to a wife. The suitors are accepted or rejected by a person having authority, and this authority introduces an interesting and suggestive feature. The suitors are invited to stay or lodge in the house if accepted, probably meaning admission into the family. The girl is to "wake up," and not sleep, that is, to rouse up, be merry, dress in bridal array, and prepare for the coming festival. She is given to the suitors with "in her pocket one hundred pounds," and "on her finger a gay gold ring." This is given by the "mother" or those having authority, and refers, I believe, to the property the girl takes with her to her new abode for her proper maintenance there; the ring shows her station and degree, and is a token that she is a fit bride for a "king." Curious, too, is the "Here's my daughter safe and sound," which looks like a warrant or guarantee of the girl's fitness to be a bride, and the robbery of the bride may also have originally related to the removal of the bride's wedding-dress or ornaments before she enters on her wifely duties.

Following these definite marriage games in line form, in which previous love or courtship does not appear, we have several games formerly played at weddings, practically as a part of the necessary amusement to be gone through after a marriage ceremony by the company present, amusements in which are the traces of earlier custom.

"Babbity Bowster" (i. pp. 9-11) is an old Scottish dance or game which used to be played as the last dance at weddings and merrymakings. It was danced by two lines of players, lads on one side, girls on the other. A lad took a handkerchief—in earlier times a bolster or pillow—and danced out in front of the girls, singing. He then selected a girl, threw the handkerchief into her lap or round her neck, holding both ends himself, and placed the handkerchief at her feet on the floor. His object was to obtain a kiss. This was not given without a struggle, and the line of girls cheered their companion at every unsuccessful attempt the boy made. When a girl took the handkerchief she threw it to a boy, who had to run after and catch her and then attempt to take a kiss. When all had done thus they danced in line form. This dance took place at the time when bride and bridegroom retired to the nuptial chamber. It is probable the bride and bridegroom would first go through the dance, and after the bridegroom had caught his bride and they had retired the dance would be continued in sport. The chasing of the bride in sport by her new-made husband at the close of the marriage festivities is mentioned in old ballads.

In the "Cushion Dance" (i. pp. 87–94) we have an instance of another similar old English game sang and danced at weddings. The "Cushion Dance," though not played in line form, has two other elements of "Babbity Bowster." The description is so interesting, I will repeat it shortly here. The company were all seated. Two young men left the room, and returned carrying, one a square cushion, the other a drinking horn or silver tankard. The young man carrying the cushion locked the door, taking the key. The young men then danced round the room to a lively tune played by a fiddler, and sang the words of the dance. There is a short dialogue with the fiddler, in which it is announced that "Jane Sandars won't come to." The fiddler says "She must come, whether she will or no." The young men then dance round again and choose a young woman, before whom they place the cushion and offer the horn or cup. The girl and the young man kneel on the cushion and kiss. Here there is no capturing or chasing of the girl, but her reluctance to be brought to the cushion is stated by another person, and the locking of the door is evidently done to prevent escape of the girls.

Other line games contain the element of courting, some versions of "Green Grass," for instance (i. pp. 161–62), show boys on one line, girls on the other, inviting girls to come and dance, and promising them gifts. After the boys have selected a girl, she is asked if she will come. She replies first No! then Yes! "Pray, Pretty Miss," is similar to these (vol. ii. pp. 65–67).

The remaining line form of marriage games are probably degenerate versions of "Three Dukes," "Three Knights," except "Here Comes a Lusty Wooer" (i. 202) and "Jolly

Hooper" (i. 287–88). Ritson records the first of these two in "Gammer Gurton's Garland," 1783; the second is probably a degenerate version of the first or similar version. They are both demands for a bride.

The other important line games are "Jenny Jones" (i. 260-283), "Lady of the Land," and "Queen Anne." I refer here to the Scotch version of "Jenny Jones," quoted from Chambers, given in vol. i. p. 281, where "Janet Jo" is a dramatic entertainment amongst young rustics. Two of the party represent a goodman and a goodwife, the rest a family of daughters. One of the lads, the best singer, enters, demands to court Janet Jo. He is asked by the goodwife what he will give for Janet Jo. His offers of a peck o' siller, a peck of gold, are refused; he offers more and is accepted, and told to sit beside his chosen one. He then has a scramble with her for kisses. Versions of this game which indicate funeral customs will be treated under that head; but love and courtship appear in the game, and the courting appears to be that of a young man or young men, to whom objection is made, pretended or real; the suitors are evidently objects of suspicion to the parental authority, and their sincerity is tested by the offers they make.

In "Queen Anne," vol. ii. pp. 90–102, I have attempted a conjectural rendering of what the game might have been, by putting together the words of different versions. If this conjectural restoration be accepted as something near the original form, it would suggest that this game originated from one of the not uncommon customs practised at weddings and betrothals, where the suitor has to discriminate between several girls all dressed exactly alike, and to distinguish his bride by some token. This incident of actual primitive custom also obtains in folk-tales, showing its strong hold on popular tradition. Many a lost bride in the folk-tales proves her identity by having possession of some article previously given as a token, and this idea may account for the "ball" incident in this game. (See also "King William.")

From these games, when thus taken together, we have evidence of the existence of customs obtaining in primitive marriage, and the fact that these customs, namely, those of marriage by capture, marriage by purchase, marriage by consent of others than those principally concerned, in other words, marriage between comparative strangers, occur in games played in line form, a form used for contest and fighting games, tends to show that the line form is used for the purpose of indicating the performance of customs which are supposed to take place between people living in different countries, towns, and villages, or people of different tribes or of different habits and customs. The more imperfect games of this type, though they have lost some of the vigour, have still enough left to show, when placed with the others, a connection with customs performed in the same manner.

In "Lady of the Land," for instance (vol. i. pp. 313–20), the words indicate a lady hiring a poorer woman's daughters as servants, and, no doubt, originates from the country practice of hiring servants at fairs, or from hirings being dramatically acted at Harvest Homes. The old practice of hirings at fairs is distinctly to be traced in local customs (see p. 319), and is a common incident in folk-tales. In this game, too, actions would be performed suitable to the work the players undertake to do.

It is not necessary to mention in detail any of the remaining line games, because they are fragmentary in form, and do not add any further evidence to that already stated.

In considering this group of games it is obvious, I think, that we have elements of custom and usage which would not primarily originate in a game, but in a condition of local or tribal life which has long since passed away. It is a life of contest, a life, therefore, which existed before the days of settled politics, when villages or tribal territories had their own customs differing from each other, and when not only matters of political relationship were settled by the arbitrament of the sword, but matters now considered to be of purely personal relationship, namely, marriage. While great interest gathers round the particular marriage customs or particular contests indicated in this group of games, the chief point of interest lies in the fact that they are all governed by the common element of contest.

I will now turn to the circle games. Like the line games, this form contains games which show marriage custom, but it is significant that they all show a distinctly different form of marriage. Thus they all show courtship and love preceding the marriage, and they show that a distinct ceremony of marriage is needful; but this ceremony is not necessarily the present Church ceremony. The two best examples are " Sally Water" (vol. ii. pp. 149–179) and " Merry-ma-tansa" (vol. i. pp. 369–367).

In " Sally Water" the two principal characters have no words to say, but one chooses another deliberately, and the bond is sealed by a kiss, and in some instances with joining of hands. The circle of friends approve the choice, and a blessing and good wishes follow for the happiness of the married couple, wishes that children may be born to them, and the period of the duration of the marriage for seven years (the popular notion of the time for which the marriage vows are binding). I have printed a great many versions of this game (about fifty), and note that in the majority of them " Sally" and " Water" are conspicuous words. In fact they are usually taken to mean the name of the girl, but on examining the game closely I think it is possible, and probable, that " Sally Water" may be a corruption of some other word or words, not the name of a girl; that the word "Water" is connected, not with the name of the maiden, but with the action of sprinkling which she is called upon to fulfil. The mention of water is pretty constant throughout the game. There are numerous instances of the corruption of words in the game, and the tendency has been to lose the sprinkling of water incident altogether.

The sitting or kneeling attitude, which indicates a reverential attitude, obtains in nearly all versions, as do the words " Rise and choose a young man," and "Crying for a young man." This " crying" for a young man does not necessarily mean weeping; rather I consider it to mean "announcing a want" in the way "wants" or "losses" were cried formerly by the official crier of a town, and in the same manner as in games children "cry" forfeits; but, losing this meaning in this game, children have substituted "weeping," especially as "weeping" with them expresses many "wants" or "woes." The incident of "crying" for a lover, in the sense of wanting a lover, appears in several of these games. I have heard the expression they've been "cried in church" used as meaning the banns have been read. The choosing is sometimes "to the east" and "to the west," instead of "for the best and worst." Now, the expression "for better for worse" is an old marriage formula preserved in the vernacular portion of the ancient English Marriage Service, and I think we have the same formula in this game, especially as the final admonition is to choose the "one loved best." Then comes the very general lines of the marriage formula occurring so frequently in these games, "Now you're married, we wish you joy," &c.

In "Merry-ma-tansa" the game again consists of a marriage ceremony, with fuller details. The choice of the girl is announced to the assembled circle of friends by a third person, and the friends announce their approval or disapproval. If they disapprove, another choice is made. When they approve, the marriage formula is repeated, and the capacity of the bride to undertake housewifely duties is questioned in verse by the friends (p. 370). All the circle then perform actions imitating sweeping and dusting a house, baking and brewing, shaping and sewing. The marriage formula is sung, and prognostications and wishes for the birth of children are followed by actions denoting the nursing of a baby and going to church, probably for a christening. In one version, too, the bride is lifted into the circle by two of the players. This may indicate the carrying of the bride into her new home, or the lifting of the bride across the threshold, a well-known custom. In another version (Addenda, p. 444) after the ceremony the bridegroom is blindfolded and has to catch his bride.

These two games relate undoubtedly to marriage customs, and to no other ceremony or practice. They are, so to speak, the type forms to which others will assimilate.

In "Isabella" (vol. i. pp. 247–56) the actions indicate a more modern marriage ceremony. The young couple, after choosing, go to church, clasp hands, put on ring, kneel down, say prayers, kiss, and eat dinner. The clasping of hands, putting on a ring, and kissing are more like a solemn betrothal before a marriage ceremony.

In the other marriage games which show remains of a ceremony are those of the kind to which "All the Boys" belongs (vol. i. pp. 2–6). In this game, customs which belong to a rough and rude state of society are indicated. The statement is made that a man cannot be happy without a wife. He "huddles" and "cuddles" the girl, and "puts her on his knee."

The principal thing here to be noted is the mention in all versions of this game the fact that some food is prepared by the bride, which she gives to the bridegroom to eat. This, although called a "pudding," refers, of course, to the bridal cake, and to the old custom of the bride preparing it herself, and giving some to her husband first.

Other rhymes of this kind, belonging, probably, to the same game, are "Down in the Valley," "Mary mixed a Pudding," "Oliver, Oliver, follow the King," "Down in Yonder Meadow." In all these the making and eating of a particular "pudding" or food is mentioned as an important item; in two, catching and kissing the sweetheart is mentioned; and in all, "courting" and "cuddling"; articles for domestic use are said to be bought by the bride. The formal ceremony of marriage is contained in the verbal contract of the two parties, and the important ceremony of the bridegroom and bride partaking of the bridal food. The eating together of the same food is an essential part of the ceremony among some savage and semi-civilised peoples. The rhymes have a peculiar parallel in the rude and rough customs associated with betrothal and marriage which prevailed in Wales and the North of England.

In "Poor Mary sits a-weeping" (vol. ii. pp. 46–62) we have very distinctly the desire of the girl for a "lover." She is "weeping" for a sweetheart, and, as in the case of "Sally Water," her weeping or "crying" is to make her "want" known. She is told by her companions to rise and make her choice. In some versions the marriage lines follow, in others the acceptance of the choice ends with the giving of a kiss.

Others of a similar kind are " Here stands a Young Man who wants a Sweetheart " (vol. i. p. 204), " Silly Old Man who wants a Wife " (vol. ii. 196–99). This is a simple announcement of the young man's need for a wife or sweetheart (probably originally intended to announce his having arrived at manhood, as expressed in the expression, " he ain't a man till he's got a sweetheart and gone a-courtin' "). These verses are followed by the marriage formula. Games of this kind are used for a kiss in the ring game, without the chasing and capturing. The ordinary kiss in the ring games are probably relics of older custom. These consist of one person going round the assembled circle with a handkerchief and choosing another of the opposite sex, after saying a nominy or form of set words. This was probably originally something in the shape of a " counting out " rhyme, to obtain sweethearts by " lot." A chase follows, and capture of the girl, and the giving and receiving of a kiss in the circle. This was a method of choosing sweethearts which prevailed until quite a late period at country festivals and fairs, but at an earlier period was a serious function. It is still customary on Easter and Whit-Monday for this game to be played on village greens, and the introduction thus afforded is held sufficient to warrant continued acquaintance between young people.

In connection with this class of games I must point out that a game such as " Hey, Wullie Wine " (vol. i. pp. 207–210), though it cannot be considered exactly a marriage game, points to the matter-of-fact way in which it was customary for young people to possess sweethearts. It seems to have been thought not only desirable, but necessary to their social standing. A slur is cast on the young man or young woman who has no lover, and so every facility is given them to make a choice from among their acquaintances. In the game "King William" is a remnant of the disguising of the bride among some of her girl friends and the bridegroom's test of recognition, when that custom became one of the forms of amusement at weddings.

The remaining love and marriage games mostly consist of lines said in praise of some particular girl or young man, the necessity of him or her possessing a sweetheart, and their being married. These are probably fragments of the more complete forms preserved in the other games of this class. Marriage games, preceded by courtship or love-making, are played in the second method of the circle form.

Among the games played in the first method of the circle form, "Oats and Beans and Barley," and "Would you know how doth the Peasant," show harvest customs. The first of these (vol. ii. pp. 1-13) shows us a time when oats, beans, and barley were the principal crops grown, before wheat—now, and for some time, one of the principal crops—came into such general cultivation as at present. All the players join in singing the words and performing the actions. They imitate sowing of seed, folding arms and standing at ease while the corn is growing, clap hands and stamp on the ground to awake the earth goddess, and turning round and bowing, to propitiate the spirit and do reverence to her. In "Would you know how doth the Peasant" (ii. 399-401) we find actions performed showing sowing, reaping, threshing, kneeling, and praying, and then resting and sleeping. These actions are in both games accompanied by dancing round hand in hand. These two games, then, take us back to a time when a ceremony was performed by all engaged in sowing and reaping grain; when it was thought necessary to the proper growth of the crops that a religious ceremony should be performed to propitiate the earth spirit. I believe these games preserve the tradition of the formula sung and danced at the spring festivals, about which Mr. Frazer has written so fully.

"Oats and Beans and Barley" also preserves a marriage formula, and after the religious formula has been sung and danced, courting and marriage follows. A partner is said to be wanted, is chosen, and the marriage ceremony follows. The addition of this ceremony to the agricultural custom is of considerable significance, especially as the period is that of spring, when, according to Westermarck, natural human marriage, as also animal pairing, takes place. It is evidently necessary to this game for all the players to perform the same actions, and the centre player is not required until the choosing a partner occurs. There is no centre player in the other agricultural game, and no marriage occurs.

In "When I was a Young Girl" (ii. pp. 362–374) we have all players performing actions denoting the principal events of their lives from girlhood to old age. When young, enjoyment in the form of dancing is represented (in present day versions, going to school is taking the place of this), then courting, marriage, nursing a baby, and occupations which women perform; the death of the baby and of husband follows, and the woman takes in washing, drives a cart to support herself, and finally gets old. Here, again, there is little doubt that this game owes its origin to those dances originally sacred in character, in which men and women performed actions, accompanied with song and dance, of the same nature as those they wished or intended to perform seriously in their own lives. "Mulberry Bush" is another descendant of this custom. In "Green Gravel" and "Wallflowers" we have a death or funeral custom. Originally there may have been other actions performed than those the game contains now. These two are noticeable for the players turning themselves round in the course of the play so that they face outwards. It is this turning outwards, or "to the wall," which indicates hopeless sorrow and grief, and there is some probability that the death mourned is that of a maiden, by the other maidens of the village. The game is not a representation of an ordinary funeral.

I must here refer to the game of "Rashes" (Addenda, ii. pp. 452, 453). I have not succeeded in obtaining a version played now, and fear it is lost altogether, which is, perhaps, not surprising, as the use of "rushes" has practically ceased; but, as recorded by Mr. Radcliffe in 1873, there is no doubt it represented the survival of the time when rushes were gathered and used with ceremony of a religious nature.

Even in the extremely simple "Ring a Ring of Roses" (ii. 108–111), now only a nursery game played by very young children, there can be traced a relationship to a dance, in which the use of flowers, and all the dancers bowing or falling prostrate to the ground together, with loud exclamations of delight obtained. It may well be that sneezing, an imitation of which is an essential part of the game, was actually a necessary part of the ceremonial, and sneezing was always considered of sacred significance among primitive peoples. It is not probable that children would introduce this of their own accord in a dance and "bop down" game.

The games played in the third method of this group are also representative of custom. In "Old Roger" (vol. ii. pp. 16–24), the circle of players is stationary throughout; the circle sings the words describing the story, and the other players or actors run into the circle and act their several parts in dumb show. The story, it will be seen, is not the acting of a funeral, but the planting of a tree over the grave of a dead person by relatives and friends, and the spirit connection which this tree has with the dead. The spirit of the dead "Old Roger" enters the tree, and resents the carrying away of the fruit by the old woman by jumping up and making her drop the apples. Possession of the fruit would give her power over the spirit. That the tree is sacred is clear; and I am tempted to suggest that we may possibly have in this game a survival of the worship of the sacred tree, and its attendant priest watching until killed by his successor, as shown to us by Mr. Frazer in the story of the "Golden Bough."

"Round and Round the Village" (ii. pp. 122–143) shows us the performance of a recurring festival very clearly in the words which accompany all versions, "As we have done before." This conveys the idea of a special event, the event in the game marriage, and I suggest that we have here a periodical village festival, at which marriages took place. It is characteristic of this, as in "Old Roger," that the chorus or circle stand still and sing the event, while the two characters act. This acting is the dancing round the village, going in and out the windows and houses, then choosing a lover, and "follow her to London." It is quite possible that the perambulation of boundaries with which festive dances and courtship were often associated would originate this game. The perambulation was a recurring custom periodically performed, and on p. 142, vol. ii., I have given some instances of custom which, I think, confirm this.

In "Who goes round my Stone Wall" we find the players in circle form, standing still and representing the houses of a village (the stone wall), and also animals. The game represents the stealing of sheep, one by one, from the village, by a predatory animal or thief. In this game the circle do not sing the story. That element has disappeared; the two actors repeat a dialogue referring to the stealing of the sheep from the "wall." This dialogue is short, and is disappearing. The game is not now understood, and consequently is dying out. "Booman," another of the same kind, represents a funeral. The grave is dug in action, Booman is carried to his grave, the dirge is sang over him, and flowers are pretended to be strewn over.

There are other circle games, which it is not needful to examine in detail. They are fragmentary, and do not present any fresh features of interest. It is, however, important to note that a few examples have evidently been derived from love ballads, drinking songs, and toasts; some of the dance games are of this origin. This may be explained by the fact that children, knowing the general form of marriage games, would naturally dance in circle form to any ballad verses in which marriage or love and courtship occurs, and in this manner the ballad would become apparently a fresh game, though it would only be putting new words to an old formula of action.

Dr. Jacob Jacobsen, in *Dialect and Place Names of Shetland*, tells us that all the *vissiks* or ballads have been forgotten since 1750, or thereby. They were sung to a dance, in which men and women joined hands and formed a ring, moving forwards, and keeping time with their hands and feet. Mr. Newell (*Games*, p. 78), records that "Barbara Allen" was sung and danced in New England at children's parties at a period when dancing was forbidden to be taught in schools. "Auld Lang Syne" is a further instance.

It will easily be seen that the circle games have a distinctive characteristic compared with the line games. These, as I have already pointed out, are games of contest, whereas the circle games are games in which a homogeneous group of persons are performing a ceremony belonging entirely to themselves. The ceremony is of a religious character, as in "Oats and Beans and Barley," or "Old Roger," dedicated to a spirit intimately connected with the group who perform it, and having nothing belonging to any outside group. The position of the marriage ceremony in this group is peculiar. It has settled down from the more primitive state of things shown in the line marriage games, and has acquired a more social and domestic form. Except in the very significant water custom in "Sally Water," which I have suggested (ii. pp. 176, 177) may take us back to perhaps the very oldest stage of culture, all the games in this group are evidently of a later formation. Let it be noted, too, that the circle has deep religious significance not entirely absent from the customs of comparatively later times, among which the singing of "Auld Lang Syne" is the most generally known.

But in speaking of matters of religious significance, it is important to bear in mind that we are not dealing with the religion of the Church. Everywhere it is most significant that marriage ceremony, sacred rite, social custom, or whatever is contained in these games, do not take us to the religion of to-day. Non-Christian rites can only be pre-Christian in origin, and these games therefore take us to pre-Christian religious or social custom, and this is sufficient to stamp them with an antiquity which alone would certify to the importance of studying this branch of folk-lore.

To take now the dialogue or individual form of game, the best example for my purpose is "Mother, Mother, the Pot boils over" (vol. i. pp. 396–401). Here the chorus has disappeared ; the principal characters tell the story in dialogue, the minor characters only acting when the dialogue necessitates it, and then in dumb show. This is an interesting and important game. It is a complete drama of domestic life at a time when child-stealing and witchcraft were rife. A mother goes out to work, and returns to find one of her seven children missing. The game describes the stealing of the children one by one by the witch, but the little drama tells even more than this. It probably illustrates some of the practices and customs connected with fire-worship and the worship of the hearth. There is a pot, which is a magical one, and which boils over when each one of the children is stolen and the mother's presence is necessary. A remarkable point is that the witch asks to borrow a light from the fire. The objection to the giving of fire out of the house is a well-known and widely-diffused superstition, the possession of a brand from the house fire giving power to the possessor over the inmates. The witch in this game takes away a child when the eldest daughter consents to give her a light. The spitting on the hearth gives confirmation to the theory that the desecration of the hearth is the cause of the pot boiling over. Instances of magical pots are not rare.[1]

After the children are stolen the mother has evidently a long and troublesome journey in search of them; obstacles. are placed in her path quite in the manner of the folk-tale. Blood must not be spilled on the threshold. This game, then, which might be considered only as one of child-stealing, becomes, when examined on the theories accompanying the ancient house ritual, an extraordinary instance of the way beliefs and customs have been dramatised, and so perpetuated. Other games of a similar character to this, and perhaps derived from it, are "Witch," "Gipsy," "Steal the Pigs."

Amongst other games classified as dialogue games are those in which animals take part. In some there is a contest between a beast of prey, usually a fox or wolf, and a hen and her chickens or a goose and her goslings; in others a shepherd or keeper guards sheep from a wolf, and in animals of the chase are hunted or baited for sport. In the animal contest games, "Fox and Goose," "Hen and Chickens,"

[1] Mr. W. F. Kirby refers me to the form of initiation into witchcraft in Saxony, where the candidate danced round a pot filled with magic herbs, singing—

> " I believe in this pot,
> And abjure God ; "

or else it was—

> " I abjure God,
> And believe in this pot."

"Gled-wylie," "Auld Grannie," "Old Cranny Crow," all played in the dialogue form, the dialogue announces that the fox wants some food, and he arouses the suspicion of the goose or hen by prowling around or near her dwelling. After a parley, in which he tries to deceive the mother animal, he announces his intention of catching one of the chickens. The hen declares she will protect her brood, and a contest ensues. These games have of course arisen from the well-known predatory habits of the wolf, fox, and kite. On the other hand, the games illustrating the hunting or baiting of animals, such as "Baste the Bear," "Fox in the Hole," "Hare and Hounds," are simply imitations of those sports. "Baiting the Bear," a popular and still played game, has continued since the days of bear-baiting.

I may also mention the games dealing with ghosts. "Ghost at the Well," "Mouse and Cobbler," show the prevailing belief in ghosts. Playing at Ghosts has been one of the most popular of games. These two show the game in a very degenerate condition. I need not, I think, describe in detail any more of the dialogue games. There are none so good as "Mother, the Pot boils over," but that was hardly to be expected. The customs which no doubt were originally dramatised in them all have in many cases been lost, as in the case of some versions of "Mother, the Pot boils over."

The dialogue games appear to me to be later in form than both line and circle games. They are, in fact, developments of these earlier forms. Thus the "Fox and Goose" and "Hen and Chickens" type is played practically in line form, and belongs to the contest group, while the "Witch" type is probably representative of the circle form. But they have assumed a dramatic character of a very definite shape. This, as will be seen later on, is of considerable importance in the evidence of the ancient origin of games; but I will only point out here that this group has allowed the dramatic element to have full scope, with the result that a pure dialogue has been evolved, while custom and usage has to some extent been pushed in the background.

The next group is the arch form of game. This I divide into two kinds—those ending in circle or dance form, and those ending with a contest between two leaders. Of this first form there are several examples. "London Bridge" (i. pp. 333–50) is possibly the most interesting. Two players form the arch, all the others follow in single file. The words of the story are sung while all the players run under or through the arch. The players are all caught in turn in the arch, and then stand aside; their part is finished. In some cases the game begins by all forming a circle, and the verses are sung while the circle dances round. The arch is then formed, and all run through it in single file, and are caught in turn by being imprisoned between the lowered arms. Also, we find the circle-dancing following the arch ceremony. In my account of this game (vol. i. pp. 341–50), I have drawn attention to the incident of a prisoner being taken as indicative of the wide-spread custom known as the foundation sacrifice, because of the suggested difficulty of getting the bridge to stand when the prisoner is taken. I have given a few instances of the custom, and the tradition that the stones of London Bridge were bespattered with the blood of little children, and that the mortar was tempered with the blood of beasts. In stories where a victim is offered as a foundation-sacrifice, the victim, often a prisoner, is sometimes forced to enter a hole or cavity left on purpose in the building, which is then walled or built up, enclosing the victim. In some, recourse to lottery is had; in others, as at Siam, mentioned by Tylor (*Primitive Culture*, i. 97), it was customary, when a new city gate was being erected, for a number of officers to lie in wait and seize the first four or eight persons who happened to pass by, and who were then buried alive under the gate-posts. After these customs of human sacrifice had ceased to be enforced, animals were slaughtered instead; and later still the ceremony would be performed, as a ceremony, by the incident being gone through, the person or animal seized upon being allowed to escape the extreme penalty by paying a money or other forfeit; and it may be this later stage which is represented in the game. The dancing in circle form, which belongs, I think, to the original method of play, shows us a ceremony in which people of one place are concerned, and would supersede an older line form of game, if there were one, when the custom showed a real victim being taken from outsiders by force, who would resist the demand. The circle dance would follow as the completion of the ceremony. The "line" form would also be the first portion of the game to disappear when once its meaning was lost.

The game, "Hark! the Robbers" (i. 192–99) may be a portion of "London Bridge" made into a separate game by the part of the building being lost, or the children who play both games may have mixed up the method of playing; but as it ends in some places with a contest and in some with a dance, it is difficult to say which is right.

"Thread the Needle," played by all players running through an arch and then dancing round, is a game well illustrated by customs obtaining on Shrove Tuesday in different parts of the country. All the children play "Thread the Needle" in the streets of Trowbridge, Bradford-on-Avon, South Petherton, Evesham, besides other places, in long lines, whooping and shouting as they run through the arches they make. After this they proceed to the churchyard, and encompassing the church by joining hands, dance all round it three times, and then return to their homes. Here is the undoubted performance of what must have been an old custom, performed at one time by all the people of the town, being continued as an amusement of children. It was played at Evesham only on Easter Monday, and in three other places only on Shrove Tuesday, and another correspondent says played only on a special day. In other places where it is played the game is not connected with a special day or season. The circle dance does not always occur, and in some cases the children merely run under each other's clasped hands while singing the words. In the places above mentioned we see it as a game, but still connected with custom. It is a pity that the words used by the children on all these occasions should not have been recorded too. "How many Miles to Babylon (vol. i. pp. 231–238) may with good reason be considered a game of the same kind. It represents apparently a gateway of a town, and a parley occurs between the gatekeepers and those wishing to enter or leave the town. Small gateways or entrances to fortified towns were called needle's eyes, which were difficult to enter. But notwithstanding these apparent identifications with the conditions of a fortified town, I think the practice of going through the arch in this and in the previous game relates to the custom which prevailed at festivals held during certain seasons of the year, when people crept through holed stones or other orifices to propitiate a presiding deity, in order to obtain some particular favour. This would be done by a number of people on the same occasion, and would terminate by a dance round the church or other spot associated with sacred or religious character. "Long Duck" is another probably almost forgotten version of this game.

"Draw a Pail of Water" (vol. i. pp. 100–108), though not quite in accord with the arch form in its present state, is certainly one of the same group. This game I consider to be a descendant of the custom of "well worship." In its present form it is generally played by children creeping under the arms of two or four others, who clasp hands and sway backwards and forwards with the other children enclosed in them. The swaying movement represents, I believe, the drawing of water from the well. The incidents of the game are :—

(1) Drawing water from a well.
(2) For a devotee at a well.
(3) Collecting flowers for dressing the well.
(4) Making a cake for presentation.
(5) Gifts to the well [a gold ring, silver pin, and probably a garter].
(6) Command of silence.
(7) The presence of devotee at the sacred bush.
(8) The reverential attitude (indicated by the bowing and falling on the ground).

I can now add another incident, that of the devotee creeping through a sacred bush or tree (signified by the creeping under or getting enclosed within the arms of the leaders). These are all incidents of primitive well worship.

I have from many different versions pieced together the lines as they might appear in earlier versions (i. p. 107).

This restoration, though it is far from complete, shows clearly enough that the incidents belong to a ceremonial of primitive well worship. Dressing holy wells with garlands and flowers is very general; cakes were eaten at Rorrington Well, Shropshire, and offerings of pins, buttons, and portions of the dress, as well as small articles worn on the person, are very general; silence is enforced in many instances, and sacred trees and bushes are to be found at nearly all holy wells. Offerings are sometimes hung in the bushes and trees, sometimes thrown into the well. Miss Burne records in *Shropshire Folk-Lore* (pp. 414, 433, 434) that at Rorrington Green, in the parish of Chirbury, is a holy well, at which a wake was celebrated on Ascension Day. The well was adorned with green bowers, rushes, and flowers, and a maypole was set up. The people used to walk round the hill with fife, drum, and fiddle, dancing and frolicking as they went. They threw pins into the well for good luck, and to prevent them from being bewitched, and they also drank the water. Cakes were eaten. These were round flat buns, from three to four inches across, sweetened, spiced, and marked with a cross, and were supposed to bring good luck if kept.

Instances of similar practices at holy wells could be multiplied, and they are exhaustively examined in my husband's book on *Ethnology in Folk-Lore*. Halliwell records in his nursery rhymes what is perhaps the oldest printed version of the rhyme. He says the children form a long string, hand in hand; one stands in front as leader, two hold up their clasped hands to form an arch, and the children pass under; the last is taken prisoner. Though this way of playing does not appear to be used now—no version, at least, has reached me—it is clear that the game might be played in this way, probably as a commencement of the ceremonial, and then the other positions might follow. Halliwell may not have recorded it minutely or have heard of it as a whole, or the version sent him may have been in degenerate form. It is, however, clear that the arch form here indicates a ceremonial, and not the taking of a prisoner.

"Oranges and Lemons" (vol. ii. pp. 25–35) is the best-known

game of the arch form, followed by the contest or tug-of-war. In this game two players, sometimes chosen by lot, clasp hands and form an arch. They have each a name, which is secret. One is called "Orange," the other is "Lemon." They sing the words of the game-rhyme, and the other players run under the arch in a long line or string. At the close of the verses which ends with the line, "Here comes a chopper to chop off your head," one of the string of players is caught and is asked which she prefers, orange or lemon. She chooses, and is told to stand behind that leader who took that name. This is repeated until all the players have been separately caught, have chosen their side, and are standing behind the respective leaders, holding on to each other by clasping each other's waists. A line is then drawn on the ground, and both sides pull; each endeavours to drag the other over the line. The tug is generally continued until one side falls to the ground. Now this is an undoubted contest, but I do not think the contest is quite of the same kind as the line game of contest and fighting. The line form is one of invaders and invaded, and the fight is for territory. In this form it seems to me that the contest is more of a social contest, that is, between people of the same place, perhaps between parishes and wards of parishes, or burghers and apprentices (townspeople) on one side, and the followers of lords or barons (military power) on the other, or of two lords and barons. The leaders are chosen by lot. Each leader has a "cry" or "colour," which he calls out, and the other players run and place themselves under the banner they choose.

In my account of this game I draw particular attention to the following details :—The game indicates contest and a punishment, and although the sequence is not clear, as the execution precedes the contest, that is not of particular importance in view of the power of the old baronial lords to threaten and execute those of their following who did not join their armed retainers when required. All rhymes of this game deal with saints' names and with bell ringing. Now, the only places where it would be probable for bells to be associated with different saints' names in one area would be the old

parish units of cities and boroughs. The bells were rung
on all occasions when it was necessary to call the people
together. The "alarm" bell tolling quickly filled the open
spaces and market-places of the towns, and it is a well-known
fact that serious contests and contest games between parishes
and wards of parishes were frequent. The names "oranges"
and "lemons," given to the leaders in the game, usually considered to be the fruits of these names, are, in my opinion, the
names of the "colours" of the two rival factions.

The passing under the arch in this game is not absolutely
necessary in order that the players may exercise their choice
of leaders, nor is the "secrecy" which is observed necessary
either. Even this may have its origin in custom. It may
signify the compulsory attendance of a vassal under pain of
punishment to serve one side, or the taking prisoner and con-
demning to death for serving on the opponents' or losing side.
An idea is current that it represents cutting off the last person's
head, the last of the string or line of players, and in some
places the last one in the line is always caught instead of one
whom the leaders choose to enclose in their arms. Of course
a "laggard" or late arrival would be liable to suspicion and
punishment, and this idea may be suggested in the game;
but I do not think that the game originates from the idea of
catching a "last" player. The passing under the arch can
also be attributed to the custom of compelling prisoners to
pass under a yoke to signify servitude, and the threat of
execution would follow attempt to escape or disobedience.
Again, prisoners were offered life and freedom on condition
of joining the army of their opponents.

The other games of this method of play, "Three Days'
Holiday," and "Tug of War," are the same game under other
names, with only a nominy surviving, and the method of play.
Several games entered under the title of "Through the Needle
Eye," are really the "arch" type with the "tug," that is the
"Orange and Lemons" game, instead of belonging to the
"Thread the Needle" or first form of arch type, as they are
usually considered. The Scottish form, described by Jamieson
(ii. p. 290), is an exception which should have been in-

cluded with "Thread the Needle," to which group it belongs. The other games, "Through the Needle Eye," have lost a portion of their play, which probably accounts for the mixture of name with the "Thread the Needle" games, because of both containing the arch form. "Namers and Guessers," "Fool, Fool, come to School," "Little Dog, I call you," practically versions of one and the same game, which I have classed in this type because of the "tug," have an additional element of guessing in them. The leader or namer on one side and the guesser on the other take sides. All the players have names given them, and it is the first business of the guesser to guess which of the players has taken a particular name. If he guesses correctly, he takes that player on his side; if incorrectly, he stays on the namer's side. After he has "guessed" at all the players, the "tug" follows, and the beaten side has further to run the gauntlet between two lines of the successful side. This game, having all its players chosen by guessing, by what might have been originally choosing by "lot" or by magical powers, may have an entirely different meaning, but it is clearly a contest game, although there is no indication as to the why or wherefore. The punishment of "running the gauntlet" is found in the game, which again indicates military fighting.

This group of games, though small, is perhaps one of the most indicative of early custom, for beyond the custom which is enshrined in each game—foundation sacrifice, well worship, &c.—it will be noticed there is a common custom belonging to all the games of this group; this is the procession under the arch. The fact that this common custom can also be referred to primitive usage, confirms my view that the particular customs in each game owe their origin to primitive usage. Mr. W. Crooke has very kindly supplied me with some notes on this interesting subject, and I gladly avail myself of his research :—

"In Cairo, women walk under the stone on which criminals are decapitated, in the hope of curing ophthalmia and getting children. They must go in silence, and left foot foremost."—Lane, *Modern Egyptians*, i. p. 325 ; Hartland, *Perseus*, i. p. 163.

"Rheumatism and lumbago cured by crawling under granitic masses in Cornwall."—Hunt, *Popular Romances*, p. 177.

"Passing children under bramble to cure rupture."—*Ibid.*, pp. 412, 415.

"This cures chincough."—Aubrey, *Remains*, p. 187.

"In Scotland, sick children are passed through the great stones of Odin at Stennis, and through a perforated monolith at Burkham, in Yorkshire."—Rogers, *Social Life in Scotland*, i. p. 13.

"Barren women pass their hands through the holes of the Bore Stone at Gask in order to obtain children."—*Ibid.*, iii. p. 227.

"Similar rites prevail in Cyprus."—Hogarth, *Devia Cypria*, p. 48; Gardner, *New Chapters in Greek History*, p. 172.

"This again gives rise to the use of the gateway through which pilgrims pass to temples. Such are the Indian Torana, in this shape, which are represented by the Torio, so common in Japan.

"The Greeks had the same, which they called Dokana (δόκανα, from δοκός, 'a beam'). With them they represented the Dioscuri —Castor and Pollux. They are described by Plutarch."—*De Amor. Fratr.*, i. p. 36.

"Similar arches, covered with charms, were seen at Dahomi by Burton."—*Mission to Gelele*, i. pp. 218, 286.

"Women in England creep under a gallows to get children." (I .have mislaid the reference.)

"There are many 'creeps' or narrow holes in Irish dolmens certainly used by people, who had to creep in to worship the ghost or bring offerings. Captives intended to be slaughtered had to creep through such places."—Borlase, *Dolmens of Ireland*, ii. p. 554.

"Barren women pass their hands through such holes."—*Ibid.*, ii. p. 650.

"A good picture of such a stone from France."—*Ibid.*, ii. pp. 626, 700, 702, 707.

Mr. Albany F. Major has also kindly drawn my attention to the following interesting passages from the sagas, which Dr. Jon Stefansson has kindly translated as follows:—

"In old times this had been the custom of brave men, who made an agreement (pact) that the one who lived the longest should revenge the other's death. They were to go under three earth-sods, and that was their oath (eiðr). This ceremony (leikr) of theirs was in this wise, that three long earth-sods (turfs) should be cut loose. All the ends were to be fast in the ground (adhere to it), but the coils (bends) were to be pulled upward, so that a man might go

under them. This play Thorgeir and Thormod went through."—
Fóstbrædra Saga, ed. 1822, ch. i. p. 7.

"Now is spread about this report of Thorkell and his men, but
Gudmund had before told [the story] somewhat otherwise. Now
that tale seemed to those kinsmen of Thorarins somewhat doubtful,
and they said they would not put trust in it without proof, and they
claimed for themselves [to share] half the property with Thorkell,
but Thorkell thought to own it himself alone, and bade go to ordeal
after their custom. This was then the [form of] ordeal at that time,
that they should go under an earth-belt, that is, a sod [which] was
ripped up from the field. The ends of the sod must be fast in the
field, but the man who was to perform the ordeal must go there-
under. Thorkell of the Scarf somewhat suspects whether the death
of those men can have happened in the way that Gudmund and his
men had said the latter time. Now, heathen men thought that they
had no less at stake, when they had to play such a part, than
Christian men think nowadays when ordeals are held. Then the
man who went under the earth-belt was clear if the sod fell not on
him. Thorkell took counsel with two men that they should let
themselves fall out about something or other, and be there standing
near at hand when the ordeal was being performed, and should
touch the sod so hard that all might see that they brought it down.
After this the man who was to perform the ordeal starts, and as soon
as he was come under the earth-belt those men who were set to do
it sprang to meet each other under arms, and they encounter near
the bend of the sod and lie fallen there, and the earth-belt fell down,
as was to be expected. At once men spring between them and
separate them; that was easy, because they were fighting with no
risk to life. Thorkell of the Scarf asked what people thought of the
ordeal; now all his men say that it would have done well if no one
had spoilt it. Then Thorkell took all the loose property, but the
land is joined on to Hrappstead."—*Laxdæla Saga*, ch. xviii.

"Berg gave notice of the blow for the Hunawaterthing and began
the lawsuit there. As soon as men came to the thing they tried to
arrange a settlement. Berg said that he would not take payment in
atonement, and would only be reconciled under these terms, that
Jokull should go under three earth-belts, as was then the custom after
great transgressions, 'and thus show humility towards me.' Jokull
said the trolls should take him before he thus bowed himself.
Thorstein said it was a matter for consideration, 'and I will go
under the earth-belts.' Berg said then would the matter be paid
for. The first earth-belt reached to the shoulder, the next to the

waist-belt, the third to mid-thigh. Then Thorstein went under the first. Then said Berg: 'Now I make thee stoop like a swine, who wast the loftiest of the Vatnsdale men.' Thorstein answers, 'That hadst thou no need to say, but this will be the first return for those words, that I will not go under any more.' Finnbogi said, 'That is clearly not well said, but then not much comes in repayment for Berg's wrong, that he gat from Jokull, if the matter shall here come to a standstill, and everything seems to you lowly by the side of you Vatnsdale men, and I will challenge thee, Thorstein, to holm-gang a week hence by the stackyard which stands on the island down before my farm at Borg.'"—*Vatnsdæla Saga*, ch. xxxiii.

These significant customs, I think, bear out my theory as to the origin of the games played in the two methods of the arch form.

Lastly, I come to the "winding up" games. "Eller Tree" (i. p. 119) and "Wind up the Bush Faggot" (ii. pp. 384–387), show a game in which a tree or bush is represented, and is probably indicative of tree worship. The tallest player represents the tree, and all the other players walk round and round in line form, getting closer and closer each time, until all are wound round the centre player. They call out when winding round "The old tree gets thicker and thicker," and then jump all together, calling out "A bunch of rags," and try and tread on each other's toes. This last action is evidently performed from not understanding the action of stamping, which is, without doubt, the object of the players. It is probable that this game descends from the custom of encircling the tree (Mr. Addy suggests the alder-tree) as an act of worship, and the allusion to the "rags" bears at least a curious relationship to hanging rags on sacred trees. A ceremonial of this kind would probably take place each spring, and the stamping on the ground would be, as in "Oats and Beans and Barley," a part of the ceremony to awake and arouse the earth spirit to the necessity of his care for the trees under his charge. The connection of all the players, by means of the clasped hands, with the central figure or tree, may also be considered a means of communicating life and action to it; the tree requiring contact with living and moving creatures to enable it to put forth its leaves. In a version of this game from Lincoln, called the "Old Oak Tree" (ii. p. 386), we find practically the same words and same actions, the dancing round and jumping up and down are constant features of this game. It remains in some degenerate versions from Scotland (*ibid.*), where the game has assumed the modern name of "Rolling Tobacco." In "Wind up the Bush Faggot" we have again the tree or bush suggested, and the dancing and jumping, or stamping up and down. In Shropshire it is the closing game of any playtime, and was played before "breaking-up" at a boys' school in Shrewsbury in 1850–1856. This tends to show that the game had originally been played at a special time or season.

For an example of this custom I may repeat (from ii. p. 386) that in mid-Cornwall, in the second week in June, at St. Roche and one or two adjacent parishes, a curious dance, like a serpent's coil, is performed at the annual "feasts." The young people are assembled in a meadow, and the band plays a lively tune. The band leads, and all the people follow hand in hand. The band or head keeps marching in an ever-narrowing circle, while its train of dancing followers becomes coiled round it in circle after circle. Then the band, taking a sharp turn about, begins to retrace the circle, still followed as before, and a number of young men, with long leafy branches in their hands as standards, direct this counter-movement. Although there is no mention of a tree in the account round which this ceremony is performed, the custom is so striking as to leave very little doubt of their connection. Lady Wilde (*Ancient Cures, Charms, and Usages of Ireland*, p. 106) says, "On May-Day in Ireland all the young men and maidens hold hands, and dance in a circle round a tree hung with ribbons or garlands, or round a bonfire, moving in curves from left to right, as if imitating the windings of a serpent." This is a closer parallel to the game still, and leaves no doubt as to its connection with custom. There may be, too, some connection between these winding-up or serpentine dances and the Maypole dances on May-Day in England.

The detail into which I have gone in the case of these games makes it, I think, unnecessary that I should enter into equal detail in other customs mentioned in the classification. Thus, with regard to the funeral customs indicated in "Jenny Jones," we have not only a ceremony of burial, but the courting of a maiden or maidens by a band of suitors, the opposition of the mother or guardians to their suit, the putting forward of domestic occupations as pretexts for refusal; there is also the illness, dying and death of the maiden, the manner of her funeral indicated by the colour selected for her burial, followed by the burial itself, the singing of the lament or funeral dirge, and, in some versions, the rising of the ghost or spirit of the departed. This game in its best versions is played in line form. But in those versions where two children only play the parts of "mother" and "Jenny Jones," there is also evidence of the tendency of the game to develop into the individual form.

Again, those games in which "guessing" occurs remind us of the important part that guessing or chance plays in the beliefs of the savage and uncivilised. A person who, by a guess, discovers a special person out of a number, or the exact number of articles concealed in a hand or under a foot, has something of the supernatural or witch-element about him. This is largely the foundation of the belief in witchcraft and the sorcerer. It is not surprising to find, therefore, the guessing-element largely extant in the dramatic game. The "guesser" is usually chosen by lot by means of the counting-out rhyme; the leader then proceeds to confuse the guesser's or witch's mind by re-naming secretly the rest of the players. He calls the "guesser," and in a doggerel rhyme (the remains or imitation probably of an incantation), tells him to pick out or name a certain person or thing. If the guess is correct, the "guesser" takes that person to his side, indicating power over that individual or thing. If the "guesser" is unsuccessful, he is scouted, mocked, and ill-used.

I now proceed with the second classification referred to on p. 461. Of the games classified on pp. 461–470, *ante*, it will be found on examination that nearly all of them are dramatic in form. This leads me at once to suggest that so important a phase of their character needs separate investigation, and this I proceed to do.

In the first place, it will be found that certain of the games are wholly dramatic whatever may be the customs or rites they imitate. These games are of two classes—first, where dramatic action is complete throughout the whole game, that is where singing, action, and words are represented; secondly, where singing has dropped out, action and words only remaining.

These two classes are as follows :—

DRAMATIC GAMES.

(1) SINGING (*containing words, tune, action*).

All the Boys.
Babbity Bowster.
Booman.
Curly Locks.
Cushion Dance.
Dillsie, Dollsie Dee.
Down in the Valley.
Down in yonder Meadow.
Galley, Galley, Ship.
Glasgow Ships.
Green Grass.
Green Gravel.
Hark the Robbers.
Hear all ! let me at her.
Here comes a Lusty Wooer.
Here comes a Virgin.
Here I sit on a Cold Green Bank.
Here's a Soldier.
Here stands a Young Man.
Hey Wullie Wine.
Isabella.
Jenny Jones.
Jolly Fishermen.
Jolly Hooper.
Jolly Miller.
Jolly Rover.
Jolly Sailors.
Keys of Heaven.
King William.
Kiss in the Ring.
Knocked at the Rapper.
Lady of the Land.

Lady on the Mountain.
London Bridge.
Mary Brown.
Mary mixed a Pudding.
Merry-ma-tansa.
Milking Pails.
Mulberry Bush.
Needle Cases.
Nettles Grow.
Nuts in May.
Oats and Beans.
Old Dame.
Old Roger.
Oliver, Oliver, follow the King.
Oranges and Lemons.
Poor Mary sits a-weepin'.
Poor Widow.
Pray, pretty Miss.
Pretty little Girl.
Queen Anne.
Queen Mary.
Ring me Rary.
Rosy Apple.
Round and Round the Village.
Sally Water.
Salmon Fishers.
Silly Old Man.
Soldier.
Soldiers.
Three Dukes.
Three Knights.
Three Old Bachelors.

Three Sailors.
Wallflowers.
We are the Rovers.
When I was a Young Girl.

Widow.
Wind.
Would you know how doth the Peasant?

(2) DIALOGUE AND ACTION (*no singing*).

Auld Grannie.
Barbarie, King of the.
Chickens, come clock.
Deil amo' the Dishes.
Doagan.
Draw a Pail of Water.
Dumb Motions.
Eller Tree.
Fox and Geese.
Ghost at the Well.
Giddy.
Gipsy.
Gled-Wylie.
Hen and Chickens.
Honey Pots.
How many Miles to Babylon.
Jack, Jack, the Bread's a-burning.
Keeling the Pot.
King of Barbarie.
King of the Castle.

Lady on yonder Hill.
Lend me your Key.
Mother, may I go out?
Mother Mop.
Mother, Mother, the Pot boils over.
Mouse and Cobbler.
Namers and Guessers.
Old Cranny Crow.
Old Dame.
Rashes.
Shepherds and Sheep.
Steal the Pigs.
Thread the Needle.
Three Jolly Welshmen.
Tower of London.
Trades.
Who goes round my Stone Wall?
Willie Wastell.
Witch.
Wolf.

Nearly all the remaining dramatic games form a third class, namely, those where action remains, and where both words and singing are either non-existent or have been reduced to the merest fragments.

In order to complete the investigation from the point we have now reached, it is necessary to inquire what is the controlling force which has preserved ancient custom in the form of children's games. The mere telling of a game or tale from a parent to a child, or from one child to another, is not alone sufficient. There must be some strong force inherent in these games that has allowed them to be continued from generation to generation, a force potent enough to almost compel their continuance and to prevent their decay. This force must have been as strong or stronger than the customs which first brought the games into existence, and I identify it as the dramatic faculty inherent in mankind.

A necessary part of this proposition is, that the element of the dramatic in children's games is more ancient than, or at all events as ancient as, the customs enshrined in the games themselves, and I will first of all see if this is so.

With the child the capacity to express itself in words is small and limited. The child does not apparently pay as much attention to the language of those adults by whom he is surrounded as he does to their actions, and the more limited his vocabulary, the greater are his attempts at expressing his thoughts by action. Language to him means so little unless accompanied by action. It is too cold for a child. Every one acquainted with children will be aware of their dramatic way of describing to their mother or nurse the way in which they have received a hurt through falling down the stairs or out of doors, or from knocking their heads against articles of furniture. A child even, whose command of language is fairly good, will usually not be content to say, "Oh, mother, I fell down and knocked my head against the table," but will say, "Oh, I fell down like this" (suiting the action to the word by throwing· himself down); "I knocked my head like this" (again suiting the action to the word by knocking the head against the table), and does not understand that you can comprehend how he got hurt by merely saying so. He feels it necessary to show you. Elders must respond in action as well as in words to be understood by children. If "you kiss the place to make it well," and if you bind up a cut or sore, something has been done that can be seen and felt, and this the child believes in as a means of healing. A child understands you are sorry he has been hurt, much more readily than if you *say* or repeat that you are sorry; the words pass almost unheeded, the action is remembered.

Every one, too, must have noticed the observation of detail a child will show in personifying a particular person. When a little child wishes to personate his father, for instance, he will seat himself in the father's chair, cross his legs, pick up a piece of paper and pretend to read, or stroke an imaginary beard or moustache, put on glasses, frown, or give a little cough, and say, "Now I'm father," if the father is in the habit of indulging in either of the above habits, and it will be found that sitting in the chair (if a special chair is used by the father to sit in when at home) is the foundation and most important part of the imitation. Other men of the child's acquaintance read papers, smoke, wear glasses, &c., but father sits in that chair; therefore to be father, sitting in the chair is absolutely necessary, and is sufficient of itself to indicate to others that "father" is being personified, and not another· person. To be "mother" a child will pretend to pour out tea, or sew, or do some act of household work, the doing of which is associated with "mother," while a lady visitor or a relative would be indicated by wearing hat or bonnet or silk dress, carrying a parasol, saying, "How do you do?" and carrying on conversation. Again, too, it is noticeable how a child realises a hurt if blood and swelling ensues after a knock. This is something that can be seen and shown.

When wishing to be an animal, a child fixes at once on some characteristic of that animal which is special to it, and separates it from other animals similar in other ways. Children never personate horses and cows, for instance, in the same manner. Horses toss their heads, shake their manes, paw the ground, prance, and are restless when standing still, gallop and trot, wear harness, and their drivers have reins and a whip. When a child is a cow he does none of these things; he walks in a slower, heavier way, lowers the head, and stares about as he moves his head from side to side, lies down on the ground and munches; he has horns, and rubs these against a tree or a fence.

A child of mine, when told that he must not run in the gutter when out of doors, because that was not the place for little boys, replied, "I am not a little boy now, I am a dog, so I may run in the gutter." When he came into the path again he became a boy.

Again the same child, when called by his name and told to come out from under a table, a round one, under which he was lying rubbing his head against the pedestal centre, because under the table was not the place for little boys, said, "But I'm not [   ], I'm a cow, and it's not a table, it's a tree, and I'm rubbing my horns."

Again, when personating a train, the actions used are completely different from those used when personating an animal. The child moves at a steady rate, the feet progressing without raising the legs more than necessary, because engines only have wheels, which keep close to the ground; they don't jump up like feet do, the arms are used as the propeller, and the puffing and screeching, letting off steam, taking in water, are imitated in sound to perfection. This is entirely on the child's own initiative. When children play in groups the same things occur. Instances could be given *ad nauseam*. It cannot, therefore, surprise us that in these games children should be found to use actions which indicate to them certain persons or things, although the words they use may render action unnecessary, as action is to them most important. Children, when acting these games or dramas, appear not to need the element of dress or of particular garments to indicate their adoption of certain characters or characteristics. To display your heels and look down at them while doing so signifies a man who wears spurs, a knight; to prance along as if a horse, shows a man on horseback, a duke a-riding. A child lies or stoops down and shuts her eyes, she is dead; if she is passively carried by two others a little distance, she is going to be buried. The child, by standing still, becomes a tree, a house, or a stone wall. If an animal is required to be shown, down goes the child on hands and knees, bends her head down, and the animal is there. If a gate, fortress, or castle is wanted, two children join hands, and their arms are raised or lowered when required for opening the gate, &c. If one child is to personate a "mother," one or two or more smaller children are placed behind or beside her as her children, because "mother's have children," and so on. Many other examples could be given from these games of the same kind of thing. There is, then, no difficulty as to the reason why children should have continued playing at these games when once they had seen their elders play them or similar performances, nor why children should not have embodied in a game or play some of the manners and customs which were constantly going on around them in olden times as they do now, imitating the habits and customs of

the men and women and animals by whom they were surrounded.

We know from the evidence of those who have collected the
games that many were played as amusements by young men and
women up to a few years ago. Some are still so played, and
some years further back it was a general practice for men and
women in country districts to play these or similar games at
fairs and festivals; it is unlikely that adults would play seriously at children's games, but children having seen their elders
playing at these amusements would adopt them and use
them in their turn, until these amusements become in turn too
frivolous and childish for them. It is not so very many years
since that the then educated or cultured classes amused themselves by occupations now deemed silly and unfit even for
children of the uneducated class—witness practical joking, cock-
fighting, &c.

The natural instinct to dramatic action in children is paral-
leled by the same instinct in grown-up people when in a state
of culture where they are chiefly dependent upon their natural
capacities for existence. Thus evidence of the natural dramatic
power in savages and in semi-civilised races is abundant. The
dances of savages are strongly dramatic. They advance in
lines dancing, gesticulating, and singing, while others sit and
look on; they dance in circles joining hands, they go down on
all fours imitating animal postures and noises, they wear
masks, special dresses and ornaments, and these have significance for their audience. Some of these dances are peculiar
to and only witnessed by men, others performed by men are
witnessed by both sexes. These ceremonial dances are performed principally at the celebration of the initiative rites, but
some also represent other customs periodically performed.

Catlin's (*North American Indians*) description of the Buffalo
dance among the Mandan Indians shows the dancers wearing
masks made of a buffalo's head and horns, and a tail hanging
down behind. The dancers went through the actions of
hunting, being shot with bow and arrow, skinned and cut up,
accompanied by singing and yelling. This dance was performed
as a ceremony when food was required and the hunters were

at a loss, and would continue until a herd of buffalos came in sight on the prairie.

Mr. W. E. Roth gives dances accompanied by songs and pantomimic action and games practised by the N.W. Central Australian aborigines.[1]

In "Secular and Ceremonial Dances" of Torres Straits (*Zeit. für Ethnogr.*, vi. 1893, p. 131), Dr. Haddon describes a "saw-fish dance" performed by natives. He says "the advent of different seasons of the year is celebrated by ceremonies amongst most peoples; the most frequent of these are harvest festivals, or periods of rejoicings at the abundance of food. Very frequent also are ceremonies which relate to the preparing for crops or the inauguration of a season which promises abundant food supply. The saw-fish dance belongs to the latter class." Dr. Haddon visited the men, and saw the making of the masks which he describes at length. These were worn by the dancers, and consisted of an imitation of a human face resting on a crocodile's head, and surmounted by a figure of a saw-fish represented in a traditional method. The dance, which lasted for hours, was accompanied by singing a chant, the words of which served as a description of the meaning of the dance. This dance is performed to ensure a good harvest from the sea.

He also refers to dramatic death dances and war dances, and describes some interesting forms of other dances, one in which crabs are represented. He says, all the men dance in single file, and each man during the dance performs some definite movements which illustrate an action in real life, such as agricultural, nautical, or fishing employments; for example, a man would crouch and move his hands about as if he were planting yams or looking for pearl shell at the bottom of the sea. These movements are known to the spectators, though the foreign observer may not catch the allusion. Probably most of these actions have become more or less conventionalised during innumerable dance representations, just as some of the adjuncts to the dance are degenerate representations of objects used in

[1] *Ethnological Studies among the N.W. Central Queensland Aborigines.* By Walter E. Roth. 1897. London.

everyday life. In the war dance the actions illustrate the method pursued in war, ending with an evolution which represented the successful warriors threading the heads of the slain on the rattan slings which always hung on their backs when they went out to fight.

Mrs. Murray-Aynsley in a paper on the secular and religious dances in Asia and Africa (*Folk-lore Journal,* vol. v. pp. 273, 274), describes an aboriginal dance which still takes place annually in certain villages in the Khassia and Jaintia hills. It generally takes place in May. The special reason of the dance is the display of all the unmarried girls from far and near to choose, or be chosen by, suitable parties, and from description it is probable that the girls choose. Many marriages result from this one annual dance. The dances take place in a circular enclosure which is set apart for this annual feast. The musicians sit in the centre, and the girls form a large circle round the musicians, and behind the girls, holding hands in a larger circle, the men dance and go through their part of the performance. The girls perform very quiet movements and dance slowly, while the men jig, leap, hop, and wave their arms, legs, umbrellas, and *daos* in the wildest confusion, accompanying their movements with the most savage war-whoops, signifying nothing. It is also usual for the men to dance when one of their tribe is buried.

In the Kulu district at Sultanpore is held the feast of Rugonath, the chief god, when the gods belonging to every village in the valley are bound to appear and pay him respect. There is feasting, and the men dance round and round the palanquins containing the inferior gods. When the excitement is at its height the temple attendants seize the palanquins and dance them up and down violently, and make the godlings salaam to each other and to Rugonath, the chief god.

In Spiti, a valley in the Western Himalayas, the people frequently dance for hours for their own amusement. Men and women dance together, all join hands and form a long line or circle. They commence by singing, then dance to the accompaniment of their own voices, and the fun speedily becomes fast and furious (*ibid.* p. 281).

Amongst the Lamas there are also religious and secular dances performed at their feasts or fairs, the religious dances by the Lamas, the secular by men and women together, or by each sex separately. In one dance those who take part form themselves into two long lines. Each dancer holds on to the one in front of him, as in our game of "Fox and Goose." The two strings of dancers wind in and out, then divide and dance opposite each other, advancing and receding with a slow undulating movement, which gradually becomes more energetic. Mock sword fights then take place between two combatants, also sword dances, with two crossed weapons laid on the ground, and precisely like those performed at our Highland gatherings. In the religious dances each man wears a gigantic headpiece, which comes down as far as the shoulders. Some of the masks are ornamented. They perform several different dances, in which separate characters are performed, one a Chinese mandarin and his wife, another, two actors wear masks resembling ferocious-looking dogs, one places himself against the entrance door, the other guards the door of exit. They remind one, says Mrs. Murray-Aynsley, of the divan-palas, or doorkeepers, whose statues are seen placed as guards on each side of the shrine of some old Hindu temple. In Algeria the dancing at weddings is performed by men and women. Before each woman went out to dance she was enveloped in a garment which covered her from head to feet, her hands even not being visible, the sleeves being drawn over and tied at the ends so that the hands and arms were enclosed as in a bag. This was apparently a form of disguise, as one woman was sent back because her husband had discovered her. At a funeral also hired female mourners were dancing on the surface of a newly-made grave and uttering wild shrieks.

An interesting account of the war-dance of the Coorgis is also given (*ibid.* p. 251). "The Coorgis assembled in a clearing in the natural jungle. The forest was only illumined by jungle. The torch-bearers formed a large circle; within the open space, in the centre, were the musicians. One dance was very peculiar, inasmuch as it seemed to be a remnant of a period when every man's hand was against his brother's.

The performers may consist of any equal number of persons; they always dance in pairs. Before they begin each man is given a bundle of sticks or bamboos. This he holds in his left hand, and a stouter stick is given him in his right hand. At first all the men dance round and round, with head erect, as if going to war. Presently they narrow the circle and assume a crouching attitude, their eyes glancing here, there, and everywhere. The respective adversaries have been singled out; the intending aggressors make a feint or two, then bend their knees so that they are only about two-thirds of their ordinary stature; at the same time they place their feet together and make a succession of bounds, or rather hops, like a frog, and with the sticks the attacking party aim cuts at the legs of the men whom they selected as their adversaries. The latter now takes up the same attitude; he wards off attack, and returns the blow if he can. Whether intentionally or not, one party is victorious in the end."

"A curious dance is also executed by Hindu women at Sagar, in the Central Provinces of India (*ibid.* p. 253). Men are present, but as spectators only. Some little time before preparations have been made for this feast. Wheat or other grain has been sown in earth placed in pots made of large leaves, held together by thorns of a species of acacia. The richer women walk along, followed by their attendants carrying trays filled with such pots; the poorer people carry their own plants. As soon as each procession arrives at the ghât, or flight of steps leading down to the lake, every family-circle of friends deposit their pots on the ground and dance round them. After a time the dancers descend to the water's edge, taking their pots of earth and corn with them. They then wash away the soil from the plants, and distribute these amongst their friends. The whole of the ceremony is observed by the men, but they take no part in it. It probably fixes the season for sowing some particular crop."

These amongst others are all dances of semi-civilised peoples, and these dances, being all of a ceremonial nature, are probably derived from older customs, and performed in commemoration of these.

There are also surviving some ceremonial dances, such as the singular ceremony observed at Echternach, in Luxemburg, on Whit-Tuesday, in which ten or fifteen thousand pilgrims take part. Professor Attwell thus describes it in *Notes and Queries* of May 17, 1890:—

"Early on the morning of Whit-Tuesday pilgrims arrive at Echternach from the neighbouring villages, some alone, or in little family parties, some in small bodies personally conducted by their *curés*, singing litanies in honour of St. Willibrord. At about eight o'clock the bells of the parish church begin to peal, and the clergy, intoning the 'Veni Creator,' and preceded by numerous banners, issue from the principal porch and march along the bank of the Sure to a stone crucifix, near which, from an extemporised pulpit, the crowd is addressed. The short sermon ended, the procession begins. It is headed by a choir of some hundreds of voices chanting antiphonally with the clergy the litanies of the saint. Then come numerous ecclesiastics, followed by a band playing the cadenced music of the dance. The pilgrims are headed by young children and men and women belonging to the parish, after whom comes the throng, in groups of from three to six persons of either sex. The dancers take three jumps forward and one backward, or five forward and two backward. It is, of course, impossible for a moving crowd consisting of many thousands to keep anything like time, save those who are near one of the many bands of music, which, at irregular intervals, accompany the procession. No special order is observed, but there is no confusion. Poor mothers with sickly children in their arms jump side by side with young well-to-do girls; old men, broken with toil, jump in step with vigorous fellows in the heyday of youth. Water and wine are freely offered by the townsfolk to the pilgrims, many of whom sink exhausted under the unwonted effort. It sometimes happens that sick persons get paid substitutes to perform for them the expiatory jumping. The distance traversed is less than a mile, but the time occupied is fully two hours. Before the church can be entered sixty-four steps have to be mounted. But the singular backward and forward movements and the accompanying music are continued, not only while the steps are ascended, but during the circumambulation of the church, beneath the altar of which is the tomb of the saint. On reaching the hallowed shrine the devotees manifest their enthusiasm in various ways, kneeling before the altar, which is surrounded by votive offerings, with sobs and gesticulations. When the whole of the immense multitude has passed the shrine, the clergy ascend the altar, the 'Salve Regina' is sung, the Benediction is given, and the imposing ceremony is ended."

Grimm also records the fact that about the year 1133 in a forest near Inda (Ripuaria) a ship was built, set upon wheels, and drawn about the country by men who were yoked to it, first to Aachen (Aix), and up the river to Tongres, Looz, and so on, everywhere with crowds of people assembling and escorting it. Wherever it halted there were joyful shouts, songs of triumph, and dancing round the ship, kept up till far into the night. This Grimm describes as a recollection of an ancient heathen festival. It was utterly repugnant to and opposed strongly by the clergy as a sinful and heathenish piece of work. On the other hand, the secular power authorised and protected it (*Teutonic Mythology*, i. 258).

The story of the pied piper of Hamelin probably commemorates a procession similar to the Echternach (see *Folk-lore Journal*, vol. ii. 209).

With this may also be noted a dance recorded by Mr. Newell (*Games of American Children*, p. 89), who states that the name "Threading the Needle" is given to a dance in which hundreds take part; in which from time to time the pair who form the head of the row raise their arms to allow the line to pass through, coiling and winding like a great serpent. When a French savant asked the peasants of La Châtre why they performed this dance, the answer was, "To make the hemp grow."

I remember when quite a small child planting hemp seeds in a patch of garden ground, and being told by a maid-servant, an illiterate country girl, that the seeds would not grow well unless we danced, we joined hands and danced round and round in a circle, then stooped down and jumped about, saying, "Please, God, send it all up," then again danced round.

This may have been said only to amuse us, but it may also have been the remains of an old festival dance. I believe there were more words, but I cannot remember them. Hemp seed is associated with ceremonies of magical nature, being one of those used by maidens as a charm to enable them to see a future husband.

Representation in pantomime of the different actions used in the ceremonies of sowing the grain, its growth, and the consequent reaping, binding, and carrying the grain, are practised in different parts of the globe. This is brought down to later times by the custom noted on p. 319, vol. i., where from *Long Ago* and Best's *Rural Economy of Yorkshire* (1641), instances are given of it being customary, at harvest-homes, to give representations of "hirings" of farm-servants. The hiring of a farm labourer, the work he had to do, his terms of service, and the food to be supplied him, were dramatically performed, showing clearly that it had been customary to go through this sort of thing, in earnest of what was expected—in fact, a sort of oral contract, in presence of witnesses.

I will conclude this part of my evidence by a summary of the conclusions arrived at by anthropological authorities.

Sir John Lubbock, in *Origins of Civilisation* (fifth ed., p. 257), says, "Dancing among savages is no mere amusement." He quotes from Robertson's *America* (iv. p. 133) as follows: "It is an important occupation, which mingles in every occurrence of public or private life. If any intercourse be necessary between two American tribes, the ambassadors of the one approach in a solemn dance, and present the calumets or emblem of peace; the sachems of the other receives it with the same ceremony. If war is denounced against an enemy, it is by a dance expressive of the resentment which they feel, and of the vengeance which they meditate. If the wrath of their gods is to be appeased, or their beneficence to be celebrated; if they rejoice at the birth of a child, or mourn the death of a friend—they have dances appropriate to each of these situations, and suited to the different sentiments with which they are animated. If a person is indisposed, a dance is prescribed as the most effectual means to restore him to health; and if he himself cannot endure the fatigue of such an exercise, the physician or conjurer performs it in his name, as if the virtue of his activity could be transferred to his patient."

Sir J. Lubbock mentions some special dances practised among different peoples, and gives an illustration of a circle dance practised by the natives of Virginia round a circle of upright stones (p. 268).

Dr. Tylor (*Anthropology*, p. 296) says, " Savages and barbarians dance their joy and sorrow, love and rage, even their magic and religion. The forest Indians of Brazil, rattle in hand, stamp in one-two-three time round the great earthen pot of intoxicating kawi-liquor ; or men or women dance a rude courting dance, advancing in lines with a kind of primitive polka step ; or the ferocious war-dance is performed by armed warriors in paint. We have enough of the savage left in us to feel how Australians leaping and yelling at a corrobboree by firelight in the forest can work themselves up into frenzy for next day's fight. But with our civilised notions it is not so easy to understand that barbarians' dancing may mean still more than this ; it seems to them so real, that they expect it to act on the world outside. Such an example as the buffalo dance (given *ante*, p. 518) shows how, in the lower level of culture, men dance to express their feeling and wishes. All this explains how in ancient religion dancing came to be one of the chief acts of worship. Religious processions went with song and dance to the Egyptian temples, and Plato said all dancing ought to be thus an act of religion. . . . Modern civilisation has mostly cast off the sacred dance. . . . To see this near its old state the traveller may visit the temples of India, or among the Lamas of Tibet watch the mummers in animal masks dancing the demons out or the new year in, to wild music of drums and shell-trumpets. Remnants of such ceremonies come down from the religion of England before Christian times are still sometimes to be seen in the dances of boys and girls round the midsummer bonfire or mummers of Yuletide."

Dr. Tylor continues: "At low levels in civilisation it is clear that dancing and play-acting are one. The scenes of hunting and war furnish barbarians with subjects for dances, as when the Gold Coast negroes have gone out to war and their wives at home dance a fetish dance in imitation of battle to give their absent husbands strength and courage. . . . Historians trace from the sacred dances of ancient Greece the dramatic art of the civilised world. Thus from the festivals of the Dionysia arose tragedy and comedy. In the classic ages the players' art divided into several branches. The pantomimes kept up the earliest form, where the dancers acted in dumb show such pieces as the labours of Herakles, or Kadmos sowing the dragons teeth, while the chorus below accompanied the play by singing the story. The modern pantomime ballets which keep up remains of these ancient performances show how grotesque the old stage gods and heroes must have looked in their painted masks. In Greek tragedy and comedy the business of the dancers and chorus were separated from that of the actors, who recited or chanted each his proper part in the dialogue."

Grimm (*Teutonic Mythology*, i. p. 43), says, " Easter fires, May Day fires, Midsummer fires, with their numerous ceremonies, carry us back to heathen sacrifices, especially such customs as rubbing the sacred flame, running through glowing embers, throwing flowers into the fire, baking and distributing loaves or cakes, and the circular dance. Dances passed into plays and dramatic representations."

It is then clear that dances accompanied with song and pantomimic action have been used by men and women from the earliest period of which we have record, at all times and upon all occasions. In times of joy and mirth, sorrow and loss, victory or defeat, weddings and funerals, plagues and pestilences, famine and plenty, civilised and savage alike dance, act, and sing their griefs and their joys. The gods of all nations have been worshipped by pantomimic dance and song, their altars and temples are encircled by their worshippers; and as the occasion was one of fear or joy, and the god entreated or terrified by his followers, so would the actions and voices of the dancers be in accord. When once certain actions were recognised as successful, fitting, or beautiful, they would tend to become repeated and stereotyped, and the same form would be used for other gods, other occasions, and other customs where the requirements were similar or the same.   The circle dance, for instance, after being performed several times would necessarily become a part of the religious customs or ceremony, and form a part of the ordinary religious observance.   It would become particularly associated with the place where it was first instituted, and might be used to inaugurate other festivals. We know that the early Christians when taking over to their use the temples and altars of their so-called heathen predecessors, or when erecting a church where a temple had previously stood, held their worship there and performed their dances to their God as the heathens had done to theirs.   The custom of encircling a church on its festival day existed until lately in several parishes in England, and this could only be a descendant of the custom once held sacred by all the followers of one belief, demonstrating by their action in group form the fact that they all believed in the same thing and held together, by the clasp of hands and the dance round, their determination to hold to and keep to it.

If these customary dances obtained and have survived in religious ritual to the present day, is it not to be expected that we should find survivals in dance form of non-religious customs which also impressed themselves strongly on the minds of the people ? Births, marriages, deaths, the sowing and gathering in of the crops ; the protection of cattle from disease and animals of prey ; the necessity for water and fire ; the protection of the house and the village—have all helped to surround these events with ceremonials which have lasted, and been transmitted from generation to generation, altering to suit later ideas, it is true, but preserving through all some trace of the events which first called them into existence.

It is because of this tendency to believe more in the power of expression by action, than in the power of expression by language alone, that dramatic action and gesture have formed such a necessary part of representation of custom as to become an integral part of it.   Limited as is our knowledge of the popular plays performed about the country by troops of strolling players before the age of the written play, we know that their chief attraction must have been the dramatic rendering of characters and events personified by certain well-known actions of the actors, accompanied by special style of dress, or portions of dress, which were recognised as sufficient in themselves to show who and what was being personified. The story was shown more by action than by words; the idea being to present events to the onlooker, and impress them on his mind. It is in these dramatic performances of what was expected we have the germs of the dramatic art that afterwards developed into the regular play or drama. Every important custom of life was probably depicted by pantomimic action. We have, first, words, describing the events, sung or said by a chorus of onlookers and dancers, afterwards a short dialogue between the chief characters taking the place of the chorus, and then, as the number of characters were increased, the representations become something that could be performed independently, without the need of a particular season or custom to render it intelligible.

At this stage of the primitive drama the characters merely present actions of the *dramatis personæ* time after time, always performed in the same manner, and this would produce conventional methods of presenting certain events. We know that events of a religious nature were presented in the same manner by the Church. This must have been in consequence of the attraction plays possessed as depicting pagan religion and events of ordinary life and manners and customs. It is easily conceivable that before the era of books and literature, a rough sort of presentation of life, present and past, would be eagerly welcomed; and it would not be until the advent of a writer who developed the individual acting, at the expense of the event depicted, that what we know as a play could be written.

Mr. Ordish, in his study of Folk drama, published in the Folk-lore Society's journal, has conclusively proved the development of the drama independently of the miracle and mystery plays of the Middle Ages, or from the old Greek plays, and this development has taken place through the action of the people, always accustomed to the influence of dramatic representation. Hence in the remains of the traditional games we have preserved a form in which we can see the beginning and early development of the drama. When once the line form was firmly established as an indication of two opposite parties, it would be used for such indication wherever it was required, and thus it became the common property of the children's game and the early stage. The remains of the line and circle form, as denoting opponents and friendly communion can, I think, be traced in old plays and old methods of acting.

In old pantomimes, the demons or evil spirits and their followers enter on one side and stand in lines; the good fairy and her followers enter on the opposite side and stand in line; the principal characters advance from the line, and talk defiance to each other. We do not have a circle form on the stage, but a half-circle, seated on the stage, is or was until comparatively lately a method of representing a social or family party. Every one who has seen a mummer's play performed, either in or out of doors, will be aware that the same method obtains in them—the performers are all on the stage or stand together at once, walking forward as each one's name is mentioned, saying his allotted part, and then standing back again, while the next player has his turn.

The action in these plays has remained in stationary form; as far as the method goes there has probably been very little difference in the manner of presenting them for a long period of time.

These traditional games are valuable, therefore, for the information they afford in a direction not hitherto thought of, namely, in the study of the early drama. If the drama can be seen in its infancy anywhere, surely it can be seen in these children's plays.

The study of children's games takes us, therefore, into several departments of research. Many traces of customs that do not belong to modern life, customs that take us back to very early times indeed, are brought before us. The weapons are bows and arrows, the amusements hunting and hawking; animals are found in such close relationship with human beings, that only very primitive conditions of life would allow : contests between men and women occur in such a way that we are taken back to one of the earliest known customs of marriage, that known as marriage by capture—then from this stage to a later, where purchase or equivalent value obtains ; then to a marriage with a ceremony which carries us back to the earliest forms of such ceremonies. That such customs can be suggested in connection with these games goes far to prove that they, in fact, originate the game—that no other theory satisfactorily accounts for all the phenomena.

In looking for the motive power which has caused the continuity of these customs to be practised as amusements, we have found that the dramatic power inherent in mankind supplies the necessary evidence, and from this stage we have been led to an interesting point in the early history of the drama and of the stage. It is not, therefore, too much to say that we have in these children's games some of the oldest historical documents belonging to our race, worthy of being placed side by side with the folk-tale and other monuments of man's progress from savagery to civilisation.

ALICE B. GOMME.

THE END